Glimpses of a Biograp

Also by Gordon Bowker:

- 1993 - Pursued by Furies: A Life of Malcolm Lowry
- 1996 - Through the Dark Labyrinth: a Biography of Lawrence Durrell
- 2003 - George Orwell
- 2011 - James Joyce. A Biography

- Under Twenty (editor)
- Freedom: Reason or Revolution
- Race and Ethnic Relations: Sociological Readings (editor)
- Beelzebub's Barbs: A Cynic's Dictionary
- Malcolm Lowry Remembered (editor)
- Malcolm Lowry Under the Volcano – A Selection Of Critical Essays

Glimpses of a Biographer's Diaries
1961 – 2000

By Gordon Bowker

*To Clare
My dearest best friend
Thank you.
Ramdei xx*

Edited by Ramdei Rhoda Bowker

PUBLISHED by Ramdei Rhoda Bowker

Copyright © Ramdei Rhoda Bowker 2025 All rights reserved

No part of this publication may be copied, reproduced in any format, by any means, electronic or otherwise, without prior consent from the copyright owner and publisher of this book.

ISBN: 978-1-0684423-9-1

Cover design by Guy Loftus

To my wife, Ramdei Rhoda

Remember Me

Remember me when I am gone away
Gone far away into the silent land;
When you can no more hold me by the hand,
Nor I half turn to go yet turning stay.
Remember me when no more day by day
You tell me of our future that you plann'd:
Only remember me; you understand
It will be late to counsel then or pray.
Yet if you should forget me for a while
And afterwards remember, do not grieve:
For if the darkness and corruption leave
A vestige of the thoughts that once I had,
Better by far you should forget and smile
Than that you should remember and be sad.

Christina Rossetti

'I have always imagined that Paradise will be a kind of library.'

Jorge L Borges

'…*if you love a writer, if you depend upon the drip-feed of his intelligence, if you want to purse him and find him - despite edicts to the contrary - then it's impossible to know too much…*'

Julian Barnes, *Flaubert's Parrot*

Foreword

On the 14th January 2019, my husband Gordon Bowker, a biographer, journalist and lecturer passed away leaving behind a body of work that scrupulously unpicked and exposed the inner worlds of some of our great literary elite. In his sights were Malcolm Lowry, Lawrence Durrell, George Orwell and James Joyce - authors my husband didn't just pick from his book shelf for their celebrated body of work or indeed their hell-raising antics or uncompromising politics, but for something much more personal. Gordon saw in them something of himself. They were all exiles from their homeland. Exile wasn't to last for Gordon.

Born in 1934, his world was shaped by war, adventure, celebrity and three early brushes with death. Growing up amidst Birmingham's bomb sites and educated at King Edward VI Camp Hill School for Boys, it was an unwanted family move to Stoke Gabriel, South Devon, which prompted the 16 year-old Gordon to buy a one-way ticket to Australia. Buoyed by one of his favourite books - Conrad Aiken's *Blue Voyage*, this Ten Pound Pom sought adventure, and a chance to prove himself to a doubting father. But exile wasn't to last. The harsh realities of sheep farming quickly turned dreams to dust, and it was to take two more years of hard graft before the young explorer had the money, paperwork, and fortitude to make the six-weeks return journey home by sea.

Undeterred, Gordon embarked on a new adventure. After a brief experience as an electrical engineer in Egypt and Cyprus with the Royal Air Force (1952-1955), he sure-footedly set his sights on a literary career. His love of books had already been the mainstay of his young life, and the chance to write came through teaching. By the early 1960's after gaining a teaching certificate from Saltley College, a degree from the University of Nottingham, an M.A., and later a PhD from the University of London, a lectureship at Goldsmiths' College beckoned. He was to work at Goldsmiths from 1966 to 1991. But life was not without further headaches. On 24th March 1961, a nagging ankle pain disguised a life-threatening medical condition. So serious was it, that doctors informed him that he would have been dead within three days, had it not been for the round-the-clock medical and nursing care from staff at London's Westminster Hospital, his writing career would have been curtailed before it had started. Thankfully, undaunted by this second setback, he launched himself into life again.

Between 1961 and 2000, he set about not just honing his lecturing experience, but his journalism, writing literary criticism, books and education scripts for radio, television, magazines, and newspapers. The Observer commissioned him to write film location reports on John Huston's *Under the Volcano*, and Bertolucci's *The Last Emperor*. And in 1985 came *Malcolm Lowry Remembered*, a step towards his very first literary biography.

Much more before, and after was to follow, against the backdrop of a post-war London embracing the Swinging Sixties, the rise of celebrity. Fearing the dark shadow cast by the Cold War, Gordon was not blind to all this, nor was he a shrinking violet when it came to a damned good party. He loved to talk to me about these times.

His stories painted a picture of literary adventures and encounters with the Who's Who of London society at the time. It was in these heady times that I first met the man who would become my life partner and husband. Gordon always wanted to be a writer, which for him meant acquiring a quiet, secure and comfortable home. So, while he was working as a senior lecturer at Goldsmith, he earned extra money during the holidays in Canada as a visiting professor. In the summer of 1980, he exchanged houses with my cousin whilst lecturing in Ontario, Canada. I visited his house in London and my cousin was quite keen for me to meet him. I did loan my cousin a set of pots and pans, which she left at Gordon's house before returning to Canada. In December 1980, Gordon rang me to find out when I would collect my pots and pans. He invited me to dinner, and, on 19th December 1980, over Coq au vin washed down with champagne, I think we fell in love. Instantly it felt like we were old friends, laughing and joking at his adventures until tears run down our cheeks. Earlier in our friendship, I knew that he was busy, had many acquaintances and kept diaries. I told him not to mention me in his diaries. By 1983, we were partners and I gave him permission to write about us if he so wished.

Tears still run down my cheeks today but for a different reason, because the man I spent nearly forty years with travelling and researching the next great biographic work is no longer with me. But, thankfully his diaries, stories and escapades are. While Gordon achieved his ambition as an author and biographer, it is his own thrilling life-story that has remained untold - until now.

Gordon told me that glimpses of his life through diaries and stories gave a more immediate account of how he felt about things each day's events, as he strove to achieve his ambition to becoming an author.

He added: 'In these diaries and stories of my life, some names have been changed in accordance with the Data Protection Act and, in some cases, to avoid embarrassment. Conversations are reconstructed from memory, notebooks, diary entries, old passports, letters received and letters unsent, a somewhat battered press-cutting album, a box of old photographs, conversation with friends, families, nurses, doctors, and the public records do help, reminding one of how memory loses its grip on the facts, and how times change. The idea of starting with nothing and seeing how far I could get was, however, deeply appealing to me, and now a free man, I feel immensely optimistic.'

Before his death, Gordon wrote twelve books including: *Under Twenty* (1966), *Malcolm Lowry Remembered* (1985), Edited, *Malcolm Lowry Under the Volcano – A Selection Of Critical Essays* (1987), *Pursued by Furies A Life of Malcolm Lowry* (1993), *Through the Dark Labyrinth A Biography of Lawrence Durrell* (1997), *George Orwell* (2003), *Inside George Orwell A Biography* (2003), *James Joyce A Biography* (May 2011). Also, he had been working on a few novels and short stories. He left two completed unpublished novels and drafts. He was not satisfied with some of his stories.

Through his diaries and short stories, I have pulled together what he started, but sadly did not have a chance to finish: an exhilarating, humorous and true account of a raconteur, who dodged an early death three times, and went on to fulfil his literary ambitions on a grand scale. The task has not been an easy one though. I have been deeply affected by his passing, but I had a great deal of help; from my dearest friends, Clare Huffington, a writer; Dione Venables (20. 10. 1930 -12. 09. 2023), novelist, broadcaster, publisher, editor, air-hostess, artist and mother. Quentin Kopp, chairperson of the George Orwell Society, who were patiently committed to reading , making changes and correcting the edited *Glimpses of a Biographer*, Gordon Bowker, Diaries. 1961-2000; from Gordon's niece, Carole Lochhead, who read this introduction; from Andrew Lycett, biographer (and so much more), who was patiently committed to reading this edition and made constructive suggestions; from Puresha Ahanghama who originally formatted *Glimpses* read it and made some suggestions and Apple Support Staff, who resolved my many problems with my laptop and from Louise North and Katie Ankers, BBC archivists, who made kindly suggestions and invited me to the BBC archives and finally Guy Loftus who converted *Glimpses* for publication for paperback and on Kindle. I hope I have produced a finished version that Gordon would be proud of.

Ramdei Rhoda Bowker, Kensington, London, March 2025

LIST OF PHOTOGRAPHS

1 - Mike (centre walking towards the camera with shoulder strap) with Gordon in Cairo 18
2 - The Bowker family from the top left Ivy, Gordon, Leonard, Brenda and Lucy, 1950, not long before Gordon left home for Australia 54
3 - Nurse (Diana) Peters 74
4 - Gordon, Cyprus 86
5 - Woodbury Down Primary School, with Head Miss Philpott and Gordon Bowker back right 100
6 - Leonard Bowker 1914 120
7 - Cathy, 1964 137
8 - Family Bowker circa 1939 from the left Ivy, Leonard, Gordon and Lucy 180
9 - Leonard and Lucy Bowker 183
10 - Portrait of Malcolm Lowry hanging in Notting Hill 236
11 - Gordon and Rhoda, Mexico 25th September 1983 250
12 - Jan Gabrial, Encino 269
13 - Gordon with Odile Hellier and Raul Ortiz outside the Village Voice Bookshop, Paris 282
14 - Portrait of Durrell hanging in Notting Hill 287
15 - Portrait of Orwell hanging in Notting Hill 308
16 - Gordon with Cecily at her flat 342
17 – Gordon Robinson and Sheila Robinson 356
18 - Portrait of Joyce hanging in Notting Hill 427

TABLE OF CONTENTS

Foreword	i
PART ONE	1
Chapter 1	1
In London, in Hospital and at Death's Door	1
1961	*1*
Chapter 2	17
In Hospital and Recovering	17
	33
Chapter 3	33
Preparing for Discharge	33
	51
Chapter 4	51
Ready to Meet the Sound of Roaring London	51
	59
Chapter 5	59
Chelsea: My Garden of Eden!!!	59
	81
Chapter 6	81
Job Hunting	81
1966 1962	*83*
	99

Chapter 7 99
   Journalist and School Teacher 99
   1962-1963 99
      1963 .... *108*
      115

Chapter 8 115
   Part-Time Lecturer, Reviewer and Feature Writer ... 115
   1963-1965 115
      1964 .... *124*
      1965 .... *138*
      151

Chapter 9 151
   Full-Time Lecturer; TV Script Writer; My First Book 151
   Published, with Another on the Way 151
   1965-67 151
      1966 .... *152*
      1967 .... *160*
      164

Chapter 10 164
   Teaching in Canada and Damsels in Distress 164
   1968-69 164
      1969 .... *170*
      182

Chapter 11 182
   Meeting the Famous and Travelling in the United States of America 182
   1969-72 182
      1970 .... *184*
      1971 .... *186*
      1972 .... *191*
      198

GLIMPSES OF A BIOGRAPHER'S DIARY

Chapter 12   198
The Loss of a Close Friend, Several Narrow Escapes in Boats, and My Own House at Last   198
1973-79   198

1974   *205*
1975   *206*
1976   *208*
1977   *209*
1978   *210*
1979   *216*
    219

Chapter 13   219
Life as a Broadcaster: Research Trips to Germany, The Arctic Circle, Poland, and exploring the Life of Malcolm Lowry   219
1979-83   219

1980   *223*
1981   *226*
1982   *230*
1983   *232*
    240

Chapter 14   240
Biographer by Way of Journalism   240
1983-1987   240

1986   *252*
1987   *257*
    260

PART TWO	260
Chapter 15	260
My First Biography	260
1984-1993	260
1985	*262*
1986	*263*
1987	*263*
1988	*268*
1989	*281*
1990	*283*
1991	*284*
1992	*285*
1993	*287*
	290
Chapter 16	290
My First and Second Biographies	290
1993-2000	290
1993	*290*
1994	*294*
1995	*299*
1996	*303*
1997	*309*
1998	*331*
1999	*360*
2000	*389*

INDEX	**Error! Bookmark not defined.**
BIBLIOGRAPHY	I
Works:	I
TV BROADCASTS	III
Rediffusion Television	III
Thames Television	III
British Broadcasting Corporation (BBC)	IV
Canadian Broadcasting Corporation (CBC)	IV
RADIO BROADCASTS	VI
OTHER WORKS	X

PART ONE

Chapter 1

In London, in Hospital and at Death's Door

1961

That day in London, 23 March 1961, I had no idea that I could have less than three days to live. I was aware, of course, that since leaving University the previous July, weighed down by the nagging belief that I had fallen well short of what I might have achieved, I had been neglecting my health. But the idea that it might go into a steep nosedive had never entered my head. The bad things that happened to others didn't happen to me. If a cowl skeleton, carrying a huge scythe, had appeared in front of me at midnight, I would have imagined he had come to the wrong address.

The mild shakes, sweats and the nagging ankle pain I'd had for the past week hadn't bothered me that much. I had put them all down to cross-country running - a pointless activity I had taken up quite recently in a half-hearted attempt to forget that, having landed myself in a small country town too far from the madding crowd, I was feeling isolated from the rest of humankind and desperate to escape from a lousy dead-end job in a dead-end school. These stabbing pains at my lower joints would, I felt sure, gradually wear

GLIMPSES OF A BIOGRAPHER'S DIARY

off after I returned to my attic flat in Torquay. But, not for the first or last time in my life, I was deluding myself.

Friday, 24 March. In London early afternoon. Everything has gone wrong. This is not how it was supposed to be. I am as close to being depressed as I can remember. It's a feeling of sadness, of loss, as if something which had once offered the prospect of intense, long-lasting contentment, had suddenly been snatched from me. A bed in a cheap hotel is not the best place for anyone in pain and I barely slept all last night. The aching joints have become worse, the ankle has seized up and I've been dragging myself along ever since I arrived in London. Somehow, the sense of failure, which has been haunting me for the past nine months has come to rest in my lower limbs. The right leg now belongs to someone else; the pain, however, is all my own. Yet, despite this, I've no sense that there's anything very seriously wrong. I've had a badly-sprained ankle before; in a few days it'll be fine.

I twiddle my thumbs, count backwards from 100, silently recite Shakespearean soliloquies, relive scenes from favourite films, then idly try to piece together the events of the day so far. Just a few hours ago, I'd hobbled from the underground station at Westminster into the St. James's Park. The early spring weather had lured the lunchtime crowd - mostly civil servants from Whitehall offices, I imagined, soldiers from the nearby barracks, and a few wide-eyed visitors like me - to bathe in the gentle warmth of a pale midday sun.

To the amusement of a handful of curious passers-by, just across Birdcage Walk, on their parade ground through the trees, a small detachment of guards in scarlet tunics and tall black busbies marched stiffly to and fro like clockwork manikins, shouted at by other manikins in scarlet tunics and tall black busbies. Suddenly, at a word of command, they turned on a sixpence, rifles at the slope,

1961

hobnail boots crashing onto tarmac, and marched stiffly back the way they had come. The people in the park - the soldiers, the civil servants and their typists - were parading along pathways or reclining on manicured lawns, taking the air or lolling around in deckchairs - the men with their sleeves rolled up, eying the girls basking and blinking at the sun or posing like film stars for imaginary cameras. Gents in bowlers, proudly swinging furled umbrellas, strode purposefully along. Perambulators propelled by neatly-uniformed nannies, glided to and fro. But for now, it was a well-rehearsed drama to be watched with amusement - St James's theatre in the park. Then, suddenly, between Horse Guards Parade and the lake, a jazz band of undergrads in straw hats struck up - swingin' the blues - vo-de-o-doh, the Theme Park Dream Park Green Park Rag. It was one of those days to lift the heart and lighten the step - a fairy tale world of trees and flowers, duck lake and real chocolate soldiers: an idyllic day - sunshine, gentle breeze, and dancing music. I must have been the only one around, who didn't feel buoyant - hungover and cloaked in gloom as I was that day, and for the worst nine months of my life.

University was meant to be the springboard from which to vault off in pursuit of a dream - in my case a life in books: a writer of books, surrounded by books - instead of which I had belly-flopped, gripped by a misplaced sense of familial duty and pitched headlong into a slough of despond. In other words, at a key moment in my life, I had completely screwed up - an indifferent degree, a dutiful but demoralising return home, and finally that school in Paignton where I was teaching and from which I had given in my notice because I was so unhappy and dissatisfied.

My feet dragged me across the park, past the duck lake to a deserted green-painted bench onto which I sat exhausted, looking on in slightly dazed wonderment at the passing show. To me, nervy, perspiring and unsteady on aching limbs as I was, this festive Shangri-la of girls and jazz and soldier-boys seen as if through smudged lenses, was no more than a scene conjured from some long-forgotten cinematic reverie or a painting once seen in a Paris art gallery. I glanced at my watch and left the green bench to hobble back along Birdcage Walk. The ankle pain was still there - intensifying, nagging at my nerve endings - so that reducing it to a dull pulsating ache would require a concentrated effort of will.

Big Ben struck the three quarters and there was barely time to make it to Old Queen Street. The world was just slightly out of focus. I stood stock still at the edge of the park. Where was I going exactly? I took the letter from my pocket to check the address and the map provided, then moved off. I tottered across Birdcage Walk and walked gingerly down the steps. Then there was the sign - 'Old Queen Street'. Further along, and finally, I spied the sign for Tothill Street. Where was I was supposed to be heading? Caxton House? And there was Caxton House. My head was full of strange voices - echoes from the park, echoes from the hotel, echoes from long-ago. But now I heard the heavy, ominous creak of the black-painted door in front of me. Rusty hinges. Inside, a handwritten sign saying, 'Medical Research Council Interviews: Top Floor'.

I arrived, panting. Stand still. Let the pain subside. Slow deep breaths. Sit where told to sit and wait until called. From beyond the door to the left came mumbling - a rival being politely grilled. The voices paused and a woman in severely-cut grey suit emerged to stare at me briefly from behind pebble glasses, before leaving without a word, her heels clattering down the stairs until the big street door banged behind her. Another pause, then a man in a neat black suit emerged to usher me inside. I stood up, braced myself and, trying with a great effort to look smart, stepped through the open door.

1961

Inside was a stage set - an audience of five waiting behind a long, polished table with a solitary seat placed in front for a solitary performer. From stage left a somewhat haggard young man, his face drained of blood, had entered, holding himself very upright, as tense as a prisoner about at last to put himself up into the dock. I sat and faced the panel. In the distance I could hear voices questioning; the thin murmur of my replies. I was droning on a bit too much, but oddly enough, from the faces of the interviewing committee, I seemed to be making some sort of an impression. Even so, I was well aware that I was burning up what final reserves of adrenalin I still had in me. The interview was over, and, amazingly enough, it seemed to have gone well, though by then I realised I didn't actually want this job. Three men and two women (all doctors and medical research staff, I imagined) were scribbling importantly. After a while, the chairman looked up, smiling. 'One final question, Mr. Bowker. How is your health?'

'Fine,' I said.

'Well, thank you for coming.'

I stood up, gasped and promptly collapsed, my face contorted. The ankle had exploded. I had become deaf with pain and surrendered gratefully to the pull of friendly gravity. The faces behind the table gazed down at me in astonishment. Then they came hurrying over with cries of concern - the chairman of the committee, the two women and the other two men gathering round, murmuring, looking anxious.

'What is it?'

'My ankle,' I said, pointing.

One of them phoned for a taxi and I was helped down the stairs. In no time a taxi drew up.

GLIMPSES OF A BIOGRAPHER'S DIARY

'Take this man to the nearest hospital,' said the chairman. The next thing I knew, I was sprawled in the back of the taxi. I glancing weakly over my shoulder at the faces on the doorstep. That's the last I would see of that committee, I was sure - the last I'd hear of their job in far-flung Aberdeen. I was beginning to fall asleep when a voice shook me awake. Westminster Hospital. Accident Admissions… Nothing to pay guv,' said the taxi driver, helping me out.

Diary: Now, here I've been waiting for two hours on a hard bench in a long corridor. I'm quite alone. The only person I have seen so far is the nurse who took my name and told me to wait. No accidents to admit this afternoon, it seems; no emergencies to bring the nurses and doctors running. It's 24 March 1961, or so an abandoned newspaper along the bench reminds me. 'Born this day,' it says at the bottom of a column, 'Harry Houdini.' I'm trembling slightly, but for me there's no escape. A nurse in a smart blue uniform wearing a starched white cap comes towards me. 'Is there a doctor?' I ask.

'Oh, there's a party this afternoon. But I expect he'll be along soon.'

The pain in my ankle is now getting worse. The whole leg is throbbing and I've broken into a sweat. For no reason in particular, I feel close to tears. I am trying to forget the wasted months - the torture of Paignton - the school for unteachables - an overwhelming sense of impotence and failure culminating in that histrionic fall from the lowest rung of the educational ladder. After a long time counting the minutes and the seconds, a young house doctor in suede shoes, shows up, still struggling into his white coat, and slightly drunk. He's about my age, I suppose.

'Been waiting long?' he asks.

1961

'A couple of hours.'

'Sorry, Friday afternoon is usually quiet around here.'

He invites me into a curtained-off cubicle - a short journey, yet I barely make it. I sit down on the edge of a sort of operating table.

'What seems to be the trouble?'

'My right ankle.'

'Let's take a look. Take off your shoe.'

I do so with difficulty. That shoe had been tightening slowly but surely, and my foot feels as though it's been suddenly released from the deathly grip of a monstrous python.

'Can you wriggle the foot?'

'It's very stiff and painful.'

'Strip off and lie down,' he says. 'Here's a gown.' He throws me a sort of nightgown and leaves.

When he returns I'm lying in this flimsy garment on an examination bed. He takes my pulse and temperature then starts to prod around my stomach and groin. Quite suddenly he seems awake and sober.

'Just a minute. I'll get a colleague to take a look.'

He leaves and I am again left wondering.

The young houseman returns. This time he brings in another doctor - similar age, also in a white coat, with a stethoscope around his neck. The two of them converse in whispers, glancing sideways in my direction. The second man prods where the first one had prodded. They go outside. More hushed mumbling.

GLIMPSES OF A BIOGRAPHER'S DIARY

When the first doctor returns he asks, 'Where do you live, Mr. Bowker?'

'Torquay,' I tell him. 'I'm up in London for a job interview.'

He places his stethoscope on my chest. 'Do you have to go home tonight?'

'You've found something, haven't you?' I say.

'We can't find your spleen,' he murmurs in a voice that sounds remarkably offhand, and he smiles as if sharing an interesting observation with a colleague. 'What does that mean?

'I think it'd be better if you stayed with us tonight, just for observation.'

'But I'm supposed to get the seven-thirty train from Paddington.'

'I wouldn't worry about that,' he says. 'You can always go back home tomorrow.

Is there anyone who should be informed that you'll be staying here overnight?'

'No. I live alone.'

'Your parents?'

'Certainly not!'

He seemed slightly surprised at my tone, so I say, 'Neither of them is well and they're bound to come up here, which would do no good at all. Anyway, I'll be returning home tomorrow.'

I give them my friend, Michael's, number. It's the only one I've remembered.

'What about your job?'

1961

'I've just resigned from teaching. I'm a free man.'

He smiles faintly and says, 'Don't bother to get dressed. We'll get you to a ward.' If he asks me to walk now I'll probably collapse again. My right ankle is throbbing and there are shooting pains all along my leg. Two porters lift me onto a trolley and I'm wheeled down corridors and taken into a lift. Finally, I'm in another curtained-off cubicle with a pretty nurse poised over me, wielding a hypodermic syringe and needle. When she jabs it into my buttock I scream. My whole body - skin, muscle and bone - has turned into a raw nerve, alive to the slightest touch, and the needle, a red-hot dart, strikes like the fatal sting of an angry Triffid.

'What is that stuff?' Now I'm shaking as well as sweating. The nurse smiles faintly. 'Penicillin,' she says. 'You'll get used to it.'

'Get used to it! But I'm supposed to be going home tomorrow.' She smiles again and says no more.

Now, suddenly my wrists are aching and I can do nothing with my hands. What's happening to me? Something is taking me over, and my whole body seems paralysed with pain. Movement has become excruciating and agonising. Shortly afterwards, the nurse is sitting me up and holding out a small dish with two large pills and what looks like a little sideways teapot. She asks me to pop the pills in my mouth then proffers the teapot spout, saying, 'Drink and swallow.' Meekly, I obey. She leaves the cubicle and by the time she returns I'm already feeling low.

'What's wrong with me? Do you know?'

'You'll be all right,' she says.

By this time, I don't care anymore and the pains in my wrist and ankle seem suddenly to have left me. But sweat is streaming out of me and dripping from my face. As consciousness slowly fades, I want to sleep forever.

25 March. Wakefulness comes only gradually. I try to sit up but can't. In fact, I can barely move. I'm trapped, with arms and legs suspended from straps attached to bars at the sides of the bed, which have now been raised to form a kind of cage. I'm pinned down, peering through bars. The bed, has been transformed into a cot, a baby's cradle, and I'm tied down like Gulliver in a real-life Lilliput. Houdini would have known how to get out of this, I'm thinking. A needle has been inserted into a vein on the back of my left hand and a bottle suspended above my bed. Three doctors in white coats and a middle-aged nurse wearing a pretty lace cap stand looking down at me, conversing in low voices. I can now see that the blind is drawn behind my head. It must be night. I hear the faint rattle of cutlery.

I want to speak but my mouth is dry, like old parchment.

'Doctor,' I croak.

One of the three turn to me.

'Yes, Mr. Bowker?'

'I'm supposed to be getting the train back to Torquay today. When can I leave?'

He gives me the faint smile, 'You're not very well. Best thing is for you to stay here with us for a little longer.' The doctors leave, still conversing in low voices. The older nurse wearing the lace cap calls in a younger one, 'We're putting you into a single room, Gordon,' she says. 'You need complete rest and quiet. If you need anything, there is a bell right beside you. On no account must you try to reach for a glass of water or anything else for that matter. The nurse will bring whatever you need.' She turns to the young person standing beside her.

'Make sure he doesn't exert himself, nurse.'

'Yes, Sister.'

I am wheeled into a single room just inside the entrance to a large ward but shut away from it. The nurse charged with my care hooks me to a drip, pours water from a jug on the bedside table into a cup with a spout, then offers me a handful of pills to swallow and a swig of water from the spout to wash them down. She lifts my gown, produces a hypodermic syringe and needle from a bowl on the bedside locker, and jabs. This time my scream is muffled.

Then, 'Drink this,' she says.

I say. 'It's foul. Good God! The poisoned cup!' She removes the medicine dispenser gently from my clenched fist.

'What is this stuff?' I ask.

'Iodine – for your thyroid.' She is busily straightening my bedclothes.

'My thyroid! What's wrong with it?'

'It's got just a little out of control.'

'God!' My voice is suddenly weak. Weariness has begun to overcome me. 'I … I'll never get that disgusting taste out of my mouth - never …never.' Strength is ebbing. Words are mumbled, low moans transform into heavy sighs. The nurse produces a dish with more pills and the glass of water to wash them down. I can barely swallow. I feel myself drifting in a dream I see more nurses gathered in a corner of my room, backs turned. Sister is joined by two doctors. They mutter together in hushed voices. Occasionally they look over their shoulders in my direction. One shakes his head. Slowly I become stupefied. I drift into a world of ghosts. Dead friends and dead enemies rise from their graves and bear down on me. Hands reach out to seize me and I scream. But my scream is silent. The whole world has gone silent. Everything is white, white light. Faces converge, heads shake. Now slowly the light is fading and faces are engulfed in shadow. The pain has gone and I am drifting on a sea of darkness, slipping down into that nothingness, drowning in it, drifting quite naturally but barely perceptibly upwards towards an ever-receding surface.

26 March. Suddenly, I'm struggling to sit upright - as upright as my strapped limbs permit. 'Torturers!' I yell. The same doctors are still standing by the door, poring over a chart. They glance over at me. The sister comes across and gently lays me back against my damp pillows. One nurse comes to the other side of my bed. 'Hush,' she says quietly. Sweat-soaked sheets … wrestling with invisible presences … pain. A new nurse looms, injection at the ready. She hovers hawk-like, then stabs.

Day becomes night and night becomes day. Again, sleep closes in. I'm being borne along on a dark cloud … a peaceful suspension… deep in a happy, thoughtless sleep … hanging … weightless … breathless … floating through time … a silent ship … a black sail … a voyage of no return … drifting off into night … drifting down into the heart of darkness.

30 March. I'm wide awake and no longer sweating. Sunlight is slanting in from the window behind me. 'How's the miracle man?' Sister asked taking my pulse. She's wearing the pretty lace cap. Her sleeves are short, her arms look strong and brown and she wears puffy starched white cuffs just above her elbows.

1961

'Open,' she says. A thermometer is shaken then popped into my mouth. She takes my wrist, looks at her watch then writes on a clipboard, frowning slightly.

'We thought we'd lost you.' Her voice is matter-of-fact, but tinged with wonderment. She removes the thermometer, reads it and jots something down.

I laugh weakly. 'Lost me? I can't go anywhere tied down like this.' She looks pleased and bustles off.

Two young nurses remain. They stare and smile. The one in glasses says, 'Sister told us last night not to be upset if you weren't here this morning.' The other, with blonde curly hair arranged in a halo, says, 'We thought the porters would have wheeled you away.' The nurse in glasses says, 'I prayed for you all last night, in the chapel.'

'Prayed for me? But I'm an atheist.'

'More reason to pray,' she says, and produces a fully-charged hypodermic syringe and needle. The pain of the jab hardly registers. In slow motion the blonde angel frowns and turns her back. A sense of deep pleasure slowly envelopes my whole worked-out body, knowing that the porters hadn't wheeled me away.

1 April. The blonde angel wakes me with a brisk 'Good morning, Gordon. How did you sleep?' I open my mouth to reply and she pops in a handful of pills.

'Drink this!'

Obediently I swallow water from the glass. I see that my straps have been removed. The good Lilliputians have set me free. 'Can I sit up?'

GLIMPSES OF A BIOGRAPHER'S DIARY

'Not yet.' She is business-like and puts a gentle hand on my chest. 'Please lie still. That's why we've left your legs tied down. If you need anything, remember, just push the bell that is beside you.'

'No more of that poison you were forcing me to drink, I hope.'

'No more of that. It did its work.'

'Which was what?'

'Dampened down your thyroid.'

'The flaming thyroid has been dampened.'?

'It has.' She smiles.

'Thank God!'

She produces the syringe and needle. 'Now it's cortisone.'

'What's that?

'Doctor's orders,' she says brusquely.

I wince. 'Can I pass off the injection for once?'

'The doctors will be around soon. You don't want them to be told you are refusing treatment.'

I groan. 'O.K. I surrender. What have I got exactly?' My voice sounds faint, the words slurred and distant.

'You'll have to ask Dr Tonkin,' she says. 'He's only one of the best in the country. You're lucky to have him looking after you.'

Something is puzzling me. 'What brings on this thyroid business?'

'Stress mostly,' she says.

'God! That figures. Those bloody school kids! 'At least I didn't have a nervous breakdown,' I say.

'Well no. But that's how it is with some people. You broke down physically rather than mentally.'

'Lucky old me!' I say, in what is meant to be a self-mocking tone.

'You are lucky!' she says. 'I'm not supposed to tell you, but you're the first patient we've ever known to go into Cheyne-Stokes breathing and survived.'

'What?'

'Heart failure,' she says, breathing deeply and desperately to demonstrate.

'For a while you were dead.'

That silences me and I remain silent as she gives me a bed bath.

'How often have you done this?' I ask, finally and weakly.

'Every day since you were admitted,' she says.

I blush. 'I never noticed.'

'You were usually half asleep.'

She runs a comb through my hair and tidies the bed. I'm still trying to take in what she told me about my being dead when Dr Tonkin and his entourage appear. He's a tall man with an air of serene self-confidence and inner certitude that radiates, as probably it acts on all his patients, like a gentle tranquiliser. I smile up at him.

'Can you tell me what's wrong with me, Doctor?'

'You've been very ill indeed, Mr. Bowker. You have had a thyroid crisis complicated by acute rheumatic fever and acute carditis.'

GLIMPSES OF A BIOGRAPHER'S DIARY

'Good God! How does one get such things?' I ask.

'Over-active thyroid most likely from passing through a period of stress; acute rheumatic fever and acute carditis from the streptococcus bacterium. Have you had a sore throat recently?'

'Yes, I had a raging one a few weeks ago. My GP told me to go away and suck a throat pastille.'

His smile turns just a fraction frosty and he says, 'Well, we're taking care of you now,' and very briskly he and his entourage pass on.

———

Chapter 2

In Hospital and Recovering

Mike (my old National Service chum) visits, bringing with him our mutual friend James Thurber, famous American cartoonist, and is now perched on my bed wearing a knowing, half-mocking smile. Mike and I did our time together in Egypt, camped out alongside de Lesseps' Suez Canal, with grains of sand dancing and swirling along, about, above and beneath everything. Grains in your hair, in your eyes, inside your ears - like swarming flies, omnipresent, relentless, impossible to brush away. Another needle. I drift off into a sandstorm of memories, and Mike, like a phantom, drifts into view, kitted out in tropical khaki, ready for inspection - small beads of sweat forming on his brow, glistening - a halo of diamonds. I'm humming along with him - an air from La Bohème. I catch the blonde nurse also humming along. She looks down at me and winks.

'What's this?' I wake with a start. The red-faced houseman, Dr Chester, is holding up Mike's present between finger and thumb. 'Thurber!' he sneers. The contempt in his voice cuts through the sound of the hospital stirring. His voice is shrill. 'Are you a lefty?' He glances down at me as if I have no right to be where I am. 'If any of these peacenik marchers and their lefty friends come in here with sore feet they'll get short shrift from me.' The voice turns more threatening. 'You should read something improving - like Ian Hemingway's James Bond.' If I were to laugh out loud I'd probably do myself an injury, so I content myself by just laughing to myself. Ian Hemingway's *James Bond*!

1 - Mike (centre walking towards the camera with shoulder strap) with Gordon in Cairo

There's a new nurse. She has a radiance and is very beautiful and smiling, and in some form Asian. Nurse Peters is a mixture - 'a bit of this and a bit of that', she explains. She seems to have read my mind about Dr Chester, telling me that I owe a lot to the irritable young houseman. 'He sat up all night working on your drugs chart - working out the doses,' she says. 'Then, suddenly, around four o'clock, he realised he'd got something wrong, so he just tore up the whole chart and began all over again. He probably saved your life.'

I think, 'God! I owe my life to an angry young fogey of the fascist persuasion, who thinks a man called Hemingway wrote the James Bond novels!'

But the doctors all say, 'You owe your life to the nurses.'

I'm thinking, 'Angels of mercy in blue uniforms and frilly white caps.'

'Tell me about your white caps,' I say.

'We're Nightingale Nurses,' says Nurse Begley, the angel with glasses who prayed for me all night. There's a note of pride in her voice as she says this.

'Nurse Begley's father's a vicar,' says the sweet young probationer, when she is left alone with me for a moment. She's Welsh and her name, she tells me, is Molly.

'What's your father?' I ask.

'He's a coal miner.'

'So, they both spend their lives on their knees trying to bring warmth to us shivering sinners,' I say, and she giggles.

Nurse Begley returns to give me yet another injection. It's still unspeakable agony but now I'm more resigned to the pain. It's becoming a companion, almost a friend.

GLIMPSES OF A BIOGRAPHER'S DIARY

'More of the same?' I ask.

'It's cortisone. The same as usual,' she says

'And what does cortisone do exactly?'

'It's for the inflammation.'

'What inflammation?'

'You've got acute rheumatic fever,' she says. 'All your joints are inflamed.'

'And Dr Tonkin and Dr Bayliss think that living where you do probably hasn't helped,' says Nurse Begley.

'Bayliss?'

'The endocrinologist, who saw you when you first came in.'

'So what's all this about Torquay?'

'It's the Mediterranean climate in that part of the world - heat and moisture. That's what they think could have helped bring it on. Anyway,' she says, straightening my blankets, 'rheumatic fever is rheumatic fever, wherever it comes from, at whatever age and that's what we're treating you for.'

'That and the thyroid?'

'That had to be dampened down before the other could be dealt with.'

'Quenching the flames, eh? But how can I tell if it's working? You have strapped my legs down.'

'You are not supposed to exert yourself. It's to rest your heart.'

'Surrounded by beautiful nurses?' I say 'Impossible.'

1961

The vicar's daughter frowns, disapproving.

'So, when do I get out of here?'

'Not just yet. But the good news is, no more injections from today.'

'Alleluia!'

'It will be just pills from now on.'

'From now on till when?'

But she's gone, and my question remains unanswered. What I really want to know is when will I be free to walk back out into the teeming, sunlit jazz-band playing in London of which I'd had just the briefest glimpse.

For the time being, routine prevails - pills and potions, nurses and needles, doctors' rounds and rounds and rounds, and visits from various women with mobile heart machines, and brisk men asking for blood. And so, life creeps by, slowly, invisibly, silently, relentlessly and with interest.

9 April. Today, everything changes. The doctors seem pleased, the nurses seem pleased, even the cardiographers seem more cheerful. Without much warning, I and my bed are wheeled out into the regimented chaos of the general ward - called Austin Taylor after some Liberal worthy, who put up the money for it, according to one of the nurses. But my first impression is how organised, and how disciplined it all seems - this small army of nurses straight out of bandboxes, not a hair out of place - blue uniforms, black belts, black stockings, flat sensible shoes, starched white aprons and white caps. And there goes the frilly Nightingale hat, worn by the head nurses. Hovering over them, Head of House in dark blue, is Sister, bustling no-nonsense Sister. Head Mistress is Matron - stately, who sails occasionally into view like a ghost ship, moving

mysteriously in and out and around, looming like the eminence she is. When she is spotted on the horizon even Sister stops bustling and pays attention.

The presence of so many young nurses is a shock, albeit a pleasant shock, to my nervous system. Angela had been my girl for eight years, but when that entanglement ended in a maelstrom of misunderstandings, I had been lured away to hopeless and pointless duties in distant Paignton. Once I had departed the scene it didn't take Angela long to find a stand in. Life for me had become a celibate desert, without even a mirage of female presence for consolation in sight. Now suddenly, in a flash, I was surrounded by feminine divinities, ministering readily to my every need. At the same time, I was being enjoined by doctors to rest my heart. Where was the injection against inflammation of the passions?

As I'm wheeled through the big ward door, still hooked to a bottle, heads turn. An old man with one eye waves from his bed in the middle of the ward and grins, revealing a single tooth; a middle-aged man lying flat, turns his head to take in this new arrival, then smiles wanly, offering a feeble salutation; a young fellow chuckles and says in a broad Yorkshire accent, 'Here comes another wounded soldier.' Then it's my turn to grin warmly and offer a wave. In here, men of all conditions are lying - the unfortunate and the wretched – levelled by fate or misfortune to the strange camaraderie of men struck down by age or virus, organ-failure, from a life-long pursuit of pain or pleasure, or both.

My destination is a bed tucked away in the far corner at the end of the ward, next to the window. For the time being I'm parked in this hideaway probably, because I'll be here for longer than most of the others. From somewhere nearby comes an organ concerto of wheezing and coughing. Next to me (or so it seems from the fruity accents) is a big man with a red face gives me a cheery 'Hello there,' in broad cockney. In an inner square of beds I see a tall bearded figure, then to the right a very blonde middle-aged man, and over there to the left, sitting on his bed, a stocky, bald-headed figure with large tattooed arms and his girlfriend. I shall call him the Pirate King. He's perfect for the part. Now, finally, I can take in the whole ward, my new world, the moving scene I could only imagine in the seclusion of my side ward, listening to distant noises and voices and rattling trolleys.

Nurses bustle around purposefully. Morning routine - crack of dawn - woken by lights and yawns and grunts and murmurings - bed-pans and bottles, mouthwash, soap and flannel, face-wash, tooth-brush, shave, then, for those of us forbidden to move, the bed bath by a business-like nurse, who, in a final ritual, hands the flannel to the patient for him to 'finish off'. Shortly afterwards, breakfast is delivered by jolly women, fluent in the art of cockney badinage. 'You've got no meat on your bones, love,' says one. 'We're going to have to fatten you up.' She laughs. Beds are stripped and remade. Fresh sheets, fresh bodies, fresh aches and pains. Afterwards, things begin to speed up. Beds are pushed to the middle of ward, floor is swept, washed and dried, the strong odour of disinfectant lingers in the air. All this in preparation for the daily grand inspection by the big chief in the white coat.

The red-faced gent in the adjoining bed, reeking of hair-oil, is Bill, a tic-tac man from a London dog track. He's been treated for stomach ulcer, but is being kept in with unusually high blood-pressure. As soon as my curtains are finally drawn back, he greets me and almost at once regaling me with tips about greyhounds, gambling, bookies, betting, and advising me that I'd do very well for myself by taking up a career like his. What's more, he offers to teach me the business, sitting on the edge of his bed waving arms, juggling fingers and thumbs in a mystifying display, and bursting a blood vessel in the process, shouting the odds by way of translation. But I am hardly an apt pupil; I have barely the strength to raise a finger. Bill is forbidden alcohol, his medicine of choice, so his good wife smuggles in bottles of vodka that he has cunning means of concealing and which, he slyly informs me, with a heavy wink, leaves not a sniff on his breath nor a whiff of it in the air around. Bill's persistent high blood pressure mystifies both doctors and nurses. I could enlighten them, but am not going to snitch on this jovial, good-hearted bookie. 'Honest Bill' teaches me how to make a Bombay Oyster - hair of the greyhound - raw egg and vinegar, swallowed at one gulp. And every morning, even on the ward, this sick man, banned from booze, still downs one vinegary 'oyster' with almost religious ceremony. Bill talks about being in the Palestine Police and waxes salacious recalling a busty Jewish girl, who visited him daily at his camp. He finally leaves us when the nurses and doctors give up on him. Off he goes with his vodka, his tic-tac talk, his high blood pressure and his cockney wife, not to mention his lurid memories of old Jerusalem. He leaves the echo of a broad London Cockney behind him.

12 April. Someone on the ward reads aloud from a newspaper. 'Russians send Yuri Gagarin into space, so trumping Americans and their dummy sent up in early March.'

'Blimey! What a turn-up,' says the gentleman who is a heart-case in the next row.

'Another American triumph,' mutters his neighbour.

Bill's bed is taken by a grinning, young medical student called Geoff, from up Yorkshire way. Geoff's eyes light on me and then light up behind his heavy horn-rimmed spectacles. He reveals a set of exceedingly white teeth and laughs loudly and sadistically, as if anticipating some fun to lessen his boredom. Geoff has suspected

1961

glandular fever, but he's up and about most of the time, sidling up to the nurses and teasing them in the gently thuggish way of a man drunk on a cocktail of oversized ego and exaggerated bonhomie. Suddenly, he turns his attention to the chart hooked to the rail at the foot of my bed. He snatches it up and starts reading it. His eyes open in exaggerated horror, and he begins to laugh out loud.

'I know what's wrong with you,' he chortles, shaking his head and grinning. 'I must take a look at your notes sometime.' Later, somehow, he does manage to peek at my notes and comes back into the ward gloating.

He sits on the edge of my bed and shakes his head. 'Rheumatic fever, Eh?' He's trying to look and sound doctorly, but in a slightly exaggerated, pantomimic way. 'You'll begin having heart attacks by the time you're forty,' he says. 'After that, you could snuff it at any time - just like that. Poof!' He snaps his fingers, beaming and leering and staring - hoping, no doubt, for a reaction. What did I do to deserve this? I give him a resigned look, but Geoff hasn't finished with me yet.

'Thyroid out of control as well as the rheumatic fever, if I'm not mistaken. No wonder you look so skeletal. You're just a bag of bones, really. I'd keep away from mirrors if I were you.' He pauses and smirks knowingly. 'And,' he says, delivering this last salvo with barely-suppressed delight, 'they've also given you a Wassermann Test. Aha!'

'What's that?'

He shakes his head, trying to look grave. 'No, it'd probably give you that heart attack if I tell you.' He grins smugly and starts ogling the nurses, swaggering round the ward like Mr. Punch on vacation, reading patients' charts and laughing to himself. He's decked out in a jazzy pair of pyjamas and an equally colourful dressing gown.

'Come live with me and be my love.' Geoff howls out his love call to a passing nurse who gives him a cold stare.

'Fine words butter no parsnips here, Geoff.'

'Like to bet?' He flashes his perfect incisors, faces me from the edge of his bed, and starts showing off his newly-acquired medical wisdom: 'Know the worst branch of medicine?'

'No idea.'

'Neurology.' He laughs. 'Why? No cures,' and he laughs even louder

I pretend to be impressed.

'Know the secret of good medicine?'

'Haven't a clue.'

He slowly intones the answer, 'The secret of all good medicine is diagnosis, diagnosis and diagnosis.'

But then his attention is distracted.

'Look at her!' He drools at the sight of the new young nurse. 'I could do things with

her.'

'What are the causes of glandular fever, Geoff?'

'It's the kissing disease,' says the Sister who has just arrived on the scene.

'Now, Geoffrey, just behave! And keep well away from my young nurses!'

1961

Geoff subsides onto his bed, grinning sheepishly. To everyone's relief, next morning his test results are through. Suddenly he's dressed and on his way, with a cheery wave.

Sunday, and hard on the heels of the bed bath, in comes the Padre, bringing glad tidings of great joy to his captive congregation. He's smoothly dressed, shaven, and is famous. 'The BBC Padre', they call him. He circulates round the ward, from patient to patient, perching on beds, nodding, murmuring, bestowing blessings. I can see that it's a routine with him. He could probably do it in his sleep. 'Hello, and how are you today?'

How many wards will he pass through this morning, I wonder? He pauses at my bed, glances at my chart, sees that at the top of it is written 'RELIGION: NONE', then, smiling smoothly, he passes on.

I call him back. 'Padre. Why did you pass me by?'

He smiles broadly. 'Your chart tells me you're an unbeliever. Are you not?'

'I am. But isn't it your job to at least attempt to save sinners like me from the bottomless pit - just in case I shuffle off this mortal coil unshriven, which I could at any moment - or so I'm told?'

The smile remains, frozen. 'I'll drop by to see you tomorrow,' he says, and, smiling fixedly, sails smoothly on.

The tall haggard-looking man with a black beard from the row in front of me approaches and settles himself on the end of my bed.

'Know what's wrong with me?'

I shake my head.

'I'm dying of cancer, and I only got married three months ago.'

GLIMPSES OF A BIOGRAPHER'S DIARY

'Oh! I'm sorry to hear it.' I say.

'They're sending me home this weekend.'

'That's good news, isn't it?'

'Good news!' His laugh is hollow and his face remains expressionless. 'I used to be a journalist with the News Chronicle - even published a couple of books. I overheard you and the Padre, so I thought this might interest you.' He has a slim volume in his hand, which he offers to me.

'Thank you. Thanks very much.'

The book has a blue cover. I glance at the title. It's called Catholic, Protestant or Jew. The name beneath the title tells me he is Frederick Lorimer. He smiles sadly and retreats to his bed. Later, his wife arrives to take him home. She's wildly pretty, looks about eighteen, and very soon, it seems, she'll be a very young and a pretty widow. After Frederick has gone, one of the nurses is straightening my bedclothes and I ask her about him. 'It's a very sad story,' she tells me in a low faltering voice. 'He's a Catholic and believes he was meant to suffer for past sins, so he refuses analgesics. He must be in the most excruciating pain. We've sent him home because he has so little time left, and there's nothing more we can do for him.'

'It's called mortification of the flesh,' I said quietly. 'It goes with certain beliefs.'

Molly, the young probationer, on night duty for the first time, comes over for a quiet chat in the middle of the night. She's very sweet-natured as well as very Welsh, a favourite among the men on the ward. She's happy to park herself on the end of the bed and exchange gossip in hushed whispers during the night. She's especially friendly with the Swede at the end of the row in front.

1961

He comes to see me one evening. He's just been allowed up, and is walking around talking with whomsoever is inclined to listen. I am deeply envious.

'My wife and I have plans to travel,' he says. He looks too sleek and well-fed to be ill.

'How exciting. Where do you plan to go?'

'We thought we might try Japan. My wife's a keen photographer.'

He talks of plans and places I can only dream about. I see his wife at visiting time - a handsome young woman gleaming with health and vitality.

I'm waiting for Molly as usual. Tonight, she's late. The ward is deathly silent except for the heavy breathing of the men in the two middle rows - all of them heart cases. Very late, almost at daybreak, Molly arrives and sits on my bed.

She's shaking.

'What's up?'

'It's Mr. Peterson.'

'Yes.'

She begins to weep. 'He just died. Right in front of me. He asked for a glass of water, took one sip and just died. And I've never seen a dead person before.'

She's shaking convulsively, and trying desperately to suppress her sobs. I try to comfort her, but I'm also shocked to hear about the Swede.

As dawn slowly starts to penetrate the darkness, the ward begins to stir. One of the first arrivals is the large Jamaican woman who sweeps and cleans the ward every morning. She's very popular, especially with the heart cases at the centre of the ward. 'Hello boys!' she always shouts. They love to tease her, and clearly enjoy her banter and uninhibited whoops of laughter. But this morning, on waking, they've noticed the empty bed from which the lifeless Swede has been silently removed by the porters during the night. The heart boys are unnaturally silent. However, the jolly Jamaican lady doesn't notice anything amiss till she spots the empty bed.

'Where's my friend, Mr. Peterson?' she asks in a loud jovial voice.

It echoes back to her through the silence. No one breathes and finally the penny drops. Her eyes widen, the grin fades and her mouth falls wide open.

'Oh my God!' she screams and quietly leave the ward.

The Pirate King's girlfriend wanders over.

'My Monty wants a word with you,' she says, on her way to the corridor for a fag. Monty lumbers across. He's a bear of a man - looks much too tough and tanned to be a heart case or a diabetic, or anything else for that matter.

'Ere, you look like an educated man. What d'yer think's wrong with me, then?'

'I'm not the best person to ask.' I say. 'I'm not a doctor.'

'Doctors!' he sneers. 'What do they know?'

'A lot more than I do.'

'I bin 'avin' these blackouts, see.'

'Oh, too bad.'

1961

'I dunno what's behind it. My girl's a doctor's receptionist. She wants to look it up in one of 'is medical books.'

'Is that a good idea?' I ask.

'They won't tell me anything, so what've I got to lose?'

Two days later. The Pirate King has been taken to the far end of the ward. He's tied down and the sides of his bed have been raised. But the reality of the ward snaps me out of my reverie. 'What happened to the Pirate King?' I ask.

'Sad story,' says the pretty blonde Nurse. 'He asked his girlfriend to look up his symptoms in the books on the shelves of the doctor she works for, and they pointed to a brain tumour.

When she told him, he had a nervous breakdown, and now the Doctors can't tell whether his symptoms are from the breakdown or from the tumour.'

'Tragic,' I said.

Later, I hear him screaming. I can just make him out at the far end of the ward, tethered to the raised sides of his cot and struggling to free himself. A nurse with a bowl, a towel and a raised syringe attends him. He is sedated and goes limp. Next day, he's raving again, and finally he's wheeled away in the night by the porters. A newly-made bed quickly replaces him.

Today, there's a new presence in my life, the Lady Almoner, Miss Alice Fairfax - comely, handsome, blonde, a gentlewoman of the county set - and she is here, it seems, just for me. She appears to find my case particularly fascinating in fact - listening attentively, beautiful eyes wide open, hanging on every word.

GLIMPSES OF A BIOGRAPHER'S DIARY

'Tell me your story - Gordon, isn't it?' Seductive voice, seductive words. I know she understands and cares, even in my still shattered and vulnerable state. She wants to know all about me and how I came to be admitted to the hospital. 'Well, it's a long story,' I say. But she's so very interested and so very patient, I tell her all. She takes it all in, every detail. She finally left.

Chapter 3

Preparing for Discharge

Mike has visited every day. Good man, Mike! He's brought another book. Wells' Tono-Bungay is sitting at my bedside. He also brings me two notebooks and two new ballpoint pens. I'll make notes and write stories. I ask him to bring me Orwell's essays, the collection which includes a piece on how the poor died gruesomely and by numbers in a pauper's hospital, once upon a time in not-so-good old Paris.

Dr Tonkin is due on his rounds this morning. If blood pressure and pulse are normal, I have been told, I'll be finally scheduled for discharge, back into the roaring streets and out of this Neverland of endless distractions. Two letters came for me. One is from the chairman of the selection committee - a kindly letter, wishing me a swift recovery and saying they would like me to remain in touch for the future. The other begins: 'Dear Gordon....' That handwriting makes my heart freeze and misses a few beats. The pulse is now galloping. The letter, full of memories both painful and delicious, folded back into its envelope, is slipped inside the drawer of the bedside locker - now a chest of lost and stolen dreams.

GLIMPSES OF A BIOGRAPHER'S DIARY

Before Dr Tonkin arrived, Miss Fairfax, Lady Almoner, came and is listening to the story as I retell it. She's been working on my depleted budget and has found ways and means of managing my debts - back-rent for my Torquay attic flat, unpaid instalments for the furniture I acquired on hire purchase, that endless book bill from the university bookshop. I show her Angela's letter.

'Do you still love her?' she asks.

'Love Angela? How could I now? Anyway, she's got herself some Highlander.'

'Can you think why she should write to you now she's married?'

'No.'

She nods. She understands so well. I'm left with Angela's ghost and a racing whirlpool of emotions, memories and imaginings, not all of them very noble. Nurse Begley has come to check my pulse, temperature and blood pressure, while I summon up the effort to forget the haunting Angela, trying by the might of mind over matter to keep my turbulent feelings in order. And here comes Dr Tonkin, at the head of his entourage - Registrar, Housemen, Matron, Sister and Staff Nurse, all here now to pass judgement on this disconcerted medical wreck.

'Good morning Mr. Bowker.'

'Morning doctor.' I'm shaking, dammit.

'And how are you today?' Now being handed my chart. 'Your pulse and blood pressure are quite high this morning, I see.'

'I had an upsetting letter, Doctor.'

'Well, it's our job to make sure you're well enough to receive upsetting letters without your pulse and blood pressure soaring away.'

'So there's no chance of my being considered for discharge today?'

The warm smile conveys fatherly amusement. 'We'd better keep you in a little longer.' He nods his goodbye and sweeps off, drawing his retinue after him as if on invisible strings.

Vernon, who has a heart condition, comes over and sits on my bed. He must be well into his seventies with the voice and command of a man used to being attended to, never questioned or contradicted. He is, beyond these hospital walls, the big Park Lane car dealer and master of hounds. Now he's a worried man. Why? The patient at the end of my row is the source of his concern. A seaman called Potterton, a stoker, is gasping out the last days of a tough life and refusing treatment. The Nurses put an oxygen mask around his neck and over his nose and mouth, and Potterton yanks it off. He doesn't want to live. His lungs are choked with coal dust from a lifetime of feeding the hungry furnaces of rusty freighters on endless seas and oceans linking together a dying Empire. 'Why?' asks Vernon, 'Why doesn't this man want to live? I'm told he's only forty-seven. I just don't understand.'

'Vernon,' I tell him, 'he's spent his life slaving away down inside stokeholds of salt-caked steamships; his lungs are all shot; they won't work. Would you like to live like that?' He looks thoughtful, but still puzzled and, shaking his head, shuffles sadly back to his bed. Vernon's been given the green light. So, now he's ready for 'the off', enjoined by doctors and nurses to take it easy. However, it's obvious, even to me, that he won't. He'll be back in his showrooms in Park Lane tomorrow, driving through his luxury car sales, and trooping off to the country to join the Sussex drag at the weekend. Bon voyage. Vernon goes home next day.

We all listen to the stoker's rasping lungs - like an expiring church organ - hanging on every painful inspiration and wheezing expiration. Suck-blow-suck-blow. His ship is listing and lurching. Port in, starboard out. Then suddenly the lungs are swamped, the heave-ho stops and the nurses quickly draw the curtains round his bed-space. The porters arrive and the no-longer able seaman Potterton is spirited away to join the jolly-rogered Pirate King.

Since Angela's departure, my heart has been left in turmoil and now I've fallen for a new vision. My new focus of fascination is full of charity, bonhomie and strangely infectious laughter, and on top of that she wears the frilly Nightingale lace cap like a veritable halo.

'She's a Bourney,' I'm told by one of her admiring juniors.

'A Bourney?'

'The chocolate people. Famous Quaker family - and prison reformers.'

I am positively fixated on the gorgeous Nurse Bourney. In fact, I am both mysteriously and decidedly besotted. This must be what schoolgirls call a 'crush' and I am well and truly 'crushed'.

'She's very religious,' says the junior.

'I don't care,' I tell myself.

I start talking to her and asking her about herself. She's thinking of leaving nursing and going for a missionary, she says. That would be taxing my love for her exceedingly. She's still talking. She's been for an interview with the London Missionary Society but been turned down. Within days she's confiding to me her great secret.

1961

She got mixed up with a patient, a diabetic and a criminal – a thorough-going bad 'un.... Having attended to his medical ills, Nurse Bourney felt compelled to attend to his spiritual needs - a sinner in need of redemption. They had prayed together over his sickbed and when, after his discharge, he invited her to dinner, she hoped to finally bring him to the faith. They'd knelt together in prayer, and one thing led to another. She had no idea how, she said. Now she had sinful thoughts and she understood therefore why she had not been considered pure enough to meet the uncompromising standards of the Missionary Society Selection Committee.

'How on earth did they know?' I ask.

'I had to tell them,' she replies, on the verge of tears. 'What I'll do now I don't know.'

'No redemption for the sinner?' She has no answer for that sad question.

I write something for her - a long confession of my unbelief, which I hope will arouse her true missionary instincts. I just can't get her out of my feverish mind and find myself watching out for her, with a strange unholy obsession. When will she come? Is she off duty today? The smiling nurses cannot or will not say. No one seems to care. I suffer in silence, pulses racing. Got to keep the rate down or they'll never let me out. But my heart is thumping, too, and I'm sweating. I do worry briefly about this obsession and wonder if there is something strange in that cocktail of pills I am swallowing daily. Is it possible that someone out there is experimenting with me and my still-unstable emotions? Lying in bed all day such idle thoughts do come and go. A jolly laughing nurse is at my bedside with a cup of tea and a large envelope. 'Nurse Bourney asked me to pass this to you.' I grab at the envelope and tear it open. Her eyes grow big. 'Oh,' she says - just like that - and smiling, turns away. Foolscap writing paper crammed with tiny writing. I begin to read. About half way down page one I see what this is - a lengthy refutation of my carefully reasoned justification of disbelief. I plough on. Slowly I begin to grasp her logic - one just has to accept her scriptural premises. 'St Peter says' - and next it's 'according to St Paul'. And now it's the irrefutable word Christ Jesus or God Himself. Just believe them and everything follows.

Come, to your senses for heaven's sake! The nurse is here to take your blood pressure. Nurse Begley, glasses twinkling, stands at my bedside. 'Give me your arm, Gordon.'

Now I'm imagining Nurse Bourney, but allowing nurse Begley to embrace my arm with her blood pressure sleeve. She sets up her gauge, then, squeezing with intense delicacy the bulbous air ball, she inflates the sleeve with slow measured puffs, staring intently as the mercury rises. A slow hiss as the air is released and Begley's eyes sharpen. Finally she unwraps the deflated sleeve.

'Okay?'

'Yes. A little high, but not too much so.' A restless evening and I have to ask for a sleeping pill.

'Hello, Gordon.'

Nurse Bourney! My heart takes a giant leap. Oh, I've missed you!

'Did you read my letter?'

'Several times over.'

'Good. Well, I hope it helped.'

'I'm already rethinking my position.'

1961

'Good. Try to pray for God's help.'

I'm nodding vigorously. There she goes. She floats around the ward, seraphic in her Nightingale cap, a halo of white lace. But she's off on her duties and I'm just one stop on her various rounds. All too often she's not even on the ward. At end of day, as shifts change over.

The procession of bodies flowing through the next bed space has slowed. Now here comes Harry, the man from the City, a smoothly-shaven dealer in money, stocks and shares, in a world of pricey commodities and inflated accounts. Harry is asthmatic. A bad attack. Doctors attend him behind drawn curtains. He seems nervous. As he recovers, he wants to talk. He's tall, handsome, South African and scared of people knowing where he is.

'God, I hope no one finds out.'

'Oh? 'I smile and raise an eyebrow.

Harry is suddenly sitting bolt upright, like a startled rabbit.

'They mustn't know.'

'What?'

'That I'm here.'

'Who?'

'My bosses.'

'Why not?'

'I'd be fired.'

'Fired - for being ill?'

'Yes. You have to be needle-sharp in this business, Gordon. You're fit and razor-keen or you're out! No room for invalids.'

'Good God! But won't they be missing you?'

'I took annual leave at short notice to come in today. They think I'm in Brittany. I just need to be out of here by Monday.'

'Will you be well enough?'

'I'm getting over this attack already. This latest treatment's very good. I'll just leave when I have to.'

I'm stricken with wonder. 'You're a gambler, Harry.'

He doesn't smile, but quickly changes the subject. 'What is it that you do, Gordon?' he asks, focusing his gaze on me

'Schoolteacher,' I say.

'What do they pay you for that?'

I tell him.

'Good God!' He looks genuinely astonished. 'I earn five times that much for doing my entirely worthless job. It's a crime, isn't it?'

I completely agree, but I have other plans now.

My morning pill dish is now quite full, but at least I'm not in pain, and today I'm allowed to sit up and reach for things from the bedside cabinet. Soon, I'll be allowed to sit out of bed, and later, they'll allow me to walk around. Then, who knows where I'll be able to sneak off to?

Gilbert, the new arrival, is in pain. Concerned nurses tend to him.

'What's up, Mr. Haroldson?'

'My heart, nurse. Help me, please!'

'Have you had this pain before?'

Now he's writhing and struggling. The nurses wrestle to hold him down. But he's fighting mad and the young house doctor is called in to help pin him down.

'What do you normally have?'

He mumbles.

What a sad case! We are all straining to hear, listening in to Gilbert's story.

'Nurse! What is it?' I whisper.

Nurse (very harassed): 'Too busy to talk now.' She passes on.

'I see,' says the young doctor. 'Classic symptoms.'

A powerful odour permeates the ward.

'What's that, nurse?'

'It's for Gilbert. It's called paraldehyde.'

'Poor man!'

'It'll settle him. I think he's had it before.'

There are murmurs of sympathy from all around. He may be a toff, but he's a fellow sufferer.

Next day, the doctors are clustered around Gilbert. Even the portly Matron has turned up to add her weight to the occasion. There seems to be much talk and cross-examination. Quite suddenly the porters arrive, and Gilbert is hauled struggling and shouting onto a trolley. He's protesting loudly and a third porter is holding him down as he is roughly and noisily ejected not just from the ward but also from the building itself, apparently. He leaves behind a sad, bad reputation and a lingering whiff of paraldehyde.

Begley is straightening my bedclothes. She looks strangely sad.

'What's happening, nurse?'

'It turns out that Gilbert is blacklisted at just about every hospital in London. We were the only one that didn't have his name in our records.'

'Blacklisted? Why?'

'He's an addict, addicted to paraldehyde, and he knows exactly how to fake the symptoms in order to be given the drug.'

Tomorrow, after doctors' rounds, will no doubt come the routine words about slow progress and more months of bed rest ahead. But I can hardly believe the joyful news - from Dr Tonkin's own lips - the news that, today for a change, perhaps, I can sit out of bed after lunch! My needles and drips have been long removed. Feelings of undiluted and unalloyed jubilation are suddenly overtaken by gloom.

Bourney, I'm told, is off-duty today, so I can't leap up and embrace her with the good tidings.

Now, into Gilbert's empty bed comes Mr. Parsons.

'What's his problem nurse?' I ask the Nurse.

'Diabetes,' she says sadly, then adds more cheerfully. 'But he's so sweet. A real old- fashioned gentleman.'

'What does he do?'

'He's a bank clerk, I think.'

1961

'Well, he's come to the right place then.' She smiles coldly and hurries off.

Bourney is back today! When she comes within hailing distance, I ask her nicely to do me a favour, and she agrees to shop for some pyjamas and a dressing-gown so that I can rid myself of this shapeless hospital gown, and appear more human - less like a bedridden zombie. And, for when I eventually go out, perhaps she could find a shirt with a collar large enough to conceal my overgrown thyroid – oh and a street map of London. I give her some of the money got for me from The National Assistance Board by Good Lady Almoner Fairfax. She flashes that lovely Bourney smile and bustles off on her kind mission.

Mike has brought me Orwell's essays and I return his Wells. The doctor has decreed that I can walk a few steps at a time, up and down the ward under the watchful eyes of a physiotherapist. Marion is rather brusque - no nonsense with her. Best foot forward and, back in bed, exercises to get the legs pumping and the blood racing. That's the way! Standing to my full height at last I feel like a man reborn. I'm bigger than I remember. Wasn't I once slight, haggard, fragile, emotionally vulnerable and anxious? Is that a true or false shadow of a memory? Medicines and now exercise have rendered me a more assured, less agitated being. At least that's how it feels as I stand surveying the sick and dying inmates of Austin Taylor ward from an upright vantage point. Now, I'm more up than down, circulating - passing, visiting, saluting some, exchanging quips or platitudes with others. Lucky old you, they say, watching enviously as I take my tottering steps past them. Occasionally, I stop for a joke. Sick jokes, no cure except laughter. Ironic, hollow, helpless hooting, shuddering laughter. Ripeness is all. And, even among the ailing and failing, unless despondency has them in a fatal grip, cheerfulness keeps breaking in. They shudder and shake and attempt a smile as I pass.

There's an outburst of curses. 'Get your fucking hands off me, you fucking bitch.'

It's sweet old Mr. Parsons. What's got into him?

'Nurse, what's up with Mr. Parsons?' I ask.

'I told you he's very ill. It's the diabetes speaking … Untreated that's what happens eventually.'

'Eventually? That sounds hideously final.'

'Afraid so.'

'Morning Mr. Parsons.' says the Nurse

'Bugger off! '

'Can't do that, Mr. Parsons. I have to care for all the other men in the ward.'

'Bugger them as well!'

'Oh! Mr. Parsons, that would be extremely difficult for me, now don't you think? You're quite a joker, though, I'll give you that.'

Now coma descends. The nurses and doctors are fighting a losing battle. So, it's no surprise, when eventually the porters come to take the sweet little old bank clerk, Mr. Parsons, to the great counting house in the sky.

I want to get out and to see Nurse Bourney, to make an assignation. She has a flat in a nurse's hostel in Vincent Square. She put the address on that long epistle she sent me. Now my fantasy is firmly fixed on that address. I see it in my mind's feverish eye. I've noticed that sometimes patients are judged well enough to sit out in the garden, which separates the hospital building from the nurse's quarters and the medical school. I ask Sister how soon before I can go out to get some fresh air.

'You've got to get just a bit better, I think. You don't realise how ill you've been, young man.' She smiles a motherly smile.

Jacky, (Mr. Wilkinson), a particularly filthy tramp, has been stretchered in straight from the Embankment. He's brought his foul tongue with him, cursing the nurses telling them to f-off, and mumbling even fouler things than that into the pink ears of our tender angels. But they're clever as well as tender. They turn the other cheeks and are extra kind to this sad, broken-down wretch, addressing him politely as 'Mr. Wilkinson'. They seem to know him. An old favourite. He has pneumonia.

'Back again, Mr. Wilkinson,' says one, kindly young nurse

'You gonna give me a fuckin' cuppa tea, then?' His voice is weak despite the strong language. He spits into a water glass the nurse has offered to him, and one wonders what kind of a man this abandoned pile of rags and bones must once have been.

'I gotta get back to my bench or that thieving git'll take it over.'

It's a scene from *Down and Out in Paris and London.*

But Mr. Wilkinson will not go back to his riverside bench. He fights the nurses and the doctors, he curses blue and purple streaks, he spits out his medicine ... and one night the porters came, and he is wheeled off to that shadowland of cheerless flophouses reserved for all of us.

Like a vision, Nurse Bourney suddenly appears - just back on duty. She's delighted to hear I've been getting out of bed at last. She has a packet for me. It's my pyjamas, a tastefully but attractively patterned pair. She draws my curtains so that I can change. There's also a dressing gown - colourful and jolly - and finally that shirt with a large collar, and an old street map of her own which, she said, would save me a few shillings.

She's looking rather happy. 'I'm invited to a party in Chelsea tonight,' she says.

God! That'll be with her sick irredeemably delinquent diabetic ex-patient of hers, I've no doubt.

Harry is packing to go. 'You're looking glum, Old Man,' he says.

'My favourite nurse is off to a party tonight. I feel abandoned.'

'Where's the party?' asks Harry, packing his shaving tackle and zipping up his holdall.

'Maybe I'll join her.'

'It's in Chelsea.'

'Ah,' he says, as if savouring the name, 'Girls with long blonde hair and Flaxman telephone numbers.'

I stare at him. 'Really?' I asked.

'Oh! and poets and painters with long hair and tuberculous coughs, I suppose.'

That sounds like the place to live, I tell myself. I watch Harry put his money and keys into his pockets.

'Has the doctor said it's OK?' I ask.

'What?'

'You just leaving like that?'

1961

'I'm not hanging around waiting for him. I must get back to the office in the morning, Gordon, or I'm screwed.' He buttons up his jacket. 'Bye old sport!' He shakes my hand, heads off towards a side door and disappears.

It's a while before anyone notices he's missing. 'He's very silly,' says Nurse Begley.

They wheel in Mr. Brokenshaw (Mr. B.). He says that he worked all of his adult life as a psychologist, devising experiments - gentleman experiments, of course, and tells me long yarns of experiments in laboratories, in factories and in hospitals. So, no home-made rockets to Mars, but finding out how managers and workers, nurses and doctors, officers and men might work harder, produce more, and be best disposed to interact favourably with one another. 'I was very busy during the war,' he mentioned. He advises me to study psychology, and said, 'You write to the Institute of Industrial Psychology. I have friends there'. It sounds a bit - how shall we say? - 'industrial' for me. I'm being moved from the corner by the window to the other end of the row, wave my goodbyes to Mr. B. and his experiments. I'm now next to a doorway onto a corridor and, opposite that, a swing door which leads to another ward - a mysterious world where strangely-ill patients and qualified doctors carry out strangely-devised treatments. Like Alice, I'm tempted to go through it to the other side - just to find out what's there and what those strange passing sounds might intimate.

Hm. This new mattress seems uncomfortable. There's a plaque on the wall behind the bed-head. I sit up to read it. 'This bed has been donated to the Westminster Hospital by the Portland Cement Company.' I laugh and suddenly the mattress doesn't seem that bad. I wriggle my toes and scribble in my new notebook.

GLIMPSES OF A BIOGRAPHER'S DIARY

The figure of Pete, the handsome newcomer, who has moved in beside me now, comes into focus. His attractive girlfriend fusses around him - glamorous lovers from a technicolour world. Pete's quite chatty, - 'I am a racing driver,' he says. 'But I keep losing control of my hands, and my feet turn numb. All feeling goes. Just like that. Sometimes I shoot round the track at some insane speed and suddenly I can't feel the steering wheel or the pedals.' 'I am bound to crash and that's me for the scrapyard,' he says. The doctors are carrying out tests. Meanwhile he's forbidden to smoke. As a hundred-a-day man he's bereft, and soon fidgeting, groaning, swearing and writhing on his bed - gripped by withdrawal symptoms. The girlfriend ministers to her glamour boy. Apart from the horror of his encroaching illness, Pete has another obsession - the physical attributes of the nurses. 'I'd like to give her one,' he says, or 'Look at the headlamps on that model. I could make a pit stop for her.' Through the window, which runs the length of the far side of the ward, we can see the nurses' home which is beyond the public garden below. Pete has noticed that after dark, one or two of the nurses leave their curtains undrawn, so their evening activities and rituals are on show to all who care to watch. Pete cares and one nurse rivets his attention. Each evening she prepares for bed with an extraordinarily sensuous striptease, almost as if she knows she's performing for an audience. Pete is always at the window ready for the show. Off will come one piece of clothing - then she'll carry on with something else. Pete gives a running commentary - 'There goes the uniform.' 'There goes the vest.' 'Wait for it' - 'Wow! There goes the bra. Have you ever seen anything like them? Now she is discarding what else she's wearing.' He gets himself a little more heated as his commentary wears on. And one could never tell whether or not the girl is conscious of the fact that she's being ogled by at least half of Austin Taylor men's medical ward - the half, that is ambulant enough to make it to the

1961

window side of the ward, drawn there by Pete's salacious commentary.

Bourney is too busy to stop by for a chat. This morning she pauses on her way past my bed. 'How was the party in Chelsea?' I ask. She smiles enigmatically. 'Interesting,' she says.

After Dr Tonkin's round, Sister stops by briefly to tell me that perhaps I can sit out in the garden in a few days-time, after I've practiced walking out along the corridor. Marion, the physiotherapist, quickly appears and takes me through my tentative paces, preparing me to be able to stand and step along steadily enough to enable me to walk out down the corridor and back. Looking out through the side door, I see the hospital world beyond the Austin Taylor ward for the first time. Nurses, doctors, ladies pushing little trolleys, peddling newspapers, library books for lending, sweets, and chocolates to sweeten the bitter taste of dying, or rattling along with meals on wheels to fatten up the lucky living. At the end of the corridor to the right, by a window overlooking Page Street, there's a small television set. It's tennis from Wimbledon and a few men and women in institutional dressing gowns sunk into armchairs watching the ball pass up and down the court, up and down, up and down, back and forth, back and forth, heads barely moving or eyes swivelling. Bodies permanently at the slump, staring. Here they can smoke, and a thin veil is drawn over their faces. They utter never a sound. I wander on, past the open doors of wards for women, for children, for patients with eyes bandaged, for people hobbling on crutches and for mothers with their babies clasped to their breasts. Doors bang shut, nurses troop along, white coats sweep past, a sister hurries by, the electrocardiogram woman trundles her monitor and the Padre passes, failing to recognise the atheist he has still failed to convert

- abandoned to the fires of Hades. I smile. I retreat to the ward and sink back onto my firm bed of Portland Cement.

Pete has tests for his numb extremities. 'They think it's my smoking,' he tells me. Like the rest of us, he's now quite suddenly an expert on his own condition. 'The capillaries at the far end of my limbs have narrowed, thanks to my years of puffing the poison weed.' He says.

'So, what's the cure?' I enquire.

'Stop smoking for a start,' he says. He's even caught the doctor's demeanour and intonation. The glamorous girlfriend is on hand and seems suitably impressed.

Chapter 4

Ready to Meet the Sound of Roaring London

It's another day. My outdoor clothes are brought to me from some cupboard. In one of the suit pockets I find the unused return ticket to Torquay. I tear it up. My clothes are laid out piece by piece on my bed. Slowly I put them on. It's like being reunited with old friends. But I have filled out, and when I stand, I can see that I'm an unfamiliar figure, unfamiliar to me, at least – gone is the narrow-shouldered scrawny character, who hobbled into the hospital, and the body I have now been given is bulkier and perhaps more commanding. I'll buy some more fitting clothes first chance I get. But finally, walking rather cautiously and well-draped in my clothes, I am ready to meet the sound of roaring London.

Once outside, I feel like running. But Sister has issued strict instructions. I am warned to go gently, and just to walk and sit quietly in the garden for the time being. The ward windows overlook the little square of mostly flowers and shrubs, so I'll still be under observation. I sit on a bench, admiring the daisies and trying to settle my thoughts. My suit is rather formal for a summer's day but I'm determined to surprise my angelic at her Vincent Square hideaway looking my very best in parsonical grey. Thanks to her London map, I know exactly where I'm planning to go and when I have to take off. I have to pick my moment - imagine when Sister is off the ward, well away from those overlooking windows, then make my move.

I sidle from seat to seat towards the garden gate, slip out onto Page Street, past the nurse's home, around the medical school into Horseferry Road, and then I am off on my pathway to heaven. I pass shop windows like decorated grottoes. I am tempted to step into this one or that - especially the gents' outfitters selling smart shirts and suits, and the bookshops with the latest novels on display (There's Camus, *The Plague*, another of those Egyptian novels from Lawrence Durrell, and - Good God - an unexpurgated *Lady Chatterley's Lover* on sale in England! Oh, of course! Last year's court case!)

I pause for a breather. But I daren't linger long. Love and desire call me onwards, and I again start moving at a steady determined pace. 'Farewell Sister Ashley, Farewell Austin Taylor ward, I go to seek my fallen angel [the hopeless object of my desires.]' Somewhere I take a left turn, and there's Vincent Square stretching ahead of me - a square of handsome Georgian buildings standing tall around it and a fenced-off garden with seats, and, at its heart, surrounded by greenery, a small hut for the gardeners, like a tiny country cottage. There's even a bed of roses.

'Gather ye rosebuds while ye may, Bourney,' I hum. But I don't seem to have the Sam Pepys luck with ladies. I trail along, counting down the house numbers. Ticking them off one by one. Then, at last, there it is. The address I'm looking for! What next? I could just lay siege to it and wait for that all-too-familiar figure to move into sight. But I can't wait. The prominent black knocker on the front door tempts me. I quickly ring the bell. I know exactly what I'll say to her. I've rehearsed it over and over, like a parrot.

1961

Footsteps approach and the heart pounds to match them. I am not supposed to let it pound. Doctor's orders. The door opens. I shouldn't be here. A strange nurse stands there, still in uniform. Someone else is supposed to be standing before me. I am confused and I stutter, 'Is Nurse Bourney in?' Grey eyes look me over and their owner shakes her head. 'She's on duty.' The door closes and I retreat to a bench on the green - just to get my breath back. A car slowly circles the square. Does Big Sister Ashley have a car and is she watching me? And am I about to be found out? By a supreme act of will I make myself invisible.

I have to get back to the ward before I'm missed. As I hurry back, I meet Nurse Peters coming in the opposite direction. She beams at me. 'Lovely to see you up and about.'

'I am not supposed to have left the hospital garden. You won't tell Sister, will you'?

'Of course not.' And I believe her. She has a simple candour and a hint of devil-may-care in the wide-open brown eyes. Her laughing smile could easily enchant me. I barely make it to my bed before Sister is there, arms akimbo, demanding to know where I have been. I suspect she knows but pretends otherwise. 'No more sitting out in the garden for you, young man.' she says. I am to be confined to quarters.

12 July. I'm anticipating discharge. Finally, I've written to my parents, and suddenly there they are in the ward, sitting beside my bed. My mother looks anxious; my father looks angry. He thinks I have been living a life of dissipation and I can see there's no point in trying to convince him otherwise. I once thought I was doing a kindness moving in with them in that house into which they had moved to that picturesque but remote village in South Devon. The air of despondency eventually got to me, so I had found my attic

flat in Torquay and ended up teaching English to rowdy, uneducable yobs at Paignton. No thoughts of dissipation cross my mother's mind. To her I am now just a broken reed. 'Will you be able to live a normal life?' she asks, before they leave to catch their train - she now so sad-looking, but once so lively and pretty; he now so frail and resigned, but once my strong silent soldier-hero, who had fought in France with the Royal Welsh Fusiliers along with Robert Graves and Siegfried Sassoon and had the record and medals to prove it.

2 - *The Bowker family from the top left Ivy, Gordon, Leonard, Brenda and Lucy, 1950, not long before Gordon left home for Australia*

Harry's back, just for a check-up, he says, and comes over to sit on my bed for a moment.

1961

'Did your boss ever find out that you'd been in here?' I ask.

'No, thank God,' he says. 'Look, old man, when you get out eventually, give me a ring and we'll get together for a drink.' He scribbles down his address and phone number and is gone. I'll miss Harry. I ask the nurses if the address he gave me - Dolphin Square - means anything to anybody. 'Luxury,' says Sister Ashley, raising her eyebrows.

16 July. Sunday and the ward is visited by the Salvation Army with heavy weaponry! And we sit or lie, mostly confined to bed. It's as well that Bourney has melted my ice-cold heart a little. I'm no more the hard-nosed argumentative atheist; I'm a soft-nosed, pensive atheist. But no one joins in the hymn singing and the Army withdraws in the face of silent suffering.

Bourney may have been tipped off that I came visiting and has made herself scarce. Where is she? She's always on the women's ward or off-duty when I enquire. I am slowly transferring my affections. Now I am looking hopefully for little Peters of the devil-may-care laugh and no religious hang-ups - as far as I know. When Bourney does finally show up on the ward I am careful to be cool but friendly, and she in turn seems quite relieved by this.

'When you go out, where will you stay?' she asks.

'No idea.'

'You could try Red Shield House. Buckingham Gate.'

'Sounds very grand.'

'It'll serve you while you're finding your bearings,' she says, giving me that lovely smile for one last time.

GLIMPSES OF A BIOGRAPHER'S DIARY

The doctors are reluctant to let me go. 'We'll see you from time to time in our outpatients clinic, and you'll have to take it easy and come back in a year's time for an operation,' says Dr Tonkin.

'An operation?'

'To put this illness permanently behind you.'

17 July. The day arrives when Dr Tonkin and Baylis arrive simultaneously at my bedside, smiling, and in the nicest possible way give me my discharge papers from the ward. They want me to attend outpatient clinic every three months and return after a year for the operation to excise that part of my thyroid gland which needs trimming back. I gather my few belongings together, pack them into a carrier bag and do the rounds of the Nightingale angels, shedding a friendly tear and thanking them for their multiple kindnesses. In my pocket I have the few pounds Lady Fairfax has got for me from the National Assistance Board and Post Office Savings Account with a small unspent sum. In my notebook, I have four phone numbers - South African Harry's, South Wales's Nurse Molly's, Parsons Green's Nurse Begley, and Pimlico's Nurse Peters. When I find a place to stay in the great metropolis I will invite them all to a party. I have finally had to exorcise the seductive spirit of Nurse Bourney. That was how it was, that long day's journey into night and back out again. The unbelievable present was no longer suspended. It now returned, quite correctly, to the past where it belonged.

As I walked out of the front door of the hospital, I felt that from this point onwards I was living on borrowed time. I made my way along Horseferry Road, across Victoria Street and saw that full ahead lay Buckingham Gate. Down on the right stood Red Shield House. I suddenly recognised the symbol above the entrance. It was the escutcheon of the Salvation Army. The red brick gothic lent the place a suitably Victorian air, and the odour of carbolic assailed me as I pushed open the door at the main entrance. It was the next thing to a workhouse casual ward - what Orwell called 'the spike' - as one was likely to find. I approached the gentleman at the reception desk. 'A room, please.' 'One and sixpence.' I handed over two coins, was led up some stone stairs and down a long narrow corridor of cubicles to a door, which admitted me to one of these compartments. My guide jerked his thumb. 'Bathroom and toilet at the end of the corridor.' He handed me the key and I was left alone to slump onto the narrow bed and contemplate. The smell was overwhelming – (carbolic was now added a strong pervading smell of stale body-odour), the walls stared gloomily back at me - an institutional dark green. Orwell again jogged my elbow. This was how the dispossessed lived in down-and-out London, but unlike him I was not a comfortably-placed public schoolboy masquerading as a tramp with a book to write; I was actually, for a day or two at least, the real such person.

I repaired to the nearby pub and was followed by an individual, who had latched onto me coming out of the Red Shield House. He parked himself beside me in the bar and I bought him a half of mild. He offered me a squashed Woodbine, looked around and began to sort out the other drinkers.

'I'm, over there.'

'What about him?'

''e's one.'

'One what?'

'A screw!'

'A screw?'

'A fuckin' off-duty warder.'

'Oh.'

'And them two over there.' He jabbed a finger. 'And 'im.' Another jab.

'I am impressed.' I told him. 'How can you tell.'

'I know, you see. I just got out.'

So, my new 'chum' was an ex-con.

By way of conversation I mentioned my recent stay in hospital, my looking for somewhere to live, and Harry, who had a flat in a luxurious complex called Dolphin Square, just along the Embankment in Pimlico.

'Let's give 'im a call. We can go round to see 'im.'

I pretended I didn't have his number and we drifted back to the 'workhouse'.

———

Chapter 5

Chelsea: My Garden of Eden!!!

18 July. Nurse Bourney had told me that in the Evening Standard there were columns of advertisements for vacant rooms and flats, but the best ones were quickly snapped up. So, I rushed out early this new day to buy a copy and ran my eye down the columns. It lit on a small ad. headed 'Chelsea, bed sitting room £1.7s.6d per week.' There was a Flaxman telephone number, and alluring visions of girls with long blonde hair came vividly to mind. I found a telephone box and quickly dialed the number. A young cultivated voice answered. 'Yes, it's still vacant.' I promised to be there within the hour and dashed for the underground, using Bourney's map as my guide.

A Circle Line train took me from Victoria to Sloane Square and I emerged into what I at first mistook for a part of Paris. Plane trees fringed the paved square with a fountain playing at its heart. Around this centre-piece stood shops, hotels, a pub and a glorious-looking theatre - the Royal Court! Luther by John Osborne, was playing. Chelsea meant poets and painters as well as their muses and models. I really was in heaven - or the nearest thing to it - my Garden of Eden.

Along the King's Road the ebb and flow of men in bowler hats, sporting umbrellas, and young women of the utmost beauty, many with long blonde hair, and, no doubt, those exotic telephone numbers. I had been wafted at the drop of a sixpenny tube train ticket from the grim carbolic hostel for down-and-outs to a dreamland of deodorised stockbrokers, perfumed actresses, exquisite model girls, and, with luck, also the poets and painters who made up the picture book Chelsea of my imagination.

I had come home, and could have lived here quite happily till I dropped, and even into the great beyond for that matter, if there was a Chelsea in the sky, that is. Everything along that road drew me to it - a trattoria; a smart department store; barracks belonging to the Grand Old Duke of York; an arty-looking pub; a cheerful eatery, the Chelsea Kitchen; an antique shop with a window display like the stage set for a Victorian comedy of manners; a very stylish boutique called Bazaar; a bookshop; a pawnbroker's shop with the traditional three brass balls dangling above the doorway; an old-fashioned grocery store, shelves stacked high behind the spacious counter and assistants wearing striped aprons; an even more antiquated gents' tailor; a Classic Cinema; a pub called The Chelsea Potter; a Chinese restaurant; the offices of a local newspaper, the Chelsea News, and a poets' café called the Picasso.

And here was my turn off. Somewhere along Shawfield Street stood the house where the woman with the cultivated voice was waiting for me. Handsome terraced houses lined the street down to where small rows of post-war prefabs stood on either side just before No 61, which stood tall, like a sentinel, at the very end of the street. Obviously, during the blitz German bombs had straddled the street at this point, so that, after its lucky escape, No

1961

61 huddled close to its Siamese twin (No 59) for company. Five steps led up to the doorbell. I gave it a swift jab, as if fearful that someone might suddenly reach over my shoulder and get there first. There was a long wait. Finally the door was opened by a smartly-dressed young woman, who might have been a sister to Lady Fairfax - long blonde hair and accent to match. After all, this was Flaxman country. She asked, 'Are you Gordon?'

'Yes.' I said and she invited me in.

The vacant room was on the top floor. Two flights and there was the room I recognised immediately as mine. There was a shabby brown carpet and a single bed, a gas fire, a gas ring with a battered-looking kettle perched at a drunken angle on top of it, and, standing demurely behind a curtain, a wash basin with an Ascot heater. In front of the window, overlooking a tiny walled garden, was a small table covered with a chequered oil proof cloth. The bathroom on the landing below was shared between seven tenants, three of them female. It was narrow, with a frosted window at the side, and a huge, menacing geyser at the far end.

'I'll take it,' I said promptly.

'One pound seven and six a week,' she said, 'and the accommodation bureau, which placed the advertisement will want the same from you for their services.'

'Of course,' I said, and swiftly handed over the cash for two weeks' rent, overwhelmed by the strange joy of having a place of my own, a comfortable place to lay my head, a London address with a Flaxman telephone number, a place of sanctuary, a base from which to make a fresh start, a new beginning, a new page, a new chapter - a launch pad into the future. She handed me two keys - one for the front door and the other for my own attic sanctuary.

GLIMPSES OF A BIOGRAPHER'S DIARY

I said a polite fare-thee-well to her, retreating back along Shawfield Street to the King's Road, where I dropped into the poet's café, the Picasso. It was just my kind of place - cheap and friendly - Formica-topped tables, artistic photographs and pseudo-modernist paintings around the walls, the aroma of brewing coffee and hot rolls. This was exactly where I'd scribble verse and fill pages with endless prose. A large man with an Italian accent served a frothy coffee and a sandwich. I lounged at a corner table and wanted something to write on, but hadn't a scrap of paper in my pocket - I had left even my pen behind in the Salvation Army 'Hotel' in Westminster. There were several poets hovering over empty cups, blind to all around them in prayerful concentration. I could see pencils at work and notebooks slowly filling. There were odes and satires being dashed off, novels and symphonies under construction, masterpieces being contemplated behind furrowed brows and uncombed, uncut hair.

This was the place! Dylan, the Welsh conjurer, might have sat here, summoning forth a whole blitz of a poem, MacNeice might have lounged in this corner penning a surrealist line, or George Barker romancing his latest muse. And didn't bold Samuel Beckett write a novel - Murphy in these parts and the play Waiting for Godot? Furthermore, it had to be noted that the great Eliot used to live but a few streets away, scrawling stanzas beside the ponderous Thames. I'd write about it. Poets With Flaxman Telephone Numbers, I decided to call it. And naturally, I was already planning a book of poems of my own. If I'd been Danny Kaye in that film about Walter Mitty it'd be out and I'd be enjoying rave reviews in the TLS and profiles in the Observer and Sunday Times.

Outside, I took in my new neighbourhood in more detail - a Choy's Chinese restaurant opposite, the Chelsea Potter, with a sort of conservatory frontage projecting onto the pavement, along to the right, that Classic Cinema and an intriguingly mysterious place next to it called The Pheasantry, a club of some sort hiding shyly behind a wall and a wrought-iron gate surmounted by Regal Archway gate. Further down the King's Road stood another pub with a conservatory frontage - the Markham Arms. Both the Potter and the Markham seemed like perfect vantage points from which to observe the passing scene. On my way down to Sloane Square tube station, I called at W.H. Smith's and bought copies of the London Magazine and New Statesman to read for the short Circle Line journey back to Victoria tube station.

At the Red Shield House, I climbed the steps, checked myself out, retrieved my carrier bag and finally left, heading off to Victoria. Along the way, I picked up a canvas holdall, crammed it full of my few belongings and disposing of the carrier bag.

As I returned to Chelsea, I inhaled deeply at slow intervals, clearing my lungs, wiping slates clean, rewinding the clock for whatever lay ahead. Then, back in Sloane Square, I became someone else - Spring-heeled Jack, Rimbaud the mad poet, Oscar the wild Irishman, Tom Jones fielding a long hop, skip and jump. I walked lightly in step with artistic ghosts of the imagination - drunk on words that didn't belong to me exactly. Well, will anyone care about yet another young Chelsea hopeful with literary pretensions? It was still only a few minutes after eleven-thirty. I saw a life of art, leisure and enlightened self-indulgence stretching ahead of me. All I needed now was the outfit, the clothes befitting a poet and novelist - a corduroy jacket, a check shirt and some suede shoes for a start. I was now the proud tenant of a top floor bedsit in Chelsea. The landlady, I learned, was a Mrs. Henkey; and the cleaner, who also collected the rent, was a Mrs. Burgess.

20 July. It's summer, and there was something fresh and sparkling in the Chelsea air. Two girls passed me in Sloane Square, looking

stunning in dresses so imaginative I could barely refrain from gawping. I overheard a woman's disapproving mutter, 'Art students!' and quickly came up with a new mantra, 'Art students with long blonde hair and Flaxman telephone numbers.'

An old university friend, Eric, well set up for the past year lectureship at some Welsh university, had moved my goods, chattels and miscellaneous personal effects up from Torquay in his new station wagon. My small bedsit was now home to a large radiogram, a small pile of records, a stack of books, a heavy barely portable typewriter, a miniature tape recorder and some half dozen tapes. I arranged the books neatly along the mantle shelf over the gas fire. There were my first editions of Durrell's *Justine* and Pasternak's *Dr Zhivago* (translated), my Penguin Book of *Contemporary Verse* (still bearing a few grains of desert sand between its pages), a *Concise Oxford Dictionary*, a Faber Collected Eliot, 1909-1935 in its lovely yellow dust jacket, Joyce's *Ulysses* in its olive green one, 's *Burmese Days* - a 1944 Penguin paperback, a Pelican edition of *The Decameron Nights*, Amis's *Lucky Jim*, Lawrence's *Sons and Lovers* and *Women in Love*, hardback editions of Hardy's *Return of the Native* (from student days, still smart in its unspoilt dust jacket), Sillitoe's *Saturday Night and Sunday Morning*, Hoggart's *Uses of Literacy*, well-thumbed, some copies of Penguin *New Writing*, eight copies of the London Magazine, including the January 1957 issue with Cocteau's inspiring Oxford Lecture on Poetry, a little book of Wordsworth's lyric poems and a couple of school prizes, including Chesterton, a passion of my young teenage years. I perched my Picasso, Matisse and Van Gogh reproductions on top of the row of books.

Now the room was beginning to look a little less austere and more like a sanctuary of cultural enlightenment, I was pleased to tell myself. I could relax by lying flat on the threadbare carpet and listening to a selection of my discs piled on the spindle of my radiogram - my Schubert's Unfinished, Overtures from Wagner, Olivier's speeches from Henry V, Anthony Quayle's Othello speeches, and Dylan Thomas's A Child's Christmas in Wales. Eric decided to give me a crash course in how to eat healthily on next-to-nothing. His tips included such culinary delights as boiled egg for breakfast, green salad for lunch, and for dinner a mixture of carrots, onions and chopped cabbage added to a pan of mincemeat, all boiled up and served with sliced potatoes. Once boiled that would last me several days, he said. Afterwards fruit - apples, oranges, grapefruit from the market, but no bananas - 'filling, but not good food value', he declared, in the voice of 'one who knows'. I think I can just about manage his mouthwatering suggestions on my pittance.

Over the next week, I met the other inhabitants at no 61. Mr. Sweeney, the gentle Irishman, employed to scout for books and ideas for films by a big American production company; Muriel and Jacqueline on the floor below, who worked as secretaries; a darkly-bearded BBC television director and the girl with the cultivated home county accent, who occupied the basement front and back flats.

An unexpected visitor arrived, who looked as though he didn't agree. A man from the National Assistance Board. I had refused help from my parents, who finally reconciled themselves to the fact that I might not be a permanent invalid after all. Out of pride, I had also declined a fund-raised in my name at my university - which now seems like idiotic posturing. The sum collected was instead, at my suggestion, to form the basis of a fund at the university for necessitous students. The idea of starting with nothing and seeing how far I could get was, however, deeply appealing to me, and now a free man, I felt immensely optimistic.

GLIMPSES OF A BIOGRAPHER'S DIARY

So, the man from the National Assistance was here to look me over. I invited him to remove his raincoat and take a seat. He preferred to remain draped and upright. I offered him tea, but he preferred nothing, thank you very much.

'What do you pay for rent?'

'One pound seven and sixpence a week.'

His eyes widened; he pursed his lips, shook his head and walked over to look through the window and then peered closely at the Ascot and gas ring. 'We don't normally pay these inflated rents,' he said sternly.

'But,' I said 'I am just out of hospital after a long stay. I came as close as it is possible to being wheeled off to the mortuary by the porters.' He was frowning. 'What on earth was I talking about?' he was thinking. But I couldn't believe he was doubting my story. 'Brilliant doctors have just saved me and I owe it to them to live somewhere well away from falling plaster and rising damp.' It took him a while to digest all this, sucking his lead pencil and scribbling importantly in his big notebook. Finally, he muttered, 'Alright.' The notebook snapped shut and he left without a word of goodbye. Two days later, I received a book of slips, each for the princely sum of five pounds to be drawn weekly on signature at a Post Office, subject to medical review.

I celebrated at the Picasso with a supper of Veal Holstein - veal with a topping of fried egg crucified beneath two anchovies - as a finishing touch. It was undoubtedly the most scrumptious meal I'd had up to that point - except, perhaps, for that spaghetti Bolognese I'd had with Mike at that Italian café in Cairo, and the country pub meal at Henley-in-Arden with Angela. Today, as I ate, I was reading the Guardian. All that seemed to obsess the Americans in those days was space travel and the Cold War.

1961

4 August. Eric phoned. He was leaving London, but there was someone he wanted me to meet before he left. I travelled over to the address he gave in Marylebone, I was let into the flat by a beautiful young woman in a maroon jumper and blue jeans. There was Eric with a secretive smile and a seriously otherworldly demeanour. He introduced me to Nick and said, 'Nick is putting on open evenings at his house in the Fulham Road.' 'Would you like to come?' asked Nick. 'Yes. Where's the Fulham Road?' I asked. 'A short walk from where you're living,' said Eric. Nick added, 'Every other Tuesday after seven - starting next week. No booze, just black coffee on the house.' 'A place for making contacts,' said Eric. 'And friends,' said Nick. 'Do come. It's number 415.' It was my first invitation to a party in Chelsea.

6 August. I met Nurse Molly at Sloane Square. She had been invited for lunch, my first guest. We walked down the King's Road. Molly was captivated by the parade of shop windows. She had never seen their like before. It was magic for her, as it still was for me. Lunch was cold chicken and salad. There was wine, too, but Molly preferred water. Afterwards we sat on my divan and reminisced about poor Mr. Peterson, Molly dabbing the tears that came at the memory. We talked about her schooldays, her first boyfriend, her Welsh village and the characters therein. It wasn't exactly Under Milk Wood but couldn't have been that far away over the next hill. I walked her back along the King's Road to Sloane Square and thanked her again for those kindly midnight conversations on the ward.

8th. Nick's open house had gathered in London's better class of odds and sods, some quite toffish. The young woman in the maroon jumper and jeans was the only person I recognised. Nick's black coffee was bubbling away in a great vat like a witches' cauldron in his kitchen. A cup, a ladle, and a place to stand was all there was. The hard drinkers didn't linger. 'Show us the way to the next whisky store...' and off they sped, muttering. But it was a chance to meet rich layabouts, or exchange small talk with other small talkers, chatting about films, fashion or food we'd enjoyed; or big talk with other big talkers - boasting of books we'd never write or films we'd never make. There were the few whose careers were poised for take-off. With this journalist it was chasing celebrities and celebrity, with that daughter of a Labour M.P., it was Westminster politics, with these thespians it was the Royal Shakespeare Company, with this linguist it was a career in publishing. 'Come to my exhibition opening at the Jermyn Street Gallery at 7.30 on Tuesday.'

'I'm in publishing - we're looking for horror novels.'

'Come to a party - Albert Finney will be there.'

'I'll call you sometime. Let's swap phone numbers.' I must buy an address book to store all these names and numbers in alphabetical order. In the back room I found young men talking of Soho eccentrics they knew, or sleazy cabarets they frequented, or young women trying to out-do each other with wilder and wilder stories.

'My dream is to sing in a nightclub.'

'I did go to that kind of party once.'

'I had a story published in Cosmopolitan.'

'What about?'

'My rape.'

'How exciting, darling!'

You wouldn't know it, but Nick was the youngest son of the knighted head of a university college, an old Victorian martinet by the sound of it. The house and the money to fund his relaxed life style was his mother's gift to him. He was very likeable - laid-back, raffish and full of idle curiosity.

I discovered a great bookshop - John Sandoe's, in Blacklands Terrace, a narrow street off to the left just before Sloane Square. It was an Aladdin's cave. There sat Lawrence Durrell's *Clea*, the second book in his *Alexandria Quartet*, Malcolm Lowry's stories, wonderfully-titled *Hear Us O Lord from Heaven Thy Dwelling Place* (which spoke to my once-Methodist soul) and his *Selected Poems* smiled so enticingly that I weakened and surrendered. There was also a stash of periodicals in the same rack, some obscure, some long-established. I chose Encounter magazine, which was edited by Stephen Spender, this issue carrying a contribution from Durrell. And there was an old copy of the New York Times dated 3rd July 1961 which caught my eye. I bought it out of curiosity.

With my tiny cash reserve now further depleted, I headed back towards Shawfield Street, and on the way glanced at the New York Times. I read: Hemingway's obituary on the front page:- HEMINGWAY DEAD OF SHOTGUN WOUND; WIFE SAYS HE WAS CLEANING THE WEAPON. On the 2nd July 1961, Ernest Hemingway was found dead of a shotgun wound in his head at his home. His wife said that he had killed himself accidentally while cleaning the weapon. And so now I do know for whom the bell tolled, it tolled for the man who wrote the novel. I bought a small bottle of whisky at an off licence just along the King's Road and took a slug in his honour. He was 'a real American man' who died with a gun in his hand. I added my new books to the mantlepiece collection above the gas fire. I ironed my best suit and wandered down to the Picasso for a coffee. The poets were still scribbling. Sauntering along the King's Road, I discovered a town hall to my left, a cinema, a post office and a public library to my right. I went to the library and checked its layout.

19 August. I had arranged to meet Nurse Begley at Sloane Square. She told me I looked well. I told her that Dr Tonkin was quite pleased with me. She already knew Chelsea and its churches - St Luke's in Sydney Street and the Old Parish Church in Cheyne Walk. I took her for a light lunch at the Chelsea Kitchen. This nurse who sat opposite me had saved my life with her prayers, sure as can be sure. She was happy to sample the house wine and I raised my glass to her kindly act of nocturnal devotion. She told me that Nurse Bourney had been reconsidered by the Missionary Society and was attending classes in preparation for the next step in their selection process.

'I am sure you will pray for Nurse Bourney,' I said.

'I pray for all our nurses and patients every night,' she replied simply – putting me firmly in my unbelieving place.

After coffee, I escort her all the way back to her hospital quarters in deepest Pimlico where we parted like old friends. On the way home, I reflected on this great metropolis to which I now belonged. One got to know a place like London much as one did a jigsaw puzzle. First, you learned your way around your own little patch, then got to know another, then another, until you grew familiar with other patches of the city. Thereafter, it became a question of how soon you could join the various pieces together to make up the whole picture, the greater patchwork that lodged itself permanently in the mind.

26 August. Dinah (Greenwood), a handsome, friendly person I had met at one of Nick's open evenings, has invited me to dinner with David, her beau, at her flat on St George's Square, down on the

1961

edge of Pimlico by the Embankment. 'There's someone I'd like you to meet,' she said darkly.

She introduced us. The pale thin man with a haystack of blue hair and ostentatiously applied makeup greeted me with a smile and a royal inclination of his head.

'Quentin,' said Dinah, 'lives not far from you.'

'And where are you?' asked Quentin in a strangely dreamy sing-song voice.

'Shawfield Street,' I told him. 'And you?'

'Beaufort Street,' he said, 'so not far away.'

'Quentin has a special theory about dust,' said Dinah.

'Oh?'

'Yes, I never clean. After the first four years the dirt doesn't get any worse. In fact I think dust is even healthy for you.'

'I will remember that,' I said. 'But unfortunately I have a cleaner - she comes with the rent.

So cleaning is out of my hands'

'What do you have? A service flat?'

'No, a bedsitter.'

'And what do you pay for this paradise?'

'One pound seven and six a week.'

'Ah, well, there you are,' he said. 'You pay three times what I pay - hence the cleaning lady.'

'Quentin works as an artist's model,' said Dinah informatively.

'Oh! where?' I asked.

'At various art colleges. I've done it for years. Do you draw?' He was talking to me.

'No.' I said.

David joined us for dinner. He took up the cross-questioning of their riveting dust-worshipping guest.

'Do you write poetry, Quentin?'

'No, I'm a poor poet. I stick to mundane prose.'

'Your prose is far from mundane,' said Dinah. 'I've read some of your book, remember?'

'Ah, yes, I forgot.'

'It's extremely good.'

'I'm glad you like it,' said Quentin.

'Is it a novel you're writing?' I asked.

'An autobiography.'

'A poetic autobiography,' said Dinah.

'A long confession, but no De Profundis from the depths, like Oscar. I speak more from the heights.'

'You're a philosopher as well as a prose poet, Quentin.'

Quentin shrugged and turned to me.

'Do you know a poet called Harold Pinter?'

'I know of the playwright who goes by that name but not the poet,' I said.

'He's been to visit me a few times. He's also an actor. I haven't seen his plays - my meagre earnings don't stretch to theatres. But he writes particularly good poetry.

Watch out for him, I think he'll write something quite extraordinary one day, and people will sit up and take notice.'

'Perhaps he already has,' I said quietly.

'Do you cook for yourself, Quentin?' asked David, no doubt prompted by his slightly emaciated appearance.'

'No, I don't cook. I live entirely on a baby food called pabulum. Mostly, I eat nothing else. It saves me from the chore of having to concoct meals - a mysterious art to my way of thinking - and, of course, no washing up to steal long hours away from so short a life. Oh, and I drink a glass of stout every morning, religiously.'

'I have no pictures on my walls and I hate pets.' He turned his gaze upon me. 'What pictures do you have on your walls?'

'Well, none, as it happens,'

'Excellent.'

'But I was thinking of getting one of a dog.' I said this by way of a joke which I immediately regretted. From the look of sour disapproval that flitted across his face. After dinner, he said, 'I must go. I hope you don't mind. I like to walk through London at night alone. You never know what will turn up.'

He donned a jaunty hat, threw a red scarf carelessly around his neck, bowed to the company and departed with a flourish.

Dinah smiled at me. 'Worth meeting?'

'Not half! I won't forget him in a hurry,' I said.

GLIMPSES OF A BIOGRAPHER'S DIARY

'He'd never allow it,' said Dinah, laughing.

Afterwards, whenever I passed Beaufort Street, I thought fondly of Quentin in his dust-filled attic living on baby food in a strangely reconstructed womb of a world peopled by eccentric notions of all-encompassing freakery.

1 September. I dialled Nurse Peters' number and a tired female voice answered. 'Nurse Peters? I asked. 'I think she's on duty.' She said. 'Can she call you back?' I left a message together with my telephone number. Later someone summoned me from the hallway where the phone was located, and I clattered downstairs to take the call. Patrick, the new tenant in the basement flat, handed me the telephone. It was Peters inviting me round to the house she shared with some other nurses. She was cooking a curry and I was welcome to join her. Excited, I took a bath. Late afternoon was one of the few times it wasn't occupied by the young secretaries. Before long I was on the Tube to Victoria. Now I was leaping onto a bus, which took me down along Vauxhall Bridge Road. Then there was my bus stop, just a short walk from Denbigh Mews. And there was the flat - no 6, half hidden by a milk machine outside the grocery shop below. Peters opened the door. She was still in her nurse's uniform.

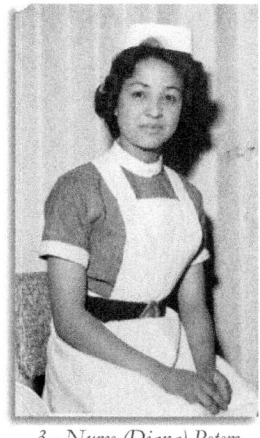

3 - Nurse (Diana) Peters

What a vision! Upstairs and inside a cavernous apartment were about half of the ward nurses - lounging, smoking, gossiping, laughing, rushing about readying themselves for dates, combing out their locks, applying a last-minute touch of lipstick or preparing to go on duty. Peters took me to the kitchen where she had the table laid for two. Very romantic. She was full of bright smiles, good humour and simple joie de vivre. I couldn't remember ever having met such an enchantress - so effervescent. Her name, I finally discovered was Diana. She asked after my health and was delighted when I told her that Dr Tonkin was quite pleased with me. 'That's great!' she said. 'He's great! The sitting room was now deserted. Peters, or perhaps I should now call her Diana, put on a record and we danced. She was a perfect fit against my right shoulder and didn't resist when I drew her close. We kissed. After coffee she saw me to the door, leaving me with the prospect of more evenings (and maybe even nights) of passion in Pimlico.

Then came my first visit to the Royal Court. Luther was John Osborne powerful drama about the German Protestant reformer Martin Luther. Albert Finney's role of Luther was vigorous and earthy.

8th. I invited Diana over for dinner. This time I was determined to impress. Candles, joss-sticks, a red paper table cloth, bread rolls, smoked oysters straight from the tin, chicken and ham pie, tomato salad, ice cream and champagne (the half bottle I could just afford). She was more spirited than ever. Her eyes flashed, she laughed, touched my arm, sipped champagne and gossiped avidly. Then we repaired to the divan. Afterwards, we laughed and lounged and talked sweet nothings and smoked Gauloises together. I saw her all the way back to Denbigh Mews.

Patrick, a very likeable gay man, was, he informed me, chauffeur to the stars, when they were in London. He reeled off a few names - Noel Coward, Boris Karloff, Elizabeth Taylor. Who needs to go to Hollywood when you live in Chelsea? He was sufficiently favoured by Mrs. Henkey to be allowed to keep a little dog down there in the basement with him - a quiet dog, even quieter than Patrick.

GLIMPSES OF A BIOGRAPHER'S DIARY

A familiar figure passed me by in the street on my way home to buy a newspaper. I belatedly recognised him as George Devine, the man who, together with Tony Richardson, ran the English Stage Company at the Royal Court. This was the man, who brought Samuel Beckett over from Paris, and discovered Osborne and Look Back in Anger. He was there in the Osborne Luther the other night.

This weekend most of the bedsitters were away. The telephone rang and I descended at top speed to grab it before it fell silent. I was hoping that it was Diana, but a soft, strangely familiar voice asked, 'Is Patrick there? May I speak to him?'

'I'll check.'

'Thank you.'

I dashed down the stairs and knocked, but there was no reply. I returned to the phone.

'He appears to be out, I'm afraid.'

'I see. Would you tell him Mr. Karloff called?'

'Er, yes.'

'Thank you.' The phone went down.

Good God! That was Frankenstein's Monster and the Edinburgh body snatcher in person.

No sooner was I back in my room than the phone rang again. This time it was Diana. She was all alone in the flat and feeling frightened. Would I go over? Would I? It was pouring rain and I had no umbrella but I dashed onto the King's Road and hailed a taxi.

1961

'Where to, Guv?'

'Denbigh Mews.'

'Where's that?'

'Pimlico.'

But then, by the magic power of pilotage which all London cabbies possess, he did get me there. The driving raindrops were sending up little fountains on the pavement and, faced with a wall of water, I was certain to get drowned unless I could get undercover quickly. Fortunately, Diana had heard the taxi and was at the door. She dragged me inside and we embraced. She was in her dressing gown and little else. She took my hand and led me upstairs to her room where she dived into bed, throwing me a towel to dry my hair. 'Come on! Hurry up!' she said.

I started getting out of my things. No pyjamas. I hesitated.

'I'm cold,' she said. 'Just come on.'

Finally my clothes were off. I climbed into bed and found that under the sheets she'd deftly shed her dressing gown. The quiet drum roll of rain against the window panes made being together in the dark even more deliciously cosy than I could ever have imagined. Dawn crept through the thin curtains.

'Come on, pig-hog,' she said, 'Fun time is over and I have to go on duty.'

A lingering doorstep clinch and I left. The rain had stopped so I decided to walk back to Chelsea - not so very far away, I discovered. As I walked, pieces of the great London jigsaw puzzle were falling into place. Denbigh Mews, Vauxhall Bridge Road, Buckingham

GLIMPSES OF A BIOGRAPHER'S DIARY

Palace Road. Pimlico Road, St Leonard's Terrace, Redesdale Street, Shawfield Street!

Next morning, life seemed very good. I looked at my desk (the oilskin-covered table by the window) and there I had everything a writer needed - an array of pens, including the Parker fountain pen that had seen me through my finals, a bottle of Quink black ink, my notebooks, a pile of pristine lined paper - foolscap, of course - pencils of different shades - HB, 2B, 4B - a favourite rubber, my old Concise Oxford and a thesaurus. To the side, on a spare chair, sat my prized portable, the Imperial, in its hard black case. I sat for a long time trying to decide which was the best way to start a great opus - a long hand draft followed by a typed one, or a draft typed straight onto the page? After much deliberation, I made my decision. I swept everything off the table, set up my typewriter with a pile of typing paper and sat down to think. Now all I needed was the inspiration to set the creative process in motion.

I had written a novel before I went up to university and sent it out, to André Deutsch in the first instance. It got the thumbs down at Deutsch but did come back with a note encouraging me to try again. This would be that second try.

The thing that would get it going was a party. The invitation came from Ursula, a girl I had met at one of Nick's evenings - tall, long blonde hair and Flaxman telephone number - and an admirably spacious flat over a corner shop in the King's Road. Back at the home pad I started a novel. It was about wild young things living in a hedonist haze. In the background the music pulsed. Nevertheless, that was my cue and soon, sat there at my typewriter, the story began merrily to flow. It never got beyond the first two chapters because other events and adventures crowded it out.

1961

14 September, Thursday. It's Battle of Britain Day on Saturday 16th. Janet, my old university friend and keen member of CND, called. 'We're having a great demonstration against The Bomb on Saturday. Will you come?'

'Of course.' I said.

She was there with her new husband, Karl. He was dynamic, very funny, a millionaire communist and main backer of Peace News! She was tall, slim with long black hair and a guitar for singing liberation songs – Joan Baez, Pete Seeger, Georges Brassens. We marched along chatting all the time - the nations of the world, whirling dervishes and all. And there were the celebrities - Michael Foot, John Osborne, Sheila Delaney, Arnold Wesker, the great Bertie Russell, and a brace of ecclesiastical worthies - Canon Collins, Donald Soper together with other vicars. Speeches in Trafalgar Square followed. Heady stuff! To the barricades, comrades! The people will prevail! Where's the guillotine? But no beheadings today. We were all peaceniks here - Christian Socialists with soft smiles, Marxists with peaceful expressions and blood red flags, the Anarchists with black flags and jolly songs, the Trots, always ready for a punch-up, though not today. Onward pacifist soldiers! Herald the new dawn! Forward to victory! ('Over my dead body!' The fascist Dr Chester must have been spitting blood over in Dean Ryle Street. 'String 'em up!') Don't listen to him. Just turn the other cheek, comrades. But if it does come to a roughhouse, the Trots will oblige. My friends were in a good mood and so was I. The singing and chanting were hypnotic.

30 October. Today, just six weeks after the big march, the Soviet Comrades let us all down with a very big bang. At the newspaper shop nearby I bought The Guardian. The headlines screamed, THE RUSSIANS EXPLODE 50 MEGATON BOMB. I rushed back to my bedsit, hoisted my typewriter onto the oilskin

tablecloth, scrolled in a sheet of A4, pulled up a chair and struck the first key. I had my title ready-made, courtesy of the Guardian - my take on that headline: THE RUSSIANS EXPLODED A 50 MEGATON BOMB TODAY. The story flowed freely - very surreal - about disconnection and disintegration in the face of impending catastrophe. When it was finished I was rather proud of it.

Diana came visiting, straight off duty. I wanted to read her my story, but she had a tale of her own to tell and started to cry. 'What is it?' I put my arm round her shoulders. Sobs heaved, shook and coursed through her tiny body. After a few minutes she took a deep breath, then managed to compose herself and began to speak in a faltering voice, dabbing away tears. 'Today we laid out a 93 year old woman, and we found she was still a virgin. Just imagine all the loving pleasure she's missed out on.' It was very touching that this young nurse should pour out her heart for an elderly patient - a sadly unfulfilled woman, as she saw it. That was empathy and it was the Nightingale in her. At that moment I could have loved her forever for her golden heart and wholehearted humanity.

2 November. James Thurber died. I had a tape recording of some American actor reading his brilliant fable, The Unicorn in the Garden – a masterly piece of comic writing which can only have come from America. Someone wrote an article in the Guardian pointing out that with Hemingway dead, closely followed by Dashiel Hammett and now Thurber, three big American writers had passed away within a few months of each another.

―――――

Chapter 6

Job Hunting
1961 - 1962

It was Christmas and I had to go home to visit my ailing mother. She and my dad had finally summoned up the good sense to escape their picturesque house in deepest South Devon and migrate back to a Midlands town house within hailing distance of old friends and their eldest daughter. But, the unhappiness of the past few years had caught up with her and all the light and life in her pale blue eyes had been slowly and sadly extinguished. I arrived full of bonhomie, certain that my cheery chatter would work the magic and summon my distracted mother back into the real world. But she was, I found, deep down in the sloughy depths, and my joviality, intended to lift her spirits high, failed utterly. Reluctantly, I took my leave of mother, then, turning at the gate, waved goodbye to my sad-looking father, and headed for the station.

I was en route back to London, where I'd planned to spend Christmas Day with my Nightingale Nurse, Diana. It was a freezing day - biting winds, train carriages like ice boxes, and now I was in the waiting-room of Rugby station. Dejected passengers, wrapped in heavy winter overcoats and swathed in woollen scarves, clustered, shivering, around a small fireplace in which a few coals glowed half-heartedly. A voice greeted me from the corner - a voice I recognised. Good God! It was the girl who had once turned heads at the university - a tall, handsome young woman always surrounded by intense-looking admirers in a corner of the students' union coffee lounge, before suddenly and mysteriously disappearing at the end of her first year. It was Prue, swathed in winter coat and scarves, huddled together with a woman I took correctly to be her mother. Prue greeted me like an old friend. She was very forthcoming; mother Pam was more reserved, but watchful. Prue was travelling to London to have her breasts reduced on the NHS, she told me. I glanced at her ample bosoms and felt sad to think that I might be seeing the last of them. We talked nonstop all the way to King's Cross, and I was invited to convalesce with her and Pam in Rugby after my approaching operation. The romance of a brief encounter in a station waiting room had not exactly escaped me, but the winter setting gave it more the feel of a novel by Dostoyevsky or Tolstoy than a one-act play by Noel Coward.

25 December. Venturing out into Shawfield Street on this Christmas morning, I was met with a remarkable scene. Snow had fallen overnight and Chelsea had been transformed into a Never, Never Land, conjured from the pen of J. M. Barrie. An Edwardian fantasy had become an Elizabethan reality. I wandered down the King's Road. No traffic had yet passed that morning, so all roads and shops were coated in white like a scene from a Rackhamesque Christmas card. Godfrey Street, Bywater Street, Jubilee Place, Markham Square and all the way round to Draycott Place and Cadogan Square had been transformed. Lovely imposing red brick houses, homes for the tastefully wealthy, blinking brightly with Christmas lights and all tricked out in the purest white. This was the land of Wendy, Peter Pan and Tinker Bell, and in all probability

1962

of Snow White, too - a pantomime setting - a transient moment, fated to melt away back into the pages of some long-discarded Victorian picture book.

And so, another Christmas became a Christmas Past, which, with its many Ghosts, slipped silently away. Diana was on duty; I was alone. I huddled close to the flaring gas fire with copies of my London Magazines for company. So, many heroic names stared out at me - Camus, dead almost two years, Graham Greene, Cocteau, Forster, Graves, Ted Hughes and Sylvia Plath still around. I knew all about being a magazine editor, was one once at my university, and anyone caring to offer me a job like that wouldn't find me hesitating for fear of any heart attacks.

A slim paperback of Lowry's poems, picked up at John Sandoe's bookshop, was in the same series as Allen Ginsberg's Howl, published by City Lights Books of San Francisco. This was so-called beatnik poetry. These were supposed to be wildly individualistic and wildly imaginative nonconformist poets, takers of mind-altering drugs who allowed their freewheeling muses to carry them wheresoever they might, unrestrained by traditional verse forms. Included in Lowry's selection, there was a picture of the bard, with neatly clipped pencil moustache, looking for all the world like a British officer - a major perhaps from some ancient regiment. His poetry, however, smacked of the sea - poetic sketches of oceanic episodes, of storms and calms, of roistering nights ashore and hangovers in strange ports of call. There were poems about alcoholics, soldiers and drunken sailors, and poems about failure.

1962

My time on National Assistance was running out. Before long, the doctors would sign me off and I'd be looking for work again. I applied for a teaching post in London and enquired about postgraduate courses at the University.

22 January. Along the King's Road I met Dave Croft, a law student at our old university when last I saw him. Now, he was attached to the chambers of Michael Sherrard, the leading counsel for the defense of James Hanratty, charged with the A6 murder. Dave stood six foot seven in his cotton socks - a giant among lawyers. He assured me that 'Hanratty is guilty for sure'. I couldn't quite believe that lawyers could defend someone whom they felt sure was guilty. Obviously I was more naïve than I imagined. Although Hanratty was found guilty and hanged, for many years afterwards leading journalists and penal reformers would argue that the evidence didn't stack up. There were several official enquiries, all of which decided that the right man had been executed, but these conclusions continued to be questioned. In 2002, based on DNA evidence, the Court of Appeal finally decided that the evidence pointed incontrovertibly to Hanratty's guilt. All those years later, my old friend Croft, by then a judge, had been vindicated.

All through January, the weather was bitingly cold – the wind had teeth that could gnaw down to the bone. As I made my way along the King's Road, my eye was caught by the window display of menswear at John Michael's boutique. At the centre was a winter overcoat of blue suede, lined with black fur, with a magnificent white fur collar to top it off. It was an article of such rare beauty that it stuck in my mind and quite refused to go away. I went back to the shop in the next few days and gazed at that coat. It remained unsold and I returned to my room and prayed that it would continue to remain unsold. One day, on impulse I went into the shop and asked to try on the coat. The assistant looked at me and smiled. Nevertheless, he took it out of the window and held it open for me to put on. It was magnificently warm and even I had to

1962

admit it did make me look good from the ankles upward – at least that's what the mirror told me. I was duly admiring myself when another customer entered. It was Lance Percival, an English actor I had seen in some recent Ealing comedy film. As he passed he shook his head. 'No,' he said. Then, looking down, he murmured, 'Nice shoes though.' I handed the coat back to the assistant and crept away down the King's Road, quietly swearing to myself that I'd be back later, hoping that the thing would still be there. The offer of a part-time teaching job at a primary school in North London came through but I was permitted to start a term late to allow time for my operation and recovery.

12 April. I was admitted to the Westminster Hospital, Surgical ward for partial thyroidectomy operation the next day. None of the nurses there were familiar, but I did have an almost constant visitor - my dear delectable nurse Diana who popped in at whatever free moment she had from Austin Taylor Ward. One of the amazing things about general anaesthetics is that, a friendly man or woman sticks a needle into your arm and you're gone, only to instantly awake, with everything fixed - an eye, a leg, heart or a thyroid gland. You'd lost hours of your life at the flash of a knife without being aware of it. Miraculous! As I woke up, there was Diana hovering over me. She stayed with me as I was wheeled back to the ward. But after only a short while I felt as though I was being strangulated. Most of my thyroid may have gone but an invisible constriction, was squeezing the breath of life out of me. I made gagging noises, and pointed to my throat. Diana jumped into action and called for a doctor. I was rushed back to the theatre to be sliced open again. Back came the anaesthetist's needle, and I was gone, there and back in a trice.

I returned to the ward where the loyal Diana was still waiting. A surgeon, standing beside her, still in theatre gown, was explaining what had happened. The drugs they had been giving me to treat my thyroid, he said, were also anti-coagulants - something they had failed to take into account when operating. So, I had what he called a haematoma - a steady seepage of blood out of the blood vessel into the surrounding tissues with nowhere else to go - a deadly necklace which had begun to compress my throat and slowly could have snuffed the life out of me. They had to bring in a blood donor to pump fresh blood directly from him into me. 'Fresh blood coagulated best,' the surgeon said. And so I was saved by an anonymous gentleman, summoned from his lunch by the doctors who had come running, bearing the fresh blood that would put a stop to the bleeding thyroid. Now, for a time at least, I prayed, no more crises. Just let me recover and enjoy the pretty and caring companion who had stayed at my side through thin blood and thick.

4 - Gordon, Cyprus

Back home to recover, I was gripped by my love affair with Lawrence Durrell's island books such as *Prospero's Cell* and *Reflections on a Marine Venus*. *Bitter Lemons* I had read avidly after returning from National Service in Cyprus – such a blissful change from Egypt. That taste for Greece had lingered on as a love affair lingers on. Suddenly, I was seized by a brilliant idea. Where else could one write poetry except beside the Mediterranean? I decided to put a small ad in the Times enquiring after the best place to settle in Greece for a writer wanting sea and sun and wine for inspiration. I thought that Diana and I would migrate there and live the idyllic life among ancient gods and olive groves. At her flat, I put the idea to her, but she misinterpreted what I was suggesting - that it was a proposal -

and hugged me in an outburst of enthusiasm, saying 'Yes, yes!' Suddenly I thought, what was I getting myself into? I was in no position to get married. I could barely support myself, and in Greece we'd both be at a loss as to how to make a living. But it was quite evident that marriage was what she wanted. 'No, no, you don't understand,' I said and she froze, then backed away and finally erupted with fury when she realised what I was really considering. It seemed so dramatically out of character that I simply didn't know what to say to her and slunk away back to Chelsea, ashamed of my utter lack of chivalry and sensibility.

Next day, full of remorse. I phoned her, but her housemates informed me that she was transferred to a hospital in Roehampton. I called Roehampton Hospital repeatedly, but she was always unobtainable. When finally, I did get hold of her she told me simply, 'I am getting married to a doctor.' To me it all seemed very suspicious – the sudden transfer and the equally sudden engagement. Had she been seeing this doctor behind my back? I didn't know and didn't ask. Our ways had parted and I could only nurse my self-inflicted wound and learn to live with my bitter regrets - after all, I had loved the girl. On the other hand, I simply hadn't known how volatile she was and realised that a future with her could be stressful to say the least especially in my present medical condition.

Fortunately, I had plenty to divert me. My university friend, Prue, from Rugby had invited me to her parents' home to recuperate after my thyroid operation. I called her to let her know that I had the operation and that the surgeons had discharged me. 'You must come,' she said. 'Pam will be away, and we'll have the house to ourselves. Is that OK?' It was an offer I couldn't easily refuse. The weather remained arctic but now at least I could wear a normal collar, a thought to warm the heart. Prue was waiting for my train and was motherly and attentive. Theirs was a terraced house in a street of terraced houses, and Prue's mother had already departed for her holiday.

She wanted me to write, she announced. 'Write what?' I asked. 'I love the sort of things you wrote and published at university,' she said - odd little stories, strange, surreal and nonsensical mostly I thought - and she wanted me to write the same for her now. She was recovering from a squalid affair, she confessed, and it would help her to engage with someone creative.

'You could always try Freud or Lawrence,' I suggested.

She flashed that enigmatic Gioconda smile which had made her so intriguing at university.

After breakfast next morning she built up the fire and gave me her instructions - 'Just sit yourself down and write while I go shopping - then we can sit in front of a roaring fire and you can read to me what you had written.'

'Have you read Metamorphosis?' she enquired

'Ah, Ovid,' I said.

'Kafka,' she replied.

'No,' I said lamely.

'You lucky man,' she said. 'You still have that wonderful experience to look forward to.' And, having delivered that pearl of worldly advice, she sallied forth to do the shopping.

I wrote another surrealistic sketch and read it aloud to her on her return. She seemed quite pleased but told me I must add further depth to it, be more elliptical, more elusive, give it even more mystery. There was a mystery about her that I was anxious to solve.

1962

How was it that she had disappeared so suddenly from university after her first year? She observed me closely, as if wondering whether she could trust me. Then she told me her story. Before the war, her father had been a Blackshirt, a speechwriter for Oswald Mosley. During the war he'd been interned. Afterwards, he had bought a farm. At home, on her first long vacation from university, her mother had asked her to take a lunch hamper to where he was working in some distant corner of the farm. She carried the hamper across the fields, looking for him. Finally, she found him under a tree. He'd hanged himself from the lowest branch - which is why she hadn't returned to university. That evening, after dinner, she invited me into her bed saying, 'I am cold.' I didn't find her at all cold. And I couldn't help thinking that that the NHS plastic surgeon had decided to leave well alone. I certainly didn't wish to leave Prue but had to get back to do some serious job hunting.

At the Royal Court, Wesker's *Chips With Everything* was playing. I'd already seen his earlier play, The Kitchen, at a Sunday Times student drama festival in Oxford. It was superbly acted, beautifully staged and choreographed like a ballet. Afterwards, to everyone's delight, Wesker came onstage to address the audience, cutting a very dramatic figure - casually dressed and full of youthful fire, with a lovely sonorous voice and real stage presence. We were riveted. Now, here at the Royal Court, he had given us a powerful play about a bunch of National Service recruits, with Frank Finlay, as the drill sergeant, a combination of caustic wit and seething contempt - a theatrical tour de force, with a memorable performance from Ronald Lacey as his pathetic victim, Smiler.

The enigmatic Prue arrived on a visit from Rugby and spent the day with me, mostly discussing literature - even the cuddle she insisted on before she left had a somewhat Lawrentian flavour to it. Thank god she didn't ask for something Kafkaesque. I wouldn't have known what to do.

May. There were shows to be seen. One of the best for my money was *Beyond the Fringe* at the Fortune Theatre, with more of those devilish clever Oxbridge grads. The Times called it 'Clowning with Distinction'. This time the distinguished clowns were Peter Cook, Dudley Moore, Alan Bennett, and Jonathan Miller. I loved the brilliant monologue by Peter Cook about being a miner who would have preferred to have been a judge - but he 'didn't have the Latin'. And a hilarious mock sermon by Alan Bennett in which the 'Reverend' attempted to draw a moral from the obscurest of obscure biblical texts and a tin of sardines.

I began writing to newspapers telling them what a good journalist I was - having read English, edited my University Literary Magazine, reviewed books, plays and films, taught, travelled and being more than ready to travel again. I followed up with phone calls. 'Is that the Daily Blaster?' 'Yes.' I make my pitch. He said, 'Are you a member of the National Union of Journalists?' (NUJ) 'No, but I'd like to join.' Man at the NUJ: 'Which paper are you working for?' 'I'm hoping for an offer.' 'Call back when you get it.' It was the same with every newspaper I tried – The Guardian, The Observer, The Times, The Telegraph, and a few others, less mainstream. Long after having given up, I received a letter from the Times Educational Supplement (TES) inviting me to meet the editor. I phoned and fixed a date.

I'd been attending the outpatient clinic at the Westminster Hospital and Dr Tonkin had decided to discharge me into the care of a trusted GP - Dr Bryans whose surgery was in nearby Pimlico Road. This bright blue-eyed doctor emphasised to me that, because I had had rheumatic fever, at the first sign of a sore throat I should see him for an immediate course of penicillin. He placed his stethoscope over my heart and declared that it sounded fine except for 'a slight systolic murmur'. I was fit to work, but still only just. My thyroid still needed the attention of a surgeon.

June. My date with the TES was suddenly upon me. A short ride on the tube by way of the Circle and District Line took me to Blackfriars Bridge - a strange bit of London, new to me. Which way was what? Ah, over there! That big block of offices sprawled across the river side of Printing House Square. I stepped boldly through the main entrance and the uniformed doorkeeper directed me upstairs and to the right. The poorly lit interior seemed endlessly labyrinthine and I had to keep asking directions as I threaded my way along endless corridors and around endless corners. I was inside the bowels of a great newspaper. Typewriters rattled in all sides. Men in shirtsleeves carried copy hither and thither. Now I was passing doors labelled 'Editor, Times, Times Sports, Times Diary, Times Foreign, Deputy Editor, Times Literary Supplement. And here at last was my door - 'TES.' Knock, knock. A voice bade me enter. The door opened onto a scene from Dickens. Manuscripts were stacked high, low and haphazardly; books were piled here and there in drunken heaps, prevented from toppling only by some invisible hand. Amid this apparent chaos, there at a desk sat an elderly gentleman in a dusty-looking dark suit, crumpled white shirt and winged collar. He was reading intently through a pince-nez. I'd stepped back into the nineteenth century, and paused in that doorway to the past, taken aback and yet drawn, as if hypnotised, through it. The elderly gentleman gestured me to a chair and I sat politely on the edge of it, facing him. He read on for a while before carefully removing the pince-nez. He coughed and looked up at me.

'Mr. --- er ---?

'Mr. Bowker.' I said

GLIMPSES OF A BIOGRAPHER'S DIARY

'Yes, quite.' He peered at me intently, then said in an offhand way, 'Are you related in any way to the secretary and recent biographer of The Lord Chief Justice,

Sir Edgar of that ilk?' I was taken aback. Not the first question I had anticipated. But, inspiration plus a rapid piece of recall came to my aid. 'My father did once tell me that there was a legal branch of the family in London, though I never met any of them.' That was enough for the gentleman. 'Do you think you could write fourth leaders for us?' he asked. I couldn't think what TES fourth leaders were, but the idea was tantalising. Unfortunately, my hesitation was noticed. 'What would you really like to write?' he asked.

'Well, play reviews or film reviews, really,' I said. He smiled knowingly and after a few further pleasantries I was bidden adieu.

After a couple of undecided weeks, I finally signed up for a postgraduate diploma in Sociology and Psychology at the Institute of Education, just to keep one foot inside the academic door.

With a career as a theatre critic in prospect - however faint - I used a few of my scarce pounds to fill gaps in my library of plays. I read most of Shakespeare, now I must devour all of Ibsen and Shaw. I stocked up on the relevant Penguin editions. My library would soon need extra space. To save money, I joined the Chelsea Public Library so that when funds ran low I could still get plays I needed to read fairly easily.

No news yet from Printing House Square, but I had not altogether abandoned my ambition of a career in journalism or even in writing fiction. There was a story I had long been wanting to write, about an experience I had at eighteen, in Colombo, the great harbour city of Ceylon while steaming homewards from Australia, where I'd persuaded a rickshaw man to swap places and let me pull him

1962

around town, that creating a mild sensation in the bazaar quarter on the way back. I finally typed up my account of this Kiplingesques escapade, and in June sent it off to the BBC. A week later, I was invited to meet a producer. The invitation came via a telephone call - the means, I discovered, whereby the BBC then checked if one's speaking voice was suitable for broadcasting.

That led to my first ever visit to Portland Place and a close up of Broadcasting House with its naughty Eric Gill stone carvings. On this visit to the heart of English enlightenment I was treading where Yeats, Eliot, Dylan Thomas and Orwell once trod. In fact, wasn't this the original model for the Ministry of Truth in Nineteen Eighty-Four?

About ten minutes after I had given my name to the receptionist, down the stairs came a smooth and smiling middle aged gentleman with the envious name of George Angel. He was a Greek expatriate and his English was immaculate. He conducted me up to his office through the serpentine interior of the nation's nerve centre. George produced a programme called Midweek which went out at precisely twelve noon every Wednesday. He liked my story about the rickshaw man, he said, but wanted me to make it even more likeable by changing the opening and closing passages slightly. He suggested giving the man a name, and having him offer me a job on the rickshaw rank at the end of our ride. I obediently moulded the piece as requested.

A few days later, Patrick summoned me downstairs to the phone again. It was a voice from the TES. Could I cover a story for them next Thursday? 'It's a book event - to celebrate the sale of the one millionth copy of the Railway Series of the Reverend Gilbert Awdry's tales about Thomas the Tank Engine. It's at the Bluebell Railway in East Grinstead. Johnny Morris, the TV Zoo man will be there. It means joining a coach party at Temple Station at 10am.'

GLIMPSES OF A BIOGRAPHER'S DIARY

Thursday. My morning at the Labour Exchange, dammit! But, how could I resist such a glittering literary occasion? I'd get there by hook or by crook. I remained calm and collected. 'Can I call you back?'

'Of course.'

I quickly dialled the Exchange, 'I've been offered a day's work on Thursday next. How early could I draw my National Assistance money?'

'We open at nine.'

'I have to be at Temple Station at ten.'

'If you come to the front of the queue, we could possibly deal with you at around ten to nine.'

'Great.' I gave my name and quickly hung up. Then I dialled The TES.

'Yes, Thursday's fine,' I said.

'Good. I'll send you your press pass.'

George Angel sent me a copy of the final approved script of my talk and a date for the broadcast on 10 August. I was now officially both a journalist and broadcaster.

At the Fulham Labour Exchange, the queue extended for some twenty yards. I was appropriately dressed in my best-suit and ready for my date at Temple. When I sauntered to the front of the queue trying to look inconspicuous, there was muttering.

'Oi! Back of the queue, you!'

'Bloody toffs!'

1962

'It's all right for some.'

An official was looking out for me and the door was unlocked. I went through, signed and collected my £5.00. Now I had to dash for that coach at Temple, but first I had to run the gauntlet of angry voices again.

More muttering. Rhubarb, rhubarb! Boo!

The Circle and District didn't let me down but I was the very last of the literary party to arrive. In a second, I was inside the coach and being shown to my seat, which was next to a rather well set up gentleman with white hair and a plummy voice. He shot out a hand. 'Jack Morpurgo, National Book League.' But that name was ringing a bell. My mind trawled back to College and an essay written for old Micky Moss, my English tutor.

'Oh, are you the Morpurgo who wrote that splendid book on Charles Lamb?'

He answered with a beaming smile. We connected. Our conversation blossomed and remained in flower all the way to East Grinstead. We parked in a field beside the Bluebell Railway Line, lovingly restored by enthusiasts. I was directed to a marquee reserved, so said the sign, for the 'Press', where my fellow journalists had foregathered. There were tables with sections reserved. Every paper in its designated place. We were made welcome with food and drink.

'Where do I sit?'

'Who're you representing?' The girl with the clipboard glanced at her list.

'The Times Education Supplement.'

She smiled and escorted me to a table set apart from the pack. The place name read, 'Gentleman from the Times.' I sat in my place of honour trying to look the part and reflected that this morning I was drawing National Assistance money at the Fulham Labour Exchange. Well, now, at the wave of a fairy wand, I'm 'The Gentleman from the Times.' This was the life! I took a tipple. The hacks took many more and became jovial.

Afterwards, I was buttonholed by the a man festooned with cameras.

'You from the Times?'

'That's right.'

'I'm taking your pics. Have you got an angle yet?'

'An angle?'

So, the gentleman from The Times had to have an angle, did he? I told him I didn't have an angle as yet. He looked mildly disappointed. Even so, he got some good background shots. So here's something to learn for the future - taking pictures to sell with articles. Photo-journalism - Cartier Bresson, Robert Capra, Lee Miller, er - Gordon Bowker.

'Why is Morris the Zoo man here?' I asked. 'Is Thomas the Tank Engine just another large mammal to him?'

'Publicity,' said the cameraman, taking a few long shots of the animated animal man. His cynicism was soon ringing true. Morris gave a short talk saying he had read every Thomas book ever published. In fact, we were told, he'd committed some of them to tape – they were like his own children, he said. Then he introduced the author.

1962

Reverend Gilbert Awdry described how he wrote the first Thomas story to entertain his children. Even the hard-bitten men from the Mirror and the Sketch offered up polite applause. Clearly the Reverend had hit a spot. He'd got it! This crowd of ill-assorted ruffians had all wanted to be little boy engine drivers before they wanted to be overgrown boozy hacks. Well, both jobs had things in common when you come to think of it - a great deal of shoveling, letting off steam and sounding off at high speed. I point this out to the man with the cameras. 'That's your angle,' he said cheerfully and disappeared off to get some 'pictures'. I hoped I wouldn't change my mind and leave his pictures looking wildly out of place. A copy of the millionth and first copy of the Railway Series, signed by the author, was held aloft by an eager young woman from the publisher's sales team. There were few takers.

We hopped aboard the Bluebell Express and seated ourselves in the quaint old-fashioned carriages. There was a whistle from the guard, and a toot and a sharp hiss of steam from an engine decked out in a spanking new coat of bright Lincoln green paint - just what the Reverend ordered. Then off we chuffed and rattled the short distance from East Grinstead to Sheffield Park via Kingscote and Horsted Keynes, through lush, leafy Sussex countryside, under a bridge, then down through a rabbit hole of a tunnel. The engine tooted again as we were swallowed up in darkness. It was all good old fashioned fun - a uniformed guard with a green flag, a smart stationmaster at all stops, and beautifully restored stations, with cast iron chocolate machines and notices advertising liver pills and enchanting holidays in places impossible to reach on this fun line.

The hacks laughed a lot and told questionable stories but were otherwise well behaved. The photographer sneaked a couple of shots of them, then popped his head out of the window to catch sight of the engine puffing round a bend ahead. After a brief stopover for tea in the station refreshment-cum-waiting room, we returned to East Grinstead and took our leave of the Reverend, the young lady from the publishers and the jolly Zoo man. On the coach journey back to Temple everyone slept. Even the Chairman of the National Book League snoozed in a gentle literary fashion.

———

Chapter 7

Journalist and School Teacher

1962-1963

Back at Shawfield Street, I slaved over my piece, picking out the letters thoughtfully on my portable, including the angle about all hacks present being little boys aspiring to become engine drivers. I then put the manuscript in an envelope, posted it off to the TES. My article on the Reverend Awdry, Thomas the Tank Engine and the animal man duly appeared in the TES, and I had the first cutting for my portfolio. Even the pictures fitted my chosen angle. A cheque for four guineas arrived in the post. It was undoubtedly the beginning of my journalistic career.

18 June. At Woodbury Down Primary School, I was a schoolteacher again - for three days a week. Returning to the classroom was not difficult to take because this time I had chosen to teach young pupils. The school was close to Finsbury Park, and I was fortunate enough to have highly civilised colleagues. This one taught music and played occasionally for the London Philharmonic; Doreen taught drama and directed Wizard of Oz at our school hall; another was a published poet and another painted.

Being North London, more than a few of the teachers were Jewish, so culture reigned and the head teacher, Miss Philpott, had decided quite deliberately to grace her staffroom with artistic colleagues. The teaching was not too onerous and I made it through my initial month without collapsing. My first pay cheque arrived and, put together with the balance in my bank account was at last beginning to look reasonably healthy.

5 - *Woodbury Down Primary School, with Head Miss Philpott and Gordon Bowker back right*

27 July. The summer vacation yawned ahead. Everyone in the staffroom looked exhausted and so was I. The class I had been given were probably also exhausted. I asked Miss Philpott, 'Would it be possible for me to take an entry class of seven year olds all the way through the school.' She said, 'I'll think about it.

1962

A colleague, Doreen, the alluring and dramatic teacher of drama, said on the spur of the moment, 'Let's go to Paris,' and on the spur of the moment, I said, 'Why not?' And so, in no time, there we were at a hotel, two rooms booked, on the Rue St Jacques just across from the Luxembourg Gardens. We breakfasted on coffee and croissants at a café overlooking the Seine and watched artists in berets and open-toed sandals painting Notre Dame. We found a wonderful bookshop along the Left Bank called Mistral (now Shakespeare and Company), run by a tall American, George Whitman, a descendant of the poet. The interior was a cavern of mysteries, a wonderland of books – books piled, books strewn, books perched on shelves, books lying flat or at drunken angles or standing to attention – on tables, on floors, in corners, on staircases, and under staircases. Books, books, books - and George, himself a book, with his indefinable American accent and that connection to the other Whitman.

After a few days, Doreen and I decided to go our separate ways, to pursue our personal tastes. Somewhere along the Left Bank, I met a handsome Russian girl called Tatiana, and made a date. Next day, over lunch at a café, we were engaged in animated conversation, and I said something that made her bristle. She leapt up and ran off, throwing a Tsarist curse over her shoulder in my direction by way of farewell.

10 August. Now it was time to get off to Broadcasting House, and into a studio with George Angel. My talk was duly recorded and, having spoken to the nation, I came away feeling that finally I had arrived. That talk brought me a merry little cheque for seven guineas which I paid even more merrily into my new account at the Chelsea Branch of the Westminster Bank.

I phoned Prue to give her the news of my success and my BBC triumph. But before I could speak she said, 'Oh Gordon. I'm engaged, so I won't be able to see you again. I met this man.'

'Ah,' I said.

'The thing is, he has an Aston Martin and I just couldn't say no to him.' She said.

Could this really be the deep and mysterious Prue speaking? I was stunned but remained strangely relaxed.

I wished her luck and could say no more. Here endeth the lesson. Well, not quite because later came news that this lovely girl had married a man called O'Connell, the man who owned the Aston Martin, I presumed, and was obviously wealthy.

3 September. Back at school, Miss Philpott agreed that I could have an entry class and take them all the way through the school to the age of eleven. It was only a small class of twenty, but I was given it on the understanding that I would take in any latecomers and any whom other teachers found difficult. On the first day, I met them they seemed awfully tiny, but very sweet and we warmed to one another from the very beginning. I always felt protective towards them and worked out a way of teaching them which was pleasurable to all. It was delightful to see how they made friends, broke up and reformed the same friendships and always they were so kind to one another. I was fortunate with this particular class of children. Perhaps there was a teacher in me somewhere after all.

One boy, who joined the class I shall never forget. His name was Ben, and he was very dark. He sat at the end of the row and spoke never a word. When I called his name from the register in the morning he just sat there, quite unresponsive. I simply noted his presence and ticked his name accordingly. Later, I called him to

1962

my desk to read, he stood there in silence while I made one-sided conversation with him. Then, he returned to his seat. I only discovered why Ben was so silent by accident. A party of children were taken for a week to Seaford. One of the supervising staff filmed them playing on the beach and the film was later shown to the school. There was a shot of Ben down at the water's edge, quite alone. He was bending down, burying his hands in the sand and holding them up in front of him. In that part of the world the rock was chalky and the sand was also chalky. And so the sand-covered hands that Ben held up were white as snow. He was clearly fascinated by this and buried his arms in the sand again and gazed at them entranced. I now saw that it was the colour of his skin that made him feel so isolated in a class of white children. But there was something about Ben that was immensely attractive - a kind of silent nobility. Very slowly and very tentatively he did begin to talk and read aloud to me at my desk. Come the end of the year we had a vote on who was the most popular child in the class. The winner by a mile was Ben.

One consequence of working with so many interesting Jewish colleagues, was that I rediscovered my fascination for Jewish writers. New discoveries for me included the whimsical Wolf Mankowitz, the intrepid recorder of Red Army cavalry, Isaac Babel, the brilliant art critic John Berger and, thanks to Prue, the inscrutable Kafka. I digested them all. Oh, and there was the young poet of whom Quentin Crisp had predicted great things - Harold Pinter. Doreen told me that she was at school with Pinter.

11 September. Lotte Lenya starred in Brecht on Brecht at the Royal Court Theatre for a four-week run. I read a review and immediately bought a ticket. It was a thrilling evening - the cabaret world of pre-war Berlin brought to life by the only living member of that magical trio, Brecht-Weill-Lenya. 'Show us the way to the next

whisky store…' and 'Mack the Knife,' evoked the haunting world of Marlene Dietrich, Christopher Isherwood, Sally Bowles, interwar cynicism, mass unemployment and the rise of National Socialism. This period and the German people of that time had long fascinated me. I remembered as a child during the Blitz wondering why the grown adults up above us in their droning aeroplanes overhead would want to drop bombs on harmless fellows crouched in our corrugated iron air raid shelters. And now there were all my Jewish friends for whom the Nazism was a lasting preoccupation. The more I learned about those times, the more I understood - or so I believed.

Not long afterwards, I was on my way home from school late. Leaving the underground station at Knightsbridge, I caught a number 19 bus to take me down to Sloane Square along the King's Road to my stop just beyond the Picasso. I sat near the door, facing the seat opposite. There, in dark glasses, across from me, sat none other than Lotte Lenya. I was surprised by how small she was. What was a star performer doing travelling by bus and where was she going? The dark glasses suggested that she wished to remain anonymous. At Smith Street, Lotte got up and I followed suit, so we ended up on the platform of the bus together. At the stop, I leapt out and offered her my hand. She smiled appreciatively, accepted the offer and stepped down onto the pavement with a quiet 'Thank you.' I had handed Lotte Lenya, widow of the great Kurt Weill and the first Polly Peacham in his Threepenny Opera, off the number 19 bus at the Smith Street stop on the King's Road, Chelsea. Not only had I touched the hem of musical genius, I had also brushed the sleeve of history. Lotte was performing in Zurich in 1915 when James Joyce was there writing Ulysses - according to the Royal Court Theatre programme.

1962

14-28 October. Cuba is in the news. Khrushchev, whom I once saw close up as he drove past my college with Comrade Bulganin in 1956, tried to send Russian missiles to Cuba, but was stopped by an American blockade. That's what I read when I caught up with the news in the Sunday papers, but it passed over my head while it was happening. Crisis? What crisis? It was probably because I had no TV at the time. I always listen to BBC Radio News. It was my class at school who converted me to the goggle box - mostly because they talked about it interminably.

The programme Saturday Night at the London Palladium was a great favourite. Clearly I needed to keep up with them, know what they were talking about and chat to them about what they'd seen.

I was living a quiet life reading, writing and contemplating my novel. I was deep into two books of which I had read so much about in the weekly reviews - Pasternak's Dr Zhivago and Gunther Grass's The Tin Drum.

*

One advantage of working at the far end of the Piccadilly Line was that it passed through Russell Square, which meant that returning from work I could hop off there to attend classes at the nearby Institute of Education, without much effort. When I obtained an MA, that would override my university degree and open the way to an academic career as a college or university lecturer. And that would leave me rather more time for writing than my present job allowed. I had signed up originally to do Psychology along with Sociology but my very first lecture decided that this was a mistake. On my way down from the Psychology lecture room in the Senate House lift I recognised Richard Peters, whom I had once invited to address our Philosophy Club at the University of Nottingham, of which I was secretary. Now he had the Chair at the Institute.

GLIMPSES OF A BIOGRAPHER'S DIARY

Oddly enough, he recognised me and asked why I wasn't doing Philosophy. Almost before I could answer, he said he would welcome me if I cared to sign up. I'd signed before the lift reached the ground floor.

Doreen told me that her sister was Arnold Wesker's secretary, and they needed help at Centre 42, his project, backed by the trade unions and dedicated to bringing high art to the masses. I volunteered my help, partly in the hope of forgetting Nurse Peters and Prue, and was soon putting leaflets into envelopes, all for the good cause. Suddenly, I was in the presence of one of my literary heroes, Arnold Wesker himself, and lots of other Jewish artists – Michael Kustow, Biba Lavrin, Bernard Kops. Wesker was in his element, a driven man - driven by good intentions and a vision, the dawn of a socialist millennium. It was heady stuff. As we got on with our various tasks, Wesker would be exuding the energy of a man possessed. A rough-hewn Glaswegian buttonholed me. 'Say, "Mary had a little lamb".' I obeyed and he then said, 'Right, You're compèring the Folk Song concert at Wellingborough next week.'

1-4 November, Wednesday-Friday. At half term, I was in Wellingborough having lunch in a pub garden with two folk singers - an American woman, Peggy Seeger, and a bearded Scot, Ewan McColl. In fact, these were enormously celebrated performers in the folksong world, she the sister of the great Pete Seeger, and he, the so-called 'Father of Folk', was the one-time husband of Joan Littlewood. Here were Socialist Royalty. Sadly, they'd found themselves faced with an abnormally ignorant folksong compère, as doubtless my efforts at speaking with them had quickly revealed. I met a whole gang of performers and musicians, including the Spinners, the great folklorist A. L. Lloyd and Francis McPeake, Irish exponent of the Uilleann pipes - all of whom were big stars in the world of folksong. It was vital to have their names tripping off my tongue and to appear familiar with all there was to do with that world, so that I could give them a sufficiently grandiose and enthusiastic build-up when I introduced them to the working men and women of Northamptonshire. 'And now, sisters and brothers, all the way from.....' Afterwards my Glaswegian promoter told me, 'You could make a career out of presenting folksong concerts, you know.' This simply wasn't my bag. Then there was Bernard Kops with a charmingly funny play - Enter Solly Gold, about a Jewish con artist, who afterwards jumped onto a convenient table and did a little jig, singing, 'Bernard Kops dances on table tops.' Bernard and I took to one another and exchange phone numbers.

I discovered a most wonderful cinema tucked away in Drayton Gardens just off the Fulham Road - the Paris Pullman - where one could see all the latest avant-garde movies from France: films by Jean-Luc Godard, Alain Renais and Agnès Varda, and from Italy by Visconti, Pasolini and Antonioni. Above all, a trip to the Paris Pullman was a trip to Paris. The whole ambience - the smell of Gauloises, the casual dress of the audience, the philosophically inspired dialogue and fleeting images from the Left Bank - was unbearably Parisian. And for us it was the dawning of the Nouvelle Vague. Afterwards, we spilled out into the cold London air, back, by contrast, to coarse reality.

The winter that year of 1962-63 was exceptionally freezing - excessive snowfalls, more than icy. By now I had worked out that with my earnings from the BBC and TES, plus a little of my savings I could afford that fur lined coat. I went to John Michael where to my surprise and delight, I saw it was still unsold. What's more, I had some new highly polished shoes to set it off. Shortly afterwards, I emerged into the King's Road in my new blue suede overcoat. I turned up the huge white fur collar and felt like a million dollars till a young woman passer-by, on the arm of her boyfriend, whispered very loudly as they passed me, 'Oh look - Father Christmas!' and began giggling. I couldn't wait to return home to take it off.

6 December. Choking fog in London. Opening the front door, I am faced by a wall of thick grey ice-cold murk. I can see no way forward. It's a pea-souper. Now I know what it's like to be blind. I'm reminded of Bleak House and Dickens's description of the city under fog, how it seeps into every nook and cranny. Only indoors can one escape the tentacles reaching out to choke the lungs. The shops along the King's Road, normally blazing brightly, are blanketed out of sight and people, blindly trying to find their way along are in constant danger of colliding. There are no buses, no Tube trains. So no school today for me. After groping my way as far as the Chelsea Potter, I fumble my way back towards Shawfield Street, depending on my memory of where kerbs were and where houses start and finish. I telephone the school and am told, 'Only half the staff are in today and just a few of the children.' Oh, well, a day at home reading suits me fine.

There were films to see. Lawrence of Arabia starring the beautiful blue-eyed Mr. O'Toole high up aloft astride a camel, bounding beautifully across endless stretches of beautifully-shot desert under blue skies with a beautiful cast of some of my favourite beautiful actors - Jack Hawkins, Alec Guinness and the splendid Claude Raines. What more could one ask for? What more can be said? It was beautiful – oh, and splendid too.

1963

February. O'Toole showed up in a London play. It was William Gaskill's production of Baal, Bertolt Brecht's first full-length play. At the Phoenix Theatre in Charing Cross Road. O'Toole played Baal with Annette Robertson, Harry Andrews, Kate Binchy and

1963

Marie Keen also in the cast. It was an afternoon performance and behind me sat two elderly women, regular matinée-goers, it seemed, who had no idea what the play might be about. They must have been attracted by the name of Peter O'Toole, who now enjoyed the charisma of Lawrence of Arabia, which the ladies had evidently seen. They chatted away merrily before curtain-up, clearly looking forward to now seeing their new matinée idol. O'Toole as the poet Baal, based on the anarchic French poet Rimbaud, made an immediate impact. At a Mayoral reception to honour him, Baal was drunk and clearly quite out of control, feeling up the women from under the table and making a blatant pass at the Mayor's wife right in front of him. The atmosphere of warmth was gradually dispelled and admiration gave way to repressed outrage. Baal went from bad to worst and was clearly destined for a bad end. The ladies behind me were stunned into silence and I felt sorry for them. Like guests at the Mayor's supper they were horrified but obviously far too polite to say so openly. They sat – no doubt tight-lipped and frozen - through all this. Then suddenly on came Harry Andrews, the good angel who had it in him to save the cursed poet, and the atmosphere behind me lightened immediately. 'Oh, Harry Andrews!' gushed one of the ladies. 'I do like him.' 'Oh, so do I,' said her friend.

11 February. Sylvia Plath killed herself at the age of 30 by sticking her head in an oven in her London home. Her children, Nicholas and Frieda slept nearby. A. L. Alvarez, her friend, published a couple of her 'suicidal' poems in the Observer. I cut them out and inserted the cutting into an anthology of contemporary poetry sitting above my gas fire.

19 March. The theatrical columns of all the papers carried rhapsodic reviews of the opening night of *Oh What A Lovely War* at the Theatre Royal, Stratford East - a musical inspired by the Alan

GLIMPSES OF A BIOGRAPHER'S DIARY

Clark book, Donkeys about the great deception and buffoonish mismanagement visited upon ordinary soldiers in the First World War. Even the Times gave it a glowing review. I have to see this, come what may.

5 April. The TES wanted me to cover a school production of Ross, a play about Lawrence of Arabia. It was by Terence Rattigan, a playwright whose reputation was beginning to falter with the arrival of the new young 'kitchen sink' dramatists. (I had seen this play with Alec Guinness as Lawrence at The Theatre Royal Haymarket in May 1960, while visiting my friend, Mike and his wife, Frances, for a few days in North London). The school now putting on the Rattigan's play was a Roman Catholic boys-only establishment. I was greeted by beaming priests and conducted to my seat beside the stage where he was plied with what must have been 'sacramental sherry'. I typed the review of the play Ross and posted it to TES.

I would like to have found a job other than teaching. I spotted a small ad in the Times. A group of Oxford graduates were planning to take excerpts from Shakespeare around the country to perform in schools, community halls and on village greens, with The Merton Professor of English Literature, Neville Coghill, to lead public discussions of the extracts. It was the posh intellectual version of Centre 42. In preparation for this, they were looking for a manager to help organise the tour. I wrote, and by return of post came an invitation to a house in Cheyne Row, just a few hundred yards from my front door, to meet the play-acting graduates. They were Richard Ingrams, Willie Rushton and Christopher Booker. We chatted very pleasantly about their tour and my reviewing for the TES. It transpired that they were wanting the appointed man or woman to travel ahead to book halls, arrange accommodation and smooth the way for the scholarly thespians. I retreated back to

1963

Shawfield Street already doubtful about the project or my suitability for the work required. Surprisingly, Ingrams sent me a postcard offering me the job, but I didn't feel inclined to take it on, mainly because of what had now begun to dawn on me - my umbilical attachment to the Westminster Hospital. What would happen to me if I ended up in some provincial workhouse of a hospital? Sorrowfully, I declined the tour. Ingrams replied saying he quite understood my decision but hoped that I might get something about them and their project into the TES.

In the Times I saw a vacancy for an editor with the publishers, Cassell and quickly posted off my CV. I was invited to attend for an interview with a Mr. Percy Brewster. Spruced up in shiny grey suit I presented myself for cross-examination. What followed was a highly-polished farce straight out of P. G. Wodehouse. The young man who sat behind the big desk was not Percy Brewster but a more literate version of Bertie Wooster. He was all smiles and affability.

On the desk in front of him he shuffled a few papers and then said, 'Well, Mr. Bowker, we don't usually have people applying for these posts with your qualifications,' he began. 'We normally take on girls straight from school with a certificate or two, but we almost never have men with degrees applying.' He chuckled and shook his head in a show of disbelief.

'This is not an intellectually demanding job,' he said, adopting a confidential tone of voice. 'Here it's more a matter of keeping yourself fit. Don't take the lift when you can walk upstairs, don't eat too many doughnuts during your coffee break. That sort of thing.'

'I see.'

He smiled. A warning note crept into his voice. 'You should see the roomfuls of editors they have at the Oxford University Press - scores of them, heads down, noses pressed to manuscripts, sharpened pencils poised. At it for hours on end they are. Extremely unhealthy.' He looked at me keenly. 'Heart attacks,' he said.

'I beg your pardon?'

'Heart attacks,' he repeated. 'From the age of about forty they keel over like flies.'

'I've heard that very thing said by a medical man,' I said, thinking of Geoff, the Medical Student, and also thinking that friendly Brewster ought to have known that flies don't exactly 'keel over' but are inclined to 'drop'. 'You'd have to edit stuff well below your intellectual capabilities here,' he said. I adopted a quizzical expression, raised my eyebrows, and regarded him expectantly.

'Yes, you'd be editing the Billy Bunter books, for example.' He looked at me keenly, as if he thought that might be the killer blow. I merely returned his gaze with the slightest of smiles. 'You'd even have to entertain their author, take him out for meals, etc. Would you be happy to do that?'

I began, 'Well, er, I - ' He interrupted and said cheerfully and finally, 'I'm very happy to offer you the job, but I wouldn't recommend that you take it.' As I walked away, I realised that I didn't want the job. So I didn't accept it.

When the ground floor flat became free, I asked Mrs. Henkey. if I could take it. She said, 'Yes', but warned me that the rent for that room would be a little higher. How much? Ten bob more. I was happy to pay, for the extra space and the room next to the telephone in the hallway. I accepted, and moved my paraphernalia downstairs with a little help from Patrick, the chauffeur. In the new room there was a locked stained glass French window which, if opened, presented a sheer drop down onto the back patio of the basement flat below - Patrick's quarters. I was now directly on a level with the walled area – an overgrown and secret garden. I opened the sash window and breathed in the Chelsea air. It was a fairytale outlook. I felt expansive and immediately began getting ideas about how to transform my new flat into a sanctuary fit for a poet.

With my new salary from teaching, I joined the British Sociological Association (B.S.A.). This yielded an almost immediate and quite unexpected dividend. I received a letter from an editor at Routledge & Kegan Paul, Brian Southam, saying that he had noticed my name on the published membership list of the B.S.A. and invited me to meet him to discuss writing a book on Social Studies. His office was in Carter Lane, close to Blackfriars Bridge. I made my way up the staircases, knocked at a door and found myself looking at pleasant editor, only a little older than myself. He was clearly a man of tremendous vitality and warmth. He wanted to talk about books for Social Studies students. I told him that I never taught Social Studies. If he was at all surprised by this news he didn't betray it.

'What have you taught?' he asked.

'English,' I said.

'Ah. From your experience, what sort of books did your English students lack but which you thought they needed?'

I thought of the pupils I left behind in Paignton and tried to imagine interesting them in any aspect of English Literature. Suddenly, I softened towards them. They were merely culturally deprived kids from homes without books. All they needed was the right kind of reading matter to bring out their finer feelings.

'I found that working-class boys could not identify with middle class literature,' I said. 'To them, Virginia Woolf, Evelyn Waugh, Thackeray and even Dickens are closed books. What they need is an anthology of working-class literature.'

Southam's eyes lit up and he seemed now more energised than ever. He leapt from his seat, picked up a large pad of paper and said, 'Come with me.'

He opened a door and took me into what looked like a small conference room dominated by a large polished table, drew up a chair, sat me down and placed the pad of paper in front of me.

'List the authors you think should be included in your anthology of working class literature,' he said and left me.

Good lord! This isn't what I expected. Here I was in the offices of a great London publishing house being asked, at the drop of a hat, to map out a book for a man I'd only just met. For the next hour I compiled my list (Alan Sillitoe, Dylan Thomas, Keith Waterhouse, DH Lawrence), while Southam popped in and out with his own suggestions (Robert Graves, Osbert Sitwell, Maxim Gorky), saying, 'We must have a few middle class writers and more women represented.') The sex balance was duly attended to and we included more overseas writers to widen the focus further, so in went Simone de Beauvoir and Muriel Spark.

Chapter 8

Part-Time Lecturer, Reviewer and Feature Writer

1963-1965

April. One morning. quite early, I was eating my favourite breakfast of escalope Holstein at the Picasso - when in walked Peter O'Toole, clearly the worse for wear after a night on the tiles, exactly as his Baal might have done the morning after the night before. He was worth examining in detail - extremely tall, a rogue lock of blond hair falling across his forehead - a strangely ethereal presence, an aura carried over from the movie - 'star quality', one supposes. I would get to know him close up much later but that was my first sighting of him out of character.

Shortly afterwards, at school I met Louise, a beautiful Rubenesque student teacher, blonde with a pale skin, shy expression and lived in Hampstead. I invited her to the theatre and dinner, then took her home in a cab - and donned my blue suede overcoat for the occasion. I couldn't afford to take the cab back to Chelsea, so I walked. At that time London at night was a silent city. It closed down around midnight, so I found myself a solitary actor on a vast film set. Traffic lights still functioned, stopping and allowing through imaginary vehicles, invisible pedestrians were beckoned across in ghostly numbers. An occasional cat ventured from behind a hedgerow then disappeared in a flash. Otherwise, all was silent and still. All that was lacking was a phantom night watchman to shout 'Two o'clock and all's well,' to complete the scene. Instead, as I trudged through Hampstead and Camden Town, I spoke the magic words in tribute to the tranquil London night. Silently I was slotting together a few more pieces in my London jigsaw puzzle.

One afternoon, during half-term, Louise invited me over to her Hampstead flat. She was a bit unwell, she said, and would appreciate a visit. When I arrived, she was in bed and simply invited me to join her. It was Prue of Rugby all over again. But with Louise it was not Kafka and writing, it was playing nurse. So, although it was she who was supposedly ill, it was I who was required to play the patient she wished to coddle and care for. Well, how could I refuse a lady? She, it transpired, was a positively voracious coddler, able and willing to devour her patient whole, a penchant for which she had never, by even the flicker of an eyelash, betrayed hitherto. If anything, she had seemed inordinately shy and virginal. But now she was a completely uninhibited nymph and could, I was to discover, coddle with equal gusto just about anywhere and at any time. After that first night, we wandered down to a nearby café for a spot of lunch. We must have looked as if we'd been dancing through thickets and hedgerows backwards because the Italian waiter sidled over to me and said in a very audible stage whisper, 'We also do bed and breakfast, Sir.'

Though I love teaching youngsters, I had long nurtured a dream of combining a scholarly life with that of writing fiction, following in the wake of great philosophical novelists like Sartre, Camus and Iris Murdoch. Now, armed with my postgraduate studies, I began to

1963

look at advertisements for lecturing posts. One I couldn't resist having a shot at was a Sociology lectureship at Hornsey College of Art. The prospect of teaching adults who wanted to learn and who had an artistic gift to unleash on the world was too much not to resist. The Sociology being taught at London's Institute of Education was far removed from what I had been fed at university. It was galvanic as taught by a charismatic genius called Basil Bernstein. In my mind I worked out a line for art based on his theory that measured intelligence is linked to the degree of verbal elaboration at an individual's disposal. It didn't, I thought, take much imagination to link it to the development of artistic vocabulary and aesthetic intelligence. At least that, if I were called for interview, was the line I was prepared to pitch with the borrowed passion of my mentor.

I'd hired a television set and noticed how it had improved since I first watched it in the 50s, and how some programmes were now quite intriguing, such as the satirical programme, That Was the Week that Was presented by David Frost. It was live television, and on one occasion life really erupted into a magnificently dramatic and delicious moment. The critic Bernard Levin was always particularly scathing in his attacks on assorted persons, institutions, books and plays. On this occasion, the object of one of those vitriolic attacks caught up with him. He was talking merrily and entertainingly, when a large well-dressed man came out of the audience and spoke to him in a rather resonant upper-class accent. 'Oh Mr. Levin, it won't take a second. Would you stand up please.' Levin looked up in bewilderment and obediently stood up. The intruder towered over him and said, 'Your attack on Savagery and Delight was not a review it was a vicious attack...' He saw that the studio minders were closing in on him and said, 'There is just one tiny thing...' He then proceeded to hit the bewildered-looking critic who staggered backwards under the blow, which caught him on the shoulder as he flinched away. Then, as his attacker was hustled out of the studio, a shaken Levin returned to the stool on which he had been perched. 'Can we concentrate on non-violence,' he said, to a storm of applause from the audience. However, the hero was surely not Levin but Desmond Leslie, the man who, it later transpired, had himself produced Savagery and Delight, the show Levin had blasted in the Daily Mail, with Leslie's wife as its star. But honour had been served; the villain laid low.

18 May, Saturday. I was invited for an interview with regard to that Sociology lectureship at Hornsey. As I waited, along with a few other, in walked the most beautiful and vivacious looking young woman, also, it seemed, a candidate for the post. I knew immediately that I had to put on my best performance. When my turn came, I could tell during the interview that I was doing well. It must have been my overpowering wish to get this particular job that gave my eloquence wings. Listening to myself I was quite impressed. Afterwards, the Head of the College's General Studies Department told me that I had given by far the best interview, but the woman candidate they had selected was better qualified and they could hardly refuse her. Later, he wrote me a loser's consolation letter: '...impressed by your articulate enthusiasm...a desperately difficult decision to take...would like to bear you in mind for occasional lectures...every probability that we shall be making further increases to the General Studies staff this time next year.'

5 June. The newspapers had just broken the story of the Profumo Affair - it was the talk of the town and far beyond. News and gossip of scandal, sleazy and sexual deviance at the highest level filled the news columns and airwaves and clogged the television screens. Headlines screamed and photographs brought us image after image of the decadent Lord, the disgraced cabinet minister, the Russian

spy, the mysterious osteopath, the glamorous prostitutes, and the gun-wielding crook - all performers in a tragi-comic melodrama which was even then shaking a wearily tottering government.

Louise read the paper carrying these many tales of posh chaps bonking working class girls and snorted fiercely. 'Quite disgusting!' she said. I reflected that perhaps the only difference between them and us was that with us no money changed hands. She was, I discovered, insanely rich while I was poor - something she had yet to discover. Now she wanted me to go home with her to meet the Daddy and Mummy. This was a situation I should have learned to avoid, but in an unguarded moment, I agreed. The visit to the country did not go well. Over dinner, Mummy said, 'I understand you live in Chelsea.' I said, 'Yes' and she said, 'Do you know Lord X and Lady Y and the Duke of Q?' To which I replied honestly: 'No'. Thereafter the atmosphere cooled perceptibly, though at the time she might have missed the subtly hostile signals given off by her mater. Shortly thereafter, Louise left her Hampstead flat, left teaching and left me too.

29 June. *Oh What a Lovely War* transferred to Wyndham's, my favourite London theatre. The press was smiling on the show. 'More Tears Than Mirth' said the Times, and the rest of the reviews were encomiastic. Luckily there was still the odd ticket. I dashed along and was immediately spellbound. Everything about this show was perfect - from the orchestra to the costumes, from the music to the mis-en-scene, from the casting to the echoing words and the panorama of moving headlines bringing the ghastly casualty figures to us directly. It was a show with a powerful impact that would haunt me for a long time to come. All the songs my father used to sing were there. I would have loved him to have seen it, but I feared that he would have left the theatre - in tears probably; after all, he was there in the trenches, and saw this kind of thing at

GLIMPSES OF A BIOGRAPHER'S DIARY

6 - *Leonard Bowker 1914*

first hand. From the outset, I was engulfed by a mixture of horror and comic nostalgia from the moment the orchestra struck up the jolly overture followed by Victor Spinetti, Master of Ceremonies, through the pierrot show to the recruiting songs and the soldiers marching and singing merrily off to war, to the gradual change in tone of the songs, the stupidity of the generals, the callousness of the war profiteers, and the final songs of sorrow and sad farewell - 'Adieu la vie,' 'And when they ask us how dangerous it was, oh we'll never tell them.' Then, as the curtain fell, the audience was sent home to the by now doubly sardonic strains of 'Oh oh oh what a lovely war!' It was where we came in and where we might come in yet again. For both my father and the others with him in the trenches, I shed a good few tears myself that night.

23 July. The TES asked me to review a play, Skyvers, by the Jamaican playwright Barry Record, featuring a young actor called David Hemmings, at the Royal Court Theatre, a play which Michael Billington, drama critic of the Guardian, called 'one of the key plays of the 1960s'. It had a strangely menacing air hanging over it, bringing my experiences in Paignton very much to mind. The play went well and received a positive review from me in the TES.

Summer (August). In the hope of reviving my passionate affair with Louise, I invited her to come to Spain where some of my university friends had hired a villa for the summer. As I had hoped, she accepted and afforded me the pleasing prospect of a cuddlesome reunion. I booked train tickets, and reserved a hotel for one night in Paris en route to sunny southern Spain. Hopefully our night in Paris would kindle the old flame, but alas Louise didn't play along and next day we were en route for the Spanish border. The rail tickets I had bought were not exactly first class, and we found ourselves sitting on hard seats opposite some Algerian workers. Unlike me, Louise did not feel this situation to be of much interest, and when one of the workers offered her a swig from his bottle of booze, she shrank into her corner of the compartment with considerable distaste. From thereon, she had to pretend to be asleep to avoid the attention of the friendly Algerians. We rattled on to the border. It was not far then to Bagur, the small fishing village, where my friends were holed up for the summer. At the villa the girls had all got together and decided there was to be no sharing of beds and that seemed to decide matters. On our first evening, at a local nightclub, Louise quickly succumbed to the seductive ambience of southern Spain, and disappeared off with one of the waiters. I felt strangely unaffected by this desertion. Several of the girls were unattached and just as flirtatious as Louise. However, I had now resigned myself to being alone with just my Penguin edition of Malcolm Lowry's *Under the Volcano* for company, which did not mean that I didn't enjoy the beach. The sea was blue, calm, warm and the swimming was an absolute delight. It had been worth getting to Spain to enjoy that sensation alone.

Next morning it was down to the beach again. Louise came down and mingled with the rest of us. The sea, warm and calm as ever, seemed to entice us to dream in a dangerously seductive fashion. The hot sand scorched the toes and although it was tempting just to flop down and enjoy the sun, we knew it wasn't wise to stay like that for long. So, to ensure that I was not exposed to the full glare of the intense midday sun, I took shelter under a large beach umbrella. Unfortunately, I fell asleep stretched out, and as the sun moved, so the shade protecting my legs also moved. I woke to find they had been thoroughly cooked, leaving them red and raw and seemingly on fire. That I realised, was the end of my time on the beach for this holiday. But other experiences awaited us - a disgusting bullfight in Girona and the marvelous dancing of the Sardana in Bagur.

The buxom Louise, seemingly driven by a compulsion to nurse, felt compelled to climb into bed with one of the university boys who happened to be suffering from Spanish tummy. But, he found he couldn't take both the bug and the bosoms together and she was forced into a retreat. Sadly for Louise, her excursions down the primrose path came to an abrupt end when she developed a rash of some sort on her face brought on by the remorseless Spanish sun. Thereafter, she withdrew herself from the beach and like the rest of us took to her bed. It was the end of the holiday for Louise. After that holiday I never saw her again, but I heard that she went into law and became a magistrate. God bless her!

November. I'd been coaxed into acting in a play at the University union - Max Frisch's The Public Prosecutor, about a stalking serial murderer, in which I played the prosecutor. But the drama onstage was about to be overtaken by a drama offstage.

On 14 December, I was about to make my entrance in an important scene when someone whispered, 'Kennedy's been shot.' The next moment I was on stage, trying valiantly to remember my lines. Afterwards, we got together. 'Let's get a paper,' I said, so we headed for Fleet Street. No papers. The street was deserted. No newspaper sellers. Then, just as we were about to give up, we spotted one - a man selling the Daily Worker. We rushed up to him.

'A Worker, please.'

1963

His face turned into a snarl. 'You only want it because of Kennedy. So, nothing doing.' And he refused to sell us the People's Paper. We were left having to crawl tiredly home and wait for the morning to learn about one of the saddest stories of the century.

After our final performance, a fellow and his girlfriend came backstage to heap praise on the cast. The girl introduced herself to me as Jane Gardner, who was working on my book, Under Twenty, at Routledge with Brian Southam. Previously she had been with Lester Clark, a script editor at Rediffusion Television and he, she said, would be very interested to meet me to discuss writing scripts for schools television.

The marvelously funny film Billy Liar, just out, was both hilarious and a sobering reminder of the youth who had left university expecting to be greeted by publishers and/or by Fleet Street editors as a young writer touched by magic. Hm. But self-delusion, it seemed to me, was a harmless enough diversion.

And here was another diversion - Poetry and Jazz Evenings at the Royal Court Theatre, with dynamic performances from Christopher Logue and Adrian Mitchell. Mitchell presented an especially dashing figure – committed, radical, denouncing advertising, the Vietnam War, capitalism in all its shapes and sizes – and doing it with originality and wit. Another star was born. It had me rushing home and scribbling furiously, with my old friend Walter Mitty, the dreamer, gazing over my shoulder.

At the end of this year, the Joseph Losey film adaptation of Robin Maugham's *The Servant* was showing locally. It gave a more sharply-focused image of modern Chelsea as a smart, sexy, arty place to live: a very particular ambience of warmth and menace subtly-distilled. There was a surprisingly brilliant performance from the onetime romantic lead, Dirk Bogarde, as the dark, devious and menacing servant, a seductively sinister one from Sarah Miles as his incestuous sister, with James Fox as the hapless aristo they plotted to take over. It was set in Royal Avenue, a few minutes from Shawfield Street. This newly-glamorous Chelsea seen through the lens of Joseph Losey's camera confirmed what I already felt, but with a freshly-minted gloss, a frisson of refined debauchery and illicit pleasure. There in Losey's film was the memorable old King's Road and the establishment of the aptly-named Thomas Crapper, bathroom throne-maker to royalty. I longed for a house like the one in the film, and any temptation to move to equally congenial parts of the city - Hampstead, Highgate, Dulwich or Greenwich - was now easy to resist.

1964

4 January. T. S. Eliot dies in Kensington. That Faber hardback of his poems was my introduction to modernism in literature along with Ezra Pound and Joyce. Eliot once lived on Cheyne Walk, a row of mansions stretching from the river to Chelsea Physic Garden, full of historical, literary and artistic echoes – once home of the Pre-Raphaelites. I had never been fully awake before, to the fact, that whenever I walked through Russell Square I was walking past the offices of Faber and Faber where the great modernist worked for so long.

12 January - 10 February. The TES sent me on my most exciting excursion to date - the launching of the new London Academy of Music and Dramatic Art's experimental Theatre in Logan Place just off the Cromwell Road. It was named after the Academy's Principal, Michael MacQwan, and had a most ingenious performance space - adaptable as a proscenium, a long-traverse stage or an arena. Seats could be wheeled in blocks to form any arrangement suitable for whatever production area was required. The evening put not just the cast but also the staging through its

paces. Everything about the event was extraordinary. A young actress called Glenda Jackson appeared in Jean Genet's scabrous play *The Screens*, which included everything the Lord Chamberlain, the Theatre's very own censor, had cut from it, by the clever device of reading out his official letter, including all the excluded obscenities. 'On page 3 line 8, cut f—k', page 5 line 6 cut 'balls', etc. Hard on the heels of that came Peter Brook's Theatre of Cruelty introducing us to the name of Antonin Artaud, the architect of the form.

The great Brook, the lofty American method guru Charles Marowitz, writer and critic Michael Kustow and other grandees of the theatrical avant garde assembled for the occasion. One play - a Marowitz production - riveted everyone. It included a scene in which a woman, Glenda Jackson, was ritually bathed by prison warders, - a metaphor for the prison system's attempts to wash away a criminal past and replace it with a respectable lily-white highly malleable character. It was meant as an allusion to the imprisonment of women, and in particular Profumo's lover, Christine Keeler, the transcript of whose court case was read over the action. In this sinister short sketch she then transformed herself into Jacqueline Kennedy at the graveside of her dead husband. Jackson performed the role with consummate skill and aplomb. I typed my review and sent it off to the TES.

For the past two years, for two evenings a week, I had been attending classes at the Institute of Education. One part of me dreaded returning to the subjects that had smothered me with boredom as an undergraduate - Philosophy and Sociology. But now Richard Peters and Basil Bernstein had fired my enthusiasm. Suddenly, everything we discussed informed my life inside the classroom, outside the classroom, and with what I attempted to do as a writer. Richard had the mind of quiet rational contemplation while Basil, far from quiet, entered the lecture room like a man possessed. His mind was on fire and in the lecture room and in seminars he ignited and gave new direction to my own more prosaic thought processes. I now saw the world as a cultural construct. Understanding it, and navigating a way through it now meant understanding and navigating a way through words. Language was the key. At the end of the course I found, to my astonishment, that I had somehow recovered my old flair for passing examinations. In fact, rather than feeling nervous, I couldn't wait to get into the examination room and start writing. I sailed through and was then poised to embark on a Master's degree in the same subjects.

One lunchtime, Brian Southam took me to Bianchi's Italian Restaurant in Soho's Frith Street, presided over by a wonderful maître d., Eleanor Salvoni. It was on the first floor and furnished like a good London club - a warm and welcoming atmosphere. Eleanor was extremely attentive, friendly and the food was exquisite. It was a place to cherish and remember, a place to which to bring special friends. You could also celebrity-spot while dining. That day Patrick Moore, the astronomer, was tucking in with a friend. On a return visit I saw the journalist Keith Waterhouse of Punch and the Daily Mirror and progenitor of Billy Liar, with a fellow hack. I had requested an extract from Waterhouse's childhood memoir for Under Twenty (the title now settled on for my book).

 The TES asked me to go down to Bradford-on-Avon in Wiltshire to cover another school play. This time it was Hamlet staged in a barn in accordance with the theories of a famous Shakespeare scholar, Leslie Hotson. Immediately it struck me that the place name was ripe with associations to the Bard of Stratford and to the schoolboy Shakespeare. I exploited this to the full, noting down not just my reaction to the play, but to word-play associated with the setting, characters, names and their resonances. My review was published auspiciously on 1st May.

Another show I felt compelled to see was Oliver!, then playing at the New Theatre, the work of Lionel Bart, who had been involved with the Theatre Workshop - another brilliant Jewish artist to emerge in the 60s. The show was stunning! The opening number (always important), the dialogue, the choruses, the solo numbers, the dances - all were superb. Tunefulness reigned. Where on earth had these tunes come from and whence came this sudden British talent for the musical? Ron Moody as Fagin - brilliant. Georgia Brown as Nancy - equally brilliant, Davy Jones as the Artful Dodger - delightful. What a cast and in Bart, what a songwriter!

March. Saturday morning along the King's Road was now Peacock's Parade. The initiative came from students at Chelsea College of Art, eager to display their imaginative designs, and introduce new fashions to the world. But it looked as though Mary Quant and Ossie Clark at Quorum nearby were also having an enlivening effect. The Peacocks were from all over, showing off their latest flamboyant outfits. Other places, such as Carnaby Street, might have been churning out some of the new gear (such as old military uniforms or Victorian feather boas), but the place to strut, the place to see and be seen, the West London catwalk, was now at the King's Road in Chelsea. Here's the most striking innovation, a revolutionary breakthrough. I've seen mention on the evening news of Quant's big creation (some say importation from France), but today with my own eyes I've spotted it - my first mini-skirt. There she was, a young woman walking along the King's Road wearing a skirt way above her knees and not far below her waist - or so it seemed.

Men too, were looking different - squeezed into 'drainpipe' trousers, bum-freezer jackets and winkle-picker shoes. Shirts often came in bright colours with matching ties. And some were beginning to tog themselves out in fancy dress. Records of the Beatles were played at parties, over the radio and on television, to which Bob Dylan's ballads were adding a gentle note of warning and sedition. There was a new and rebellious swing and swagger to the young - in Chelsea, at least - especially young women who were asserting themselves in all sorts of ways.

I'd passed through the world of a hospital ward at full stretch into the Alice in Wonderland of the London sixties at the heart of the dream – the King's Road, Chelsea.

*

Now, if I was going to become a lecturer, I needed to get some experience of teaching adults. On a tip from a friend, I sent off a CV to the Workers Educational Association, (WEA) offering my services as a Lecturer. Shortly afterwards I was asked to give a lecture at the West London Jewish Club, on Psychology, of which I knew precious little, so I quickly burrowed into those few books I had acquired for the course I'd so promptly abandoned at the Institute. Somehow I staggered through the evening, but vowed never to repeat the painful exercise. Academic Psychology was simply not my thing. My next assignment was far more satisfying. The WEA Lecturer in Philosophy at The Working Men's College (WMC) in Mornington Crescent was taking a holiday and was looking for a stand-in. George Orwell had lectured there a couple of times. The class of men at the WMC looked expectant. I smiled at them and they continued to look expectant - perhaps, as I was a new face. I launched into a cross between Richard Peters and Basil Bernstein, trying to be concise but flowery - a blatant attempt to appear riveting. Hobbes and Locke were on the agenda and I had dug out some typed undergraduate notes and old essays to give myself plenty to say. At some point, not long after I got into my

1964

stride, one of the men raised his hand and popped a question at me which stopped me dead in my tracks. I was flummoxed. Fortunately someone else chipped in and answered the question and I was off the hook. I nodded sagely and congratulated the informative interjector. It gave me a way through the evening. All difficult questions I threw back at the class. 'Now who knows the answer to that one?' Hands flew up and all I had to do was pick one. The chosen person sounded better, more fluent and more informed, than I did. 'Very good,' I said, as if I were responsible for their excellent contributions. 'So, there's your answer.' It transpired that most of them were 'regulars', signing up for the same course year after year, so, they knew as much as the Lecturer, even more perhaps.

Now the work began to flow. John Cox, an assistant producer at Glyndebourne, asked me to stand in for him at Morley College (Orwell had also taught briefly there.) I chose to speak on something about which I felt more confident – John Osborne and the theatre revolution. It was my first chance to give a lecture on a subject for which I had a current passion. I was confident and felt rather good.

27 June. I heard on the radio news that that evening was to see the last performance of *Oh What a Lovely War* at the Wyndham Theatre, I telephoned immediately and was told it was completely sold out.

'Nothing at all?' I asked. 'All we have is a box.' 'How much?'

It was more than I had ever paid for a theatre ticket several times over, but I just couldn't miss this final performance. 'I'll take it,' I said. And so I watched my favourite show from the grandeur of my own box. I could pretty well recite every scene by heart, but one unscripted incident stuck in my mind – it brought the show to an unexpected stop. After the overture, I watched an only-too-familiar scene and settled down to enjoy myself. As usual, Victor Spinetti, the Master of Ceremonies, launched into his opening speech, introducing 'The Ever-Popular War Game!'. After the first numbers, as always, he paused while the latecomers were admitted, making some quip as they filed in, such as, 'Don't worry. You've missed nothing yet,' which always got a laugh. On this last night it also got a laugh, but then, down the aisle came a solitary figure, the last man admitted - a tall, impressive-looking chap.

'You've missed nothing yet,' said Victor.

'Don't worry,' boomed the latecomer. 'I saw the show in Paris and know it back to front so I know exactly what you've been saying so far.'

This time it was the latecomer, not Victor, who got the biggest laugh. After that, on with the show …. And as usual I was left in tears – for my father and for my two uncles, Bill and Ernest, and all the others who never came back.

I was still writing off for permission from publishers and literary estates to use material chosen for my book, *Under Twenty*. Brian Southam had given me the right form of words to use. The replies were sometimes quite revealing. The Hemingway estate, for example, asked an extortionate amount for a single short story. By contrast, Alan Sillitoe – from whose *The Loneliness of the Long-Distance Runner* I requested a passage - wrote personally, enthusing about the book: 'What a great idea!' he said, and, as it was for an anthology of working-class literature he waved any fee. Just what I had expected from one of my favourite writers. I was invited to a party in Marylebone: Most partygoers were dancing, a few were talking. Among the talkers I met Rachel Longford, daughter of the Anglo-Irish Peer Frank Longford, and amused her to the point of boredom with my tedious political iterations and talk of television.

1964

At my mention of television she pointed across the room. 'That girl over there is interested in television.' She said, 'You should talk to her.' The girl indicated was alone. I crossed over and perched beside her.

'I hear you're interested in television.'

'Yes,' she said. 'Are you?'

We then launched into an animated conversation. I talked up my Scriptwriting for Rediffusion; she said she was a picture researcher for the BBC and her name was Rebecca She was chatty, pleasant and had an engaging smile. We arranged to meet for lunch at an offshoot BBC building near the Television Centre at Shepherd's Bush, where she worked. From then on, from time to time, Rebecca and I dated occasionally - for lunch perhaps or for a trip to north London to sit with a group of others at the feet of Anthony Smith, an increasingly influential figure among television broadcasters. Here in one place were some of the media's future elite.

27 July. A play by Joe Orton, a new writer much talked about, transferred from the New Arts Theatre to Wyndham. *Entertaining Mr. Sloane* was outrageously funny without using shocking language. It involved murder, homosexuality, nymphomania and sadism - the quintessential black comedy, but somehow expressive of the times. The permissive society seemed just a bit more tolerant thereafter.

12 August. I had been invited to spend part of my summer holiday with my beautiful friend Janet and her husband Karl on Karl's yacht on the Ijsselmeer, the old Zuider Zee. I couldn't wait. The cobblestones of old Amsterdam, worn smooth by centuries and now glistening with rain felt cool and comfortable underfoot. Then it was off to where the yacht was moored. It then transpired that

the 'yacht', was an old motor torpedo boat, salvaged from some wartime navy, and we guests had been invited not to spend an idle summer at sea but to be painting the yacht, and tarting it up generally. It was moored at Muiden, just a short drive in Karl's little car into Amsterdam where Janet took us to the Rijksmuseum, home to the wonderful Vermeer interiors, and great Rembrandts, including the *Night Watch*.

That summer, Karl sailed us around the Ijsselmeer. We went ashore at Haarlem and Volendam, where locals, decked out in national costumes, played up to the expectations of tourists and projected a quaint image of Dutch life - the pictures one finds on the lids of biscuit tins. Both were altogether picturesque. On the 'yacht', Cathy, Janet's sister, began to express an interest in me and, in the circumstances, had to be to be gently discouraged. Afterwards, in London, she called at my flat and we became a dating couple. She was in love with France and everything French and studying the language for her degree. She wore her hair long, eschewed makeup, and sang Françoise Hardy and Bob Dylan songs, accompanying herself on the guitar. She was quite intense with a magical smile and a warmth which radiated. When Janet found out about us she was delighted, I was pleased to say.

20 August. I had what was for me a profoundly moving theatrical experience (to add to that of *Oh! What Lovely War*) - I saw Peter Weiss's *The Persecution and Assassination of Jean-Paul Marat* as Performed by the Inmates of the Asylum of Charenton Under the Direction of the Marquis de Sade (the Marat-Sade to those of us with short memories), magically directed by Peter Brook at the Aldwych Theatre, the London home of the Royal Shakespeare Company (the RSC). That was my first sight of Ian Richardson, a strangely distant Marat, Patrick Magee, a chillingly sinister de Sade, and the exuberant Freddie Jones as Cucuraci, a character from the

1964

commedia dell'arte, there to pass satirical comments on the passing show.

The murderous Charlotte Corday, was Glenda Jackson. The script was by Adrian Mitchell, which only added to my pleasure. It was full of wonderful rhyming couplets such as, 'Crucifixion, all good Christians know/Is the most sympathetic way to go.' The whole thing amounted to a grand coup de théâtre. Unforgettable.

Charlotte, a girl whom I'd met at Nick's, was rich and idle, wanted to introduce me to her friends Henry and Sue Williamson, both of whom were in the Marat/Sade, where Sue, played Marat's mistress like a lunatic sleepwalker, while Henry played the Father - of the madly ecclesiastical sort. I was invited to their flat just off the King's Road, where Henry told me this incredible story about his old schoolfriend Harold Pinter. Pinter had mostly written poems, he said, but he, Henry, had asked him in 1957, if he could write a one act play for him to produce as a graduation production at Bristol University Drama Department. Pinter replied that he had never written a play but he would give it a try. Within days a play arrived. It was called *The Room* and Pinter the playwright's career was launched. Henry showed me a copy with Harold's inscription saying something like, 'Without you, this would not have been possible.' What a story!

Also in Summer. Another iconic film, this one directed by Peter Brook - *Lord of the Flies* - was shown at the Classic cinema, my local flea-pit – though what class of fleas you'd find in our somewhat exclusive Chelsea art house picture palace is difficult to tell. A little rough at the edges and shot in black and white, Brook's film shared some of the qualities of the French nouveau vague cinema. The boys led by Jack, who went wild on the island, reminded me of Paignton. I suppose I was the one playing Ralph, the good guy, who stood for order, but, like the boy in Golding's story, lacked the wit to know just how to hold back a rising tide of chaos.

In the Observer one Sunday I read a review of a book called *Albert Angelo*. Accompanying it was a photograph of its author, B.S. Johnson. I bought a copy, read it at a single sitting, and was transfixed by it. It was experimental, with the text switching to double column, to verse, to drama, to a page with a narrow window cut into it allowing the reader into the future on the page ahead. The narrative was also disrupted by Johnson's bold declaration that his book was all lies. Maybe, but why on earth should that worry him? After all, the book was a novel, not a work of history. Nobody's life hung on the veracity of what he wrote. The critics were divided - some saw it as a refreshing break from social realism; others were less complimentary, and even the sympathetic Observer review, concluded, 'I look forward to his next book, which will wisely be conventional.' But the subject, the grim trials and tribulations of a London secondary school teacher rang so many bells with me that I was entirely won over to this strange book and its remarkable author. Another tome to add to my shelf.

Back in July. I was asked by the news editor of the TES, a young man called Simon Jenkins (Jenkins) - my first encounter with modern front-line journalism - to do a survey of schools where staff were dealing with the arrival of immigrant children from the Commonwealth. After taking advice, I rang ahead, spoke to the local Times personnel, was given an update on the schools in the areas of concern, and the teachers to contact. This took me to Birmingham, Wolverhampton, Bradford,

Slough, Southall and London's East End to meet the teachers, and pupils – mostly from the West Indies, India, and Pakistan. I did a series of six articles and these were well regarded for me to be asked by Jenkins to cover the October general election in the West

1964

Country, where education was a big issue. It was left to me to make my own arrangements.

In Bristol, covering the general election, a casual-looking figure buttonholed me in the hotel foyer. I recognised him from my Bluebell Railway adventure. It was the Times photographer who asked me what my line was. This time he had come in a sports car and he said, 'When you go on your tour through South Gloucestershire I'll give you a lift.' I went along to the Tory headquarters to see the agent who was organising their campaign in Bristol, and because I was 'the gentleman from the Times' he let me in on their secret strategy and intended moves.

One candidate in Bath fascinated me - the Liberal called Adrian, a school teacher. He invited me to accompany him to the town square where he proposed to make a speech. We all trooped down there - he, the Times photographer and I - with a placard and the soapbox. Adrian planted his soapbox, hoisted his placard, mounted the box and began to proclaim the Liberal word. The photographer stood by waiting for the crowds to gather. A small Scout licking an ice cream stopped and regarded Adrian with curiosity. The photographer duly captured the scene. Then the little Scout was joined by a dog. The photographer snapped the dog, too, then the dog and the Scout together. Adrian rambled on making in the circumstances a rather good fist of the message he had to deliver, I thought. A few people passed by barely giving him a glance. Finally, both the little Scout and the dog lost interest and moved on. The Liberal candidate reached his peroration, but Bath had passed him by. He lost his deposit and, I presume, returned to teaching as soon as the new term began.

Finding the Tory candidate was a problem in South Gloucestershire. At each small town we enquired at the Party's offices about his location and were told in each of them that he had just left for the next village. But by the time we got to the place indicated, he'd gone. We quickened our pace and looked for signs of this elusive gentleman's whereabouts. Finally, we ran him to earth. He was, as it happened, the Minister of Housing, and we caught him, ankle-deep in a sort of quagmire, plodding in gumboots around a caravan site where people were living because not enough houses had been built during his reign as Minister of Housing. The photographer caught him emerging from a rain-soaked garden, boots caked in mud. The photographer captured the scene and the Minister's discomfiture with a few smart clicks. I typed my piece for the TES, posted it and received my cheque.

24 August. I felt I had enough TES cuttings to send to Peter Roberts, the editor of Plays &Players, which I did. I was invited for an interview. Roberts asked me to write feature articles on theatrical topics. As a first story I was dispatched to report onto backstage life in theatre - about the minions who make the theatre of illusions possible - lighting men, scene shifters, property managers, costume mistresses - with box office managers thrown in for good measure. It was far more fascinating than I had expected. Venturing backstage at the Old Vic or the Duke of York's Theatre or the Aldwych, was to enter a world of ghosts - of David Garrick, Edmund Kean, Sir Henry Irving and Mrs. Patrick Campbell. And for some theatre staff as well as performers, theatrical phantoms were palpable presences, as real as the ghost of Hamlet's father. I typed my report *Glamour And Guts* - probing into life backstage, posted it 18th September to the Plays and Players. My report was published in October.

14 December. For the first part of the Christmas holidays, Cathy was going to Paris with her friend Mary to absorb the atmosphere, culture and practice their French. She wanted me to go with them and the chance to spend time with this most beautiful girl in the

world's most beautiful city was irresistible. Our destination was St Germain, just beyond Rue St Jacques, and a small hotel, the Grand Hotel de Lima, between the Rue Monge and the Quai de la Tournelle, a short walk from Saint-Germain-des-Prés. We all stayed at the same hotel, Cathy sharing with Mary, me on the floor below and nights spent together as the feeling moved us, which it did most nights. We went to a nearby café for breakfast – coffee and croissants. Sitting there we smoked French cigarettes and watched the world go by - and the Paris world, of course, is like no other. The smells of Paris – the aroma of coffee, the scent of Gauloise, the occasional whiff of a pissoir – assail the nostrils as one settles into a frame of mind that only this city can evoke, a sort of mental smile. It is a poet's heaven. French style prevails. 'In France, they do things differently,' said Cathy. 'The shops are different, the clothes are different, the bookshops are different, the films are different, the songs are different, the wine is different, the food and the restaurants are different. It is a difference that evokes a sense of the possibilities within oneself. Vive la différence!' I now got a better sense of the place than on my previous visit - George Whitman's cavernous book shop, presently named *Shakespeare & Company* in honour of Sylvia Beach's prewar bookshop, the Luxembourg Gardens, the soaring Cathedral of Notre Dame, just opposite, and the great cafés of the Left Bank (Les Deux Magots, La Dôme, Café de Flore, and La Cloiserie des Lilas). We could only ever afford a coffee in such places but took all main meals at one of the Take-away restaurants.

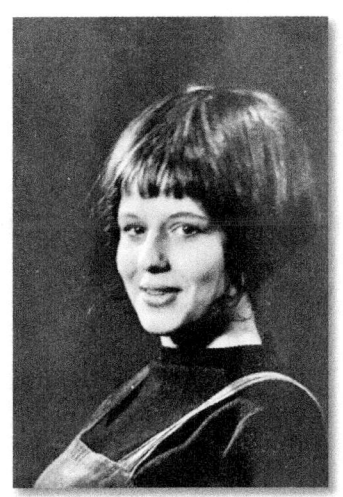

7 - Cathy, 1964

GLIMPSES OF A BIOGRAPHER'S DIARY

1965

February. The Plays and Players published my report on Plays in Prison with cartoons by Ralph Steadman which had been commissioned a few months ago.

March. One of my favourite streets in London was and still remains Villiers Street, home to the Players' Theatre. I discovered Villiers Street and the Players' Theatre on one of my meanderings around the backwaters of the Strand. There was always an old-style Victorian music hall programme playing there. I suggested to Peter Roberts that I do something on the Players' for him and was asked to do a piece more generally on the music hall revival which was a feature of London theatrical life at that time. The Players' were flourishing and *The Good Old Days* was almost permanently on television, as it had been for some dozen years past. What is more, as if to remind us that this form of entertainment was not long dead, there were some authentic old music hall stars still alive and living at Brinsworth, the Variety Artistes' Home for retired performers out at Twickenham. So, it was to Twickenham that I journeyed first to meet the old time stars, the authentic performers. Among them I found Flo Hastings and Jack Wilson. Flo was a lovely old Victorian lady of 94 who featured on music hall bills of the 1890s as 'The London Belle', well-known for her song, Just Like A Lady. She was, she told me, a friend of Marie Lloyd, with whom she did the rounds of the London halls, hurrying from one venue to another, by horse drawn cab, several times a day. Occasionally they would dine out with Marie's American friend, Belle Elmore and her charming doctor husband. 'Poor Belle,' said Flo, as if letting me into a secret, 'she was murdered by that charming husband - Dr Hawley Harvey Crippin.' She pointed to her friend Jack Wilson. 'That's Jack Wilson,' she said. 'He used to be part of the famous act – Wilson, Keppel and Betty. Then Keppel died and

Betty left him. Now he's in here. He's only 60, and he's my boyfriend!' She said this with some vehemence. Then, pointing to all the other old lady performers sitting around the room, she said, 'And they're all as jealous as buggery!' I left behind the Victorian music hall with all its passions and jealousies, and returned to the present day.

My next stop was Greenwich. The 'theatre' at the Green Man was a meeting room on the first floor over the saloon bar. For Music Hall Night there was an appropriately atmosphere full of good humour and fun. Jolly singing, joking and some jolly drinking. The patrons had brought their drinks up from the bar below. First up on the comedy bill was a pretty young lady with a sweet voice and come-hither patter of smiles and double-entendres. It was a brilliant Marie Lloyd impersonation, with all the subtle innuendos, coy glances and teasing words and gestures of the great star herself. It was hilarious and altogether a showstopper. The pretty young performer had the most beautiful eyes and cheekily radiant smile. She was utterly enchanting - a star in person, no less. In fact, I had rarely seen such a beautifully-observed performance - very saucy but with perfect timing, as all comedy should be. Her name, I saw from the programme, was Pauline Collins.

Next up, was an act that began in almost dead silence, except for an old man who dressed as a tramp and was making disgusting noises at the back of the hall. He then came shuffling down towards the stage. He was obviously in the wrong place, or some old drunk who at any moment, no doubt, would be escorted away by the pub bouncer so that the show could go on. But no, he just continued shuffling towards the front of the hall. Why was no one making a move to eject him? At the front he heaved himself, with much groaning and grunting, up onto the front of the stage, and there sat this man, in a shabby overcoat, old hat, long scarf, sniffing and shuffling and making his disgusting noises. My God! He was one of the acts. But he uttered not a word. He perched on the edge of the stage and after a few more grunts, scratches, sniffs and spits into a coloured handkerchief pinned to his overcoat, reached deep into his pocket and came out with - a banana! He was now peeling the fruit - slowly and leeringly and lasciviously - all done without a word but with many strange animal noises, obscene expressions and gestures. It brought the house down. The name on the programme said 'David Burke'. That was another name to look out for.

I could see that every performance was a drama - a story in its own right. And even behind that drama was another drama - the drama of the performance. Suddenly, I was full of ideas for future articles and any theatrical connections would be valuable. I introduced myself and we all exchanged phone numbers. I decided to start a book of show business contacts. My piece on the Music Hall appeared in The Plays and Players April 1965 issue: *Music Hall - Dead or Alive?*

May. I invited Pauline out for coffee. She had won a part in the forthcoming musical, Passion Flower Hotel, with a cast including Karin Fernald, Jeanie Muir, Francesca Annis, Jane Birkin and Michael Cashman. She told me about her training at the Central School of Speech and Drama where she had taken the teaching course and first set out to be a teacher of drama, but eventually she had taken her chances as a performer. She spoke about her agent, named Hilda Physick, and that proved to be a good topic for my next article for Players and Players.

Shortly afterwards, Pauline phoned and invited me out to dinner with a few friends. They were going to take me to a restaurant they had discovered, the 555 restaurant at 555 Battersea Park Road. She turned up with Jeanie Muir. Jeanie had a red sports car, in which

1965

we headed first for the Mermaid Theatre at Puddle Dock in Blackfriars, to pick up Peggy Mount, the comedienne. Peggy was playing in Gerhart Hauptmann's *The Beaver Coat* - an unusually dramatic role for her - in which one critic described her acting as 'just like a hurricane'. That evening the great dramatic role had taken its toll. She was feeling unwell and was getting out of London for the weekend. Even hurricanes, it seemed, needed a break between shows. As ever, it was fascinating to see the person behind the make-up. Peggy was warm and jovial in person. We were to drop her off at King's Cross station before going on for dinner. Leaving the dock area, we stopped for a red light, only to be hit from behind, with a sudden sickening crunch of metal, by someone who had applied his brakes too late. Pauline, Jeanie and I were uninjured, but Peggy had, she thought, suffered whiplash. However, she insisted we drove on so that she could catch her train. After the two drivers had exchanged names, numbers and insurance details, we headed for King's Cross, nursing our various bruises. After fond theatrical farewells, the three of us left for 555 Battersea Park Road, where a final member of the party would join us. That final member turned out to be the young actor called Edward Fox, who already had four film roles to his credit. Over dinner, a major topic of conversation was the restaurant itself. It was run by a small fat Polish chef and his tall thin Irish wife, both of whom had previously worked at the Savoy. The distinctive feature of their service was that, after diners had given their orders to the Irish waitress, they were invited into the kitchen to watch the maestro at work on their orders. It was a jolly evening.

June. I was at a Labour Party party in North London. At some point I had to nip up to the bathroom and passed the bedroom where coats, umbrellas and other belongings had been deposited by the partygoers. There, on the end of one of the beds, was a beautiful young girl in floods of tears. She told me she was sixteen and hated the party. She just wanted to go home but the person who had brought her to the party didn't want to leave.

'Where's home?' I asked her.

'Wallington in Surrey,' she said.

'Take a taxi,' I suggest.

She shook her head. She couldn't afford a cab. In truth neither could I, but her need seemed greater than mine. I called for a cab and while waiting for it, she told me her name was Jill Murphy. She was tall with long hair and had a radiant smile. Jill said she was about to start at the art school in Chelsea, just down the King's Road from me. The cab arrived and I asked the driver what it would cost to get to Wallington. 'Twenty quid,' he said. I gave her my phone number on the understanding that she would call me in the morning to let me know that she got home safely. I gave him the £20.00 and he drove away. I retrieved my coat and set off to find the nearest bus stop.

Jill and I kept in touch and when she started at Chelsea Art School she would occasionally drop round for coffee. She told me she was writing and illustrating a book for children, about an academy for young witches, based on her own Catholic convent, to be called *The Worst Witch*. She showed me what she had done. I was bowled over by what I saw - by the superb artwork, and the beautifully written story. As someone who had taught very young children, I was amazed at how instinctively she seemed to have understood the psychology of that age group. At some point she left Chelsea and went off to Camberwell. Sometime afterwards she got back in touch. She was working as a nanny, writing and married. Meantime, she was illustrating comic annuals for some outfit in Oxford Street. One day, she told me that the publisher of these annuals was not paying her - that is, not until she had delivered the drawings for the next annual. Soon after, she and Pete then disappeared off to Ghana for a year or so and I wasn't sure whether I would ever see her again.

In July Issue: My report on *Actors' Agents* with illustrations by Ralph Steadman was published in the Play and Players.

Summer. The Chelsea Classic was showing the William Wyler film of John Fowles' novel *The Collector*, with Terence Stamp as Reggie, the sinister loner, and Samantha Eggar as the unfortunate Miranda, his doomed victim. It was a brilliant study of madness and menace. I had to read Fowles's novel as soon as possible. He was clearly a writer to watch. The film was a further icon of the age.

At a meeting of the Writers' Guild, I met Bryan Stanley Johnson (Bryan) whose novel *Albert Angelo* had struck chords in my mind the previous November when I bought it. It so happened Bryan was a friend of Tony Tillinghast, who had been my deputy of the University Literary Magazine. No sooner did Bryan learn that I had known Tony than I was invited to have lunch with him and his beautiful wife Virginia at their flat in Middleton Square in Clerkenwell. The year before, November 1964, Tillinghast had died of cancer. He and Johnson had first met while editing a student poetry anthology - two weighty Londoners reading English Literature, and both avid football fans. Travelling around reporting on soccer for the Observer, Bryan tried whenever possible to detour through the Midlands town where Tony had lived. Over those last months, however, he had to watch his friend slowly waste away as the cancer advanced - the jovial Tony shrinking by degrees to a barely recognisable skeleton. To say he was deeply moved by this experience would be an understatement. He was completely devastated by memories of Tony's agonising death.

GLIMPSES OF A BIOGRAPHER'S DIARY

On the afternoon I had lunch at Middleton Square, June Tillinghast, Tony's widow, was there and we reminisced all afternoon. I recalled one editorial meeting at their house close to the university campus. We sat around drinking canned beer deciding what would go into the next edition of the magazine. The beer, no doubt, made us all rather merry, and for fun we decided to invent a student contributor called Christopher Gillimore. We wrote a spoof review of little magazines under his name, and invented stories about him, which were so absurd that we reduced ourselves to helpless laughter. That was the jovially affable man who had died. Bryan was still sadly depressed by Tony's sad end, but delighted to hear our anecdotes.

Bit by bit I took in my new friend. He was neatly turned out, taller than my six foot three, though heavily built, a beer-drinker's figure, while I was then quite skinny. He had a round cherubic face, dark brown wavy hair, and watchful eyes always ready to laugh. His voice was more tenor rather than baritone and he spoke with a distinctly London accent. As I got to know him better, I found he could be deeply sombre and hilarious by turns, though generally speaking my memory is of laughter rather than gloom. Nevertheless, one thing he was deadly serious about was the business of authorship. Tony had helped Bryan with his first novel, *Travelling People*, which had launched his novel-writing career.

Also in Summer. My friends Janet and Karl invited Cathy and me to spend the summer with them in Slovenian Istria, at the Villa Rog in Piran, a beautiful tiny town in as perfect a setting as one could hope to find - a medieval gem at the far end of a peninsula just to the south of Trieste - narrow streets, red-tiled houses piled in uneven layers, rising steeply up the little port to where it overlooks the Adriatic ('emerald-blue' not 'wine-dark', as Homer had it). The Villa Rog was built in the 1930s by Mussolini as a hideaway for him and his mistresses, or so the story went. It was a mysterious and roomy place - high ceilings, elaborately-carved mouldings, windows which opened onto a wide sweep of the sea. One day Kurt said, 'Would you like to come into Trieste and see how my boat is progressing?' He was building an altogether ultramodern yacht filled with electronic wizardry. We set off on a glorious summer's day in Karl's little car. Cathy rode in the front passenger seat while I sat in the back. Halfway to the border, I suddenly said, 'Oh my God! I've left my passport behind!' Quite unfazed, Karl said, 'That's okay, just lie as low as you can at the back of the car.' I crouched there trying to imagine spending the next how-many years of my youngish life in a communist prison cell with only the works of Marx and Engels for company.

As we approached the border with Italy, Karl said, 'Stay low. Guards don't always bother much over people leaving a country. I'll try out my Serbo-Cornflake on them.' Then as the guard approached the car, Karl wound down the window, switching to Serbo-Cornflake, and said, 'Hi there! We're from the Villa Rog in Piran. We are having a great party on Saturday and you are welcome to come along. Plenty Slivovitz, plenty girls.' At this point he grew expansive, gesturing towards Cathy who sat simpering prettily beside him. 'You and your comrades are all invited. You'll have a great time. What's your name? 'The guard gave his name and Karl repeated it. 'Great! You're invited.' The guard smiled with and waved us through. Then we approached the Italian checkpoint. I again felt nervous but Karl knew his border guards. 'Oh the Italians,' he said. 'We'll promise them plenty of wine, women and song, They'll love it. The Italian guards acted true to form and we were waived through while I kept low in the back seat.

There followed a day in Trieste enjoying the old city, and a visit to Karl's yacht under construction (so full of electronic gadgetry that, once fully installed, it would enable him to transform the deck into a large dance floor in a trice). After more chatter about yachts and travel, a drive around the ancient port city and a drop-off for coffee, we began our journey back to the border. The Italian guards seemed not to care who left their country. They lifted the barrier after a few words from Karl. Now I was then faced with the prospect of re-entering Tito's Yugoslavia without a passport. As we approached the barrier at the frontier, Karl said, 'Look, there's a queue of people going over the border on foot. You join the back of the queue and try looking inconspicuous. I'm sure you'll get across safely enough.'

I hopped out of the car, and joined the queue. All those in front of me were quite small people. I, who stood just over six foot and wore western holiday clothes, would've been as inconspicuous as the proverbial sore thumb. Taking in the situation, I panicked, back-pedalled and jumped back into the car.

'Can't do it,' I said.

'Okay,' said Karl. 'We'll try my Serbo-Cornflake again.'

By now, it was a well-rehearsed routine, and Karl performed his part to perfection. Again the cheery greeting, talk of a party and the leering gesture to Cathy, who also played her simpering part flawlessly. The invitation, the request for a name and the border guard's expected reaction. And once more we were waived through. It was unbelievable! Thanks to the genius of Karl, I had passed out of an Iron Curtain country and back into an Iron Curtain country without a passport. There's a good joke in this: 'A man walks through the Iron Curtain without a passport and a man says to him...'

But that was by no means the end of my Slovenian adventures that summer. One Saturday evening, Janet threw a party at the Villa to

1965

which all the interesting people in Piran were invited - many of them weekenders from Ljubijana. Guests of honour included the towering Davorin Ferligoj, Minister of the Interior, ex-Partisan Commander and Commissar, Mayor of Piran, now a Treasury Secretary of the Slovenian Republic, then a Judge, and finally Stojan Batič, a small but tough-looking sculptor of great monuments celebrating the regime and the triumph of the Partisans over the Nazi invaders. Much vigorous dancing took place, a lot of drink was consumed, and a jolly time was being had by all. Stojan Batič, the sculptor, asked me if I would like to visit his studio in Ljubijana. I said, 'I'd love to but unfortunately I have no transport.' He said. 'Don't worry I'll arrange something.' Then, after a while, he came back and announced that Davorin would take me if I could be up by 5 o'clock on the Monday morning. Slightly drunk and to be polite, I agreed. Janet lent me an alarm clock and the following morning I managed to be up in time. I was crammed into the waiting car along with Davorin, and the Judge.

The conversation turned to the law at some point and I said to the man sitting beside Davorin, 'What kind of judge are you?' to which he replied, 'I'm a hanging judge.' I turned my attention to the spectacular mountainous landscape through which we were passing. Every so often we passed a grand statue, celebrating the heroic Partisans. The judge pointed and said, 'Batič'. Occasionally we stopped at an auberge or taverna, had a coffee and cognac, at the next stop it would be a coffee and Slivovitz, then after that another coffee and cognac. And so we proceeded onwards towards Ljubijana. At each stop, a few more members of the Slovenian cabinet joined us, so that eventually at the last stop much coffee and spirit had been consumed.

Eventually we arrived in Ljubijana, and Davorin dropped me off at the studio of Batič. The sculptor had not yet arrived, but his young

Russian assistant was there and invited me in for a drink. We sat down to chat and, from somewhere, he produced a bottle of whisky. We exchanged anecdotes about London and Moscow and raised our glasses to art while the whisky slid happily down to hit our innards and then slid back up into our heads. My drinking partner was, he told me, the nephew of Prokofiev. We carried on, talking about art and politics, life in Moscow, and life as a student there. The arrival of Batič interrupted our merry chatter. He was in a dark and belligerent mood. Prokofiev's nephew was torn off a strip, in fact several strips - for sitting around doing no work, and for pilfering his mentor's whisky. He was put to work to wash down the walls and prepare the studio for a day's work ahead.

Batič then took me down through the streets of the lovely town. I was struck by the number of shopkeepers, cafe owners and simple passers-by who hailed my companion or even buttonholed him. Apparently, he was a great hero of the wartime resistance and bathed in the adulation of his compatriots. We went into one café after another, to enjoy a coffee and cognac or coffee and Slivovitz. There was someone special Batič wanted me to meet, he said. In a restaurant we found a handsome, grey-haired woman surrounded by a number of young men and women clustered at her table. This, it was explained to me, was an English woman, who had lived in Ljubijana for many years, including throughout the war. She was tall, elderly and spoke with a decidedly upper class Edwardian accent. She taught English at the University, she said, and loved what she called 'my beautiful Slovenes'. She interested them in Shakespeare by teaching them that the Bard had visited and was familiar with their part of the world. 'How else could he have set *Twelfth Night* on the coast of Illyria?' she asked. She was a certain type of classy English woman who, having embraced Communism, became anxious for adventure, and had convinced herself that her bearing and manner would see her through any vicissitudes she might encounter along the way. Frontiers she could negotiate, new languages she could master, Nazi occupations she could survive.

Nothing could disturb her inbred poise and certitude. We left her and her 'beautiful Slovenes' and continued on our tour.

We did finally have a good meal and some coffee which ensured, I hoped, that I would remain upright for at least the rest of my visit. Batič next took me off to the Slovenian National Theatre, where I met the company's director and his chief designer. Fortunately, their English was very good. They regaled me with stories of their many productions, walked me arm-in-arm to the theatre, telling me that their greatest wish was to take the company to the World Theatre Season held each year at the Aldwych Theatre in London. They showed me around their theatre, and loaded me up with photographs of their various productions (Brecht, Strindberg, Ibsen, Shakespeare etc.). I undertook to take them home and make a case for them to Peter Daubeny, the World Theatre director, in London. We parted with a celebratory drink of Slivovitz and hoped to meet up again in London.

Our next destination was a restaurant, in the garden of which, around a table, sat some of Batič's drinking friends. We all sat talking, about life, war, women, theatre, cinema, wine and women, and books and women - until through my alcoholic haze I realised that if I ran I would just about catch the bus back to Piran - if I wished to arrive back in time for supper. We all said jovial farewells to one another, backslapping, cheering, wishing one another well, and off I wove my way with Batič in attendance to the bus station. I certainly hoped that I could stay awake during the trip but found myself sitting next to an eloquent young man who told me in very good English that his great ambition was to go to a school for croupiers in Italy. Eventually I did doze off and woke just as we pulled into an auberge for a stop-off. As I opened my eyes I felt the compulsion to be violently sick. All that cognac and Slivovitz and whisky were now rearing up in a boiling storm to wreak its revenge on one reckless drinker. Seeing how I looked, my lovely would-be croupier friend dragged me off the bus, and ran me through the restaurant into a toilet at the back. where I brought up everything in one great heave. I then washed up and was happy to be led back meekly to the bus. The rest of the return journey to Piran was lost in the mists of a dreamless sleep. But I made it back and promised to tell the story of my day to Janet, Karl and Cathy the following morning over breakfast, hangover permitting.

27 August. The TES commenced publishing my six articles on the Education of Immigrants from the Commonwealth, mostly from the West Indies, India and Pakistan. Reactions to Immigrants 1: Frustration or Exhilaration.

Chapter 9

Full-Time Lecturer; TV Script Writer; My First Book
Published, with Another on the Way

1965-67

After the summer holiday, I realised that my job at the primary school had changed so dramatically I could no longer continue working there. A year earlier, the lovely Miss Philpott had retired and her replacement, a middle-aged man, who lacked her imagination and understanding, was intrusive and petty. Once I had to ask him politely to leave my classroom. Having seen my lovely class through to the end of its final school term, and with almost four years of postgraduate studies behind me, I now felt free to look seriously for work as a lecturer.

I sent my C. V. around and finally landed a job teaching Liberal Studies at Hendon College of Technology. At last I was a full-time Lecturer. The problem with Liberal Studies was that it was not an examination subject and students simply refused to take it seriously. Furthermore, at Hendon College the Vice Principal toured the building prying into classrooms to see that you were where you should have been. I took a term off - study leave to complete my M. A. thesis - then, when I was refused promotion, and plans to set up a Sociology degree at the College were shelved by the Liberal Studies Head, I decided to leave. My notice duly went in.

With my pending M. A. and my book: *Under Twenty* in the pipeline, I thought I stood quite good chance of a job in a college. I sent out my C. V. to various colleges already offering London degree courses, and after a week of interviews, I ended up with three definite offers. I was offered the teaching of Criminology at West Ham College of Technology, Political Sociology at Kingston and Sociology of Education at Goldsmiths' College, all teaching the London University Sociology degree. I consulted my university friend, Alan Sillitoe, who was already lecturing at Goldsmiths', and he recommended I take the job there, because, he said, there was a good head of department and the College was part of the University of London. I rather hoped that there might be the future possibility of teaching a course in the Sociology of Literature. I plumped for Goldsmiths' College.

25 October. My fully prepared script on *An Aspect of Immigration* was broadcast at 22.45 hr. at the BBC Home Service, London.

1966

20 January. A newspaper report told me that one of my theatrical heroes, George Devine, had died aged 55. I went to the Chinese restaurant and managed to get his corner table, just to mark the occasion.

In March. Peter Roberts asked me to write alternative articles in a series for Plays and Players to be called *All Our Yesterdays* in the Theatre. I first tackled 1919. The required material could be found at the Victoria and Albert Museum, in the so-called Enthoven of theatre magazines, programmes and reviews - enough for a history of 20th century English theatre let alone a series of short articles. My article was published in the Plays and Players April Issue. Also in March, I interviewed five London buskers outside the London Palladium, Soho at the Brewer Street corner of the Berwick Street Market, outside the Cambridge and the Duke of York Theatres and in the West End. Some of the songs they played were rock-n-roll,

American folk and blues and music hall songs. They were happy to go singing in the streets and I really enjoyed meeting and interviewing them. My report on *London's Buskers* was also in the *Plays and Player* April Issue.

15 April. The cover of Time Magazine carried a prominent feature headed, '*London the Swinging City*'. After that, the city, especially the 'Swinging Chelsea' bit of it, could expect an influx of Americans. Carnaby Street and the King's Road in particular were overrun by Yanks flaunting their dollars and decking themselves out with the latest London fashions. And not just the New Yorkers, but the Hollywood clique too. In one week I passed Paul Newman and Joanne Woodward in the King's Road, and Jack Palance in Sloane Square. At least, I suppose they added an element of glamour to the rather modest poets, artists, novelists and film directors who passed unnoticed in the normal way of things.

*

When Roy Thompson, the Canadian press baron, bought the Times newspaper this year from members of the Astor family, I was invited to attend the party to celebrate the hand-over. That's where I first met David Astor, editor of the Observer, a close friend of George Orwell.

The publication of my TES articles on ethnic minorities in schools led to my being asked by the BBC in the Spring to help with a television programme called *Minorities in Britain*. I prepared some notes about Indians living in Southall. The story of their presence there was fascinating. It seems that the Woolf Rubber Company was having difficulty getting men prepared to work in the intensely hot conditions there. The personnel officer, an ex-Indian Army man, remembered how his Punjabi soldiers would work and fight under equally trying conditions. He invited one of his old NCOs to Southall. That man then brought his family, and other willing workers from around his village, to join the procession to Britain. Their main spokesman was a member of a trades union, which had led to the company firing him. He therefore invited each of these men, one by one, to his home for tea and recruited them on the spot. Once he had all the Indian workers signed up, he went to the management and said, 'Now all your men are members of the union. Kindly agree to our demands or we go on strike.' I interviewed this clever union man and asked him whether he liked living in England. He said that he did. I wrote my script and posted it to TES.

In Summer. Pauline Collins invited me to a party at her flat overlooking Battersea Park. It was crowded with young theatricals. Many were from the new television series Doctor Who, a science fiction soap opera for kids, in which Pauline had been cast as Samantha Briggs, a young Liverpudlian in search of her missing brother.

To celebrate confirmation of my new job at Goldsmiths' College and the salary to go with it, I decided to splash out. At a shop called *Casa Pupo* along Pimlico Road, I saw a beautiful red Spanish carpet, and fell in love with it instantly. I went in and bought it. I then hailed a passing taxi, loaded it on board and took it straight to my flat. I quickly laid it down and in an instant the room was transformed into a sort of exotic grotto. Now at least, on my new salary I could afford to save. What I had in mind was a flat in some small corner of Chelsea.

September. I was due to start my new Goldsmiths' job. But with only a few weeks to go, I was once again struck down. Fortunately, it happened at home in my flat at the rear of number 61 Shawfield Street. As I bent to straighten the carpet, I felt as if someone drove a stiletto into the base of my spine. I hit the deck and just lay there. Once more I turned deaf with the pain and lay still - frozen. Any attempt to move or stir was agonising. I couldn't think what to do - how to extract myself from the situation - immobilised by overwhelming pain. Everyone else was away for the weekend. Finally, I managed to roll over onto my back and that seemed to ease matters, but still left me as an inert heap on my new *Casa Pupo* carpet. Any attempt to sit up was excruciating. Gradually, by degrees I managed to drag my way over to the door, and, by propping myself against it, reached up to the catch, undid it and opened it very slightly. Now, I had to puzzle out how to get through the door to the telephone to make a call. But who could I call on a Saturday? Then I thought of Joanna, a physiotherapist at Westminster Hospital – kind-hearted - and fortunately I remembered her phone number. Painfully, I managed to heave my bottom forward slightly, opened the door, then hauled myself backwards out into the hallway. How I managed to get my seat onto the chair beside the phone, I can't remember as it was so agonising. I inserted a few shillings into the telephone, dialled the number and crossed my fingers, hoping that Joanna would be at home.

Fortunately she was off duty. I poured out my sorry tale and asked her if she could possibly come and help me.

She said, 'I'll leave immediately and be with you within about fifteen minutes.'

I dragged myself on the floor again and up to the front door. It seemed an age until the front doorbell rang, but ring it eventually did. I managed to claw my way to the door catch and unlock it to let her in, then fell back so that when she entered she was confronted by a body lying prone in the hallway. Luckily, Joanna was strong enough to be able to drag me back to my room and then, with her help, I managed to get myself onto the divan.

After a few days on my back, I called a taxi and went to see my doctor.

'I think you may have slipped a disc Mr. Bowker,' he said, and when I asked him if he could send me to an osteopath, he said he wasn't allowed to do so, because of a ruling by the British Medical Association. However he did recommend that I go to St Thomas' Hospital for traction. This involved a sort of a rack which attempted to pull patients apart in the hope that this would allow their displaced discs to be sucked back into place. With me the hope was not fulfilled and I was left to climb painfully into a cab and returned to my flat as best I could.

GLIMPSES OF A BIOGRAPHER'S DIARY

I rang my new head of department at Goldsmiths' College and said, 'I am not sure I'd be able to start promptly in September because of this disc problem.' 'Try my osteopath,' he said and gave me a telephone number. Mr. Ambrose was a quietly-spoken Canadian with a very gentle manner. He was an avid student of Holistic Medicine. He read widely in the literature of alternative medicine, and he would often discuss his readings during treatment. To begin with, he would simply have his patient lying prone while he massaged the back. Then, when he judged the moment right, he would manipulate dramatically so that the vacuums between each vertebra popped off like a machine-gun fusillade. He would then explain the whole thing to me. It was, he said, 'Like the throwing up of a tottering column of dice so they fell back into a neat and orderly pile.' Well, it seemed to work with me, and I walked away from Mr. Ambrose's consulting rooms like a new man. I rang my boss, gave him the good news, and said I would be at Goldsmiths' College at the beginning of the September term after all.

Lecturing at Goldsmiths' was a joy from the very start. The students were eager to learn and were a pleasure to teach. I soon developed a teaching technique which suited both them and myself. Being first-year degree students and new to university life and studies, I had to teach them how to address a question posed, ensure the material they drew upon was relevant and how to argue a case before summing up their own words in coming to a conclusion. Once they had mastered that simple technique, it was surprising to me what good work they turned out.

Also in September. My book, *Under Twenty*, was finally published and I was sent my copies. Brian Southam told me that the idea for the cover - the title repeated and staring through a red mist - had come from a young fellow in their office. But I noticed that my name was missing. My first book, and no name on the cover! When I pointed this out, Brian was full of apologies - an inexplicable oversight, he said. I pulled a face, but was somewhat mollified by the fine page design and the fact that my passages of interconnecting commentary and lists of questions and exercises for the pupils were left untouched. And my name did, at least, appear on the title page. There was a launch party - at the flat of the very chap who had designed the cover and left off my name. He seemed a nice enough young fellow and I forgave him. News to cheer me came shortly afterwards - that *Under Twenty* had become 'a mini bestseller', whatever that meant. Then Margaret Heinemann, who taught English at Goldsmiths', said to me how much she admired the collection.

I was rather proud to have brought out this modest volume, and sent a copy to Dr Tonkin at Westminster Hospital, telling him that without his help this book would never have appeared. A few days later I received a charming postcard in response. 'Patients rarely remember,' he said. But I, for one, would never forget.

November. A letter came from Lester Clark (Lester), Jane Mercer's old boss at Rediffusion Television. He had read *Under Twenty* and wanted to meet me. He was the script editor for a series of drama-documentaries for schools based on words and, at our first meeting, he asked me if I could write two scripts for their series of Schools Television Programmes: *Ways With Words*, Title: *Trapped and Protest*. He sent me away with the scripts of a couple of previous programmes. They seemed straightforward enough and I duly sent in my final scripts with dialogues on the 30th November. Lester liked them (and they were due to be televised in the Spring 1967). I was paid what I thought were more than handsome fees, £25 per script to begin with and ending at £80 as the Writers' Guild negotiated new rates.

I was now in the mood to do more journalism. I'd always been struck by the brilliance of Irish actors. Could it be, I wondered, that there was something in the Irish soul that came through on the stage and found its greatest expression there? And what about other nations? Great Welsh actors like Richard Burton, and fine Scottish ones like Alistair Sim suggested to me that there was a story in this for Plays and Players. Fortunately, Peter Roberts agreed with me. For the Irish, the first on my list were Peter O'Toole and Michael MacLiammoir whom I had seen recently in his remarkable one-man show, *The Importance of Being Oscar*. I told Peter what I had in mind and he told me that O'Toole was not Irish but was born in Leeds. My second choice was the pixie-like Jack McGowran, the first actor to play Lucky in Samuel Beckett's *Waiting for Godot*, that I arranged, through his agent, to visit at his home in Hampstead. I arrived hotfoot at MacGowran's house at the appointed hour and rang the bell. The door was answered by a handsome Irish woman who introduced herself as Jack's wife. She then announced that he sent his apologies but he was filming that day with Roman Polanski in the North.

Michael MacLiammoir in *The Importance of Being Oscar*, had lodged itself in my memory ever since I saw it. It was an indescribably brilliant coup de théâtre - from where I sat at least. No sooner had the great actor stepped onto that stage than he commanded every inch of it. All eyes were on him and some eerie magnetism kept them pinned there. MacLiammoir's panache and extraordinarily theatrical presence, his sonorous voice and the ingenious incorporation of Wilde's epigrams into the script, left one dazzled. A magician had just breathed life into one of the icons of British theatre. Oscar had walked again. I arranged a meeting with this larger-than-life actor at his grand hotel in a square close to Hyde Park. On declaring myself at the reception desk I was asked to wait. His secretary came to find me, led me to a small lounge inside the hotel and announced that Mr. MacLiammoir would be with me in five minutes. I arranged my notes and sat there expectantly, clutching a small tape recorder and notebook. I was a fan and so of course grew a little nervous as I waited.

Then, suddenly, the door swung open and in flounced the great actor. It was a fine theatrical entrance and I was suitably impressed. He came straight over to me, followed by his secretary. We shook hands and said our hellos.

'Well now,' he said, settling himself down.

'What are we going to talk about?'

I was in awe of this mighty man of the theatre. My questions were batted away with deftness and wit and I was subjected to some of the most exhilarating conversation I had ever engaged in. As an interviewee he was worth his weight in gold. He was one of those rare characters, whom you only have to set talking and he just wouldn't stop. All his answers were delivered like lines from his play, many of which were Wildean epigrams delivered bang on cue.

'As Oscar said - I have it in my show - "There is nothing so dangerous as being too modern; one is apt to grow old-fashioned quite suddenly."' It's a great put-down line; I've since used it often. Another line quoted from the same show was, 'Every boy with the slightest ambition left Ireland as soon as he had had his first shave.' MacLiammoir said with passion. When the interview ended and I was about to shake his hand, he grabbed me by the cheeks and planted a great smackeroo kiss on my lips. When I froze, he swept out of the room. Exit Michael and exit Oscar. His secretary followed discreetly closing the door behind him.

As for the Scottish actor John Laurie, I was able to catch him at his stately home at Gerrard's Cross just outside London, I remember him mostly as the crofter in Hitchcock's 1935 thriller The 39 Steps and as the comic Scots soldier in Olivier's 1948 film of Hamlet. He was quite eager to talk about his theatrical career, especially his years at the Stratford Memorial Theatre between the wars. He had not long before appeared as the Duke of Gloucester in Peter Brook's production on King Lear at the Aldwych. Brook, he told me, was a sadist, because of the way he had had the Duke of Cornwall gauging out Gloucester's eye with a golden spur on a powerfully-lit spot downstage left. A few years later, he landed a plum part in Dad's Army, a BBC sitcom about the wartime Home Guard.

I couldn't get O'Toole, but I did manage to interview his beautiful Welsh wife, Sian Phillips, who insisted on meeting me at my Chelsea address. At the arranged time, to the minute, my front doorbell rang and there stood a uniformed chauffeur. Drawn up at the kerb behind him stood a gleaming Rolls. The chauffeur announced, 'Miss Sian Phillips is here to see Mr. Bowker.' He then returned to the Rolls, opened the rear door and the grand lady grandly stepped out. She mounted the steps to my front door with great dignity and we greeted one another politely. She swept into my flat and I said, 'Please sit down,' and she sat herself in the armchair next to my gas fire. She was striking, not to say stunning, and draped herself elegantly over the chair. We talked about Welsh theatre and acting and, when I offered her a Gauloise, she took one and lit up saying, 'Peter smokes these things.' For once I felt close to the great man himself even though at one cigarette removed. When the interview ended, I escorted her to the door, we shook hands and she left.

The Scottish, Welsh and English actors I interviewed gave me enough material for my article, but pointed to no firm conclusion as to which nation produced the best thespians, though I did favour the view that probably the Celts did have it over the English - with certain great exceptions, that is.

My report on *Nationalism and the Theatre: Paddy, Taffie and Jock*, was published in Plays and Players, December Issue

18 December. *Blow Up*, Michaelangelo Antonioni's latest movie, starring David Hemmings, was shown at the Paris Pullman, adding yet further confirmation that we lived in a new age - the era of the photojournalist and pictorial illusion, of the wild unfettered libido, the epoch in which youth rather age was seen as the repository of all wisdom, aided and abetted by the mass media.

1967

In Spring, Tom Stoppard's play *Rosencrantz and Guildenstern Are Dead* was staged at the Old Vic. What a strange play! But how ingenious and entertaining. One became slowly aware that a rare intelligence was at work on that stage. Where would the playwright go after that?

Also in Spring, both *Trapped* and *Protest* (final scripts with dialogues that were delivered on the 30th November 1966 and 14th December 1966 to Rediffusion Television) were televised, and I looked on proudly with friends. Rediffusion Television commissioned me to write three scripts to be completed with dialogues for the series of schools television programmes entitled

1967

Ways With Words, titled: *On The Move* (2) *Tricked* (3) *It's All In The Mind*. (1) *On The Move* was sent in on the 7th March. (2) *Tricked* sent in on the 14th March and (3) *It's All In The Mind* sent in on 14th April. All 3 were televised in the Summer Terms.

1 July. I flew to Venice en route to stay with Janet and Karl in Piran. Returning to Piran was a sad experience without Cathy, who had disappeared off to college. This time, instead of a hiring a large villa, my friends had rented two small adjoining ones. They lived in one and I had the other next door, reserved for their guests. That meant that I was free to spend my mornings after breakfast on the book *Teaching Immigrant Children* for Longmans Green, that I was trying to finish. Working steadfastly on it every morning, I was able to complete it within a week. (It was about the teaching of immigrant children, and was based on the research I had done for the TES on the 27th August 1965 - and which I'd also incorporated into my MA thesis.)

There were two memorable experiences for me in Piran. First, I met Janko Lavrin, a Slovenian-born Emeritus Professor of Slavonic Studies at my old university in England, who spent every summer back in his homeland. There, he had a career and reputation as a poet and novelist. As a young man, he was a newspaper correspondent in pre-revolutionary Russia and broadcast for the BBC during World War II. He had written studies of Pushkin, Tolstoy, Dostoevsky and Nietzsche – so he was a man steeped in East European high culture.

One evening, Lavrin told us a wonderful story of the time he spent with Albert Einstein after being given the job of interpreting for him during a visit to Nottingham in 1931. Einstein had told Lavrin a story against himself. It happened in Germany during the hyperinflation of the early 1920s, when the currency lost all its value and a loaf of bread could cost hundreds of thousands of Marks. Einstein wanted to go on a tram from one end of Berlin to the other. The journey involved several changes and meant having to buy several tickets, one for each section of the journey. Normally, the conductor did the calculation for the whole trip and the passenger paid up before starting. Einstein, thinking to save the conductor a chore, had done the sums in advance and when he handed the fare money to the conductor, he also showed him his calculation written down. However, the conductor, being a good German, did not trust the passenger and did the calculation for himself. Having done so, he said, 'I am sorry, Mein Herr, but you are wrong,' and he took Einstein slowly through the figures. Finally Einstein had to admit that the conductor was right and he was wrong. The man beamed and said, 'Never mind, Mein Herr. We cannot all be mathematicians.'

The other experience that lingers in the memory was of a dinner one evening at a restaurant overlooking the beach in Piran. The food and wine were perfect, and the service impeccable. Suddenly, all hell broke loose. Angry voices were raised and a great altercation erupted between a group of men at one of the tables and the waiters, which ended with a glass being thrown and shattering against a brick wall. It looked very ugly and we braced ourselves for a rumpus. The whole restaurant went silent. Then something strange and very impressive happened. Almost all the men in that restaurant stood up and formed a barrier at the entrance. The angry men sized up the situation and in a moment made up their minds that the best thing they could do was retreat while they could. They filed sheepishly towards the door and the local guardians parted ranks to allow them through. Then, when they had departed, the customers returned quietly to their seats and their meals as if nothing had happened. A man at the next table to us hissed, 'Bloody Serbs!' By the time I left for home on the 15th, I had a completed book manuscript with me on *Teaching Immigrant Children*. I could scarcely believe what I'd accomplished. I couldn't wait to post my typescript to Longmans Green. I had offered it as a book to Brian Southam at Routledge who turned it down, but he was interested in my other proposal for an anthology of extracts about democracy and revolution. I then offered the book to Longmans Green who quickly snapped it up before I went away on my holiday in Piran.

1967

A lovely Swedish film *Elvira Madigan*, based on a true story of love denied, was playing at the Paris Pullman. It was the first movie I'd seen which used classical music as a soundtrack - the andante from Mozart's Piano Concerto no 21 in C., a suitably romantic piece to heighten feelings of both delight and melancholy to accompany the story.

Rediffusion Television commissioned me to write five final television scripts completed with dialogue each having a playing time of approximately twenty minutes for series of television programmes for schools entitled *Approach to Living*.[1]

---

[1] Programme No: (1)(2)(3)(4)(5). The final scripts with dialogues: (1) was sent in on 6 December, (2) was sent in on 13 December. (3) was sent in on 3 January 1968. (4) was sent in on 10 January and (5) was sent in on 24 January. All five programmes were televised in the Spring Term.

Chapter 10

Teaching in Canada and Damsels in Distress

1968-69

28 February. The first production of *Cabaret*, the musical based on Christopher Isherwood's Berlin Stories, opened at the Palace Theatre with the bright young Judi Dench as Sally Bowles. There seemed to be no end to these theatrical delights. 13 April, I met my friend, Eric, who was briefly back in town and he said, 'Why not do Summer School teaching as a Visiting Professor in Canada?'

'How do I go about that?' I asked.

'I'll give you an address to write to,' he said.

The next day, I wrote to the Professor of Sociology at the University of New Brunswick in Fredericton, enquiring about Summer School. He replied by return: 'You're down on the programme to teach Introductory Sociology. We look forward to meeting you.' All I had to do was present myself at the Canadian border, show this letter to immigration officials, and proceed to Fredericton ready to start teaching.

July. I bought a ticket on a cheap student flight from Gatwick to New York and one for an Air Canada flight from there to Montreal with a connecting flight to Fredericton. I couldn't wait for college term to end so that I could hop on the plane from Gatwick heading off to sunny North America.

24 August. I had met Barney at one of Nick's open evenings. He was a busy chap, exuding enthusiasm and curiosity about things and people. He was very bright, not long down from Oxbridge and had got his foot on the publishing ladder. Now he was planning to marry and had called round to talk it over. Was he doing the right thing, he wanted to know? I played it along the lines Richard Peters had once played it for me - when I couldn't decide on the job I was offered in Belfast - listing all the pros and cons and then leaving it to him to decide. It seemed to work and he was, apparently, reassured that he was doing the right thing. As we chatted, there was a sudden frantic hammering at the front door. When I opened it, a young woman rushed past me as if pursued by the hounds of hell. She dived into my flat and flung herself onto the divan sobbing while Barney sat there quite as bemused as I was.

'What is it? Can we help?'

'They're chasing me!'

'Who?'

'These men!' She was clearly distressed.

As her sobs subsided, she gasped out her story. Some man had invited her to a party in Chelsea. She was quite enjoying herself when suddenly another man picked on her and accused her of stealing. To her horror he said he was going to call the police and in a panic she'd fled with the man and his friends in hot pursuit. She had seen a light behind our front door and was seeking sanctuary from her pursuers. Now she sat up and turned to us, pleading. 'You won't let them get me, will you?'

She had touched us with her story and we told her not to worry. We'd make sure they didn't 'get' her.

GLIMPSES OF A BIOGRAPHER'S DIARY

'Thank you so much.' Big brown eyes widened in gratitude. She was rather beautiful-looking, and we both felt quite heroic to have helped this maiden in distress.

'Can I make you a coffee?' I asked.

'I have to go,' she said, 'but I'm still scared. Could one of you escort me to a bus stop?' Barney said, 'I have a car outside. I'll give you a lift.'

Her relief was palpable.

'Where are you parked?' she asked, still anxious.

'Right outside,' he said.

'Good. Can we go now?'

'I'll be back,' said Barney. I offered her the best of luck and they left.

What now? I wondered, but it seemed like no time when there was another ring at the door. Barney was back. That was quick. 'She asked me to drop her just a few streets away, then she took the first cab that came along.' he said.

We began our post mortem. Imagine, we said. It could have happened to anyone.

Terrible to be accused of something you haven't done. We went on for a while before the subject began to change. But we were not allowed to continue. The doorbell rang again.

'Surely she can't be back.'

'Only one way to find out,' I said and went to the front door.

Outside was a well-dressed man with a distinctly public-school accent.

'Has a girl with long brown hair been here?' he asked.

'There was a girl, but she's gone.'

1967

'You let her go?'

'Why shouldn't we?'

'Can I come in?'

Perhaps he suspected she was still with us. If this was her accuser, her pursuer, it'd be interesting to hear from him anyway, I thought, so I said, 'Sure. Come in.' He came in, looked around suspiciously for a while, then, satisfied that his victim was no longer there, sat on the edge of the divan.

'What did she tell you?'

We repeated her story while he shook his head and looked grimly amused.

'Want to know the truth?' he said.

'Go on,' said Barney.

He lived just around the corner in Redesdale Street, he began. 'It was a wedding party, and this couple arrive, uninvited.

'Party-crashers.'

'Exactly!' he said. 'She acted wildly, even outrageously while the man disappeared. Because of this girl's over the top behaviour, no one noticed her companion's absence, until my wife disturbed him rifling through her room with a suitcase full of our wedding presents. He bolted past her into the street and, by the time we made the connection to the girl, she was also slipping away. We gave chase around here and suddenly she disappeared. Now we're going from house to house. Do you know where she went?'

'I drove her down the King's Road and she took a cab where I dropped her off.' Said Barney

'God,' he said. 'What a team!'

'She took us in,' I said, smiling weakly. 'Sorry.'

'You weren't to know,' he said.

GLIMPSES OF A BIOGRAPHER'S DIARY

'Have you told the police?'

'They've been called, and are probably over there now.'

He departed and we went back to our post mortem. What Barney drew from all this about marriage I don't know, but a week later I receive an invitation to his wedding.

September. When I first saw a copy of my book from Longmans Green, I was concerned about the title chosen for it. *The Education of Coloured Immigrants* was certainly not my choice. The word 'coloured' concerned me. But, apparently, the publishers had complete control of the book title. So, I just had to live with it. Fortunately, no one ever picked me up on this.

However, the book produced several invitations to talk about young immigrants. I gave a lecture to just about the whole of Goldsmiths' College staff in the main hall one Monday morning. I was invited to speak to a number of undergraduates at Oxford on the same subject, and was also asked to lecture to a class of Birmingham University extramural students at Stratford-upon-Avon. I had only ever been to Stratford-upon-Avon as a boy, to go boating on the river with a friend, and as a student to visit the theatre with Angela. Now I was going to deliver a lecture, clutching a copy of my book and trying to look and sound professorial. It turned out to be an odd occasion. I finished my talk and invited questions. After a few simple points and enquiries, a loud voice piped up from the back of the class which I recognised instantly. It was the stentorian voice of my old drama teacher, David Turner, who, it transpired, lived in nearby Leamington Spa and was now making a reputation for himself as a playwright.

After the class he and I repaired to a pub. There he told me about a recent question and answer session in which he had taken part with Christopher Fry, the dramatist, at a literary festival, and said that, without his memory of the essay I had written for him as a student on Fry's *The Boy With The Cart*, he would have been unable to contribute much to the discussion. These were flattering words indeed coming from a personal hero of mine. He told me some lovely stories - how he'd been thrown off the BBC radio series, *The Archers*, for pushing his socialist views onto Phil Archer and then told of his tussles with moral crusader Mary Whitehouse. He was proud to claim that he had been mentioned more often in Whitehouse's books than anyone else. He told me all this with barely suppressed laughter after which his nervous bellow burst into an unconfined guffaw. It was a strange and memorable encounter, and I was determined to renew our friendship and get to know him even better.

When my book, *The Education of Coloured Immigrants* was published, Janet threw a party. I met her schoolfriend, Rosemary, who happened to be secretary to Douglas Hyde, the journalist. Hyde had once been News Editor of the Communist Daily Worker, but had left the Party in a blaze of publicity for the Catholic Church. I'd read his book, *I Believed*, in which he told that strange story. Rosemary told me that Douglas had read my book and would love to talk to me. I was invited to meet him. He was an extraordinary man, small, immensely friendly and intensely religious. His Methodist beliefs had led him into the Party and it was the dishonest conduct of its leaders and the promiscuity of its members that led him out of it into the arms of the Catholic Church. Douglas told me about Eddie Linden, a gay Glaswegian Catholic-cum-communist, who was starting up a poetry magazine, *Aquarius*. I gave him a call and invited him round to Shawfield Street.

Rebecca and I were to meet up for dinner. However, she rang ahead and asked, 'Do you mind if I bring a friend along?.' 'Not at all,' I said. In fact she brought along two friends. One was a chap who seemed to be somewhat attached to her; the other was a younger woman who it transpired had been brought along as my dining companion. The male - introduced to me as Milton - was an expansive type. He was clearly building empires - saying at one point that they were going to make a star out of his dining companion. He then commenced to regale us with salacious stories about sexual goings on at ITV. Rebecca and Milton seemed to be very much in love.

GLIMPSES OF A BIOGRAPHER'S DIARY

John Fowles had put in another appearance. In 1965, his novel *The Magus* had been panned by the TLS as 'silly', but now is regarded as an extraordinary work, *The French Lieutenant's Woman*, as 'a tour de force', a brilliant piece of meta-fiction written in the style of Thackeray with nods in the direction of Freud, Marx and 'certain historians'. Fowles's juggling with time and narrative voice was what I found so intriguing. I added a first edition to the now groaning shelves of the wall library which I had installed above my bed.

1969

1 May. I decided to visit Paris, on my own this time. I stayed at the Grand Hotel de Lima again, and lived cheaply, eating at takeaway restaurants, Chinese restaurants and pizzerias when not with my friends. This was to enable me to stay one single night at an expensive hotel afterwards. My first choice was the Hotel Georges V in Avenue Georges V. Sadly, that was full, so I turned to the next best place which was the adjacent Prince des Galles. It was everything I could wish for in a sumptuous Paris hotel. The fixtures and fittings were elegant, and the furniture was Louis XIV. The trimming and pipings were in gold, as were the taps and fittings in the most exotic bathroom imaginable. I settled in. It was a warm evening, I went out for a stroll and then wandered past the crowded cafés and restaurants along the Champs Elysées in leisurely fashion, enjoying the perfumed ambience and the thought of a luxurious evening ahead. I turned off the Champs Elysées and returned down the Avenue Georges V to the Prince des Galles. I took a leisurely shower, and then sauntered down to the foyer to sit and observe the comings and goings. After supper, I returned to my princely bedroom to reflect on how to achieve my burning desire to become a writer and to buy my house. I spent time visiting my friends, bookshops, Luxembourg gardens and restaurants e.g. La Coupole, La Closerie de Lilas in Montparnasse, Les Deux Magots and Café de Flore in Place Saint-Germain des-Prés with my friends before returning to my flat in Chelsea.

1969

June, and I was preparing myself for the summer's teaching as a Visiting Professor in Canada. Charlotte had invited me to a party at her parents' Sloane Square apartment. It was crowded with minor celebrities, of the transatlantic variety. Ethel Gray, a elderly woman but full of American fizz, once managed the tennis star, Little Mo' Connolly, and spoke seductively of California and the charms of Hollywood where she had her home. 'When you come to Los Angeles you must stay with me,' she said, handing me her card. I was flattered and thrilled. My tentative summer itinerary suddenly included a trip to L.A. Alessandro, a New York dress designer, a small dark Sicilian, and his wife, Sharon, tall and blonde, a walking testimony to the latest 1960s New York style. We talked a lot worth remembering and I was invited to dinner at a King's Road restaurant along with Charlotte. There were about ten people in our party that evening, all seated around one large table, and again the conversation was memorable until Alessandro, looking at the bill - which must have been enormous - produced with a grand flourishing gesture a long book under our noses and announced with a laugh, 'My Cosa Nostra cheque book.' And one could almost have believed it was true. Before the evening was over, Alessandro, or maybe it was Sharon, said to me, 'If you ever come to New York you must stay with us.'

Before embarking on my trip to Canada, I called Alessandro long distance, announcing that I would soon be hitting the streets of the Big Apple. He sounded enthusiastic and said, 'You must stay with us, of course.' I bought two airline tickets – one to New York and one, for ten days later, from there to Montreal. When I arrived at JFK, I was overwhelmed by the sense of uncontrollable movement - nothing permanent; everything on the move; nothing still, no tranquility - airport buses coming, company buses going, cars sweeping in and out and past, and people bustling to and fro. I was on the bus heading towards the megaliths of Manhattan, this city of sky-scraping monuments to capitalism. I somehow made my way to West 67 Street and there was my destination, right across from the Lincoln Centre. Suddenly I was in a world of luxury. It was all-pervasive - the finely chosen fittings, elegant furnishings, princely wallpapers, tasteful gold-framed mirror over marble-topped occasional table... and that was just in the foyer of the apartment block.

When I gave my name to the janitor, I was announced to my hosts and welcomed by them via an intercom. Then into an elevator. The doors closed silently, rose imperceptibly, and when they opened, there stood my 'friends' welcoming me loudly. Now it was all adventure with Alessandro and Sharon. She was his third wife and they had only been married eight months. Their apartment was a cathedral: a triplex, stained-glass windows overlooking the rooftops of Manhattan. I was settled into a small top floor bedroom.

As the honoured guest, I found myself fussed over with the metaphorical red carpet rolled out. Seated beneath the high, stained glass window I clutched a highball laced with ice and pineapple. Laughter, bonhomie, the pursuit of pleasure, anything legal to buoy us aloft, to float us over the skyline stretching upwards, like Peter Pan or Mary Poppins, reaching for more - the ultimate heaven maybe, forever out of our grasp. This city sends the mind running, streams of consciousness tumbling over and swamping the imagination. On my very first night, Alessandro took me to his favourite restaurant. He, Sharon and I walked to the nearby Ginger Man, an Irish restaurant on W. 64th Street, with an Irish-American proprietor, the actor Patrick O'Neal. It had a charm and style of its own. Waiters in waistcoats and shirtsleeves reminded me of Paris. The atmosphere was highly congenial and Alessandro was obviously something of a celebrity in this affluent and affable company. People came across to the table to greet him and exchange a word; he went across to greet others.

The days passed in strangely routine merriment. Every morning the marriage chamber's door was left ajar and, with the husband away at his studio, I was called in to help Sharon organise her day. That invariably meant shopping expeditions along Fifth Avenue. We headed first for Saks, where Sharon spotted a sleigh bed. She went into ecstasies and bought one in a flash, without even glancing at the price. At Tiffany, it was a diamond-studded bracelet. Then on she went to pick and choose antiques, dresses, blouses and bracelets - whatever caught her eye. If Brecht's *Alabama Song* went 'Show us the way to the next whisky store,' Sharon's Manhattan song went 'Show me the way to the next jewellery store.' We headed off for lunch. At some fine food bar, Sharon ordered a huge Caesar salad, but left most of it uneaten. Out of habit I finished what was on my plate. Then we set off in pursuit of more acquisitions. The evening routine was cocktails, out to dinner and early to bed for the industrious Alessandro and the exhausted Sharon. Sometimes the pattern differed, but always those evening drinks.

One evening I was taken to the Electric Circus, a nightclub and discothèque in the East Village, where the New York equivalent of San Francisco's flower children hung out. There we met with wondrous flashing lights and explosive music - my first encounter with the surreal world of psychedelia, distortion and disorientation - the drugless high.

Sharon had been bubbling since I arrived about a proposed trip to St. Tropez. Of course, she had to find clothes for that bonanza and where else to find them but Fifth Avenue? Our daily spending spree therefore took in all the fashions. I stood patiently, like a good escort, and admired Sharon in this outfit and that as she bobbed in and out of changing rooms and fancy cubicles. She twisted and twirled while I hummed and hawed and complimented. I seemed to be quite good at it because she rewarded me with a particularly sumptuous lunch at the Regency Bar and Grill.

Back at the apartment when Alessandro came in from work, the atmosphere of endless bonhomie and emotional high continued. Up in the marital bedroom they were talking. Apparently, Alessandro's designer had walked out on him on the eve of his summer show. Understandably, he felt a bit low. I went to my room. Later we were all downstairs. Over cocktails, I talked about 'shows' and Alessandro talked about his day at work. Over dinner, there was pleasant conversations as usual and then we left for the theatre where Alessandro and Sharon sat either side of me. Next morning, I went downstairs and the bedroom door was closed. No planning with Sharon that morning. I got out into the street with a sense of relief. On my return that evening, there was a note saying simply, 'We've gone to our ranch. Stay as long as you like. Make whatever use of the apartment you care to make.' And so, for the rest of my stay in New York, I had a luxurious base from which to explore the city.

Out of sheer curiosity, I trotted along to Radio City Music Hall at the Rockefeller Centre where NBC were recording their Janet Leigh extravaganza. It was a music hall setting with a noisy, crowded auditorium. Suddenly the lights went down, the band struck up, and hubbub gave way to an air of intense expectation - the Janet Leigh Fan Club had turned out in full force, I guessed - the curtain went up, and a chorus line went through a gymnastic routine. Then, on a very high note, in swooped the star to deafening applause and cries of adoration. The fans all rose, applauding and whooping at the sight of their own star in the flesh. Some of these people had travelled miles to see her and there she was - Janet - hoofing it up in great style - high kicks, twirls, pirouettes, taps and soft shoe shuffles - vo-de-o-doh, boo-boopy-do-dum-dey. The fans clapped and stamped their feet. This was their Janet, this was their show, this was their theatre!!!

All of a sudden something went wrong. A voice through a megaphone shouted 'Cut!' and the dancing came to a sudden dead stop. 'Let's do it again,' said the voice and the star and the dancers all casually trooped off stage. The audience paused. The fans subsided. What had gone wrong? The band struck up again. Clearly this must herald the second scene to follow the first. But no. The curtain rose, the chorus line went through the same gymnastic routine, then, on a very high note, in swooped the star - this time to a more muted round of applause and fewer cries of appreciation. All proceeded as before. Same old hoofing, high kicks, twirls, pirouettes, taps and shuffles - vo-de-o-doh, boo-boopy-do-dum-dey. The fans clapped but there was little stamping of feet. This might be their Janet, but they had already seen this routine. Again the voice through the megaphone shouted 'Cut!'

and the show ground to a halt, the curtain fell and the band struck up. Again the curtain rose and in danced the chorus line. By now some voices were raised in protest. Did they buy tickets and come all this way to see the same little scene repeated over and over? By the fourth shout of 'Cut!', even the most hardened fans were up in arms and revolution was breaking out in the ranks. They were shaking fists, threatening to smash up the theatre, burn the place down, lynch the megaphone man who kept shouting 'Cut!' and wishing a bad end to NBC and all its works. Some were now leaving the theatre in disgust. They had been set up, they shouted. The man with the megaphone on stage tried to calm things, but he was much too late. Finally they gave up and closed the show. In the foyer the disgruntled fans were milling around, demanding their money back. I left them to it. A story to remember and savour.

But now I had to turn my mind to Summer School. Among the people I met at University of New Brunswick last summer of 1968, was one very remarkable character - Nels Anderson, an elderly American Sociology Professor for whom the department head had arranged a retired professor position. Once I had reason to fire a student teaching assistant, Randy, assigned to me for the summer. Attracted by the sound of raised voices, Nels arrived outside my door just as I was expelling Randy, who, out of sheer laziness had just dished out marks for a multiple- choice test without reading the answers the students had been given. I had unmasked the wrongdoer by marking a sample myself.

'What's going on? 'Nels asked. I told him. 'Ah yes, Randy, 'he said, 'but, he will get on,' he said then turning on his heel he quietly returned to his office. And so it was. (Randy had been appointed Assistant Professor at a University in Quebec).

After I'd finished teaching at Fredericton, I stayed for a time at the Laurentian Hotel in Montreal. One afternoon, in the hotel bar, I found myself talking to Adriana, a Canada Air hostess. Noting her strongly European accent, I asked its origin. 'I am from Romania,' she said. We got onto the subject of writing, and she told me that she wrote poetry. When I said, 'I'd like to read some of it,' she immediately broke into verse. I sat bewitched until she had finished. It was fraught with the powerful but sickening imagery of casual violence and motiveless murder.

'Where on earth did that come from? 'I asked? 'I was born in Auschwitz,' she said simply. I sat there, stunned. All I could say was, 'Great Heavens!' Then I heard her story. Her Romanian mother had been sent to Auschwitz, and had given birth to her just before she died. Her poetry was certainly haunted by the ghost of that hellhole. The lovely Adriana had lived with the barbaric truth of her birth, and had transformed a filthy cruel world into the saddest most vehement language imaginable - and recited with such moving eloquence there in the foyer bar of the Montreal Laurentian.

Adriana invited me to meet her cousins. The following day we all met up at the house of her aunt and uncle. They were very charming people but like Adriana, I discovered, also survivors. Adriana's cousins, two boys, lived on the basement floor of the house, in an apartment of their own. They were into drugs, and orgiastic sex. They even, I was informed, injected heroin. 'Why do you do it? 'I asked. One of the boys pointed to the ceiling. 'Them up there, 'he said. 'Here we are living every day in Auschwitz.' I suddenly saw that the Holocaust did not only have its terrible after effects on the survivors, but on the following generations, too.

I returned to Manhattan and checked into the Taft Hotel in Times Square. Now I was free to explore Manhattan. Somehow I found myself in a bar next to two young Americans and we were soon on old buddy terms. They were newly-weds, Jack and Cinders. He was a newly-qualified doctor with film-star looks - as so many American boys were, or so it seemed to me; she was exquisitely beautiful – as so many American girls are. They knew just the place to go on to. It was a club in Harlem and there we drank and danced through the late evening to what seemed to me to be authentic and therefore exquisite trad jazz - vo-de-o-do. Then, suddenly, they were gone and I was alone, needing to get back to my hotel. Out there was big bad New York City with its reputation for muggings and killings, but somehow I felt I could walk alone and make it safely back to the hotel. I strode back to Times Square down the sidewalk beside Central Park without feeling once in danger, but trying to look both fit and determined for safety's sake. At the Taft I said to the porter, 'I just walked all the way back from Harlem, along the side of Central Park, and never felt scared for a moment.' The threat of violence in this town was greatly exaggerated, I decided. Next morning, the Bellboy said, 'You were lucky. Last night, just after you got back, a man was shot dead right outside this hotel.'

After a few more days in Manhattan, I re-joined the students at JFK on 28 August, for our return flight to home, London. They were full of the places they had been to: LA, Texas, the Grand Canyon. Visiting America was a kind of joyride, a white-knuckle affair, and it was good to have braved it but doubly good to get one's feet back on terra firma and have something interesting to look back on. That's not to say one would hesitate for too long if offered a return trip.

29 September. In Chelsea, I had two strange visitors who become unexpected overnight guests. I was walking down Shawfield Street towards home one night when a pretty girl emerged from the shadows. She spoke with a refined public schoolgirl's accent in a voice like a bell. 'Do you have a bed for the night?' she asked. I'd only been propositioned by a lady of the night once before, in the back streets of Naples (a proposition I politely declined), but here was a well-spoken English girl in the darkening streets of Chelsea. 'Well, yes. I do have a spare mattress.' She looked over her shoulder and said, 'OK Bruno. I've found you a bed for the night.' From the shadows, Bruno emerged - a large shaggy figure in a woolly pullover, more a bear than a boy. The joke was on me.

'That's a trick to remember,' I told the girl and she seemed happy to accept the compliment. Fortunately, Bruno was not the threatening oaf he at first appeared to be, but a highly intelligent young man just about to go up to read Philosophy at Oxford. Since that was still my field, along with Sociology, the evening descended into a prolonged tutorial over multiple cups of coffee. In the morning, Bruno left to team up again with his pretty companion. Good luck at Oxford, young Socrates!

October. On another occasion, wandering along the King's Road past the Picasso one evening, I was buttonholed by a couple of cockney lads. They had a diminutive, very black young girl in tow, clutching a baby to her breast. 'Do you know where she could find a bed for the night, mate? 'one asked. Alarm bells rang. Bruno was one thing, but, this tiny young lady and her child were another. I suggested the YWCA.

'They won't have her.'

'I think theres' a woman's hostel round in Sydney Street, 'I ventured.

'They've thrown her out of there.'

'Well, I'm sorry, I have no other ideas, 'I said, planning to walk off smartly.

'Do you have a place nearby? 'asked the chirpier of the two.

'Yes, but…'

'It'd only be for one night, mate. She has a place for tomorrow.'

I shuffled my feet. I was an obvious mark for this kind of thing. I hummed and hawed, then came grudgingly to a decision. 'Well, for just one night only' I said quavering slightly at the sound of my own voice. What was I letting myself in for? But the girl's face had lit up with such pleasure, what could I do? I said, 'This way' and turned off down Shawfield Street at the head of a small procession - myself, the young lady, the baby, and the two Cockney lads all in a line.

1969

'She could have stayed in our garden shed at home, 'said one of the lads, 'but my Mum would not understand and she'd have thrown her out.'

They all followed me into no 61. I made them all a cup of coffee and pushed back the furniture. The lads helped me remove the 'guest 'mattress from underneath mine and I dug out some spare sheets and blankets. The girl handed her child to one of the boys and insisted on making up the 'spare bed 'herself.

' She'll be all right here, won't she, mate,' he asked the bigger of her two escorts, clearly concerned, yet with an edge of menace to his voice.

'We'll be back to check on her in the morning' he said, as they departed.

My guest for the evening quickly made herself at home. 'I'm Daisy, 'she said, as she took various items from her bag - a packet of nappies, a tin of baby powder, a packet of baby food, a baby bottle and a toilet bag.

'I'm Gordon. What's the baby called? 'I asked.

'She's not been christened yet but I call her Daisykins.' She was delightfully self-contained and matter-of-fact, busying herself and quite relaxed as if we were old friends. As she changed the baby's nappy, she told me her story. A salesman at Harrods fell for her and wanted to marry her, but his family objected, so he dropped her. Unfortunately, she was pregnant by that time and was thrown out of her lodgings. She went to a hostel and, once her baby was born, she was thrown out of there, too. Others simply turned her away. That was when she met the two boys, and after hearing her story, they had promised to find her somewhere for the night. She'd be staying with friends at King's Cross tomorrow, she said.

GLIMPSES OF A BIOGRAPHER'S DIARY

8 - Family Bowker circa 1939 from the left Ivy, Leonard, Gordon and Lucy

I just sat back, watching her chatter on. This tiny girl attending to her small baby reminded me of my little sister, Brenda, playing with her doll. I don't know why. She warmed the bottle and fed Daisykins. Then she asked if she could bathe her in my washbasin. I said, 'Why not? 'She filled the basin with lukewarm water and with great delicacy got to work, soaping, washing the baby and finally wrapping her in a towel. After settling her in the bed she flopped back, obviously tired. Would she like to take a bath, I asked. 'I'll take care of the baby. 'She would, she said. I gave her directions, a clean towel and pointed her in the direction of the bathroom. The baby was asleep and looking after her was no problem. I changed into my pyjamas and prepared my bed.

Daisy reappeared, duly bathed, full of thanks for the bath and full of merry chatter. She got into her nightie and snuggled in beside her baby. I wished her goodnight and turned off the light. In the morning she told me she was surprised I hadn't tried to get into bed with her. She busied herself, cleaning and feeding Daisykins and it was clear that she was more than able to look after her baby - a highly competent mum, impressively so and charming with it.

We had breakfast - an egg, toast and coffee - and discussed the best way for her to get to King's Cross. It happened to be on my way to work, just a few stops further along the line. We headed down to the King's Road where I hailed a passing cab and we headed north. The cab set her down at her new home near King's Cross Station. She stood at the door, clutching Daisykins and looking a little forlorn - a scene from a Victorian novel came to mind. When the door opened we exchanged waves and I told the cabbie to drive on.

Not long after I got home from Goldsmiths', the two cockney lads called round and I invited them in for coffee. Their young friend was uppermost in their minds. 'She was all right last night,' they asked with emphasis. I knew what they meant and assured them, describing how she'd handled the baby, had a good night's sleep and was duly delivered to her new front door. Next day she called and invited me to where she was staying in King's Cross. I made my excuses.

Chapter 11

Meeting the Famous and Travelling in the United States of America

1969-72

November. I was in Paris for the weekend with friends. One day, I was roaming around the UNESCO Headquarters building in the Place Fontenoy. On that occasion, I wandered into an assembly hall to find the auditorium full. The chairman was introducing someone as the new Assistant Director General. It was none other than Richard Hoggart, another literary hero of mine - author of *The Uses of Literacy* (1957) a fine book on W.H. Auden which I had consumed at college. He was also, by all accounts, the man who had helped swing the court in favour of the publication of *Lady Chatterley's Lover*. I sat at the back and absorbed his message about the civilised power of education.

Back at my flat, Malcolm, a Scottish lawyer who was waiting to get married, had taken the front ground-floor room at Shawfield Street. He saw me in the front hallway and invited me in for a drink. Whisky was Malcolm's tipple of choice, and the conviviality of the man drew me gently into the arms of John Barleycorn. Malcolm

1969

invited me to meet his fiancée - Christine, a beautiful county girl with a difference. She had a boundless enthusiasm for travel, a wanderlust which led her and Malcolm to choose an unusual way of deciding whether or not they were suited. Each set off to circumnavigate the globe in the opposite direction. If they still felt the same about one another when they met back home again, they would marry. That moment was about to happen and I was given an invitation to the great occasion, which took place at Hurstpierpoint, not far from the Bluebell Railway where I had begun my latter-day journalistic career as 'the gentleman from the Times'.

*

I can't help feeling extremely sad about my late parents' death. They both died - my mother of brain haemorrhage on 1st April, my father of lung cancer on 31st August. He had dodged German bullets during the Battle of the Somme but the good old British fag did it for him in the end. He had spoken little about his war but had opened up from time to time with short accounts of incidents: the memory of which made him chuckle, until the chuckle died away as the story grew dark; - a man standing next to him had taken a

9 - *Leonard and Lucy Bowker*

bullet to the head after telling a joke; another shot by firing squad in front of the regiment for having deserted the trenches from sheer boredom at the lack of action, a bullet which took off the end of his bayonet during a charge 'over the top', a commanding officer wearing a monocle who went over carrying little more than a walking stick and had been shot before he even reached the top of the parapet. I made a list of all these memories after he had died, but then wished I'd talked to him more about his 'Lovely War'. But at least he had also entertained us from time to time with his songs from the trenches. Now I had to travel home twice to see both him and my mother, buried in the same plot in a lovely English country churchyard. At least he had escaped the fate of so many of his friends, buried under the mud of Flanders fields, and she had avoided the fate of some of hers, buried under the bricks and masonry of a bombed-out city.

1970

1970 was memorable for three separate events: (1). My new Routledge *Anthology, Freedom, Reason or Revolution* came out on 22 February. (2). At the same time I was informed by Routledge that *Under Twenty* had become 'a mini-bestseller' - whatever that might mean. (3). David Turner produced a stunning television adaptation of Jean-Paul Sartre's *Roads to Freedom* – a thirteen-part drama serial broadcasting on BBC 2 and was released on the 22 September.

*

2 July. Thames Television commissioned me to write two final television scripts completed with dialogue, each having a playing-time of approximately twenty minutes for a series of television programmes for schools entitled *Living Now/This Is Life:* (1) *Love* and (2) *Cruelty*. The final scripts with dialogues for Love were sent in on 15 October and for Cruelty on 29 October to Lester Clark. Both programmes were televised in the Spring Terms 1971.

3rd. I flew from Gatwick, London to New York, and from there by Air Canada to Montreal with a connecting flight to Fredericton for my Summer lecturing at the University of New Brunswick (UNB).

1970

September. Back in London, there were great and haunting theatrical experiences: My friend, Henry gave a stunning performance as the foulmouthed, shamelessly lewd central character in Heathcote Williams' *AC/DC* at the Royal Court. I told him truthfully that he was wonderful. He then invited me to see him in Kaspar, Peter Handke's play about the German wolf-child, Kaspar Hauser – that was full of sombre echoes of Germany's immediate dark past. Henry had tremendous comedic focus and brought great conviction to the role. He asked, 'When you come to see the show come backstage and see me.' So I did just that. He was brilliant and it was easy to tell him what I thought. He said, 'Would you like to meet Harold Pinter? He's in the pub across the road.'

'God! Of course, I'd love to meet Harold.' In the pub, at a long table, there was Henry's friend, surrounded by fans - mostly of the female gender. Henry introduced me. 'This is Gordon. He writes plays.' Pinter turned his attention to me. 'Oh? What plays do you write?' I said, 'Plays for television.' 'What kind of plays?' 'Plays for schools,' I said. Pinter's interest evaporated in an instant, and he turned back, without even a pause, to his female admirers.

One night, on the 'God Slot' on Thames TV, I saw Lester Clark presenting a programme on Greek drama. When we next met I asked him about this. It was obvious from what he told me that the 'God Slot' had become the 'Godless Slot' and the programme no longer needed to mention 'God', only to raise moral issues.

'Could I do that?' I asked. 'Of course you could,' he said,

I sent in a proposal for a series on actors who had played Christ. The commissioning group came back with something on representations of religion on the stage and TV with the title, 'God and Greasepaint'. I spent time perfecting my questions and

GLIMPSES OF A BIOGRAPHER'S DIARY

Thames TV arranged for me to visit Dame Sybil Thorndike at her flat in Chelsea Manor Street.

Visiting her was a rare experience. Here was a woman who had known George Bernard Shaw and Mrs. Patrick Campbell, and had been acting in Shakespeare long before the First World War. She was 90 when I met her - an impressive and gracious lady with a beautifully musical Edwardian accent. When I invited her to talk about Shaw, she did so eagerly, telling me how one day she had received a postcard from him saying, 'I want you to play Dolly in *You Never Can Tell.*' Later he wrote St Joan with the starring role reserved just for her. What could you say to that except, 'Wow!'? I couldn't wait to do our interview.

1971

19 April. Just before the filming, while receiving the attentions of a make-up lady at the studios, I met Michael Parkinson, also being beautified for the small screen. 'Who are you interviewing?' he asked. I reeled off my list. 'Oh,' he said, 'Give my best regards to Dennis Potter, will you?' The interviews were as follows on the studio set:

Day 1. 19 April at 16.00 hours: I interviewed Sally Miles about her production of the Wakefield Mystery Plays at the Mermaid Theatre.

Day 2. 20th. At 14.15 hours: I interviewed Ted Childs about his TV documentary on the Pope.

Day 3. 21st. At 15.30 hours: I interviewed Dennis Potter about writing The Son of Man. His appearance was riveting - sandy red hair combed straight back, inquisitive eyes and hands that seemed somehow distorted. He soon lit up a cigarette, handling it in a strange way by hooking his hand and smoking it through the back of his fingers. It was his painful psoriatic arthritis which he spoke about by way of explanation. Although we had never met, contact was instantaneous and intense - though I felt certain that he had the same effect on everyone he met. Not only that, but so ardent and focussed was he that any prepared questions were immediately abandoned and one was simply drawn by the concentrated brilliance of his thinking. Clearly I was in the presence of a very fine mind. All I needed to do was suggest a point and Dennis would pick up the ball and run with it.

Day 4. 22nd. I interviewed Dame Sybil Thorndike about playing 'St Joan'. She was as riveting as I had expected she would be. Curiously enough, after I had interviewed her, the floor crew simply would not let her go. They all gathered around and bombarded her with questions about Shaw. What was he like? Was he as funny as he is said to have been? How much of a socialist did she think he was? Transmission date commenced on 19th May.

After five years at Goldsmiths', I qualified for a sabbatical year and arranged to spend it at the University of New Brunswick (UNB) in Fredericton, Canada. My annual earnings would make all the difference between what places I could then afford and that house or flat in Chelsea I had set my heart upon.

2 July. To get to the Summer School at UNB, I found a cheap student flight to New York with Laker Airways from Gatwick. If I made it to New York at the promised hour, I'd be in good time to catch my connecting flight to Montreal with Air Canada. Well, the flight took off a bit late, but we were told, 'Don't worry. We'll make up the time as we cross the Atlantic.' As the flight progressed I began to feel more and more anxious. I'd never missed a connection and couldn't imagine what would happen if I did. I'd be cutting matters fine because I was due to start teaching the following day. Halfway to New York, there was an announcement: 'Mr. Freddie Laker is on board and would be happy to talk with

you. He's easy to recognise - he's the chap in the red shirt.' I had no wish to speak with him, but on a trip to the toilet I passed the steward's station where drinks could be obtained, and there, at a window seat, clutching a glass of alcoholic, was the gentleman in the red shirt. On an impulse, I said, 'Mr. Laker?' He stood up and said, 'How can I help?' 'Well,' I said, 'I have a connecting flight to catch in New York and I'm worried we won't arrive on time. We're a bit behind as it is.' I glanced at my watch. He exploded. 'My planes ALWAYS arrive on time!' he bellowed.

I just didn't know how to react. The smell of alcohol warned me that it was probably best for me to quietly return to my seat. As I turned away, Laker slumped back into his seat, grabbing at his glass and knocking back the contents in one go.

We arrived at JFK late, and of course, my connecting flight had long gone. When we disembarked, there was no sight of Mr. Freddie Laker. Meanwhile, I was stuck in the airport. Air Canada, fortunately, were enormously friendly and helpful and said they would try to fit me onto their first flights to Montreal next morning. 'Do you want to check into a hotel?' I was asked. 'No,' I said. So, I decided to spend the night at the airport. I watched as the airport passed the night away, and slowly woke as a new day dawned. Finally, the Air Canada staff arrived and I walked up to the desk. 'Anything doing for me?' I asked.

The pretty uniformed young woman behind the desk activated her computer and studied what I suppose was the state of availability on the first flight to Montreal. Her face told me what she finally said. 'Nothing at all in economy class.' I was about to ask about the next flight when she said, rather apologetically, 'There is one seat I could offer, but I'm not sure you'd want it.'

I couldn't think what she meant. 'What seat?' I asked.

1971

'I'm afraid it's in Business Class,' she said.

I pulled a face. 'Out of interest what would that cost?'

'Oh, nothing,' she said.

It took a while for me to take this in. 'Nothing at all?'

'That's right.'

'Well,' I said, 'it's not what I booked, but in the circumstances I'll take it.'

'Oh good,' she said, adding, 'Sorry about this.'

'That's alright. Thank you,' I said

And that's how I found my way into a Business Class seat on a flight from New York to Montreal. At first I had two seats to myself and chose to sit away from the windows and read a book. No sooner had I settled down than I was asked if I wanted something to drink. I said I would, only because I wanted to sample the full delights available to someone into Business Class seat. They were about to close the plane doors when a latecomer was allowed on board. It was a dark-haired youngish man with a single piece of luggage which he stowed overhead, and I made way for him to sit next to the window.

After a couple of minutes, my neighbour introduced himself - sort of. He gave no name but simply said he was on his way to Montreal. I recognised that same Sicilian New York accent that I remembered from my first visit to the United States, from my friend, Alessandro. I told him, 'I am over here from London to teach at a Canadian university for a year. 'What is the purpose of your journey to Montreal?' I asked. 'Strictly business,' he replied. 'I'll be flying straight back to New York tonight.' I feigned lack of interest, went back to my book and fell asleep until jolted awake by the air hostess telling me: to buckle up my seat-belt for landing

I was very late and the chances of me getting to my first university class were a bit remote. At the airport I enquired about the next flight to Fredericton and fortunately they had a vacant seat. I called ahead to friends asking them to meet me at the airport and take me straight over to the department. Everything went to plan. I made it to the department with seconds to spare.

'Where am I holding my first class?' I gasped to the secretary who said something like 'Room M453.'

'Thanks,' I replied, dumping my luggage, and just ran.

Thank God, I knew the building and quickly found the correct floor. I looked at my watch. With luck my class wouldn't have all left yet. There it was - Room M453. Just in time. I took a deep breath and opened the door. It was a broom cupboard! By the time I did find my class, the students had all departed and I was free to go and relax for the rest of the day in my room in one of the student residences.

For one year after this Summer School, I was moved into the house of a staff member who was himself away on sabbatical leave. There I spent the rest of the warm Canadian summer, and later the freezing Canadian winter. I remember waking one morning to find my bedroom white with an unearthly glow and, when I pulled back the curtains the whole scene outside was revealed - a blanket of snow with a filigree of forest of fir and maple in the background. It was the most magical of magic-shows I remember witnessing, like that Christmas when snow transformed Chelsea into a picture postcard wonderland. This was breathtaking because it was so unexpected - the enchanted forest, silent and awe-inspiring.

1972

*

There was a postal strike in Canada that year, and no mail came in or went out. That was a pity because, as I discovered on my return, that a French friend, Martine, had rung me several times at my Shawfield Street, saying she was coming to London, but the secretaries at No. 61 simply said I wasn't there, without mentioning where I was. Sadly, Martine gained the impression that I didn't want to speak to her, which was unfortunate because I'd told her I was going to be away for the year. But things were going on in her life that she may have wanted to discuss with me.

1972

I passed an eventful Summer Term, a year and another Summer Term - 3 July 1971 to 11September1972 - at the UNB as a Visiting Professor in Sociology.[2] I was free afterwards to travel before

---

[2] When I was at UNB in Fredericton from 3 July 1971 to 11 September 1972, I was commissioned by the Canadian Broadcasting Corporation (CBC) to research and prepare full scripts with dialogues for the three part series on: Bush and The Salon for Radio Programmes Canadians at War - based on letters, diaries and memoirs of Canadians who had served in the three wars: The Boer War, The First World War and The Second World War - and to be backed by materials from other sources: newspaper reports of the period, speeches, dispatches etc.

(1) 4 April 1972. I received my first CBC contract to research and prepare an one - hour radio script to be used in the Corporation's programmes series *Bush and the Salon* on the subject of William Cobbett (19/03/1763 -18/06/1835) - Title: *How Peter Porcupine Acquired His Quills* - a full and fair account of the early life and adventures of William Cobbett as ploughboy in England, soldier in the North American Colony of New Brunswick and as pamphleteer in London and Philadelphia wishing to make a fortune. His first work was published under the pseudonym 'Peter Porcupine.' That was broadcast in October.

(2) 20 April. I received my second CBC contract to prepare a thirty-minutes original television scripts. Title: *Separate But Equal*. Televised on 28th April 1973.

(3) 22 August. I received my third CBC contract to prepare a drama documentary entitled: *The Ordeal of John Gyles*, intended for use in the Corporation's Programme Series *'The Bush And The Salon.'* - that concerned with a tale from:

(4) '*Memoirs of Odd Adventure and Strange Deliverances in the Captivity of John Gyles, Esq*, - his capture by the St. John River Indians as a nine-year-old in 1689 until his return from captivity in 1698 - an account originally described by himself when commander of

returning home with my earnings to buy a house - or at least a decent flat in Chelsea - one of those little houses in Godfrey Street was my ideal, but a flat close to King's Road would suit me admirably.

11 September. However, before returning home, there was that trip to the US West Coast I had been promising myself. I called Ethel Gray, the tennis coach in Hollywood, announcing my impending arrival there. 'You're very welcome to come,' she said. 'However, I have to tell you I've recently had a heart attack. I'll talk to my friend, Gerald. He's British and has an apartment nearby. Perhaps you can stay at his place, too.' It all sounded fine to me and, as I packed my bags, I couldn't resist a burst of 'California here I come!'

12 September. However, I decided first to go by train to see Canada from the comfort of a railway carriage and to visit my friends, Christine and Malcolm, who were now living in Kamloops, British Columbia. I booked on Canadian Pacific, and enjoyed the fast-moving landscape, taking in long stretches of plains and mountains between east and west Canada. In Kamloops, a low-lying city overlooked by gently-rolling mountains, Malcolm was practising as a lawyer. A friend of Christine's from California, Pat and her daughter, Sandy, were staying with her and Malcolm. They were from San Francisco, and I was invited to stay with them whenever I got there. I said, 'That's where I am heading,' Pat said, 'Fine. Do look us up.' Christine said that her friend, Brenda also lived in San Francisco and she was sure she'd love to have me stay with her for a while.

---

the garrison on Saint George River in the District of Maine and was published in Boston in 1736.' Broadcast on radio in August 1973

1972

I flew from Vancouver to Los Angeles and called Ethel from the airport. She told me how to reach her. I called a cab and headed off towards Hollywood. Arriving at Ethel's, I saw what she was saying about being ill. She looked wretchedly frail and skeletal compared to how she had been when I last saw her in London. But she then cheered me up by saying that I had been invited to a party the following day. I thought how wonderful! I'd no sooner arrived in Hollywood that I'm invited to a party. Ethel said, rather cautiously, 'I have to warn you that it's a gay party.'

'Ah,' I said, a little disappointed. Then I brightened. 'Well, I'm a writer and a sociologist, and I'd probably quite enjoy going along and observing events.'

Ethel looked serious. 'I wouldn't do that if I were you. If you are propositioned and say, "No, I'm just here to watch," some of those guys will get very angry. People have been murdered at these parties.'

My curiosity switched off and I said, 'Thanks for telling me. I won't go then.' I wanted to see America but not through the back end of a glass coffin.

Now, she said, 'As I'm not well, a friend of mine, Gerald, will put you up at his place if I can't manage.'

I eyed her cautiously. 'This friend, Gerald - he isn't gay is he by any chance?' She looked thoughtful, then said, 'I think he is what you call AC/DC. But I'm sure you've nothing to worry about. He's English and he's lived here for years.' I went off for a shower and to unpacked my toothbrush and pyjamas.

Next day, Gerald turned up promptly, straight after breakfast. He was a sandy-haired, chunky man of around thirty or thirty-five perhaps. And he had plans to take me all around Los Angeles. I repacked, said my thanks and goodbyes to Ethel, and left with Gerald. He took me on a long-long trail around Los Angeles - up avenues, along boulevards and down canyons. He kept up a running commentary, informing me of the cleverness and ingenuity of 'The American Way'. Every time we came to a supermarket he led me into it, then through it, expounding on the wonders of the wealth and range of food and the variety of all other goods. In particular, he was in enthrall to the various gadgets on sale - clever corkscrews, ingenious can openers, inventive nutcrackers, novelty egg-whisks - hanging at the end of each aisle. 'I'll bet you don't find these in England,' he said, almost gloatingly.

Back at his apartment, he showed me to my bedroom and said he would call me when dinner was ready. I scribbled a diary-entry in my notebook: I just didn't feel comfortable here. However, I unpacked my pyjamas and a toothbrush.

Finally, Gerald knocked on my door and conducted me into the living room where a table was laid for a candlelit dinner. The meal - Coq au vin - was accompanied by Californian wine and he was trying to entertain me with stories of his first arrival in the States and the various astonishing places he had been. He spoke with awe of this great country he had stumbled across. 'Then tomorrow,' he assured me with great emphasis - 'We will be going to Disneyland!' The prospect left me cold. The wine of California consumed, Gerald finally announced he was going to bed. I thanked him for dinner and retreated to my own room, which, like my host's, opened off the living room. But before I had a chance to even undress, I heard him shouting, so I went to his room. The door was wide-open and there, on his bed, stark naked, lay Gerald in all his glory.

'This,' he announced grandly, 'is the body they're all going crazy about!' 'Gerald,' I said, 'I'm very much into ladies.' Surprised, he threw the bedclothes across himself and said in a somewhat petulant voice, 'I wanna go to sleep.' And with that, he buried his head under the bedclothes and waved me away. 'Good night then, Gerald,' I said politely, and retired to my own bed. It was all so absurd. No way was I going to stay here. I would leave in the morning.

Next morning, I got up, took a shower, got dressed, packed my pyjamas and toothbrush and went into the living room. Gerald was pacing up and down like a caged leopard. 'I haven't slept a wink all night,' he whined. 'I've been calling my mother. I feel so humiliated.'

'I am very sorry, I said. I'm leaving this morning to stay with friends.' No more was said, and I retreated to the bedroom, picked up my suitcase and returned to the living room where Gerald was on the telephone, no doubt calling his mother again. He looked up and I asked, 'Where can I find a phone to call a cab, Gerald?' 'There is a drugstore at the end of the block.'

I thanked him, lumbered out with my luggage, hauled it down to the drugstore, made my call, got myself into the cab and headed for the airport.

From there, I phoned Brenda in San Francisco and said, 'I am on my way.' She sounded delighted. I stayed with her for several days - without a car, spending most of my time listening to her music or wandering down to a nearby MacDonald's and acquiring a lifelong distaste for fast food and such eateries - before moving on to stay with Pat and Sandy in Sausalito. More village than town.

Sausalito was in Marin County, in sight of the Golden Gate Bridge and Alcatraz island, both of which I wanted to see at close quarters. I took the bus into San Francisco, crossing the Golden Gate Bridge in the process. I loved the streets of San Francisco running steeply

GLIMPSES OF A BIOGRAPHER'S DIARY

downhill towards the Bay, with rows of colourful period houses spilling over the brows of hills, then sweeping downwards. The trams which hauled themselves up the hills and slid smoothly back down again, allowed me to see the passing sights and get a fuller, richer feel of the city.

Out in the Bay, the forbidding island prison of Alcatraz had, until recently, been occupied in a protest by native Americans. Now it had become a tourist attraction. I chose a cruise taking me around the island - tours of the disused prison had yet to be properly arranged. This gloomy place had been home to Al Capone, Machine Gun Kelly and, of course, the legendary 'Birdman of Alcatraz'. The rocky terrain and boulder-strewn shore shows why so few escape-attempts seem to have worked. A few days later, Pat and Sandy drove me to the airport, we said goodbyes, and I left for London.

*

September 1972. I found that 61 Shawfield Street was practically closed down. Mrs. Henkey was dead, the lease was up, and we all had to move out. Mr. Henkey had put some of my furniture and books into storage, and I had to find somewhere else to live. A huge pile of letters awaited me, thanks to that Canadian postal strike. I sorted through them, and found a sad letter from my French friend, Martine, writing broodingly about death and quoting Rimbaud. But the next letter, quite a small one, which, when I opened it, was simply a card bearing the ominous message, 'Amis pour toujours?' I heard her voice and felt a chill. Then I froze. There on the pile lay a black-bordered letter from France inviting me to her funeral. 'Died by accident at home,' it said - the Catholic French code for, 'Died by her own hand'. I sat on my bed and wept.

1972

There was a sense that this chapter of my life was about to close. Around me including the old King's Road, there were signs of change. Women and girls were striding about in hot pants or split skirts, while men and boys were abandoning drainpipes and winkle-picker shoes in favour of bellbottom trousers, which I considered decidedly inelegant. But my greatest shock was to find that my hopes of buying my little house in Chelsea had been decidedly dashed. The new Prime Minister, Edward Heath, and his chancellor, Barber - in an excess of enthusiasm for an economic theory called 'monetarism', had released a mass of money into the economy, and the price of property had zoomed. Houses I should have been able to afford were now selling for prices well out of my reach, even the price of the little studio in Cheyne Row, once used by Clint Eastwood, on which I had had my heart set before leaving, had skyrocketed. If I'd bought it earlier I would have been a little wealthier now. My lawyer actually apologised for giving poor advice.

I found temporary lodgings in a block called: Chelsea Cloisters, 502, Sloane Avenue, SW3, where you could rent a self-contained bedsit by the week. From there I sallied forth to view flats in Chelsea, Earls Court, and Fulham. It was obvious that I'd have to venture further afield for what I could afford.

Chapter 12

The Loss of a Close Friend, Several Narrow Escapes in Boats, and My Own House at Last

1973-79

1 February. I found a two-bedroom ground floor flat in Westbourne Terrace, Bayswater. It had some merits, but a few faults and inconveniences. The master bedroom was a strange elongated shape with a walk-in store cupboard the size of a small guest room but full of shelving for storing luggage and boxes of one shape or size. There was another smaller square room with black and white tiles that looked perfect for a study. Along a parquet-floored corridor, reaching from the front door to the back of the flat, were a bathroom to the right, a small kitchen to the left, opposite a series of floor-to-ceiling cupboards. Finally there was a generous living-room beyond. The main drawback of the lounge, second bedroom and kitchen, was that sunlight only penetrated for about one hour in the afternoon because of the height of the houses across the street opposite. The new flat was adequate but it was clear that I would have to spend another sabbatical year in Canada to put me back within reach of that house in Chelsea I so hankered after.

1972

I painted the walls of my new home white, and with the three long Mucha reproductions I had hung on the wall and the newly acquired bookshelves I'd lined with my most precious possessions, together with decorative fern-like plants, the room seemed to brighten considerably. I finished off the scene with a glass-topped coffee table and two elegant basket chairs - my latest acquisitions from Habitat. My Casa Pupo carpet was draped over a trunkful of books to lend my strangely-shaped bedroom a touch of class.

Having my own kitchen at last inspired me to shop for cook-books. I settled on Len Deighton's *Action Cook Book*. Once I'd mastered his coq au vin, I felt I had arrived as a chef. My dinner guests could always be assured of one thing - their main dish would always be a memorable coq au vin. My culinary ability stopped at that, although I did once or twice substitute beef for chicken and served it as Boeuf Bourguignon.

Henry came to christen the new flat, and I invited my beautiful friend, Jade, whom I had met at Nick's and seen a few times, to join us for a small party. Henry arrived with Heathcote Williams, author of the 'outrageous' *AC/DC* in which Henry had played the 'outrageous' lead. Heathcote arrived first, clutching eight bottles of brown ale. Henry, as usual full of bonhomie, he embraced Heathcote. Jade was beauty and glamour personified. Soon we were swilling champagne - my usual welcome cup. Thereafter it was food and wine. The brown ale sat forlornly in my kitchen. After a while, Heathcote began to act even more strangely than usual and asked for seclusion. I took him to the bedroom where I had an inflatable mattress and he sank into it, asking me to put out the light. I left him in darkness to his own strange devices. Later in the evening I thought I should see what had happened to my guest, Heathcote. He was thrashing around in the darkness and muttering, 'I'm wrestling with the Devil.' I dragged him away from his hell. As we re-joined the others, he cast an appreciative eye over Jade and whispered, 'We'll have an orgy tonight.'

He was a member of the Magic Circle and ended the party by demonstrating his conjuring and mind-reading skills. I was the victim of one trick in which he drew a circle in the middle of a blank piece of paper and asked me to write a word in it. He then took the paper from me, tore it up and burned it in an ashtray. Nothing more happened and we gossiped our way to the end of the evening. Then, just before my guests took their leave, Heathcote asked me to look at a book on my bookshelf which he named, and to turn to a particular page which I did. There, tucked away, I found the torn centre of the paper in a circle on which I had written my word. By that time the magician had left, along with my other visitors.

Also in February. The publishers, Allison and Busby threw a party to launch Bryan Johnson's posthumous anthology of National Service Memoirs, *All Bull*. There I met Lynn Alison, the publisher's wife, who told me that she had been given the role of setting up a children's list. I told her that I had just the book to get it started - a book about a school for witches by a brilliant young artist and writer I knew. She was intrigued, and when I got back home I wrote a letter to Jill in far-off Ghana, telling her to send her book to Lynn. Things were about to look up for Jill Murphy as her book *The Worst Witch* was published by Allison & Busby the following year, 1974. Jill sent me a copy with a personal dedication, thanking me for helping her to get it published. She also sent me a beautifully-painted card bearing much the same message. They remain amongst my treasured possessions.

There was a new editor at Plays and Players, and I persuaded him to allow me to review a play. David Turner's take on Molière's *The Miser* was about to open at the Birmingham Rep, and I was commissioned both to review the play and to interview the playwright. Everything was booked - David was alerted to my coming to Leamington Spa, and I set out, with my tape recorder fully-charged, for one of my favourite Midlands cities. The Birmingham Rep was a theatre I knew from my early twenties. David's take on *The Miser* placed the play in a Pakistani immigrant household. The immensely ambitious central character sets out to marry off his daughter in an arrangement for money. Today, no doubt, the ethnic setting would excite controversy, but for David in 1973, it was the only community in which arranged marriages took place in Britain and that's what he needed for his play. The production worked well, and I said so in my review.

Next, I travelled down to Leamington Spa to interview David. As usual, he was both tense and intense. At times, talking about his life and work, he became extremely excited and burst into compulsive peals of laughter. It quite overwhelmed him when he told me about writing an episode for the BBC television series *The Edwardians* - an episode in which Edward VII did unmentionable things with a fifteen-year-old girl, and in which his mistress, Daisy, the Countess of Warwick, who had become a communist, invited the king into her bed, saying, 'To each according to his needs; from each according to his ability. You have the need, and I have the ability,' before mounting him. The executive producer came to him having read the script and said, 'We can't have this, David. The people upstairs won't stand for it.' So, he said, 'If I can have Daisy Warwick, you can have the fifteen-year-old girl.' He got his way. My article about the background to his writing *The Miser* appeared together with the review.

One day, over the phone, Bryan Johnson told me that he and Virginia had just returned from a visit to Samuel Beckett in Paris. He then informed me that he was unable to get a commission for further novels from Hutchinson, as he had hoped, and talked gloomily of having to return to supply teaching. I thought it was an outrageous thing to happen to an author of his stature. I managed to get him a commission to write an essay about his troubled schooldays for: Education and Training, to which I had contributed, and for a television series for Thames Television, about a secondary modern class of C streamers about to leave school. It took him back to the dreaded classroom of *Albert Angelo*. In return, Bryan put me in touch with Nicholas Whines, a BBC

GLIMPSES OF A BIOGRAPHER'S DIARY

producer, who commissioned me to write a series of history programmes for Schools Radio.[3]

Summer. Miles Tomalin, whom I had met at a meeting of the Society of Authors, invited me to go with him, his Hungarian wife, Madeleine, and assorted friends on a boat trip along the Regent's Canal for an island picnic. It sounded fun. I went over to his house in Gloucester Crescent and, along with a complement of intrepid sailors, boarded the good ship, Nancy en route for an island that lay just through and beyond the Islington tunnel. The boat, I noticed, was little more than a dinghy with an outboard motor attached to its stern. We set sail and chugged happily along for a mile or two, then headed into the half mile of pitch blackness of the tunnel with not even a flashlight to brighten our darkness and just a small patch of light at the far end to show us that we were where we thought we were. Back in sunlight, we found a little island on which we sat down to our picnic lunch - bread, cooked ham and wine. We attacked the government and the food with equal relish, then we re-boarded the boat and set off back into the tunnel heading for home.

We were fut-futting merrily along in friendly darkness when suddenly an invisible shape loomed up from behind us, our boat was turned upside down and we were instantly all flung overboard into the filthy waters of the Regent's Canal in the pitch darkness of its longest tunnel. From the water we watched in disbelief as the stern of a huge barge disappeared ahead of us towards the far end of the tunnel. I had gone under and resurfaced close to the tunnel wall. Next to me was Miles, gasping for breath and shouting, 'Save the women!' I ignored this call to action. Miles had a heart condition and I decided that ensuring his safety was my immediate

---

[3] 9 March. The BBC commissioned me to write a fully dramatised script Entitled: *Soldiers' Diary* for Radio 4 schools programme series *History - Not So Long Ago* for broadcasting on the 5th February 1974. I sent in my fully dramatised script.

13 June. The BBC Commissioned me to write another fully dramatised script Entitled *Fresh Air And Entertainment* for Radio 4 schools programme series *History - Not So Long Ago* for broadcasting on the 17th March 1974.

1972

priority. I managed to insert my fingers between two bricks in the slimy concave wall and got a grip of some sort. That enabled me with my free arm to keep him afloat. One of our party, a young woman, bravely swam to the far end of the tunnel and raised the alarm. After ten minutes or so, a boat slid out of the darkness towards us, picking up our party and took us back out into blessed daylight.

We all collapsed on the canal bank at the bottom of Miles's garden, the point from which we had all set out so gaily for a sunny day's boating. When we finally dragged ourselves indoors, Miles's journalist son, Nick, and his beautiful daughter-in-law, Claire, arrived and arranged for us to go to the local hospital for anti-tetanus jabs. Afterwards, Nick drove me back to Westbourne Terrace. I knew that he was a journalist working for the Sunday Times, who had produced prize-winning reports from Vietnam. In Westbourne Terrace, he parked the car and we sat for an hour or so chatting. He talked about his foreign assignments and his book about Donald Crowhurst, the fraudulent round-the-world-yachtsman; I talked about my journalistic efforts and mentioned my offer of a job on the Times. He urged me to consider photo-journalism – something for the Sunday Times or Observer Colour Supplements perhaps. I wanted to keep in touch with him and we exchanged phone numbers. A couple of months later he was killed by a Syrian missile on the Golan Heights while reporting on the Yom Kippur War for the Sunday Times - a heat-seeking rocket, I later learned. I was very sad. I liked him a great deal and had hoped to think that our friendship would have strengthened.

14 July. I went to Canada, to UNB in Fredericton to lecture on sociology for the summer. Stimulating as usual.

14 November. Lester Clark called with the agonising news that Bryan Johnson had committed suicide. Over a long weekend he had phoned various friends to discuss a crisis in his marriage. His adored Virginia had left him and taken the children. He was in despair. No comforting words would console him. On the 13th he was found dead in his bath, with his wrists slashed. The sense of

loss was greater than I would have imagined. Bryan, to me, was nothing less than a man of burgeoning talent with a great lust for life, utterly sure of himself - a man with a literary oeuvre to make any writer envious (six novels published and seven films produced), a man with everything to live for. Then, I recalled our brief conversation at the National Film Theatre, and the grim message of his film, and I remembered the man who had been so obsessed with the death of Tony Tillinghast. I was trying to understand that Bryan Johnson was capable of ending his own life, but making sense of his death was difficult. It struck me that he was probably being slowly crushed under the weight of his own mortality - like his schoolmaster in his film *You're Human Like the Rest of Us*, he was too conscious of the process of slow physical decay. Perhaps he foresaw the demise of his own creativity in the same way - the Hutchinson rejection somehow signalling the decline of his talent. Later, I heard from Virginia that Bryan had, in his last months, fallen under the spell of an occultist (according to Jonathan Coe, Johnson's biographer, a homosexual man called Michael Bannard), who seemed to exercise a strange power over him. At home he might jump up suddenly and leave the house, saying that he 'knew' this man wanted him. His behaviour had become increasingly bizarre, and he had even started talking to Virginia about their committing suicide together. It was at that point that she took their children and fled.

Bryan was a man deeply concerned about his art and about the conditions of his fellow writers, a political fighter as well as a cheerful pugilist, an angry man who never showed his face of anger to me, a deeply depressed man whose depression I only once glimpsed in person, though I felt it through his art. Perhaps he found his own atheism unbearable. He shared Beckett's sense of despair, but unlike Beckett he grew tired of waiting for nothing. A very good friend of his, the actor Neville Smith, swore to me that on the day he died, Johnson went to see Chelsea play for the last time, as though himself playing out a carefully calculated endgame.

Lester Clark asked me if I would take on the television series which Johnson had begun. As I'd been there when the programmes were

1974

first discussed, I agreed, though somewhat hesitantly in the circumstances.

30 November. I was sent a contract by Thames Television to write six final television scripts, complete with dialogue, each having a playing time of approximately twenty minutes, for the television Programmes for Schools Series, that was entitled: *You and Your World*. I was also sent Johnson's notes and drafts for the six episodes commissioned. For the first episode, there were even some lines of dialogue. Here again was the world of *Albert Angelo*. A supply teacher has taken over a C-stream secondary modern class. The kids want to know what happened to their previous teacher. The answer is - he has committed suicide. It was uncanny to read these lines, which only hinted at what must have already been playing on Bryan's mind when he wrote them - composing, as it were, his own final scenario. I sent in my final draft on the 7th January 1974, and that was broadcast in the Summer 1974. The series went well. Although we were given a joint credit, I insisted that his name precede mine, and it was a tribute to Bryan that it was nominated for the Japan Prize for Educational Broadcasting. 28 December. I received a contract from The Canadian Broadcasting Corporation to research and to prepare a one-hour radio documentary script, with working title: *Canadian Soldiers at War: That I May Not Weep* - for broadcast in the CBC National Series *The Bush And The Salon*. The final documentary script was sent in on 12th September 1974 and duly broadcast on the 11th November 1974.

1974

12 March. Children at School, a fully dramatised script for the BBC Radio 4 school series: History: Not So Long Ago, that was broadcast on the 19th. Victorian Entertainment, a fully dramatised script for the BBC Radio 4 schools series *History: Not So Long Ago* was broadcast.

Also on 19 March, my birthday, Anna, a handsome young Polish woman, moved into a flat next to mine. She introduced me to her best friend, Sarah, the daughter of a famous Polish nuclear scientist, who had been part of the team that produced the atomic bomb. Sarah, was a dark, remarkably handsome and quietly animated young woman. She had left her job in Warsaw as a newsreader on Polish television. She had left, she said, because she had got fed up with having to repeat Party propaganda over and over all day long. She had a young son whom she'd left with her family in Warsaw but was now anxious to bring him over to England. She was highly intelligent and, beautiful with a gentle and sensitive nature.

One day, out of curiosity, I took her to an evening laid on by some self-proclaimed young gurus of arcane wisdom. Their 'session of enlightenment' involved the usual: Tarot cards, numerology, a pinch of necromancy, and a few other items of occultist claptrappery - all strung together with a persuasive patter designed to seduce the unwary and emotionally needy.

'What did you think?' asked Sarah afterwards.

'Rubbish!' I replied.

'I thought it was very interesting,' she said in a dreamy voice, and I knew she had been well and truly hooked. Sadly, it also meant that we would drift apart.

Summer, as usual, I went to Canada as visiting professor lecturing on sociology for the summer term.

My six final television scripts, completed with dialogue, and entitled: *You And The World* for Thames Television schools series were televised in the Summer.

1975

In Summer. My four final Thames Television scripts, completed with dialogue, and each having a playing time of approximately twenty-minutes entitled: *You And The World for Thames Television Programmes* schools series were televised.[4] 1st July. As usual, I went

---

[4] My final four twenty-minutes each, fully dramatised scripts, entitled: (a) The Search for the North West Passage. (b) Francis Drake. (c) Sir Richard Grenville and (d) The Spanish Armada for the BBC

1975

to Canada as visiting professor, lecturing on sociology for the summer term School.

5 September. Sarah was walking along Park Lane. She had just returned from Warsaw bringing her young son back with her. Now, she wanted to call Anna. Where, in Park Lane she wondered, could she find a phone? Then she recalled an evening she had spent at the Hilton Hotel. In the foyer stood a row of telephones booths separated by just small partitions at head level. She went through the revolving doors into the foyer, slipped into to one of the telephones booths and dialled Anna's number.

'Sarah here. I'm at the Hilton,' she said. Then a bomb went off and the lights went out.

Two people were killed and 63 injured. Sarah's left arm had taken the full force of the blast, and was left hanging by a mere shred of skin. Anna called to give me the news. Sarah had been rushed to St George's Hospital at Hyde Park Corner where surgeons were treating her as an emergency.

After a few days, I was able to visit her. She had a bed in a bright ward overlooking the Park. The surgeon, a deeply concerned young Scot, I recall, came to visit, and afterwards I asked him about her prospects. He took me aside. 'Sarah's arm was so damaged - dangling by a mere shred of skin,' he told me, that he should have amputated, but when he saw this beautiful young woman in such a condition he decided on radical experimentation. He repaired the shoulder as best he could, then attached her arm to her womb, the flesh of which had great resuscitating powers, he told me. Later, when she was about to leave the hospital, I visited her again. Her arm wasn't completely back to normal but not bad considering. What amazed me, was that she bore absolutely no animosity towards the men who had planted the bomb. I might not have admired her newly-acquired mystical frame of mind, but I certainly

---

Radio 4 schools series *History: Not So Long Ago*; were broadcast on (a) 25th February 1975. (b) 4th March 1975. (c) 11th March 1975, and (d) 18th March 1975.

did her acceptance of the world and of her cruel fate. There, I thought, lies a woman destined for happiness.

Sarah had found a small flat in my favourite street, the King's Road, Chelsea. It was above Joanna Booth's antiques shop. When I tracked her down to that address she'd moved on, this time to a place in Soho, in a house which catered for young female teachers of French, lady masseuses, administrators of punishment to naughty schoolboys and their kind. I entered this establishment with avid curiosity, but did finally find Sarah in a sparsely-furnished top floor flat. She seemed to find it a great joke to be living there, chatting away merrily about her colourful neighbours. In an odd way she didn't seem at all out of place.

22 September. My article *You Always Remember The First Time* was published by Quartet.

1976

5 April. The brilliant Harold Wilson was defeated and James Callaghan became Prime Minister.

11 May. My twenty-minutes, fully dramatised script entitled: *Dr Barnardo's Children* for the BBC Radio 4 school series *History: Not So Long Ago* was broadcast.

18th. My fully dramatised script entitled: *At School* for the BBC Radio 4 school series: *History: Not So Long Ago* was repeated. 1 July. I went to Canada as visiting professor, lecturing on sociology for the summer term school.[5]

---

[5] 6 June 1979. I granted permission to repeat my script: *Dr Barnardo's Children* for the BBC Radio 4 schools series, *History: Not So Long Ago*. That was broadcasted on 13th November. Also on 6th June. I granted permission to repeat my script: *At School* for the Radio 4 schools series *History: Not So Long Ago*. Broadcasted on 20th November.

24 July 1979. I granted the renewal of the rights to my script: *At School* (HEA245J814) for the Radio 4 schools series *History: Not So Long Ago*. That was broadcasted on the BBC Education Programme for Radio 4 on 20th November.

1977

1977

24 May. After I had received permission to take another sabbatical year in Canada, I had to attend the Outpatient Clinic at the Westminster Hospital for my annual check-up. There, I discovered that Dr Tonkin had left and my new consultant was the great Sir Richard Bayliss, the endocrinologist who had first seen me at the hospital in 1961. He greeted me with great interest, especially when I asked if it were possible to have a year's supply of thyroxine to see me through my upcoming sabbatical year. He made out the prescription on the spot. He was about to address a group of medical students, he told me, and would I be prepared to join him to have my case discussed? I readily agreed. After all, I owed my life to this hospital and felt morally obliged to do whatever they asked of me. Sir Richard, in his genial and expansive fashion, asked the students what they thought thyroxine cost the NHS. No one knew, and he then quoted an astonishingly low price. Having surprised them with that piece of news, he then announced that; here before them, they saw a young man who had come into the hospital at death's door; acute rheumatic fever, acute carditis and thyroid crisis, and had been pulled back from the very brink. Now he was about to take off for Canada for a year as a visiting professor and he had just prescribed him a year's supply of thyroxine. Put like that it did seem impressive - but any achievement in survival was to the credit of the nurses and doctors, including himself, and certainly not to me. When I left, I was just delighted to have got my prescription for a year's supply of the pills that kept my thyroid from taking me over again.

---

14 January 1980. I granted the renewal of the rights to my script: *Soldiers Diaries* (HEA246N200) for the Radio 4 schools series: *History: Not So Long Ago*. That was broadcasted in the BBC Education Programme for Radio 4 on the 25th March.

30 June 1980. BBC Copyright Department requested to repeat each of my final fully dramatised scripts: (a) The Search for the North West Passage. (b) Sir Francis Drake. (c) The Spanish Armada ,and (d) The First English Colonies for the BBC Radio 4 schools series: *History: Not So Long Ago*. Those were broadcasted on 27th January, 3rd , 10th ,and 17th February 1981. Also the licence covering repeat broadcast of these materials had now expired. I gave permission for the above and for the renewal of the rights.

GLIMPSES OF A BIOGRAPHER'S DIARY

4 July 1977 to 3 July 1978. My sabbatical year was spent at the University of Alberta in Edmonton as a professor. It was a curious year and I never got used to the sociology department ruled by statisticians. In Alberta, measurement ruled! Even the level of salaries was fixed by measuring the length of articles and books published over the past year. This led to some strange practices. I put in for a small grant to do a small piece of research, and was turned down. Then a teacher in the department came up to me and said, 'I was on the grant committee, and it was because you were a visiting professor that you didn't get the money. If we could put this in as a joint piece of research, I'm sure you will get what you want.' In that moment I saw how it was done. A student presents an original piece of research to his teacher. The teacher, then says, 'If we put this forward as a joint piece of research, I'm sure we can get it published.' And so, a few more inches of text published under the teacher's name contributed towards his annual increase in salary. Sam Goldwyn, Polish-American film producer, wise words gave me my ready-made excuse - 'Sounds like a great idea. Include me out.'

1978

The Commonwealth Games 1978 was held in Edmonton. Suddenly, writing a Freddie Forsyth-type thriller excited me, and it wasn't long before a plot was conceived in my mind and I got a Canadian publisher interested. He was confident they would want to bring it out to coincide with the Games. All I needed next was to do the leg work to research the operation of the Games - where the Games village would be, what was its layout, which teams would be where, and what security arrangements would be in place. This involved me not only looking over the stadium and its surroundings but visiting the television studios. I also decided to look over the gambling casino installed in the city for the occasion. At the casino, a young Canadian was designated to show me around. One of the first people I met was an American from Las Vegas brought in to help set up this gambling den. I learned what the various games on offer amounted to - roulette, baccarat and blackjack. I asked my Canadian guide specifically about blackjack and how a character in my book might attempt to cheat at it. The man from America overheard this exchange and suddenly I heard the unmistakable intonation of the Sicilian American I had met in Business Class in the plane in 1971.

'Who is this guy?' he asked in a voice edged with menace. 'We ask him in here as our guest, give him our hospitality, and already he's asking questions about how to cheat at blackjack.' I assured him and my guide that I never gambled anyway so any secret would never be used by me. But I could see that he was still unhappy.

'So why the questions?' came to the voice laced with threat. I decided to say no more. My guide led me away, but I felt the eyes of the Las Vegas man riveted to my back. If I wanted to write a thriller, I was certainly getting the sense of menace that Ian Fleming brought to the world of Bond - James Bond, that is.

4 July-13 August. I stayed on to teach Summer School in a flat that had no air-conditioning. The weather was intensely hot, and so was the flat I had rented from a student. To keep me going at my typewriter, I found that a bottle of whiskey close beside me worked wonders. I didn't get so very drunk either, because I sweated it away even as I typed out the copy. When I had finished, I was really rather proud of what I'd written. I had no wish to remain in Edmonton, so quickly sent the manuscript off to the publisher in Toronto. He got back to me almost immediately, saying that they had reconsidered the position and thought that, because the Games would soon be a thing of the past, the book would soon be without any reason to exist. I quickly swallowed my pride and simply sent it straight off to Harvey Unna, my literary agent in England.

After the summer school and before returning home, I felt I needed a change of scene. My friends Christine and Malcolm had separated, and Christine was now living with their three children at a village in Nanaimo Bay, Victoria Island looking out across the Strait of Georgia. I telephoned and told her that I wanted to see Vancouver again. As I would be there in a few days, could I come across and visit her? She was quite enthusiastic, and, remembering that I used to teach in a primary school, said, 'The girls would love you to read stories to them.' I found the idea immensely appealing, but there was a problem. When I tried to book a passage to the Island I found that the ferries were all on strike, and the airlines were all booked up. I called Christine and explained the situation.

'Don't worry.' she said, 'I'll get my friend George to bring you over in his yacht.' Later she called me back. 'George says that's fine.' She gave me his address and phone number and I called George. He sounded warm and expansive.

'Come for dinner tomorrow. If the weather's good we'll cross the Strait in the morning.' George was, as I'd guessed, a generous host. A millionaire, he owned a beautifully-designed house overlooking Vancouver Harbour. 'If we can see the Harbour Bridge from my back porch in the morning,' he said, 'It'll be a fine day and plain sailing for Nanaimo.' Christine would meet us on our arrival.

George was overweight, and trying manfully to recover from an alcohol problem. His cure involved drinking bottle after bottle of tonic water. He had a crate of them beside him and drank almost continuously. Nevertheless, we enjoyed a congenial evening, and I listened to his stories of adventures at sea, including several round the world yacht races. I got in a good night's sleep, woke early, took a shower, dressed casually and went down to the kitchen where George was sitting, reading a paper and drinking tonic water. He immediately took me to his back porch overlooking the Harbour. 'Look,' he said, with a gesture, offering me a pair of binoculars. 'Look. The Bridge is perfectly clear. The sea will be calm, and we'll have an easy crossing, like we're sailing on glass.' He called Christine to tell her we were on our way.

After breakfast, we piled into George's estate car, and I saw he'd packed a few dozen crates of tonic water, and we sped off down towards the yacht basin. The yacht was impressive, a 40-footer at least. George unloaded the wagon, and I helped him carry his cases of tonic water on board. Then, he cast off. Despite his bulk, George nipped around the yacht with all the nimbleness of a younger slimmer man. That was lucky, because I was no sailor, and George, after all, was an international yachtsman who had, he assured me, sailed several times around Cape Horn. I had nothing to fear. The sea, as he had predicted, was like glass and in the company of several other yachts we sailed smoothly under the magnificent Vancouver Harbour Bridge out into the Strait beyond.

I breathed in the sea air while George drank bottle after bottle of tonic water. He knew just what he was up to, I decided, and watched with admiration as he adjusted a sail here, pulled on a rope there, his eyes scanning the water ahead from time to time. There was a pleasant breeze on our backs, the sails billowed, and the air was suffused with the healthy tang of sea-brine as we skimmed across the calm seas on a westerly course.

While enjoying the sight of the other yachts in our company, I noticed that the breeze had stiffened somewhat, which only added to the excitement. One could turn one's face into the wind and feel the fresh air rippling across one's face and through one's hair. This was the life! I could almost grow to enjoy open-sea sailing. Then I noticed that the water was getting a little choppy and the wind had become friskier. The yacht began to pitch a little more and roll a little more. George began to move around the deck a fraction more vigorously. Gradually I realised that the sea was getting quite heavy. Some of the other yachts were now heading back towards the harbour. George, however, ploughed on. The sea had clearly woken the international yachtsman in him and he was once again heading for Cape Horn.

'Are you okay George?' I shouted. 'I'll get you there!' he yelled back. I wasn't so sure. I hadn't exactly banked on this kind of adventure, nor yet reached the point of panic but I did find myself clinging onto the rails more firmly. Heavy spray had now begun to drench me and I was soon soaked through. George battled on grappling with a swinging yardarm, and flapping sails - pulling on ropes, tying, and reefing the sails. Now we were the only yacht sailing out across the Strait. All the others had turned back to the safety of the harbour.

GLIMPSES OF A BIOGRAPHER'S DIARY

'Are you sure we're okay, George?" I shouted.

'I'll get you there!' he yelled, grappling with ropes and downing yet another bottle of tonic water. By this time the sea had become quite angry and the troughs between waves were reaching new depths. The yacht rolled like a lurching drunk. Then I noticed out towards the horizon the wave that I knew was going to get us. It was rolling quite rapidly in our direction and I could see it swelling and gaining height and momentum with devilish determination as it approached us. George seemed oblivious to our peril, and continued to dash around the deck consuming tonic water and determined to live up to the reputation he had given himself.

Then, the inevitable happened. The giant wave broke over the boat with a shattering thump and we were completely soaked and almost dislodged from the deck, clinging on wildly while the boat itself keeled over so dramatically we could very easily have turned turtle. Now I did panic. Supposing George had been washed overboard, how the hell would I get out of this? At last my captain emerged into an upright position and simply said, 'Right!' And without further ado he turned the yacht around and we headed back towards the Harbour and the calm waters of the Fraser River. We sailed sadly but majestically back under the Bridge and upriver to an anchorage where George left the yacht and found a phone.

When he came back, he said, 'I've fixed for a float plane to pick you up and I called Christine to let her know where to meet you.' I thanked him and wondered what to expect next. I parked myself and my luggage on the dockside. George clambered back onboard, wished me a happy week on the island, weighed anchor and, as he smartly manoeuvred the yacht back out towards the harbour, I waved him and his cargo of tonic water a fond farewell.

After a while, a smart-looking float plane wafted silently down and chugged up to the anchorage. The pilot opened the door and came out to help me. He took my suitcase and stowed it. I clambered up into the cockpit and, as instructed, sat next to him. The intrepid aeronaut seemed very young to be in charge of even a tiny craft

1978

such as this. He made sure my seat belt was fastened and taxied us out into the harbour for a smooth take-off. I was impressed at just how easily we rose over the land and the seascape under the clearest of clear blue skies to take in the panorama of the Strait of Georgia across to Victoria Island. Now at this height it did look as narrow as it had on the map. Surprisingly, the pilot had no charts but seemed to know just where he was heading. Down below was the sea that George and I had attempted to navigate. It didn't appear rough at all, but I saw very few boats heading out towards the island. 'How do you get to where you want to go without a chart?' I asked. The pilot grinned. 'I do this all the time,' he said. 'I know these waters and that coastline like the back of my hand.' 'Really!' I said, suitably impressed. The island loomed ahead. The pilot sent the plane into a downward glide. Suddenly he pointed. 'I think your friends are probably just over there!' I followed his finger. All I could see was a tiny speck.

As the plane put down and taxied towards it, I saw a car and a tall woman, with three small girls gathered around her. Joyfully I said, 'Good God! It's Christine and the girls!' And so it was. I wished farewell to the clever young pilot and stepped ashore to greet my waiting friends. I spent a lovely week or so driving round the island with the family and entertaining the girls with stories so exaggerated and absurd that they were reduced to giggling heaps.

September. Now, back in London, I could finally afford the sort of house I wanted. But first I had to sell my Westbourne Terrace flat, valued at £20,000. I decided to advertise it in the Sunday Times, featuring it as 'writer's flat close to Hyde Park'. This produced many people wanting to view the place. However, just three of all those people made offers. One was a busy little man who phoned some city property outfit to describe the flat saying it looked like a distinct possibility; another man said he had money coming from South America - would I mind cash? The other one made an offer just short of the target sum. This last customer decided to send a surveyor and I arranged for him to come at 3 o'clock which was the time the flat often looked at its best - flooded with a sort of angled sunlight from over the top of the tall buildings opposite. The gentleman arrived, the sun duly smiled and so did he.

1979

February. The offer was confirmed. Now I had to find my new home.

There was a brief moment of excitement when I made an offer on a little terraced house in Bywater Street, Chelsea. I was told that if an earlier viewer failed to sign up by 12 noon the following day the house was mine. At five minutes past 12 o'clock I phoned and was told that the other party had signed just one minute short of the deadline. And so my dream of a place of my own in Chelsea was extinguished yet again. I then saw a house near Notting Hill Gate for sale and arranged a viewing. I loved the neighbourhood at first sight. I looked at the house and noticed a worrying crack running down the outside wall. The agent met me on the doorstep and announced that the house had just been sold but I wasn't particularly worried. 'There's one just down the street which came onto the market only this morning,' he said, pointing at his clipboard. 'Let's take a look at it,' I said. The house had three floors and was next to the end of the terrace. When we arrived a woman answered the door. She was young with a slightly melancholy air but brisk enough to want to show me around the house. At the rear of the ground floor stood a grand piano; at the front was the living room with a pretty tiled fireplace as its centre point. Down below was a kitchen and bathroom and, at the rear, a dining room with a chandelier on a brass fitting with French windows opening onto a small patio dominated by a beautiful honeysuckle creeper. Back upstairs on the top floor, there were two bedrooms one with a fitted wash-basin, but no upstairs bathroom - the house's one big flaw. I told her I wasn't sure and would get back to her. But there was something about the house that had hit the mark with me - its cosy country cottage air and secure sense of enclosure.

My next stop was Hampstead - a house next to the Heath. It was as large, a bit more expensive, but had five bedrooms, two

1979

bathrooms and two large living rooms, together with a long garden. If I wanted to sublet to students I could easily repay the extra mortgage, I figured. The owner, Celia, showing me around was pleasant and young with an indefinably theatrical air. She obviously loved the house, and said they were only moving because they needed to pay off a large tax bill. We had reached one of the first floor bedrooms and she said, 'I hope you don't mind but this is where my husband is working.' She knocked and we entered. At the desk sat a man writing in longhand. He looked up to exchange pleasantries and I recognised him immediately. It was Adrian Mitchell, one of my very favourite poets- the man who had written the magnificently versified script for the Marat/Sade. We had met quite recently over dinner at Miles Tomalin's. Indeed we had sat exactly across from on one another. There was much affability as recognition dawned. They said they'd love me to have the house. I made an offer which they accepted. Celia rang to say that someone had turned up on her doorstep with a bag of money and they couldn't resist the fact that, with a cash deal, things would go through very quickly, whereas waiting for me to get a mortgage could drag on. I expressed regrets but said I quite understood.

I hurried back to Notting Hill Gate and to my relief, the house I had seen earlier was still unsold. I quickly made an offer and the deal was done. All I now had to do was to find a mortgage big enough to move me up from a flat in Bayswater to a house in Notting Hill. A friend told me that the local council gave out mortgages on properties in the locality, so, on the off chance, I phoned the Town Hall and asked for the Housing Officer. He, an affable gentleman by the sound of it, said I had called at just the right moment. 'I have all this money left,' he said, 'and if I don't get rid of it by the end of the month, it will all go back into central funds.' How much did I need, he asked. I told him and he said, 'That shouldn't be a problem.' All I had to do then was to complete the appropriate forms and pray. I didn't have to wait long; the decision came through. I had my mortgage and I had my house. My lawyer did all the conveyancing and I asked him this time to send the bill. It was about time he did. For the eight years or so he'd been acting for me and hadn't sent me an invoice. It was always that, 'All in good time, Mr. Bowker,' and then nothing happened. So, when the sale finally went through, and I received his final statement for the transaction, I could scarcely believe what I saw. One item had been included - for work done since 1973 - an astonishingly modest sum. I had never before paid a bill so happily. When I received the deeds to my new house, I saw that the owner before last was none other than my first editor and publisher of Under Twenty - Brian Southam. One further event connecting my home to a book and its publication, would remind me what a lucky house it was.

19 March. My Birthday, I decided to move into my first house and I never look back. I still love my house.

4 May. Margaret Thatcher became Prime Minister of the United Kingdom and served until 28th November 1990. She was the first woman to hold the position and the longest serving Prime Minister. Also, she was the first ex-Prime Minister in British history to be honoured with a Statue in the Houses of Parliament.

Chapter 13

Life as a Broadcaster: Research Trips to Germany, The Arctic Circle, Poland, and exploring the Life of Malcolm Lowry

1979-83

I was anxious to show off my home to friends. Amongst them, was Claire Tomalin whom I invited round for lunch and to see the house. Fortunately, she loved it and thought it one of the best small houses she had seen. We discussed our different tastes in fiction. I told her about my passion for novels by mostly European writers and writers working and living in exile. I reeled off a few names - Kafka, Conrad, Grass, Sartre, Camus and, of course, Lowry - about whom I waxed lyrical. 'Are you not interested in English writers such as Jane Austen, Dickens, Iris Murdoch, and Angus Wilson?' She asked. At that time I wasn't and so I shook my head. I mentioned the influence her husband Nick had had upon me, encouraging me into journalism.

We didn't keep in touch much after that, but we did meet again some years later, at the Royal Society of Literature where the erstwhile Mistress of Girton College Cambridge, Muriel Bradbrook, was about to give a talk. Muriel and I had met through a mutual interest in Lowry; Claire was to introduce her to the gathered assembly. We bumped into each other in the street just outside and she said, 'Gordon Bowker! What are you doing here?' Then she recalled. 'Of course - Malcolm Lowry!' She gave Muriel a brilliant introduction, recalling her own time at Girton and the debt she owed her. Muriel, in turn, gave a very engaging talk, recalling her days as an undergraduate in Cambridge, at a time which coincided with Lowry's at St Catherine's. She mentioned with some reverence the occasion on which Virginia Woolf visited Cambridge in 1928 to give the students of Newnham and Girton Colleges a series of talks on the need for a woman wanting to write, to have a room of her own and money to support herself, talks which form the basis of her classic essay.

I was delighted when Harvey Unna, the literary agent, to whom I had sent my Commonwealth Games thriller, sent me a note to say he thought it excellent. It had, he agreed, clearly missed the boat once the Commonwealth Games had ended. 'But,' he said, 'if you can do me an outline for another thriller, I'll try and find a publisher for you.'

I dreamt up a suitable story about an attempt to kidnap Adolf Hitler and embarked on a research trip to Germany to check out pre-war Berlin and, Berchtesgaden in Bavaria, where Adolf had his Berghof at Obersalzberg. Before flying to Berlin, I visited the Imperial War Museum to obtain a copy of the 1939 map of Berlin with all the places marked, such as Gestapo headquarters and Nazi Party Headquarters. Fortunately, I was able to bring away a first-rate photocopy. I also obtained once-secret information on the men Hitler intended to rule Britain in the event of a successful invasion. Then there was the famous list of people in Britain who were to be targeted for not-so-friendly visits from their local Gestapo.

25 August. In West Berlin, where I landed, there was plenty to take in - the ruined Kaiser Wilhelm Memorial Church in the Breitscheidplatz on the Kurfürstendamm (K'damm), for example, named after the father of the barbarous 'Kaiser Bill'. Between wars, along the K'damm, Christopher Isherwood and his mates once flirted, and Sally Bowles kept the city entertained while Brownshirts went barging, butting, and strutting along its crowded streets. I

wandered on. There was the Reichstag, or what remained of it. There was the Tiergarten, restored to its pre-war perfection. There was the ironically-named Victory Column, a rearing gold-tipped phallus, still where the defeated Nazis left it at the centre of a great crossroads standing between the former Berlin City Palace and the Eastward-road to Brandenburg Gate. Now, this part of the city was limping along, still cut off, not just from the communist East but also from the capitalist West - cut off by a monstrous frieze of defiant slogans - the Berlin Wall. I spent a good couple of hours photographing it from different angles: The graffiti was modern art, a latter-day 'Guernica', inscribed in wild strokes by unacknowledged Picassos, moved to leave their mark by what? – anger, frustration, pity, sorrow? It was an expression of exasperation from both sides.

I was still in the mood to ask in my silent way of every man of a certain age, 'What were you doing in the War, then?' I looked out along Prinz-Albrechtstrasse, where the Gestapo had its fearsome headquarters, the anguished screams from inside it muffled by concrete. Be taken into their cellars and you could kiss goodbye to sweet or even not-so-sweet life. I found myself staring at the ground. What horrors were hidden under those flagstones? And there was the Wall itself. The path which ran beside it, a favourite with joggers, was what was left of Hermann Goering Strasse. The shadow of the demented Austrian seemed still to hover around in this city. I found my way to the old Berlin Olympic stadium, where he had declared the 1936 Games open, and where he'd later stormed off, after Jesse Owens beat his German supermen in the 100 and 200 metre sprints. Now, this circle of crumbling concrete, once built to project Hitler's power, stood deserted, but for a few sightseers such as myself.

It was easy, I found, to cross over to the Eastern Communist-controlled section of the city on foot as a tourist. I managed this quite successfully, even being allowed to take my camera with me. The difference between the two sides of the city, however, couldn't have been starker. Compared to the neon-lit, pulsating and modern city of West Berlin, this Eastern sector was shabby and rundown, therefore photogenic and worthy of comment. The armed guards were noticeable and, as I began to point my camera in the direction of the Wall from that eastern side, two of them came towards me signalling to me to desist and with a 'No no' gesture. Rather than seeing the inside of an East Berlin jail, I complied with a smile.

After the entertaining displays of the West, the absence of advertisements was a noticeable and shop windows were remarkably empty. There were scarcely any cars about, and the few people I saw, seemed poorly dressed. I spotted an open-air café, went in and found a table from which to survey the surrounding life. I glanced at the menu and saw listed a small bottle of Henkell Trocken, which I knew in England to be a relatively cheap sparkler. A sly-looking waiter appeared and I ordered it. At a nearby table I got into conversation with a group of Dutch tourists. They were communist themselves and having a wonderful time visiting the 'socialist paradise' of East Berlin.

'Such few cars there are!' said one with an expansive gesture of pleasure.

'Yes,' echoed the others at the table.

'And so few advertisements!' This was obviously a big day for them, and they sat back in the afternoon sunshine and basked in the ambience of equality and sensory deprivation. I called the waiter and asked for the bill. He produced it with a flourish. I was staggered by what I'd been charged for my Henkell Trocken and queried it.

'But,' said the waiter in perfect English, 'that's what you ordered - champagne.'

I looked into his face. Quite suddenly I wanted to laugh, and didn't. I then said, 'You have to come to a communist country to be ripped off in good capitalistic fashion.' He smiled. And I saw then that in reality the East Germans were nothing less than secret capitalists at heart.

1980

Down to Bavaria and on to Berchtesgaden where that feeling – a confusion of angry impulses to wring necks and shed a tear - intensified. I ventured out to see the Berghof, out at Obersalzberg, that dramatic setting for Hitler's mad nightmare played out to the sound of Wagnerian trumpets - the summons to Hell and back. To reach his 'Eagle's Eyrie' there was a tunnel to the centre of the mountain at the end of which there was a mirror-lined elevator - its shaft, 120 metres deep, hacked out by slave labour under the supervision of Martin Bormann. In the teahouse at the pinnacle, that sense of having the world in your hands, inspired by the sweep of country before you, was overwhelming. Very tempting, I'm sure, to little men with little moustaches dreaming of global mastery….. I brought back a wealth of notes, brochures and photographs for my researches. However, the Hitler thriller was soon abandoned and I used my research materials for a different project later.

November. *Amadeus* was playing at the National Theatre on the South Bank, superbly acted by Paul Scofield as Salieri and Simon Callow as Mozart. The playwright, Peter Shaffer, was a new name to me, but the English theatre was forever on heat, it seemed to me; English theatrical talent was second to none and was currently producing some of its most prolific of geniuses in all departments.

1980

Having been unable to drive in America, back in London I was determined to acquire a licence. Jill Murphy said she had been taught by a brilliant woman instructor, a Geordie, and I was delighted when she took me on. She was indeed brilliant. Having passed my test, I acquired a car which only led me into more strange adventures. On one memorable occasion, having entertained a friend to dinner, I decided to drive her back to her home in Pimlico. On my return journey, I drove across Buckingham Palace Road - the best and easiest a way for me to get to Ebury Street, and from there back to Notting Hill Gate. But it wasn't to be. Just as I passed over the road, I was stopped by a policeman and, even before he spoke to me, I realised what had happened. I'd driven the wrong way up a one-way street. And so, I was put through what I imagined was the usual routine.

'Been drinking, sir?'

'Just a little, over dinner.'

'Would you please blow into this bag – blow until I tell you to stop.'

I took a deep breath and blew. The good man examined the instrument and said that I had failed the test. I was over the limit, he told me, and was under arrest on suspicion of drunk driving and he then read me my rights. There would be a second test to decide my guilt or innocence on the more precise breathalyser at the station. I was taken from the car and placed in a police van.

'What about my car?' I asked.

'Don't worry, sir,' he said, 'We'll look after that for you.'

We sped away and suddenly I remembered, reading somewhere that the way to beat the breathalyser was to take deep breaths, before you were tested for a second time. And so I began some silent heavy breathing.

We arrived at the famous Rochester Row Police station. I was duly presented to the sergeant behind the desk as under arrest on suspicion of drunk-driving. After that, I was led to where the big, more reliable breathalyser was located. All this time, I had continued my deep breathing. It was explained to me that I would have to blow over the limit twice more for a charge to be brought. I sat down and blew, then blew again. I passed and silently congratulated myself on remembering the deep breathing story. A distinctly disappointed PC told me I would not be charged and directed me to sit on a bench to await transport back to my car. There was a small desk in front of me on which stood a big old-fashioned manual typewriter. On the front of it on an embossed metal strip I read the immortal words, 'For Sergeants Only'. It might just have been a scene from Carry on Constable. At any

1980

moment I expected, Sid James or Hattie Jacques to come in with Kenneth Williams in handcuffs, protesting loudly.

A journalist friend had told me you could get free flights sometimes if you were commissioned to write a piece of travel journalism. Then I discovered that Des Wilson who used to run Shelter, the charity for fighting homelessness, was now assistant editor of the Illustrated London News (ILN). They had recently been running a series called; *'Letter From'* and I suggested a 'Letter From Canada'. My proposal was accepted and I was determined to write a piece for them, illustrated by my own photographs when I went off to teach Summer School in July. I phoned the Air Canada Press Office, explaining my commission from the ILN to write a travel article. Was there any chance of my getting a complimentary return ticket? 'There might be, if you are going to mention Air Canada', said the woman at the other end of the line. I assured her that I would do so. Later, I received a phone call. I could pick up my tickets from their office or they could mail them to me.

August. After teaching summer school as a visiting professor, I contacted Travel Ontario and told them I was in Canada for the ILN and would like to do a travel piece on the province. They quickly agreed, and a package of tickets and list of hotel bookings was sent to me. Within no time, I found myself speeding north on the Ontario Northland Railway's 'Polar Bear Express', heading towards the Arctic Circle. We passed through small remote towns and vast forests of boreal Canada – endless acres of spruce and pine trees, a primitive landscape stretching far beyond the horizon of any eye. St James Bay was as close as I got to the Circle, but the sense of remoteness was overwhelming. The old native tribes who had lived by hunting were now reduced to sad, impoverished town dwellers. They had in many cases lost their hunting skills and every week there were suicides among the young men there. I left that settlement with a feeling of immense sadness. Returning to the balmy south, I did get to an Indian pow-pow - probably put on mostly for tourists - and got some wonderful shots of children

GLIMPSES OF A BIOGRAPHER'S DIARY

dancing in their colourful Indian costumes. All went into my piece for the ILN.[6]

1981

25 March. I again went to Berlin - this time to write another piece for Des Wilson (Des) in the ILN, this one focussing on the Wall, and using my earlier notes and recordings as background. Suddenly, as my preparations were almost complete, Des told me that the Army had long wanted the magazine to do an article on their occupation of the British sector of the city. If I agreed to do that, they'd pay expenses. I was reluctant - preferring to act as a free agent rather than a someone's press officer - but finally decided that there could be good experience to be had from such an arrangement. I interviewed the jolly general in charge of the British Occupation Force, a captain from the Army Press Corps and an American Army liaison officer. Then a tough soldier from the Royal Green Jackets took me up into a Wall-side watchtower and pointed over to the East where communist troops manned towers opposite. He said, 'They hang nooses over the side,' and shouted, 'This is for you when we come across. So, we hang nooses over for them.' It was good to know there was a cordial reciprocity between opposite armies.

Before returning home, I met and interviewed people who had been woken one morning by the sound of the Wall being built right outside their bedroom window, and the Jewish man, who escaped the city ahead of the Nazis, then returned as a colonel in the US Army to become Mayor of West Berlin. My article *'Twenty Years of the Berlin Wall'*, appeared in the ILN on 26 September.

Also in March. The TES asked me to report on the Sunday Times Annual National Student Drama Festival held this year at Hull

---

[6] 26 December. TES published my report *On Theatres and Education: Raw Issues in the Round*.

TES published five of my articles on: (1) 2nd January on *Look Round in Anger* at The Royal Court Young People Theatre Scheme, (2) 9th January on some recent radio documentaries *Agreeable Retrospection*, (3) 30th January *On and Off the Wagon - on Alcoholism*, (4) 20th February on radio documentaries *A Dreadful Litany*, and (5) 10th April on theatre and education *Walking the Tightrope*.

1981

University from the 9th April-15th. It thronged not just with student actors, directors and designers but also, with various literary and theatrical luminaries; the playwrights John Godber and Alan Plater, the poet, James Fenton, and the actress, Janet Suzman, were all there to offer advice and criticism. Suzman, like a stern headmistress, tore into a production of Chekhov's: *The Three Sisters*, which would have been fine for a performance by a cast from the RSC, but, for a student cast it was, I thought, unnecessarily harsh and soul destroying. John Godber, who would go on to found the Hull Truck Company, won the prize for outstanding production for his play *Cramp* and a clever young student, Rebecca Harbord, won best actress for her portrayal of the eighteenth-century actor, Sarah Siddons. Luckily for her, she did not appear in the Chekhov play. The TES published my article on the Annual National Student Drama Festival *Stage Planks into Springboards* on the 24th of April.[7]

Sarah, my Polish friend, was eager for me to go to her homeland where Solidarity were struggling for freedom from the communist

---

[7] 13 May at 21.30 p.m. In a live broadcast, Paul Vaughan, a man with a voice like honey, quizzed me about my trip. Afterwards, Sarah said, 'I cried when I heard your Polish story.' Also on the 13th at 21.30 hr. BBC Radio 4 transmitted my report and interviews: Title: Kaleidoscope; entitled *Special report from Poland on the State of the Arts including interviews*.[7]

12th June. TES Art published my script on *Do Put Your Daughter on the Stage* at the Leicestershire Festival of Dance and Drama.

17 June. I gave permission for the BBC copyright department to renew the rights and to repeat my fully dramatised scripts: *Dr Barnardos* for Radio 4 schools series: *History: Not So Long Ago* on 6th October.

19 June. I gave permission for the BBC copyright department to renew the rights and to repeat my fully dramatised scripts *At School* for Radio 4 schools series *History: Not So Long Ago* to be broadcasted on the 13th October.

5 July at 21.30hr. BBC Radio 4: Woman's Hour: Sue MacGregor introduced *Rodeo Women* and I talked to some of female participants in Rodeo - one of the fastest growing sports in Canada and North America.

11 September. TES published my article on: *Myths Polished off*.

4 December. TES published my review on George Orwell *The Road to 1984* by Peter Lewis *Swimming against the Current*.

government. She gave me the phone number and address of a good friend of hers at Polish radio. I phoned her from London and she readily agreed to give me bed and breakfast for the duration of a visit to Warsaw. I also phoned the BBC World Service and managed to speak to Tim Sebastian, who had been covering the rise of Solidarity for BBC news. I asked him whether he had covered any of the activities of artists in Warsaw during that period and he said he had been too busy with strictly political events and, if I wanted to do a programme on Polish artists, he was perfectly happy for me to do so.

I spoke to Des at the ILN and persuaded him to commission me to write a report on my adventures behind the Iron Curtain. But more important was the piece I had in mind for my BBC Radio 4 documentary.

16 April. I flew to Poland and, no sooner was I out of the airport, than I discovered I had left my camera behind, probably at the Customs desk. I managed to borrow one from a young man in Solidarity and asked him to send the prints on to me. However, they did let me take my bulky Uher tape recorder in with me. It enabled the radio journalist in me to come to the fore when I went along to the Easter service at the Cathedral, where the archbishop was due to conduct the service. My tape recorder was switched on and well concealed in a satchel when I entered the church. I'd placed the microphone in a little pouch just beneath a flap hanging outside sufficiently to pick up all sounds. I sat at the back of the church and, to my delight, at some point the congregation rose to sing their Polish National Anthem. Then the archbishop began to preach and I managed to record the whole service.

Sarah had told me that the food in Poland was terrible and the only place you could get a decent meal was the Hotel Europejski. It was evident from the empty shops that food distribution in Poland was not just bad, it was worse than bad. My Polish friends directed me to the Hotel and I went in looking for a good lunch. The dining room was very imposing - clearly a grand salon, a hangover from the previous century. The tables with their starched white tablecloths were all neatly laid out. Around the room, stood waiters, formally attired, with white napkins folded over their arms. All that was missing were customers. The whole scene was both impressive and amusing. I took a seat, consulted the menu, and one of the waiters came over immediately to place bread rolls on the table and pour me a glass of water before retiring. I can't remember the menu in detail but I do remember ordering the rabbit. I had eaten it before - during the War - and enjoyed it. Now, with a decent helping of vegetables, this was going to be my first enjoyable meal since arriving in Warsaw. I looked around and saw that I was not alone. At a table just behind me sat another guest. We exchanged glances and nodded to one another. After the meal – when the coffee arrived, it seemed only polite to turn to my neighbour again. Fortunately, he too was English, so conversation flowed readily. He was, he said, the European correspondent of the Christian Science Monitor, and covered all of the Iron Curtain countries. Like me, he found the Europejski quite amusing - the palatial dining room, the waiters and the empty tables. It was, he assured me, the same all round Eastern Europe. These were hotels mostly patronised by foreign visitors. When the waiter came with the bill, he bent down and whispered, 'Would you like to exchange some pounds for zlotys?' The man from the Christian Science Monitor saw this and shook his head but I did.

Members of Solidarity sat around at their headquarters cracking Polish jokes. 'What is a Polish cow? One that's fed in Warsaw and milked in Moscow,' 'What's the difference between an optimist and a pessimist? The optimist says, "The Russians will invade tomorrow, then put us all on trains and ship us off to Siberia." And what does the pessimist say? The pessimist says, "They'll make us walk."' I bought my Solidarity lapel badge and said a fond farewell to the party workers I had got to know. Finally, through my hostess, the radio producer, I contacted the artists and writers I had come to Poland to interview - a film director, a poet, a dramatist - all had been subject in one form or another to state persecution and censorship. The film director's works were sitting on shelves not shown; the dramatist's plays had never been staged, the poet's verses remained officially unpublished. In a totalitarian society, you didn't need to be in prison to be separated from your fellow man. When I went to the airport to return home, I enquired about my camera and, a smiling woman customs officer handed it to me. I thanked her and set off to return home.

10 May. In London, The Sunday Times published my piece *Censors are the Poles' New Target*. But more important to me was to get some of my tapes played on BBC radio. I parcelled them up and mailed them to the editor of the arts programme Kaleidoscope. To my delight, a few days later, I received a phone call from an editor called Clare Selerie-Grey inviting me to go in to the Broadcasting House to talk to her. She was a Russian speaker and fascinated by Eastern Europe. She liked the tapes, she said, and suggested that I wrote a script for a piece, about my visit to Poland for the programme. My script *Special Report from Poland on the State of the Arts + Interviews* was written and delivered to Clare.

1982

10 January. I gave permission for the BBC copyright department to renew the rights in my fully dramatised script: Soldiers' Diaries for the Radio 4 schools series *History: Not So Long Ago*. That was broadcasted on the 9 February.

19 February. TES published my article on Ideas in Action on the Newham's Second International Festival of Theatre-In-Education.

March. Yet again, the TES commission took me to Newcastle. The Royal Shakespeare Company out on tour at the Theatre Royal were visiting schools, hoping to spread interest in the Bard around Geordie land. I tracked them down to a classroom and saw them in action. Sheila Hancock, Harriet Walter, and Eileen Atkins spoke enthusiastically to the children and acted out a few scenes but, when they called for questions, they found, the kids' Geordie accents all but impenetrable, as did I. I suspect it worked the other way too, so that trying to sell Shakespeare, of all playwrights to kids who had no idea of what was being said, just as adults who had no idea either, made it a hard sell to say the least. My article on Northern Lights on the RSC's educational activities in Newcastle was published by TES on the 19 March.[8]

28 March. Now what can I say: I am doing reading and teaching sociology? All along I wanted to write novels, but have been constantly distracted. Now I gather myself together to return to my true path of Literature. Everything I do now must reassert this total intention and commitment. Working at my craft of writing must supersede everything else. It will take time, patience and steadfastness.

Lawrence Durrell had begun sketches for his Alexandria Quartet when he was around thirty-five and published the first volume at forty-five so now, only a little past that age, I didn't worry too much that I had not embarked as yet on my great novel-writing career. I had completed one when I was twenty-two but, when two publishers turned it down I cast it aside instead of carrying on till I found one wanting to bring it out. When I realised that I had passed the Durrell date without even a short story in print, I took to drink - though not in a way that made it at all obvious to me. I merely continued a habit brought back from North America - the bourbon or whisky in the evening after work, followed by a hungover next morning. Dylan Thomas fell into hard drinking in much the same fashion in the U.S.A. Finally, I got out of this pernicious habit and dreamed up a book - an updating of Ambrose Bierce's Devil's Dictionary. This year, I'd been idly scribbling down what I thought were humorous definitions for some time past. Soon I had enough materials to fill a small book. I sent them off to Harvey Unna. He thought it would make a series of daily items in some newspaper, calling them Beelzebub's Beastly Bards, A Cynic's Dictionary. But no newspaper was interested. So, I showed them to Giles Gordon, whom I had first met when he was an editor at Penguin Books. Now he was an agent. Giles sent them out to a

---

[8] 16 April. The TES published two of my articles:(1) Impossible, but Impressive at the National Student Drama Festival and (2) Force for Peace.

19 April. The TES published my article on Winning the Derby.

couple of publishers, but they landed fairly heavily and promptly on their rejection pile. That's when I decided to publish them myself.

It needed a series of cartoon-like illustrations. I set up a large work desk in my living room and churned out endless funny drawings. Finally, I had enough to illustrate my book. I got a young typesetter with a base in Clerkenwell, and the cover I had designed by Nicola Lane, who had done a superb cover one the new edition of Alternative London. December. I called my book Beelzebub's Beastly Barbs.

9 December. I first publicised my book at Birmingham Evening Mail, on Colmore Circus, Birmingham where I was interviewed by Fred Norris at 10.30am. From there, I drove to BBC Radio Derby at 56, St Helen Street, where I was interviewed by Jon Barton. Later, I went to the Derby Evening Telegraph, and was interviewed by Geoff Hamerton at 13.30pm. I then headed to BBC Stoke On Trent, Conway House, Cheapside, Hanley and was interviewed by Ian Strachan a 16.30pm. I proceeded to Manchester to stay the night at the Piccadilly Hotel, Piccadilly Plaza.

10th. I drove to Radio Trent, Castle Gate, Nottingham and was interviewed by David Lloyd at 15.00 p.m. Later, I carried on to Centre Radio, Granville House, Granville Road, Leicester and was interviewed by Brigette Blair at 16.15 p.m.

13th. At Radio London, I was interviewed by John Wait at 08.00 a.m. Then, proceeded to L.B.C, where I was interviewed by Bob Holness at 09.00 a.m. Later, at 11.00 a. m, I was interviewed by Rick Davies at Capital Radio, London. At 12.00 noon, I was interviewed by Tommy Vance at British Forces Broadcasting, London.

1983

February. After many more promotions for my book, on a whim, I prepared a press release boosting my book as an antidote to the sugary excesses of Valentine's Day.

1983

14th. I was invited to be interviewed by David Frost on TV-AM - Good Morning Britain. I made my way to Nathan's, the theatrical costumiers, and hired a black cape and hat, plus a Groucho Marx face-mask and so transformed myself into Dr Dick Diabolus, author of this devilishly comic dictionary. My attempt to torpedo Valentine's Day by going on about the heightened chances of being impoverished and even murdered if you're married quite amused Frost.

Also on the 14th, my next stop was Broadcasting House - for Start the Week, eight or nine guests were gathered around the circular tables there. In the chair sat Kenneth Baker, and beside him Kenneth Robinson, a smart and cutting cross-talk duo. Then, who should be sitting down next to me but my friend Rebecca, the onetime picture researcher, with her own TV show. That included all sorts of novelties and she now seemed fascinated with my dictionary, quoting from it. Suddenly, I became worried that she might want to invite Dr Diabolus to appear on her show. To avoid this, at the end of the programme, I revealed myself to her. She looked furious and promptly took off. Later, when we passed in a corridor, she gave me the coldest shoulder imaginable. I think, I did well to keep out of broadcasting as a career. Publishing too, because my book was by no means a bestseller, though it did get the occasional good review. The best I could say for it was that I recovered my costs - mainly due to the fees from these last two appearances into broadcasting.

17 February. Kurt Vonnegut Jr. was in conversation with Martin Amis at the Institute of Contemporary Arts. It coincided with the London publication of his latest novel, Deadeye Dick. He was as wry and amusing as one could have wished him to be. Afterwards I managed to speak to him, telling him about my Ambrose Bierce-inspired dictionary. It was clearly as much a favourite of his as it was mine. I told him about Beelzebub's and he thought it a great idea - although probably he was being kind. Afterwards, I mailed him a copy care of his publisher and duly received a marvellous letter saying that he would be quoting from it at parties from then onwards. Whether he was much of a partygoer I don't know, but

his elaborate signature was a wonder to behold - like a sketch by Picasso.

*

27 March. Today, eight days after my forty-ninth year, I dedicate myself steadfastly to writing. Now, all energy must be concentrated to that end. All else must take second place.

*

22 May. At 2.30 p.m. for thirty-minutes on BBC Radio 4: I presented my script for the Food Programme featured On the Diet of the Canadian Plains Indians.

In the Guardian, I read about a BBC man, Roger Laughton, taking over responsibility for setting up the corporation's daytime television service. Laughton, it reported, was on the lookout for one-off social documentaries, and I thought I was just the fellow he was looking for. I sent him a proposal for a programme on National Service. He replied, inviting me to Television Centre to discuss the idea. In fact, he talked a lot about daytime TV and listened to what ideas I might have - as no doubt he asked just about everyone else he thought worth talking to.[9] He was clearly keen to do the National Service programme. Next time I saw Roger, he introduced me to the director and his assistant, and I was asked to do the picture research for the programme, even though I was hoping to write the script and read the narrative. The picture research took me to both the BBC and Pathé Archives, as well as to the National Film Institute. The list of contributors we drew up included Michael Frayn (who was taught Russian as a National Serviceman), and Paul Foot (who served in Jamaica where his father was Governor). I interviewed him and Freddie Truman on 24 June, Auberon Waugh, son of Evelyn (who managed to shoot

---

[9] 13 July at 13.20 p.m. for half-an-hour, BBC Radio 4 Woman's Hour transmitted my script: Feature on the *Rodeo Girls in Canada and North America*.

6 September. BBC Radio 4 Woman's Hour transmitted my script entitled: *She's My Antibiotic*.

himself accidentally in the stomach in Cyprus) on 28th. Later, I interviewed Bob Monkhouse (the comedian who consulted his joke book before our interview) and Leslie Thomas (author of Virgin Soldiers, a comic autobiographical novel on National Service) on 4th July. They all laughed it off as a waste of valuable time, except Freddie Truman, the cricketer, whom my two directors treated as a sporting hero. We toured the country and I did the interviewing. The final programme was well received, the only criticism coming from the Tory press who thought it frivolous.

I was looking for a writer on whom to base a forty-five minute BBC radio documentary. I knew that the BBC liked anniversaries. How long is it since a certain book was published, what famous person was born or died 50 or 100 years ago? It was coming up to 75 years since Malcolm Lowry was born, so, I put that forward to the BBC. It was only when I made contact with someone in the Education Department at the Langham Place that matters moved forward. They, it seems, were allowed one documentary slot every few months, and I was told they'd be happy to let me have the next one. A young director, Michel Petheram, was appointed and we set to work, with me given the task of writing a script which traced the author's drunken ill-fated life. This was to include inserts from my recorded interviews.

I managed to interview Arthur Calder-Marshall, John Sommerfield, and other old friends of Lowry's, plus Malcolm Bradbury, Professor Muriel Bradbrook and Anthony Burgess who had expressed enthusiasm for his work. I met Bradbury at his home in Norwich. It was a long but pleasant drive over the lovely flatlands of Cambridge and Norfolk, and I found Bradbury an affable man and relaxed company. He was sitting on the sofa ready to be interviewed. We'd talked for only a few minutes about Lowry when he suddenly jumped up and said, 'Excuse me.' He was away for five or ten minutes and came back downstairs with a pile of books in his arms, each with a page marked with a slip. He put them next to himself on the sofa and indicated that he was ready to be interviewed. Bradbury gave me a beautifully fluent interview and left me with at least one vivid image – 'the lunatic city' - depicted in Lowry's brilliant novella *Lunar Caustic*, in which the lunacy of the snake-pit psychiatric ward becomes a metaphor for the madhouse of the modern urban maelstrom.

10 - Portrait of Malcolm Lowry hanging in Notting Hill

Michel, my BBC producer, discovered that Anthony Burgess was staying at a London hotel in the throes of promoting his latest novel, *Enderby's Dark Lady*. We were early and had to wait. Finally, in breezed Burgess with his publisher's minder, and we were soon audience to a bravura performance from an obviously intense and driven man. Questions were barely out of my mouth when he launched into an almost endless monologue on the virtues of Lowry as a novelist. The way this man savoured words and relished his understanding of other writers was deeply impressive. Burgess was not just a writer and critic; he was a most engaging entertainer.

Through Muriel Bradbrook, I was able to contact Malcolm's sole surviving brother, Russell, who still lived on the Wirral where they had grown up together. He agreed to talk, and, I was soon driving up the motorway to spend a day with him. It was fascinating, and not only did I get a fairly interesting account of Malcolm's young life and a sense of his hostility towards his parents, but also towards him, Russell. He shared his younger brother's antipathy towards their mother and father, but for different reasons. First, they stopped him marrying the girl he loved, then forced him to work in his father's office on a very modest salary, while the sometimes drunk and violent Malcolm was paid handsomely to stay away from home. A perfect family portrait of respectable Wesleyan Methodist misery. I visited Russell many times, and I thought, I had a very good knowledge of the family and especially of Malcolm.

I visited the Leys School, Lowry's alma mater in Cambridge, and was given copies of memoirs of masters who had taught him and, interestingly enough, boys who had been with him at the school. Russell told me of the son of the Australian ambassador, who had turned the awkward little boy into a young ruffian, by encouraging him to 'rough it'. I sent his name to the Australian High Commission asking to be put in touch with the man if he were still alive. Several months later, out of the blue, I received a letter from an old sheep farmer in remotest Queensland describing the Malcolm, and the school he had known back in the early twenties. He knew nothing about the long-dead writer Malcolm Lowry and ended by saying, 'When you next see Malcolm give him my best regards.'

Two other school chums stood out from the crowd. One called Thomas Hardy (a name that no doubt would have immediately attracted the literature-mad Malcolm), sent me a phone number to call and a precise time to call him. It transpired that he lived remotely in the Highlands of Scotland, and the only telephone to which he had access was a pay phone in a call box some miles from where he lived. So, he had to come down from the hills and wait at the phone box in order to receive my call. Surprisingly, I got through to him at the very first attempt. According to Hardy, he had invited the fourteen-year-old Malcolm to spend one half-term break at his home in Nottingham, and had driven the Hardy family mad strumming away on his ukelele. Then, when Thomas invited him to watch England playing Australia in the Test Match at Trent

Bridge cricket ground, he disappeared off, only to reappear outside the ground as the day's play ended. 'He was,' said Hardy, 'weaving all over the road, drunk as a lord, but he had produced screeds of writing at the local pub.'

One of the Leys School's most celebrated masters was William Balgarnie on whom another Leys boy, James Hilton, the novelist, based the character of Mr. Chips. 'Chips' took a shine to the wild, insubordinate, accident-prone Lowry who contributed comic stories and reviews to the school magazine which the master edited. Sadly, the real Chips existed only in the memories of a few remaining 'Very Old Boys,' like Russell Lowry, and in the pages of Hilton's novel. But he also comes through as a distinctly humorous character in Malcolm's own schoolboy short stories.

I organised a Saturday class on Lowry at Goldsmiths'. I invited Ron Binns, an independent scholar, who had just produced a short book on Malcolm Lowry, to join me. On that occasion, after Ron had given a fascinating lecture on Lowry and details his book, we showed the Canadian film *Volcano* about Malcolm's calamitous, self-destructive final months in Mexico in 1938 on which he drew in copious detail for the book. The reception was so enthusiastic, I asked whether there would be any interest in a longer conference to be arranged for later. There was such a burst of enthusiasm from the audience that I said that I'd try to get one organised.

It was, I thought, important to think big. I wrote to Anthony Burgess, who had called *The Volcano* "a Faustian masterpiece", inviting him to speak at our grand Lowry Conference, offering him a taxi from his hotel plus a substantial fee. Sadly, he could not attend, but Stephen Spender, who had written a preface to a later edition of *Under the Volcano*, agreed with polite enthusiasm. We also managed to sign up the novelist and critic Arthur Calder-Marshall, who knew Lowry in his twenties, and Muriel Bradbrook, Mistress of Girton College, Cambridge, a great Shakespearean scholar, whose passion for Lowry led her to write a biography of his early life.

1983

When Anthony Burgess wrote, turning me down for the Lowry's Conference, he added, 'Did you see that John Huston is to film *Under the Volcano* in Mexico?' It was news to me. But oh! to be there, to see the novel's anti-hero, the ex-British Consul, Geoffrey Firmin, Lowry's alcoholic alter ego, actually in action under Popocatépetl! And who on earth would and could play the part? There was no doubt that I had to see the filming of the great novel, *Under the Volcano*.

Not only was John Huston directing it, but the role of the Consul had gone to Albert Finney, the first actor I had seen performing after my near-death experience at the Westminster Hospital in 1961. He would now move from 1 Sloane Square to acting under Popocatépetl.

Chapter 14

Biographer by Way of Journalism

1983-1987

September. Masquerading as a journalist, I set out to cover the making of John Huston's film *Under the Volcano*, and to continue the process of converting myself from lecturer to biographer, by way of journalism. But first, I needed someone from a newspaper to commission me to go to Mexico to cover this film. I aimed at the Fleet Street colour supplements which had become highly fashionable following the launch of the Sunday Times Magazine in 1962. Since then the Times Magazine's contributors had included the likes of Ian Fleming, Martin Amis, Bruce Chatwin, Zoe Heller and Nick Tomalin. Who would not wish to join them? But how?

I remembered what Nick had told me, sitting in his car outside my Westbourne Terrace flat - that the trick was to cast your net as wide as possible. 'Type up a proposal of around 250 words, have multiple copies made, then do the rounds of all the Sunday papers with supplements, deliver them to their room desks or through their letterboxes and follow up a week later with a phone call.' I typed out and photocopied the proposal, and duly did the round of Fleet Street offices, offering my Mexican story to the Sunday Telegraph, Sunday Times, Observer, and a couple of others.

No replies came. A week later I made my follow-up phone-calls, as advised. The Sunday Times said they already had someone covering the story, the Telegraph said they were not planning to cover it. The Observer, to my delight the good angel who answered, an editor called Polly Pattullo, said, 'We're interested, but we don't know your work and wouldn't be able to pay your fare.' Did I care? Not a bit of it. I was simply astonished at how easy it had been.

I was now a commissioned Observer journalist. I booked, and included Ramdei Rhoda, my beautiful partner since 1980, on my airline tickets for Mexico City and made a hotel reservation the same day. Recalling Lowry's picture of Mexico in *Under the Volcano*, I also felt sure that I could bring back some good enough sound recordings to place at least a couple of programme items with the BBC.

I called the production company in Hollywood and was given a number for the location office in Mexico. John Huston was based in Cuernavaca. The publicity man I spoke to there, was not encouraging; in fact, he was very rude and as good as told me that I would be most unwelcome but, if I wanted to come he couldn't stop me. And so, I decided to go there on spec. I had nothing to lose, except a fee for a non-existent story. With a hotel room booked, I let Polly know when and where I would be heading to, and prepared for my second venture into big-time photo-journalism.

21 September. Arriving in Mexico City, Rhoda and I took a taxi from the airport and were deposited at the Hotel Continental on Pasao de la Reforma in the city centre. I immediately called Huston's production office and found myself speaking again to the angry American.

'Not another goddam journalist! We're crawling with them here!' he snarled.

'I called from London and was told it was OK to come.' I said. 'Listen. We have reporters here who came for a couple of days from Hong Kong or Rome or some other goddamn place, who have been hanging around here at our expense for more than two weeks. I just sent the man from your Guardian newspaper back home without a story.'

'Well, I've travelled a long way and really want to do this story,' I said, trying to sound very British, very polite and very reasonable.

You can come if you like, but we can't give you a room at the Racquet Club, and all the other hotels here are booked out.' The snarl had subsided fractionally to a growl, which I regarded as encouraging.

'I'll be there tomorrow,' I said.

'It's your choice, buddy.' The phone went down.

'That's OK,' I told Rhoda. 'They're expecting me tomorrow.'

'I'll do some sightseeing here in the city,' she said.

I spent an afternoon visiting contacts in Mexico City. The Central America correspondent for the Economist, recommended to me by someone at the BBC World Service, offered a lead to a woman in Cuernavaca, who had known Lowry there in the 1930s. She was the widow of B. Traven, author of The Treasure Of Sierra Madre, I was told.

Next day, the people on the bus to Cuernavaca were mostly Mexican peasants, some with livestock accompanying them, mostly chickens. At the first stop in town I found myself fortunately close to the enchanting Racquet Club where the film crew was based. I ventured into this wonderfully exotic building, a world of its own, and found my way through a courtyard of palms, fuchsias and bougainvillea. At the end of a long veranda was what was now home to the film's publicity unit. A tall young man with a fraught expression, busying himself at a desk, turned his head. He was not happy to see me.

'Yea? What do you want?'

1983

I recognised the voice of the angry American I'd spoken to from London and again from Mexico City. I could see that he was in no mood to be interrupted. I decided to play the ultra-polite Englishman.

'I'm from London, from the Observer and the BBC. We spoke the other day on the telephone.'

'And didn't I tell you not to come? There's no room here.'

'Oh. Is there anywhere else I could stay?'

'What you think this is?' he snarled, 'A goddam tourist office?!'

'I quite understand,' I said in a voice which was part Laurence Olivier and part Uriah Heep. He now turned fully to face me, still in threatening mode, his face darkly thunderous. 'Listen,' he snarled, 'We have journalists from the whole goddam world, crawling all over us like fucking flies. We don't need any more.'

'I can see that that must be quite a problem for you,' I replied meekly, 'but, I did come all this way at my own expense after Anthony Burgess told me about it and I did speak to you first.' I could see that he couldn't quite make me out. Why aren't I snarling back at him, Hollywood-style? At a loss for any stinging comeback, he took a deep breath and snapped, 'OK. But there's only one place that might have a room and it's way out on the edge of town.'

'That's fine,' I said.

'But let me make one thing clear.' He's switched now to a menacing growl.

'You speak to nobody without my permission. If I see you talking to any of the stars, you're off the set! Got it?'

'That's quite understood,' I said.

'And you don't speak to Albert Finney at all!!'

'If you say so.'

'I fucking well do say so. Albert's sick to the teeth with journalists. He refuses all further interviews. If you speak to Albert, I'm fired. That's me finished! My job, my salary... my watch!' He drew a finger across his throat, then tore the watch from his wrist and flourished it in front of my face. He was getting himself nicely worked up into a boiling rage.

It was a wonder to behold - a scene from some Hollywood movie about Hollywood. I was the trembling hack being bawled out by the wrathful mogul. It was a great performance, worthy of an Oscar, but I smiled and nodded and said in a voice of the utmost reason, 'I'll most certainly do as you say.'

He was totally disarmed. He scribbled down a phone number. 'They might have room there.'

I took it. 'Thank you,' I said in the humblest voice I could manage.

'We start filming at eight. There's only one bus and that leaves at 7am. Report to Tom Shaw.'

I phoned and arranged to get transported to the other hotel later, but for the moment I was free to look around the Racquet Club. In a spacious room off a veranda, around a little courtyard, I saw filming in progress and dared to enter. A tall handsome young man came up with his hand outstretched. 'Hi! I'm Danny Huston. ,'

This, I decided, must be the son of the great director. 'We're working on the credits,' he explained. 'You're welcome to watch.' Danny had assembled a cast of puppets dangling from strings - figures from the Mexican Day of the Dead, floating and dancing skeletons - meant to give the film's opening sequence a haunting atmosphere, like a sequence from such German Expressionist chillers as Nosferatu and The Hands of Orlac, which so influenced the young Lowry. Now, it was being suggested, these figures were the furies of delirium tremens tormenting and terrifying the drunken Consul. I told Danny,, 'I hope to see you again later.' Then, I went off looking for the transport to my hotel.

1983

My new home for a couple of days was a newly-built place, with none of the charm and character of the Racquet Club, but good enough. The hotel foyer was expansive, with lots of black leather seats. Lounging around on these were many youngish Mexican women and girls, rather revealingly clad, I thought. They seemed remarkably welcoming, and I was flashed some enticingly inviting smiles. I caught some of them gesturing towards me. Later, I went down to the bar and met a man who said he was there covering the filming for the Boston Globe. 'What are all these women doing here,' I asked. 'Is there a women's conference or something?'

He laughed. 'They're all whores.'

'What!'

'Huston has recruited them from a Mexico City brothel to perform in his film.'

'Good God! So that's where all those inviting smiles and gestures came from.'

'That's it.'

My story was already beginning to write itself.

I barely slept that night, so excited and anxious was I not to miss the next day's filming. The words, 'Only one bus' keep echoing through my head. I drifted off and woke with a start. I groped about for my watch, but seemed to have misplaced it. It must be late and I needed to be picked up early in order to catch that bloody bus.

Tom Shaw was the man to contact. I called the Racquet Club and asked for Shaw. A drowsy voice answered.

'Yeah?'

'Mr. Shaw?'

'Yeah. What the hell d'yer want?'

GLIMPSES OF A BIOGRAPHER'S DIARY

'I was wondering if the bus for the location has left. I need transport to get me there.'

'What!' He was now awake and his voice was thunder - a bellow reminding me of Ernest Borgnine as the menacing sergeant in From Here to Eternity.

'I was wondering...' My voice had become suddenly pathetic and weak.

'Do you know what fucking time it is? It's goddam 4 am for Christ sake!' The telephone crashed down. I was exhausted from lack of sleep, and now reduced to a jelly, but didn't dare doze off in case I missed that bus. Somehow I made it to the Racquet Club, caught the bus, and finally got to the film set, all the time trying to avoid Tom Shaw's eye, even though he wouldn't have known me from Adam. I found myself in what was a quite a spectacular setting, high in the Sierra Madre. A cantina had been constructed beside a great gorge - where the drunken Consul, intent on getting himself shot, picks a fight with a policeman and gets his wish - first taken outside to be blasted by the cop and then pitched into the ravine. In the novel, set in 1938, with the world teetering on the very edge of an abyss, we are let into the Consul's dying thoughts - foreseeing the holocaust to come. The film crew had searched across that part of Mexico for an appropriate gorge for weeks.

Finally, they had found this spectacular barranca, perfect for the film's finale. Clearly it would be a breathtaking ending to a great movie.

Another bus arrived and the brothel girls disembarked, casting their enticing glances around as if by instinct fishing for punters. They drifted onto the set where Finney was rehearsing a scene in the bar of the cantina with John Huston. The set was a scene of chaos. Various members of the crew - journalists, photographers, sound men, costume people, make-up artists, extra barflies and prostitutes milled around, while documentary makers jostled for a camera angle. Amidst all this apparent confusion stood the tall, stooped figure of the great director. I ventured into this bedlam, then decided to retreat to the periphery. As I did so, I found myself confronted by Huston himself. He caught my eye and smiled.

'Oh, hello Mr. Huston,' I said, 'I'm here for the London Observer and the BBC. I hope you can find time for a short interview.'

'Why sure,' he said. 'Catch me later.' And he returned to directing the movie.

Suddenly, I was grabbed from behind by a furious hand. 'Did you just speak to John Huston?' a voice screamed. It was my old friend, the publicity man. He was glaring at me, but it was clearly fake fury - Hollywood hysterics. I smiled apologetically and said, 'Sorry about that. I simply asked him for a brief interview.'

'You do that through me and only through me!' He had turned the volume down slightly, but his eyes were still glaring and his hands still hovered close to his gun belt. He was waiting for me to make a move, but I disappointed him by giving him my David Niven-cum-Hugh-Grant Englishman again. Once-more, he melted in the face of this unexpected display of Old World courtesy. 'Well,' he grumbled, 'just remember!'

The scene proceeded. Inside the ramshackle cantina, Buñuelesque ruffians, sinister policemen and brightly-painted women lounged at tables, drinking and gambling. The brothel girls, sworn to chastity for the duration of filming, were still slyly practicing their nods and winks as they waited for rehearsals to begin. Others gyrated slowly to barely-audible music. Press photographers, television cameramen and film crew milled around the set. A carpenter hammered at a loose board in the ceiling. It was hot, noisy and shambolic.

Huston looked on silently. Now in his late seventies, he had acquired an ethereal aura. It wasn't just the halo of white hair and the beard; his tall frame was whittled and gaunt, and he was racked by emphysema. He spoke only when he had to, and the effort left him coughing and breathless. Now, crouched at his video monitor, he was listening courteously to the suggestions of the film's three young German producers who clustered around him. Then, seemingly having made up his mind, he quietly murmured instructions to his production supervisor, Shaw, who sprang to life and placed a bullhorn to his lips.

'Silencio!' he bellowed, and miraculously, order was restored and silence descended.

'Action,' said the director, in a quiet almost casual voice.

From a dark passageway at the back of the set, Finney emerged as Geoffrey Firmin, the drunken Consul, whose disintegration was now all but complete. In the previous scene, he had been tumbled by one of the girls in a squalid back room overlooked by a candlelit figure of the Virgin. His white suit was dishevelled and stained. He paused, then walked across to Huston. Filming had stopped.

'John,' he said, 'when I left the room back there my flies were undone. You don't like that sort of thing, do you?'

Huston nodded. 'No, I think we'd better take the lipstick off the flies and do them up.'

The dress was cleaned, adjusted and the action resumed. Around the room, photographers jostled with television cameramen for the best angles.

During a break in the filming, I got my interview. Publicity Man gave me my cue and I approached Huston at his monitor. Close up, I saw why he'd been instructed to keep interviewers at arm's length - advanced emphysema had left him breathless after even the slightest exertion. Publicity man had had one final word of instruction to me. 'You talk to Mr. Huston for no more than ten-minutes.' The director had not stirred from his seat at the monitor, and ignoring the melée that had returned to the set, responded to my questions in the most thoughtful fashion. How did he get involved in this project? He remembered reading Lowry's book when it first came out, he said. Then, over the years, scripts had been sent to him, none of which he thought filmable – that was until this one came along.

Huston engaged one like an old friend in a warm conversational manner. I was struck by the timbre and recognisable musical lilt of his voice – something from the American past. I was carried away by our conversation, and so engrossed in it, that when I suddenly looked at my watch, I realised that I had already run just over the ten-minutes to which I'd been limited. I was also concerned that I was making him too breathless, so, I thanked him and drew the interview to a conclusion. Shortly afterwards, I was buttonholed by a television producer from Central Television back home. 'You got the best interview out of Huston so far, from what I hear,' he said. 'Could we borrow a tape of it for our programme?'

I said, 'Yes, as long as I get paid for it.'

Outside with Danny, we encountered Albert Finney taking a break after shooting that cantina scene, and emerging into the open beside a mountain pathway at the rear of the set. 'In there,' he muttered to no one in particular, 'there are people making documentaries about this film, and there are people making documentaries about those documentaries. There are even people making documentaries about the people making those bloody documentaries. It's a madhouse!'

Danny introduced us and, I asked the irritated Finney what impression he had gained of Lowry. He kicked at a stone. 'What a life! He must have been a right pain in the arse.'

Danny said, 'Gordon's here from the Observer,' and Finney exploded.

'Another bloody journalist!' He kicked at a second stone.

At that moment, a little Indian girl came along the path with her mother and, as if to prove that he was a very different man from the drunken Lowry, he threw open his arms and cried, 'Hello, darling!' The child screamed in terror. The dishevelled Consul looked pained and backed off.

'Behind this face of stone,' he declaimed to her, 'there lies a heart of - of stone!' It sounded very Lowryesque.

GLIMPSES OF A BIOGRAPHER'S DIARY

I interviewed the rest of the leading cast members, including Jacqueline Bissett and Anthony Andrews, who was playing the Consul's half-brother, Hugh. He was looking cool and composed, sitting in a canvas chair a short distance away from the set. 'The part has taken Albert over, absolutely,' he told me. 'I just don't know how he does it.' Bissett, equally cool and composed, said, 'Most of the time, when he's not on set, Albert sits alone in a tent ministered to by suppliant maidens.'

With all that material safely in my tape recorder and the many strange events of the day's filming fixed in my memory, I retreated back to the Continental hotel and my lovely Rhoda. She had gone on a day trip to Taxco and the Cathedral. So, I waited for her in the lounge. On our way to a restaurant, a well-dressed man tried to steal her handbag. Being Rhoda, always in charge of herself, she hung onto it and he fled. We were both quite shocked by this incident but Rhoda calmly remained unruffled. We had a wonderful evening and memorable days for the rest of our stay in Mexico.

24th September. Following the lead I'd been given in Mexico City, I called the widow of B. Traven and she invited me to tea. She was a very dignified woman, who told me a compelling story of how Traven and Lowry had been good friends - had admired each other's work and often got together. She told me how much she liked him although, she said, he did drink rather too much. I had seen no mention of this friendship anywhere else, so, it could have been a

11 - Gordon and Rhoda, Mexico 25th September 1983

1983

great discovery of mine. I returned to our hotel and set to transcribing my tapes while waiting for Rhoda.

Next morning, I returned to Cuernavaca, bade farewell to the angry publicity man, Danny and others, before having a leisurely walk with Rhoda around the Racquet Club.

28th. After thanking the staff, we left our hotel by taxi and made for the airport, en route to Heathrow and home.

29th. Back in London, I sat down to compose my first article for the Observer Colour Supplement. I conjured up a small procession of travel-writers and journalistic Muses - Nick Tomalin, Graham Greene, Martha Gellhorn, Lawrence, Hemingway and Lowry himself - then started writing, reworking the mass of material I had brought home for the BBC.[10]

---

[10] *Through A Glass Darkly*, a location report on the filming of *Under The Volcano* in Mexico, appeared in the Observer Magazine on the 15th May, 1984.

2nd November. I presented my prepared and scripted package from the set of John Huston's film *Under the Volcano* (which included interviews with, for example John Huston, Guy Gallow the writer and Anthony Andrews) on the BBC Radio 4 arts programme Kaleidoscope.

I conducted two interviews on location in Mexico and in Autumn of 1983, was subsequently interviewed and recorded live in the studio: Mexico/London for Meridian on the BBC World Service: transmitted on two consecutive days: 14th January, twice that day, and 15th 1984. I also prepared programmes to be broadcast on the CBC and ABC.

31 March 1984. CBC: My one-hour radio script for Atlantic Airwaves, entitled: *The Captivity of John Gyles* in the series *The Bush and the Salon* was aired throughout the maritime region.

28 July 1984. I wrote and presented my first forty-five minute documentary for BBC Radio 4 medium wave on *The Lighthouse Invites The Storm*, Malcolm Lowry and *Under the Volcano*. They were repeated on 1 August, followed shortly by an article in the BBC's news and *Profile on Malcolm Lowry* in The Listener on Thursday, 2 August.

1 September 1984. When I was interviewed about the film *Under the Volcano* by Sarah Dunant for the BBC World Service, I found her refreshingly enthusiastic about it.

The final version of the film *Under The Volcano* was released at the end of 1987. When Danny Huston invited me to a private showing of the film. I was very regrettably obliged to made my excuses due to a prior engagement.

GLIMPSES OF A BIOGRAPHER'S DIARY

1986

30 July. I read in a movie magazine that Bernardo Bertolucci was to film the Life of Pu Yi, the last Emperor of China. What was more, Peter O'Toole was to play the emperor's tutor, Reginald Johnson. I rang the press office of Columbia Pictures, the production company in Hollywood, and was sent enough material to produce a solid proposal which the Observer took and a trip to China was on the cards. Full of anticipation, I went to their Embassy to obtain necessary visas, and to the newspaper to collect my Air China ticket - First Class this time.

28 August. BBC Radio 4 programme Kaleidoscope engaged me to write, present, script and package a piece on work in progress on Bertolucci's film *The Last Emperor in China*. Work included collecting interviews.

31 August. I embarked on my trip to China, on the other side of the world, finally to get my interview with Peter O'Toole. Next day, my first evening in Beijing, staying at the Beijing Hotel on Tiananmen Square, the film's publicity team announced that they were taking me for 'a real Chinese meal' at a nearby restaurant. The food was magnificent, and so was the rice wine. By the time I got back to the hotel, my head was reeling slightly. My publicity friends left me at the entrance. The foyer of the Beijing is a long one and, as I made my way towards the lift, from a bar on the right came an easily recognisable figure. The rice wine propelled me forward and I called out greeting.

'Peter O'Toole!'

He turned towards me. 'Yes, dear boy?'

'I'm here from the Observer to cover the film but I'm told that you won't give me an interview.' He beamed at me as one drunk to another. 'Of course I will, old boy. Come and see me in my caravan at 3 o'clock tomorrow afternoon.' And, with a pat on the arm and a cheery wave he wove his way off towards his bed. I had my interview date and wove my way on towards my bed.

1986

2 September. Watching Bertolucci at work was a revelation. Deep inside the labyrinthine Forbidden City, in the open space between of the Great Hall of Eternal Prosperity and the Halls of Cloudless Heaven and Earthly Tranquillity, princes, mandarins, eunuchs and banner men were drawn up in serried ranks - all members of the People's Revolutionary Army, decked out in heavy costumes from the China's Manchu past. A quiet word from the director was then bellowed forth in Chinese through a megaphone, taking the gathered company through its paces as the cameras rolled. Bertolucci, observing the action through his lens, resembled a monk at prayer. 'I feel a bit like Cecil B. de Mille,' he said aloud to one of his assistants.

I made my way past three huge mobile generators with Roma number plates, imported from Italy by Bertolucci, and found Peter O'Toole's caravan parked in one of the many courtyards around the Forbidden City. The actor was in a scholarly mood. The interior of his temporary home was both a place to take a nap and also a study. He sat at a desk wearing a pair of gold-rimmed reading glasses, looking like a bookish don. Before him he had a copy of the autobiography of Reginald Johnston, the Emperor's tutor - his character in the film - and he referred to it frequently. He had clearly thought deeply about the part and happily gave me an interview expounding on it and expressing his appreciation of Bertolucci's directing technique. 'Watch him. He doesn't sit in his caravan as some do. He sets up every shot himself. And when that is in the can, watch where his eye goes - straight to his viewfinder for the next shot.'

He was right and that evening the viewfinder was at work again. The Peking Opera was being filmed in the quaintly named Building For Seeing Opera, the Royal Theatre of the Forbidden City. Black-clad Mongolian princes in fur hats with red feathers clustered around the stage. On cue, the performers slid easily into their spectacular routines, cymbals clashing, drums drumming, the picturesque characters weaving and tumbling, their decorated staves swinging, their curved blades flashing in that breath-taking display of ritualistic acrobatics which was their hallmark. The cameras whirred and wove, the Mongolian princes watched on stolidly. However, they were meant to react. Shooting them later, Bertolucci cavorted across the stage waving an old jumper to get their eyes and laughter to follow the action. Some sacrilegious journalist standing nearby applauded. 'Last Tango in the Forbidden City,' he sniggered. At around 1.30am, after some six hours of shooting, he called for another take. But, the translated direction was too late to catch the remaining group of Chinese extras. It is long past their bedtime and they'd disappeared.

Talking to the Chinese actors was a story in itself - actors who had, or whose ancestors had, left their ancient birth-place to live in America and were thoroughly delighted to be back to their roots, drawing on them with relish and undisguised excitement. Jon Lone, Victor Wong and Joan Chen were enjoying visiting their homeland as much as filming with Bertolucci. I found them in the morning in a Beijing park where they had joined the locals in the gentle choreography of Tai Chi, the slow-motion Chinese exercises which spoke of Confucius rather than Bertolucci.

Next day. I had my questions prepared to interview Bertolucci but was told by the publicity people to wait until they called me. On the 5th the call came. I was led to a quiet courtyard where chairs had been set out for us. After a short wait, Bertolucci arrived, straight from the set. The friendly smile set the tone for the interview. It was as though he was sharing confidences with me and spoke of his films as he might have spoken about poetry. Every shot, every movement of the camera, the play of darkness and light within each movie contributed to the experience he wished to create for the viewer, he told me. The filming of *The Last Emperor* was set out for me in the context of the lighting for his whole oeuvre. Bertolucci spoke eloquently about *1900*, *The Conformist*, and *Last Tango In Paris* - the camerawork and lighting and the meaning he attached to them. It was a brilliant essay in the art of movie-making from one of the genre's greatest practitioners. As we ended, I thanked him profusely for what was a fascinating interview. Then, I glanced down at my tape recorder: to my horror the 'Pause' button was on. The tape hadn't moved an inch. He saw the look on my face.

'You didn't get any of that did you?' he asked.

'No,' I replied thoroughly pathetically.

He smiled broadly. 'Let's do it again,' he said in the most matter-of-fact way. We did the whole interview all over again, and he was just as brilliant as he had been the first time. I can't imagine anyone else I ever interviewed who would have pulled that off with such aplomb, and this was a film director in the middle of making a highly complicated movie with a huge cast. If there are great men, I thought, my vote goes to Bernardo Bertolucci.[11]

He introduced me to his friend and mentor, the elderly Alberto Moravia who walked with sticks, still suffering from the results of a childhood illness, apparently. But his blue eyes were clear and busily taking in everything around him, not needing a notebook or tape recorder like me. I remembered reading *The Woman of Rome* as an undergraduate, and regarded him with some awe. Bertolucci's film *The Conformist* was based on one of Moravia's well over thirty novels.

While in China, there was another riveting story I wanted to chase up. I had been told about the Western communists, who had chosen to live in Mao's China and had even been given a few leads by a producer for the BBC's World Service. His father was David Crook who worked at the Foreign Languages University in Beijing. The list I took to China, thanks to this contact, included an American with a Chinese wife, an English woman with a Chinese husband, and a man who call himself British but had never set foot in the country, having been born and educated in Shanghai. They ranged from hard-nosed, fanatical communists to those for whom their Marxism was a secular version of Christianity. A number of

---

[11] 14 October. (This is supplementary to contract dated 28 August). I received additional fees from BBC Radio 4, Kaleidoscope for writing, presenting and scripting a piece on work in progress on Bertolucci's film *The Last Emperor In China*. Broadcast on 6 October and repeated on 7 October.

them were children of missionaries who had chosen to stay on after Mao took over in 1949.

5th. I also called the Observer in London, outlining the story, and they agreed to extend my ticket and hotel accommodation for a further week. My first interviewee, David Crook, had been converted to communism while studying at New York's Columbia University in the 1930s. In 1936 he had gone to Spain to fight with the International Brigade. One thing he told me during our interview stayed in my mind. 'I fought in Spain, and came East after reading Edgar Snow's Red Star Over China.' (That remark gave me the lead to a great story about Orwell when I came to write his biography sixteen years later). After being wounded at the Battle of Jarama, Crook had been recruited by the NKVD to spy on the English Trotskyists with whom George Orwell was fighting. Orwell and his wife had to leave Spain in a hurry to avoid arrest and possible execution by the communist secret police, and it was Crook's reports that put them in the greatest danger. (I knew nothing of this at the time, and only found out about Crook's involvement with Orwell much later when writing his (Orwell's) biography.) But, talking to the British Marxists, including Gladys Young, proved to be one of my most fruitful adventures. I managed two full length documentaries for BBC radio, and items for ABC radio, the CBC radio, and an article for the BBC's weekly review, The Listener.

In my Observer article about the filming, I tried to capture the atmosphere and the spectacle of Bertolucci in action, as well as the experience seen through the eyes of some of his leading crew, players and members of the numerous company this brilliant director had mobilised for the creation of the movie. The Forbidden City, the presence of so many actors and creative crewmen with the great Bertolucci orchestrating the intricate action was a remarkable sight.[12]

1987

3 April. Gaythorne Sylvester called, saying he would like me to cover the filming of a BBC drama, *The Vision*, for the Observer.

'In what exotic location is this to be filmed,' I asked.

'Swindon,' he said.

Two weeks later, Gaythorne asked me to cover another filming, this time of Hanif Kureishi's *Sammy and Rosie Get Laid*. I interviewed Kureishi, at his West London flat. Like me, he had read for a degree in philosophy, but was committed to writing novels. However, he had succeeded where I had not. He was very straight, honest about his work and one of the easiest people to interview. *Sammy and Rosie Get Laid* was recorded (CBC Radio) on the 1st September.

18 September. I recorded interviews, writing and presenting script for BBC Radio 4 on *Stepchildren of the Dragon*.

*

Before I set out on my great journey in search of *The Vision*, I had to speak to the man ultimately responsible for this project – Michael Grade. I rang the BBC, hoping to catch Mr. Grade in his office with a spare moment for a chat. Instead, I was told he would call me back and of course he did so, when I was least expecting it, catching me completely on the hop.

26th May. Michael Grade filled in the background to the film for me. The fear was that some independent television company with oodles of money would buy up all the sports events, and leave

---

[12] My Observer article on *Fall of the House of Manchu* appeared in the Observer Magazine on 23 November, and *Bertolucci Brings Back Imperial China*, in the New York Times on 1 February, 1987. (BBC World Service, Title: Meridian, I wrote and presented *The Last Emperor* on Saturday, 27th February 1988 with three repeats.

others with nothing. In this story, they were bought up by an American fundamentalist Christian sect, intent on getting its message across. The play would star Dirk Bogarde and the female interest would be provided by Lee Remick, Eileen Atkins and Helena Bonham Carter. I'd grabbed a pencil and scribbled down Grade's words as best I could, but in future I'd have to find a means of recording telephone interviews directly.

I drove down to Swindon and found my way to the film set. It was a huge aircraft hangar, with helicopters flying noisily overhead. I met the screenwriter, William Nicholson, who had already written several play scripts for the BBC, including most notably the screenplay for *Shadowlands*, which later became a movie. David M. Thomson, the film's producer, took charge of me and arranged the various interviews. Lee Remick, a very engaging woman, living with her husband in a caravan on the set, gave me an extremely informative interview, as did Helena Bonham Carter. My final interview was with Dirk Bogarde. Thomson told me that Dirk was very reluctant to speak to the press but finally, he had been convinced to talk to me. He chose to meet me just inside one of the hangars and that interview was almost drowned out by hovering helicopters. As we talked, I gained the impression that, he had chosen this noisy spot deliberately, so that, the recording could never be used for broadcasting. He had some rather eccentric ideas, I thought. There were forces, represented by the mass media, that were threatening to take over the world, he suggested, quite seriously. This film was a warning. His whole attitude was strangely gloomy, almost bitter. Afterwards, I tried to get him talking about his literary life in France, especially in Paris, but he was not in any mood to talk further. We shook hands and parted. I discovered later that his partner, Tony Forwood, then living in France, was extremely ill with Parkinson's disease. And Bogarde himself was unwell (he suffered a minor stroke shortly after the filming). Under those conditions, I too, would have been a little more than grumpy.

1987

It was the last filming I covered for the Observer.[13] Both the editor and Gaythorne had moved on, and I got caught up in other matters to achieve my aim; on becoming an author, with the support of my partner, Ramdei Rhoda.

---

[13] *In The Beginning Was The Vision* had appeared in the Observer Magazine on 13 December.

PART TWO

Chapter 15

My First Biography

1984-1993

This section of my Diaries will have to begin in 1984 when I was still a senior lecturer at Goldsmiths' College. I stopped going to Canada as a visiting professor. My partner, Rhoda (later my wife), and I planned to take early retirement so that I could become a full-time author.

30th March to 1st April. I planned and organised the First International Malcolm Lowry Conference at Goldsmiths' College, University of London. Paul Tiessen, Professor at Wilfred Laurier University, Waterloo, Ontario, Canada, generously publicised it in the Malcolm Lowry Newsletter in Canada. Paul and I found ourselves playing hosts and joint editors of the proceedings.

The idea for a Goldsmiths' conference on Malcolm Lowry began on 3rd November 1983, after a Saturday afternoon class which involved a lecture from Ron Binns, a writer, and the showing of the National Film Board of Canada's documentary feature film *Volcano*. Some sixty people attended and their enthusiasm for Lowry led us to believe that a conference would attract a keen audience. Ron Binns and I set the programme, and I began to get the organisation going at Goldsmiths' College.

However, a weekend long conference on Malcolm Lowry presented certain problems, but this I did with the valuable help of

1984

Peter Bindley, Deputy Dean of Adult Studies at Goldsmiths' College. Paul's generous publicity of the conference in the Malcolm Lowry Newsletter brought in expressions of interest from Lowry scholars: from Canada, United States of America, Brazil, Belgium and Japan, as well as England, Scotland and Wales. We christened it the *First International Conference on the Life and Work of Malcolm Lowry*, 1984.

After, he left UNESCO, Richard Hoggart became Warden of Goldsmiths', and I got to know him fairly well. He was interested in my Lowry project and agreed to open our conference. Being a Northerner like Lowry, I think he had a partiality for him, even though Lowry was not a working-class boy like himself and had lived on a private income. He took a particular interest in the family photographs that I had pinned up at the entrance to the conference hall, and gave a perfectly judged speech of introduction, welcoming visitors from abroad as well as from Britain.

One day, who should turn up from California but Danny Huston and his mother who were in London for the London première of *Under the Volcano* in May. A bottle of Mezcal, the drink to which Lowry was addicted, sat on the chairperson's table throughout the proceedings and was appropriately consumed on the final day.

Arthur Calder-Marshall, an English novelist, essayist, critic, and biographer, rang me a day or two before the conference and, making a great point of it, asked me to ensure that there was a jug of water and a glass on the table from which he would be speaking.

6 July. With all this under my belt, I wrote out a proposal and sent it to Jonathan Cape, Lowry's publisher. To my delight, I was invited to meet Senior Editor, Liz Calder. She expressed great interest in my proposed book and Tom Maschler, she said, wanted me to write a specimen introductory chapter. I didn't really feel up to doing anything of the sort because, at that stage, I didn't have all of the material on Lowry that I needed to reflect back and forth on his life. I started working steadily, especially on Russell Lowry's

notes on his brother Malcolm for Tom Maschler. I did what I could and sent in my introductory chapter.

31 July. I was invited a second time to Cape's headquarters in Bedford Square and there again I met Liz Calder. After a pleasant preliminary chat with her, Tom Maschler, tall and immensely self-assured, came striding into the room with my introductory chapter his hand. 'Well,' he said. 'This is very boring.' What he had been hoping for, he said, was something along the lines of George D. Painter's *Marcel Proust; A Biography*. I sat there toughing out the rest of the interview, but I didn't feel like trying particularly hard for Jonathan Cape. Tom Maschler asked me to write another specimen chapter. I said I would and wished him and Liz Calder goodbye. I found out afterwards that Painter's biography of Proust was one of the greatest in the English language. In the circumstances, it wasn't difficult to decide what to do. Returning to Maschler with another specimen chapter at that stage, and having at the same time to compete with one of the greatest biographers of all time, was as grim a form of torture as anyone could have devised in times of peace. However, I eventually sent Tom Maschler another specimen chapter.

1985

1 January. I am at the brink of taking a gamble - to retire early as soon as is possible to catch the freedom that had eluded me for so long. I will have to dedicate myself to writing or abandon the idea for ever. There can be no more excuse that I lack experience. I have had several life times of that which many successful authors have gone through. Now I read. Now I write. I discussed this idea of course with Rhoda who supported me fully.

8 August. *Malcolm Lowry Remembered* was duly published by the BBC, attracting some decent reviews in the press - especially the Guardian and the Listener. It was certainly a step towards my very first literary biography. 25th. I am working steadily on Russell Lowry's notes on brother Malcolm for Cape.

1986

30 November. I organised and chaired a study conference at Goldsmiths' College on: *Teaching Under The Volcano*, that involved a lecture on the novel *Under The Volcano* from Dr. Duncan Hadfield, a writer. Some fifty people attended and they were very enthusiastic.

1986

10 April. Rhoda and I went on the trail of Malcolm Lowry in Paris. On the next day, we made our way to the Luxembourg Gardens in search of the Statue of George Sand where James Stern says Malcolm Lowry lay down and drunkenly serenaded her after a twenty-four-hour alcohol parade through Paris in 1933. Unfortunately, we didn't find the Statue of George Sand due mainly to the weather. Two days later, we went to Chartres and it snowed a blizzard (almost). This 13th century cathedral with intricate stained-glass window was impressive, but cold, dark and somewhat empty interior. Not empty, of course, but had strange Gothic stone carvings and the so called 'Veil of Mary'. Rhoda lit a candle to the 'Veil of Mary.' I had a sense of long history of religious persuasion in Europe. It was still snowing outside, and we returned promptly to our hotel. Among the many places we visited, was the Marie of the Fourteenth Arrondissement where Malcolm and Jan were married on the 6th January 1934. Julian Trevelyan was best man and his beautiful girl friend, Louise Scherpenberg, a New York artist, was the bridesmaid. We then walked to the Villa Brune off the rue Des Plantes, where Trevelyan was living with Louise. A wedding breakfast was held at Trevelyan's studio.

15 April, Jean Genet, a French novelist, playwright, poet, essayist and political activist, died.

23 April. The day we left Paris, Simone de Beauvoir died.

1987

18 April, Unfortunately, my proposed Malcolm Lowry biography had been gently turned down by Maschler at Jonathan Cape.

GLIMPSES OF A BIOGRAPHER'S DIARY

Also on 18 April. I wrote in my diary, 'Today, I have decided to abandon Lowry's biography in favour of writing a novel. It isn't the first time I've made that decision, but it does take the weight off my mind.' I discussed my feelings and my decision with Rhoda. She is a very good listener, and, without realising it, she was counselling me. After that discussion, I decided not to abandon the biography. I had been on Lowry's trail too long now, interviewing his brother, Russell, many times, many of his friends, colleagues, as well as collecting materials, letters, photographs and actually I had immersed myself too deeply and must continue. After that, I made a vow to get an agent and go on from there.

8 May. I travelled from Gatwick to Vancouver for the Canadian Malcolm Lowry Conference to which I was invited to present a paper on Lowry. It was held at the University of British Columbia's (UBC) enormous campus. About 150 international academics from Australia, New Mexico, America, Japan, Germany, Belgium, Spain, Britain and, of course, Canada. This conference was held in Vancouver where Lowry wrote his final master piece *Under the Volcano*. Actually, he conceived and began it in Mexico in 1938 and, it was then typed by his first wife, Jan. When he was living in his 'beloved shack' among a colony of squatters' huts at Dollarton, just outside Vancouver, the many drafts were typed by his second wife, Margerie, and it was published in 1947. The discussions that followed the papers presented with pleasure and anticipation, were of a very high quality, exciting, vigorous and continued at mealtimes, and in residences. I spent some time researching Lowry's special collection at the UBC Library. I met the archivist, Anne, many of Lowry's heavyweight scholars and writers including David Markson who, when age 23 and writing a thesis on *Under the Volcano*, had met and stayed with Lowry and Margerie at Dollarton. Malcolm and Margerie had corresponded regularly with David. At this Conference, I gained tremendously useful information from talks, knowledgeable discussions, debates and at the UBC Library.

16 May, I returned home with the sense that, 'I am getting to know this genius more and more, and it was a good feeling.' Back home, I felt sympathetic vibes coming from Liz Calder at Jonathan Cape,

and thought it was a pity that it wasn't up to her to give me the commission. Later it was announced in the press that she was one of a group who were about to set up a new publishing house to be called Bloomsbury.

18 May. I sent her my proposal with a note saying, 'No more specimen chapters.' Soon after, I received a letter from her accepting the proposal, hinting at an advance, and summoning me to Bloomsbury's temporary offices in Bloomsbury Square. I was early getting there and, so, took a stroll along Southampton Row where, I came upon a bookshop – a place always difficult to resist. On entering, one of the first books I spotted on prominent display, was a new book by Malcolm Bradbury entitled: *No, Not Bloomsbury*. Lowry would have instantly regarded that as an omen, a cryptic warning worth heeding.

Liz was in a cheerful mood and told me that they were able to offer me an advance for the world rights. But, the words 'world rights' worried me. I told her that I would be bringing in an agent to which she replied, 'Why would you need one? You've already got your publisher.' She said, 'You should talk to our rights manager,' and, then took me upstairs to another office, leaving me there to discuss rights with one of her colleagues. The rights manager was a pleasant young American lady. She ran me through what the firm intended, which was to sell the American rights to a US publisher. None of that money would come to me but, would repay them for the advance they were giving me. That idea just didn't appeal and I said simply that I would think about it. Nevertheless, Liz followed up our meeting by putting her offer in writing to me. Much later, we met and, I explained why I had rejected her offer. She was friendly and understanding as usual.

I found an agent through my good friend, Neville Braybrooke, an ebullient writer I had met at PEN's Writers' Day on 22 March 1986. He recommended me to Bruce Hunter who, acted for him at David Higham. I wrote to Mr. Hunter, sending him my CV, and a copy of *Malcolm Lowry Remembered*. These were passed on to a younger member of staff, Anthony Goff, whose job it was to bring on new young writers. I was, it was decided, an acceptable client.

4 August. My new agent, Anthony Goff, invited me to meet him. When I showed him my letter from Bloomsbury with its offer of an advance, he said that he would ask to see the proposed contract and discuss it with Liz Calder. But for some reason or another, Liz did not return his calls, and he asked me if I would mind him offering it to someone else. It wasn't long afterwards that he phoned to say he had had an offer from William Collins to match the one from Bloomsbury. Collins were asking for no more than UK and Commonwealth rights, leaving Canadian and US rights free for us to sell. Of course I agreed.

11 September. I went to Collins to discuss my Lowry biography with Ariane Goodman, the editor. She was a very good listener, patient, encouraging and helpful.

3 December. Anthony sent me my Lowry biography contract with Collins which I signed and returned. I prepared myself to write my first biography, to be called *Pursued by Furies, A Life of Malcolm Lowry*.

Lowry was quite a commitment. When I informed an American friend about the commission, he said, 'Congratulations. But did you know that the first two biographers of Lowry committed suicide? They blew their brains out, like Hemingway.' I thanked him for his words of encouragement and said, 'I'd keep my shotgun firmly locked away, together with the rest of my extensive gun collection' (I have no shotgun nor any gun collection).

I had done a lot of research and interviews already for my radio programme and on my BBC book: *Malcolm Lowry Remembered*. Also, in 1987, my book *Malcolm Lowry Under the Volcano*, A CaseBook Series for MacMillan Education was published. But, there was far more to be done, an incalculable amount in fact. So, I was quite keen to meet Malcolm Lowry's first wife, Jan Gabrial. David Markson, the American novelist, whom I had met at the Malcolm Lowry Conference in Vancouver gave me her phone number. He had got it from one of the directors of that Canadian film *Volcano* -

the man who had tracked her down but, was too late to put her into the movie. David had been sworn to secrecy but, for a friend, he said, he would let me have it.

Some time back, an American woman, whom I had met in London wanted an Englishman to squire her around town. I did accompany her once or twice, and she invited me to visit her whenever I was in Los Angeles. So, I rang and informed her that I would shortly be going to L.A. and, she invited me to Hollywood.

28 December, I rang Jan and she invited me to stay.

30 December. I flew out from Heathrow to Los Angeles, planning to visit the Huntington Library, which housed some Conrad Aiken and Lowry materials, and to go on afterwards to Jan Gabrial. On the plane coming over, the in-flight movie had a character saying, 'Go to a party in Hollywood and everyone there is a producer, all with proposals for the greatest movie ever and it's always starring Faye Dunaway.'

Back again in Hollywood, when I had once left in haste, I checked into a hotel and rang Jan to let her know that I would be on my way on the 1st January 1988. I then rang the lady whom I had squired around London just to say, I was there and would be staying with other friends after a night or two in town. She told me, 'This evening I am going to a party for Oscar screenwriter winners and would you like to accompany me?' Would I not? 'Of course,' I said. Many of those present at the party were producers hoping to pitch a new film to one of the studios. Circulating at the party, I found myself in conversation with a couple of young partygoers, a man and a woman. After the introductions, the woman said, 'What are you doing here?' I told her that I was a guest of one of those with an invitation. 'And what is it that you do?' she asked.

I said, 'I am a writer.'

I asked, 'And what about you two?'

'We are producers,' she said.

Her colleague chipped in. 'We have a great proposal which we are trying to sell here. It stars Faye Dunaway.'

I hope that I concealed my amusement and tried to look suitably impressed. Well, I thought, that's Hollywood for you, and wished them the best of good luck.

My squire returned. She asked me, 'Would you like to meet one of the screenwriters of Casablanca?' 'I most certainly would,' I replied. Julius Epstein was about 80 years of age, that was a decent age for someone who had survived the rough and tumble of so many Hollywood years. He had written the screenplay for Casablanca in 1942 with his brother, Philip, who had died in 1952. 'It was nothing special,' he told me. 'It was just another movie as far as we were concerned.' And they hadn't needed Faye Dunaway; they had Ingrid Bergman, not to mention Humphrey Bogart.

1988

1 January. I hired a car and drove to Encino, L. A. to meet Jan Gabrial, as planned. (Jan and Malcolm Lowry were married in Paris on 6th January 1934 and divorced in 1940.) I found my way along the concatenation of freeways and, at a drugstore, I stopped the car and phoned Jan, informing her where I was. Encino is a friendly little town, with villas spaced out along streets lined with hedgerow plants fringed with bougainvillea and overhung by genuflecting palm trees. Here, at the end of a short drive, in a handsome bungalow, lived the first wife of Malcolm Lowry, my mad, drunken subject and author of some of the most beautiful, rich and ornate prose to have ever fallen from an English pen.

Now here was a woman he had loved to distraction and, to whom he had penned a multitude of letters pleading his undying devotion and displayed his genius in the process. This was the woman whom, he had dazzled, ensorcelled and tempted into marriage, much to the dismay of his friends, who saw him as the last man any woman would be advised to hitch herself to.

Arriving at her house, I found her waiting for me. As I climbed out of the car she called to me, 'Were you ever in theatre, Gordon?'

1988

She asked. 'Well, not since I was a student', but, like many others, an actor-manqué who as a journalist and hunter of London theatre, had rubbed shoulders with the best thespians then around.

12 - Jan Gabrial, Encino

She was a small woman and, even at 77, still very pretty. I could well imagine young Lowry being bowled over by her when they met in Granada, Spain in 1933 at the Villa Carmona pension. Jan had a lovely architect-built house in the Mexican style, with an outdoor swimming pool and a large games room which had doubled as her late husband's study. She said, 'That is now my study.'

Jan made me very welcome and, after a cup of coffee we sat in her dining-room, talking about her life with Malcolm and, she showed me an album of photographs. 'Some pictures of Malcolm.' She said. Those were amazing images completely new to me. I was particularly taken by three of him; one on board the Norwegian ship that took him to Oslo in 1931, where he met Nordhal Grieg, the Norwegian novelist, whose influence on his first novel *Ultramarine* is palpable; one of him at Chartres and another in his room in New York in 1935. They were gold dust for biographer.

'Oh!, I said. 'I'd love to use these three in my book. Can I get a copy of each?' She snatched away the album.

'No,' she said - rather curtly, I flinched.

I have brought my tape recorder. Could we do an interview sometime before I leave?

'No,' she snapped.

She left the room. I sat there. Clearly I had brought too much expectation with me. I sat twiddling my thumbs, trying to remember the photographs, glimpsed all too fleetingly: the young man in a sailor's jersey on the deck of the *Favervik*, casually posed one hand on a piece of rigging; the young man sitting at a cafe table in Chartres and, another in his room in New York. Could I conjure anything from such lightening-flashed revelation of a long-dead ghost?

She came back and, invited me to join her for cocktails. We found ourselves chatting away. It was as if she was getting something off her chest after a long period of self-restraint. We found we were agreeing about politics. After cocktails, came dinner with good Californian wine. Then, she regaled me with stories about her tumultuous marriage to Malcolm, their meeting in Granada in 1933, his pursuit of her in brilliantly lyrical letters full of poetry and passion as she carried on journeying around Europe. The next day, she carried on from where we left off yesterday. She told me about their reunion in England when, she discovered his alcohol compulsion, their marriage in Paris, their briefly idyllic creative work in New York, disrupted when, he again took to the bottle and, ended up in Bellevue Hospital's psychiatric ward, their escape to Mexico and the stormy end to the relationship as fiery Mexican liquor left him raving and violent, her escape to Los Angeles and the end of the affair. She had supplied me with enough new material to make my book distinctive. All I had to do was to get her to tell the story over again into my tape recorder. In the evening, she showed me some of the notebooks and letters she had, which Malcolm had left behind at her mother's house after they had separated. Also, she showed me a copy of *Ultramarine* signed by Malcolm, a present to her mother and, a notebook which he had taken into Bellevue Hospital in 1936 and, in which he had written notes under the title: *Delirium on East River* that would one day emerge from a long process of writing and revision as *Lunar Caustic*.

I said, 'Could I possibly look through them?'

'No,' she said sharply.

Well, nothing like being direct, I thought. When she told me later that she was herself writing *My Life with Malcolm Lowry*, the penny dropped. Of course, she wanted the material for her own book and, so, I didn't press her after that to let me see them. But, I did talk her into giving me four long interviews about her marriage to Malcolm and their lives together, which she did quite willingly and graciously. Later on, she gave me the photograph of Malcolm on board the Norwegian ship, and even allowed me to see Malcolm's notebooks and letters (which, she later sold to me.)

Next morning after breakfast, she went out for the morning and gave me the run of the place. After lunch, we began talking about Malcolm in particular and about world events in general. Her views were distinctly left-wing and, I said to her that in many books about Malcolm she was described as a communist. She bridled at that.

'I'm a liberal!' she snapped, and I later discovered why she was so touchy on the subject. When she and Malcolm divorced in 1940, she had joined the *Anti-Nazi League*. At some point during the war, she had agreed to bear witness for a union leader threatened with deportation. She showed up at the court playing the part of the 'glamorous woman of mystery'. The judge, or so, she recalled, was rather taken with her and, the man was let off. However, in 1947, after she had remarried, she received an early morning visit from the FBI who, questioned her about her politics. Her husband, a wealthy real estate gentleman, said, 'We have to get this stopped,' and managed to get her FBI record destroyed. Nevertheless, she still didn't want it thought that she was a communist.

4 January. I headed off to the Huntington Library, threading my way through the spaghetti junctions and, along the spidery freeways of Southern California to San Marino where, the library was housed in a handsome building in 120 acres of botanical gardens. There, I found a large collection of letters and material relating to Conrad Aiken, Lowry's dark angel, who encouraged some of the worst aspects of young Malcolm's delicately-balanced personality, especially his drunken rowdiness and tendency to plagiarise. It was worth the trip and, I came away with several photocopies of letters

and materials which, I thought, threw light on the wayward Englishman's teenage years.

On my return to Encino, in the driveway of Jan's house, I saw a parked police car bearing the logo of the LAPD. Inside the house were a couple of tough-looking female cops, who brought to my mind *Cagney and Lacey*, the two tough LA law officers in the television series of that name. Jan told me that while she had been out that day, the house had been burgled – a ring which Malcolm had given to her in Mexico had been stolen. My first thought was that I had brought her terribly bad luck. However, what riveted me was that one of the policewomen, standing at a table, was loading a revolver, methodically inserting bullets into the chambers and then spinning it with a professional flick of her wrist.

'Is that the revolver they issue you with at the LAPD?' I asked.

Jan butted in. 'No, that's my gun and from now on I'm sleeping with it under my pillow,' she said.

Any idea of searching to take a peep at her letters in the middle of the night, was promptly banished from my mind. Confronting a trigger-happy Jan at midnight was the last thing I wanted, just as we'd become friends. At breakfast one morning, Jan said, 'Having these conversations with you reminds me of conversations I had with Malcolm.' That came as a big surprise, but I knew that this friendship, much as I was coming to value it, was very important for my book. She had other surprises in store for me, telling me that she had seen the Huston movie of *The Volcano* and, had found Finney's performance as the Consul uncannily accurate - 'It was exactly Malcolm as I knew him,' she said.

5 January. We had an enjoyable supper at Café Casino. When we arrived home, I discovered that I had left my raincoat behind. So, I rang the Café. The check-out young lady answered the telephone and I informed her that I had left my raincoat hanging up there when we left the Café. She told me to hold on, she returned and said, 'The raincoat was found and it was given to the manager. Better collect it tomorrow as we are about to close.'

1988

Next day, 6th, was Jan and Malcolm's Wedding Anniversary. We decided that we would go out and celebrate, especially as I was going to write my biography on Lowry and she was writing her own book. However, at 9.30am, I first went to Café Casino to collect my raincoat. When I arrived, I said to the man at the counter, 'I have come to collect my raincoat.' He went away and returned saying, 'the coat is not in the manager's office.' He called the checkout young lady from the night before who confirmed that she had given it to the manager. He was not there. I returned at 5.30pm, to pick up my rain coat and the manager said, 'It's been stolen.'

'But last night,' I said, 'when I rang, I was told that it had been given to the manager.'

He said, 'No, the checkout girl saw it hanging up and when she turned her back, it was taken.' I did not believe him. I told him that I would report this to the police, which I did. I rang Rhoda at home and told her about this incident. She said, ' you won't get your raincoat back. Forget it, and, buy another coat.' Wise Rhoda.

I was determined not to allow this incident to mar Jan's celebration. So we went out to a restaurant and had a delicious dinner. It was a lively talkative evening. So much to talk about.

7th, I went to the Los Angeles Police Department, made my statement, received an incident report, paid $8.00 for the report and left, taking Rhoda's advice and buying myself a new coat. Returned to Jan's house, I spent the day putting all my collections from the Huntington Library together, making records in my note-books, having lively talks and discussions with Jan and making notes of these later in my room. Jan, of course, was writing her own remarkable stories about talented Malcolm and the highs and lows of their marriage. At the same time, she was quite happy to tell me more about their lives together for my book.

On the 11th. I rang Rhoda to let her know that I would be leaving Los Angeles Airport at about 17.45pm and, hoped to arrive at

GLIMPSES OF A BIOGRAPHER'S DIARY

Heathrow at about 12.00 next day. She was at the airport, we collected our car and drove home - to blessed peace.

I began my book on the Amstrad computer and, abandoned my trusty old electric portable and heavy German typewriter, both of which, had seen me through all my past efforts at journalism. I typed every letter, every document and every interview of Lowry onto the new Amstrad, together with every other document I could find - birth, marriage and death certificates, newspaper clippings, memoirs and reviews.

24 March. I travelled from Heathrow to Vancouver for three weeks to continue my research on Lowry's special collection at the University of British Columbia (UBC) Library. This time, I was invited by Anne Yandle to stay at her home. This UBC Library houses a remarkable collection of Lowry materials. Anne was an outstandingly helpful professional archivist and, had the library's best interest at heart always. I met more enthusiastic scholars and writers.

13 April. Loaded with Lowry's documents and letters etc., I left Vancouver by Air Canada for Heathrow via Amsterdam. Rhoda was waiting for me, and again we collected our car and, I drove us home.

Back home, I embarked on more serious research for my book. Once again, I interviewed Professor Muriel Bradbrook at her home in Cambridge and, visited Cambridge University and Library. Also, I interviewed Dr Kathleen Raine, Anthony Burgess, visited the University of London Library and Colindale to collect photocopies. I met and interviewed more friends of Malcolm Lowry: Carole Phillips and her brothers, Sue Vice, Roger Davenport (John Davenport's son), Neville Braybrooke and Jim Hepburn and, of course, Russell Lowry and his son Colin among others.

21 May. I rang and spoke with Priscilla Bonner, Margerie's sister, a silent-screen actress as well, during Margerie's times there. I told her that I would visit Los Angeles later in the year to continue my research and, would like to interview her, to which she agreed.

1988

Just as I was embarking seriously on my research, a very sad event occurred. On the 4th October. Betty Moss, a compassionate woman, who had been caring for Margerie Lowry, Malcolm's second wife, who had been ill since suffering a stroke many years ago, phoned me.

She said, 'I have some sad news. Margerie is dead. She died on 28 September.'

I was lost for words.

'I'm with her at Heathrow,' she said.

'Oh,' I stuttered, now quite mystified. 'How did you travel?'

She said, 'We flew. Margerie's in "Freight" until I can arrange for her to be buried. She wants to be buried in the same grave as Malcolm. I'm planning to call the vicar and make the necessary arrangements, then go down to Ripe for the burial. Once, it's been fixed up, will you accompany me?'

I naturally said, 'Of course. Call me when you have the date and time and I'll meet you at the churchyard.' Betty was on her own in London for this very sorrowful event and I felt that I must be there to support her.

Next day, she called again. 'I've spoken to the vicar. Burying her in Malcolm's grave would mean disinterring him,' she said, 'and that would be a long process getting permission from police, magistrates, archbishops and, I don't know who else, so, I've arranged for her to be buried in a new grave not too far from Malcolm. The burial is in two days' time at 9.30am.'

'Sounds fine,' I told her and said, 'I will meet you at Ripe churchyard in East Sussex.'

It would involve getting away from London early, before the morning traffic become too heavy.

7 October. I made it in good time and met the coffin bearers waiting in the churchyard with a large shiny metal coffin. A plaque

on the side of it read, 'Made from Genuine Chicago Steel.' Inside lay the body of a mummified Margerie. I was very moved and felt quite sad not to have met her in life. Betty duly arrived and, the ceremony began - a short service in which the vicar read the eulogy handed to him by Betty. Margerie was a faithful and loving wife of a genius. She was buried a short distance away from Malcolm.

Sybella, one of the two ladies who were present at the funeral invited Betty and I to her house for tea, where we met her husband and her daughter. After a relaxing chat, she took us to the White Cottage, where Malcolm and Margerie had lived and where Malcolm died, and we were shown over the house. I was so pleased that Betty had seen this house. When Betty had had enough, we went to the Yew Tree for drinks and, then to the Metropole on Brighton seafront for lunch. She was a very compassionate, gentle and kindly person and I could not resist commenting 'Now, I have met Lowry's first and second wives.' We just looked at each other. Soon afterwards we said our goodbyes, and I told her that I would be visiting New York, Los Angeles, Mexico and Vancouver later this month. We agreed to meet in LA for an interview.

On my last trip to L. A. on 1st January to stay with Jan, she graciously gave me at least four interviews which I recorded. Even though she was still writing her own memoirs, she was prepared to let me have as much information as possible about Malcolm and their lives. I told her, 'I will return later this year to carry out further research in New York, more at UBC Library, Vancouver, to the Huntington Library and Mexico. Ever generous, she invited me to stay with her.

Now that Jan knew that on my next visit I would be going to New York, she told me about Malcolm's arrival on the 2nd August 1934 to New York to join her. She said, 'Malcolm was in his Herman Melville period and had planned for us to sail at once to New Bedford.' They went to New Bedford, found the place depressing and left immediately for Cape Cod. They stayed at an hotel in Martha's Vineyard where they had a lovers' reunion after weeks of separation. They used to wander many mornings to the pier watching newcomers disembark. Ten days later, they moved to Provincetown where they took a small cottage on the beach at 447 Commercial Street and their stay there was idyllic. Lowry had brought along his Paris Stories and the notes for *In Ballast to the White Sea*. He worked on these steadily, discussing them at length with Jan. Jan herself was working on her book called *I'll See You in Paris*. After this, they spent some valuable time with her mother at Bayside on Long Island. She said, 'That Fall we returned to New York and leased an apartment at 99 Perry Street, Greenwich Village.'

14 October. I flew from London Heathrow at 13.00 hours, arriving at J. F. K New York at 15.45 hours. I checked in at the Sea Shell Hotel overnight and, then went to Cape Cod to see where Malcolm and Jan stayed at the hotel in Martha's Vineyard. The next day, I went to Provincetown. I can well imagine Malcolm being in his element, living by the sea with the ghost of one of his literary heroes in close attendance. The following day, feeling satisfied with my visit to Cape Cod, I travelled to Greenwich Village to meet up with David Markson, the writer I met earlier, and we explored the area where Jan had found a small cosy apartment at 99 Perry Street. Here to Lowry's delight, they were just a few blocks south of Gransvoort Street where Herman Melville had worked as customs inspector. It was a good base from which to launch themselves on to the literary scene. We also explored all the other places mentioned in his notes, talked about Jan and Malcolm, about his many books, about Rhoda and my life in London, went to restaurants, cafés, Central Park and to the library. I visited Bellevue Hospital where I met a doctor who, informed me that Bellevue was, up to 1936, the alcoholic admission hospital and had a reputation for medical and psychiatric care. Later, it had been a pioneering hospital for medical research and provided mental health services for children, adolescents and adults. I felt that I had quite a lot of information here about Jan and Malcolm's life in New York that would be very useful to me when visiting the places she had mentioned to me in January and the many discussions I'd had with David.

GLIMPSES OF A BIOGRAPHER'S DIARY

21 October. I flew from New York to L. A. where I hired a car and drove to Jan's house. As usual, she made me feel very welcome. After a late light supper, we sat talking about my visit to New York. She was engrossed in my findings. She said, 'I told you about our lives when you were here in January. Now, I shall fill in some of the gaps.' She painted a vivid picture of their lives in New York. Later on in my room, I included the gaps in her last interview onto my laptop. During the following days, she talked more about their meeting in Granada, Spain, Paris, London.

On Monday and Tuesday, 24th and 25th, I went to the Huntington Library to continue my research into Conrad Aiken and Malcolm. I came away with further copies of letters and documents that threw more light on the wayward Malcolm's teenage and later years.

Jan knew that I was going to visit Mexico again. She was thinking of coming to Mexico with me but got cold feet at the last minute. I thought, 'She does not want to relive their high and low lives by visiting the place again. It might well be too painful.' However, she agreed to go to Paris with Rhoda and I sometime, to show us over the city where she and Malcolm had married on 6th January 1934.

27th. I met up with Betty Moss. It was good to see her again. She told me about Margerie's life after Malcolm's death which I entered in my note-book. The next day, I met and interviewed Margerie's elderly sister, Priscilla in L.A., a star from the old silent movie days. She would not hear a word against Margerie and, told me all about their family history and time together in Hollywood. 'This would be the last interview on my sister and her drunken husband.' She added, 'Margie pleaded with me never to read Douglas Day's biography of Malcolm, so, I never have.' I urged her to read it, all the same.

Saturday, 29th. I made my second trip to Mexico, taking me back to Cuernavaca, 'under the volcanoes - Popocatépetl and Ixtaccihuatl', the scene of Malcolm and Jan's final fateful months together between 1936 and 1937.

31ˢᵗ. I went to Oaxaca, to the Church of La Soledad where Lowry spent time praying to the Virgin of Soledad, 'the Saint for those who have nobody' as he called her. The ambience there was an artfully-achieved kind of holiness - colourful and gilded icons, beautiful hangings and Churrigueresque architecture. At the high altar, I saw an Indian woman and her small child who was watching her mother closely and, copying her every movement. When, the mother made the sign of the Cross, she made the sign of the Cross. When the mother knelt down to pray, she did the same. When the mother stood up and, again made the sign of the Cross, the child stood up and, made the sign of the Cross too. They departed hand-in-hand. It had been a very lovely glimpse of a perfect mother-child relationship, an indelible memory. It almost moved me to gentle religiosity.

In Oaxaca, on the Day of the Dead I visited the cemetery. There are two days of the Day of the Dead in Mexico: All Saints Day, is from midnight on the 31st October and last for 24 hours. Mexican Indians believe that the spirit of dead children can re-join their families and, their families welcome them back.

From midnight on the 1st November for 24 hours, All Souls' Day, is the day when adult spirits can do the same and, are welcomed back by their families. These two days are Mexican holidays celebrated throughout Mexico. In the Day of the Dead practice, people bring water, food, fruit, wine, bread and other offerings to the graves of their loved ones. On All Souls' Day, families would cover the graves with gay flowers and light candles to illuminate the dead souls' way back to their homes on earth. This is an occasion for remembering and celebrating those who have passed on from this world, while at the same time portraying death in a more positive light, as a natural part of human experience.

3ʳᵈ. I returned to Guernavaca to absorb the culture and the atmosphere of the place. On our last visit to Mexico on the 21st September 1983 for a week, I visited these places when, I was covering the filming *Under the Volcano*, and, where Rhoda had been such a help. It was the town, its hotels, the volcanoes and the barranca that gave Lowry the topography of the fictional town of Quauhnahuac in which to set the story of the violent and dramatic last days in the life of the drunken ex-Consul, Geoffrey Fermin. Calle Humboldt where Malcolm and Jan lived for thirteen-months, became the Calle Nicaragua and, the street at the top which took me to Calle de la Casas became the Calle Tiero de la Fuego. By the time I left Mexico on 5th, I had a strong sense of the spirit of the place which I hoped would infuse that part of my biography of Malcolm Lowry.

From Mexico City Airport, I flew to L. A., hired a car and, drove to Jan's house. She was most curious to hear all about my visit to Mexico. We talked into the night. I felt that she was quite happy to share with me all those details about those places and their lives. She celebrated her birthday on the 6th and, we talked about her book, I gave her as much help as I could. We also discussed my life with Rhoda, with whom, I shared my many calls while I was away. I typed all my findings onto my laptop. sold me lots of materials and books that I shipped home.

8-18 November. I flew to Vancouver to stay with Anne, the archivist, and, to continue with my research at the UBC Library. Once more, I visited Dollarton, interviewed some of Malcolm's neighbours and friends especially Earle and Esther Birney and, saw again the place: shoreline dilapidated old shack - where Malcolm and Margerie had lived and, he wrote the final version of *Under the Volcano*, that Margerie typed, and which became a masterpiece.

16th. I left Vancouver for New York, hired a car, drove to Cambridge, Massachusetts and, booked in at the Holiday Inn. Malcolm came here on 28th July 1929 to be tutored and stay with Conrad Aiken and his wife, Clarissa, in their apartment at 8 Plympton Street. He had been stunned to find someone old enough to be his father with whom, he could talk so explicitly about books, sex, matters scatological and, with whom, he could happily drink himself unconscious. Aiken wrote to a friend shortly afterwards: 'Lowry is a nice chap, but incredibly sloppy and helpless. Writes exceedingly well, should do something undoubtedly, very companionable and trifle vague.'

18th. I flew from J. F. K. Airport to Heathrow, arriving at 08.00am and Rhoda was there to meet me. We collected our car and headed for home,

Shortly, after I returned home, I received a phone call from Betty Moss. Priscilla had decided that she would give me another interview, she said. I flew straight out to LA. Priscilla's whole demeanour had changed from what it had been at our last encounter.

She had read Douglas Day's book, she said, and, having now seen what her sister had told him about her and her family, she was incensed. 'It was all lies,' she said. Then she gave me a picture of a vain teenage flibbertigibbet, who, had little or no 'acting talent, whose first marriage was a disaster as much as her second. And 'Malcolm Lowry,' she said, 'He was a walking disaster - drunk and offensive.' She and her husband had thrown him out of their house when last they visited, and, she never wanted to hear about him again. This went so much against the version of Margerie that so many of the Lowry scholars accepted, and, I realised that this was biographical gold dust.

Now back home, I wanted not only to enter all my most valuable Lowry's materials and letters into my laptop, but, to get on with my lecturing at Goldsmiths'. By then, I was also lecturing on Biographer Studies. Rhoda, bless her, typed some of Lowry's materials and letters into my laptop, whenever she was off duty.

1989

17-19 March. Even though, we had been to Paris often, we decided to go over there again for the weekend. We arrived early on the 17th, and checked in to one of our favourite hotels, Hotel Le Clement at 6 Rue Clement. After a large and delicious coffee and croissant, we left to visit the Mairie of the 14th Arrondissement where Malcolm and his first wife, Jan, were married on the 6th January 1934. We, then headed for the Jardin du Luxembourg in

GLIMPSES OF A BIOGRAPHER'S DIARY

13 - Gordon with Odile Hellier and Raul Ortiz outside the Village Voice Bookshop, Paris

search of the statue of George Sand and, we found it. James Stern, a writer, and Malcolm's friend, told me, 'Malcolm Lowry laid down and drunkenly serenaded her after a twenty-eight-hour alcoholic progress through Paris in 1933.' We had our photographs taken as a memento of this visit to Paris. Next morning, we visited the Village Voice Bookshop, met with Odile and Michael and, among the many issues we talked about, was my pending biography of Malcolm Lowry. We walked to the Cathedral Notre Dame. It is spectacular. Of course, Rhoda lit candles. Notre Dame is renowned for its Lent sermon. We crossed to the Shakespeare and Company Bookshop, one of our favourite haunts, met George Whitman, and after endless talk, he invited us to the regular Sunday tea the following day. The shop sells new and second-hands books, and housed aspiring writers and artists in exchange for helping out around the bookshop. The following day, we walked once again to Shakespeare and Company. I was asked to talk about my forthcoming book, and was invited to return, give a talk and to sign books after publication day. Eventually, it was time to take our flight home. Rhoda and I were very happy that we made this quick trip to Paris especially as I planned to visit Jan again in June to clarify some points.

In May. Rupert Murdoch's Harpers took over William Collins and I lost my outstanding editors.

22 June to 10 July. Even though I had been treated for osteoarthritis of both knees and hips, I visited New York, Boston, L. A. ., the Huntington Library, and UBC in Vancouver to continue my research. I was given permission to use these for my biography, taking in the scenes of the years in which Lowry wrote

1990

Under the Volcano. When, I told Jan that Rhoda and I had been over to Paris to visit the Mairie and Jardin du Luxembourg, her eyes lit up. Most days were given up to Jan's reminiscences of their marriage in Paris, living in London, New York, Mexico and Hollywood. I was overwhelmed.

Returning home, not only were Rhoda and I typing the abundant notes, recordings and letters onto my computer and laptop, but I found I needed to pay another visit to Lowry's brother, Russell, whom I had already met several times at his home. I rang and arranged to meet him at his home on 29 July at 11 a.m.

26 July. We were staying, on this occasion, at the Queens Hotel in Chester as I had arranged to visit and interview on the 27th July, Carole Hyde and her brothers, Lowry's very close friends in their teens. Meeting them was extremely interesting. They had so much to tell me, enabling me to have a clearer picture of the teenage Lowry. They gave me photographs, materials and letters. The following day, we visited Russell at his home. He and his wife were most welcoming as usual. He gave more insight of the teenage Malcolm's life, photographs and correspondence from him.

1 November. Radio 3: I wrote and presented my interview with Jan Gabriel *Love and Grief Under the Volcano. The Life and Work of Malcolm Lowry*.

9 November. The iconic Berlin Wall was breached in the afternoon and starting at midnight, citizens became free to cross the country's borders. They were drunk with the prospect of their new freedom. It seemed that a profound shift in world history was imminent.

1990

8 June, after parking our car at Heathrow, we flew at 4 p.m. instead of 2 p.m. by British Airways to Madrid. As a result, we missed our connection from Madrid to Granada. BA staff put us up in Madrid overnight and early next morning we caught a flight to Grenada. My left hip was rather painful due to my osteoarthritis, but after a

rest, we left our hotel for the Villa Carmona pension where Jan and Malcolm first met on 19th May 1933. We wandered around the area to get the feel of it, aware of its peace and serenity. Later, despite my painful hip, we tackled the steep road to the Generalife Gardens of the Alhambra where, we sat and enjoyed the splendid scenery. The leafy tree-lined walkways provided pleasant shade, enhanced by the abundance of water flowing in the nearby stream. We returned to the hotel, and I had to rest my aching left hip, feeling that despite my problems, we had enjoyed this day.

The following morning, after breakfast, we went to the Alhambra Palace. The Palace is a glory of majestic rectangular court-yards and fountains, especially the Court-yard of the Lions with its fountain. The feeling we had, walking through the Palace and the Gardens was overwhelming - perfect and breath taking. We were mesmerised by its beauty of art and creativity. Next day, after an early breakfast, we headed for to the airport, flew to Madrid, made our connection in time to Heathrow, collected our car and drove home. This, I thought, might be my last trip abroad until after my left hip replacement operation.

7 November. Lawrence Durrell, 78, British novelist and poet died of an emphysema - related stroke at his house in Sommières

20 December. I also wanted to see the original Cape contract for *Under the Volcano,* and letters between Cape and Lowry. The librarian at Reading University, where the Cape Archive is stored, told me that contracts for their books still in print were probably at Cape's offices. I rang the publisher, and an editor replied that she had had instructions not to help me. I thought this must be a misunderstanding, so, I wrote to the Chief Executive, and got an immediate reply from his assistant saying, 'Of course, you can have a copy of the contract.' She added a PS; 'I used to live at your house.' And I did remember her name on a couple of letters that I had earlier forwarded on to her.

1991

9 April. Stuart Proffitt took over as new director at HarperCollins

1992

31 August. I took early retirement from my senior lecturer post at Goldsmiths' College and, found freedom at last to fulfil my dreams in becoming a full-time author. I had been planning this day since 1988 with Rhoda, ensuring that our financial situations were stable. We both had planned to retire early but, the earliest Rhoda could do would be in another three years. I had a great deal to cover in that time, getting Lowry's biography properly written up before I sent it to my publisher. That day, we went to the Hilton Hotel to celebrate and, mark the day as a very special occasion. I was at the beginning of becoming a full-time author. We were both very excited by the thought and hopeful.

1992

It took me longer than planned to write the book - too long, with months of combing through the interviews, letters, documents, and notes from various note-books. Twice, I postponed the deadline. I ended up with a book way beyond the length for which I had been contracted but, when I could cut no more, I printed it out, took it early on the 9th March to my publisher, and prayed.

From there, Rhoda and I went straight to the Westminster Hospital for my admission, and having a total un-cemented left hip-replacement operation on the 10th March.

My new hospital experience began most interestingly. I had just been admitted, we were sitting on a bed, waiting for the admissions nurse to return. Glancing around, I saw, on the next bed, a thick file of my medical notes. Here was my chance to settle the nagging question that that medical student, Geoff, had planted in my mind all those years ago. I looked at the first page of notes. There I read '24 March 1961 - admitted in a bad state,' then '(25th) deteriorated,' then '(26th) very poorly,' then '(27th) semi-conscious - 12 hours later - thyroid crisis, acute rheumatic fever and acute carditis - desperately ill,' then '(5th April) remarkable improvement,' then '(6th) looks well,' then '(10th) feels quite well'. Tests administered included - let me see - yes, a 'Wassermann Test'. My pulses quickened. 'Result: negative!' So, Geoff, the medical student, had simply been tormenting a suffering soul, as I had suspected all along.

In hospital, I recovered well, having intensive physiotherapy daily. By the 28th March, I was fit to go home. Rhoda, who had taken 6 weeks to look after me, came to pick me up and take me home. I had to rest my new hip for a few weeks before returning to the Westminster Hospital's Orthopaedic Clinic to be formally discharged. Rhoda had carefully arranged the house for me to recuperate in a secure and safe place, bed raised, loo had an added seat, handrail, and chairs were raised. Under her care, I recovered quite well.

22 April. I received a letter from Stuart Proffitt, informing me that my manuscript was far too long, and should be cut by half.

15 June. With Rhoda's help, we managed to cut down to 750 pages. I informed my agent, Anthony Goff, who was a tower of strength. He was very patient, sympathetic, encouraging, supportive, and put up with my endless telephone calls.

7 July, I delivered it to HarperCollins.

Anthony sent my manuscript to Random House of Canada, Toronto. I had been given permission to quote by everyone, but I had to cut my quotes on Lowry to 4,000 words and paid $750 to the Estate.

4 September. I received complimentary messages from HarperCollins and Random House of Canada.

10 September. I said to Rhoda, 'I must decide what's next. I have been thinking of writing another biography, but whom? I thought of Lawrence Durrell, Albert Camus and D. H. Lawrence. I have given each lots of thought, and have decided on Lawrence Durrell. I first discovered Durrell while serving as an electrical engineer in Egypt with the Royal Air Force at a desert outpost in 1953, when I came across a volume containing some of his poems. Later, I spent six-months in Cyprus while he was Director of Information there. In London, when I read *Bitter Lemons*, it seemed to me the perfect

account of that lovely island at a tragic and explosive period of its history, and one of the best sustained pieces of poetic prose I had then read. When Justine appeared shortly afterwards, I was hooked on Durrell, and have remained so ever since, though not everything he wrote afterwards recaptured the magic of those earlier works. I read all his books and most of his writings.

Rhoda said, 'I must now read all his books so that, we can discuss them on your new enterprise.'

14 - Portrait of Durrell hanging in Notting Hill

1993

25 January. I delivered the Malcolm Lowry typescript to Collins and, on 29th to my Agent. 14th March, Anthony sent it to Canada. 27th May, I sent in photographs to HarperCollins. 14th June, I sent in photographs to Random House of Canada for my book. 15th June, I returned finished proofs to HarperCollins.

26 January. Back on Lawrence Durrell's trail. I wrote to his schools; the Jesuit-run College of St. Joseph at North Point in Darjeeling in India; St. Olave's and St. Saviour's Grammar School in Tooley Street, Bermondsey, South Bank, London, and St. Edmond's School in Canterbury. I, also, wrote to the University of Illinois and Durrell Centre in Sommières.

GLIMPSES OF A BIOGRAPHER'S DIARY

1 February. I received brochures from Durrell's Centre. On the 9th. I got a letter from Sommières suggesting a stay from 5 to 29 April. I did more work on my Durrell's chronology. "I feel that Durrell is taking me over. I must always remember that Ian MacNiven was appointed by Durrell to be his biographer. 11th. I rang and informed Anthony that 'I want to write a biography of Lawrence Durrell, but Ian MacNiven was appointed by Durrell to be his biographer, and I am staying at the Durrell's centre from 5th -29th April". He said, 'I will talk to Collins about it'. By 24th. I had read all of Durrell's books: *Bitter Lemons, Prospero's Cell, Pied Piper on Lovers, Panic Spring, The Black Book, Cefalu, White Eagles Over Serbia, Justine, Balthazar, Mountolive, Clea, Tunc, Nunquam, Monsieur, Livia, Constance, Sebastian, Quinx, Reflections on a Marine Venus, Spirit of Place, Sicilian Carousel, The Greek Islands, Caesar's Vast Ghost* and his Plays *Sappho, An Irish Faustus* and *Acte*. 'Now, I must continue reading his books, plays, poems, essays, comic stories, his recordings and other writings. Also must read Anais Nin (21.02.1903 - 14.01.1977), French-born novelist and short story writer, and Henry Miller (26.12.1891-07.04.1980) an American writer and artist and others. And others who, had written about him. A very aspiring list'.

4 March. I rang the Durrell's Centre, and booked my stay from 7th-21st April, which I did.

1 April. I heard from Durrell's schools in England, and arranged visits.

24 May. I sent in my Durrell's proposal to Anthony after, I had done a lot of research especially at the Durrell's Centre, reading and interviewing some people face-to-face, on the telephone, and sending and receiving letters.

31 May. I took Durrell outline to Anthony's office.

17 July. I am working steadily on Durrell. 21st. Anthony send my proposal and outline to Christopher Sinclair-Stevenson, whom I saw on 12th of August at his office, Michelin House. We had lively talks and discussions. He is such a charming and civilised

gentleman, who is extremely keen on my Durrell Biography. We agreed on 400 pages. I told him that, 'I need to make trips to Illinois, and to other libraries to complete my research on Durrell, as they had masses of his materials.

24 August. Anthony rang, and informed me that Christopher made an offer, and agreed 150,000 words.

29 September. Anthony sent me the contract from Christopher for my biography of Lawrence Durrell *Through the Dark Labyrinth*.

Chapter 16

My First and Second Biographies
1993-2000

1993

4 October. My hardback book of *Pursued by Furies, A Life of Malcolm Lowry* was published in Great Britain by Harper Collins, and simultaneously by Random House of Canada, Toronto. When my copies of *Pursued by Furies* arrived from the publishers, and I held one in my hand, I felt for the first time that finally I'd fulfilled my dream. My friend David always said: 'Books survive longer than magazine and newspaper articles, and don't disappear into a black hole like film or radio tapes.'

He also said that, 'This is a form of life after death.'

That's good enough for me.

Pursued by Furies was launched with a party at the Mexican Embassy thanks to Raúl Ortiz y Ortiz, the Mexican translator of *Under the Volcano*. I took along a bottle of Mezcal. There was a warm assemblage of Lowry aficionados, as well as persons from the publishers, the press and assorted Mexican embassy staff. I was prevailed upon to introduce my book, which I did hesitantly and not a little nervously, ending with the quotation from Fray Luis de

León: 'No se puede vivir sin amar' (One cannot live without loving) which features so prominently in Lowry's masterpiece.

The reviews of *Pursued by Furies* were rather kinder than any Lady Fairfax, at the Westminster Hospital in 1961, might have anticipated. According to the Guardian reviewer, it was 'a fine, intelligent biography.' Ian Hamilton on the Sunday Telegraph called it 'a cool, thorough and not uncritical appraisal of a dreadful life,' while Martin Amis in the Independent on Sunday provided a perfect quotation for the front cover - 'The biography is thorough, and thoroughly engaged; it is both gripped and gripping. It won't have to be done again.' Did I need any more than that?

I did the publicity rounds - with warmly-received presentations especially in Lewes, West Sussex, at South Bank, London, The Village Voice bookshop and Shakespeare and Company in Paris.

Giving a talk at a bookshop in Cambridge, who should show up but Margaret, the woman who was about to marry a vicar, and had come to Shawfield Street to see my first TV programme. She appeared when I was signing copies, and we met briefly afterwards. I asked after the vicar.

'Oh,' she said, 'that ended a long time ago.'

'What happened?' I asked.

'He was entirely unpredictable, and one day he just took off for South America with a backpack. Eventually I divorced him and remarried.'

'Another vicar?' I asked. She laughed. 'No, and a genuine pacifist this time.'

Unfortunately, I was not now allowed to feel pleased with myself for long. I was invited to Swansea to give a talk about Lowry at the Arts Centre there - a good opportunity, I thought, to talk about Lowry and Dylan Thomas. Quite a sizeable audience, mainly men, showed up. About twenty-minutes into my presentation, when, I thought it was going well, a man put his head through the door and shouted, 'Bar's open, boys!' and, just about every member of the audience rushed out. My talk, by any standards, collapsed with a slow flop. I probably looked on with my mouth open, as the hall almost emptied. Afterwards, when I went to the bar several drinkers came up to me, and apologised, saying, 'Sorry about that boyo, but most of us are only here for the beer.' Another came up and said, 'We had that Kenneth Griffith here talking about Dylan. He was bloody marvellous as you were!' I drove back from my visit to Swansea properly chastened, with the words of the boyo rather than Dylan's or Lowry's words ringing in my ears. Perhaps I should have told them that, I had a Welsh grandfather. That might have held them for another five-minutes.

4 October. My books, both hardback and paperback, on Malcolm Lowry were published separately by Random House of Canada, Toronto.

7 October. I signed and returned Lawrence Durrell's contract to Anthony,. Also, I booked 8th – 22nd November for my trip to the University of Illinois library in Chicago, to spend times researching their very large collection of letters, documents, newspaper clippings, memoirs, reviews and photographs. I came away with lots of photocopies of the above which threw much light on Durrell. I typed every letter and every document on my Amstrad. I returned to Illinois a few more times and to other libraries.

13th. I was invited to talk about my book *Pursued by Furies* at the Harbour Front International Writers Festival. Rhoda came with me. We stayed at the luxury hotel in Toronto, where most of the writers attending the Harbour Front Readings were staying.

17th. We stepped into an elevator en route to delivering my presentation to a hopefully expectant audience, when who should join us, but Anne Fine, the children's author. She looked at me.

'Did you write that?' she asked, pointing to the oversized tome I was clutching.

'Afraid so,' I replied.

1993

'A friend of mine read that book,' she said, 'and when he'd finished it, he felt like cutting his throat.'

The presentation was a success, and discussions which followed were of very high quality. I signed many books, met up with friends, and celebrated well into the night. I was interviewed by the press, radio stations and the CBC. Anne Fine was at CBC as well, on the day I went there. It was great to meet with other writers internationally, who were so passionate and enthusiastic about writing. This book festival generated much excitement and delight among its participants. We were well taken care of and entertained.

20th. We flew from Toronto to Vancouver, where I was invited to talk about my book at their International Writers Festival. We were booked in at Hotel Vancouver by Random House of Canada, Toronto. We checked in, and were met by the organiser of the Festival. They had a well organised and entertaining programme. I gave three talks. All were well attended. I was interviewed, and had stimulating, enthusiastic and lively discussions with other writers. Rhoda loved the Beat Poetry evening best. It was very pleasant to meet Anne Fine again. On the 24th. We returned to London.

7-18 November. I flew by American Airways from Gatwick Airport, London to Dallas. Arrived late and missed my connection. Fortunately, I was put on the next flight to Chicago. I hired a car at the Airport, and drove to St Louis in the dark and managed to get to my hotel.

Next day, I drove to Southern Illinois University Carbondale, that is a public research university. I was informed by helpful staff that McNiven had been asked by Faber and Faber to get his biography manuscript ready by the end of the year for publication next Autumn. Gosh! Now I must move fast.

The following day, I was told that; I could not double up copies, and to count them as one. God help me!! During the rest of my time here, I researched tirelessly, and seemed to have got all I came for, pretty much. Other things, I can get in the U.K. for example, birth, marriage, divorce, death certificates, newspapers and magazine stories, voting lists, telephone directories, radio and television recordings. On the 18th. I was ready to leave. I must say, it would be lovely to see little Rhoda.

31 December. The difficulty of getting lots of Durrell's letters, and talking to various of his people had turned out to be a problem. Fortunately, I taught Biographical Studies at Goldsmiths' before my retirement, and covered such eventualities. As such, I ploughed through the archives, libraries, knowing that handling original letters, diaries and note-books were infinitely preferable to study them in print. In an original letter, one can read the handwriting, the inserted afterthoughts, the marginal scribbles and tea-cups or wineglass-stains, and, importantly, becoming aware of letters that had gone missing. Any of these scribbles and hieroglyphics could provide clues to the hidden story. In addition, I worked on readings that others wrote about Durrell, interviewing people not only face to face, but by telephone, letters sent and received, paraphrasing and quoting from Durrell and others. To have depended excessively on the Complete Works would have been a less exciting way to proceed. I had to put in a good deal of legwork before I could even start; 'The Trail That Never ends.' Durrell was quite a commitment.

1994

7-18 January. Today, I went to the India Office Library, and got birth, marriage and death certificates for Durrell's family for their India days. On the 11th, India Office found Lawrence Durrell's will. 18th. I went to St. Edmonds, Canterbury. It was a single faith school, and the prevailing theology was Anglican. Durrell was duly instructed, and on the 3rd December 1926, was confirmed with twenty other boys by the Archbishop of Canterbury in the school chapel. The Chaplain was very helpful. He gave me a grand tour, photocopied many items for me from his life. He also, gave me names and addresses of contemporaries of Durrell whom I contacted later.

1994

9 February. My paperback proofs of *Pursued by Furies* from Flamingo, London arrived. I checked them. Apart from the odd things, all corrections seemed to have gone in, and my book was published in London in 1994. 11-13 March. Rhoda and I drove to Bournemouth for useful research in Kelly's and voting lists to trace history of the Durrells in the town. We drove to Donhead, St. Andrew, near Shaftesbury in Dorset to visit the small cottage that his friend, Diana Ladas, lent him. It was a charming cottage set over a rushing stream, and buried deep in the countryside, well away from prying eyes. He was completing *Bitter Lemons*. Claude had finished her novel about Ireland, and submitted it to Faber.

21 April. More birth, marriage and death certificates - nine in all came, including Mrs. Durrell's.

3 - 10 May. Rhoda and I went to Corfu for a week to continue on Durrell's trail. We stayed at the White House apartment on Kalami Bay. The view over the encircling bay towards Albania was idyllic. The present owner and Tasso Anastasiou were very helpful and polite. He even sent me a copy of a Durrell's photograph for my book cover. After, we checked in and settled in our two-bedroom apartment, we went walking, exploring the neighbourhood, and especially the bays where Durrell and his friends loved to go swimming. We had supper at the White House tavern. We ate delicious sword fish meals washed down with Ouzo for me, and orange juice for Rhoda. Next day, Wednesday, we went to Danilia in Corfu for a Greek evening of dancing, eating and drinking. We met a very charming and jolly couple, Bryan and Lynette. We had a truly pleasant evening. The following day, we booked a trip to Achillion. We saw the mountains, monastery and a bit of old Corfu. The Greek tour guide took us to an expensive tavern at Bella Vista, and to a souvenir market at some obscure village. On Friday, we travelled by bus to Corfu centre. It was raining heavily. Later the heavens opened, lightning flashed and thunder roared. Rhoda was a bit cast-down especially as she lost her lovely red scarf. We went to the old city and found charming little squares. We returned to the town centre, did some shopping and went to the church and lit candles. Then, we returned to the coach to get the

GLIMPSES OF A BIOGRAPHER'S DIARY

2.30 p.m. bus. By now, I finished re-reading Durrell's *Prospero's Cell* and, began *Colossus of Maroussi* by Henry Miller. I cooked supper for us washed down with a bottle of white wine. Lovely. Next day, we spent a leisurely day in Kassiopi, Kalami and, had supper at Kalami beach. It was a glorious day. Tuesday, 10th. We packed and said our goodbyes to the staff. Once again, Tasso Anastasiou promised to send me Durrell's photograph for my book cover, which he did. We left for the airport and for home. Kalami is one of Corfu's most picturesque spots.

17 to 22 May. We returned to Paris. 19th. I was invited by Odile to talk about my book *Pursued by Furies a Life of Malcolm Lowry* at the Village Voice, an English Language bookshop at the heart of Saint Germain -des -Prés – (It was closed on 31st July 2012. Very sad.) My talk was a great success. Afterwards, Odile took some of us to a French restaurant, where we continued our talks and discussions about my book, ate and drank delicious French wine.

On the morning of 22nd, I gave another talk about *Pursued by Furies* at Shakespeare and Company book-shop. George Whitman (12.12.13-14.12.2011), an American bookseller, who was the founder and proprietor of Shakespeare and Company, another English Language bookshop in Paris Left Bank, knew Lawrence Durrell very well and gave me a very good talk about him. I miss George very much.

Also, I wanted to clarify some points about Durrell with Cecily

Mackworth, Ghislaine Durrell and Diane Deriaz. We visited 21 Rue Gazin, where Durrell and his first wife, Nancy lived. Then, headed for the Villa Seurat. Afterwards, we met with friends at our favourite cafés, restaurants before leaving Paris for London.

26 June. Our friend, Cecily Macworth, came to lunch at our home in London. We spent all afternoon talking about Lawrence Durrell among other issues. We had passionate and enthusiastic discussions. Certainly a very fruitful day.

1994

5 July. Letters and papers from University of California at Los Angeles (UCLA) arrived. Rhoda scanned and typed all these onto our computer. Bless her.

20 August. I went to interview Beatrice Dennis at her home, London. Beatrice and her late husband, Dennis, the playwright, were very good friends of Lawrence Durrell. I left with masses of material, letters, photographs and newspaper cuttings. All went on my computer with Rhoda's help as usual. .

30 August. Rhoda retired. The staff held a delightful party for her. Lots to eat and drink, much talking and many speeches followed by a farewell presentation. We stayed at Rhoda's flat for her last night at St Georges' Hospital and left for home the following day. We are both free now. Wonderful.

Over the years, Brian Southam, now running his own publishing house, had been suggesting that I should go to Frankfurt with him and his wife, Doris, to visit the famous Book Fair. Finally, with *Pursued by Furies a Life of Malcolm Lowry*, I was looking for an American publisher, So, I agreed to go to Frankfurt. Brian gave me a ticket. Rhoda became enthusiastic. She put together what amounted to a brochure of positive reviews, and with that, and copies of the great opus, I set off on the 5th October.

The Frankfurt Book Fair was a remarkable event. In a vast hall, the stalls were laid out with books, books, books - book posters, book covers and book reviews. Publishers, editors and sales persons mingle and gossip, haggle and slip away to talk business together. It was a rare cultural event, dedicated to books and readings. The whole point here, is to sell books for overseas publication, for translation, and for adaptation.

Using Brian's stall as a base, I began to circulate, looking for a publisher, who might be sympathetic to a book about a brilliant literary alcoholic or just one that published long biographies. I chatted, schmoozed and attempted to project myself. Finally, at the stall of St Martin's Press, I spotted a large biography of Thomas Hardy by Martin Seymour-Smith, that ran to 896 pages. There was a charming young man at the stall, and I asked him whether the person, who had edited that book was around. He said, 'He is off to lunch. Can I help you?' 'I have a bulky biography of Malcolm Lowry for which I'd like an American publisher,' I said.

'I'd be interested,' he said. 'I recently published a book on Lowry - *Malcolm Lowry: Eighty Years On*.'

'I contributed an essay to that book,' I said, unable to conceal my surprise.

'Would you let me take a look?' He asked. How could I resist? I gave him a copy with Rhoda's brochure to accompany it. 'I'll read this tonight,' he said. And I thought, 'Not if you want to get in a good night's sleep, you won't.'

Next morning at the fair, he hurried up to me and said, 'I read half of your book last night. Who is your agent?' I told him. He, Garrett Kiely, editor, and I, had a most useful discussion. I left Frankfurt on the 9th after thanking my good friends, Brian and Doris, and returned home.

9 November. I went to Eton, invited to give talks on *Pursued by Furies* and on *Under the Volcano*. House Master, Michael Grenier, and his pupils in very elegant uniforms, met me. We had very good discussions on *Under the Volcano*. Then, I went to the Library, and was shown manuscripts by Michael Meredith, an enthusiastic librarian. After dinner, I met with about twenty members of The Literary Society. We had very good discussions and lively debates on the above topics. After the next speaker and coffee was served, we said our goodbyes and left.

21st. Rhoda and I went to Oxford Street, London, to buy a new photocopier. On our way home, Rhoda hit her head in the taxi. Next day, she was in bed with a headache. The following day, she was feeling better.

2 December. I was working tirelessly on the Durrell's book every single day. Rhoda helped, of course. On the 7th. In London, I met and interviewed Sir Steven Runciman, who ran the British Council

in Athens in 1946, and Durrell met him there. They were good friends.

21st. Anthony received 2 offers for *Pursued by Furies* from USA. One from St. Martin's Press, and the other from Harcourt Brace. We accepted St. Martin's Press, of course.

22nd. UCLA papers arrived. I had masses of papers to read including a chronology. Rhoda scanned and typed all of these on the computer. Bless Rhoda. Thus enabling me to concentrate on with my many readings and writing my book.

1995

4 January. I wrote letters to Desmond Tester in Australia, David Hughes and Henry Woolf, friends of Durrell. They replied.

12th. Deal agreed with St Martin's. I put my heart and soul every day to complete my Durrell's book. On the 13th, I wrote to Leslie Durrell's neighbour, John, who agreed to talk with me about Leslie later. On the 17th. Almost, all letters and interviews, including all Audrey Beecham's letters, and all material from the Cyprus period, were copied mainly by Rhoda.

31st. Gerald Durrell died age 70 on the Channel Island of Jersey. Lawrence Durrell said that his brother, Gerald, wrote about animals. He began his animal escapades in 1953 in The Overloaded Ark. He wrote 32 books. He was one of the most popular authors of animal stories. He founded the Jersey Zoo, dedicated to breeding endangered species.

16 February. My agent handled the correspondence thereafter, and kept me informed of work-in-progress every step of the way. Bless . The contract for *Pursued by Furies A Life of Malcolm Lowry*, arrived. I signed and returned same to Anthony, who sent it to Mr. Garrett Kiely, who informed me by fax that he would use the cover and all photographs of the present *Pursued by Furies* for US editions.

On 28th. I met, and interviewed John Brahe at 10.30 a.m. at his home. He gave a very good interview about Leslie, his neighbour.

GLIMPSES OF A BIOGRAPHER'S DIARY

Also, he told me that Gerald and Lawrence Durrell did not speak to Leslie, after he got a Greek maid pregnant, and refused to marry her in 1950. I came away with books and photographs. Very good morning.

18 March. I attended PEN Writers Day at Café Royal. Richard Holmes was in the chair. Michael Holroyd and Margaret Drabble spoke on Facts or Fiction. I met Mr. A. Blokh, who knew Durrell in the Palais de Justice in Genova. He gave me useful information for my book.

26th. I received good material from Somerset House and St Catherine's House; including Claude's marriage and divorce, and Leslie's marriage to Doris certificates

4 April. I went to the BBC Written Archives, and found some excellent material, that I photocopied, brought home, and Rhoda entered them onto my computer. On the 6th. I gave a talk on *Pursued by Furies* at the Royal Festival Hall, South Bank Centre, London, in the evening which was a great success. Christina Pallisani, who invited me, seemed delighted with my talk and discussions. This gave me a great boost and confidence on Durrell, and how I can write a good book.

4-7 May. I went to Paris again, and booked in at the Royal Hotel, 212 Boulevard Raspail, to check out some information on Durrell. Rhoda was with her sister in London. Hence no Rhoda on this visit. I visited Cecily Mackworth at her home, and after an enlightening discussion and giving me letters, papers and photographs, we went to the Brasserie Lipp for supper.

On the 5th. In the morning, I went to the Bibliothèque Nationale at Pompidou Centre, and obtained valuable photocopies of Durrell's material. In the afternoon, I visited and interviewed Ghislaine Durrell at her flat. She told me fantastic stories of love and cruelty of their marriage for 3 hours. Wow!!. In the evening, I had dinner with Elizabeth Braillé, a French writer, at the Lipp.

Next day, I returned to the Bibliothèque Nationale at the Pompidou Centre in the morning, and then, went to Cecily for lunch, and back to the Bibliothèque Nationale at Pompidou Centre in the afternoon, and in the evening, had dinner with Diane Deriaz at the Closerie des Lilas. She gave me much valuable information about Durrell. I am exhausted!

7th. I was so glad to be back home. Rhoda and I continued to work tirelessly typing, photocopying, scanning letters and materials, transcribing tapes and reading. Also, I was writing stories to relax and maybe for a future project.

23rd. I had a discussion with Anthony about another biography. We talked about various authors, including George Orwell.

29th. All UCLA letters were on my computer.

13 June. I wrote to Ruth Speirs, who knew Durrell since their days in Cairo. Also, I wrote to many other friends whose replies were always very nice and informative. On the 21st. I spoke to John Craxton, an English painter, who was a very good friend of Lawrence Durrell, and interviewed him on 24th. He gave me an excellent interview, and led me to Daphne Fielding and Paddy L. F.

26th. I continued on my novel set in Paris.

28th. I met with Ghislaine for a drink at the Forum Hotel, Cromwell Road, London. She answered all my questions and promised to talk with Penelope, Margo and Eve to talk with me.

9 July. I met Desmond Hawkins, an author, editor and radio personality, at his home. He was very generous with his memories of Durrell, and people connected with him. I left with contact names, copies of letters and material.

On 10th. Rhoda and I went to the University College London (UCL) to continue with my research. Valuable material and document.

GLIMPSES OF A BIOGRAPHER'S DIARY

16th. Stephen Spender, an English poet, novelist and essayist whose work concentrated on social injustice and the class struggle, died on the 18th.

27th. I saw Mary Trevelyan at her home. She was delightful, gave me an excellent interview, and names of two further contacts of Durrell. I received many valuable replies. Feeling good.

31st. Met Alan Ross (06.05.1922 - 14.02.2001) gave me an excellent interview, as he did few times before. Alan was always charming and helpful. I do miss him very much.

August. I am really extremely busy writing my Durrell's biography.

3 September. BBC Radio 4 announced they were broadcasting some of Lawrence Durrell's stories every morning next week. Gosh! I must listen to each one and make notes.

On 9th. We had a very enjoyable dinner with Doris and Brian Southam, publisher, and friends. It was a very pleasant evening indeed.

On 14th. I interviewed Sir Bernard Burrows, who promised to ask friends of Durrell to see me, and to send me copies of photographs and letters.

On the 19th, I had lunch with my London editor, putting her in the picture, and she agreed to postpone the delivery date to March 1996.

2 October. I met Garrett Kiely at the Ritz for dinner. He was very charming, talked easily, very courteous, pleasant and helpful. He asked searching questions, and listened to my answers politely. Of course, we talked a lot about my books. Certainly. a very good evening. 14th. Anthony talked to Garrett about my Durrell book.

23rd. My hardback book *Pursued by Furies, A Life of Malcolm Lowry* was published by St Martin's Press, New York. This book received very good reviews, and became a NY Times Notable Book of the Year, and appeared on their bestseller list for three weeks running at the end of 1995. Rhoda and I celebrated this auspicious occasion at the Ritz.

Diary. I am moving very fast in writing my London, Durrell's book, with Rhoda's help in typing, scanning materials, letters and transcribing.

8 November. Garrett Kiely was interested in my Durrell's book, and wanted to see some chapters. On the 15th. The cover for my Durrell's biography came. We liked it very much indeed. 20th. I had already got ideas for my next book.

1996

7 January. I delivered the first three chapters to Anthony for Garrett, that he requested on the 8th November 1995. I still have more to cover, getting the biography written up prior to going into hospital for my right knee-replacement operation next month. I am in a lot of pain, and am writing tirelessly on my book, before sending it to Anthony,, and to my editor. It took me longer than planned to write this book - too long, with months of combing through interviews, letters, documents and notes from various notebooks. Twice the deadline was postponed. Now, I completed a book way beyond the length, for which I had been contracted.

28 February. When I could cut no more, I printed it out, and took it early to my editor at Michelin House even though, I knew that there was some writing, I was unhappy about. From there, we went straight to the Chelsea and Westminster Hospital. I was admitted to David Evans ward. I am second on the list for an operation tomorrow morning. Rhoda beautifully and lovingly helped me to settle in, and prepare me for tomorrow. 29th. Shortly, after returning from the operating theatre to the ward, I had a bad reaction to morphine, and I stopped breathing. Rhoda was at my bedside luckily, and shouted for help. Kate, the physiotherapist, phoned for the Emergency Team (Resuscitation Unit), who gave me oxygen and drugs to counteract the effect of morphine. When I came round, Rhoda was still by my bedside, holding my hand and very concerned. She stayed all night to make sure that I kept

breathing. (Apparently, morphine can make you forget how to breathe).

1 March. Rhoda went home to sleep. When she returned later, she was very happy that I was breathing normally and smiling. The following day, my drip was removed, but the urinary catheter was still in situ. I was seen by my doctors and physiotherapist.

On 3rd. Sitting out of out of bed, the physiotherapist got me going with my exercises and walking. I continued to receive twice daily physiotherapy, was seen by doctors and nurses, so that, I could go home to recover, and to get on with the correcting of my Durrell's manuscript. However, Rhoda brought in the first eight chapters, for me to get on with the corrections.

On the 6th. She took in those corrected chapters to Michelin House. She continued to bring in more chapters for me to correct. 9th. The ward sister agreed, that I could go home by 13th after receiving more daily physiotherapy to enable me to be fully mobile with my right-knee.

Over the weekend, my right-knee was swollen, and I had to stay in hospital longer to continue receiving twice daily exercises. Lying in my hospital bed recovering from right-knee replacement, I was watching a woman on the telephone at the nurses' station - to her lover. She was trying to avoid her husband. What is the story behind that?

15th. I was fit to be discharged and went home, to return to the physiotherapy department on 18th, twice a week until 13th May. I commenced hydrotherapy treatment weekly for 6 weeks, and was to continue with my exercises at home with Rhoda's encouragement. 26th Rhoda and I bought a second-hand Amstrad, but found that the printer was useless. So, we took off the hard-drive and circuit from the machine, and transferred them into our old Amstrad. Amazingly, it worked, and we had a working Amstrad with our old printer. Excellent!! I continued correcting the remaining chapters, and Rhoda took them to Michelin House.

1996

4 April. My editor rang, and told me that she found my book very interesting. However, she wanted some more cuts and a few changes. I said, 'Fine.' So, I continued with the cuts and changes.

Diary. 16th. Now, I have been working through my manuscript and preparing myself for my literary way ahead. There are novels to be read, a style to be found, a theme to focus upon, I must pick up from where I left off back in 1957, when I wrote a novel and the first publisher, though finding it interesting, did not publish it, but advised me to continue writing. It seems as though, I have been deflected for three decades, and more by the 'pop' sixties, the dissolute seventies and the money-making eighties. My two biographies have been serious attempts for me to return to that inspiration. Perhaps, I had read, and should have read more books that inspired me most: Orwell, Camus, Sartre, Dylan Thomas, Dostoevsky, Hardy, Shakespeare, Grass, Boris Pasternak, Nabokov, Mann, Hemingway, Kafka, John Fowles, William Golding, Julian Barnes, D. H. Lawrence, Joseph Conrad, Cocteau and many others. Also I began writing a story: *Soliloquy and Solitude*.

On 19th. My editor told me that she was 2/3 way through my book.

2 May. I was still combing through my manuscript, checking on all quotations and paraphrases, ensuring that, I stuck to 'fair usage policies.' 13th. I finished checking all paraphrases, and quotations, and started revising all chapters.

14 June. I had gone through and corrected my manuscript. A few loose ends to be done. I took it in to my editor. I started writing off for permissions. 25th. I met with Anthony,, and we discussed future books among other issues. From there, I went to the Chelsea and Westminster Hospital for my weekly hydrotherapy treatment in the pool.

16 July. I went to Michelin House, to add in some changes, so as to avoid putting them in at proof stage. I met my editor and we had a productive discussion. However, I continued going through my manuscript, checking especially paraphrases and quotations,

and still applying for permission to quote. 26th. Photo caption completed and sent to my editor.

5 August. Proofs arrived, and I am scrutinising them to ensure that all changes sent in are included. On the 11th. Finished proof reading, and would start the index on the next day. On the 21st. Index completed, and faxed them off to my editor. Of course, I continued checking for last minute changes through the text, so as, to make it safe.

1 September. I completed, and faxed all last minute changes to my editor. On the 14th. Our friends, Brian and Doris came to dinner. Brian, always a cheerful person, talked easily, fluently, asked searching questions, and listened to answers. It was a lovely evening.

18 September. Our friend, Rosemary, rang to inform us that our dear friend, Douglas Hyde, had died in hospital early this morning. She was deeply upset, needed friendship, support and being there for her. He was so well, and in such good form, when Rhoda and I saw him a couple of weeks ago. Very sad. Douglas was an English political journalist and writer, a communist and the editor of the Daily Worker. He resigned in 1948, and converted to Catholicism. He wrote *I Believed*, his autobiography. He illustrated, both his political and personal journey as a Communist.

20th. (as planned). We drove to France for one week. Then move on from Calais to Dijon. After a good meal and sleep, we drove to Lyon where we got lost, but eventually got to Orange to see the crématorium where Lawrence Durrell was cremated. We continued our journey to Nîmes and then to Sommières, where we checked in at a chateau - a large old room (just right for my novel). After baths, we rested and walked around Sommières, we enjoyed a delicious gourmet meal washed down with good French wine. The following day, after a good breakfast, we proceeded to Arles, parked our car near the Church St. Trophime, a Roman Catholic Church, and then booked into St. Trophime. We had a happy and relaxing holiday in Arles and surrounding areas. It was truly wonderful. We, then made our journey home to London. 30th. I sent Garrett Kiely blurbs for my Durrell's book. His assistant thought it would be due out in April 1997. Hope springs eternal.

1 October. I immersed myself in my story and reading Swift, Thackeray, Dickens, and Shakespeare. Later, I delved into Browning, Yeats, Swinburne, Wandsworth, Shelly, Keats and Eliot.

11th. My hardback book *Through the Dark Labyrinth A biography of Lawrence Durrell* from Sinclair Stevenson arrived. It looked lovely, but some words, I asked to be removed, had been left in, and in photo captions in particular, one or two words had not been corrected. I couldn't celebrate with Rhoda, because I was dining out with Garrett at the Ritz, as previously arranged. He congratulated me on my book being out and said, 'I and everyone at St Martin's are very excited about the Durrell book.' We talked about my next book. He was not sure about John Osborne, but keener on Orwell. Perhaps I am, too. I should look more closely at Orwell. I had read all his books and most of his works already. Currently, I am rereading my new Durrell book to identify errors etc. On the 15th. I made a list of changes required. The next day, I sent correction list to Garrett in New York.

17th. I asked Anthony about doing Orwell's biography and discussed other issues. In my youth, I always wanted to be a writer. I saved my pocket money to buy books at country house book sales. At fourteen, I left school to work in the local public library. There were first editions of Orwell's books on the shelves. I discovered those stylish Gollancz and Warburg editions in the fiction section of the library, sitting quietly between Baroness Orczy and Ouida. Around the same time, in the sixpenny-box outside a Torquay bookshop, I found a second-hand copy of the Penguin *Burmese Days*, which today stands happily next to my first edition of Inside the Whale. Later, as a student journalist, I was able to write about Orwell and, later still, reviewed books about him for the Times Education Supplements and London Magazine.

GLIMPSES OF A BIOGRAPHER'S DIARY

15 - Portrait of Orwell hanging in Notting Hill

After completing my book *Pursued by Furies, a Life of Malcolm Lowry* in 1993, I wanted to tackle Orwell, but Michael Sheldon's 'authorised' biography of George Orwell the previous year seemed to preclude another for some time ahead. I, therefore, opted for Lawrence Durrell, who happened to feature in my PhD thesis. The approach of Orwell's centenary, then, offered another chance to take him on. I began spending times at London University College, noting letters and anything else, that caught my eye in the Orwell archive. I will come back to this later.

*

18th. Garrett rang, wanting a cover photograph for the Durrell book. I sent him my negative, and a list of further corrections. 19th. Rhoda and I entertained my friend, Alan and his wife, Elaine, to dinner. Much catching up and discussions. They were very happy of course about my Durrell book being out. Truly a very pleasant evening. Alan and I have been friends since university days.

24th. My free ten copies of the Durrell's book arrived. I had been writing stories and continued doing so.

6 November. A contract from St Martin's Press, New York, arrived. Same signed and returned to Anthony,. My London books are in my local Waterstones bookshop. On 8th. I collected another ten free books from Michelin House, got back my transcript, photographs, and some discs. On the 10th. I looked through the transcript and noticed five instances, where editing had robbed a good opening, and one, where a word had been changed rendering the sentence into falsehood. I would try to get things changed for St Martin's Press.

Diary. On 28th. At the moment I have to consider my next biography. I am re-reading all works by George Orwell and writing my novel.

5 December. I attended Hatchards at Piccadilly, London, to my book signing *Through the Dark Labyrinth A biography of Lawrence Durrell* by Sinclair Stevenson, at 5pm.

I received very many nice telephone calls and letters regarding my book.

19-24 December. We took another trip to Paris to meet with our friends, eat well and relax. 25th. Rhoda and I had a lovely Christmas Day. Well deserved.

1997

1 January. Happy New Year. Will my 'novel' emerge in any recognisable shape or form this year? 2nd - 11th. I am still writing my novel on *Crime and Punishment*, but my priority is to reading and researching more on George Orwell for my next biography.

16th. Durrell contract from St Martin's Press arrived, which I signed and handed over to Anthony,, who then forwarded it to Garrett. Also, I faxed a list of corrections to Garrett. 20th. I bought a new Toshiba laptop. 22nd. Eugene sent me a copy of a letter from

GLIMPSES OF A BIOGRAPHER'S DIARY

Margot Durrell saying how much she regretted the family not helping me.

27th. I wrote to Anthony again suggesting Orwell for my next biography, and on 29th, he suggested that I do an outline.

5 February. Doreen, my friend since 1962, came for lunch. We had very pleasant talks about old times, and catching up with recent news. She liked and enjoyed reading both of my books. 15th. We went to see Henry 1V part 1 at Old Vic. Samuel West was well cast as the prince. Timothy West was a good Falstaff. He looked the part and got the laugh, but it was not as full blooded a performance as it might have been.

16th. Garrett rang and informed me that all other errors have been corrected in my paperback book *Pursued by Furies and Through the Dark Labyrinth*.

20th. I was invited to write a piece for the Updated Oxford Dictionary of National Biography and agreed to do it.[14]

March was a very good and happy month for us. My paperback book *Pursued by Furies A Life of Malcolm Lowry* was published by St Martin's Press, New York.

9th. We saw the film *A Portrait of a Lady*. Disappointing but good central performance from Nicole Kidman. In the evening, we saw *The English Patient* at our local cinema. Very good, lovely photography, and excellent performance from Ralph Fiennes and K. Scott Thomas.

27th - 29th. I spent my time mostly converting my Word document to Word Perfect.

---

[14] March 7th. I signed and returned contract for The Updated Oxford Dictionary of National Biographies that was published on 23rd September 2004: 60 volumes and outlines with 50,113 biographical articles covering 54,922 lives including Malcolm Lowry. The biographies are full of interesting details. I recommend them.

30th. We saw the film: *Shakespeare's Romeo and Juliet* this afternoon at our local cinema. Rhoda loved it.

31st. I am exhausted and not feeling well at all. Rhoda gave me tender loving care.

April, also, was another very good month for us. My hardback book of *Through the Dark Labyrinth a biography of Lawrence Durrell* was published by St. Martin's Press, New York.

19th. Dinner at Brian and Doris to celebrate the publication of my books from St. Martin's Press.

26th. We saw Simon Callow, an English actor, director and writer, in *The Importance of Being Oscar*, a homage to Oscar Wilde and it was truly very good.

4 May. We attended the birthday party of Eddie Lindon's, a Scottish Poet and literary magazine editor, who published and edited the poetry magazine Aquarius. We met many interesting people including Jim Campbell from The TLS, whom I know very well. However, I got £30. parking ticket for parking our car outside on a Sunday. Westminster of course.

14th. Kathleen Raine, a British poet, critic and scholar, urged me to write a Biography of the poet, David Gascoyne. We would be visiting him and his wife, Judy, who lived in the Isle of Wight soon. How can I gracefully wriggle out of this? I am heavily involved in research on Orwell, and I do not feel like taking on another - too much exhausting commitment.

17 May. Garrett sent me the cover for *Through the Dark Labyrinth* together with a complimentary review of it by Shelly Cox in the Illinois Library Review. So generous.

21st. I entered the Asylum Club, London, where I met Susan Chitty, an English novelist and writer of biographies, and Mrs. Martina Raymond, Dr Raymond's wife. We talked about Gascoyne and my books, of course. Delicious lunch and jolly friends.

GLIMPSES OF A BIOGRAPHER'S DIARY

24th. Garrett sent me twelve copies of my hardback book *Through the Dark Labyrinth a biography of Lawrence Durrell*. Also, I sent off to a draft letter to the Orwell Estate. He phoned me with sensible suggestions about an approach to it.

25th. We drove to the All Saints Church, Sutton Courtenay, to pay homage to George Orwell. It was a secluded peaceful churchyard and grave backed by cypress trees, and near to the grave of Herbert Asquith, Liberal Prime Minister, UK, 1908-1916.

30th. Alan Ross wrote accepting Diane Deriaz's memoir of Lawrence Durrell. I wrote to her publisher for permission to quote. Same was given.

1 June. I started on the Orwell trail. We drove to the tiny Hertfordshire village of Wallington to see the shop that Orwell and his first wife, Eileen, kept in 1930's, and met the lady, who knew Orwell, and whose mother helped in the shop. She gave me a very good interview. Also, we saw Manor Farm - Orwell's name for Animal Farm. The farmer kept pigs and other animals. We took photographs of the farm, the church, the shop, but the pub next door, where he drank was no longer there. A valuable trip!

3rd. I went to BBC Archives, which housed lots of material on Orwell.

5th. I started drafting his chronology.

7th. Interviewed Margaret Hepburn, friends of Eileen and Orwell. Continued building up his chronology.

11th. I received a reply from the George Orwell estate informing me 'that a huge scholarly edition of all Orwell's work is planned for next year. Until that is published, access to it is not granted.' This is all right with me. I understand. I can get on with my research on Orwell as I have been doing. However, I'll discuss this matter with Anthony,, of course.

15th. I drove to Desmond Hawkins' house to interviewed him as arranged. I had interviewed him before on Lawrence Durrell, and he did an excellent interview, together with names of contacts. Today, here I am again interviewing him, but on George Orwell. We talked at length about Orwell, Dylan Thomas, Eliot, Waugh, Green, Barker, Gascoyne and others. He gave me an excellent one-hour interview on Orwell, and names of his contacts. Long drive there, and back and heavy traffic. Rhoda transcribed my tapes. After this interview, I asked myself the following questions: Why did Orwell co-operate at the end with MI5? Why were his friends so suspicious? Did he realise the depth of his hatred of Communism? For many on the left, the Russian Revolution, even today, was, though brutal, a beacon - a light showing the way ahead. To have been so fiercely against it, as Orwell was, put him beyond the pale. Animal Farm and Nineteen Eighty-Four showed the strength of his feeling, and how he viewed the danger. The years 1947-1950 were perilous. Orwell didn't belong to any political party, and so could not be said to betray any group. But who is on the list? Were they the people, with whom he was friendly? It seemed, as if, he had turned on his impeccable police background. I asked myself many such questions, and now I must find the answers.

16th. Writing another story. Also, I spoke to Garrett about my Orwell's book.

17th. Digging into Orwell's noble past was not difficult. In Burkes Peerage and Landed Gentry, it was easy to find Lady Mary Fane, youngest daughter of the Earl of Westmorland, who married Charles Blair, Orwell's great grandfather, in 1765. Like most landed gentry, the Fanes were keen field sportsmen - their ranks included Masters of Hounds, army cavalrymen and even, curiously enough, a one-time commander of the British Army in Burma. Orwell's enthusiasm for hunting and the East were long-entrenched family traditions, it seems. A short visit to the Dorset village of Milborne St Andrew, where his paternal grandfather was once a vicar, produced at last one interesting further piece to the jigsaw. According to the parish magazine, Thomas Blair was, like his grandson, an eccentric figure quite prepared to risk public hostility - in his case, by rebuilding his vicarage at great expense to the parish in the teeth of much local opposition. Orwell's Anglican heritage, that the Milborne visit highlighted, made his attachment to the church (despite his unbelief) that much more comprehensible. Other ancestors, also, left their marks on him. He cherished the memory of his great-uncle Horatio Blair, a naval captain, whose travelling library he inherited (his niece still has it). According to a press cutting in the archive, 13 January 1911, Captain Richard Charles Blair of the 6th Gurkha Rifles, one of Orwell father's cousins, sailing home from India through the Red Sea, and suffering from depression, walked on the deck one night and quietly jumped overboard - an incident Orwell looked to have considered, and incorporating it into his unfinished novel, A Smoking Room Story.

As to the Limouzin history, some of their documents are in the India Office Records section of the British Library, Thacker's India directory, archive, and public library local history section. These are a great source of biographical data. Henley Library kept pre-1914 Kelly's Street Directories. There, I discovered the Convent des Ursulines, a private boarding school for girls at 23 Station Road. To authenticate this, I rang the Church House Library in London, and asked if they had any knowledge of an Anglican convent in Henley during the years in question. After checking, the librarian reported, that no such record had been found. A call to the Catholic Church's Central Library quickly produced the information, that the Ursuline convent listed in Kelly's had, in fact, been registered with them. The nuns, I was told, had moved to London after religious education was banned in France. Young Eric had been taught at a convent, as he said he had, it was this Catholic convent of French Ursulines, which could well explain his overt hostility towards Catholicism. (He recalled as a child helping to make up stories about nuns being raped and murdered).

Living at Kensington, I often pass Mall Chambers on Kensington Mall at Notting Hill Gate. Mall Chambers was a block of low-rent flats provided mainly for artisans, and Eric rented a flat there. Also, I passed 22 Portobello Road, where he lived in a room so cold, that he had to warm his hands over a candle flame, before he could start writing in the morning. I often passed 23 Cromwell Crescent, Earl's Court, where his mother moved from Henley to London to do war work for the Ministry of Pension, renting a pied-à-terre. Now, I wanted to locate the house of his Aunt, Nellie Limouzin, who had also lived in the neighbourhood. Ida Blair's address book (also in the Orwell archive) located Nellie at 195 Ladbroke Grove. At the local history section of Kensington Central Library, combing through old street directories, electoral rolls and rate records, I finally discovered that Nellie had lived there from 1911. In her top-floor flat, and she was supposed to have held a library salon at which Humphrey Dakin, Orwell's brother-in-law, claimed to have met G. K. Chesterton, and where Jacintha Buddicom reported Eric saying he had met the socialist and children's author E. Nesbit. I, then, found that Conrad Noel (a good friend of Eric, according to one of his ILP friends) was at that time a curate of nearby St Mary's, Paddington Green. What is more, he spent his spare time visiting spikes and workhouses dressed up as tramp, which opened the fascinating possibility that Eric had picked up the idea of roughing it around the dosshouses from Noel.

20 June. We took another visit to Paris on the Orwell's trail, and to meet friends. We checked in at our usual Hotel Le Clément, 6 rue Clément. In the evening, we had dinner with our friend, Elizabeth B, a writer, at the restaurant Wepler, in Paris that serve very good food. We talked of many things including my books and hers. I was exhausted afterwards and had a good night's sleep.

21st. We went to the bookshop Astebi in the Forum des Halles. From there, we headed for 6 rue du Pot de Fer in the Latin Quarter, where Orwell stayed in 1929-1930. He made this hotel famous as Hotel des Trois Moineaux in the rue du Coq d'Or in Down and Out in Paris and London. Number 6 is now a Patisserie. I was very tired walking, and had to sit every so often. Rhoda was very patient making sure that we stopped at cafés and restaurants on our return journey to our hotel.

22nd. After breakfast, we visited our friend, Cecily Mackworth, for lunch. She told us about Inez Holden, who hankered after Orwell, and was incensed when he married Sonia Brownell. She, also, knew Celia G. who lived in Cambridge. (I must telephone to interview her). Cecily told us about many people, who knew Orwell, and gave me a list of names and addresses to contact.

Afterwards, we made a quick visit to Hospital Cochin, a pauper's hospital in the fourteenth arrondissement, where Orwell was admitted in March 1949 with bronchitis and coughing up blood. The hospital is no longer the wretched place it was in Orwell's day. The authorities, there, kindly provided me with his medical record which bears his hospital number - 3058. This otherwise trifling scrap of information acquires new and sinister significance on rereading the scene in How the Poor Die in which a grim fellow pronounces 'Numero 57' as Blair ('Numero 58') sees that the emaciated man in the bed opposite has finally expired. A 1920's map of Paris shows the hospital backing onto the mental asylum of St Anne's and La Santé Prison, the Paris home of the guillotine. The hideousness of the old institution is further intensified by Camus' description of it as 'the barracks of poverty and illness....its wall drip with the filthy humidity that belongs to misfortune.' Its soulless ambience, as captured by Orwell, clearly foreshadows that of the Ministry of Truth, and the little operating room from 'dreadful screams were said to issue' sounds uncannily like Room 101 in embryo.

Later still, on the 22nd , we went to Pompidou Centre for 31 July 1914 to do research on Jean Jaurès, French Socialist Leader, who was assassinated on that day.

23 June. We headed to Montparnasse Cemetery to pay our tributes to Simone de Beauvoir, an author and feminist, and to Jean-Paul Sartre, a philosopher. They were laid to rest in the same tomb. Then, we proceeded to Samuel Beckett's grave. From there, we returned to Hospital Cochin again (with benches along the way). We made a break for lunch at restaurant, Belfort. Then, we got to Centre Pompidou, where I copied from Le Monde the 1st August 1914 an account of the assassination of Jean Jaurès. By now, I was

truly exhausted. We returned to our hotel where we had dinner in our room.

24th. We wound up at the café restaurant de Croissant where Jean Jaurès was assassinated on 31 July. We sat at a table by the door. On the opposite side of the door stood a bust of him, photographs and copies of press reports, especially L Humanité of 1 August 1914 about the account of Jaurès' murder. A plaque on the floor beneath my chair was where he was assassinated. The madame patron gave me a very good account of the assassination. We had lunch, and then walked to Shakespeare and Company bookshop, where we met a member of the Lawrence Durrell Society. He gave us the latest account about the Durrell Centre that had been sold. A remarkable story. We left and made for the Bibliothèque Nationale de France where I looked up some of Orwell's material and journals. I ordered materials and Le Monde. We returned to the Café Restaurant de Croissant for dinner and left for our hotel.

25th. To the Bibliothèque Nationale de Franc to find Orwell's article in Le Monde. Eventually, after some formalities, I entered the reading rooms, read the articles and had them copied to take away.

26th. We returned to the Pompidou Centre to carry on Orwell's trail, and then headed for home in London. Many letters to be read awaited me etc.

27th. Back home and after a good night sleep, I updated Orwell's chronology.

30th. I had flu symptoms and stayed in bed under the tender loving care of Rhoda.

2 July. I am rereading Bernard Crick's biography of George Orwell and hope to finish it by Friday.

4th. I consulted Bill Hamilton, Orwell's Agent, about undertaking another Orwell biography, and found him quite encouraging. However, he suggested I wait until Peter Davidson published his Complete Works of George Orwell about which I had not previously heard. Meanwhile, I decided to keep going rereading Orwell and about Orwell, going to Libraries, archives, and interviewing people who knew him.

5th. I received a letter from Lewes Live Literature inviting me to a literary festival and to contribute to a magazine - all about Malcolm Lowry. I accepted of course. Furthermore, Sue Hewitt, a friend and author, sent me interesting printouts about Lowry, Durrell and Orwell. This cheered me up no end. 10th, 14th, 21st.24th. I went to University College London (UCL) researching Orwell. Everything about Orwell is here. Real gold dust. I saw, read and copied many documents and letters including one to Celia K, a friend and an editor, he sending her the 35 names of suspected fellow travellers. Now how do I proceed with Celia? How to get the full list of these suspects? Apparently Orwell kept a list of 85 names of such people in a notebook. Can I get access to that notebook? Would the journalist who quotes some names tell me where he got them and I could therefore get them?

13th. I sent the Orwell proposal to Anthony,. I was busy reading and typing Orwell's letters and materials on my computer. Rhoda was a great help.

20th. My paperback book *Through the Dark Labyrinth a biography of Lawrence Durrell* by St Martin's Press, New York was published. Rhoda and I celebrated at the Hilton Kensington. I wrote many letters and posted books. Also, I wrote another story *Terrors, Experiences and Understanding One's own and Other People*.

22nd. Ten books arrived from St Martin's Press.

23rd. After a good night's sleep, I received another ten books from St. Martin's Press. How gracious!! Of course Rhoda and I read my book with joy. We continued updating our records on Orwell.

28th. Am writing a story on *Passion*.

30th. I received letter from Lewes about accommodation and the Lewes Festival 31st. I read and scrutinised my book *Through the Dark Labyrinth a biography of Lawrence Durrell* and made a list of corrections for the paperback and sent it off to the publisher at Pimlico, London.

3 August. Entertaining Rhoda's relatives from Atlanta, United States.

4th. Copied notes today from Richard Aldington, English writer and poet, *Death of a Hero* and stared on another story about 2 brothers.

8th - 11th Rhoda went to Paris with her sisters, Margaret and Mary and her family. They had a wonderful and memorable stay sightseeing in Paris, visiting Sacré Coeur in Montmartre, Eiffel Tower, Louvre Museum, Notre Dame cathedral, dining on a Seine Cruise and eating good French food. Rhoda said, 'We had fun a time.'

11th. Anthony rang this morning and was quite encouraging about Orwell.

14th. Pimlico publisher informed me that all corrections would be included in the paperback. 15th. spent a very fruitful morning at the Orwell archive.

19th. I received a letter from Jan Gabriel, Malcolm Lowry's first wife, informing me that she was in hospital but was recuperating at home and writing her book *Inside the Volcano*. Jan didn't have an agent. She asked me to be her agent. I said, 'I have never been an agent, and I am very busy researching my next biography.' She said, 'You published one book on your own.' I could see that she really wanted me to help. She had given me such a lot of information about her and Malcolm's life together from 1933 to 1940, that I felt I must help her. I told her to let me know when she had finished her book, by then I should be able to visit her and we could go through the manuscript together. 20th. I did a fantastic amount of work on 1914 novel. I hope to get down to it next week.

22nd. I had Lunch with Michael Estorick, an author and chairman of the trustees for the Estorick collection since 1995, at his club. We ate well, drank well and had a spirited conversation about

Malcolm Lowry and Lawrence amongst others. He gave me 3 copies of Lowry letters and Christmas cards and I came home at around 7.30 p.m.

29th. We drove to Ipswich, checked into our hotel and then drove to Southwold, Suffolk. After parking our car, we walked to number 3 Queen Street, the third Southwold home of Orwell and his family, near to a fish and chip shop where we had lunch. My arthritic hip and knee were painful. So we drove around the town and along the beach. Southwold is a charming seaside town. It is known for its colourful beach huts and the beach stretching all up and down the coast, from the harbour to the pier and beyond. We returned to our hotel. Noisy night, sleep spoiled by noises of traffic from A12.

30th. Today changed room for hopefully a quieter one, and afterwards drove to Walberswick ruined church where he claimed to have seen a ghost. We walked all around and inside this ruined church, but we saw no ghost. Walberswick had a stunning coastal view and beach and is a nostalgic English seaside town. Afterwards, we returned to Southwold - to the library, museum, walked, with the aid of a walking stick, to the pier and then to the lighthouse where we also enquired about his sister Avril's Copper Kettle Tea Room. We were given directions, came to the site but of course the teashop was no longer there. The lighthouse is a Grade II listed and has a spiral staircase with over 100 steps leading to the top. One can tour the building and take in the view along the coast. Beautiful. We returned to our hotel.

31st. Early this morning, Diana, Princess of Wales, 36, died from injuries she sustained in a car crash in the Pont de l'Alma tunnel in Paris. Her partner, Dodi Fayed, and the driver of the Mercedes-Benz, Henry Paul, were pronounced dead at the scene. Their bodyguard, Trevor Rees-Jones, was seriously injured, but survived the crash. Her death caused an unprecedented outpouring of public grief in United Kingdom and worldwide. We were transfixed to our radio 4 and TV, listening to memories of Diana. A very sad day. Before leaving Ipswich for home, we walked along the River Orwell.

1997

1 September. Patrick McCarthy, author, came today and we had lunch at the Topo Dora Odeon, Notting Hill Gate. No Longer there. Afterwards, came back to our home for coffee. Good talk about Malcolm Lowry, James Joyce and Samuel Beckett. Mid-afternoon, Anthony rang wanting a new print out of the Orwell proposal for an editor at Fourth Estate publishing which I took in to him. Sometime, I feel quite uncertain about my writing ability when I make mistakes. But next time I will not rush anything. If it is to be Orwell, I'll have to restart reading him through, letter by letter, review by review, essay by essay, novel by novel and works about him. I am still trying to ignite the spark, to get the flash of inspiration. I need to look for themes, even for the big themes!!

On 7th. Listening to Madame Bovary on tape followed by reading Robert Graves *Goodbye to All That* were truly joyful.

On 8th. I received contract for the Lewes Festival, looked good, signed and returned. I got down to writing up my talk on Malcolm Lowry. What's more, I got a letter from Pimlico Press informing me that all corrections are included in my paperback book *Through the Dark Labyrinth a biography of Lawrence Durrell*, and proofs should be ready by the end of the month.

On 9th. Anthony rang and told me that Fourth Estate publishing is interested in Orwell, but wanted it for 2000. I suggested 2003, his centenary year.

10th. I was writing a story about *Saints: Heroic Virtue and Miracles*.

11th. We went to Eastbourne Library, where the local history section did not disappoint. It held reports of the Eastbourne Workhouse (not far from St. Cyprian's, an English preparatory school, to which Orwell attended at age eight) showing Mrs. Wilkes (the formidable 'Flip'), the school's part owner and head, listed as a Guardian. From memoirs kept in a bulging file on the school, I saw that a boy was said to have been bullied by young Blair, who was called Burton (the name Orwell often used when tramping around spikes), and that a bad tempered maths teacher at the school was called Ellis (the name Orwell gave to an equally unstable character in Burmese Days). The use of these particular names for a vagrant and a racist villain exemplified one of Orwell declared 'great motives for writing' - revenge!! I copied most material in their Orwell archive, requested some more and photographs. En route from Eastbourne, we called in at Ripe to see Malcolm and Margerie Lowry's graves. Their headstones were greatly weathered and difficult to read. The inscription on Margerie's headstone read: Come to me my Love, as once you did in May. How appropriate!

17 September. I attended a seminar on Reading at the British Library. All very good.

18th. Microfilm came from the Lilly Library, Indiana University in Bloomington, United States, - 90 letters from George Orwell to his agent, Leonard Moore. I listened to Madame Bovary on tape, part 2, followed by reading Robert Graves' *Goodbye to All That*.

22nd. Received fax from Lilly Library waving $5 fee for a single photograph. How noble! Worked on Lowry article for Lewes Festival, and had my weekly French lesson at home.

25th. Finished reading *Goodbye to All That*. I wrote off for permission to see Orwell, Sonia and Cyril Connolly letters.

28th. I did lot of work today - completed article and talk for the Lewes Festival, completed translation of Blair/Galsworthy, and typed out all Eastbourne notes onto my computer. Rhoda helped, of course. Our friend, Cecily Mackworth, rang for a chat, and to informed us that her book *Lucy's Nose* with a French Translation would be published shortly.

1-9 October. I was busy typing, scanning, transcribing material and tapes, writing and receiving letters, reading, entertaining friends, writing short stories and my novel; Lewis Luton,[15] and visits to theatres and cinemas. Rhoda was a great help as usual.

---

[15] Lewis Luton was the name of the main character in Boker's finished and unpublished novel *Lunching With Lucifer*.

1997

10th. We drove to Portsmouth, got the ferry to Isle of Wight, then drove to our hotel in Ryde; overlooking the Solent - a pleasant place to stay.

11th. In the pouring rain, we drove to Newport to visit Judy and David Gascoyne (10.10.1916-25.11.2001). David was an English poet, and associated with the Surrealist movement, in particular the British Surrealist Group. We ate, drank and talked a lot about various writers, especially Lawrence Durrell, whom he knew very well. He gave me food for thoughts, especially about his version of existentialism. On returning to our hotel, I entered my notes onto my laptop and we enjoyed the rest of the evening.

12th. We headed for Sandown to pay a visit to Edward Upward (09.09.1903-13.02.2009), a British novelist and short-story writer. We had tea and talked mainly about his friends, Christopher Isherwood, an American novelist and W. H. Auden, a British-American poet. From there, we proceeded to Cowes to dine with Neville Braybrooke (30.05.1923-20.08.2001), poet, novelist, essayist and a biographer. Neville cooked, and we ate, drank, talked, especially about his wife, June, better known by her pen name, Isobel English, who died in 1994.

13th. We returned to mainland, after visiting Roman villa in Newport. On our return journey, we called at Winchester, especially to see the Cathedral and burial place of Jane Austen, the English novelist. Rhoda lit candles, of course. We arrived home around 5.30 p.m. and had a relaxing evening.

16th. Wrote thank-you letters to my friends in Isle of Wight, and many to libraries in America for Orwell materials and letters.

18th. Received letters, very nice letters from my friends in Isle of Wight, and including notes about Orwell.

19th - 27th. Reading, typing Orwell notes and letters onto my computer, relaxing, going to cinemas and theatres, and continued with my novel on Lucifer; making it more introspective about his love life, and the world he was leaving behind, trying to give more of a picture, about his life he ordinarily lived; and - his work, where he lived. Rhoda enjoyed reading this novel so far.

28th. Proof of my paperback book for *Through the Dark Labyrinth* arrived from the publisher. Delighted. All changes including stylistic ones were put in. I wish I had added back more quotations. Returned same.

29th. Writing an article about the *Last Days of Malcolm Lowry. How did he die?*

31st. Revised Lewes Festival talk. Wrote off to The Berg Collection, New York Public Library, and Huntington Library Los Angeles.

1 November. I must finish the proof of my paperback book (received on 28th October).

2nd. The Day of the Dead. We arrived at Lewes Festival hall - good exhibition of paintings inspired by Lowry. My talk on Malcolm Lowry went down well. Afterwards, we all went to the pub, and then to the studio drinking and talking where a woman who was drunk tried to kiss me. Stayed up late talking with Phil and Kathy Myles, whose house we stayed for the night. Next day, we returned home.

4th. Editor from Pimlico informed me that I could make further changes to my book. Wonderful.

5th. Bonfire night. I must mention the Lewes Bonfire night celebration. Lewes Bonfire is the home to the largest and most celebrated of festivities in the Sussex Bonfire tradition. There are seven societies putting on six separate processions, and firework displays throughout Lewis on the 5th November. As well as this, 25-30 societies from all around Sussex come to Lewes on this date to march the streets. Should the 5th falls on a Sunday, in which case, it would be held on Saturday the 4th.

6th-8th. Our builder and decorator, Reg, had been putting tiles on our bathroom walls. When finished, they completely transformed our bathroom. It looked so good, I was ashamed of my earlier doubts about how it would look. He removed an old tank from our roof, and kindly took it away.

11th. I took corrected proof of my paperback book to the editor at Pimlico. He seemed very relaxed about number of changes and quotations. Very gracious. 14th. Anthony rang informing me, that he had given the Orwell proposal to Roland Phillips at Hodder, who wanted to know about Orwell archive.

15th. Rhoda was away at Margaret's, her sister. I had a very grim night with stomach pain, feeling sick, and almost fainted. I managed to get from the bathroom to the guest-room down-stair, and flung myself into bed. After an hour, I felt slightly better. I went to the kitchen, made myself tea and toast, felt better. Next day, though feeling wretched, I drove to the London Library to pick up the Maurice Cardiff book and several other books, and photocopies of Orwell. Rhoda returned. Bless her. I told her about last night. She was very concerned of course and pampered me no end. Lovely. Stomach much better but still tender. Rhoda was at home and all's well.

15th - 26th. Busy updating Orwell material and letters onto my computer, and rereading works about Orwell, especially Bernard Crick, Michael Shelden, and Stansky, Peter and Abrahams William.

On the 26th, I had one tag/mole removed from my neck, and a tiny one on my left eye at the Chelsea and Westminster hospital, skin clinic.

30th. I did some more work on my novel. Now up to 19,000 words. Then listened to more of Proust on tapes.

1 December. Anthony rang informing me, that Hodder had turned down my Orwell on the grounds, that people were still digesting Michael Shelden's biography on Orwell (1991), which Roland Phillips thought was very good, and he believed that only academics would find the archive interesting. Rejection often has the opposite effect to that intended, and naturally I ploughed on through the

archive, collecting material, letters, and interviewing Orwell's many friends. Also, I did some more work on my novel.

2nd. Paperback proof of *Through the Dark Labyrinth* arrived from the publisher at Pimlico, London. Delighted. All, but a few of very last-minute changes were in. Anthony telephoned - will try Orwell on Weidenfeld & Nicholson. Fingers crossed. Met new neighbours this afternoon. They seemed affable enough.

3rd. We went to the Chelsea and Westminster Hospital at 8.30 a. m. for total left- knee replacement operation tomorrow early afternoon. As usual Rhoda got me settled and prepared for tomorrow and left at 8.00 p. m. Fasted from midnight.

4th. Slept well. Rhoda came early. I was prepared by the nurses for the operation, and seen by the anaesthetist, who explained the procedure and possible complications. I signed the consent form, and was given premedication of temazepam, and was soon feeling drowsy. To operating theatre. 'Operation went well,' said the doctors. I returned to the ward. My beautiful Rhoda was at my bedside waiting for me. Felt fine and slept most of the day. All my observations were satisfactory and Rhoda left at 10 p. m. Unfortunately, just after midnight, I had a bad reaction to the antibiotic injection the young doctor was giving me. I recovered, after I was given chlorphenamine and cortisone injections. I told the staff not to inform Rhoda as she needed her sleep, and I was well after the injections were given.

5th. Slept well, seen by the physiotherapist, who gave me some exercises, got me out of bed and I sat by my bedside on a comfortable chair. Rhoda arrived and was happy to see me sitting out of bed, and doing my leg exercises. She brought me my mails. I received proofs on Writing Writer Lives for Lewes Live Literature, and proofs for Eastbourne article. I told her about my experience last night and she was quite concerned. Later, the porter took me to the X-ray department. After being X-rayed, I felt a bit woozy, and was returned by the porters to my ward. The nurse took my blood pressure reading, told me it was on the low side and

I must press the nurses' call bell should I want to get out of bed. Of course, Rhoda, being a retired midwifery manager, was very concerned and wanted to stay the night by my bedside to take care of me. But the nurses reassured her that she did not have to stay, because the nursing staff would look after me. She left later.

6th. I had a night of broken sleep, felt tired but was more alert than yesterday. I must make an efforts to get up today. Rhoda came at 2.00 p.m.

7th. Slept well and felt good. Unfortunately, my blood pressure was still a bit low. Must finish proofs by 15th. Physiotherapist came to see me and encouraged me to do my exercises. She helped me out of bed, we took a walk around the ward, I felt tired and returned to bed. Rhoda arrived at 2.00 p. m. Later, she took me to the bath room and gave me a shower. I felt better, returned to my room, sat out of bed until supper time, did some exercises and continued reading my novel. Rhoda liked it, and left after getting me back to bed.

8th. Slept well until 1.50 a.m. when woken by night staff talking quite loudly. I asked if they could keep it down. The male nurse told me, 'We have to communicate.' But I couldn't get back to sleep till around 5.00 a.m. At 6.15 a.m. I had a wash, my blood pressure was taken, and I slept. The nurses left my drugs on my bed-side table without disturbing me. I wanted to go home very soon, and to Rhoda, who would care for me.

9th. Excellent. Different staff on duty.

10th to 12th. Normal hospital routine and I wanted to go home.

13th. I was seen and examined by the doctors, who discharged me home under the care of Rhoda and my G.P. So very good to be home and with my lovely Rhoda.

14 December. My piece on The Sunday Times! Amazing boost to my ego!! Stayed up till two in the morning, correcting proofs.

GLIMPSES OF A BIOGRAPHER'S DIARY

15th. I typed up all corrections for my Durrell's book, and sent them to my editor at Pimlico, London.

16th. I felt a bit better, though leg felt quite unstable. Wrote letter to Jan, Michael Beasley and few other friends. Cancelled my dental appointment for tomorrow until I feel safer on my feet. Feeling increasingly disillusioned with the government.

17th. Snow last night. Sleep somewhat broken but adequate. Lots to do today. 18th. Sent off corrected proof to Lewes. District nurse came and removed clips from my knee. Some slight infection. She will come on Monday to remove the remaining clips. Got back to my novel, and wrote treatment of Lowry film.

19th. Encyclopaedia Britannica, Media 98. It seemed to promise multi-media features, but when I tried to activate them, I was informed that I needed to be on the Microsoft internet in order to receive it. My editor from Pimlico rang me and said, 'too late to incorporate your changes.' However, I sent him a list of a dozen essential changes. They were one letter alterations - not word changes. 'I don't know. I will see!'

Also, on the 19th. My left-knee was clicking this morning with some pain. I hoped that it would be temporary, possibly muscular, which could go as the swelling subsided. The pain under my patella on raising my leg had died down. I ordered a new cartridge for my Epson printer. In the afternoon, I notice that the infection was still in my left-knee incision.

20th. Knee felt slightly better in the morning, but was rather painful at night. Rhoda gave me two tablet of Co-dydramol 10/500 mg, and applied cold compress as required, which helped and I slept.

21st. I stayed in bed mostly resting my knee, doing my exercises and rereading Orwell's *Nineteen-Eighty-Four*. However, we did venture out in our car to collect my photographs.

22nd. Rhoda posted one of my photos to Lewes. Nurse came, examined my knee incision, saw that it was still infected, cleaned and applied fresh dressing. Rhoda rang the ward at Chelsea and

Westminster Hospital to find out the result of the swab taken on the 13th before I was discharged from hospital. She was told that the swab showed Staphylococcus infection. I rang my G.P. surgery and spoke to the manager, who informed me that she would check with my doctor and ring back.

23rd. In the morning, my doctor rang, checked on my health and informed that she had written a prescription for my knee infection and it was at the reception. Rhoda went, collected it, took it to the pharmacy, brought the seven-day course of Amoxycillin 500mg three times a day, and started the treatment straight away.

Also, she gave me two tablet, of Co-dydramol 10/500 mg, and I went to sleep for couple of hours. I can now prepare for Christmas with my beautiful girl. In the afternoon, Colin Russell (Lowry's nephew) rang and informed me that the Lowry material from Rose Cottage had gone to University of British Columbia, Canada. Also, a technician for the Encyclopaedia Britannica rang and went through setting up and managed to get sound and film but not animation to work on my computer. Restarted entering Orwell material and letters so far collected onto my computer and Rhoda entered some on the laptop.

24th. Continued from yesterday until evening when we relaxed and enjoyed our Christmas eve. Of course, Rhoda prepared the turkey ready for tomorrow. Wonderful!

25th. As usual, everything is very special from morning tea to night cap at bed time. Rhoda always makes Christmas Day very happy. I could not drink champagne, because I was taking antibiotics. However, we made an exception, and, so washed down the turkey lunch, after the Queen's speech, with champagne. We watched some television programmes, including a fabulous French film *La Reine Margot* about St Bartholomew's Day Massacre. Superb acting and directing. Shows what American cinema can do. Also, we saw Simon Callow as Dickens in very fine form. I must return to treatment, and novel, and my article on *In Ballast to the White Sea* for The Times Literary Supplement (TLS).

26th. Quiet day. Watched some television programmes, including *Dances with Wolves* and *Strauss Salome*. Must start reading and writing tomorrow.

27th. My leg seemed much improved over last two-three days. I did exercises without much pain. After doing some work on Orwell, we watched *Shallow Grave* on television. Very good film indeed. Must try to get to sleep earlier.

28 December. By now, I was better acquainted with the new Encyclopaedia Britannica, and read all of Orwell's works and some works about him: *Down and Out in Paris and London, Burmese Days, A Clergyman's Daughter, Keep the Aspidistra Flying, The Road to Wigan Pier, Homage to Catalonia, Coming Up For Air, Inside the Whale, The Lion and the Unicorn, Animal Farm, Nineteen-Eighty-Four, The Collected Essays, Journalism and Letters of George Orwell, George Orwell: A Life* by Bernard Crick, *George Orwell, A Literary Study and Orwell* by Michael Sheldon, and getting on with the rest.

29th. Poor night's sleep. To bed too late. Antibiotic seemed to be working. Operation wound appeared to be more healed over. After completing the course of antibiotic the next day, I must get back as much as possible to normal, continue with my exercises, and rest my knee as often as I can. In the afternoon, I typed up *In Ballast to the White Sea* article for the TLS. To bed early.

30th. I listened to Proust side 4 A, again. Continued reading works about Orwell and was happy with my public lending rights - the British Library account for year:

1997: £49.49, *Pursued by Furies A Life of Malcolm Lowry* was borrowed 680 occasions, *Through the Dark Labyrinth a biography of Lawrence Durrell* was borrowed 1685 occasions, *Freedom, Reason, or Revolution?* 25 times, *Malcolm Lowry Remembered* 51 occasions and *Under the Volcano* 11 times.

31st. New Year's Eve. We were determined to see 1997 out, and welcome the New Year. We had a very good day, ending it with drinking champagne and watching the fireworks. However, at

11.30 p.m., someone rang our door bell, I looked through the curtain and saw two cars parked outside in the middle of the road with doors opened. We heard a voice saying, 'Someone just looked through the window.' Then there was talk of meeting at Lancaster Gate, and both cars left. We wondered what that was all about. Rhoda said, 'New Year's Eve!!'

1998

1-3 January. Happy New Year! Two years to the millennium. I made no resolutions, but was determined to commit myself to literature, for example, to George Orwell, my novel, complete my article for the TLS and then, the film treatment about Malcolm Lowry. Rhoda didn't say whether she made any resolutions or not. We had a delightful New Year's Day as usual, ending by washing down our supper drinking champagne. Promising!! 3rd. Feeling poorly – probably, due to a disappointing 1997, and too much excitement. Felt better after doing a bit of work on Orwell.

4th-13th. I had a broken night's sleep. Rhoda just left me to sleep till 11.30 a.m. My left- knee's wound had improved, but still looked inflamed. Rhoda kept a close eye on it. I didn't seem to be getting back to work properly yet. Must do something to ensure a decent sleep at night, and to have my tooth extracted.

5th. In the morning, I rang my G. P's surgery, and informed the receptionist that my left-knee is still inflamed, and I wanted the doctor to visit me at home. She came in the afternoon. After discussing my health, saw and examined my left-knee, she put me immediately on the same antibiotics, and arranged for me to see my surgeon the next day. I was impressed with her and her duty of care. Well done. Rhoda took the prescription to the chemist, returned with the antibiotics and started me immediately on them.

6th. We went to the Chelsea and Westminster hospital to be seen and examined by my surgeon, who was happy with my knee and my progress, continued with the antibiotics, and to see him in three weeks. The receptionist gave us the appointment date in writing, and we returned home.

GLIMPSES OF A BIOGRAPHER'S DIARY

9th. My knee was still swollen, felt hot and inflamed. My G. P. rang this morning and gave me advice. Need to rest my knee. So, I slept downstairs to avoid climbing up and down the three sets of stairs.

12th. The nurse came, checked on my health, saw and examined my left-knee, ran and spoke to my G. P., who decided that no further action was needed. However, she said that, should it flares up again, to ring her and go to the hospital.

14 January. Anthony rang me this morning and informed me that Weidenfeld & Nicolson said 'no' to Orwell. We talked about other authors. Another rejection. I spent a lot of time researching Orwell, and I knew that he was the author I wanted to write about. I would not give up on him. I discussed this matter with Rhoda and we agreed not to give up on Orwell. She herself had been reading Orwell's works. She even said that if I had to self-publish, so be it. Bless Rhoda. I could make use of the work I had done on Orwell. I could even make it a Testimony of George Orwell. In the afternoon, I sent Anthony a revised Orwell's proposal, stressing the psychology about his father insisting that, he should miss Oxford, and told him, 'Go to India' after Eton. He went to Burma.

15th. Anthony rang, and told me that he had sent revised Orwell to Bill Hamilton. Also, he let me know that Dylan Thomas's publisher would probably want a new Dylan Thomas biography. Both Rhoda and I had read Dylan Thomas' works. I had a lot of his books on the shelves, but I thought, 'He never went to France.

17th. Reading The Death of Dylan Thomas. 18th. I felt a bit gloomy about doing him. I couldn't decide whether I could live with him or not. Do I care enough or feel empathetic? I had a headache. I talked with Rhoda. She is a very good listener.

18th. We went to my dentist for a tooth extraction. Poor and tired day.

19th. Began a proposal outline of Dylan. I continued with my novel and was enjoying it.

1998

22nd. Carried on reading The Death of Dylan Thomas. 25th. Finished reading Dylan, and started reading Caitlin Thomas *Leftover Life to Kill*. Added slightly to Dylan. Continued with Dylan proposal and outline.

28th. Received cheque for £300.00 from The Sunday Times.

29th. Attended the Chelsea and Westminster for physiotherapy.

31st. Reading Fitzgibbon's on *The Life of Dylan Thomas*. We went to our local library, and brought home some more of his books.

2-6 February. I received a fax from BBC TV Bookmark, who were doing a TV programme on Lawrence Durrell to which I contributed. I asked the staff at David Higham Ltd to settle a fee for any contribution that I might make to it.

3rd. Jo from David Higham rang and briefed me that she gave the Bookmark woman my phone number before coming with a deal with her of £100. - consultation fee for £75. and short TV interview for £25. I said, 'Say £150.' She came back to say that the BBC stuck at £100. but only if they used me in the interview. I said, 'No'. So, the programme would have to be made without me. Jo left a message on my answerphone to say, 'No contract, no deal.'

5th. I agreed to meet Julie Heppenstall from Bookmark at my home at 2.00 p.m.

6th. Julie came, interviewed me, which went well. We said our good-byes, and she left.

8 February. I received a letter from my friend, David Markson, an author based in Greenwich Village, New York, saying that he had a couple of Dylan stories. I rang him later, and we discussed them. Continued working on my novel, and up to 24,000 words. It was going quite well, but would get difficult later. Reading more of Dylan's works.

14 February. Continued writing my novel, up to nearly 30,000 words and I am enjoying it. We had a delightful and happy Valentine's Day at home.

GLIMPSES OF A BIOGRAPHER'S DIARY

16th. Slept quite well. It was possible to find a style for Dylan, which could captured his inner life - the creative id, and the other many facets - the self-confidence, the careless scrounging, the harsh judgemental disposition, the lustful womaniser, the alcoholic, and the bohemian.

I had physiotherapy at Chelsea and Westminster Hospital at 4.30 p. m. Continued with my novel and up to 31,000 words.

17th-19th. Writing my novel and up to 47,000 words. Of course, I was reading Dylan's works.

20th. The Editor of Halliwell Filmgoer's Companion (now published as Halliwell's Who's Who in the movies) wrote thanking me for my update on Malcolm Lowry, and on my suggested entry on Lawrence Durrell, which he said he would incorporate in a future edition.

23rd. My paperback book of *Through the Dark Labyrinth - a Biography of Lawrence Durrell* - arrived and was published. Its arrival was timely with the BBC TV interview on my Lawrence Durrell book coming up on the next day. The Duff Cooper Award at Mayfair was interesting occasion.

24th. I won't give up on Orwell. The BBC TV film crew came as planned at 4.30 p. m. to interview me for the Bookmark programme on Lawrence Durrell. They rearranged the furniture and set up lights. I was interviewed by the producer, Nadia Haggard, at great length, especially about Sappho, Nancy, Lawrence Durrell's sexuality, and about Durrell and Henry Miller. Then, they shot me working at my computer. They said that I was great. But who knows? Before leaving at 7.00 p. m., Nadia said that she would be sending me a contract. In the evening, Rhoda and I went to our local Greek restaurant, and had a delicious meal washed down with red wine. We had a good time and spent the evening relaxing.

25th. Anthony rang in the morning to let me know that the Orwell proposal had been turned down yet again. Also, he didn't like the Dylan Thomas proposal. What can I say? Over coffee, Rhoda and

1998

I had a post mortem. I would continue with my novel and Orwell, and would have to read other biographies.

26-28. Ploughing through Dylan, and writing my novel. Up to 54,500words.

1-18 March. I spent most of my time continued to reading Dylan, and writing my novel - up to 86,000 words. Finished 1st draft and checked novel for corrections. I thought about my next novel. It could be: *A Man Searching for George Orwell in Paris*.

19th Rhoda and I visited Paris again by Eurostar. I read a good brief article in the Eurostar magazine about Julian Barnes and how popular he was in Paris. We stayed at our favourite hotel: Le Clément on the left-bank. Our Paris plans were to visit scenes from my novel, to check authenticity of descriptive passages, places, associations and to revise the novel on site as it were. In the evening, we headed for our dinner at the Alsace restaurant. A guy, next to our table, talked about food - food they had, and food they liked. I'd forgotten how many Crêperies there were along Rue du Bucci, Blvd St Germain, St Michel and student's cafés. Before leaving St Michel, we saw a man stripped to his waist, and performing oriental dance. Delightful.

20th. We called on Odile Hellier and Michael at the Village Voice bookshop. We talked about the Lowry and Durrell books, which they said they loved. Of course, I gave talks on both my books at this bookshop. I told them about my novel, and we had some enlightening discussion. Then to Montparnasse, and had lunch at Le Dôme café, green leather and polished wood, red walls with drawings, portraits and photographs of famous clients/customers, arts nouveau lamps and so on. Opposite Le Dôme café, is the La Rotonde restaurant. At Montparnasse Cemetery, many messages were left on Simone de Beauvoir's tomb: 'Thank you ever so much, your words have given me endless joy.' 'You are beautiful.' 'Your words were so beautiful.' 'I love you, my darling.' 'Bonne Nuit.' Many more tributes: flowers, more messages, some scribbled on the back of a Metro ticket, small pebbles and more. At Samuel

GLIMPSES OF A BIOGRAPHER'S DIARY

Beckett grave, a single stone was left. Then, we went to L' Odéon, by Metro, where the imposing statue of de Danton was pointing mysteriously to the Seine'

20 March (continued). We walked up Boulevard Monparnasse, passed la Coupole restaurant on the left and Le Select on the right. Then, in the other direction, we walked to Closerie des Lilas, and sat at the table of Edvard Munch for late tea. Then round to the corner, were tables of Max Jacob, Struulltberg and André Bréton. Other tables carry small brass plaques to Man Ray, Simone de Beauvoir and some others. It was said that here Hemingway wrote The Sun Also Rises.

In the evening, we attended a talk by David Leavitt, an American novelist, short- story writer and biographer, on Prayers to Demigod at the Village Voice bookshop - very simple and direct prose. After his talk, Odile introduced me to him. He was surrounded by many of his friends and Kathleen Spivack, an American poet. I met many others. Later, we went out for dinner, but he made an excuse not to attend. Odile invited me to talk again about both of my books. Maybe I will.

21st. I had a poor night, due to my neighbour coming in late, and turning on his television. We headed to our friend, Cecily Mackworth, for lunch. Delightful. She knew Dylan Thomas and Vernon Watkins very well and gave me useful information. I told her about my novel, and we had some fruitful discussions. We returned to our hotel for dinner, and I reread my novel to Rhoda, who enjoyed it very much.

22nd. To the market for food, back with them to our hotel, then to Montmartre - first to the cemetery, and saw graves of Emile Zola, La Gouline, Frederick Leinditre, Heinrich Heine, Dumas Filo, Stendhal, Clougets, Truffaut, and some family graves were built like small temples. Then, to Place Blanche and the Moulin Rouge, where a crowd had gathered, and circus performers mixed with the crowd - stilt walking, unicyclist, jugglers and more. We headed for coffee at Le Chat Noir. Then, proceeded to the Pigalle and the

Sacré Coeur. Many police about. So far, I had to correct some places where my character, Luxton, had travelled. We made a break for a light lunch at L'Impérial, then, to the Ritz on Place Vendôme. Afterwards, we went to the Hotel Lotti in Rue Castiglione, where Orwell worked in the kitchens as a plongeur and Hôtel Crillon at La Place de la Concorde. Finally, back to Sèvres Babylone, walking a bit more, observing and checking places before returning to our hotel.

23rd. We paid a visit to Hôtel le Royale, where Luxton stayed in room thirteen, which energised him. We proceeded to the Banque de France to change some old French notes, and then to Saint-Germain-des Près, where we had coffee and croissants at Les Deux Magots, there taking in the scenery. Continued on Luxton trail and ended up at St Michel, close to the 1998 Alsace restaurant, where we had lunch. Then walked along the Seine, passed Bouquinistes to the Notre Dame Cathedral, where Rhoda lit candles. We, then, proceeded to Shakespeare and Company bookshop, having a look around and chatting to George, especially about my books and my novel set in Paris. He was interested, and we had some enlightening discussion. Also, we continued to keep notes of all the places along the way to St Michel and our hotel. After supper, I updated my novel. Rhoda read and enjoying it so far.

24th. We returned to the Village Voice bookshop, said our goodbyes to Odile and Michael before leaving for home by Eurostar to Waterloo, London. Back home, amongst my many letters, I received a good one from Nadia Haggerd about Bookmark. I restarted revising my novel and reading *The Great Gatsby* - fine fluent style. We relaxed.

25th. Revised chapter two of my novel. Toner for our printer arrived. I wrote and sent off letters. Despite sleeping in late this morning, I fell asleep this evening. Finished reading The Great Gatsby.

GLIMPSES OF A BIOGRAPHER'S DIARY

26th. Ten copies of my Durrell's biography arrived. I listening to Proust tape, side 7A - Swann in Love. Will listen to Proust tape, side 8A tomorrow. Rhoda finished reading *Luxton* and she liked it.

2 April. I finished correcting my novel, and delivered one copy together with my paperback copy of Durrell's to ,.

3rd. Rhoda and I drove to Dover to catch the ferry to Calais, where we continued our journey to France, Béthune, then to Neuve Chapelle. Very flat farming country, and heavy-looking reddish dark soil. We arrived at the Memorial Neuve Chapelle, saw a small number of tombstones, a monument and several graves with simple marked names, A Soldier of the Great War Known Unto God. All graves have daffodils, primroses, cornflowers, lilies, beautifully kept, well-tended, stones pristine and were well preserved. We then walked to the Indian War Memorial bearing hundreds of names of soldiers killed in battle, especially at the battle of Neuve Chapelle. We had great difficulty finding a hotel, and when we found one, we had our supper, discussed our experiences and went to sleep.

4th. We headed for Arras, wanting to see my father brother's, Uncle Bill, grave. We got lost, but finally found Duisans British Cemetery. It lies in Étrun but takes its name from the nearer village of Duisans. Duisans and Étrun are villages in the Department of the Pas-de-Calais, about nine kilometres west of Arras. Some graves were a little apart, others joined together, no space between tombstones. Uncle Bill's grave was in a row, a little separated from his neighbour. He died of a wound on 23/03/1918. The Royal Garrison Artillery was his Regiment. A very sad day for me, all sort of emotions. I wept and Rhoda planted roses. From there, we drove to Bapaume, then to Thiepval Memorial, which is north of the Albert-Bapaume Road. We proceeded to the German War Graves, they were in black and on the battlefield. Also, we saw a French Memorial Cemetery, before returning to our hotel in Lille. It was a very memorable day in our lives.

5th-6th April. From Autoroute south from Lille on the N29, we headed for Amiens south of the Somme. At the river crossing teenagers were fishing. The 1916 boys of that age went fishing with something a bit different from a fishing rod. On the road to Amiens, the woods crowd the hillside like gathering armies. We saw houses with different roofs, pitched at different angles, some half-timbered, some large iron gates, and so on. On the horizon, some church spires were noticeable. Remembered that in this part of France, there are public displays of faith: crucifixes, crucified Christ and effigies outside churches as at Neuve Chapelle.

Houses on roadsides in towns and villages: some single-story, some with decorated facades, mostly checker-board pattern, occasional barns and factories. Now to Rouen. 6th. We drove from Rouen up the autoroute to Calais, where we took the ferry to Dover and home.

7 April. Back home, many messages on answerphone, and letters waited. One was from Anthony saying that he had received the Durrell's book and would read it over Easter. Another from Sophie at Pimlico Press informing me that BBC Radio Jersey wanted to interview me. I arranged interview for next Tuesday.

8th. Revised my novel up to chapter fourteen. I felt bad about sending early chapters to Anthony, for there was some bad writing, but it got better from about midway. I was very tired.

9th. Continued revising my novel, ordered fifteen more copies of Durrell's book from my publisher, prepared five for friends and Rhoda posted them. I was tired again. I must make an appointment to see my G. P.

11th. Among letters received was one from Mulk Ray Anand (12/12/1905-28/09/2004), who was a prominent Indian author of novels, short stories, and critical essays in English, editor and journalist. Rhoda posted a copy of my Durrell's book to Anand and Judy Anderson.

12th. Listened to Proust part two, side 1A tape, and printed out complete 4th draft of my novel.

GLIMPSES OF A BIOGRAPHER'S DIARY

14 April. BBC Radio Jersey interviewed me at BBC London in the morning.

15th. Reading *The Magus* by John Fowles telling the story of Nicholas Urfe, a young British graduate, who is teaching English in a small Greek island. Very good indeed.

17th. I received an invitation to Lewes for my Durrell's paperback book launch on the 25th. We attended, and I gave my talk, stayed for another talks, had much discussion followed by much eating, drinking, talking and laughing. It was a very satisfying day.

29th. I saw Anthony at 11.00 a. m. at his office. He had read my novel and Dylan Thomas proposal. He liked the novel, but it needed tension throughout to keep the readers involved. He suggested, that he could give it to an independent reader, or I could revise it. I chose to revise. Then, he told me that he would show Dylan Thomas proposal to his boss. After further discussion, I left. I continued this discussion with Rhoda when I got home. We went out for dinner at our local Greek restaurant and were merry.

1 May. BBC contract for Bookmark programme on Durrell arrived, and was scheduled for 15th August. Rhoda went to her sister in London for the weekend.

2nd. I finished rewriting my novel. Now to concentrate on my writing.

6th. I received a letter from Mulk Ray Anand - mostly about Indian philosophy and western writers, and said that he would review my book in India. I spent most of the day on Thomas Dylan proposal, and redrafting my novel.

7th May - 24th June. In addition to reading Dylan, and redrafting my novel, I listened to Proust *Swann's Way* tapes, reading Cocteau's *Opium*, Nabokov *Transparent Things*, and other books, writing stories and letters, continued researching Orwell, listening to radio 4 literary programmes, out for dinner, to theatres, local cinema and relaxing at home with my beautiful Rhoda.

1998

24 June. Anthony telephoned and agreed we could try Orwell again. I would have to revise my proposal in the light of the new archives.

25th. I wrote my article for the Times Literary Supplements (TLS) on *In Ballast to the White Sea*.

30th. Alan Ross told me, that he would like me to review *Orwell's Complete Works* for his London Magazine. I accepted, of course.

3-12 July. I was mostly immersing myself in reading; *George Orwell's Complete Work* edited by Peter Davison, making notes and entering them on my computer.

6th. The Orwell's Archives arrived. Fascinating!!

13th. We travelled by Eurostar to Paris to make more notes on the Orwell trail, and on: Orwell The European for Prospect Magazine. We checked in at the Hôtel le Royale, Boulevard Raspail, Montparnasse. Then, proceeded to the Le Dôme café for lunch, bought some food at the Spar supermarket, and telephoned our friend, Cecily Mackworth. Later, we had dinner at the Closerie des Lilas. returned to our hotel, relaxed, read and sleepy.

14th. We started our day at Shakespeare and Company bookshop, signed copies of my Durrell's and Lowry's biographies. Afterwards, we went to Pompidou Centre, but found it closed. So, we returned to the Le Dôme café for lunch. Then, in the evening to Cecily for dinner, and collected her door keys, because we would be staying at her very pleasant and comfortable flat from 16th.

15th. For the second time on this trip, we headed for the Pompidou Centre on a fool's errand. Yesterday closed, today not fully operational, because of renovation and repairs. So, we went to Place du Panthéon on Bibliothèque St Genevieue to see Le Figaro for 1928 - 1929. On our way back, at a crossing at Châtelet, an Arab man on a motorbike, shouted at Rhoda. I shouted back at him, and he rode off with an obscene gesture. As we were crossing, he turned, and headed back straight for us. Fortunately, some people beside us were shielding us. As he passed, he spat at me, but hit Rhoda instead. My poor inoffensive Rhoda. Very upsetting. I took her to Les Deux Magots for coffee, and she went to the washroom to wash her face. Then, we walked to Saint-Germain-des Près church to light candles and pray. Rhoda felt better. We returned to the Place du Panthéon on Bibliothèque St Genevieue and saw Le Figaro for January to June 1928 - very anticommunist, got the idea of what the political background was. Returned to our hotel, Rhoda had a shower and sponged down her coat to rid herself of the last trace of the Arab man's spit. We had room service for dinner. Tomorrow, we move to Cecily's flat.

16 - Gordon with Cecily at her flat

16 July. We checked out from the Hôtel le Royale, and walked to Gare Montparnasse to check out bus services to Cecily. Decided that it was too far to walk from the bus stop. So, we would travel by train. Went to the Le Dôme café for coffee, croissants, wrote post cards and posted them. Then, staggered off to the cemetery to pay our respects to Baudelaire and Beckett. Afterward, we

hobbled off to the train station, took a train to Rue du Temple, walked to Cecily's place and collapsed.

17 July. Once again, we headed for the boarding house above 6 rue du Pot de Fer, where Orwell stayed, whilst working as a dishwasher at Hotel Lotti. We walked around the area, had lunch and tried to feel the spirit of the place. Then, returned to Cecily's flat, had tea and read. Later, we dined out at a Moroccan restaurant. The food was truly delicious. Slept well.

18th. We returned to the Place du Panthéon on Bibliothèque St Genevieue to see Le Figaro from 1928-1929, photocopied pages of relevant materials. Also, we saw *Les Amis du Peuple*, the Farthing newspaper for which George Orwell worked for G. K's weekly in 1928. Then, to the Odéon for lunch, afterwards, bought food at the shop, too tired to go to bookshop, and so, returned to Cecily's. Ate in, discussed events, read, made notes and slept well.

19th. Walked to the Picasso Museum, at 5 rue de Thorigny, an art gallery dedicated to showcasing the paintings, drawings, engravings and sculptures of Picasso. A very good overview of his life's work. Returned to the flat and reading more of Orwell, and Rhoda reading Stuart Gilbert on James Joyce and *The Untouchable* poem by John Banville. Had dinner at the very good local Moroccan restaurant.

20th. We left Cecily's keys with her neighbour, headed for the Gare du Nord station, and caught the Eurostar to London. Later, we went to our very good local Greek restaurant for supper.

21st. Hangover, but worked on Orwell's proposal. Spent much of the next day at the Chelsea and Westminster hospital for various investigations and physiotherapy. In the evening, after supper, we looked at Anais Nin video obtained by one of Rhoda's patient's working at the Daily Mail. Bless her.

23-31 July. Continued reading Orwell's Complete Works, making notes on my computer, reading reviews, revised my article for Alan Ross' London Magazine, entertaining friends and neighbour, listening to Proust tapes, writing letters, starting a new novel, cleaning and preparing our car for MOT.

1 - 8 August. I continued reading, making notes on my computer from *George Orwell's Complete Works*, listening to Proust tapes, with the occasional visit to our local cinema and dining out.

9th. Headed for Hayes and Uxbridge, looking for material on Orwell's days as a school teacher. He taught at the Hawthorns High School, a private prep school for boys in Hayes from 1st April 1932. There were only 14 to 15 boy pupils and one other teacher. In June 1933, he left the Hawthorns to become a teacher at Frays College, in Uxbridge. I met one of his ex-Frays College pupils, who told me that he had a motorcycle, and took trips through the surrounding countryside. He added that, on one of these sightseeing trips, in the heavy-rain, he became very soaked, caught a chill, that developed into pneumonia. He was taken to the cottage hospital in Uxbridge, where he was so seriously ill, that his life was thought to be in danger. When he was discharged in January 1934, he never returned to teaching. Apparently, he went to his parents to convalesce. He mentioned that one of Blair's colleagues at Frays, Henry Stapley, was still alive and living in Chesterfield.

Later on, I travelled north to see him. Henry was 86 and blind, had taught maths and geography at the College, and had some wonderful stories to tell me about his 'Bolshy" colleague, Blair - how the man, who appointed him, was a Mosley Fascist called Donovan, and how, openly flouting the rules; he had smoked his pungent tobacco at the refectory high-table. Once, Stapley and his wife invited him for dinner, and were presented with a book called: *Down and Out in Paris and London*, which he was pleased to announce he had written. 'But this is by George Orwell,' said Henry. Blair smiled and said, 'That's me.' He, also, confirmed what the ex-pupil told me about Blair's motorcycle trip, when he caught pneumonia, and ended up in hospital never to return to teaching at Frays College. All very interesting.

1998

10th. Completed and printed out another revision of George Orwell's *The European* for Prospect magazine. Started to revise my article on: In Ballast to the White Sea for the TLS, but more work needed to be done on it.

12-14 August. Rhoda away with her sister, Margaret, and their friend, Val, on a weekend girls' outing. I continued reading Orwell's *Complete Works*, and making notes on my computer, writing stories, received proofs of Orwell's *Complete Works* from Alan Ross, revising drafts of my novel.

15th. Durrell programme on Bookmark went out on BBC TV.

18th. I delivered my article: *Orwell; the European to Prospect in Bedford Square*.

22nd. Rhoda's nephew, Gabriel, was married to beautiful Leyla, and there were lots of family celebrations before and after the wedding. Rhoda and I had great fun on the wedding day eating, drinking and dancing.

26th. Wrote to Odile Hellier at Village Voice bookshop, Paris, accepting the 19th November to talk on Lawrence Durrell in Paris.

31st. Rhoda returned home after all the family celebrations and her 2 sisters and brother and families returned to Canada and Atlanta, USA.

1-12 September. I continued reading, making notes on my computer on Orwell's Complete Works, and writing many letters.

5th. Went again to see *Oh What a Lovely War* with Rhoda. Started another story about a young poet going to university, finish off revising my novel that I delivered to Anthony,, booked another driving trip to France and having car serviced.

9th. We saw *Lolita* by Vladimir Nabokov with Jeremy Irons at ABC cinema, Piccadilly, London, and preparing for our trip to France.

13th-14th. We left home at 5.30 a. m. for Dover, missed our Sea France ferry by ten minutes because a woman before us was discussing her ticket. So, we bought The Observer and The Sunday Times and read, took the next ferry to Calais. From there, we drove briefly to Béthune, which is between Arras and St Omer just off the A 26 motorway, then to Camdrin in pouring-rain, visiting the two cemeteries used for Commonwealth burials. We proceeded to Quincy, a village in the east of the Loire, afterwards to Festubert, the village was on the Western Front during the First World War, but was largely destroyed in the May 1915 Battle of Festubert. Then, we drove on to pay our tributes at the Indian Memorial Neuve Chapelle, and headed to Arras, where we booked at the Moderne Hotel for two nights. We were tired, had room service, watched a bit of TV, reread Chapter One of: *Keep the Aspidistra Flying*, prepared for bed and slept.

14th. Woke up at 6.00 a.m., had breakfast at 7.00 a.m., and then drove around Arras, saw Grand Place, one of two fabulous squares in Arras, mostly built following their destruction during the War. Very impressive with loads of places to eat and drink, with underground parking as well as parking on the cobbled-street level. Arras is well known for its architecture, culture and history. We headed for Duisans British Cemetery, parked our car and walked to my Uncle Bill's grave again. This time, the weather was beautifully sunny, but still a whipping wind. The trees at the end, now in leaf, obscured the barbed-wire-like-fencing. Uncle Bill's grave (Row E5, Grave 48) now had blooming yellow roses that Rhoda had planted. On the road to Aubigny British Cemetery and Loos, a French city, where we had coffee and cakes. Then made for La Bassée and Lavonte. Parked our car in the square, had lunch, listened to Kenneth Branagh reading Wilfred Owen poems. Made me weep, as usual, especially the one about the young soldier blinded. La Bassée and Lavonte were mentioned by Graves in *Goodbye to All That*. Leaving Lovante, we visited German Cemetery again briefly, and headed for Vimy to pay our respects to the Canadians and other soldiers, who died there. The Canadian National Vimy Memorial is a War Memorial in France, dedicated to the memory of Canadian Expeditionary Force members killed during the First World War. It was established by the Canadian Corps after the successful storming of Vimy bridge on April 9, 1917. We saw an exhibition and videos, visited trenches and tunnels, sandbags and duckboards. But the tunnels were very realistic and eerie. Below the first level down was a locked iron door, with a set of holes like a grill to look through, and saw barely lit steps going down to a tunnel. It was an uncanny replica of the door leading to the bunker beneath the Villa Luxton, I dreamt up for my novel. Then back to Arras.

15 September. After a good night's sleep, woke up early, had breakfast at 7.00 a.m., and checked out. We drove to Bapaume, to Albert, and to Pozières visiting the Pozières British Cemetery. The Pozières Battle (23 July-3 September 1916) took place around the village during the Battle of the Somme, and this Cemetery is enclosed by the Pozières Memorial. We proceeded to Fricourt and Mametz, and visited the Fricourt British Cemetery (Bray Road). This cemetery contains graves in which more than one casualty is buried, and on which more than one headstone is erected. Each grave has a single number. One of the burial is unidentified and an, special Memorial commemorates, casualties whose grave could not be found. I wonder, could it have been around here that my Dad was wounded. Afterwards, we made for Amiens Cathedral and walked to Place Gambetta, a building at Gambetta Square in the city centre with lawns, paddling pools and deck chairs in the summer.

After a good French lunch, we returned to the Cathédral, which was cold, deserted and dreary. Rhoda lit candles, of course. We made a break for Giverny to Claude Monet's house and the most famous gardens. He had a passion for gardening. Most of his paintings were his colourful gardens and, especially the famous Water Lily ponds. We bought cards, had coffee and cakes before leaving for Rouen. After initial problems finding our hotel and parking place, we went out for a delicious French dinner, washed down with Morgan red wine. Rouen is situated on the banks of the River Seine, and is Normandy's vibrant, historic and cultural capital, famous for its Cathédral and for many fine museums. Joan of Arc met her death in the French city of Rouen.

16th. After breakfast, we checked out and set off for Beaune at around 9.30 a.m. Got lost in Rouen, and found ourselves on an Autoroute going north. Luckily, we found our way out of a small town, and were back to Rouen, which led us fairly straight to the Autoroute to Paris. We needed the A6 to take us to Beaune, but had great difficulty finding our way through Versailles and Rambouillet until, by some fluke, we found ourselves on the right route. A long haul to Beaune, so we stopped once, slept for half an hour en route, had French coffee and cakes, of course. Beaune is a lovely walled-town at the centre of the Burgundy wine-making region of France. It is surrounded by the Cote d'Or vineyard, and the cobbled town is renounced for an annual wine-auction on the third Sunday in November. We stayed at Inter Hotel Relais Motel 21. This charming and traditional hotel had every modern amenity for a comfortable and relaxed stay, with free car park, fully enclosed, and code-controlled gate. After lunch and a rest, we walked around this charming town, visited the museum, park and garden, had afternoon tea, and later a stunning dinner. It was truly wonderful. Tomorrow, to Santenay and to try to find my friend's, Martine, family grave. Martine died in 1970 when I was a visiting professor in Canada.

17th. We got up late. After breakfast, we left our hotel around 9.45 a.m., and went to the Beaune tourist office. We found our way out along Chalan Road to Santenay. There, we asked direction to St. Jean Church. It was a long, winding- country road out to Santenay le Haut. Got to the church, and find it closed for repair. As we were about to enter the churchyard, it began to rain and soon it was bucketing down. Rhoda said, 'Martine is crying, because you are here after twenty-eight years. She is crying for her lost life, the years untried.' It was about 11.30 a.m., and we decided to go back to the village square to wait for better weather. Had lunch and explored Santenay. We found a large camp site, visited the Casino, and lost sixteen francs. We saw another church, and Rhoda lit candles. Santenay is a lovely village, with mansions and château in the heart of the vineyards. Quite a pleasant and tasteful place really. On our way up to St. Jean church, we found the Château de la Crée and got a map of the village. Now, the sun was shining and we returned to St. Jean Church, hoping that the good weather would hold. Rhoda and I began to look for the family grave. Finally, we found it, a brown marble slab, with a cross upon it and in gold letters, chiselled along the sides the names of various family members. First was Martine from - to - , followed by the rest of the family. She came from a family blessed by longevity, but died, aged twenty-eight, more than twenty-eight years ago!! How sad to see one member of the family - perhaps Martine's grandmother lived to be one hundred and three, and perhaps her grandfather lived to be ninety-three. Rhoda is so very understanding, empathetic, comforting and supportive. She left me alone beside the grave for a time. I spoke to Martine about my regrets, my thoughts about her, and I explained exactly, how it had been that her letters had gone unanswered – (me away in Canada lecturing, a postal strike and me only getting to read them on my return - too late!!!) I took in the beautiful setting, a hollow scooped of rock, leaving cliffs above, towering over the church and cemetery, lined with trees, shrubs and more. I would like to have wept, and feel the occasion more deeply as I did when I returned home then from Canada, and read her letters, especially her family one with black-bordered envelope notifying me about her death. When I read that letter I wept and wept. But, even though I thought of her often, after all these years, it was just a moment of sad reflection. I photographed the grave from every angle and left my message on a postcard in a sealed-clear sleeve, that Rhoda happened to have. I said my goodbyes and we left. Workmen at the church allowed us to see the church briefly. 'This is where Martine's funeral took place. Could her family ever forgive me? Did they, I wonder, blame me in any way for her death? I blamed myself certainly. How would they react to my visiting her grave? So many unanswered questions!!!' Later, at a post office in Santenay, I was told that a family member aged about fifty lived close to the church at St. Jean. Perhaps, she would find my postcard. Rhoda persuaded me to have coffee and cakes to eat before returning to Beaune. Bless her. In our room, Rhoda read and left me to my thoughts. I started writing a story entitled: *The Wrong Man*. Later, we went out for dinner washed down with red Morgan wine.

18 September. After a good night's sleep and breakfast, we checked out, and from Beaune, we drove to Reims via Troyes where we had our lunch. Afterwards, took a short tour of this charming, very pleasant old town, with narrow cobbled-street lined with colourful half-timbered houses. Went to the Cathédral, which has striking stained-glass windows. Rhoda lit candles. Then, on to Reims, checked in at this peaceful Hôtel Les Réflets Bleus, room 34. Rhoda was taken by the fact that our room was number 34, my birth year. Outside, rosemary grew like those at Martine's grave. We were both tired and had tea in our room; I read *The Road to Wigan Pier* and Rhoda *The Clergyman's Daughter*. Had an amazing dinner at the hotel. Very enjoyable.

Next day, after breakfast, we wrote postcards, checked out, drove into Reims, and went to Reims cathedral. Rather striking and empty-of-life, but has some beautiful features. Posted our cards. From there, we drove to Laos. Another lovely Cathédral, but high up on a small mountain, which you had to climb on foot. My knees and hips would not make it. So, we drove on, and skirted St Quinton, and Abbeville, and then on to Montreuil, where we booked in at the Hôtel La Peuplerale and had a real taste of family cooking.

20th. After a good night's sleep, the morning fog forced us to check out and leave late. Drove to Berck and Le Touquet, which has the best beach in France and lively night life. Rhoda is very impressed with this classy resort. Then via Bologne to Calais, where we took the ferry to Dover in the afternoon. We drove to Dover St. James' Cemetery and found my Uncle Ernie's grave after much searching. He was wounded in the First World War. More than 700 servicemen and women are buried in this Cemetery. Throughout both World Wars, Dover was a hub of military activities, with hundreds and thousands of soldiers embarking for and returning from Europe. Throughout the First World War, more than six million wounded servicemen were brought ashore at Dover, and during the Second World War, the Dunkirk evacuation was coordinated from here.

Arrived home at 5.30 p.m. Lots of letters and messages to deal with.

21-30 September. Back home, Martine was so much in my thoughts last night, that I felt, I had to read through her surviving letters, and the old diary for the period 1967-70. Prospect Magazine appeared not to have used my Orwell's article. Received copies of my Durrell's book from Pimlico. I attended TLS evening reception at Hatchards, Piccadilly. Bought books and videos. Very good as usual. Alan Ross published my Orwell's article in his London Magazine. Received letter from Penguin Books asking for 3000 words introduction to: Malcolm Lowry; *Hear Us O Lord From Heaven Thy Dwelling Place and Lunar Caustic*. I accepted and asked them to send my contract to Anthony,. Received a letter from Margaret Crosland, an English literary biographer and translator, offering to read my novel, that was turned down. Finished reading *A Clergyman's Daughter*.

1 October. I drove to Uxbridge Local History Library, to continue my research on Orwell. Discovered some more interesting material, and that the owner of Hawthorns High School for Boys was called Robert and not Derek. Also, there was a woman, who remembered Orwell (Blair) at Frays College. Afterwards, I went to interview Geoffrey Stevens, a pupil at Hawthorns, who was taken with teacher, Blair, and confirmed that the owner of Hawthorns was called Robert. He gave me a very good interview indeed. What's more, before leaving, he gave me some new material about Orwell.

5th. Anthony rang informing me that he had agreed £1,000. and Penguin's contract to follow. Also, he also told me that he had forwarded a reader's report on my novel, which was thumbs down again!!

6 -13 October. However, I received a friendly and encouraging letter from Margaret Crosland. Later on, I went to see my friend,

Eddie Linden, owner of Aquarius, at St Mary's hospital, sitting out of bed in grand style in a side ward. We had interesting conversation about Orwell and my novel. Lovely to see Eddie again. Watched video of Henry and June, writing stories, did a little more work on my future Paris talk about Lawrence Durrell, booked again for our Isle of Wight trip to visit friends, Anthony telephoned me, and said to do the Orwell proposal again. We had a lively talk. I finished reading *Keep the Aspidistra Flying*.

14 October. Tomorrow, Rhoda and I would drive to the Isle of Wight to visit friends again for five days. I listened to David Gascoyne interviews I did on my last visit.

15th. We drove to Portsmouth, took the Wight Link Ferry to Isle of Wight, proceeded to Shanklin, where we checked in to Luccombe Hall Hotel, that had a breathtaking sea view and direct access to sandy beach. In the afternoon, we visited David Gascoyne and his wife, Judy. His friends Kathleen Raine, poet, and others wanted me to write his biography. We talked mainly about his life and works, covering some more grounds not included on our last visit. Bought a copy of his Selected Prose. Of course, they wanted to know about my biographies, and we talked a bit about them. Also, they asked about my novel. Sadly, I told them that it was turned down. They, like all my friends, were encouraging me to 'persevere with it, because there is a publisher out there somewhere, who would be proud to publish it'. I thanked them, of course. After a very pleasant afternoon, we left and explored Shanklin. This is a popular family resort that offers all the traditional seaside treats including a long sandy beach, safe bathing, restaurants, pubs and tea shops. We dined out of course. Lovely.

16th. Drove to Cowes to visit my friend Neville Braybrooke, author, at his house. Later, we all went to the local pub, and had a wonderful time eating, drinking, talking mainly about our work and about the biography he was writing *A Life of Olivia Manning*. Of course, like all my friends, he encouraged me to persevere with my novel. Delightful as usual. Then, we returned to interview Gascoyne again. Very good interview. Afterwards, we returned to our very pleasant hotel, transcribing the interviews on my laptop, and had room service.

17th. We headed for Sandown to visit my friend, Edward Upward, a British novelist and short-story writer, at his house. He looked as good as ever for a man of 95. We talked about his life, his friends, and about life in general. After tea, we drove around, and explored Sandown, the magnificent and safe sandy beach, where one can enjoy great sea bathing and all kinds of water sports. The town is lively with plenty of shops, tea houses, restaurants and bars. Returned to our pleasant hotel, relaxed, transcribed the tapes on my laptop and dined out.

On Sunday, 18 October. We returned to Gascoyne's and Judy's house for lunch. After lunch, Rhoda and Judy went to the kitchen to talk and washing up, while I interviewed David once again, covering some more points, because he had so much to say about his life and works. Judy and Rhoda joined us, and the conversation became general and light hearted. Judy loaned me two tapes about David's life and work to record. Very generous and we had a pleasant time. On returning to our hotel, I recorded the two tapes and transcribed them on my laptop. Later, we strolled along the beach and dined out.

19th. After breakfast, we checked out of our very pleasant hotel and drove to Ventnor, a Victorian spa town with a Mediterranean feel, the sunniest spot of the island. The town was built on terraces, and offered a good selection of antique and other interesting shops, a seafront with a superb bathing beach, cafes, pubs and promenade. Nearby, is the famous Ventnor Botanical Gardens. Then, we headed for Northwood to return the tapes to Judy. After that, we drove to the ferry for Portsmouth. En route, we made a detour to Winchester cathedral to pay our respect to Jane Austen, buried in the north aisle of Winchester cathedral. A magnificent cathedral. We didn't go on the tour and exhibition, but Rhoda lit candles. Home after shopping en route.

GLIMPSES OF A BIOGRAPHER'S DIARY

20th. Returning home, letters and answerphone messages awaiting, especially from the man, who knew George Orwell at Fray's college and from Penguin about *Hear Us O Lord From Heaven Thy Dwelling Place and Lunar Caustic*. Wrote thank-you letters to my friends in the Isle of Wight.

21 October. Wrote letters to people, who knew Eileen Blair, George Orwell's first wife, at University College, London (UCL). Went to UCL library to continue my research on George Orwell, and Eileen Blair; reading and making notes from papers, scripts of recorded interviews and other material. I had been to UCL library many times before, but had to go there more often. Of course, continued rereading *The Road to Wigan Pier*.

23rd. I received and responded to many letters, fax and telephone calls including one from my friend, Cecily, who had had a heart attack and was still not well. We hoped to visit her soon.

24th. Received articles from Geoffrey Stevens about local Uxbridge paper on Orwell. Betty Moss, who brought Margerie Lowry to England to be buried at St John the Baptist churchyard near to her husband, Malcolm Lowry's grave, wrote to inform that she was selling Malcolm Lowry's first editions of *Ultramarine* and *Under the Volcano*.

25th. Interviewed Tony Hyams, a pupil of Orwell, at his home. He remembered him as a very pleasant, easy going teacher, who, when exasperated would say, 'Oh Lord! You'll drive me to Hanwell!' - a local mental asylum. It was a very good interview about Orwell as a school teacher.

26th. Wrote, asking editor of Prospect Magazine to return my article, if he would not be using it.

27th. I sent off Orwell revised proposal to Anthony,. Received a letter of thanks from the National Portrait Gallery telling me that Malcolm Lowry should go well into their Fitzrovia book.

28th. Ted Hughes, British Poet Laureate, 68, died of cancer peacefully at his home. Augusto Pinochet, former President of

Chile, won ruling from the High Court that he was released on grounds of ill health, and was not liable to prosecution under English law, and eventually returned to Chile on 3rd March 2003.

Next two days, I did some more work on Durrell's talk for Paris, and wrote to UCL library regarding Orwell's Archives, reading and updated entry on my computer.

1-6 November. Received letters, faxes, answerphone messages and replied. I am still angry, that I did not negotiate a price with Prospect Magazine, and got a commission in writing. I received letters from various people, who knew Orwell. All very helpful. I entered them on my computer.

7th. Again, I headed for Chesterfield to interview Mr. Stapley at his home. He confirmed what Orwell's pupils told me, and added a few more pieces of information. He gave me a photograph of Frays College. It was a good interview.

8th-10th. Rhoda and I drove to our friends, Gordon and Sheila Robinson, at Shepshed Loughborough in Leicestershire. We sat up until 3.30 a.m. putting the world to rights. Next day, we had a country pub lunch, and talked about my novel and Orwell. Gordon Robinson was one of my very good friends, who always acts as my sounding board. Very gracious of him. Later, we left for home. We saw a moving programme about the First World War on television. The following day, my tooth was so painful, I had to have it extracted by my dentist.

GLIMPSES OF A BIOGRAPHER'S DIARY

17 – Gordon Robinson and Sheila Robinson

11th. Eightieth anniversary of the First World War. My father told me so many stories about this war. I just wept. A very emotional day. Cecily rang. She had been asked by Odile to introduce me at the Village Voice bookshop, Paris, and asked me some more questions. Of course, I answered her questions, and must get on with the preparation of my talk on Durrell's for the occasion.

17th. I had my BT Broadband set up, exploring it and comfortable using it. Very excited.

18th-22nd. Rhoda and I travelled by Eurostar to Paris, booked in at the Hotel Apollinaire in Montparnasse, spoke to Cecily and Odile, dined at the Closerie des Lilas and discussed my talk for tomorrow with Rhoda, my sounding board. Next day, in the morning, we went to Shakespeare and Company bookshop, had a lengthy talk with Carl and George about David Gascoyne, signed some more books, returned to our hotel after lunch and rested for a couple of hours. Afterwards, I read my talk once again with Rhoda. At 6.30 p.m. we arrived at the Village Voice bookshop, and were made very welcome, as usual. There were police around the area. Cecily explained that the police were there not to control the crowds of fans, but because the third Thursday of November is Beaujolais Nouvelle Day, and friends gathered with a few bottles of this very mediocre-wine to celebrate the annual arrival of the season's Beaujolais - much drinking, an excuse for a mid-week of fun and drinking freely in the streets of the city.

About twenty people gathered for my talk. Cecily's introduction was charming, though she exaggerated my achievements shamelessly, making it difficult for me to keep a straight face. Talk went well, I think, followed by the lively questions and discussions. I signed about thirty books. Suzanne Kim, a friend, came to the talk, and invited us for dinner on Saturday. Marthe Nochy invited us to visit her libraire at 93 rue de Seine and gave me an Oscar Epts poster inscribed: 'Lawrence Durrell dévolle les peintures. Oscar Epts.'

After that, Odile, Cecily and Michael went to dinner washed down with Beaujolais, we returned to our hotel at midnight.

20th. Slept well. Headed for Marthe Nochy gallery. She spoke lovingly about Durrell, showed me her file of press cuttings, his photographs and hers, and gave me an Oscar Epts painting. She was sad about her lost friend. She met him at UNESCO when she was a translator. She gave me a small card advertising Epts exhibition. She said that she'd never been a lover of Lawrence Durrell, never been to Sommières, because he expected everyone to drink along with him, and she did not drink. I bought a French translation of *Reflections on a Marine Venus* by Lawrence Durrell for Cecily. She gave me an interview. Very pleasant. We then made for Cecily's home, gave her a bottle of Beaujolais Nouveau, and the French translation of *Reflections on a Marine Venus*, which she had not read. She said how much she enjoyed my talk. We discussed Orwell, my novel and her works. We went for a late Moroccan lunch, and after tea, we left for our hotel and snoozed and had room service supper. Rhoda had bought bread, cheese, butter and croissants for breakfast. Smart girl. Next day, to the Gallery

GLIMPSES OF A BIOGRAPHER'S DIARY

Lafayette via the local Saturday morning market and bought Christmas cards. Proceeded to Lafayette in Boulevard Haussman, its flagship store, then to Madeleine and back to our hotel. In the evening, we went to dinner at Suzanne Kim's flat. She offered to translate *Pursued by Furies* my biography of Malcolm Lowry if I can find her a publisher. We talked about many issues that interested us, especially on Malcolm Lowry. We had a very lovely day. Came to our hotel late and slept well. The following day, 22nd. We went to the local market and the shops. But it was so cold, we dashed to the Dôme for lunch and coffee before returning to our warm room to read and relax. In the afternoon, we made for Shakespeare and Company bookshop for tea and to talk about my Durrell's book. I told some stories as well, and everyone had some good laughs. I signed few extra books, and George sold further copies and we headed for our warm hotel.

23 - 30 November. After checking out from our pleasant hotel, we headed for home by Eurostar arriving around 3.00 p.m. Gosh!! the house was so ice-cold. Fortunately, we had two large heaters, switched them on, while the boiler started to heat the house. In the mean-time, we drank hot tea with French cakes, had hot baths and switched on the electric blanket. Lots of letters and answerphone messages to respond to later. Some were very helpful with added information about Orwell. Now, that I have my Broadband, I gave out my email address, so all information would be on my computer and laptop ready for me to work, especially whenever we returned after being away from home. I had a slight sore throat and not feeling too well. Rhoda told me that I might be having the flu. Of course, being an ex-nurse/midwife, she commenced treatment straight away. Good to be pampered. For the next few days, I was mostly in bed, and whatever I needed Rhoda ensured, that it was at hand, and I worked from my bed as much as possible.

27th. Feeling much better, but Rhoda insisted, that I spent most of the day in bed. Started reading *The Counterfeiters* by André Gide, spoke to Eddie who was suffering the effects of the treatment he received.

29th. I took Rhoda to hospital, visited Eddie and we had an enlightening conversation after talking about how he was feeling and his treatment. I then returned to collect Rhoda. I wrote to my friend, Cecily, asking her to mention my interest in Orwell to her friend, Celia K., because I wanted to ring and make an appointment to interview her. In the evening, we saw a very good interview with Pinter on the South Bank show.

30th. Still learning about the internet, sending out emails, reading mainly Orwell works, about him and updated my computer.

1st-9th December. Receiving and sending out emails, saw Eddie in hospital, keeping on with Orwell's trail, finished reading *The Counterfeiters*, and started reading *Through the Panama* by Lizzie Josephson, and writing my short-stories. Still learning about the internet, making mistakes and correcting them with BT support team, who were very helpful.

4th. To Fray's College to meet Tony Hyams and saw the dormitories, the schoolroom and Orwell's bedroom, where he finished *Burmese Days*. Back home, I continued to work on my Lowry's article for HVOL, and did some extra work on the internet including archives search.

6th. Frosty morning with ice in the air, stunning breath, nipped nose and fingers, sky-blue, pure and perfect. Finished reading *Through the Panama*, and started on *The Name of the Rose* by Umberto Eco, to be followed by Charles Dickens, George Eliot, Browning, *Strange Comfort Afforded by the Profession*, on the internet daily, getting on with my Orwell's research and writing my short-stories.

10th December. In the morning, Jan rang and informed me, that she didn't have an agent. I discussed it with Rhoda, who suggested, 'Later, go and visit her, bring her manuscript home, and I'll type it on the laptop for her.'

Also, on the 10th. In the afternoon, I went to the BBC writers' meeting at the Duke of York Theatre. Inspired as usual. I felt like wanting to write plays, films, and so on, but I knew the feeling would wear off. Rhoda had her friend visiting for dinner. Afterwards, I excused myself, read Malcolm Lowry's Pompeii story, and wrote notes on my computer.

11th-16th . Once again, I was feeling rough with influenza, stayed mostly in bed, and being pampered by Rhoda's tender loving care. Continued with Lowry's article for HVOL, rereading *The Counterfeiters* by André Gide, wrote Christmas cards that Rhoda posted, went to Christmas party with Rhoda and had very pleasant times with her previous boss and colleagues.

25th. We had a wonderful Christmas Day, as usual.

31st. Delightful New Year Eve, seeing the New Year in with goodies and champagne. Farewell 1998. What a challenge 1998 was?

1999

1-27 January. Happy New Year! What lies ahead this year? Our New Year resolution: to work harder and be there for each other. I continued researching and visiting the Orwell's archives, and reading, interviewing and updating my Orwell's notes on the computer. I am comfortable with and like the internet. I sent and received letters, revised my novel, wrote short-stories, read, kept abreast of current affairs, went to the local cinema, theatres, ate out, being visited and entertained friends.

28th. Took Orwell proposal in to Anthony, who was going on holiday.

29th. Sketched out *Show of the Century*, and we saw *Shakespeare in Love*.

31st. Neighbours came to drink and we all had a merry evening. 1 February. Brian Murphy came at 12.45 p.m. and we had good talk about the theatre, Joan Littlewood and actors and actresses. A fascinating hour of recording. He was excellent to interview, very fluent and had a good strong voice.

2nd. Installed free Microsoft online, put in a new Internet Explorer and tried to find out, who to approach with my BBC series ideas.

1999

3rd. Good day. Made contact with Guy Young, BBC Scotland, who expressed interest in *Pursued by Furies*, and in *Show of the Century*. Let's hope for the best. I sent in my article on Orwell, The European to The Observer.

4th. Wrote and received letters and emails, and sorted out my receipts for next year's tax returns.

5th. Writing a story on *Death - the world of dreams and the world of death*. When we dream do we visit the land of the dead? Is a dream a preview of the experience of being dead? Wouldn't that be strange?

The next few days, I spent times sorting out my finances, and spoke to friends. The National Portrait Gallery wrote asking, who to send review copies of Fitzrovia to, and I suggested Alan Ross at London Magazine and The Malcolm Review in Canada. I might have to think of a new proposal for *Show of the Century* to include the Brian Murphy interview. Making more notes on my computer on Orwell.

14th. Made up my Valentine card for Rhoda on my computer, and we had a very pleasant and fun day ending by going to a restaurant with a dance floor. Super.

15 - 21 February. Reading Iris Murdoch's *Under the Net*, her first novel, set in London, a story of a struggling young writer. Fascinating. Wrote and received lots of letters including one from Ruth Pitter giving a good insight on Orwell. Watched Bookmark programme on Iris Murdoch. She spoke fascinatingly about the unconscious, and that was very good. I was writing a story about Englishness. Still researching Orwell in Paris 1928-1929. Read my copy of The TLS, and did The Times crossword puzzle. Listened to Radio 4 and news, keeping abreast of current affairs regularly. Telephoned UCLA, Huntington Library and New York public library. Continued with my story on Englishness.

22nd. Celebrated Rhoda's birthday with supper of Coq au Vin and champagne and later watching Midnight in Paris. It was a fun-day.

25th. Began adapting *Pursued by Furies* for radio, may even offer it to The Independent.

GLIMPSES OF A BIOGRAPHER'S DIARY

Next few days, continued writing my story on Englishness. Guy Young, BBC Scotland, said 'No' to *Pursued by Furies*, and passed *Show of the Century* to Feature editor. Reading Kathleen Raine *The Land Unknown*, and telephoned friends.

1 March. I sent suggestion for a repeat of *Love and Grief* to the Controller of Radio 3. Also, sent tape to Feature editor in Edinburgh about the proposal of *Orwell the European* to Robert McCrum, English writer, editor, journalist and broadcaster on BBC Radio four.

2nd-7th. Anthony rang and informed me that Penguin said 'No' for Orwell, but he would send it to three other publishers. Bought Edmund White's *Proust*, and spent most of the day reading it. Sent Cecily a copy of *Hear Us O Lord From Heaven Thy Dwelling Place and Lunar Caustic*.

8th. Continued on my Orwell trail. I telephoned Jan, and she informed me that she was as well as could be expected, but she was as lively as ever to talk to. I said, 'I will be coming to see you in two weeks' time and will discuss your book with you.' She said, 'I look forward to that. You will stay here, of course.'

For the next few days, in addition to reading Orwell, I was putting my notes, letters and interviews on my computer daily, and writing another story on *What Motives?*

16th. Rhoda and I discussed my trip to visit Jan. I would travel on the 19th, stay at The Hampton Inn on the first night as I would arrive late, drive the next day to her house, work with her on her book, bring notes back home for Rhoda to put on the laptop, and return with the disk to Jan.

17th. Writing another short-story on; Fables, and finished reading Edmund White's; Proust, a beautifully judged, poised account of Proust's life and career. Rhoda and I went out to dinner.

Next day, we prepared for my trip making sure that I left enough space for Jan's book. I was quite busy on the internet, replied to letters and emails.

1999

19 March. Drove and parked my car at Heathrow, and boarded Virgin Atlantic to Los Angeles. I checked in at the Hampton Inn, where I spent the evening watching television, rang Jan and arranged for the next day.

20th. Went to Hertz to pick up the car. Paid $9. a day extra for the Toyota Camry. Very good car. To Encino, did some shopping, and headed for the American Express. Then, drove to Westlake in the evening and got lost. The gentleman at the real estate office gave me direction and a map. I arrived safely. Jan was in good form, showed me photograph of Lowry and Carole Landis. Sad moving story of her death by suicide at age 29. After dinner and too much booze, especially brandy, that I brought, I went to bed.

Next day, hangover, but went to Jan's friends, Marilyn and Jim, lovely house overlooking sea and mountains, for late lunch. Afterwards, we went shopping, and returned to Jan's house. I was so tired, that I went to sleep. Had sandwiches and tea before bed.

22nd. In the morning, after working on her book: story about her and Malcolm's life, we drove to Hearst Castle. What can I say? Had dinner at Westlake and return to Jan's.

Next day, I drove to the Huntington Library, saw many letters from Arthur Lowry to his son, Malcolm Lowry, not seen before, also, saw several books about Orwell - privately printed, copies of reviews by Orwell, Koestler, Inez Holden and some of Orwell's other friends. Back to Jan for dinner and worked with her on her book.

The following day, I went to the bank, spoke to Rhoda and all was okay at home. We worked on Jan's book most of the day, but she got tired and had to rest. Later, I took the book to bed and read it, very impressive, needed only a small amount of work to be done now, made copious notes as I went along.

25th. Finished reading her book, continued making notes as I went along, we talked about them, and in the evening went out for dinner. Coming out of the restaurant, Jan slipped and fell. I felt terrible. She said she was okay. And we returned to her house. After talking and had nightcap, Jan went to sleep, I read a bit more of her book, and went to bed.

26th. Leaving for home tonight with her book for Rhoda to enter on our laptop. After four hours in her study sorting out materials, that she was selling to me, she came down with them. I was so delighted, that I gave her more than agreed. She signed a transfer of ownership letters without mentioning money. There was a letter from Malcolm, 'Saying that all his manuscripts are hers,' and he had made no request for them from Jan and her mother. All he wanted from her was his college blazer, but his other things, he said, 'She need not send.' I was staggered. I departed from Los Angeles at 8.50 p. m, and arrived at Heathrow at 3.30 p.m. on the 27th. Rhoda was waiting for me. Bless her. We collected our car and drove home, and I slept in till 12.30 p. m, and we had brunch. We spent the rest of the day sorting through letters and other material, put it in cases and stored it away. Fax last week from BBC wanting to see my treatment of Lowry's story.

29th. Anthony rang and told me that Bill Swainson, senior editor at Bloomsbury, was definitely interested in Orwell book, and he had fixed a meeting for Thursday, 1st April, at 2.30 p.m. next day, we went to UCL and checked on Orwell letters, family materials, reminiscences, transcript on radio and television broadcasts. Good range. I was still finding documents not included in previous biographies, for example: Jacintha Buddicom, an English poet and a childhood friend of Orwell, remembered George Orwell's fascination with ghost-stories; his favourite stories from Poe and M R James, and also the Proctor of Eton College thought, that he would make an excellent ghost-story writer. Rhoda started typing Jan's book on the laptop, working hard at it.

1 April. I saw Bill Swainson, as planned, at Bloomsbury. He asked about Lowry, Durrell, and then about George Orwell. Got the impression that he wanted Orwell. He followed me into Soho Square, and he continued talking to me outside. Also, that afternoon, I took a copy of my Lowry's book to BBC Film

1999

Development people. Then in the evening, I rang and spoke to Jan and my friend, David Markson.

Next day. I started going through what I had of Orwell so far on my computer, and highlighted what I could include in his biography. Of course, this would take me many months, depending on my commitments of the day. In the evening, we went to my friend Doreen's house for dinner, lots of chat, remembering old primary-school teaching days, Centre 42 and more.

Following few days, I wrote letters to the University of British Columbia, Doreen, Iris Murdoch and some others.

6th. Anthony rang and told me, that another writer, who had just finished a biography, had signed a contract to write a biography on George Orwell to be published for his centenary, 2003!!! I mentioned strong points in my favour, and also, I had raced another writer successfully before. I must concentrate on Orwell, with Rhoda's help and support.

Next day. Anthony rang and informed me that Bloomsbury had said, 'No." I was very disappointed. 'Chin up and carry on'. Rhoda and I had a post- mortem over this disappointing news and planned ahead. Biography is a portrait. All portraits are subtly different, Orwell tried to cross the class-barrier one way - upwards embracing philosophical fascism; he tried to cross downwards, embracing socialism.

Rhoda had finished putting Jan's book on the laptop and on disk. I place the disk into my computer upstairs, printed all pages, wrote a letter and put both books and letter in an envelope, which Rhoda took to the post office, and sent it by special delivery to Jan. I rang and informed her that her book was on the way and she must contact my publisher, St Martin's Press, New York.

8 - 14 April. We visited UCL archives, and many more times; mostly looking and copying more letters to and from Orwell, materials, reviews, what others wrote about him, collected photocopies previously requested, looked at Jacintha's and

GLIMPSES OF A BIOGRAPHER'S DIARY

George's relationship, St Cyprian, and the many aspects of Orwell. I asked myself, 'What was the Ghost at the Orwell Feast?' In Paris, he strove to gain inspiration for great novels and poems; his sense of injustice soon took over, and he found himself writing instead about social injustices. I visited the new British Library many times, looking up Orwell, and entered new material, letters, reviews, what was written about his fiction, repression, freedom, political views and more on my laptop, They were very impressive.

15 - 23 April. I had a good meeting with Michael Fishwick, publisher and novelist, at HarperCollins. 17th-23rd. Had influenza, and was mostly in bed receiving tender loving care from Rhoda, reading, updating Orwell on my computer and still highlighting what more I should include in my biography of him.

24th. The lady from Edinburgh rang regarding the: Show of the Century. She would try for an afternoon fifteen-minute slot.

27th. The National Portrait Gallery informed me, that they had no photographs of Lowry, and the exhibition would not be mountable until 2000. That's okay by me. I would give them one.

29th. Anthony rang informing me the Michael Fishwick turned down the Orwell proposal. It turned out that another writer had a contract to write a biography of George Orwell. His wife worked at HarperCollins, and was present at the board meeting concerned. I felt a little crushed. Meanwhile, I kept on fervently with my Orwell research.

Jan rang and told me, that she had sent her book with all corrections inserted to St Martin's Press, and they were interested in her book. I told her that, I would bring the disk, when I visit her in June. She had been and is ill, and wanted to see her book published. We understood, and I would visit as soon as I could.

1 May. Spoke with Jan, she was still so excited about St Martin's Press interest in her book.

2nd. Began entering notes of Orwell's Collected Works on my computer, and would be doing so daily.

Next day, visited Evelyn Morrison at Star and Garter Home at Richmond. She seemed frail, since we last saw her, but pleasantly cheerful and resigned to life there. Builder, Darren, came and would be laying the floor in our attic today and tomorrow.

4th. Anthony rang to say that he would send Orwell proposal to Macmillan, Little, Brown.

5th. Received Celia's letter informing me that she would be happy to see me on 5th June at 3.30 p.m. I accepted. Also, Richard Peters' carer rang. She told me that he would see me on 9th, Sunday, at 2.00 p.m.

9th. We arrived on time, were made very welcomed. Richard and his brother, Maurice, were supervised by Orwell in Southwold in the early thirties. Both had been interviewed by Bernard Crick, but were very happy to talk again about their old 'tutor.' Richard, who, strangely enough, had once been my philosophy professor, came up with one story not recorded by Crick. During his father's absence (he was a policeman in India) old Richard Blair, Orwell's father, came chasing after his mother, and whenever they saw him approaching their cottage, the boys and their mother hid behind the sofa till he went away. Orwell and his father, it seems, were not so very unlike. He gave me a good interview about Orwell and his parents. Also, he gave me his brother, Maurice's address and telephone number. I would write with a view to interview him soon. Orwell was with the Peters' boys of the comic book age - boys he perhaps enjoyed having around.

21st. We set off for Bournemouth, arrived at hotel around 5.30 p.m. After supper, we listened to my interview with Richard Peters. Would meet his brother tomorrow at 4.30 p.m. Next day, We visited Maurice Peters, a retired Naval Intelligence officer, thought Crick (who failed to use his testimony) had a left-wing axe to grind, and ignored what he had to say, because he regarded Orwell as an anti-Communist rather than a socialist. He told me that in 1935, he had visited Booklover's Corner to consult Blair (Orwell) about joining the Navy, and the 'pacifist' Eric told him that it was a very good idea. Perhaps, it was the spirit of the good Captain Horatio Blair speaking. He told us many jokes about Orwell. From there, we drove to Dorchester, visited Hardy exhibition at the County Museum, saw his study, with his desk and books. Then, to a bookshop in town, bought *1940 Horizon* with an Orwell's interview in it, and returned to our hotel in Bournemouth. The following day, we checked out of the hotel, drove to Dorchester, then to Hardy's house, Max Gate. Not much to see, just two rooms, conservatory, the garden, his pets, albums of photographs going back to his youth as an apprentice architect and pictures of his mother. Certainly, there was a sense of the period and of him. Then, we returned home, and continued on the Orwell's trail, reading and making notes on my computer, especially of his *Complete Works*, receiving and replying to letters and emails.

1 June. Spoke to my friend, Cecily, in Paris, who had a heart attack, but was in good spirits.

4th. After taking Rhoda to hospital, I drove to Cambridge.

Next day. I went looking around Cambridge, then to Fitzwilliam Museum, the art and antiquities museum of the University of Cambridge, that has an amazing variety of beautiful artefacts, and art from around the world. In the afternoon, to Celia G's. house to interview her. Charming woman, who gave me a very good interview not only on Orwell, but also on others well known to him. We will meet again. Headed for home. Rhoda's friend, Bonnie, collected her from hospital, and was in good spirits. Began transcribing Celia's tape, and entered more ideas and notes on Orwell on my computer.

7th. Anthony telephoned this afternoon to tell me that Little, Brown's editorial director said that he would like to publish my Orwell's biography, but wanted to take it to a board meeting, and so needed reviews of my past two biographies. Straight away, I assembled the reviews, sent one copy to Little, Brown and one to Anthony.

1999

8th. Celia found my Orwell's note-book, that I left behind. How very embarrassing. I rang my friend, Cecily, in Paris, but received no reply. Worried about her. Rang Odile at Village Voice bookshop. She would check on Cecily. Wrote her a letter, and Rhoda posted it by special delivery. We prepared for my Los Angeles trip tomorrow. Jan and I had a good conversation in the evening. I told her that, I would do the shopping on my way to her house tomorrow.

9th. I drove to Heathrow for the 9.45 a.m. flight via United Airways to Los Angeles. The plane was half full. I read and slept. The steward gave me a bottle of Chilean red wine on disembarking. How gracious? I collected the Toyota Camry, drove to Encino, did shopping, rang Rhoda, who was very happy that I arrived safely and would continue working with Jan on her book. Then to Jan's house. She appeared well despite her illness. We had a pleasant evening, eating, talking and drinking a bit. I was tired and went to bed.

Next day, she gave me photograph of Lowry to have copied, which I took to the photographer, and would be ready the following day. We had a lovely lunch and talked a lot on various issues. I slept in the afternoon and woke up at 7.00 p.m. She cooked steak for supper to be washed down with champagne. Pre-birthday celebration. Early to bed and to read her book.

11 June. Happy Birthday, Jan! I slept heavily, due to the heat last night and woke up with a headache. I collected Lowry's photographs. After lunch, we got down checking her book, and made a few more changes. I would take it home, Rhoda would enter it on the laptop, and I would send it to St. Martin's Press, New York. We talked a lot about other issues, which she wanted to sort out before I left. She kept on saying, "I am old and ill." I listened to her. (I learnt from Rhoda.) In the evening, we went to her friends, Marilyn and Sidney, to celebrate her birthday. Much eating, talking and drinking. Excellent day and happy birthday for Jan. Afterwards, she almost collapsed on our way to the car, but recovered quickly. We arrived safely to her house.

GLIMPSES OF A BIOGRAPHER'S DIARY

Next day. After breakfast and much talking, we went to Marilyn and Sidney's house, and then out to lunch and jolly talking. Excellent company. When we returned to Jan's, I was tired due to the heat. After a strong cup of coffee, she brought out various materials, that she wanted me to have. Of course, I paid for them, but she would only take so much, wrote out a receipt, but would not enter the sum of money. She insisted. She read some of hers and Lowry's letters to me. They were very moving. We had steak again for supper. I was so tired.

Jan spent most of the following day resting, and I read *Coming Up For Air*.

Later, we talked mostly about her book *Inside the Volcano; My Life with Malcolm Lowry*. She wrote a highly readable, vividly descriptive story, about the tormented talent of Malcolm Lowry, and the highs and lows of their marriage. What can I say!!!

14th. At breakfast, she told me a lovely story about a writer. We went through her book again, and then, said that she was extremely grateful for my support, encouragement, willing her on to complete her book. She was extremely gracious. After tea, I went to collect her photograph, and did shopping.

Next day. The cleaner came, and we went shopping again and had lunch. In the afternoon, I read and Jan went to sleep. Later, we went out for dinner.

16th. I packed my case and other items for my return journey home tonight. Jan signed over to me the materials, I bought from her, and what she gave me. We went out to dinner, and I left for the airport, flying out at 8.50 p.m. by United Airways to London. On the plane, a woman was sitting with her child strapped to her. Suddenly, she started to scream and wriggle. To quieten the child, the woman threw her up and down, up and down, with vigorous jerks, explaining to the curious passengers sitting near, that this had a calming effect on the child. Amazingly, she stopped screaming. After about half an hour, she screamed and screamed, and the woman took her out of the strapping, and threw her up and down, up and down violently. Miraculously, the child ceased to scream. It was like something out of Alice in Wonderland. About half-way home point, I fell asleep and woke up to have a meal. Landed safely on the 17th at about 7.30 a.m. Rhoda was there to welcome me. We collected our car and drove home.

17 June. Back home, we had a quiet day, but started putting the material I brought in individual plastic folders. I was very tired, so we left the rest for another day.

18-19. We spent most of our time putting away the rest of the material safely. I rang my friend, Cecily, but still no reply. Rang Odile, who had no news of her, promised to let me know if anything amiss. We watched the Royal wedding of Prince Edward and Sophie Rhys-Jones at St George's Chapel, Windsor Castle. Rhoda was thrilled by it all.

Next day. Visited Eddie in hospital. He was feeling better. Rhoda and I had good conversation and put the world to rights. Rhoda and I now had all materials in steel boxes and stored them away safely. Started another novel. Now, I must concentrate heart and soul on Orwell.

21st. I faxed Mexico accepting the invitation to give two talks and participate in one discussion. Working hard on highlighting what I would use on Orwell biography.

Next day. I attended the hospital, saw my orthopaedic registrar who explained why one of my legs is stronger than the other. She said that in all knee replacements, the two inner tendons are cut. Why my left leg is stronger than my right one is a mystery. Perhaps, I had put more weight on it over time, because of my badly degenerated right-knee, even though I had had a right-knee replacement operation at the same hospital. I did some revision on my novel. I could possibly send it out under a pseudonym. Who knows? Rhoda preparing to travel on 24th to Atlanta, USA, for a month to help her sister, Mary, who had a new baby son.

GLIMPSES OF A BIOGRAPHER'S DIARY

The following day, in addition to sorting out my computer on Orwell, I started reading Ford Madox Ford's novel *The Good Soldier*, and Orwell's essay *Such, Such Were The Joys*.

24th June. I drove Rhoda to Heathrow Airport and saw her off on her happy trip. On returning home, I found a fax from Mexico offering $2,500. plus all expenses for 2 talks and one discussion - participation. (It seemed I can't leave Lowry behind. I won't be allowed to do so.) Anthony rang and informed me that Little, Brown had made an offer. I agreed with it. Working tirelessly, putting my heart and my soul on Orwell. Continued reading *The Good Soldier*. In the evening, I rang Rhoda, who arrived safely, and was very happy being with her sister and her family. I emailed St Martin's Press about Jan's book.

Next day, I transcribed the Peters brothers' and some of Celia G's interviews on my computer, and started copying Jan's book. In the evening, rang Jan, who was still not feeling well, and informed her that I had emailed St Martin's Press. She was quite relieved.

The following day, I went to my local Kensington Library and the London Library to return all Dylan Thomas' books, and take out all Orwell's. Continued copying more of Jan's book, and transcribed more of Celia G's. interviews.

27th. Rhoda and I went to Lewes, met our friends, Marc Cooper and Peter Masser, then drove to Ripe to pay our respects to Lowry and to spray his grave and headstone with special cleaner. Returned to Lewes to eat, talk a lot and had few drinks before returning home later.

29th. It rained all day, stayed indoors, completed transcribing Celia's interviews, copying Jan's book, and began amending notes to it. Reading and highlighting Orwell material and letters on my computer for his biography daily.

30th. Ready to send off Jan's manuscript with notes to St Martin's Press.

1-12 July. Anthony rang. Little, Brown agreed to share permission cost of up to £1,000, length 120,000 words and delivery date 31st December 2001. Can I do justice to my subject? Here we go, full speed on. Sent off Jan's manuscript with notes to St Martin's Press.

Next few days. To TLS for introduction to online archives. Very interesting. Collected Lowry photograph for the National Portrait Gallery. Rang and spoke to our friend, Cecily, at last in Paris. She was okay and staying at a friend's house. Went shopping, bought food, bookcases, and a paper trimmer. Celia rang and invited me for lunch and to look through Inez's diaries. Got car washed and changed tyres. Sent off many letters including one thanking Maurice Peters for sending me a good photograph of the Peters boys. Wrote another short-story, put up two more bookshelves, editor at St Martin's emailed to acknowledge receipt of Jan's book. Began reading George Gissing *The Private Papers of Henry Ryecroft*.

12th. Left early for Cambridge and to Celia's house at 11.30 a.m. I visited her on three occasions. On this, my second visit, she kindly agreed to let me see the diaries of her sister, Inez Holden, writer and journalist, also a friend of Cecily. Fascinating day reading through Inez's diaries and typing relevant passages onto my laptop. In one entry she described how, after 'a charming day' at the zoo, 'I went back and had tea at his flat, and then, just as he was dressed up in his Home Guard uniform and ready to go off to his parade, he more or less "pounced". I was surprised by this, by the intensity and urgency.'

Next day. He invited Inez to tea and 'explained the situation at home.' She did not mind, because she found his explanation 'helpful and clarifying', seemingly to confirm that by now, he and Eileen had worked out some form of open relationship, at least, Orwell thought they had. What he said was not recorded. It speaks volumes about Orwell's attitude to casual sex and probably to the attitude of upper-class women like Inez to being 'pounced on'. That evening, he and Eileen took her out to dinner. 'There was rather an atmosphere of submerged strain,' she wrote. 'Might be worth writing a short-story about this sort of thing. Also, almost subconsciously [Orwell] seemed to have disappeared as if to disassociate from the whole story.' I thought that it might have been a story he had already composed in his head, so that George the 'pouncer' was just a 'character' from, whom he could readily distance himself. They became very close, though he was happily married to Eileen, who knew about their relationship. Celia gave me lunch, tea and supper before I left for home. At tea, Celia told me about her relationship with Orwell. After Eileen's death on 29th March, 1945, Orwell took care of Richard. Later, he wanted to marry, so that, when he died, his wife would bring his son up. When they returned to London in 1946, he invited Celia to tea. She saw him bathing Richard and was impressed by how he handled and cared for the little boy. He told her that he had bronchiectasis and sometimes had lung haemorrhages. He proposed to her and they had a good discussion.

A few days later, she invited him to lunch at her Chelsea flat. She said, 'He asked me again, whether I would consider marrying him, or at any rate having an affair with me. I was awfully worried about this last, as he made it somewhat difficult to refuse. I told him the only reason I had for refusing was that I was not in love with him, but I could see that it was going to be more and more difficult to cope with him if I continued to see him, which of course I did.' He felt very sexually attracted to Celia, and wrote her a letter so explicit in his desire for her, that she could not bear either to show it to anyone or even talk about it. She preferred rather to think of him as a friend and a brilliant mind, and ignore the animal side of his nature. This left her feeling even more confused. She said, 'So, I wrote back to George some rather ambiguous letter. Anyway, it got sorted out.'

13th-15th July. I was updating, ploughing through and highlighting my notes on Orwell. Rhoda rang, was travelling with her family to California and New York and enjoying herself. Her sister, Margaret and her husband, were there as well. What fun-times!!!

16th-19th. The editor from St Martin's Press emailed that she liked Jan's book, needed some more work and wondered about quotations from Lowry's letters. I offered to do all. Listened to David Copperfield's tapes. Kathleen Raine informed me that she would publish Lowry's poem.

20th. The editor from St Martin's Press telephoned. We agreed to work together to get Jan's book out. How gracious and charming. I would interview Jan if necessary to get more information, the letters would be paraphrased and maybe cut somewhat. I started printing out transcript of various interviews with Jan which I posted by special delivery to St Martin's Press.

22nd. I collected Rhoda from Heathrow Airport. So very good to see and have her back at home. She was full of stories of her adventure and I took her out to the local Topo Doro, one of our favourite restaurants, for supper.

24th. We drove to Ripe, headed for Lowry's grave to pay our respects and left flowers. Then to Lewes, checked in at our hotel above a lovely pub on the high street. After tea and rested, we walked to Marc for dinner with Peter and his wife, Margaret, Marc's artist friend, and few others. Jolly good time eating, talking and drinking.

Next day. A little hungover, after a good English breakfast, we said our goodbyes to our friends and left for home. Quiet evening, still reading *The Private Papers of Henry Ryecroft*.

Next few days. I received letter and photograph from Celia. Spoke to Kathleen Raine, who seemed determined to bring out Lowry's poem, took car for service and MOT at Sidcup.

30th. Fixed our flight for Mexico. Visited Mary Treadgold, author, at 5.00 p.m. as arranged. She used to be literary editor at the BBC World Service and knew Orwell in 1941-42 period. She said some interesting things about him.

31st. Spent most of the day reading Orwell's memoirs and entered notes on my computer.

1-8 August. Rang and spoke to Jan. She was happy for me to send transcript of my interviews with her to St Martin's Press. Put some of Lowry's and Durrell's papers in the attic.

Next day, I sent off Jan's transcripts and cassette of *Love and Grief. Under the Volcano* to the editor.

The following day, I interviewed Kathleen Raine as arranged at her house and she spoke glowingly about David Gascoyne. Working steadfastly on Orwell.

11th. My Orwell's contract from Little, Brown came. There were few questions I wanted to raise with Anthony.

13th. Received a message from the editor at St Martin's Press saying that she wanted to agree a contract with Jan and me. Anthony's assistant rang to answer my various questions about the Little, Brown contract. I signed and returned it.

Next day, we entertained our friends, Brian and his wife, Doris, for supper. Very good food, talking and drinking. I discussed many issues with Brian that concerned me.

16th. I spoke with Anthony on various matters. He received the contract, and forwarded it. I emailed Garrett at St Martin's Press with news of Little, Brown. He emailed back hoping that he and the editor would receive a copy of my proposal on Orwell. He also suggested the title: *Inside the Volcano. My Life with Malcolm Lowry* for Jan's book.

17th. Spoke with Jan, keeping her up to date with news about her book. Also, told her that we were going to France for a week on Orwell trail and on holiday.

18 August. Set off for Dover at noon, took the ferry to Calais. Then to Arras booked into hotel Le Carnot Astoria. Lovely dinner and pleasant evening.

Next day. Long drive from Arras to Avignon, but there was no room at the inn, so we drove to Orange and found a motel. Gosh!! I was rather stressed and tired.

Rhoda didn't like this long drive. After lunch and a rest, we visited the Orange Hill Cemetery. This cemetery was made by the Canadian Corps after the Hill was taken for the second time at the end of August 1918. So tranquil and peaceful.

Returned to the motel, rested and did some work on Jan's book. Rhoda reading *Down and Out in Paris and London*. After supper and some more reading fell asleep.

20th. Booked in at Hôtel D'Angleterre at Salon de Provence, drove to Marseilles, saw the old port where Orwell stood in 1927, on his way home from Burma and might have seen the devastating execution of Nicola Succa and Bartolomeo Vanzetti. The port is surrounded by a lovely marina, and known for its hotels, waterfront cafes and restaurants. We went to one of these waterfront restaurants, enjoyed the scenery, had lively conversation, ate delicious fish and laughed a lot. Very hot day and rather tired after walking through the market where Rhoda bought scarves and slippers. Returned to Hôtel D'Angleterre. Did some more work on Jan's book, and read more of Orwell's *Complete Works*.

21st. After a good night's sleep, a very good French breakfast, left for Troyes and checked into Hôtel de Troyes. It is an old town with narrow, cobbled streets lined with colourful, half-timbered houses and is famous for its vineyards and champagne. Before going out for dinner, we rested, and I did a bit more work on Jan's book. Rhoda still reading *Down and Out in Paris and London*. We had champagne at supper.

Next day. We drove around Troyes before heading for Boulogne, where we booked at the Hôtel Lorraine. We dined at an Italian restaurant down by the harbour. I continued working on Jan's book and Rhoda carried on reading *Down and Out in Paris and London*, afterwards collapsed into bed.

23rd. After breakfast, I did a bit more work on Jan's book while Rhoda packed for our leaving. En route to Calais, we stopped at the supermarket to stock up. From Calais, we took the ferry to Dover and drove home.

Back home, lots of messages and letters, putting aside those needing to be entered on my computer, and ones to be completed the same day.

The next few days were spent mostly reading Orwell's *Complete Works*, and making notes on my computer and had two new tires fitted to car. Rhoda put Jan's book on disc, friends visiting, had dinner, drinks and jolly talking.

30th. Rhoda busy putting Jan's book on disc for St Martin's Press. I rang Ian Angus, author and scholar on George Orwell and he promised me names and addresses of people still alive, who knew Orwell and transcripts of various interviews with people.

31st. We were both mostly busy with Jan's disc and Orwell's *Complete Works*. Rhoda, of course, had other daily work to do. Bless her.

1-2 September. Three months to the new Millennium! Sad to see the old century go. There were times of peace and tranquillity which may never return. I fear a more brutal world of more brutal people doing their own brutal things. I finished itemising contents for the first twelve volumes of Orwell's *Complete Works*.

3rd. Sixtieth anniversary of Britain's declaration of war on Germany. Almost nothing about it on television or radio. However, some programmes earlier and a few later did mention it in passing, but one programme raised the question of whether we should have entered the war at all!!! The past is not only another country but a better one.

4th. Cheque from Little, Brown (first half of advance) arrived. Rhoda's friends came to dinner, eating, drinking, talking and laughing. Lovely.

The following few days, I interviewed many people, who knew Orwell including Peter Vansittart, an English writer, at his house. Very pleasant gentleman. Interview was completely marred by continuous bell ringing from neighbouring church. We dined out at our local Greek restaurant. Visited Ian Angus and his wife at their house. I was very impressed with what he said about Orwell. Excellent. He lent me three books and notes on him, and gave me a list of people he knew with their address. Charming, very generous and gracious.

Next day. I prepared for my trip to Cologne on Orwell trail. Rhoda wanted me to tell her again why I was going to Cologne. I reminded her that David Astor had asked Orwell to act as war correspondent for The Observer to cover the liberation of France and the early occupation of Germany. In the second week in March 1945, he set off to keep up with the War. 'Where did he stay?' She asked. I said "He used the Hotel Scribe in Paris as his base, until the fourth week of March when he went off to Cologne". She was happy with my explanation and so I set off on Orwell trail.

12 September. Left home at 09.00 a.m. and got to Dover at 11.15 a.m. Took the 12.15 p.m. ferry to Calais and travelled to Cologne, stopping at hotels en route. On my way to Chartres, took wrong turning and ended in Amiens, returned to Abbeville and booked at a hotel for the night.

Next day. After breakfast, I headed for Chartres booked, at a hotel for the night, then visited the Cathedral and went to dinner. The Cathedral seemed less gloomy than before.

The following day, drove to Arras to interview a lady living near Arras, who knew Orwell. I rang and spoke to her and arranged to see her for lunch the next day. I checked into Hotel Moderne ,and went to Neuve Chapelle visiting war graves. Returned to my hotel, had dinner in the square. Excellent.

15th. Visited the lady, who knew Orwell. After lunch, we talked about Orwell, but she knew nothing new, and gave me a contact, who could give me more information. To Frommel War Museum. Fascinating artefacts - recovered mostly from the fields around. Returned to hotel, rested, read volume 13 of Orwell's *Complete Works* then to dinner at the hotel.

GLIMPSES OF A BIOGRAPHER'S DIARY

16th. Headed for Cologne. Arrived at 3.30 p.m. and checked in at the Holiday Inn. Went to the library and looked for 1945 records when Orwell was in Cologne for The Observer, met some very helpful ladies, who recommended city archives.

Next day. went to the city archives where the women were very interested in my research, helpful but doubted whether any records survived from 1945, except maybe in England. They gave a contact name and address of a woman, who did a book on Cologne in March 1945 which mentioned Orwell in passing. Back to hotel and checked out. Set off for Arras, parked car, checked in at the Moderne Hotel by the station and rang Rhoda.

18th. Checked out and made for Calais, first to the supermarket to stock with goodies, especially Morgan red wine. Got 12.30 p.m. Sea France ferry to Dover and to home. Lot to do especially with Jan's book and her contract, and I must get my head down on Orwell. Lovely evening and dinner with Rhoda at home.

19th. Replied to letters and emails including one from Mexico for next month's talk. Posted many letters.

20 September. Jan's contract came from St Martin's Press. Did a small amount of work on my novel, and entered my Cologne trip notes onto my computer.

21st. Anthony rang. St Martin's Press made an offer for the Orwell book. I asked him about Jan's contract and he smoothed away my concerns.

Next day. We went to the hospital for physiotherapy. It seemed that the weakness in my right-calf was connected to the numbness down the right-side of my leg - probably nerve damage. Rhoda had put up to page 200 of Jan's book onto disc.

23rd. To Mexican Consulate for work permit. I interviewed John Craxton, an English painter. He gave a very good interview on Orwell that I enter onto my computer as soon as I arrived home.

Next day. We entertained friends and relaxed a bit.

27th. Spoke to Jan and sent editor's letter and contract to her by special delivery. Made appointments and wrote more letters to people, who knew Orwell and interviewed some of them on the telephone and face-to-face in the coming days including Denzil Jacobs and his mother, Kay Ekevall, who knew Orwell very well when he was working at Booklovers' Corner. She read literary books and would do typing for writers. She met Orwell in 1934 when she went to the bookshop. She was happy to have met him, a boy who was jolly to talk to, to walk with and to make love. He did not talk to her about his writing, but she later discovered about it. She met and mingled with writers and talked about their lives. They both gave very good interviews and told some lovely stories. When she told me that she and Orwell were lovers, she did so with a wink and a pleasant smile.

1-2 October. Busy working on Orwell. Spoke to and informed Jan that Rhoda and I were going to Mexico from 3rd to 10th.

3rd. We flew by United Airlines from Heathrow, London to Washington, then from Washington to Mexico City. Carlos and Mariyo from the Centro Nacional de las Artes met us at the airport, and drove us to hotel Real del Sur where we were warmly welcomed.

4th. I slept badly last night due to heavy traffic on the road. Mariyo came and drove us to the Centre. It was a day of interviews, one journalist after another, had lunch with our translator, then Mariyo returned us to our hotel. We changed room, to a quiet one, so that I could sleep well. After a rest, tea and shower, I was interviewed by another journalist on Malcolm Lowry in our room. Then, we went for a delicious Mexican supper.

5th. Got to bed before midnight after brandy to induce sleep. At about 5.00 a.m. the telephone rang - an early call for someone in another room. Afterwards, I could not sleep. In the morning, I went through my lecture with Rhoda, especially, as I learned that it would be simultaneously translated. After lunch, I was interviewed by Channel 22 at 1.30 p.m. in our room. At 5.00 p.m. Mariyo came and drove us to the Centre to give my lecture at 6.15 p.m. Amazingly, I realised as I listened to one interviewer that he referred to me, as 'Maestro' - for the first and no doubt last time in my life. (Mariyo was our driver throughout our stay). My talk was on the Life and Work of Malcolm Lowry, seemed to have gone extraordinarily well. Lots of challenging questions and delightful discussion. We were entertained at dinner. The director, Roberto, a charming man, liked it very much, and so did Raul Ortiz, a friend. It seemed Rhoda was a great success.

6th. Relaxed and read until 5.30 p.m. when driven to the Centre, listened to other speakers including Herman L. Zavala, a Mexican novelist, literary critic and an academic at the university. He was very good on Lowry's poems.

Ortiz, Cultural Attache at the Mexican Embassy in London, and the translator of Malcolm Lowry's novel *Under the Volcano*, gave a very good talk on Malcolm's Lowry's Correspondence.

7th. After tea with Roberto and Carlos at the Centre, Herman and his wife, Aida, drove us to a restaurant for a Mexican cuisine, apparently a favourite place for writers to congregate and socialise. Herman, a charming, warm and intelligent man. Aida was tall, statuesque, very beautiful and a translator. Jokingly, I said she should translate my Lowry book. To our surprise and delight, she took up the idea with great enthusiasm and so did Herman (she did translate my book that was published in Mexico in 2008). Herman drove us to the Centre at 5.00 p.m. for me to deliver my talk on *Writing the Biography of Malcolm Lowry*. It went very well, though I went over time - not rushing matters for the sake of the translator. Warmth and enthusiasm on all sides. A student came up to me after my talk, and gave me a pencil portrait he had drawn, while I was speaking. He was very good and was chuffed, when I expressed my pleasure and congratulated him. Then Herman and Raul joined me for the round table talk. Lots of lively talks, questions and challenging discussions.

8th. Herman and Aida drove us to a lunch reception at Raul's at 3.30 p.m., with many others attending. Delightful and very friendly. Afterwards, Roberto drove us to our hotel, and after much talking, he treated us to dinner. He was very charming and gracious. Nothing was too much for him.

Next day. Valenti and his wife, friends of Raul, took us to Cuernavaca for the day, showed us the city including the Cathedral, the Palace of Cortés and the market, where Rhoda bought some dresses. Then to their villa in a gated residential area for a late afternoon lunch party. Met pleasant and friendly people. Brought back to our hotel by Fillipe, his wife and three lovely ladies.

10th. We checked out and Mariyo drove us to Mexico Airport. We said our goodbye, we checked in and flew at 10.40 a.m. by United Airways to Washington. A good flight. The air-hostess gave us a bottle of red wine for our lunch. How gracious! We arrived at Washington at 3.46 p.m., collected our cases, went through customs and security, checked in our cases and left Washington Dulles at 6.00 p.m. by United Airways for Heathrow, London. Good flight. Arrived on the 11th at 5.30 a.m. A very pleasant and memorable trip.

11 October. After resting and recovering somewhat from the flight, read emails and letters received including one from Anne Dunn, entered notes onto my computer.

12th. To hospital. The physiotherapist informed me that she thought the femoral nerve was damaged, and degeneration of leg-muscles would probably be permanent. Gosh!!! I would be seeing the neurologist sometime.

14th. We went to The Institute of Contemporary Arts. We saw three of Bryan S. Johnson's films: *The Unfortunates*, *You're Human Like the Rest of Them* and *Fat Man on a Beach*. Then to our local Greek restaurant for supper and drank too much.

Next day. I was very hungover. Rhoda finished Jan's book on the laptop and disc.

GLIMPSES OF A BIOGRAPHER'S DIARY

17th. Finished off Remembering Bryan S Johnson for Alan Ross.

21 - 22nd. We worked on Jan's book together. Packard Bell computer was playing up. Informed John Lewis, London. Engineer came and put it right. Fortunately, we had the laptop.

23rd. We entertained our friends, Mike and his wife, Frances, for supper. Lots of talking, reminiscing, laughing, eating and drinking. All very merry and happy. Over the next few days. I rang friends, wrote and posted letters and sent out emails, mainly regarding Orwell.

31st. Did some more work on Jan's book, mostly inserting editorial notes and suggested changes, cut down some quotations or paraphrased them and kept Jan up to date about her book.

1 November. Worked all day on Jan's book with Rhoda.

2nd-9th. Signed and posted my contract to St. Martin's Press by special delivery. Still reading Orwell's *Complete Works*, making notes and transcribing interviews onto my computer. Sending and receiving letters, emails and interviewing many more people, who knew Orwell.

10th. Jan's book was ready for she and I to work through.

11 November. After observing one minute's silence at the eleventh hour, we headed for Heathrow Airport, London. After saying bon voyage, I went through customs and security, flew to Los Angeles. Arrived late, hired a car and drove to Jan's house at about 6.30 p.m. Jan was very tired and went to bed early.

Next day. We discussed her book. We spent a week reading and correcting it many times. She signed the contract.

13th. We visited her friends, Marilyn and Sidney, and dined out. It was a delightful evening.

17th. We finished her book and had a pleasant evening. She talked mostly about her illness, her life, her books and just unburdened herself of various issues. I listened.

18th. Packed and put her manuscript in my case. I bought some more books from her, but she refused to give a receipt. I did shopping for her before I left. In the evening, I headed for Los Angeles Airport, returned car, checked in, went through customs and security and flew by British Airways to Heathrow, London. Arrived on 19th around 2.00 p.m. Rhoda met me at the airport. Bless Rhoda.

19th. I had a brief look at Jan's manuscript. We had a pleasant afternoon and evening.

20th. I cleaned up the script and began printing.

Next few days. Rhoda proofreading manuscript and finding errors. I got on with my research on Orwell.

22nd. I was down with a touch of flu and jet lag. Spent most of the day in bed, putting more information received about Orwell onto my computer.

24th. Dispatched Jan's contract to the editor at St Martin's Press.

25th. Interviewed Janetta Parladé, a friend of Sonia Orwell, at her house. It went very well, although I wished I had read David Cesarani on Arthur Koestler because, from our conversation, I gathered that she obviously had been his lover. She said that she would mention me to Robert Kee (an ex-husband of hers), who was visiting her this evening.

Next day. I drove to Firle near Lewes to interview Anne O. Bell, who edited the diaries of Virginia Woolf. Very interesting interviews but nothing new. Concentrated more on researching Orwell.

30th. To UCL to look up David Astor file, and then to view Arena production of programmes on Orwell: *The Road to Wigan Pier*, *Nineteen Eight-Four* and *Such Such Were the Joys*.

1 December. Felt rather weak following the flu. I spent most of the day in bed reading *The Lion and the Unicorn*, and preparing to interview David Astor tomorrow.

GLIMPSES OF A BIOGRAPHER'S DIARY

2nd. Visited David Astor at his house at 3.00 p.m. He was a fine, charming gentleman, who thought very highly of Orwell. They obviously had a deep, respectful and reliable friendship. We talked for about three hours. Then drank cherry. He told me how Orwell was refused burial by the vicar at Cliveden, and how he had to approach the vicar at his local church at Sutton Courtenay.

3rd. I visited Gordon Dunstan, who told me how he persuaded one reluctant member of his churchwardens' committee, a farmer, to agree to the burial by showing him a copy of *Animal Farm*. He also pointed out that a family of gypsies and the old Liberal Prime Minister, Herbert Asquith lie buried close to Orwell on either side of his grave.

4th. Hungover most of the day. I read *The Gentleman from San Francisco* by Ivan Bunin. I can see why Lowry loved this book.

5 - 11 Tidied Orwell discs. Found a list of articles on Orwell on the internet, which I then printed up. Wrote and posted thank you letter to David Astor, checked on how many people I had interviewed so far, and made sure that Rhoda or I had written up all transcripts. I received and wrote many Christmas cards and letters about Orwell to Douglas Moyle, Richard H. Blair, Jane Morgan, Henry Dakin, Lucy Dakin, Quentin Kopp, David Astor, Susan Watson, Diana Witherby, David Sylvester, Dr Kenneth Sinclair Loutit, Fay Evans, Janetta Parladé and many more to his friends, family and people I interviewed. Continued reading Orwell's *Complete Works* and making notes onto my computer. Rhoda scanned Ian Angus' notes onto her computer. (We have two computers).

12th. Celia rang and gave me some more interested information about Orwell that I entered onto my computer. I wrote letters to Robert Kee, Adrian Fierz and Sir Steven Runciman. Rhoda finished reading *More Modern Short Stories* and commenced *Orwell: Fugitive from the Camp of Victory* by Richard Rees.

Next few days. I read *Burmese Days* again. Received Hemingway's letter from Boston. Michael Sayers from New York rang and left a message on my answerphone. He once shared a flat with Orwell in Kentish Town.

15th. Rang Jan, who informed me that she received her cheque from St Martin's Press some time ago, and looking forward to see her book published. She asked about her contract. I reminded her, that she signed the contract on my last visit and it was sent to the editor. Rhoda and I are so very happy for her.

16th-19th. I rang and spoke to Michael Sayers, who wanted me to interview him at his home in Manhattan. He told me that Orwell was deeply depressed over Eileen's death. Also, he said what Orwell feared most was that the 'new streamlined news' would change his old England beyond all recognition. I spent some time on the internet tracking down books, dates and so on. I finished reading Rayner Heppenstall's: Four Absentees and entered some into my Chronology.

18th. I Interviewed Adrian Fierz, who knew Orwell very well, at his home. He gave me a fascinating interview, found Orwell quite engaging, and thought that 'George' came from his father's habit of applying it to casual acquaintances. Also, he told me that his mum, Mabel, had said she had an affair with Orwell. Once, Orwell wrote to his mother inviting her to spend a day in the country. Her reply suggested that she knew exactly what he had in mind: 'Darling, how splendid! 2.30 then at Hayes Station on Monday. Take me there by the quickest route to a punt on the river. I adore a warm sunny day in a punt by the river. I will punt you carefully along the prettiest way and not upset your male dignity into the Thames! Take your costume in case we find a suitable place. I hate the usual swimming bath. It will be nice. Not as you say a decent walk. I prefer the opposite. If it rains. Well, we will visit the pubs in turn. The great thing is to walk as little as possible, so try and find out the route....'

He said that it was not unusual for his mother to take a lover; his father merely turned a blind eye to all her amours. I imagined that a seductive afternoon on the river or out in the country was the sort of idyll of which Orwell dreamed. It was sad for him that the girl he really pined for, Brenda, was not so readily seduced. Before I left, Adrian loaned me Arena programmes one to three, video and tapes to copy. I entered his captivating interview and stories onto my computer.

20 December. In the late morning, Robert Kee rang and talked about Orwell and Sonia's wedding and Orwell's funeral.

21st. Good day. Friends came bearing gifts, ate and talked, were merry and in a celebratory mood. Great fun.

Next day. Rhoda was coming down with flu, was resting and taking medication. Fortunately, she did finish all Jan's typing and saved it on disc for her and St Martin's Press.

23rd. We did our last-minute shopping for Christmas. Afterwards, she was still unwell, went to bed and slept. My turn to give her tender loving care.

The following day. I continued entering interviews on my computer. Read a bit more of *People of the Abyss*. Rhoda up and about, though not fully recovered. We watched Orwell's Arena programmes. Very good indeed. Made notes.

25th. Happy Christmas Day. We both prepared and cooked turkey, sprouts, baby carrots, roast potatoes, pudding and so on. After the Queen's Speech, we had our late Christmas delicious dinner with champagne. Lovely day as usual. Rhoda slept for an hour or so, but feeling better. I finished transcribing Anne Dunn's interview and started on David Astor's interview. Wrote letters. When Rhoda woke up, we had a lovely evening, but to bed early for she needed to rest and sleep.

The next few days. Worked on Orwell's chronology, completed making notes on *The People of the Abyss*, began rereading Jeffrey Meyers' *Users' Guide to George Orwell*, some excellent stuff there, transcribing interviews, carried on saving Orwell's *Complete Works* notes, receiving and sending letters.

29th. Rhoda felt better and was up and about. I did some more transcribing on Astor's interview and saved Orwell's *Complete Works* notes on my computer.

30th. Dispatched Jan's manuscript, disc, photographs and captions to St Martin's Press. Received lovely letters and cards from our Mexican friends. We went to the London Library and did some more shopping.

31 December. Happy New Year's Eve. Unfortunately, I seemed to be coming down with the flu. Started taking medication. We had a lovely day as usual. I worked a bit on Orwell's *Complete Works* note. We saw the New Year in style drinking champagne and eating snacks. Rhoda said that the champagne is good for my flu. We talked, laughed, looked at television watching the spectacular way each country welcomed the millennium.

2000

1 January. Happy New Year. A better one we hoped. Every day, I read and made notes on Orwell's *Compete Works* on my computer with Rhoda's help. Every so often, I worked on my novel, sending, receiving, replying to letters and emails, and entering transcripts onto my computer including some more of Astor's interview. I told Rhoda, "I am over-weight." She started me on a diet as she did before. I enjoyed her cooking.

2nd. Rhoda's sister, Margaret and her family came to dinner. Delicious food, merry company, much talking and laughing. Wonderful day.

3rd. Re-reading the first chapter of *A Passage to India* for inspiration. A magnificent piece of evocative description, encompassing a time and a landscape. I decided to re-read the entire book. Not all at one go, but dipping into it from time to time. Reinstalled McAfee Virus scan on my PC.

Next few days. I did a bit more work on my novel and felt that it was improving. In the evening, we watched a video of Rhoda in the U.S.A. She is very photogenic, unlike me. Rhoda helped putting Orwell's letters on disc. Books I ordered: *Orwell's Critical Heritage*, B. S. Johnson's *Everyone Knows Somebody Who's Dead*, Reginald Reynolds *My Life and Crimes, Cambridge Poetry 1930, Life and Letters, July 1934*, Oxford Anthology of English Literature volume two arrived. I rang and spoke with Jan, who was looking forward to seeing her book published. Rereading Orwell's *Burmese Days*. He shared with E. M. Foster the same subversive attitude towards British India. In *A Passage to India* there are features, which Orwell also incorporated in Burmese Days.

13th. Anthony rang. We would go ahead with St Martin's Press deal on Orwell. Reliable publisher.

14th. Rhoda went to her sister, Margaret, for the weekend.

15th. Took Mira, an author, to dinner at Hillgate Street. Towards the end of the meal, my then next-door neighbours, Jo and Amanda came, said "Hello." Jo looked embarrassed, as if he had caught me out in an infidelity. I introduced Mira and they left. Funny really!!

I must work at a style to get the right opening for my Orwell's book.

17th. Faxed The Independent suggesting *Orwell: The European*, and they asked to see it, but I was not too hopeful that they would like it. I collected Rhoda from her sister's house. She had fun time with her family, as usual. She was very pleased that I continued with my healthy diet.

20th. The Independent turned down my article on the grounds that their Literary pages had done something recently on Orwell.

Next day. I received an invitation from Penguin to a party to launch the new Penguin Classics next month. They also sent proofs of my introduction to Malcolm Lowry *Hear Us O Lord From Heaven Thy dwelling Place and Lunar Caustic*, that I returned a week later. In the evening, we watched a television programme on Englishness.

29th. Natasha Spender rang, and we had a very pleasant chat about Orwell and Sonia. We would talk again in ten days' time.

Next day. We saw *Time Regained*, (French: *Le Temps Retrouvé*). A French drama film based on the final volume of Marcel Proust's epic *Remembrance of Things Past*.

31st. Almost, at the end of my first month into the Millennium researching Orwell. So far, going well, though still lots to do. Spent most of the day reflecting on what I have to date gathered about Orwell's life and works. A productive day as Rhoda would say.

1 February. Alan Ross rang to say, among other things, that my Bryan S Johnson's article would come out in June. Spoke to Jan. She wanted to change a few things in her manuscript. I made a note of her changes, would look at them later and come back to her.

Next day. On my return from hospital I went to Pan's bookshop, bought books and tape of Anthony Powell's *A Dance to the Music of Time*, the first of his twelve novel sequence.

5th. Still copying with more letters to Orwell. Received St Martin's Press contract for my input on Jan's book.

8th. To hospital. Not impressed by the neurologist, who examined me and said that he thought that my back pain was due to my right-leg problem. Would preferred a different consultant. Spent the afternoon on Orwell's letters, listened to audio tape of *Down and Out in Paris and London*. In the evening, I attended Penguin party to launch the New Penguin Classics. I met some interesting writers and two pretty girls. Charming. Good talk. I feared that a photographer I specifically asked not to take my photograph, sneaked up and snapped me when I was talking to a fellow-writer just before leaving.

11th. Malcolm Muggeridge's diary arrived. Some marvellous material on Orwell for my book. Muggeridge stressed self-pity and egotism as his predominant characteristics. In the afternoon, I interviewed Natasha Spender. A lively, voluble and animated woman, who began talking at length about her husband, Stephen, the CIA and Encounter, as if defending him against an accusation which I had not raised. However, she was annoyed at Stonor Saunders for interviewing her very briefly, inadequately and then refusing her final manuscript. She wanted me to let her see what I intend to write from our talk. Came home, looked at Stephen Spender's Journals and saw that he rather contradicted what she told me about Sonia. I'll send her the pages and invite her comments.

Next day. We went to the London Library. Anthony Powell's diaries are excellent. When Orwell wrote about England, he was writing about himself.

14th. Happy Valentine's Day. Fun day as usual. Next few days. I was very busy reading, interviewing, transcribing more notes and letters onto my computer.

17th. We went to see *The End of the Affair*. It is based on Graham Greene's novel of the same name. A British-American drama romance film. It was charming, and the plot was cleverly revealed with stirring chemistry between the lovers.

23rd. We went to see *American Beauty*. Rhoda enjoyed it, of course. Books ordered came.

29th. Leap Year. We pledged our love over a bottle of red Morgan wine. In the evening, we watched *The Red Balloon*. Lovely day and drank too much when I should be losing weight.

1-18 March. Every day, Rhoda and I concentrated on Orwell and his *Complete Works*. I have almost finished volume 13. Has taken me too long. I received an email from the editor at St. Martin's Press informing me that she spoke to Jan and they were working on the changes. Great news. Michael Sayers emailed saying that he could not reply to my Orwell questions by email and wanting me to go to his home in Manhattan, to interview him.

3rd. Pinochet left for Chile yesterday. When he arrived today, he jumped out of his wheelchair and walked unaided. Wow!!!.

9th. Worked till 3.00 p.m. Some good ideas arising out of what I had read so far. We went to see *The Talented Mr. Ripley*. It was a great performance, brave and complex, all the actors were perfectly cast and stylishly wrapped.

11th. Pleasant evening with Brian and Doris at dinner. I found myself hotly arguing with Doris about capitalism and socialism - she was making me out to be saying what I was not saying all the time. I probably drank too much. We were and are great friends.

13th. Reflecting on Orwell in Barcelona in May 1936. Little did they know that this minor operation would spawn *Animal Farm* and *Nineteen Eighty-Four*. Read Orwell's Partisan Review article for August 1942, and his *Reflection on the Spanish Civil War*. They were extremely revealing. Now, I know more about his thinking. Also, read passages on Orwell in Mark Benney *Almost a Gentleman* and this gave me some more good ideas.

16th. I had a good day at Orwell's archive. Saw some documents, birth, marriage, death certificates, Indian Police forms, army medical records and much more' which got me very excited. I went to bed late, after gathering all these together onto my computer.

17th. Rhoda was at her sister's home. I returned to the archive and saw Orwell's death certificate, Eileen's birth and death certificates, PEN membership card and Eileen's correspondence, including some letters from Georges Kopp addressed care of her brother in London. I felt very tired, and went to bed early.

Next day. Reflected again on the Spanish Civil War and its effects on Orwell and Eileen. We celebrated my birthday today at the Café Royal, because it would not be opened tomorrow.

19th. Happy Birthday to me. Hungover from last night. Rhoda reading *George Orwell* by John Atkins and scanning Orwell's letters. We watched Michael Sayers' video again. Some good stuff there.

22nd. I received a strange telephone call from David Sylvester. He said that he had spoken to Ian Angus, who spoke warmly of me. So, he decided that he would talk to me as well as the other Orwell's biographer. That's all. And the telephone went down. Then to the archive to copy Ida Blair's diary for 1905 and looked at microfilm of Tribune. Very good stuff there.

23rd. Entered notes onto my computer. In the afternoon, I had tea with Ian Angus at his house. Good talk and got answers to most of my questions. But I feared I gave a few information away. He had already met the other biographer, and would probably see him again. However, I had said that "I'm not going in competition with him. I wish him well." Rhoda had finished the letters in Volume 10 of the *Complete Works*. What a girl!

24th. Good day. At the UCL, Orwell's archive, I saw the medical report from Preston Hall. Orwell had had pneumonia four times in 1938. I had been reflecting about his illness recently in the process of putting my notes in order onto my computer. Fascinating stuff. Very busy on my book during the weekend.

27th. To the archive again to look up some more letters and various transcripts. Then to The Imperial War Museum to listen to Stafford Cottman tapes on The Spanish Civil War 1936-1939. Very enlightening. Good questioning.

28th. To the Orwell's archive for an hour of transcripts. What a mass of material!!! Then prepared for our trip up North, interviewing and relaxing.

29th. We set off on another Orwell trail. First stop was at Hopwood to interview Douglas Moyle, who fought in the Spanish Civil War and was an Independent Labour Party member. He gave a very good account of events during the War. Left at 3.30 p.m. for Keswick, Cumbria, where we checked in at the Queens Hotel, Main Street. We did not sleep well because of the noise from the pub and the hotel alarm went off at 6.00 a.m.

Next day. After breakfast, we changed room and explored the town centre. Rhoda wanted to stay and enjoyed the town centre further, while I went to interview Henry Dakin, Orwell's nephew, at his home at 2.00 p.m. He was very pleasant and welcoming.

Gave a very good interview about the life and works of his uncle. I left and went to meet Rhoda. We drove around Keswick. Picturesque lakes, quaint villages, beautiful walking routes, climbing spots, mountains and hills. After supper, we returned to our hotel.

31st. We had another rough night due to noise from the radiator. After breakfast, we checked out, drove to Jane Morgan and Lucy Dakin (Orwell's nieces) to interview them at their home. They were charming and welcoming and gave me a very good interview about their uncle Orwell. Some very good pointers for my Orwell book. Left at about 6.00 p.m. for Gretna Green and checked in at the Welcome Lodge, large and comfortable. We went out for supper, returned to the Lodge, entered a small part of the interviews on my laptop.

1 April. Slept very well. What a difference! After breakfast, we drove to interview Sir. Steven Runciman in Dumfriesshire, Scotland. He had spoken to me at his club in London about Lawrence Durrell, whom he had known in 1945. This time we met at his castle. Aged 97 and still the epitome of Eton charm. (Rhoda did not want to come in. She preferred to enjoy the charms of the surrounding and read). He kindly gave me tea, and afterwards, during a longish interview, told me that the 'received' story of him and Orwell making an image of a boy out of soap, was inaccurate. Because the perpetrator of this false account (Christopher Hollis) had failed to correct it, as he had promised to do, it had remained in circulation. Sir Steven's 'corrected' version was that after a boy had insulted him, Orwell suggested making a wax effigy and spearing with pins. Sir Steven thought that too drastic, so they broke off the leg. Later, to their horror, the boy broke his leg, and shortly after that he died. At first reluctant to name the boy, he wrote later to inform me that it was Philip York. But, he and Orwell were convinced they had killed York and even at his advanced age, Sir Steven told me that he still felt extremely guilty about what they had done. With his heightened sense of guilt, one can easily imagine how Orwell would have felt, something hinted in his subsequent writing. Sir Steven gave some very good points for my book. We left at 12.30 p.m. and returned to Gretna Green

GLIMPSES OF A BIOGRAPHER'S DIARY

Welcome Lodge, had late lunch and checked out. Drove to Newcastle to pay our respects to Mrs. Eileen Blair at St Andrew's and Jesmond Cemetery. Her headstone read 'Here Lies Eileen Maud Blair, Wife of Eric Arthur Blair, Born Sept. 25th 1905; Died March 29th 1945. The burial spot had been found by Orwell, who ordered a gravestone on which he approved a simply-worded engraving, similar to the one he later requested for himself. We left and drove beyond Preston to the Welcome Lodge Charnock Richard. We checked in, lovely and comfortable. Went out for dinner. Returned to our room and had a good night's sleep.

2nd. After breakfast, we checked out and drove all around Wigan, especially Wigan Pier, a sort of Orwell theme park - stretch of canal with pubs and a museum. Then to Warrington Lane, Darlington Road, the Trip Shop, but it was knocked down and no sign of it. Wigan Pier had photographs of Orwell. Wonderful. After lunch, we headed for Orwell's aunt's, Nellie Limouzin's, house at 195 Ladbroke Grove, Portobello Road. Aunt Nellie was his closest female relation after his mother. She gave her second name, Kate, to his goat. In her top-floor flat she was supposed to have held a literary salon at which Humphrey Dakin, Orwell's brother-in-law, claimed to have met G.K. Chesterton, and where Jacintha Buddicom reported Eric (Orwell) saying he had met socialist and children's author, E. Nesbit. An Esperantist contact sent me a photograph of Nellie posing with Sylvia Pankhurst and friends on the Sphinx which stood on the Thames Embankment between 1900 and 1909. Sadly, Nellie's face was obscured by her hat, and the picture was considered too poor to go into my book. But it offers further proof that she moved in radical circles. I then found that Conrad Noel (a good friend of Eric's, according to one of his ILP friends) was at that time curate of St Mary's, Paddington Green, and certainly himself knew Sylvia Pankhurst. What is more, he spent his spare time visiting spikes and workhouses dressed as a tramp, which opened the fascinating possibility that Eric had picked up the idea of roughing it around the dosshouses from Noel. Later, as a revolutionary vicar of Thaxted, Noel flew the red flag above his church, a story incorporated into Robert Shaw's absorbing novel *The Flag*. Ruth Pitter remembered being taken by Eric to Nellie's flat to have dinner with her and what she called 'some old Anarchist', presumably the esperantist Eugene Adam. From there, we returned home and later went to our local Italian restaurant, Topo Dora, which is no longer there.

3rd and 5th April. My visits to Orwell's nephew and nieces, energised me greatly. I went to the archive often, to examine more transcripts including Brenda Salkeld saying that Orwell told her that he expected to die in Grantham. Bill Dunn, (Avril's husband) had good stories about him, Eric, Avril, his sister, and Richard, his son, went for a picnic to Scarba, a neighbouring island. Well, the first living thing they met on stepping ashore was an adder. Eric put his foot on it, just behind its head. They expected him to bash it with the other foot or a stone or something, but surprisingly he deliberately took out his penknife and opened it and slit the snake from top to bottom. He gutted it, filleted it...." Rhoda scanned more letters onto the computer.

6th. Spent day transcribing Sir Steven's and David Astor's interviews onto my computer. Cecily rang from Paris. She is still unwell. We had pleasant talk. Photographs arrived from Jane Morgan, and later I returned them, sent thank you letters and my books: *Pursued by Furies* to Jane and *Malcolm Lowry Remembered* to her brother.

7th. Today a young girl, who tried to queue-jump in the Post office called me "a senile old git". Probably she was right. All I did was to raise my eyebrows when she looked at me.

Next few days. I received, replied, wrote and transcribed letters and entered more material onto my computer.

13th. Sent thank-you letter and returned papers to Douglas Moyle. To the archive in early afternoon, and interviewed Frances Partridge at 4.00 p.m. at her home. We had a very good discussion on Sonia Orwell. A fine and delightful lady. She gave me tea.

14th. I wrote and thanked her, and sent a few more questions to Sir Steven Runciman. Rhoda was not well, so I encouraged her to go to bed and rest in the afternoon. After spending most of the day at the computer, we relaxed watching *Madame Bovary* on television.

16th. Sorted out papers, organised some folders in chronological order, and continued reflecting on Orwell's life and his *Complete Works*.

17 April. Sir Steven Runciman replied, very good letter and informative. Orwell's contract from St. Martin's Press arrived, signed and returned to .

19th. Natasha Spender telephoned to thank me for sending her husband's material and gave me further information.

Next few days. I had my head down focussing on my Orwell's book.

23rd. More work on chronology, copied letters from notebooks, reading and entering Orwell's Eton stories. Rhoda's friends came to supper bearing presents. We all had a very pleasant evening and Rhoda was quite happy.

24th. Slight hungover and feeling unduly tired. Spent day putting more touches to the chronology, work done by Rhoda on disc from Orwell's *Complete Work*, sorted out all letters to Orwell and painted a new bookshelf with Rhoda's assistance.

Next few days. I continued going to the archive, saw and made notes on Prosper Buddicom's diary. They threw more light on Orwell. Continued working on Orwell's *Complete Work*, chronology, writing, receiving and replying to letters and emails, did some work on my novel, keeping in contact and entertaining friends.

1 May. We toured around some sites where Orwell lived in London. He lived in a series of short-term lodgings in the area around Hampstead. From August 1941 to August 1943, he lived at Dorset Chambers in Chagford Street; 77 Parliament Hill;

Longford Court in Longford Place, here, he was commemorated with a blue plaque; and 10 Mortimer Crescent in Kilburn; from June 1944, he lived at 222 the Strand; from 1944-47, he lived at 27 Canonbury Square in Islington, where he was commemorated with another blue plaque. Returning home, I continued working at my computer on Orwell's *Complete Works*, my novel, sorted out more papers and books.

Next few days. I was busy reading Orwell's *Complete Works*, making telephone calls, mostly to clarify various issues, more work on his chronology, receiving and sending letters and emails, and started reading Vanity Fair.

9th. Copy-edited manuscript of Jan's book arrived from St. Martin's Press. Looked like a fair amount of work to be done. I may have to go out and worked through them with her again. Rang Jan. We had a good discussion. Faxed Matson for permission to quote from Lowry's letters for Jan's book.

10th. I bought a new personal computer, printer and scanner, and familiarised myself with them.

12th. We drove down to Eastbourne Library and photocopied all St. Cyprian Chronicles from 1914-1919. Afterwards, we drove to Dr. Howard Nicholson's cottage to interview him. He was a junior consultant physician in Dr. Andrew Morland's team at University College Hospital, London. Dr. Morland was a leading authority on pulmonary tuberculosis. Dr. Nicholson noticed how old and wizened Orwell looked sitting in a chair in the corner of his room. He spoke so interestingly about tuberculosis and gave me good ideas and a vivid picture of a dying man. Then, to Lewes and checked in at the Castle Hotel.

Next day. We returned to Eastbourne Library to look at Eastbourne Union Workhouse records. Found some more interesting material, made notes on laptop. Arrived home by 5.30 p.m. Later, we went to our local Greek restaurant for pleasant evening dinner.

GLIMPSES OF A BIOGRAPHER'S DIARY

15th. Cheque, first advance for my Orwell's book, arrived from St. Martin's Press.

16-17 May. Heard end of *Animal Farm* tape. Very good and gave me another approach for my book. Planning my trip to Los Angeles from 26th May - 1st June. I rang Jan and encouraged her to be prepared to work on her book. We had a good talk.

18th. Listened to side 1 of *Nineteen Eighty-Four* and made notes on my computer. Excellent read by Timothy West. Later, we attended TLS party at Hatchards bookshop. Very interesting as usual. Bought books and videotapes. On returning home, I caught up with work on my book.

19 – 20 May. Reflecting on Orwell's life: From the age of eight until twenty five, he lived within a structured system of authority, in which he had to learn to survive. Also, he managed to retain a sense of his own creativity, a free inner-life like Winston Smith, rebelling silently and promising himself that one day he would live differently. Listened to side two of *Nineteen Eighty-Four* this morning. Very good. Made more notes on computer. Rhoda did some scanning and booked my B. A. flight. Tomorrow, I will book a hire car in Los Angeles. Scanner seemed not to be very good on photographs. I spoke to our friend Cecily. She was better and her audiotape finally arrived.

22nd. In the morning I returned scanner to John Lewis and bought another one, which worked very well. Rhoda continued scanning Orwell's works and material.

Next day. I took Rhoda to hospital for investigation. Got photographic papers for new printer. Returned to hospital to collect Rhoda.

Next few days. I listened to more of *Nineteen Eighty-Four* on tapes. Very impressive. Did more work on scanning Orwell's *Complete Works*. Rhoda's nephew, Gabriel, and his wife, Leyla, came to dinner. Lovely relaxing evening. Rhoda off to conference. I was busy working on my computer, reading and preparing for my Los Angeles trip.

26 May. To Los Angeles (L.A.). Quiet flight and got some sleep. Two hours to get through U.S.A. Immigration at L.A. and two hours' drive to Westlake. Jan was in good spirits, but did not appreciate the urgency of what we were doing. She spoke of going to Encino tomorrow to buy a new word-processor, so that she could type out her book again! I was stressed. I said, "No book by fourth of June; no Autumn publication!". I felt the message got home. Exhausted and went to bed.

Next day. She was eager to get on with her book. She started typing up and denouncing some suggestions as a demand to rewrite her book. I jollied her along and before much time had elapsed, we had done 100 pages. She insisted we stop at page 130 or so. We did that, then we drove to Encino to American Express. It was very hot and Jan began to feel the heat. So, we returned to Westlake, did some shopping before coming to her house. She insisted we had some champagne with our meal. Then hurried back to her manuscript to press on, wanting to finish before I leave. At around page 150, I started falling asleep. I had to go for a lie-down, and slept for one and a half hours. When I got back, and saw that ink was splashed just about page 156. I was angry with her for spoiling the manuscript. But, although we proceeded amicably, the atmosphere was poor and after dinner, I retired to bed.

28th. A better day. We finished her book. Pleasant dinner and talk.

29th. Got on with correcting her book on disc. Put up to page 130 onto it. Jan's friends, Marilyn and Sidney, were invited to dinner. Jan cooked steak for her and for her friends and salmon for me and nothing else. She forgot to cook vegetables, potatoes and make salads. When her friends arrived, she gave them Champagne and tried to be jovial. They then finished the cooking in the end and produced a sort of sweet. Humour saved the day.

The following day. We worked steadily putting her book on disc, just 38 or so pages to go! Marvellous. I must get her to sign Matson contract for permission before I leave. Or else, I would have to return. I rang Rhoda. Be calm!!!

31st. Jan was in one of her strange moods. I said that I would probably finish the manuscript of her book by 12.00 noon. It was bizarre. She wanted to buy an electric typewriter. Went to Staples and bought one. Returned via bank and food store. Got to her house, and I wanted her to sign Matson's contract. She talked and said she wanted a copy. I went to the pharmacy and did a photocopy. Returned. Got her to sign the contract. I told her that I would pay Matson for permission to quote from Lowry's letters which I did. She didn't want to dine out tonight. So, now I prepared for home and Rhoda. She must be at her friend's, Val, place, because her sister, Mary, and the children were coming today from Atlanta, U.S.A. Rhoda and Val would collect them, and stay at Val's place for the night. More fun to come. Rhoda's nephew, Trevor, was getting married on the 11th of June, and relatives would be arriving from abroad for this joyous occasion. I guess I won't be seeing much of Rhoda. She is a family person.

1-2 June. Before going to the airport, I went to Bank of America in Westlake and opened an account. Returned car. Flight home, I sat in a pool of orange juice on my seat. Moved to Business Class. Changed into clean clothes, and travelled home in style on the 2nd at 3.00 p.m. Rhoda met me. Lovely girl. She had been cleaning, shopping and getting excited about her nephew's wedding. Most of her family would be there.

3rd. I must put my heart and soul into my Orwell's book. Spent some time in the morning reading letters and emails received, replying and sending out letters. In the afternoon concentrated on Orwell's *Complete Works*.

Next few days. Copied emails and letters received on Orwell's, including one from Sir Steven's, onto computer, and sent him a letter and Hollis chapter on Eton. Rhoda and I had a discussion about time with her family and parties to attend. We agreed that I would take her and her friends, Bonnie and Val, to the wedding, stay to non-alcoholic party and drive them home afterwards. Of course, there would be alcohol there. I always want her to be happy, and that she should spend most of her time with her sisters and their family. Wrote to Mr. Matson asking for rights in all languages. Jet lag catching up with me, plus all that drinking in Los Angeles, Rhoda said.

7th. Rhoda's sisters, Margaret, Mary and her family came. I played with the children colouring in stencils and telling stories and they roared with laughter. So much fun. Unfortunately, Margaret's chair collapsed, we all jumped up and prevented her falling. Felt awful. Probably need new chairs. Rhoda went off with her family to Margaret's place to help preparing for the wedding, the many family gatherings and parties. Rang and received many calls including one from Celia G. about my visit to her house in two weeks' time to look at more of Inez's diaries and further talk on Orwell, and another from Margaret Crosland, who remembered being almost drowned in Orwell's extraordinary sea-blue eyes. She told me that she wrote a few reviews for Orwell for Tribune, when he was literary editor there.

8th. To hospital to see the consultant neurologist, who examined me, and discussed my medical history, and informed me that he thought my back pain was at the source of my leg and ankle problems. To have more tests and to see him on 28th September. Received fax from Mr. Matson agreeing permission to quote for all languages. Wrote to New England Review offering HVOL introduction. Reflecting to Orwell politics.

Next day. I drove to Professor Dunstan in Exeter. Charming man. Good interview. Pleasant wife, who treated me to tea. Long drive down and back, 405 miles, round trip. But worth it. Rhoda came while I was away, hoovered, dusted, cleaned the house, brought lovely fruits, cooked and left food for me to last a few days. Bless her.

10th June. Spent the day working hard on my book. In the evening, I went to the pre-wedding party, had a wonderful time meeting most of Rhoda's family, lots to eat, dancing music and so on. Brought her home.

11 June. The wedding day! Rhoda looked gorgeous. Sunny, warm and lovely weather all day and night. We went to the wedding at Grim's Dyke Hotel - Trevor and his wife, Deepal, were just handsome, very beautiful romantic setting, tranquil woodlands, stunning blossom trees, cameras as usual, tried to avoid them, but Rhoda's sister, Mary, photographed me. Rhoda made an eloquent speech and had lots of fun-time including dancing. She has dancing feet. Later, we left by taxi, first to Bonnie's, then to our house to collect car and drove Val to her beautiful flat. It was an enjoyable and happy day all round.

12th. Post-wedding day and grand celebration at Margaret and Peer's big house and lawn. I took Rhoda and collected her later. I did more work on my computer and scanning.

13th. Reflecting on Orwell, the realist - a poet trying to escape. Received a good letter from Sir Steven Runciman giving me permission to use the interview and the story he told me on my last visit.

14 – 19 June. Margaret and her sisters, Rose, Rachel and Mary, together with Mary's family went to Wales and Ireland to continue the wedding celebration. Rhoda did not go, because she had hospital appointment for a 48-hour recording of her blood pressure, which she kept.

Next few days. Rhoda and I slogged away at my book. Spent most of the time on Orwell's *Complete Works*.

19th. Heard from New England Review about introduction to HVOL, wanted to see it. Rhoda had completed scanning up to volume 16.

20th. She went to Margaret's to spent the night with her family.

Next day. Mary, her husband and their children returned to Atlanta, U.S.A. After seeing them off, Rhoda returned home. She had a happy and memorable time with her family. She was a bit sad too.

27th. Good day. Visited Celia G. and did a very useful interview with her. She clarified certain things, and told me a few new stories for my book. I looked at Inez's diaries and got some more information for my book, as well. Returned home, entered interview and further information from diaries onto computer.

Next day. Visited John Russell, a friend of Sonia, in London. According to him, she was so profoundly Frenchified, that for many years she really had trouble reading English authors. She might have found Orwell's Englishness unappealing. He was well read in French literature and had his own French cast of mind.

30th. Drove to Birmingham to attend the Saltley College's reunion. I checked into the hotel, had shower and dressed for the occasion. I joined my colleagues for pre-dinner drink and dinner. So good to see them after all these years. Very pleasant, lots of chatting and reminiscence. Got back to my room by midnight. I rang Rhoda, who had been scanning volume 20 most of the day, told me that a fax from Mr. Matson's office came, accepted the amount offered and all permissions given for Jan's book. Hallelujah! Great news. She rang Matson's office in New York and informed them that I would be in touch on Monday.

1-5 July. Will now sleep happily and enjoy tomorrow. However, I slept badly. Riotous noises from the street at 4.00 a.m., with what sounded like road cleaning vehicles. Also between 5.00 a.m. and 6.00 a.m., the man in the next-room was either having a heart attack or a noisy orgasm. Almost certainly the latter. Had breakfast with my colleagues. Then to Saltley College. The area around it was un-recognisable, and now settled by large number of Muslims. Half-way up the College Road was a large Mosque. A different area all together. Saw my old College, which brought back happy memories and met old pals again. Next, we all went down to the Parish Church for service to commemorate 150th anniversary of the College. Well attended, excellent choir, well-judged sermon by the Archdeacon of Birmingham. Good hymns to sing. Back to College briefly, saw old refectory - just as it was, old small hall where we did drama, the field at rear was now used by the locals, especially the youngsters to play. Also, saw exhibits of old photographs, plays and some good shots of David Turner. After lunch and much talking and laughing, we said our goodbyes, and I left for home. Rhoda had been busy not only meditating on Psalm 23 and praying for Mr. Matson to respond favourably to my request to grant permission for Jan's book which he did, but had done a huge amount of scanning. Lovely angelic girl.

Next few days. I listened to more of *Nineteen Eight-Four* tapes. Filled in and returned St. Martin's Press questionnaire on Jan's book. They wanted her to do press, radio and television interviews in Los Angeles. I informed Jan. I received and sent letters and faxes to my old chums and people known to Orwell. Reflecting often on his thoughts, feelings and actions in the process of gathering and entering information onto computer. Had new neighbours, Diana and Hugh, in for snacks and drinks, joined later by their friend, Sarah. This went on from 6.00 p.m. to 10.30 p.m. We drank at least four bottles of champagne. Rhoda was beautiful. Diana was an advertising copywriter and he a composer of electronic music. It was a very enjoyable evening. Neighbours delivered thank-you card plus flowers and chocolates. How gracious!!

6th. I download FBI file on Orwell from the internet. Next, I wanted to see Orwell's elusive KGB file, rumoured to be somewhere in Moscow. In James K. Hopkins' book *In the Heart of Fire; The British in the Spanish Civil War*, he mentioned having seen Orwell's file. He had no detailed notes on it, he told me, but referred me to the New York Tamiment Library, which held a number of KGB files on Westerners. I contacted them. Sadly, the library only had files on Americans, who had served in Spain with the Abraham Lincoln Battalion. But to my delight, they had the file on David Crook, who, although born in London's East End, had been recruited to the Party as a student at New York's Columbia University. Since he had held an American visa, his file was there among the Americans. It duly arrived, and there was Crook's reports to his handlers in Barcelona after being arrested on a trumped-up charge to preserve his cover as a Trotskyist sympathiser. He had got to know the Blairs (Orwells) and McNair after meeting Eileen Blair (Orwell's first wife) at a café. While the ILP (International Labour Party) offices were deserted at lunchtime, he had photographed their documents and taken the film to the Russian Embassy. He spied separately on Eileen at her hotel and reported that he was 95% sure that she and Georges Kopp, Eric's commander, were intimately involved. Astonishingly, I saw that the party contact to whom he passed information was code-named 'O'Brien'! When the Blairs later visited Kopp in prison, they found Crook in the same cell, and Eileen promised to forward Kopp's mail and kept him supplied with cigarettes. (Crook, his file revealed, had in fact been imprisoned with Kopp in order to spy on him.)

Also, Tamiment sent me the file of another shady figure, David Wicks. He, too, had spied on the Blairs for Communist spymasters in Albacete. His file contained a letter to Eileen revealing that he had made overtures to her, and pleading with her to understand him. And there was more. Looking for back numbers of the Daily Worker at the Mars Memorial Library in Clerkenwell, I dug out a report by the British Communist commissar, Walter Tapsell, about meetings with British POUM (Partido Obrero e Unificacion Maxista)-ists on leave in Barcelona, indicating that some, including Blair, were willing to defect to the Communist-led International Brigade. Only when Communists turned on the POUM, did they change their minds. None of this had found its way into the Orwell's story previously, but it does demonstrate that if he was paranoid, as some claimed, he had good reason to be. It also throws light on the indictment of the Blairs and McNair for treason, unearthed in 1988, which evidently drew on reports from both Wicks and Crook.

7-12 July. I continued slogging away on my book, including going to the British Library to look at electoral rolls and found very useful information on William Phillip, his family and friends at Callow End; information on Henley-on Thames,

Wallington. The Limouzins' documents in the India Office Records section of the British Library indicated roughly when they had arrived in Burma, where they lived, whom they married, what children they had and when and how they died. Their history proved especially revealing - numerous deaths from lung conditions and several off-springs from interracial liaisons. Thacker's India Directory indicated when Ida Limouzin, Orwell's mother, left Burma to become a mistress in the girls' department of a boys' school in Naini Tal, a hill station over six hundred feet above sea-level in India's North West Province. She met Richard Walmsley Blair, a civil servant from Gaya, and there in June 1897, they got married. Also, Thacker's showed that Richard had not languished at the very bottom of the promotion ladder, as some had claimed, but had risen from sub-opium agent class 6 to sub-opium agent class 1 at his retirement. I interviewed Diana Witherby and Michael Sayers among others on the telephone.

13th. Mailed off Mr. Matson cheque.

17th. Copied letters into and updated chronology. Listened to more of *Nineteen Eight-Four* tapes.

20th. I spoke with Paul Crook, David Crook's son, in London. He confirmed that his father did spy on the Orwells, McNair, Kopp and other Trotskyists in Spain.

21st. Rang Jane Morgan and her brother, , to clarify some points, and Henry sent me a photocopy of the Orwell family tree.

22nd. St. Martin's Press rang to say that proofs of Jan's book were on the way. As soon as it arrived, I started reading and noting changes and so on. Rhoda, who had been scanning books, letters and material onto the computer, and transcribing tapes, had flu on the 24th and to bed.

28th. Joe and Amanda came in the evening, and we had a very pleasant time drinking, eating and chatting.

30th. Unbelievably, Rhoda was better and finished scanning *Down and Out in Paris and London* in one day.

31st. I listened more to *Nineteen Eight-Four* tapes, read more *New Grub Street*, scanned letters, including some more from Celia to Inez.

1 August. Continued reading, entering notes onto computer, putting more letters and material into chronology, transcribing interviews from tapes and rang Michael Sayers, Jane Morgan, her sister, Lucy, and her brother, Henry Dakin, amongst others.

2nd. I spoke to my friend, Cecily, in Paris and she pretty well eliminated Inez as a model for Julia in *Nineteen Eight-Four*. Also, spoke to Christopher Date at the British Museum. He would look up Orwell's application to its reading room. Our friend, Sattie, from Sweden came to late lunch and tea. Very jolly catch up.

3rd. To hospital for an EMG nerve test on my right-leg. I had to attend St Mary's Hospital, Paddington, for three weeks of physiotherapy treatment. A nice young Chinese doctor treated me with great consideration and respect and said that it had been a pleasure to meet me. In the afternoon, I started on index for Jan's book. Received letter from Faber and Faber and many others giving permission to quote.

4th. Christopher Date rang from the British Museum informing me that George Orwell applied for a reader's ticket in February 1928 from 22 Portobello Road, and in August 1937 from Wallington. Good discovery. This meant that Orwell, like Durrell and many others; took the British Library as their university.

Next few days. Rhoda finished scanning *Burmese Days*, and I completed Jan's index and editing of her manuscript. Continued chasing up last minute permissions, faxed alternative epigraphs and got Jan's proofs off to St. Martin's Press and a copy to her. Jan wanted me to handle everything regarding her book as she was not well. Of course, I will, with Rhoda's help.

10th. Rhoda finished scanning *The Road to Wigan Pier*. She has extraordinary application and stamina. What a lovely creature! Reflecting on what I had done so far on my book and on making notes. Orwell always claimed that Eton had no influence on him whatsoever. But, in *Burmese Days* he had John Flory saying that 'The chief virtue of the great public school (with their traditions of High Anglicanism, cricket and Latin verses…[is]…their atmosphere of literary scholarship…and…masters… the kind from whom one absorbs wisdom unawares.' This suggested to me, that probably much that made Orwell tick was to be found at Eton. More in hope than in expectation, I wrote to visit the College.

11th. We drove to Epping for lunch with our friends, Frances and Michael Beasley. We had very pleasant time. Then drove to Lewisham to visit Margaret, Rhoda's sister, and then returned home. A long drive.

13 August. We drove to Callow End. Following clues and picking up associations are all part of the thrill of biographical research. Writers, after all, pick up names and places and incidents wherever they can find them. During the war, Orwell took a fishing holiday at Callow End in Worcestershire. I had noticed that one of Orwell's Eton contemporaries was William Lygon, the 8th Lord Beauchamp, who lived at Madresfield, the grand riverside manor at Callow End, which stands at the confluence of the Rivers Teme and Severn—excellent for fishing. In his wartime diary, Orwell mentioned drinking at the Blue Bell Inn (often closed due to beer shortages) and staying at Beauchamp Court Farm, itself part of the Beauchamp Estate. Furthermore, the Beauchamps were childhood friends of the Yorkes, and July 1942 was the twenty-fifth anniversary of Philip Yorke's untimely death. Perhaps for Orwell, this was a pilgrimage of atonement.

I sat in the Blue Bell trying to conjure up the ghost of the 39-year-old Orwell, joining the locals for a pint. They had never heard of him or of his novel, but they talked about fishing, Madresfield and Beauchamp Court farm. One told me that the ex-Mayor of Malvern, Rachel Clapton, had worked at the farm as a wartime

2000

land-girl and had written an article about it at the local paper. When I contacted her, she told me about the farm, William Phillips, his wife, Florence, the farmhouse, and how well they had treated their workers. We drove from the pub down a lane to Madresfield, but found no one at home, but the front door was opened. We ventured inside shouting 'Hello'. No one answered, but along the river a group of youngsters were playing loud music, laughing and chattering—probably young Lygons. We didn't invite ourselves to the party, but retreated to the car. Driving back along the lane in Callow End, we noticed an ancient brick barn with the date of its building inserted in dark bricks in a red wall—1894! Was this the conception of 1984?

14th. Proofs for BS Johnson article for the London Magazine arrived. Also, a fax from Michael Meredith, the Eton College librarian, arrived saying I would be very welcome to visit the library to see what records Eton had on Orwell. I arranged to go from Wednesday 16th.

16 August. I spent three months at Eton College Library. Michael is the most unusual gentleman, who brings an immense enthusiasm to whatever he does. He placed in front of me every conceivable record in which Blair (Orwell) is named - College Annals, The Eton College Chronicles, A.S.F. Gow's mark-books and various ephemeral publications to which he contributed. It was all uncannily revealing. For example, articles in The Eton College Chronicle strongly suggested the sometimes quirky essays he later contributed to Tribune, and the satirical cast of his contributions and the rebellious attitude he and Cyril Connolly adopted towards the College Officer Training Corps, foreshadowing his later sceptical attitude policing in Burma. The 'Tory Anarchist' may have been born at St Cyprian's, as Connolly hinted, but was certainly fully-fledged by the time he reached Eton. After visiting the College mostly daily for three months, I was convinced that Orwell's time there was an important key to understanding a good many aspects of him, the man.

GLIMPSES OF A BIOGRAPHER'S DIARY

Through Michael Meredith, I also met Robbie Watkins, the young contemporary of Orwell mentioned in his scurrilous mock advertisement in *The Eton Ephemeral College Days* as the subject of 'overfond' attentions of John Grace, the College Master. Watkins was 95, a great 'Mr. Chips", who had spent his working life teaching at Harrow. Like Sir Steven, he was happy to talk, and from him I discovered that Orwell's tyrannical 'fagmaster' at Eton was Godfrey Verrall, and I was told about Marjoribanks, the sadistic School Captain. (An unpleasantly snobbish 'Verrall' shows up in *Burmese Days*, and the debauched Old Etonian, 'M' in *Down and Out in Paris and London* strongly suggests the cruel School Captain.) Watkins recalled Orwell making cheese in his room, and spoke revealingly about the atmosphere of the College and the masters who taught him - Crace, Alington, MacNaughton, Gow and Huxley, and, last but not least the great 'Monty' James.

17th. To Eton again. Found good article/BBC talk by Malcolm Muggeridge about Orwell and some reviews of the magazines to which he contributed at Eton. Saw photographs of Orwell's contemporaries, including Philip Yorke, who died so suddenly after possibly black magic and some amusing background details, like the visitation from seventeen elderly Etonian generals after Armistice Day, when speeches proclaimed that the Great War had been won on the playing fields of Eton. At home, I found Rhoda had finished scanning *Animal Farm*, and later finished *Nineteen Eighty-Four*. So all *The Complete Works* of George Orwell were now scanned in !!! Amazing girl!!!

18-20 August. Took Bryan S. Johnson's script to the London Magazine. Started entering Eton notes onto computer, and later went to the London Library and shopping with Rhoda. Felt exhausted, not well and to bed early.

21st-22nd. To Eton College Library (ECL). Took laptop. Copied reviews of College Days and a few other materials, I saw some rather Orwellian items on Bubble and Squeak dish. Michael supplied Society books and photographs of Ronnie Watkins, another scholar and contemporary of Orwell. I was very struck by the cloistered life in College, isolated in what Connolly called an 'intensive intellectual forcing-house.' My article on Bryan S Johnson goes to press today.

23rd. To Ronnie Watkins at his home. An elderly gentleman with a very sweet nature and the recognisable Etonian charm and courtesy I have so far found in my three Eton subjects. He gave me a very good interview, but not a lot on Orwell. In the evening, I transcribed Watkins' interview onto computer.

24th. To Eton. Good material on games. Orwell played a great deal. Not always well thought of as a player. At home, Alan Bradshaw at St. Martin's Press and I went through Jan's book on the telephone.

25th. To BBC Written Archives Centre at Caversham to look up Orwell's file. The archivist seemed quite excited to see me. 'You are in luck,' he said.' 'The Orwell files have been released to us only today.' They were brought to me and I spent the day gorging myself on what was there. Found rich source of new material, apparently not seen before. Reports on Orwell, including one from his BBC superior saying that he was not, I discovered, first choice for the post was Stephen Spender, and two others had already been considered. On his application form, he mentioned having 'lately done one or two odd jobs for the Ministry of Information,' and there, in a separate file, were all those glowing annual reports from his head of department, as well as reports of others trying either to get him fired or brought to heel. Also, there were references, medical certificates and much more. Very good material. Over the weekend, got on with my notes, scanned more of Ian Angus notes, finished transcribing Watkins' interview, re-reading *The Unknown Orwell* by Peter Stansky and William Abrahams, wrote, received, sent letters and faxes.

28th. Alan Bradshaw from St. Martin's Press rang with the good news that 'All done with Jan's book.'

GLIMPSES OF A BIOGRAPHER'S DIARY

1-20 September. Updating notes on computer: continued scanning letters, and other material; transcribing interviews from tapes; writing, receiving and sending letters, especially concerning Orwell.

2nd. At Family Records Office, I found Philip Yorke's death certificate, confirming cause of death as Lymphatic Leukemia. I requested a copy, which I received two days later. Rest in peace George Orwell!! I could not trace Brenda Salkeld's death certificate.

5th-7th. To Eton. More valuable details.

6th. Found tremendous diary entry from Roger Senhouse, English publisher and translator, about Orwell which I started entering onto my laptop.

8th. To Henley Library. Found some good documents about Ursuline Convent For Girls. I did a lot of research on this subject. Orwell's mother's diary for 1905 mentioned walks to a convent at Henley-on-Thames, where she had settled, the first clue I had to where she might have sent her children to school. Jane Morgan, Orwell's niece, confirmed her hunch that her mother, Marjorie, had been educated by French Catholic nuns at a convent in Henley.

11th. To Eton. I did a little more from Roger Senhouse's diary, and from Cyril Connolly writing about St Cyprian's school onto my laptop. I informed Michael that I saw and received a copy of Philip Yorke's death certificate confirming cause of death as Lymphatic Leukemia.

12th. Mostly at home, working on Orwell's *Complete Works* and chronology. Read *Enemies of Promise* by Cyril Connolly —analysing his time at Eton and gave a good insight into the world of Eton.

Next few days. I spent three days at Eton, Michael asked me to address The Book Collecting Society at Eton. An honour, of course. I accepted. Saw more fascinating stuff, including character reference of Orwell and others from St. Cyprian's to Eton, very good photograph of Orwell and his contemporaries and many letters commenting on him. Sorting out Eton notes and ensuring that most were entered onto my computer.

Rang Michael Sayers about my trip to New York, and he gave me dates and times for interviews. We would be staying with Rhoda's sister, Elizabeth, and her family in Queens, New York, U.S.A.

21 September. We parked our car at the long term car park at Heathrow Airport, London. Flew at 09.50 a.m. via British Airways to Newark, New Jersey. From there, we headed to Rhoda's sister and were greeted very warmly by the family. Jolly evening. I rang Michael, and we confirmed our meeting for the next day at 2.00 p.m.

22nd. Michael Sayers had managed to evade all previous biographers, I found on an old membership list of the Writers' Guild. In 1935, Michael, as most Orwellian's know, shared the same flat as Heppenstall and Orwell at the time of the shooting-stick incident. I was amused to find him referring to his friend 'Orwell'. I had to fly to New York to get his story. After an early lunch, I travelled by train to 59th Street, exiting at 57th Street. Rang Michael, and no answer. Went to a coffee shop, had coffee and read. I rang again at around 3.50 p.m. He answered and said that his wife asked if I could come at 5.00 p.m. for dinner at 7.00 p.m. I explored the surroundings and a bookshop. At 5.00 p.m., arrived bearing gifts of malt whisky, wine and chocolate for his wife. Then gave him a copy of Rayner Heppenstall's book *Four Absentees* plus his reviews of *Burmese Days* and *A Clergyman's Daughter*. Then he said, 'I don't want to be interviewed about Orwell today.' He just wanted to get to know me. Ugh!!! He would talk about Orwell tomorrow at 3.00 p.m. So, we talked about everyone. Luckily, I knew a good few people he knew and shared a similar political outlook. He told me how he found Orwell reading Swift's *A Modest Proposal* and Somerset Maugham's *Ashenden*, then copying passages from memory, attempting to create a new and simpler style, a wonderful vignette, which also brings the partially-evolved Eric Orwell wonderfully alive. But it got dark and I had to call Rhoda's nephew, David, to pick me up and drive me to Queens. Rhoda and her two nephews came, drove me home and we talked late. I now collapsed into bed and hoped for a more productive day tomorrow.

GLIMPSES OF A BIOGRAPHER'S DIARY

23rd. A day of disaster! After breakfast, Rhoda left me to rest and prepared for meeting with Michael at 3.00 p.m. She went with her nephew, Frederick and his wife, Indra, to the flea market. They returned bearing gifts. After lunch, I left to interview Michael. Got to 57th street early. Went to a coffee shop. Suddenly found I had left my tape-recorder behind. Horror! After some difficulties, I eventually found a shop, bought a tape recorder and batteries. Then to Michael. Couldn't get recorder to work. Back to the shop. Apparently, I had pause button on. Returned and we got on with the interview. Then they invited me to dinner. I rang David to collect me later. Being Saturday night, he had a few drinks but had back-up. His wife, Shanta would drive if necessary. Rhoda and Frederick came too. Got home safely. Chat till 12.30 a.m. and then to bed.

24-25. After a good night's sleep, socialising and a late lunch, David drove us, with his daughter, Diana, and Elizabeth to Newark Airport, New Jersey. Said our goodbyes and left. Flew at 6.35 p.m. with British Airways to Heathrow, London. Arrived at around 06.45 a.m. on the 25th. Good flight and grim end to it. We were very tired. After collecting our cases, we headed for the airport bus. As soon as we came out of the airport, the bus was coming and we hurried and put our cases and hand luggage in the bus. On our way to the car park, I became aware that we left my hand luggage behind. We collected our car and returned to the airport. Rhoda looked for it without success and went to the lost property office. There was a long queue. She saw a policeman, reported the loss and together they went to the lost property office. He spoke to the gentleman, who told them that no one handed in any lost luggage. They went looking where we were sitting and were unsuccessful. He informed Rhoda that the hand-bag was stolen. He took our particulars and made a report. Only, by the grace of God, I had put the tapes of Michael's interview in my jacket inside-pocket. The loss included the cassette recorder I bought in Manhattan. When we arrived home, Rhoda reported the loss to American Express, who made a refund. No fuss. What a trip! Happy to meet and be with the family. Loving family.

26th. Cover to Jan's book arrived. I rang her and she liked it. She now wanted to hold her book in her hands. She was so excited. Rand and spoke to Rhoda's family in Queens, New York.

Next few days. I did work on *Nineteen Eighty-Four* notes and started transcribing Michael's interviews. Rhoda scanning onto the other computer. Rang Ian Angus, who informed me that I could hang on to his notes. How generous. London Magazine arrived with Bryan S. Johnson's article and Fitzrovia review.

30th. Spent most of day working on David Turner's profile.

1-2 October. I finished and polished David Turner's piece. I would try it on The Guardian, The Independent on Sunday newspapers, then the London Magazine. Faxed The Independent on Sunday Review proposing it for 10 December, the date David Turner died. I can't wait to start Orwell's book. Now I feel ready to start.

3rd. To Eton. Michael showed me his copy of Jeffrey Meyers' book on Orwell. It was a straightforward biography with some extra material. Can I do something entirely different? See it (George Orwell's life) as a stream of consciousness, a kaleidoscope, or a hall of mirrors. Can I conceive his life poetically or romantically? We shall see. Michael gave me the date to address The Book Collectors Society —10 November. I accepted. Reflecting on Orwell as I started gathered my notes together, I got his ideas into more or less chronological order.

4th. Faxed from St. Martin's Press. Jan's book, *Inside the Volcano: My Life with Malcolm Lowry*, is out. It would be featured in Elle magazine with a photograph of Jan. Rang her. She was ecstatic. She asked me to visit her soon. Rhoda agreed that I should visit her.

5th. Went to UCL and saw reminiscences of two men, who knew Orwell in Spain. Some good ideas. Then to the London Library for article to photocopy. Took Rhoda to her sister, Margaret's house for the weekend.

GLIMPSES OF A BIOGRAPHER'S DIARY

7th. Very tired all day, hardly worked.

Next few days. Rhoda returned home, more transcribing of Michael Sayers' tape. Spent days at Orwell's archive looking at more letters, note-books, manuscript and reviews of his work. Kept in touch with my friends, wrote to Sir Steven and informed him of the cause of Philip Yorke's death. Beatrice Dennis gave permission to see Nigel Dennis' letters to Sonia. Many of Orwell's contacts gave me permission to quote from letters, interviews, manuscripts and books. Received many positive emails and telephone calls from friends about my piece on Bryan S. Johnson.

14th. Spent too much time today trying to arrange our Jura trip, but weather forecast heavy rain, gales and rough seas —put us off. Received many letters, telephone calls, emails, including a letter from Sir Steven. Charming gentleman, so courteous, kind and informative. Email from St. Martin's Press that cheque and Jan's books coming soon. Spoke with Jan. She had her books and was thrilled. Finished transcribing Michael Sayers' tape. Some very good ideas for my book. Now working to finish David Astor's tapes.

21st. Reading *The Quest for Corvo* by A. J. A. Symons. Jan received her second cheque.

23rd. Telephone call from New England Review, decidedly wanting my article on HVOL, said so beautifully written. Good boost to the ego. A bit hungover today and got little work done.

27th. To UCL. Saw Nigel Dennis' letter to Sonia. Very steamy! Sonia was very good and loyal to her women friends, but with men she had great problems. She could plunge into a relationship, but would then withdraw violently if she felt the man was getting close to her. After Orwell's death, she became an editor with Weidenfeld & Nicolson.

31st. More reflection on Orwell — a writer of fiction and social prophet and therefore not an unimaginative author. It was not difficult for him to imagine himself in Trotsky's shoes and to face the very danger Trotsky faced. With Trotsky, it was an ice pick, for so many others it was the lead slug. To arm himself as he did, to remove himself to the distant Hebrides, to have seemingly an overreaction to the arrival of a communist companion — he feared a Trotsky death. Another figure hidden in the biographer's shadow was Rodney Phillips, who funded *Polemic*, the magazine to which Orwell contributed between 1945 and 1947, and for whom Celia G. once worked. While talking to Celia and Janetta Parladé Phillips' name came up, and they told me that he lived in Spain and gave me his telephone number. I called him and found him surprisingly ready to answer questions. He told me that he had pulled out of *Polemic* after becoming exasperated over having to settle the huge lunch bills run up by the magazine's editor, Humphrey Slater. Then, as an afterthought, he said, 'Oh, by the way, I sold Orwell a pistol — a Luger I'd brought back from the war. I think I sold it for £5.' I was taken aback. This extraordinary piece of information fitted neatly together with several other facts about Orwell — his fear of being targeted by the communists, especially following the assassination of Trotsky; Anthony Powell having found him during the war, armed with what he called 'a Bowie knife'; and Hemingway's claim that, on his journalistic visit to Paris in 1945 Orwell had asked the loan of a pistol. Then, while in Jura, he had asked his friend Michael Sayers to obtain ammunition for him in London, and Susan Watson, Orwell's housekeeper, mentioned him keeping a gun behind the door at Barnhill. All this made more intelligible his suspicion of David Holbrooke, then Susan Watson's boyfriend, when he learned that he was a party member. After all, Trotsky's assassin had got into his house through a friendship with his daughter.

1 November. Finished transcribing David Astor's tapes. Reading essays of William Hazlitt and Charles Lamb to see where Orwell fits into tradition. Hazlitt was placed in the company of Samuel Johnson and George Orwell.

2nd. Sir Steven Runciman died yesterday. A charming gentleman. A man of great learning and refinement. He was an English historian best known for his three-volume *A History of the Crusades* and was a strong admirer of the Byzantine Empire.

Next few days. Began transcribing Henry Dakin's tapes. I was trying alternative ways of writing my Orwell's book. Michael Meredith rang reminding me of my Eton talk on the 10th and dinner. Spoke to Jane Morgan and Margaret Crosland to clarify certain points. Booked my flight to Los Angeles to celebrate Jan's book. (Rhoda and her sister, Margaret, booked their flights to Atlanta, U.S.A. to support their sister, Mary, who has now separated from her husband.) I went to US Embassy to take in form for tax identification number. To the archive to copy some of Nigel Dennis' letters to Sonia. Threw fascinating light on Sonia. Some of which I mentioned above. Received letter from Little, Brown asking about progress on my book and I replied.

10th. To Eton to talk to The Book Collecting Society, dinner and after dinner discussion. Great success, it seemed. Good response. Everyone stayed afterwards, much talk and many thanks. Stayed talking until 11.30 p.m.

13th. Flew to Los Angeles and drove to Jan's house in time for dinner and champagne.

14th. After helping her to sort out her affairs, we went shopping for food and wine.

15th. Rhoda and Margaret flew to Atlanta, USA, to support their sister, Mary.

16th. Went to Barnes and Noble in Encino, where Jan's books were on sale. Took her to see her previous house and then to Westlake, did more shopping, returned to her home, and dined out later.

Next day, I had a hangover and did very little.

18th. To some more bookshops. Jan was very excited to see her book in all the shops. I Spoke to Rhoda. She told me that yesterday, she, Margaret, Mary and the children went to Mary's cottage at Hartwell Lake, and today would spent the day in Charlestown visiting Magnolia Plantation, shopping and dined at a special seafood restaurant. The next day, they would return to Atlanta and to a pool party.

19th. I drove Jan to the supermarket, where she found the December Elle magazine with a very good review of her book plus her photograph. She was delighted. I continued teaching her to use her electric typewriter. She learned and promptly forgot. She would learn with time. Did some Orwell notes, read and took sun for half an hour.

Next day. We mostly talked about the book she said she had written about her early life. I didn't see it, and didn't comment, because I did not want to be involved as I am very busy with Rhoda on my Orwell's book and I had lots more to do. I continued teaching her to use the electric typewriter. After dinner, I packed and ready for departure at noon tomorrow.

21st. At Los Angeles airport, I drank milk and spoke to Rhoda. They were all at her niece's house enjoying the day and at times by the pool. I told her that I was grossly overweight. She laughed and said, 'Do what you did before'. I would be glad to be at home.

22nd. Long flight over. Chatty student next to me. Home. House very cold. Exhausted. Many mails and telephone messages. I spoke to Rhoda. She and her family were at Mary's other condominium in Clearwater, Florida, and having a good family-time preparing for Thanksgiving tomorrow.

23rd. Very good stuff from Carolyn Wakeham, an American writer, about David Crook's spying on Orwell. Rather excited about ways his story was unfolding for my book. Spoke to Jane Morgan who clarified more queries. Very helpful as usual.

Next day. Very busy on Orwell. Spoke to Jan.

The following day. Rhoda rang, she and Margaret would be leaving Atlanta tonight. Very sad leaving their sister and family.

GLIMPSES OF A BIOGRAPHER'S DIARY

26th. Met Rhoda and Margaret at Gatwick airport. Great! Drove Margaret to her house before bringing Rhoda back home. Did some work on my novel, but had my head down and tried to get on with my book.

27th. Sir Malcolm Bradbury, the author, died at his home in Norwich aged 68. Sad. Very nice man.

Next day. Re-started reading *Down and Out in Paris and London*, and continued entering notes on my computer. I received further emails with more fascinating material on *Nineteen Eighty-Four* from Carolyn Wakeham. St. Martin's Press said that Jan's book would be reviewed in The New York Times, and the first chapter would be on the website. Wonderful. Spoke to Jan. She was thrilled. Rhoda preparing for our next trip.

29 November. Good flight to Barcelona on Orwell's trail. Unfortunately my bag had gone missing. We checked in at our hotel and spoke to British Airways people three times. I was angry as I won't be having my medication, toiletries and other essentials. Cast a shadow on the day. After rest and bath, we went walking along the Las Ramblas, had late lunch at Café Moka, found Hotel Continental (where Eileen and Orwell stayed) and the Poliorama cinema. Did some shopping, returned to our hotel and had dinner. By 9.30 p.m. still no sign of my case.

30th. It arrived. Bath and I dressed in clean clothes. Then walked and took the metro to the University of Barcelona library, where two very kind, patient and helpful students tried to trace some material I wanted to see, but was not successful. To Café de L'Opera, then back to Poliorama cinema, Café Moka , Continental hotel and enquired whether we could see the room where Orwell and Eileen stayed —would see it tomorrow, to market, and the Cathedral, where Rhoda lit candles and spent some time meditating. Returned to our hotel. Spent evening reading *Homage to Catalonia* after supper. I told Rhoda, 'The trouble in Barcelona began on 3rd May, 1937 when the chief of police tried to take over the telephone exchange, which was in the hands of the anarchists.

(The anarchists had been antagonising the government by the way they ran the telephone system.) The anarchists fought back with gun fire, and in no time rumours spread that one political faction was attempting to take control of the city. So, random shooting broke out everywhere. The assault guards, who were held up at the Café Moka a few doors down from the POUM headquarters, roamed the streets trying to restore order by shooting at anything that moved. Communists fired at anarchists, who fired back, and all sides seemed to be firing at the POUM members. This chaos lasted for about four days. Georges Kopp, who had been very brave, approached the guards unarmed and reassured them that no one wanted any killing and managed to established a truce. The ILP group was sent across Las Ramblas to cover the front of the POUM headquarters.'

1 December. After breakfast, we walked to Poliorama cinema. Got permission to go on the roof, up winding stairs to gallery, where we had a very good view of the city. Then, we went to the roof where, on the 4th May 1937, for three days Orwell and a small band, including Branthwaite and Moyle, sat perched on this roof which had a commanding view of the Café Moka and the whole of Las Ramblas below. They spent their time alternately guarding any approach to the POUM headquarters, and assuring the assault guards opposite that they had no intention of firing. The atmosphere was nerve-racking. After the chaos ended on the 7th May, life in the city began to return to its usual routine.

We then made our way down the winding stairs. Thanked the girls, who administered the building, and left. Walked to where the POUM headquarters were, no longer there, but just another hotel. Eileen had worked in John McNair's office. We headed by metro to the University of Barcelona, history department where we met Susan T., specialist on Orwell and POUM. Very interesting. She was very busy, but told us where the Hotel Colon (previous Communist Headquarter) was, where the telephone exchange still is, pointed out Lenin Barracks in the hills NW of Barcelona and said that she would keep in touch. Then, we returned to the Plaza de Catalunya, saw the Hotel Colon and telephone exchange and afterwards headed to our hotel. In the evening, we went to dine at the Café Moka. Very good. Then walked to Hotel Continental, saw the Room 361 where Orwell and Eileen, his first wife, stayed —lovely and overlooking Las Ramblas. Sat on Ramblas Square enjoying the atmosphere at night. Returned to our hotel. I was too tired to write my diary. Slept.

2nd. Woken early morning by loud noisy neighbours. After breakfast, we walked to the Port de Barcelona and saw the Statue of Columbus. Walked, sat and enjoyed the view. Then to the Café Moka for lunch. Back to our hotel, checked out and made our way to Barcelona Airport. Flew by British Airways to Gatwick Airport. Collected our car and drove home.

3rd. Must put heart and soul into my book. Continued transcribing letters, emails and tapes, including Jane Morgan's onto computer, and returned telephone calls.

Next few days. More reading and making notes on Orwell's *Complete Works*. Wrote letters to Susan Watson, Alan Ross and many others. Sent a copy of Jan's book to Michael Sayers. Interviewed Richard Horatio Blair (Orwell's adopted son), Quentin Kopp (Georges Kopp's son) and Dione Venables (novelist, broadcaster, publisher and editor) at their houses. They were all welcoming, helpful, gave very good interviews, quite generous with their information and providing me with photographs. On our last trip on Orwell's trail, we drove to Gloucester to find the Cotswold sanatorium, set in beech wood at Grantham, to which Orwell went in January 1949. This was after he had finished his book *Nineteen Eighty-Four* in Barnhill on the Scottish island of Jura in the Inner Hebrides.

His health really deteriorated. He was suffering from tuberculosis. He was put in a small wooden chalet, which at first he found very grim. Part of the cure (other than rest and good food) was to be left for periods in the 'fresh air', even though in the winter this left patients shivering. However, the hut had central heating and hot and cold water, so there was a degree of comfort. Orwell tried unsuccessfully to recover at Grantham. On the 3rd September 1949, Orwell was transferred to University College Hospital, London, was married to Sonia Brownell, tried again unsuccessfully to recover and died on the 21st January 1950. He died of a haemorrhage of the lungs brought on by tuberculosis.

6th. To Cambridge to lunch with and interview David Holbrook, Susan Watson's boyfriend. Afterwards, he gave a lovely interview with a highly poetic account of his visit to Barnhill, Jura. He also said that he thought that Orwell, having been told that he was a Communist, suspected he had come to spy on him. Holbrook was not to know that Orwell had feared something even worst, which was precisely why he had bought that luger (Susan remembered him with a loaded handgun always at the ready on Jura). After all, Trotsky had been eliminated by a Communist agent, who had insinuated himself into his household. Like Susan, Holbrook had walked on to the set of a Kafkaesque drama being played out in Orwell's own mind.

Then visited Celia G. who gave me some more information for my book. Wrote thank you letters, including one to David Holbrook and one to Celia G.

9th. Alan Ross said that he would like David Turner's articles.

11th. To UCL to see letters to Sonia from Orwell's sister, Avril Dunn. Finished copying Nigel Dennis' and Sonia's letters onto my computer.

16th. Transcribed more letters and tapes onto computer. In the evening, we entertained our friends, Brian and his wife, Doris, to dinner. Good company and conversation as usual.

24th. Rhoda went to Khans for dinner with her friends, Val and Pascal. Then returned with dinner for me and drinks.

25th. Merry Christmas Day. Working at the computer while Rhoda prepared Christmas lunch and so on. Lovely dinner with champagne after the Queen's speech. Relaxed evening looking at late-night movies.

28th. Alan Ross rang, said he was very interested in my Turner's article but he was not well. We talked.

By 31st. Rhoda and I had been working tirelessly on my book. I am now ready to start writing up my George Orwell biography. Greeted 2001 with champagne.

Almost at the end of my first year of the Millennium researching Orwell. So far going well, though still lots to do. Spent most of the day reflecting on what I have so far gathered about Orwell's life and works, very busy reading, interviewing, entering more notes, letters and transcripts onto my computer. Copied letters into and updated chronology. Every day, Rhoda and I concentrated on Orwell's and his *Complete Works*. I almost finish volume 13, and all are on my computer. Had taken me too long. I must put my heart and soul into my book.

I still have to go to Orwell's archive often to examine more transcripts, letters, notebooks, manuscript and reviews of his work, writing, receiving and sending letters, especially concerning Orwell. Keep in touch with my friends. Many of Orwell's contacts had given me permission to quote from letters, interviews, manuscripts and books. To chase up last minute permissions to quote. Read proofs of my book from Little, Brown and St. Martin's Press, noting changes and corrections. To start on index Rhoda will update notes on her computer: continue scanning letters, document, material; transcribing interviews from tapes, notes and letters.

***

I am very sad to say that Jan Gabrial died on September 2001.

***

I can't help believing that the streams of experience here recalled have fed themselves in some fashion into what I've written since. My near-death experience at the Westminster Hospital in London, when I was aged twenty-seven, gave me the chance to revive my dreams. Since then, I would like to think I've got a little closer to fulfilling those dreams. Probably, that's a comforting self-delusion, and I still have my Walter Mitty moments, as, no doubt, we all do. I continued with my freelance journalism (see my Bibliography). My biography of George Orwell, hardback, was published on the 1st May 2003 by Little, Brown, London and paperback by Abacus, an imprint of Little, Brown Book Group, London on 2004. Inside *George Orwell: A Biography* was published by Palgrave MacMillan, U.S.A. in 2003. 17 Cassettes by W.F. Howes Ltd in 2003, London, and later in Spain and Mexico. My James Joyce. A Biography was published by Weidenfeld and Nicolson, London in 2011 and 2012, and also in 2012 by Farrar, Straus and Giroux, New York, U.S.A. I have written twelve books, including my four biographies.

18 - Portrait of Joyce hanging in Notting Hill

Looking back, life as depicted here is a series of stories, cabaret acts or myths created to give one man's life a meaning and himself an identity. It's the way all lives are built, all biographies composed. Our lives are created mostly in story-form by ourselves and others. Where this one will end, I don't know, though by this time I do have a very good idea how.

INDEX

A

Abrahams, William, 325, 413
Adriana (Auschwitz), 175–76
Alessandro and Sharon, 171–74, 189
Alhambra, 284
Amis, Martin, 233, 240, 291
Angel, George, 93, 101
Angela (first girlfriend), 22, 34, 36, 66, 168
Astor, David, 153, 379, 385, 386, 388, 397, 418, 419

B

Balgarnie, William, 238
Bannard, Michael, 204
Bayliss, Sir Richard, 20, 209
BBC, 27, 65, 93, 102, 107, 131, 152, 153, 159, 161, 169, 184, 201, 202, 205, 206, 208, 209, 227, 228, 230, 232, 234, 235, 236, 241, 242, 243, 247, 251, 252, 255, 256, 257, 258, 262, 266, 300, 302, 312, 333, 334, 339, 340, 345, 359, 360, 361, 362, 364, 375, 412, 413, I, IV, VI, VIII, IX, XII
Beazley, Mike, 17, 18, 33, 43, 66, 110, 384
Berlin, 103, 161, 164, 220–23, 226, 283, VIII
Bertolucci, Bernardo, 252, 253, 254, 255, 256, 257, IX
Blair, Eileen, 354, 396, 407
Blair, Ida, 315, 394
Blair, Richard Horatio, 386, 424
Bloomsbury Publishing, 265, 266, 364, 365
Bogarde, Dirk, 123, 258
Bonner, Priscilla, 274, 278, 281
Bowker, Leonard, 53, 81, 92, 119, 120, 130, 183, 356
Bowker, Lucy, 53, 54, 81, 183, 184
Bowker, Ramdei Rhoda, v, 241, 242, 250, 251, 259, 260, 262, 263, 264, 273, 274, 277, 278, 279, 280, 281, 282, 283, 285, 286, 287, 292, 293, 294, 295, 297, 298, 299, 300, 301, 303, 304, 306, 307, 308, 309, 311, 313, 315, 317, 318, 319, 322, 323, 324, 325, 326, 327, 328, 329, 331, 332, 334, 335, 336, 337, 338, 339, 340, 341, 342, 343, 345, 346, 347, 348, 349, 350, 352, 353, 355, 356, 357, 358, 359, 360, 361, 362, 363, 364, 365, 366, 368, 369, 371, 372, 374, 375, 377, 378, 379, 380, 381, 382, 383, 384, 385, 386, 387, 388, 389, 390, 391, 392, 393, 394, 395, 397, 398, 400, 402, 403, 404, 405, 406, 408, 409, 410, 412, 415, 416, 417, 418, 420, 421, 422, 425, 426

Bradbrook, Muriel, 219, 235, 236, 238, 274
Bradbury, Malcolm, 235, 265, 422
Brahe, John, 299
Braybrooke, Neville, 265, 274, 323, 352
British Sociological Association, 113
Buddicom, Jacintha, 315, 364, 396, 398
Burgess, Anthony, 235, 236, 238, 239, 243, 274
Burrows, Bernard, 302

C

Campbell, Jim, 311
Canada, 164, 175–76, 184, 187, 190, 191, 192, 198, 203, 206, 207, 208, 209, 210, 211, 225, 227, 234, 260, 261, 264, 274, 329, 345, 349, 361, VIII, XI, XII
Cathy, 132, 136, 144, 145, 146, 150, 161
Childs, Ted, 186, III
Connolly, Cyril, 322, 411, 414
Crick, Bernard, 317, 325, 330, 367
Crisp, Quentin, 71–74, 103
Croft, Dave, 84
Crook, David, 255, 256, 406, 408, 421
Cuernavaca, 241, 242, 251, 242–51, 278–80, 383

D

Dakin, Henry, 386, 394, 408, 409, 420
Danny Huston, 244, 249, 251, 261
Davenport, Roger, 274
David Frost, 117, 233
David Higham (agency), 265, 333
Davidson, Peter, 317
Devine, George, 76, 152
Dick Diabolus, 233, I
Dr Tonkin, 14, 15, 20, 33, 34, 42, 49, 56, 70, 75, 90, 157, 209
Durrell, Ghislaine, 296, 300, 301
Durrell, Lawrence, 52, 69, 86, 231, 284, 286, 287, 288, 289, 293–97, 292, 294, 296, 297, 293–97, 299, 300, 301, 302, 306, 307, 308, 309, 311, 312, **286–312**, 312, 317, 318, 321, 323, 330, 333, 334, 345, 352, 357, 395, II, IV
Durrell, Margot, 310

E

Ekevall, Kay, 381
Encino, 268, 272, 363, 369, 401, 420
Eric (friend), 65, 67
Eton, 298, 332, 364, 395, 398, 402, 410, 411–14, 417, 420, XI

F

Fairfax, Alice, 31, 34, 43, 56, 291
Fierz, Adrian, 386, 387
Finney, Albert, 68, 75, 239, 243, 246, 248, 249

Fishwick, Michael, 366
Flaxman telephone number, 46, 59, 61, 62, 64, 78
Fowles, John, 143, 170, 305, 340

G

G, Celia, 316, 368, 372, 373, 374, 375, 386, 403, 405, 409, 419, 425
Gabrial, Jan, 263, 266, 267, 268, 269, 272, 273, 268–73, 276, 277, 278, 280, 282, 283, 284, 319, 359, 363, 364, 365, 366, 369, 370, 375, 376, 381, 384, 392, 400, 401, 402, 409, 418, 420, 421, 426
Gascoyne, David, 311, 323, 352, 353, 356, 376
Godber, John, 227
Goff, Anthony, 266, 286–89, 292, 299, 301, 302, 303, 305, 307, 309, 312, 318, 319, 321, 325, 332, 334, 338, 339, 340, 341, 345, 351, 352, 354, 360, 362, 364, 365, 366, 367, 368, 372, 373, 376, 380, 390, 398
Goldsmiths, 152, 154, 156, 157, 168, 181, 187, 238, 260, 261, 263, 281, 285, 294, XI
Gordon Robinson, 355
Grade, Michael, 257
Gray, Ethel, 171, 192, 193, 194

H

Hamilton, Bill, 317, 332
Harper Collins, 290

Hellier, Odile, 282, 296, 335, 336, 337, 345, 356, 357, 369, 371
Hemingway, Ernest, 69, 80, 130, 251, 266, 305, 336
Hepburn, Jim, 274
Hoggart, Richard, 64, 182, 261
Huston, Danny, 251
Huston, John, 239, 240, 241, 246, 247, 248, 249, 251, VIII
Hyams, Tony, 354, 359

I

Illustrated London News, 225, 226, 228
Inez, 315, 363, 373, 403, 405, 409

J

Jackson, Glenda, 125, 133
Janet (University friend married to Karl), 79, 131, 132, 144, 146, 147, 150, 161, 169
Johnson, B.S., 143, 144, 200, 201, 203, 204, 205, 383, 384, 391, 411, 412, 413, 417, 418
Joyce, James, 64, 104, 124, 321, 343, 427, II, XII

K

K, Celia, 318, 359
Karloff, Boris, 76
Kee, Robert, 385, 386, 388
Kiely, Garrett, 298, 299, 302, 303, 307
Kopp, Georges, 393, 407, 423, 424
Kopp, Quentin, 386, 424

G

L

Laker, Freddie, 187, 188
Leavitt, David, 336
Lenya, Lotte, 103, 104
Limouzin, 314, 315, 396, 408
London Missionary Society, 36, 70
Los Angeles, 278, 280, 282
Losey, Joseph, 123
Louise, 115, 116, 119, 120, 121, 122
Lowry, Colin, 274
Lowry, Malcolm, 69, 83, 121, 220, 235, 237, 238, 251, 260, 262, 263, 264, 265, 266, 268, 271, 274, 280, 281, 282, 283, 287, 290, 292, 296, 297, 298, 299, 302, 308, 310, 318, 319, 320, 321, 324, 330, 331, 334, 351, 354, 358, 360, 363, 370, 376, 381, 382, 390, 397, **219–402**, 417, I, IX, XI
Lowry, Russell, 236, 237, 238, 261, 262, 264, 274, 283

M

Mackworth, Cecily, 296, 300, 315, 322, 336, 341, 342, 343, 354, 356, 357, 359, 362, 368, 369, 371, 373, 397, 400, 409
Malcolm and Christine, 182, 192, 211, 212
Margerie Lowry, 264, 275, 276, 278, 280, 281, 322, 354
Markson, David, 264, 266, 277, 333, 365
Martine, 191, 196, 348, 350, 351
Maschler, Tom, 261, 262

McNiven, 293
Michael, 335, 357
Michael, 337
Michael Shelden, 325
Miles, Sally, 186, III
Miller, Henry, 288, 296, 334
Mistral (letterly Shakespeare and Company), 101
Moss, Betty, 275, 278, 281, 354
Murphy, Jill, 142, 200, 223

N

National Assistance Board, 43, 56, 65, 83, 94, 96
New York, 290, 176, 277
Notting Hill Gate, 216, 217, 223, 314, 321
Novel writing, 78, 105, 231, 301, 305, 306, 309, 322, 323, 325, 326, 327, 328, 329, 331, 332, 333, 334, 335, 336, 337, 339, 340, 345, 347, 351, 352, 355, 357, 360, 371, 380, 389, 398, 399, 422
Nurse Begley, 19, 20, 34, 38, 42, 47, 56, 70
Nurse Bourney, 36, 37, 38, 42, 43, 44, 45, 49, 51, 53, 55, 56, 59, 70
Nurse Peters, 18, 53, 55, 56, 74, 75, 76, 77, 80, 81, 83, 85, 86, 106

O

O'Toole, Peter, 108, 109, 115, 157, 159, 252, 253
Oh What a Lovely War, 119, 129, 345

Ortiz y Ortiz, Raul, 282, 290, 382
Orwell, George, 33, 43, 45, 57, 64, 93, 128, 129, 153, 227, 256, 301, 307, 308, 309, 310, 311, 312, 314, 312–16, 317, 322, 319–22, 323, 330, 331, 332, 335, 341–45, 351, 352, 354, 360, 361, 364, 365, 366, 367, 368, 378, 388, 393, 396, 397, 407, 409, 412, 414, 415, 417, 419, 426, 427, **308–427**, II, XI
Orwell, Sonia, 316, 322, 385, 397
Osborne, John, 59, 75, 79, 129, 307

P

Paignton, 3, 6, 22, 54, 113, 120, 133
Paris, 121, 137, 170, 182, 281, 282, 296, 300, 309, 315, 319, 335–37, 341, 409
Peters, Richard, 105, 125, 128, 165, 367
Philiips, Carole, 274
Phillips, Roland, 325
Phillips, Sian, 159
Philpott, Miss, 100, 102, 151
Pinter, Harold, 72, 103, 133, 185
Polish Solidarity, 227–30
Potter, Dennis, 186, III
POUM, 407, 423
Prue (University friend), 82, 87, 88, 89, 102, 103, 106, 116

R

Random House (Toronto, Canada publishing), 286, 287, 290, 292, 293, I
Red Shield House, 55, 56, 57, 62, 63
Ross, Alan, 302, 312, 341, 343, 345, 351, 361, 384, 391, 424, 425, 426
Runciman, Steven, 298, 386, 395, 398, 404, 419
Russell, Colin, 329

S

Sandoe, John, 69, 83
Sarah (Polish friend), 205, 206, 207, 208, 227, 228
Sayers, Michael, 386, 387, 392, 393, 408, 409, 415, 418, 419, 424
Sebastian, Tim, 228
Shakespeare and Company (Bookshop), 101, 282, 291, 296, 317, 337, 341, 356, 358, XII
Shawfield Street, 60, 62, 69, 71, 78, 82, 99, 108, 111, 124, 154, 169, 177, 178, 182, 191, 196, 291
Sheldon, Michael, 308, 325, 330
Skyvers, 120
Sloane Square, 59, 63, 67, 69, 70, 104, 153, 171, 239
Sommières (Durrell), 284, 287, 288, 306, 357
Southam, Brian, 113, 114, 123, 126, 130, 156, 162, 218, 297, 302

Southwold, 320, 367
Spender, Stephen, 69, 238, 302, 392, 413
Stansky, Peter, 325, 413
Suzman, Janet, 227
Swainson, Bill, 364

T

Tamiment, 406, 407
television scripts, 163, 184, 191, 205, 206, III
the Picasso, 60, 62, 66, 69, 104, 115, 178, 343
Thomas, Dylan, 65, 93, 114, 231, 291, 305, 313, 332, 333, 334, 336, 340, 372
Thorndike, Dame Sybil, 186, 187, III
Thurber, James, 17, 80
Times Educational Supplement, 90, 91, 92, 99, 102, 107, 110, 120, 124, 125, 126, 134, 136, 150, 153, 161, 226, 227, 230, 231
Tomalin, Claire, 203, 219
Tomalin, Miles, 202, 203, 217
Tomalin, Nick, 67, 68, 203, 219, 240, 251
Trevelyan, Mary, 302
Trotsky, 418, 425
Turner, David, 168, 184, 200, 201, 406, 417, 425

U

Under Twenty, 123, 126, 130, 152, 156, 157, 184, 218, I

Unna, Harvey, 211, 220, 231

V

Vancouver, 193, 211, 212, 213, 290, 264, 266, 274, 276, 280, 282, 293, XII
Venables, Dione, 424
Vice, Sue, 274
Village Voice Bookshop, 282, 291, 296, 335, 336, 337, 343, 345, 356, 369, XII

W

Wesker, Arnold, 79, 106
Westminster Hospital, 6–50, 85, 90, 111, 155, 157, 209, 239, 285, 286, 291, 303, 305, 326, 329, 334, 426
Whitman, George, 101, 137, 282, 296
William Collins (publisher), 266, 282, 287
Wilson, Des, 225, 226, 228
Woodbury Down Primary School, 99, 102, 104, 105, 108, 115, 151
Woolf, Henry, 133, 185, 199, 299

Y

Yorke, Philip, 410, 412, 414, 418

BIBLIOGRAPHY

Works:

Under Twenty, (edited: collection of passages from novels, short-stories and autobiographies). Routledge and Kegan Paul, London, 1966.

The Education of Coloured Immigrants, Longmans, Green and Co Ltd, London, 1968; and by Humanities Press, New York, 1968.

Freedom, Reason or Revolution, (edited collection of prose on topic of politics and freedom), hardback and paperback, Routledge and Kegan Paul, London, 1970.

"Sociological Afterword" to You Always Remember The First Time. Quartet Books, London, 1975.

Race and Ethnic Relations: Sociological Readings, edited with John Carrier, Hutchinson and Co LTD, London, 1976; and by Holmes and Meier, New York, 1976.

Beelzebub's Barbs: A Cynic's Dictionary, Diabolus Press, London, 1982.

Malcolm Lowry Remembered: Ariel Books, BBC, London, 1985.

Malcolm Lowry: Under the Volcano; A Case Book Series: A Selection of Critical Essays, edited, MacMillan Education, London, 1987.

Pursued by Furies: A Life of Malcolm Lowry; hardback: HarperCollins, London, 1993; hardback and paperback: Random House of Canada, Toronto, 1993; paperback: Flamingo, London, 1994; hardback 1995 and paperback 1997: St. Martin's Press, New

GLIMPSES OF A BIOGRAPHER'S DIARY

York, U.S.A.; Fondo De Culture, Mexico, 2008; Faber Finds Ltd, London, 2009.

Through the Dark Labyrinth: A Biography of Lawrence Durrell; hardback: Sinclair-Stevenson, London, 1996; hardback and paperback: St. Martin's Press, New York, U.S.A. April 1997 and October 1997; paperback: Pimlico, London, 1998; eBook: Endeavour Press, 2018.

George Orwell; hardback: Little, Brown, London, 2003; paperback, Abacus, London, 2004; 17 Cassettes: W.F. Howes Ltd, 2003; A Foreign Language Translation: Education and Culture 2000: with the support of the Culture 2000 programme of the European Union, 2004; Spanish Translation: Nakladatelstvi Lidove Noviny, 2006.

Inside George Orwell: A Biography; Hardback: Palgrave MacMillan, United States of America, 2003.

James Joyce: A Biography; hardback: Weidenfeld & Nicholson, London, 2011 (in time for Bloomsday); paperback: Phoenix, London, 2012; hardback and paperback: Farrar, Straus and Giroux, New York, 2012, U.S.A.: (it was runner-up for the American PEN.2013)

TV BROADCASTS

Rediffusion Television

(1) Trapped and Protest: Two scripts for a series of school programmes entitled: Ways with Words, each with a playing time of twenty minutes. Televised in Spring Term 1967.

(2) On The Move, Tricked and It's All In The Mind: Three scripts for a series of schools programmes entitled: Ways With Words: each with a playing time of twenty minutes. Televised in Summer 1967.

(3) Approach To Living: Programme No: (1)(2)(3)(4)(5). Five television scripts for schools, complete with dialogue, each having a playing time of twenty minutes. Televised in the Spring Terms 1968.

Thames Television

(1) Two television scripts: (1) Love and (2) Cruelty, each having a playing time of twenty minutes. Written for a series of television programmes for schools entitled: Living Now/This Is Life: Televised in the Spring Terms 1971.

(2) God and Greasepaint: a series of television programmes, 1971. Thames arranged for me to visit and interview Dame Sybil Thorndike at her flat in Chelsea Manor Street, and a further four interviews at Studio 6, Euston: 19 April. Sally Miles, interviewed about her production of the Wakefield Mystery Plays at the Mermaid Theatre. 20 April. Ted Childs interviewed about his TV documentary on the Pope. 21 April. Dennis Potter interviewed about writing The Son of Man. 22 April. Dame Sybil Thorndike

interviewed about playing 'St Joan'. Transmission date: Commenced on 19th May 1971.

(3) You And The World: six x 20 minutes plays. Written for a series of television programmes for schools. Transmitted in Summer 1974.

(4) You And The World: four x 20 minutes plays. Written for a series of television programmes for schools. Transmitted in Spring 1975.

British Broadcasting Corporation (BBC)

BBC 1. Script Consultant: Wrote material for Teachers' notes for the first programme on the Violence Series for 20th Century Focus: School Television. Transmitted on 3rd March 1969.

BBC 1, Documentary: Network Features, Television. Called Up: Impression of National Service. Tuesday, 22 November 1983.

BBC 2, BOOKMARK: Lawrence Durrell: Recorded 29th April 1998.

Canadian Broadcasting Corporation (CBC)

Programmes series: Bush And The Salon, Subject: William Cobbett's first work, written under pseudonym 'Peter Porcupine' and entitled: How Peter Porcupine Acquired His Quills. Broadcast in October 1972.

Separate But Equal. Thirty-minutes script, televised on 28th April 1973.

The Strange Ordeal Of John Gyles: 60-minutes drama documentary for programme series: The Bush And The Salon. Broadcast in August 1973.

(4) One hour radio dramatised documentary script, working title: Canadian Soldiers at War: That I May Not Weep - for CBC National Series: The Bush And The Salon. Broadcast on the 11 November 1974.

(5) 31 March 1984: One-hour radio script for Atlantic Airwaves, entitled The Captivity of John Gyles in the series: The Bush and the Salon was aired throughout the Maritime region.

(6) 1 September 1987: Feature on the film : Sammy and Rosie Get Laid: was recorded on CBC Radio Arts Programme for 1988.

(7) Feature on Europeans in China, CBC Sunday Morning, 1988.

RADIO BROADCASTS

The British Broadcasting Corporation: (BBC)

Taken For A Ride: Home Service: Broadcast on 10th August 1962.

The Immigrant at School: Educating Immigrants. fully dramatised script for Home Service: Broadcast on 25th October 1965.

Soldiers Diary: fully dramatised script for the Radio 4 School Series. History: Not So Long Ago. Broadcast on 5th February 1974.

Children at School: fully dramatised script for the Radio 4 School series: History: Not So Long Ago. Broadcast on 12th March 1974.

Fresh Air And Entertainment: fully dramatised script by me for the Radio 4 Schools Series History: Not So Long Ago: Broadcast on 19th March 1974.

History: Not So Long Ago: four x 20 minutes, dramatised scripts for the Radio 4 Schools Series: (a) The Search for the North West Passage. (b) Francis Drake. (c) Sir Richard Grenville. (d) The Spanish Armada. Broadcast on (a) 25 February 1975. (b) 4 March 1975. (c) 11 March 1975 and (d) 18 March 1975.

Soldiers Diary: fully dramatised script for the Radio 4 School Series. History: Not So Long Ago. Repeat broadcast on 23 March 1976

Dr. Barnardo's Children: 20-minutes, fully dramatised script for the Radio 4 School Series: History: Not So Long Ago. Broadcast on the 11 May 1976.

At School : 20-minutes, fully dramatised script for the Radio 4 School Series: History: Not So Long Ago was repeated on 18 May 1976.

Dr. Barnardo's Children: 20-minutes, fully dramatised script for the Radio 4 School Series: History: Not So Long Ago. Broadcast on the 2 May 1978.

Children at School: fully dramatised script for the Radio 4 School series: History: Not So Long Ago. Broadcast on 9 May 1978.

Dr. Barnardo's Children: 20-minutes fully dramatised script for the Radio 4 School Series: History Not So long Ago was repeated on 13 November 1979.

At School: for the Radio 4 Schools Series History Not So Long Ago. Broadcast on November 1979, Education Programme

Soldiers Diaries: for the Radio 4 Schools Series: History Not So Long Ago, Broadcasting in Education Programme on 25 March 1980.

Repeat dramatised scripts: (a) The Search for the North West Passage. (b) Sir Francis Drake. (c) The Spanish Armada and(d) The First English Colonies for Radio 4 Schools Series: History: Not So Long Ago. Broadcast on 27 January, 3, 10, 17 February 1981, and repeated The First English Colonies on 24 February 1981.

13 May 1981: Radio 4: Kaleidoscope - Special report from Poland on the state of the arts and interviews.

6 June 1981: On World Service, Meridian - The Arts in Poland and Interviewing J. Fuksiewicz and Jerzy Sito.

17 June 1981: Dr. Barnardo's Children for Radio 4 Schools Series: History: Not So Long Ago: Broadcast on 6 October 1981.

19 June 1981: repeat dramatised scripts: At School for Radio 4 Schools Series: History: Not So Long Ago: Broadcast on 13 October1981.

GLIMPSES OF A BIOGRAPHER'S DIARY

5 July 1981: Radio 4: Woman's Hour: Interviewed with Sue MacGregor introducing Canada's Rodeo Women.

13 August 1981: On Radio 4: Kaleidoscope: presented my special piece on the 20th anniversary of the building of the Berlin Wall, together with a report on the effect this division of a city has had on its writers and its artists: The Great Cultural Divide.

10 January 1982: Dramatised script: Soldiers' Diaries for the Radio 4 Schools Series: History: Not So Long Ago: Broadcast on the 9th February 1982.

22 March 1982: Radio 4: Kaleidoscope: I reviewed three plays at the Soho Poly:- (1) The Mission. (2) Blow On Blow. (3) Toller.

22 May 1983: On Radio 4, transmitted my script for The Food Programme featured: On the Diet of the Canadian Plains Indians.

13 July 1983: On Radio 4 Woman's Hour: transmitted my script: Feature on the Rodeo Girls in Canada and North America.

6th September 1983: Radio 4 Woman's Hour transmitted my script: She's My Antibiotic.

2 November 1983: On Radio 4 Arts Programme: Kaleidoscope: presented my prepared and scripted package of John Huston's film Under the Volcano, including interviews with John Huston, Anthony Andrews and the writer Guy Gallow.

Two interviews I conducted on location in Mexico and in Autumn 1983. Subsequently, I interviewed & recorded live in the studio: Mexico/London for Meridian. BBC World Service: transmitted on14 and 15 January 1984. Also, prepared programmes for CBC and ABC.

28 July 1984: Wrote and presented 45 minute documentary for Radio 4: The Lighthouse Invites The Storm: Malcolm Lowry and Under the Volcano, repeated on 1 August 1984, followed BBC's Profile on Malcolm Lowry in The Listener on 2 August 1984.

1 September 1984, Interviewed re the film Under the Volcano by Sarah Dunant, BBC World Service.

14 May 1985: Dramatised scripts: Dr. Barnardo's Children, repeated on Radio 4 Schools Series: History: Not So Long Ago.

1 September 1985: Radio 4 repeated The Lighthouse Invites The Storm. Subject: Malcolm Lowry, his life and Under the Volcano.

28 August 1986: Radio 4, Kaleidoscope, engaged me to wrote, present script and package a piece on work in progress on Bertolucci's film: The Last Emperor in China. Work included collecting interviews.

6 and 7 October 1986: On Radio 4, Kaleidoscope, wrote & presented my script on Work in Progress on Bertolucci's film: The Last Emperor in China.

18 September 1987: Recorded interviews, wrote & presented my script on BBC Radio 4 on Stepchildren of the Dragon.

30 January 1988: Radio 4 repeated: Stepchildren of the Dragon.

27 February 1988: Wrote & presented: The Last Emperor, three half-hour scripts on BBC World Service, Meridian.

(39) 5 April. Radio 4 repeated: Stepchildren of the Dragon.

(40) 1 November 1989: Radio 3: I Interviewed Jan Gabriel, wrote and presented: Love and Grief, Under the Volcano, The Life and Work of Malcolm Lowry.

OTHER WORKS

Edited my University Magazine.

Reviewed novels, biographies, plays, films, students dance and drama festivals, volunteered at Centre 45.

Researched on arts and culture and wrote reports on them.

Wrote reports, scripts and articles for: The Times Education Supplements, Plays and Players, Illustrated London News, The Observer Magazine, The Times Literary Supplements, The Times Higher Education Supplement, The Sunday Times, The Guardian, The Independent on Sunday, The Daily Telegraph, The listener, London Magazine, New England Review, Slightly Foxed, The New York Times, Washington Post, George Orwell Society. The Malcolm Lowry Review, Canada.

Planned and organised the First International London Conference on Malcolm Lowry at Goldsmiths' College 1984.

Introduction to: Hear Us O Lord from Heaven Thy Dwelling Place, and Lunar Caustic by Malcolm Lowry, Penguin Books, London, 2000.

Talks and my books promotion: Like all authors, I am passionate about promoting my books by giving talks and lectures at bookshops, arts centre, pubs, halls: Waterstones at Cambridge, London South Bank Centre, Brighton, Oxford College, Eton College, Liverpool, George Orwell Society AGM.

Literary festivals: in England: Letchworth on George Orwell, Lewes Live Literature, St. Ives; Guardian/Observer Seminar on 'The Influence of George Orwell on Literature, Live Literature Wallington and Oxford; Dublin; Edinburgh.

Radio interviews: Brighton, BBC Today, BBC Northern Ireland, Eiren, Kent, Radio 2 Arts Programme, Scotland and Saga Radio; Frankfurt Book Fair; English language bookshops in Paris, on the Left Bank: at Shakespeare and Company Bookshop and The Village Voice Bookshop.

Canada: at the Harbour Front International Writers Festivals, various interviews on TV and radio in Toronto, Vancouver and Mexico City.

Writing with a group of International scholars on the use of life-history research in Sociology and in the development of biographical method as a research tool. Introduced courses in biographical method on University of London sociology degree courses at under-graduate and post-graduate level.

The James Joyce: Three BBC Radio Drama Collection - and a fascinating biographical account of James Joyce Life. 2019 BBC

Annual Gordon Bowker Annual Volcano Prize organised by The Society of Authors from 2022.

Printed in Dunstable, United Kingdom

POEMS

SONGS AND SONNETS

BY

HARTLEY COLERIDGE

I write, endite, I point, I rase, I quote,
I interline, I blot, correct, I note,
I make, allege, I imitate, I feign
                       Drayton

For I, that God of Lov'is Servantes serve,
Ne dare to love, for mine unlikelinesse,
Prayin for spede, al should I therefore sterve,
So ferre am I fro his help in darknesse,
But nathelesse, if this may doe gladnesse
To any lovir, and his cause aveile,
Have he the thanke, and mine be the traveile
           Chaucer Troilus and Creseide

LEEDS
JOHN CROSS, COMMERCIAL-STREET

William Whewell.

DEDICATORY SONNET,

TO S T COLERIDGE.

Father, and Bard revered! to whom I owe,
Whate'er it be, my little art of numbers,
Thou, in thy night-watch o'er my cradled slumbers,
Didst meditate the verse that lives to shew,
(And long shall live, when we alike are low)
Thy prayer how ardent, and thy hope how strong,
That I should learn of Nature's self the song,
The lore which none but Nature's pupils know

   The prayer was heard. I "wander'd like a breeze,"
By mountain brooks and solitary meres,
And gather'd there the shapes and phantasies
Which, mixt with passions of my sadder years,
Compose this book. If good therein there be,
That good, my sire, I dedicate to thee.

HARTLEY COLERIDGE

PREFACE.

Of the verses contained in this volume, a considerable number have already appeared in various periodicals. The rest are productions, for the most part, of a later time—it may be, of less leisure. None of them, with a single exception, can claim the privilege of juvenile poems. I neither deprecate nor defy the censure of the critics. No man can know, of himself, whether he is, or is not, a poet. The thoughts, the feelings, the images, which are the material of poetry, are accessible to all who seek for them; but the power to express, combine, and modify—to make a truth of thought, to earn a sympathy for feeling, to convey an image to the inward eye, with all its influences and associations, can only approve itself by experiment—and the result of the experiment may not be known for years. Such an experiment I have ventured to try, and I wait the result with patience. Should it be favourable, the present volume will shortly be followed by another, in which, if no more be accomplished, a higher strain is certainly attempted.

As there is nothing peculiar either in the principles upon which these poems are written, or the circumstances under which they were produced, further preface would be superfluous. Wherever I have been conscious of adopting the thoughts or words of former, especially of living writers, I have scrupulously acknowledged the obligation: but I am well aware that there may be several instances of such adoption which have escaped my observation. It is not always easy to distinguish between recollection and invention. At the same time, be it remembered, that close resemblance of phrase or illustration, or even verbal identity, may arise from casual coincidence, in compositions that owe nothing to each other.

Leeds, January, 1833.

CONTENTS

	Page
To a Friend	1—3
Sonnets	3—13
On a Picture of the Corpse of Napoleon Lying in State	14
To Wordsworth	15
November	16
On parting with a very pretty, but very little Lady	17
Night	18
The First Birth-Day	19
Sonnets	20—24
From Country to Town	25—26
Sonnet	27
To Shakspeare	28
Sonnet	29—31
From Petrarca	32
Sonnet	33
To a lofty Beauty, from her poor Kinsman	34
A Task ad Libitum	37
Song	39
Stanzas	40
A Brother's Love to his Sister	42
"Of such is the Kingdom of God"	44
Written on the 1st of November, 1820	45
Epigram	46
Ballad	47
Sense, if you can find it	50
To Somebody	51
Song	53
New Year's Day	54
On a Young Man dying on the Eve of Marriage	56
To the Nautilus	57
Sweet Love, the Shadow of thy parting Wings	58
Song	59
Song	60

	Page
Epitaph on a Mother and Three Infants	60
Leonard and Susan	61
Album Verses	84
An Old Man's Wish	88
The Sabbath-Day's Child	89
May, 1832	92
Isabel	93
Reply	95
Fragment	97
To —— ——	98
Expertus Loquitur	99
A Farewell	100
Horace Book I, Ode 38	101
Death	102
Inania Munera	103
To my Unknown Sister in Law	104
A Medley	106
Thoughts	110
Address to certain Gold Fishes	113
What I have heard	115
Sonnet	118
By a Friend	119
Poietes Apoietes	120
From Petrarch	122
Regeneration	123
Blandusian Spring, more gaily bright	125
Written in January, 1833	127
The Birth-Day	128
To a Posthumous Infant	133
Homer	134
Valentine	135
The Forsaken to the Faithless	137
To the Memory of Canning	139
Liberty	140
Who is the Poet	141
The Use of a Poet	142
Young Love	143
Death bed Reflections of Michelangelo	144
Notes	145

SONNETS.

SONNET I

TO A FRIEND

When we were idlers with the loitering rills,
The need of human love we little noted·
Our love was nature; and the peace that floated
On the white mist, and dwelt upon the hills
To sweet accord subdued our wayward wills
One soul was ours, one mind, one heart devoted,
That, wisely doating, ask'd not why it doated,
And ours the unknown joy, which knowing kills.
But now I find, how dear thou wert to me,
That man is more than half of nature's treasure,
Of that fair Beauty which no eye can see,
Of that sweet music which no ear can measure;
And now the streams may sing for others' pleasure,
The hills sleep on in their eternity

SONNET II

TO THE SAME

In the great city we are met again,
Where many souls there are, that breathe and die,
Scarce knowing more of nature's potency,
Than what they learn from heat, or cold, or rain,
The sad vicissitude of weary pain —
For busy man is lord of ear and eye,
And what hath nature, but the vast, void sky,
And the throng'd river toiling to the main?
Oh! say not so, for she shall have her part
In every smile, in every tear that falls,
And she shall hide her in the secret heart,
Where love persuades and sterner duty calls
But worse it were than death, or sorrow's smart,
To live without a friend within these walls

SONNET III

TO THE SAME.

We parted on the mountains, as two streams
From one clear spring pursue their several ways,
And thy fleet course hath been through many a maze
In foreign lands, where silvery Padus gleams
To that delicious sky, whose glowing beams
Brighten'd the tresses that old Poets praise;
Where Petrarch's patient love, and artful lays,
And Ariosto's song of many themes,
Moved the soft air   But I, a lazy brook,
As close pent up within my native dell,
Have crept along from nook to shady nook,
Where flowrets blow, and whispering Naiads dwell
Yet now we meet, that parted were so wide,
O'er rough and smooth to travel side by side

SONNET IV.

The Man, whose lady-love is virgin Truth,
Must woo a lady that is hard to win
She smiles not on the wild and wordy din
Of all-confiding, all-protesting Youth,
The Sceptic's apathy, the garb uncouth,
And Cynic sneer of o'er-experienced Sin,
The Serpent, writhing in its worn-out skin.
Craving again to flesh its sated tooth,
She quite abhors   She is not fond, nor coy—
Self-seeking love, and self-appraising scorn,
She knows not   She hath utterly forsworn,
Her worldly dower of wealth, and pride, and joy—
Her very beauty none but they discover,
Who for herself, not for her beauty, love her

SONNET V

What was't awaken'd first the untried ear
Of that sole man who was all human kind?
Was it the gladsome welcome of the wind,
Stirring the leaves that never yet were sere?
The four mellifluous streams which flow'd so near,
Their lulling murmers all in one combined?
The note of bird unnamed? The startled hind
Bursting the brake—in wonder, not in fear,
Of her new lord? Or did the holy ground
Send forth mysterious melody to greet
The gracious pressure of immaculate feet?
Did viewless seraphs rustle all around,
Making sweet music out of air as sweet?
Or his own voice awake him with its sound?

SONNET VI

I loved thee once, when every thought of mine
Was hope and joy,—and now I love thee still,
In sorrow and despair —a hopeless will
From its lone purpose never can decline
I did not choose thee for my Valentine
By the blind omen of a merry season,—
'Twas not thy smile that brib'd my partial reason.
Tho' never maiden's smile was good as thine —
Nor did I to thy goodness wed my heart,
Dreaming of soft delights and honied kisses
Although thou wert complete in every part,
A stainless paradise of holy blisses
I lov'd thee for the lovely soul thou art,—
Thou canst not change so true a love as this is

SONNET VII.

Is love a fancy, or a feeling?   No,
It is immortal as immaculate Truth
'Tis not a blossom, shed as soon as youth
Drops from the stem of life—for it will grow
In barren regions, where no waters flow,
Nor rays of promise cheats the pensive gloom.
A darkling fire, faint hovering o'er a tomb,
That but itself and darkness nought doth shew,
Is my love's being,—yet it cannot die,
Nor will it change, though all be chang'd beside;
Tho' fairest beauty be no longer fair,
Tho' vows be false, and faith itself deny,
Tho' sharp enjoyment be a suicide,
And hope a spectre in a ruin bare.

SONNET VIII

Whither is gone the wisdom and the power
That ancient sages scatter'd with the notes
Of thought-suggesting lyres? The music floats
In the void air, e'en at this breathing hour,
In every cell and every blooming bower
The sweetness of old lays is hovering still
But the strong soul, the self-constraining will,
The rugged root that bare the winsome flower
Is weak and wither'd   Were we like the Fays
That sweetly nestle in the fox-glove bells,
Or lurk and murmur in the rose-lipp'd shells
Which Neptune to the earth for quit-rent pays,
Then might our pretty modern Philomels
Sustain our spirits with their roundelays

SONNET IX.

Long time a child, and still a child, when years
Had painted manhood on my cheek, was I;
For yet I lived like one not born to die,
A thriftless prodigal of smiles and tears,
No hope I needed, and I knew no fears
But sleep, though sweet, is only sleep, and waking,
I waked to sleep no more, at once o'ertaking
The vanguard of my age, with all arrears
Of duty on my back. Nor child, nor man,
Nor youth, nor sage, I find my head is grey,
For I have lost the race I never ran,
A rathe December blights my lagging May,
And still I am a child, tho' I be old,
Time is my debtor for my years untold.

SONNET X

Youth, love, and mirth, what are they—but the portion.
Wherewith the Prodigal left his Father's home,
Through foreign lands in search of bliss to roam,
And find each seeming joy a mere abortion,
And every smile, an agonized distortion
Of pale Repentance face, and barren womb ?
Youth, love, and mirth ! too quickly they consume
Then passive substance, and then small proportion
Of fleeting life, in memory's backward view,
Still dwindles to a point, a twinkling star,
Long gleaming o'er the onward course of Being,
That tells us whence we came, and where we are,
And tells us too, how swiftly we are fleeing
From all we were and loved, when life was new

SONNET XI

How long I sail'd, and never took a thought
To what port I was bound! Secure as sleep,
I dwelt upon the bosom of the deep
And perilous sea. And though my ship was fraught
With rare and precious fancies, jewels brought
From fairy-land, no course I cared to keep,
Nor changeful wind nor tide I heeded ought,
But joy'd to feel the merry billows leap,
And watch the sun beams dallying with the waves,
Or haply dream what realms beneath may lie
Where the clear ocean is an emerald sky,
And mermaids warble in their coral caves,
Yet vainly woo me to their secret home;
And sweet it were for ever so to roam

SONNET XII

Once I was young, and fancy was my all,
My love, my joy, my grief, my hope, my fear,
And ever ready as an infant's tear,
Whate'er in Fancy's kingdom might befal,
Some quaint device had Fancy still at call,
With seemly verse to greet the coming cheer,
Such grief to soothe, such any hope to rear,
To sing the birth-song, or the funeral,
Of such light love, it was a pleasant task;
But ill accord the quirks of wayward glee,
That wears affliction for a wanton mask,
With woes that bear not Fancy's livery;
With Hope that scorns of Fate its fate to ask,
But is itself its own sure destiny.

SONNET XIII

Too true it is, my time of power was spent
In idly watering weeds of casual growth,—
That wasted energy to desperate sloth
Declined, and fond self-seeking discontent,—
That the huge debt for all that nature lent
I sought to cancel,—and was nothing loath
To deem myself an outlaw, sever'd both
From duty and from hope,—yea, blindly sent
Without an errand, where I would to stray:—
Too true it is, that, knowing now my state,
I weakly mourn the sin I ought to hate,
Nor love the law I yet would fain obey
But true it is, above all law and fate
Is Faith, abiding the appointed day

SONNET XIV

ON A PICTURE

OF THE CORPSE OF NAPOLEON LYING IN STATE

Lo! there he lies. Is Death no more than this?
Is this the worst that mighty mortal can
Inflict upon his fellow? Could the man—
The strongest arm of angry Nemesis,—
The rod that routed hosts were fain to kiss,
Whom failing Faith afar with terror eyed,
And Atheism madly deified—
Could he with all his wars and policies
Effect but this? To antedate a year
That cold unfeeling calm, that even now
Blanks the dark meaning of that deep-lined brow
And from the loose lip half uncurls the sneer?
If such be Death, O man, then what art thou
That for the fear of Death would'st live in fear?

SONNET XV

TO WORDSWORTH.

There have been poets that in verse display
The elemental forms of human passions:
Poets have been, to whom the fickle fashions
And all the wilful humours of the day
Have furnish'd matter for a polish'd lay:
And many are the smooth elaborate tribe
Who, emulous of thee, the shape describe,
And fain would every shifting hue pourtray
Of restless Nature   But, thou mighty Seer !
'Tis thine to celebrate the thoughts that make
The life of souls, the truths for whose sweet sake
We to ourselves and to our God are dear
Of Nature's inner shrine thou art the priest,
Where most she works when we perceive her least

SONNET XVI

NOVEMBER

The mellow year is hasting to its close,
The little birds have almost sung their last,
Their small notes twitter in the dreary blast—
That shrill-piped harbinger of early snows
The patient beauty of the scentless rose,
Oft with the Morn's hoar chrystal quaintly glass'd,
Hangs, a pale mourner for the summer past,
And makes a little summer where it grows
In the chill sunbeam of the faint brief day
The dusky waters shudder as they shine,
The russet leaves obstruct the straggling way
Of oozy brooks, which no deep banks define,
And the gaunt woods, in ragged, scant array,
Wrap their old limbs with sombre ivy twine

SONNET XVII

ON PARTING WITH A VERY PRETTY, BUT VERY LITTLE LADY

'Tis ever thus   We only meet on earth
That we may know how sad it is to part ·
And sad indeed it were, if in the heart,
There were no store reserved against a dearth,
No calm Elysium for departed Mirth,
Haunted by gentle shadows of past Pleasure,
Where the sweet folly, the light-footed measure,
And graver trifles of the shining hearth
Live in their own dear image.   Lady fair,
Thy presence in our little vale has been
A visitation of the Fairy Queen,
Who for brief space reveals her beauty rare,
And shews her tricksy feats to mortal eyes,
Then fades into her viewless Paradise

SONNET XVIII.

NIGHT.

The crackling embers on the hearth are dead
The indoor note of industry is still,
The latch is fast, upon the window sill
The small birds wait not for their daily bread,
The voiceless flowers—how quietly they shed
Their nightly odours,—and the household rill.
Murmurs continuous dulcet sounds that fill
The vacant expectation, and the dread
Of listening night And haply now she sleeps,
For all the garrulous noises of the air
Are hush'd in peace. the soft dew silent weeps,
Like hopeless lovers for a maid so fair—
Oh! that I were the happy dream that creeps
To her soft heart, to find my image there.

SONNET XIX.

THE FIRST BIRTH DAY

The Sun, sweet girl, hath run his year-long race
Through the vast nothing of the eternal sky—
Since the glad hearing of the first faint cry
Announc'd a stranger from the unknown place
Of unborn souls. How blank was then the face,
How uninform'd the weak light-shunning eye,
That wept and saw not. Poor mortality
Begins to mourn before it knows its case,
Prophetic in its ignorance. But soon
The hospitalities of earth engage
The banish'd spirit in its new exile—
Pass some few changes of the fickle Moon,
The merry babe has learn'd its Mother's smile,
Its father's frown, its nurse's mimic rage.

SONNET XX

Whither—Oh—whither, in the wandering air,
Fly the sweet notes that 'twixt the soul and sense
Make blest communion? When and where commence
The self-unfolding sounds, that every where
Expand through silence? seems that never were
A point and instant of that sound's beginning
A time when it was not as sweet and winning,
As now it melts amid the soft and rare,
And love sick ether? Gone it is—that tone
Hath passed for ever from the middle earth,
Yet not to perish is the music flown—
Ah no—it hastens to a better birth—
Then joy be with it—wheresoe'er it be,
To us it leaves a pleasant memory.

SONNET XXI.

Love is but folly,—since the wisest love,
Itself disclaiming, would invent a use
For its free motion.—Penitents recluse,
That scarce allow the natural heart to move,
With amorous ditties woo the mystic dove,
Or fondly bid their heavenly spouse unloose
Their sacred zones.—The politic excuse
Of worldlings would to worldly ends improve
The gentle madness.—Courtiers glibly preach
How Love and Woman best rehearse the play
That statesmen act.—The grave fine-spoken leech
Counts how the beatings of the pulse betray
The sweet disease.—And all the poets teach
That love alone can build the lofty lay.

SONNET XXII

Youth, thou art fled,—but where are all the charms
Which, tho' with thee they came, and pass'd with thee,
Should leave a perfume and sweet memory
Of what they have been?—All thy boons and harms
Have perish'd quite.—Thy oft renew'd alarms
Forsake the fluttering echo.—Smiles and tears
Die on my cheek, or, petrified with years,
Shew the dull woe which no compassion warms,
The ninth none shares. Yet could a wish, a thought,
Unravel all the complex web of age,—
Could all the characters that Time hath wrought
Be clean effaced from my memorial page
By one short word, the word I would not say,
I thank my God, because my hairs are grey

SONNET XXIII

I thank my God because my hairs are grey!
But have grey hairs brought wisdom? Doth the flight
Of summer birds, departed while the light
Of life is lingering on the middle way,
Predict the harvest nearer by a day?
Will the rank weeds of hopeless appetite
Droop at the glance and venom of the blight
That made the vermeil bloom, the flush so gay,
Dim and unlovely as a dead worm's shroud?
Or is my heart, that, wanting hope, has lost
The strength and rudder of resolve, at peace?
Is it no longer wrathful, vain, and proud?
Is it a Sabbath, or untimely frost,
That makes the labour of the soul to cease?

SONNET XXIV

It must be so,—my infant love must find
In my own breast a cradle and a grave,
Like a rich jewel hid beneath the wave
Or rebel spirit bound within the rind
Of some old wreathed oak, or fast enshrined
In the cold durance of an echoing cave —
Yea, better thus than cold disdain to brave —
Or worse,—to taint the quiet of that mind,
That decks its temple with unearthly grace
Together must we dwell, my dream and I,—
Unknown must live, and unlamented die,
Rather than soil the lustre of that face,
Or drive that laughing dimple from its place,
Or heave that white breast with a painful sigh

SONNET XXV.

FROM COUNTRY TO TOWN.

WRITTEN IN LEEDS, JULY, 1832

I LEFT the land where men with nature dwelling,
Know not how much they love her lovely forms—
Nor heed the history of forgotten storms,
On the blank folds inscribed of drear Helvellyn,
I sought the town, where toiling, buying, selling—
Getting and spending, poising hope and fear,
Make but one season of the live-long year—
Now for the brook from moss-girt fountain welling
I see the foul stream hot with sleepless trade,
For the slow creeping vapours of the morn,
Black hurrying smoke in opake mass up-borne,
O'er dinning engines hangs, a stifling shade—
Yet nature lives e'en here, and will not part
From her best home, the lowly-loving heart

SONNET XXVI

CONTINUED.

Tis strange to me, who long have seen no face,
That was not like a book, whose every page
I knew by heart, a kindly common-place—
And faithful record of progressive age—
To wander forth, and view an unknown race,
Of all that I have been, to find no trace,
No footstep of my by-gone pilgrimage.
Thousands I pass, and no one stays his pace
To tell me that the day is fair, or rainy—
Each one his object seeks with anxious chase,
And I have not a common hope with any—
Thus like one drop of oil upon a flood
In uncommunicating solitude—
Single am I amid the countless many.

SONNET XXVII

If I have sinn'd in act, I may repent,
If I have err'd in thought, I may disclaim
My silent error, and yet feel no shame—
But if my soul, big with an ill intent,
Guilty in will, by fate be innocent,
Or being bad, yet murmurs at the curse
And incapacity of being worse
That makes my hungry passion still keep Lent
In keen expectance of a Carnival,
Where, in all worlds, that round the sun revolve
And shed their influence on this passive ball,
Abides a power that can my soul absolve?
Could any sin survive, and be forgiven—
One sinful wish would make a hell of heaven

SONNET XXVIII.

TO SHAKSPEARE

The soul of man is larger than the sky,
Deeper than ocean—or the abysmal dark
Of the unfathom'd centre. Like that Ark,
Which in its sacred hold uplifted high,
O'er the drown'd hills, the human family,
And stock reserved of every living kind,
So, in the compass of the single mind,
The seeds and pregnant forms in essence lie,
That make all worlds. Great Poet 'twas thy art,
To know thyself, and in thyself to be
Whate'er love, hate, ambition, destiny,
Or the firm, fatal purpose of the heart,
Can make of Man. Yet thou wert still the same,
Serene of thought, unhurt by thy own flame.

SONNET XXIX

Why should I murmur at my lot forlorn?
The self-same Fate that doom'd me to be poor
Endues me with a spirit to endure
All, and much more, than is or has been borne
By better men, of want, or worldly scorn.
My soul has faith, my body has the nerve
To brave the penance that my sins deserve
And yet my helpless state I deeply mourn.
Well could I bear to be deserted quite,—
Less should I blame my fortune were it worse,—
But taking all, it yet hath left me friends,
For whom I needs must mourn the wayward spite
That hides my purpose in an empty purse,
Since what I grateful wish, in wishing ends

SONNET XXX.

What can a poor man do but love and pray?
But if his love be selfish, then his prayer,
Like noisome vapour melts in vacant air
I am a debtor, and I cannot pay
The alms which drop upon the public way,—
The casual tribute of the good and fair,
With the keen, thriftless avarice of despair
I seize, and live thereon from day to day,
Ingrate and purposeless —And yet not so
The mere mendicity of self contempt
Has not so far debased me, but I know
The faith, the hope, the piety, exempt
From worldly doubt, to which my all I owe.
Since I have nothing, yet I bless the thought,—
Best are they paid whose earthly wage is nought

SONNET XXXI

What is young Passion but a gusty breeze
Ruffling the surface of a shallow flood?
A vernal motion of the vital blood,
That sweetly gushes from a heart at ease,
As sugared sap in spicy-budding trees?
And tho' a wish be born with every morrow,
And fondest dreams full oft are types of sorrow.
Eyes that can smile may weep just when they please
But adult Passion, centred far within,
Hid from the moment's venom and its balm,
Works with the fell inherency of sin,
Nor feels the joy of morn, nor evening calm
For morn nor eve can change that fiery gloom
That glares within the spirit's living tomb.

SONNET XXXII

FROM PETRARCA

"*Solo e pensoso i piu deserti campi*"

Lonely and pensive o'er the lonely strand,
"With wandering steps and slow," I loiter on,
My eyes at watch, to warn me to be gone
If mark of human foot impress the sand·
Else would my piteous plight be rudely scann'd,
And curious folk would stare to see the wan
And deathlike images of joy foregone,
And how I inly waste like smouldering brand,
Or I would fain believe the tangled wood
Which girds the small field on the mountain side
The one sole witness to my crazy mood·
But ah! what sandy waste, or forest dim,
My haunt obscure from love can ever hide?
Where'er I *think*, I converse hold with *him*

SONNET XXXIII

The vale of Tempe had in vain been fair,
Green Ida never deem'd the nurse of Jove;
Each fabled stream, beneath its covert grove,
Had idly murmured to the idle air,
The shaggy wolf had kept his horrid lair
In Delphi's cell, and old Trophonius' cave,
And the wild wailing of the Ionian wave
Had never blended with the sweet despair
Of Sappho's death-song · if the sight inspired,
Saw only what the visual organs shew,
It heaven-born phantasy no more required,
Than what within the sphere of sense may glow;
The beauty to perceive of earthly things,
The mounting soul must heavenward prune her wings

SONNET XXXIV.

TO A LOFTY BEAUTY,

FROM HER POOR KINSMAN.

Fair maid, had I not heard thy baby cries,
Nor seen thy girlish, sweet vicissitude,
Thy mazy motions, striving to elude,
Yet wooing still a parent's watchful eyes,
Thy humours, many as the opal's dies,
And lovely all:—methinks thy scornful mood
And bearing high of stately womanhood,—
Thy brow, where Beauty sits to tyrannize
O'er humble love, had made me sadly fear thee;
For never sure was seen a royal bride,
Whose gentleness gave grace to so much pride—
My very thoughts would tremble to be near thee,
But when I see thee at thy father's side,
Old times unqueen thee, and old loves endear thee

THOUGHTS AND FANCIES.

A TASK AD LIBITUM

TO A LADY

You bid me write, and yet propose no theme
Must I then shoot my shafts of poesy
At the vast, void, invulnerable air ?
Or lead my Pegasus a steeple-hunting ?
Or issue forth with chiming hue and cry,
With trampling feet of thorough-paced blank verse
And winding horn of long-drawn melody
In chace of butterflies ? Or shall I rather,
In gentler figure, *make believe* to hang
My careless harp upon a willow tree,
That every gale may prattle with its strings ?
'Tis strange that any bard should lack a theme
In such a world of wonders Look abroad,
Around you, and above you, and within you :
The stars of heaven (as elder sages told)
Roll on from age to age their lonely way
To their own music. So the humbler spirit
Hears in the daily round of household things
A low sweet melody, inaudible
To the gross sense of worldlings —Aye, I grant
That earth and sky are cunning instruments ;

But who may rouse their sleeping harmony,
And not torment the strings to grinding discord,
Or vex the hearers with the weary drone
Of half-forgotten lays, like buzzing night-flies
Thwarting the drowsiness themselves produce
All, all is stale the busy ways of men,
The gorgeous terrors of the steel-clad warrior.
The lover's sighs, the fair one's cruelty,
Or that worst state, when love, a rayless fire,
Is sever'd quite from hope and tenderness,
Or dogg'd by base suspicion, hurries onward,
Scared by its own black shadow —These are themes
Unmeet for thee, or old, or harsh and strange
The gentler joys, the calm sequester'd hours
Of wedded life. the babble sweet of babes,
That unknown tongue, which mothers best expound,
Which works such witchery on a parent's heart,
Turning grave manhood into childishness,
Till stoic eyes with foolish rheum o'erflow,
And fluent statesmen lisp again,—for love
Will catch the likeness of the thing beloved —
These have been sung a thousand times before,
And should I sing of thee and thy soft brilliance,
Thy tender thoughts, in reckless laughter melting,
Thy beautiful soul, that shapes thine outward form
To its own image,—thy essential goodness,
Not thine, but thee,—thy very being's being
Thy liquid movements, measured by the notes
Of thy sweet spirit's music,—the unearthly sound
Of that beloved voice, less heard than felt,
That wins the wayward heart to peace, and lulls
The inmost nature to that blissful sleep

Which is awake to heaven, and brings no dream,
But foretaste of the best reality
Then must I modulate empyreal ether
To strains more sweet than mortal sense could bear.

SONG.

The earliest wish I ever knew
Was woman's kind regard to win;
I felt it long e'er passion grew,
E'er such a wish could be a sin

And still it lasts;—the yearning ache
No cure has found, no comfort known·
If she did love, 'twas for my sake,
She could not love me for her own

STANZAS.

She was a queen of noble Nature's crowning,
A smile of her's was like an act of grace,
She had no winsome looks, no pretty frowning.
Like daily beauties of the vulgar race :
But if she smiled, a light was on her face,
A clear cool kindliness, a lunar beam
Of peaceful radiance, silvering o'er the stream
Of human thought with unabiding glory,
Not quite a waking truth, not quite a dream,
A visitation, bright and transitory

But she is changed,—hath felt the touch of sorrow,
No love hath she, no understanding friend,
Oh grief! when heaven is forced of earth to borrow,
What the poor niggard earth has not to lend,
But when the stalk is snapt, the rose must bend
The tallest flower that skyward rears its head,
Grows from the common ground, and there must shed
Its delicate petals   Cruel fate, too surely,
That they should find so base a bridal bed,
Who lived in virgin pride, so sweet and purely

She had a brother, and a tender father,
And she was lov'd, but not as others are
From whom we ask return of love,—but rather
As one might love a dream, a phantom-fair
Of something exquisitely strange and rare,
Which all were glad to look on, men and maids,
Yet no one claim'd—as oft, in dewy glades
The peering primrose, like a sudden gladness,
Gleams on the soul—yet unregarded fades—
The joy is ours, but all its own the sadness.

'Tis vain to say—her worst of grief is only
The common lot, which all the world have known,
To her 'tis more, because her heart is lonely,
And yet she hath no strength to stand alone,—
Once she had playmates, fancies of her own,
And she did love them   They are past away
As Fairies vanish at the break of day—
And like a spectre of an age departed,
Or unsphered Angel woefully astray—
She glides along—the solitary hearted.

" And the rathe primrose that forsaken dies "
Lycidas.

A BROTHER'S LOVE TO HIS SISTER

Full ill, I ween, can measured speech reveal
Or thought embody, what true bosoms feel,
For hollow falsehood long has set her sign
On each soft phrase that speaks a love like mine
The choicest terms are now enfeoff'd to folly,
To vain delight, or wilful melancholy

Oh! for a virgin speech, a strain untainted
By worldly use, with holy meaning sainted,
Thoughts to conceive, and words devote to tell
The strength divine of love, its secret spell.
Of brother's love, that is within the heart
A spiritual essence, and exists apart
From passion, vain opinion, hopes and fears,
And every pregnant cause of smiles and tears
A life that owes no fealty to the will,
Nor takes infection of connateral ill—
That feels no hunger and admits no doubt,
Nor asks for succour of the world without.
But is, itself, its own perfected end,
The one sole point to which its workings tend

A love like this so pure of earthly leaven,
That hath no likeness in the earth or heaven,

No correspondent in the world of sight,
No symbol in the total Infinite
Was ne'er engendered in the soul or eye
From ought conceived of form or quality,
He loves not right that asks, or answers why,
It is not born of weakness, common needs,
Or gainful traffic in convenient deeds
The joy, the good, that name and being owe
To sin and pain, it can and will forego,
For moral good is but the thrall of time,
That marks the bourne of virtue, and of crime
A joy it hath that underived of pain,
Its proper nature, shall for aye retain:
A good it is that cannot cease or change
With man's desire, or wild opinion's range
A law it is, above all human state
A perfect freedom, and an absolute fate.

'OF SUCH IS THE KINGDOM OF GOD'

In stature perfect, and with every gift
Which God would on his favourite work bestow,
Did our great Parent his pure form uplift,
And sprang from earth, the Lord of all below

But Adam fell before a child was born,
And want and weakness with his fall began—
So his first offspring was a thing forlorn—
In human shape, without the strength of man—

So, heaven has doom'd that all of Adam's race,
Naked and helpless, shall their course begin
E'en at their birth confess their need of grace—
And weeping, wail the penalty of sin

Yet sure the babe is in the cradle blest,
Since God himself a baby deign'd to be—
And slept upon a mortal mother's breast,
And steep'd in baby tears—his Deity

O—sleep—sweet infant—for we all must sleep—
And wake like babes, that we may wake with him
Who watches still his own from harm to keep
And o'er them spreads the wing of cherubim

WRITTEN ON THE FIRST OF NOVEMBER.
1820

Hail, dark November! spurious progeny
Of Phœbus and old Night,—thou sable mourner,
That lead'st the funeral pageant of the year,—
Thou Winter's herald, sent before thy lord
To bid the earth prepare for his dread presence,—
I gladly wish thee welcome, for thou wear'st
No flaunting smile to mock pale Melancholy,
Which ever loves its likeness, and derives
From most discomfort, truest consolation

The world is heartsick, and o'erwearied Nature
Bears, in her lost abandonment, the mark
Of ills expected, and of pleasures past,
And, like a late-repenting prodigal,
Deals out with thrift enforced the scant remains
Of lavish'd wealth, sighing to think upon
The riotous days, that left no joy unrifled,
No store reserved to comfort poor old age.
The tip-toe levity of spring, flower-deck'd,
And Summer's pride, and Autumn's hospitality
Have eat up all.

    And now her festal robes
Are worn to rags,—poor rents of tatter'd state,

Telling a tale of mad, luxurious waste,
Yet not enough to cover nakedness,—
A garb of many hues, and wretched all
There is a desperate patience in her look,
And straggling smiles, or rather ghosts of smiles,
Display the sadness of her wrinkled visage
Anon, with gusty rage, she casts away
Her motley weeds, and tears her thin grey locks,
And treads her squalid splendour in the mire ;
Then weeps amain to think what she has done,
Doom'd to cold penance in a sheet of snow

EPIGRAM

They say Despair has power to kill
   With her bleak frown, but I say No.
If life did hang upon her will,
   Then Hope had perish'd long ago
Yet still the twain keep up their " barful strife,"
For Hope Love's leman is, Despair his wife

> 'Tis silly, sooth,
> And dallies with the innocence of love
> Like the old age —

IN THE MANNER OF A CHILD OF SEVEN YEARS OLD.

An' woe betide my bonny bride.
   For war is in the land,
And far and wide the foemen ride
   With ruthless bloody brand.

Still as a dream the purple beam
   Of eve is on the river,
But ghastly bright, at the dead of night,
   A blood-red flame will quiver

Fair in the skies the sun will rise
   As ever sun was seen,
But never again our window pane
   Shall back reflect his sheen ·

For the warrior stern our cot will burn,
   And trample on the bower;
It grew for years of smiles and tears,
   'Twill perish in an hour.

Those firs were old, our grandsires told,
　　In their good fathers' days,
And my soul it grieves that their needle leaves
　　Must crackle in the blaze.

Beneath their shade how oft we played!
　　There was our place of wooing —
But now we're wed, and peace is fled,
　　And we shall see their ruin.

In battle plain shall I be slain,
　　And never would I shrink
Oh! were that all, what may befall
　　To thee. I dare not think

And our sweet boy, our baby joy,
　　He'll for his mother cry,
Till the hot smoke, his voice shall choke,
　　And then my bud will die

Green are the graves, and thick as waves
　　Within our holy ground—
And here, and there, an hillock fair,
　　An infant's grave is found

Our fathers died, their whole fireside
　　Is laid in peace together
But vile as stones, our bleaching bones
　　Must brave the wind and weather

Nay, love, let's fly, to the hill so high,
   Where eagles build their nest,
Among the heather we'll couch together,
   As blithely as the best

We'll leave the bower and tender flower
   That we have nursed with care,
But the wild blue bell shall bloom as well
   Beside our craggy lair.

We shall not die, for all birds that fly
   Shall thither bring us food,
And come the worst, w'ell be help'd the first,
   Before the eagle's brood

The mist beneath, that curls its wreath
   Around the hill-top hoar,
There will we hide, my bonny bride,
   And ne'er be heard of more

SENSE, IF YOU CAN FIND IT.

Like one pale, flitting, lonely gleam
   Of sunshine on a winter's day,
There came a thought upon my dream,
I know not whence, but fondly deem
    It came from far away.

Those sweet, sweet snatches of delight
   That visit our bedarken'd clay
Like passage birds, with hasty flight,
It cannot be they perish quite,
    Although they pass away.

They come and go, and come again;
   They're ours, whatever time they stay
Think not, my heart, they come in vain,
If one brief while they soothe thy pain
    Before they pass away.

But whither go they? No one knows
   Their home,—but yet they seem to say,
That far beyond this gulf of woes
There is a region of repose
    For them that pass away.

TO SOMEBODY.

*And the imperial votaress passed on
In maiden meditation fancy free* —SHAKSPEARE.

I blame not her, because my soul
  Is not like her's,—a treasure
Of self-sufficing good,—a whole
  Complete in every measure.

I charge her not with cruel pride,
  With self-admired disdain;
Too happy she, or to deride,
  Or to perceive my pain.

I blame her not—she cannot know
  What she did never prove:
Her streams of sweetness purely flow
  Unblended yet with love.

No fault hath she, that I desire
  What she cannot conceive,
For she is made of bliss entire,
  And I was born to grieve.

And though she hath a thousand wiles,
  And, in a moment's space,
As fast as light, a thousand smiles
  Come showering from her face,—

Those winsome smiles, those sunny looks,
    Her heart securely deems,
Cold as the flashing of the brooks
    In the cold moonlight beams

Her sweet affections, free as wind,
    Nor fear, nor craving feel,
No secret hollow hath her mind
    For passion to reveal

Her being's law is gentle bliss,
    Her purpose, and her duty;
And quiet joy her loveliness,
    And gay delight her beauty.

Then let her walk in mirthful pride,
    Dispensing joy and sadness,
By her light spirit fortified
    In panoply of gladness

The joy she gives shall still be her's,
    The sorrow shall be mine,
Such debt the earthly heart incurs
    That pants for the divine

But better 'tis to love, I ween,
    And die of slow despair,
Than die, and never to have seen
    A maid so lovely fair

SONG.

'Tis sweet to hear the merry lark,
  That bids a blithe good-morrow,
But sweeter to hark in the twinkling dark,
  To the soothing song of sorrow
Oh nightingale! What doth she ail?
  And is she sad or jolly?
For ne'er on earth, was sound of mirth
  So like to melancholy

The merry lark, he soars on high,
  No worldly thought o'ertakes him,
He sings aloud to the clear blue sky,
  And the daylight that awakes him
As sweet a lay, as loud, as gay,
  The nightingale is trilling,
With feeling bliss, no less than his,
  Her little heart is thrilling.

Yet ever and anon, a sigh,
  Peers through her lavish mirth,
For the lark's bold song is of the sky,
  And hers is of the earth
By night and day, she tunes her lay,
  To drive away all sorrow,
For bliss, alas! to night must pass,
  And woe may come tomorrow

NEW-YEAR'S DAY

While the bald trees stretch forth their long lank arms,
And starving birds peck nigh the reeky farms:
While houseless cattle paw the yellow field,
Or coughing shiver in the pervious bield,
And nought more gladsome in the hedge is seen,
Than the dark holly's grimly glistening green—
At such a time, the ancient year goes by
To join its parents in eternity—
At such a time the merry year is born,
Like the bright berry from the naked thorn.

The bells ring out, the hoary steeple rocks—
Hark! the long story of a score of clocks,
For, once a year, the village clocks agree,
E'en clocks unite to sound the hour of glee—
And every cottage has a light awake,
Unusual stars long flicker o'er the lake
The moon on high, if any moon be there,
May peep, or wink, no mortal now will care,
For 'tis the season, when the nights are long,
There's time, e'er morn, for each to sing his song

The year departs, a blessing on its head,
We mourn not for it, for it is not dead.
Dead! What is that? A word to joy unknown,
Which love abhors, and faith will never own.

A word, whose meaning sense could never find,
That has no truth in matter, nor in mind
The passing breezes gone as soon as felt,
The flakes of snow that in the soft air melt,
The wave that whitening curls its frothy crest,
And falls to sleep upon its mother's breast
The smile that sinks into a maiden's eye,
They come, they go, they change, they do not die
So the Old Year—that fond and formal name,
Is with us yet, another and the same.

And are the thoughts, that ever more are fleeing,
The moments that make up our being's being,
The silent workings of unconscious love,
Or the dull hate which clings and will not move,
In the dark caverns of the gloomy heart,
The fancies wild and horrible, which start
Like loathsome reptiles from their crankling holes,
From foul, neglected corners of our souls,
Are these less vital than the wave or wind
Or snow that melts and leaves no trace behind?
Oh! let them perish all, or pass away,
And let our spirits feel a New-Year's day

A New-Year's day—'tis but a term of art,
An arbitrary line upon the chart
Of Time's unbounded sea—fond fancy's creature,
To reason alien, and unknown to nature
Nay—'tis a joyful day, a day of hope!
Bound, merry dancer, like an Antelope,
And as that lovely creature, far from man,
Gleams through the spicy groves of Hindostan,

Flash through the labyrinth of the mazy dance,
With foot as nimble, and as keen a glance—

And we, whom many New-Year's days have told
The sober truth, that we are growing old—
For this one night—aye—and for many more,
Will be as jocund as we were of yore,
Kind hearts can make December blithe as May.
And in each morrow find a New-Year's day

ON A YOUNG MAN DYING ON THE EVE OF MARRIAGE

With contrite tears, and agony of Prayer,
God we besought, thy virtuous youth to spare,
And thought, Oh! be the human thought forgiven,
Thou wert too good to die, too young for heaven—
Yet sure the prayers of love had not been vain,
If death to thee were not exceeding gain.

Tho' for ourselves, and not for thee we mourn,
The weakness of our hearts thou wilt not scorn;
And if thy Saviour's, and thy Father's will,
Such angel love permit, wilt love us still,
For Death, which every tie of earth unbinds,
Can ne'er dissolve the "marriage of pure minds"

TO THE NAUTILUS.

Where Ausonian summers glowing,
Warm the deep to life and joyance,
And gentle zephyrs nimbly blowing,
Wanton with the waves that flowing
By many a land of ancient glory,
And many an isle renown'd in story,
Leap along with gladsome buoyance,
      There Marinere,
      Do'st thou appear,
In faery pinnace gaily flashing,
Through the white foam proudly dashing,
The joyous play-mate of the buxom breeze,
The fearless fondling of the mighty seas.

Thou the light sail boldly spreadest,
O'er the furrow'd waters gliding,
Thou nor wreck, nor foeman dreadest,
Thou nor helm nor compass needest,
While the sun is bright above thee,
While the bounding surges love thee,
In their deepening bosoms hiding,
      Thou canst not fear,
      Small Marinere,
For though the tides with restless motion,
Bear thee to the desert ocean,
Far as the ocean stretches to the sky,
'Tis all thine own, 'tis all thy empery.

Lame is art, and her endeavour
Follows nature's course but slowly,
Guessing, toiling, seeking ever,
Still improving, perfect never,
Little Nautilus, thou shewest
Deeper wisdom than thou knowest,
Love, which man should study lowly:
    Bold faith and cheer,
    Small Marmere,
Are thine within thy pearly dwelling,—
Thine, a law of life compelling,
Obedience, perfect, simple, glad, and free,
To the great will that animates the sea.

Sweet Love, the shadow of thy parting wings
Hangs on my soul like the soft shade of even
Farewell to thee, for thou art going to Heaven,
And I must stay behind, with all the things
Which thou, and thy benign administerings
Once made most sweet of sweetness now bereaven
Whose memory, as a sour fermenting leaven,
Perverts all nature with an ill that springs
From good corrupted. Oh! for mercy—Love,
Stay with me yet, altho' thy comrade fair,
The smiler Hope, be gone to realms above,
Stay with thy youngest sister, meek Despair—
For meek she is in truth, as brooding dove,
If thou with her the lowly bosom share

SONG

Say—what is worse than blank despair,
'Tis that sick hope too weak for flying,
That plays at fast and loose with care,
And wastes a weary life in dying.

Though promise be a welcome guest,
Yet may it be too late a comer,
'Tis but a cuckoo voice at best,
The joy of spring, scarce heard in summer.

Then now consent, this very hour,
Let the kind word of peace be spoken;
Like dew upon a withered flower,
Is comfort to the heart that's broken.

The heart, whose will is from above,
Shall yet its mortal taint discover,
For Time, that cannot alter love,
Has power to slay the wretched lover.

SONG.

She is not fair to outward view
   As many maidens be,
Her loveliness I never knew
   Until she smil'd on me,
Oh! then I saw, her eye was bright,
A well of love, a spring of light.

But now her looks are coy and cold,
   To mine they ne'er reply,
And yet I cease not to behold,
   The love-light in her eye:
Her very frowns are fairer far,
Than smiles of other maidens are.

EPITAPH

ON A MOTHER AND THREE INFANTS

From God they came, to God they went again,
No sin they knew, and knew but little pain,
And here they lie, by their fond mother's side,
Who lived to love and lose them, then she died.

LEONARD AND SUSAN

*   *   *   *   *   *

They were a gentle pair, whose love began
They knew not when—they knew not of a time
When they loved not   In the mere sentient life
Of unremember'd infancy, whose speech,
Like secret love's, is only smiles and tears,
The baby Leonard clapp'd his little hands,
Leapt in his nurse's arms, and crow'd aloud
When Susan was in sight, and utter'd sounds
Most strange and strangely sweet, that nothing meant
But merely joy, as in the green-wood tree
The merry merle awakes his thrilling song,
Soon as the cool breath of the vernal dawn
Stirs the light leaflets on the motionless boughs
Mute as the shadow of a passing bird
On glassy lake, the gentle Susan lay,
Hush'd in her meek delight   A dimpled smile
Curl'd round her tiny, rosy mouth, and seem'd
To sink, as light, into her soft full eyes—
A quiet smile, that told of happiness
Her infant soul investing, as the bud
Infolds the petals of the nascent rose.

Born in one week, and in one font baptized,
On the same festal day—they grew together,

And then first tottering steps were hand in hand,
While the two fathers, in half-earnest sport,
Betroth'd them to each other. Then 'twas sweet
For mother's ears, to hear them lisp and try
At the same words, each imitating each;
But Leonard was the babe of nimbler tongue,
And 'Sister Susan' was the first plain phrase
His utterance master'd—by that dear kind name
He call'd the maid, supplying so a place
Which Nature had left void. An only child
Of a proud mother and a high-born sire,
Full soon he learn'd to mount a palfrey small,
Of that dwarf race that prance unclaim'd and free
O'er the bleak pastures of the Shetland Isles
And who may tell his glory or his pride
When Susan, by her mother's arms upheld,
Sat, glad though fearful, on the courser's rear,
While he, exulting in his dauntless skill,
Rein'd its short testy neck, and froward mouth,
Taming its wilful movement to the pace
That palfrey suits of wandering lady fair.
Bold were his looks, his speech was bold and shrill,
His smooth round cheeks glow'd with a ruddy brown,
And dark the curls that cluster'd o'er his head,
Knotty and close. In every pliant limb
A noble boy's ambitious manliness
Elastic sprung. Yet child more loving, fond,
Ne'er sought the refuge of a parent's side
But Susan was not one of many words,
Nor loud of laughter; and she moved as soft
As modest Nymphs, in work of artist rare,
Seem moving ever In her delicate eye

And damask cheek there dwelt a grace retired,
A prophecy of pensive womanhood.
And yet, in sooth, she was a happy child;
And, though the single treasure of her house,
She neither miss'd a brother's love, nor lack'd
The blest emotions of a sister's soul.
She thought no sister loved a brother more
Than she her brother Leonard—him who show'd
The strawberry lurking in the mossy shade,
The nest, in leafy thicket dark embower'd,
The squirrel's airy bound   No bliss he knew,
No toy had he—no pretty property—
No dog—no bird—no fit of childish wrath,
That was not hers.   The wild and terrible tales
His garrulous old nurse o'ernight had told,
He duly in the morning told to her,
With comments manifold; and when seven years
Made him a student of learn'd Lilly's page,
With simple, earnest, kindly vanity.
He fill'd her wondering ear with all his lore
Of tense, and conjugation, noun, and verb;
Searching the word-book for all pretty names,
All dainty, doating, dear diminutives
Which the old Romans used to woo withal.

So pass'd those happy seasons, when no law
Of jealous custom, no suspected harm
Bids fresh virginity beware of man;
And, like two sexless bees, from flower to flower,
They wander'd unreproved   But soon an age
Of fearful wishes found the spotless pair,
And Susan felt, unprompted, that the name

Of sister was not hers by right of kind.
Reserv'd she grew, and though she thought no ill,
She sigh'd in fear, and strove to frame her speech
To formal phrase of maiden courtesy
Sore wonder'd Leonard at her mien constrain'd,
Her flitting blush, her intermitted words,
That seem'd unwelcome strangers to her lips,
And to her thought unknown. Why thus withdrawn
Her trembling hand, that wont in his to lie,
Still as the brooding warbler in her nest,
Close as the soft leaves of the rose unblown ?—
Why shrinks she from his kiss, his watchful gaze,
With such a faint and half-reproachful smile—
Nor longer may permit her flowing hair
To seek the pillow of his breast ? Ah ! why
Is he no more her brother ? But, ere long
New passion budding in his vernal soul,
Fill'd him with joy to think no kindred tie,
No common blood forbade the current free
Of his warm wistful sighs

      The tale is old
Of "passionate first love" with all its dreams
Sleeping and waking—all its cherish'd pains,
Uneasy raptures, quarrels, fantasies,
Quaint wiles, and riddles read by lovers' eyes,
And bland deceptions meant not to deceive
Though wooing well might seem a useless toil,
When Love, a goodly plant, in cradle sown,
Shot forth its leaves spontaneous to the warmth
Of genial youth, yet Leonard duly paid
The appointed duty of an amorous swain,

" With adorations and with fertile tears,"
And " loyal cantos of contemned love,"
As if in truth his Susan were a dame
Haughty and fierce, as Lady of Romance,
That must be woo'd with blows, and won with scars
And homicide. Sometimes a shepherd he,
And soft and silly as his fancied flock
Anon an arm'd and errant Paladin,
He talk'd of forests dark, and deserts drear,
And foes defied, and giants huge o'erthrown,—
And all for Susan's sake Young love is still,
Like Eastern sages, parabolical,
And bliss, unearn'd, scarce knows itself to be,
But by the contrast of imagined woe.
What more of patient suit and coy delay,
Or passion paid, or maiden pride required,
I pause not to relate, nor how, at last,
The seemly ceremonial courtship done,
With interchange of braided locks and rings,
And holy kiss, they seal'd their plighted troth,
In their glad parents' sight. Unskill'd am I
Such scenes to paint—to me, alas! unknown
Unmeet historian of a golden time,
I cannot give the charm of life renew'd
To pleasures long forgot, for happy days,
Unvaried save by sun, or sunny shower,
Are bare of incident as dreamless sleep,
Or sweet existence of a flower unseen.
Suffice to say, that Leonard and his maid
Grew up to man's estate and womanhood
Then pure affection, ripening with their years,
Like a bright angel's broad o'ershadowing wings,

Guarded their spirits, kept their inmost thoughts
All lovely, pure, and beautiful. Secure
In the assurance of an authorized pledge,
They, unrepining, brook'd their bliss deferr d
By charge parental, till maturer years
Should fit them for the cares of wedded life

   Alas ! too wisely spake the poet wise—
" The course of true love never did run smooth,"
How clear soe'er the stream   Though like estate,
Congenial birth, affection tried and true,
Taste, tempers, studies, finely harmonized
By sympathy in dissimilitude—
Divided excellence, that sought and found
Its full perfection in the bond of love.
Decreed the union of the happy pair,
Whose mutual passion was obedience
To those beloved parents, who had wish'd
Their offspring blended in a common stock
Ere either babe was born, yet eyeless Fate
And human baseness wrought the righteous will
Of fate-controlling Heaven   The lovely maid
Was doom'd on earth to droop, a virgin flower,
Unsoil'd of earth, to bloom in Paradise.

   Accursed faction poisons e en the fount
Of household amity. A man there came
Of dubious honour, and of race unknown,
Deep laden with the plunder'd wealth of Ind,
And he, forsooth, must shine a rising star
In Britain's senate, make and unmake laws
He learn'd but late to keep , beat down prerogative,

" And make bold power look pale"—a patriot he,
Profound economist, the people's friend,
And champion of reform.   Now Leonard's sire
Was one of ancient lineage, and estate
For many generations handed down,
Without an acre added or impair'd—
He counted a long line of senators
Among his ancestry, and ill could brook
The lineal honours of his house usurp'd
By the ill-gotten purse of yesterday.
And now the day of license was at hand,
Britain's septennial Saturnalia,
When the soft palm of nice nobility,
Ungloved, solicits the Herculean gripe
Of hands with bestial slaughter newly stain'd,
When ladies stoop their coroneted brows,
And patriotic kisses deal to churls
A gipsy would refuse; and, reeling ripe,
Big Independence, reeking as he goes
Through the rank toll-booth, works his burly way
To hiccup perjury.—O Mountain Nymph!
—O Virgin Liberty! behold thy shrine,
And send a snow-blast from thy native hills,
Or thy fat offerings will all dissolve
And choke the world with incense.—Plutus now,
And roaring Bacchus, are thy ministers,
While swoln Corruption, like a toad, half-hid
Beneath the purple trappings of the throne,
Distends her bloated features with a laugh,
To hear the many take thy name in vain

Unequal strife had Leonard's sire to wage—

Too proud to flatter, and too proud to yield
The palm to flatterers, he fondly deem'd
Hereditary gratitude—the name
Of his time-honour'd house—and all the links
That bind the present to the past, and make
Each moment sponsor for eternity,
Were barriers potent to resist the flood
Of pauper treason, back'd with traitorous gold
Hark !—the loud war proclaim'd by drum and fife
And labell'd banners, that affront the sky
With gaudy blazonry of factious hate,
Turning the innocent hues of flower and field
To party shibboleths   The clear blue sky
Frown'd on the crimson of the regal rose—
Nor spared the maiden blush. Fierce riot rung
In homely mansions, long devote to peace,
And mild, benignant mirth   From vale to vale
The uproar echoed through the spacious shire,
The clang o'erpowering of the madd'ning wheels
That glow'd incessant in the whirling fog
Of sleepy dust that courts the ground in vain.
The Sabbath bells alarm the slumbering dead
With irreligious peals ; old Silence flies
From all her hallow'd haunts, and hides her head
In the brute dumbness of o'ergorged excess :—
Talk not of Hecatombs, imperial feasts,
Or antique feats of Roman gluttony,
For every alehouse is a temple now,
And flocks and herds but half suffice to stay
The popular maw.—Not sapient Egypt's god,
The lowing Apis, had escaped the knife,
Had slavish Egypt ever claim'd the right

Of unbought suffrage and election free
Who dare deny—that beast, and fish, and fowl
Were made for man? Calves, sheep, and oxen, slain
In freedom's cause, by freemen are devour'd—
A feller fate attends the generous steed—
Outworn with toil, he gluts a freeman's cur

But Leonard—and the gentle Susan? Where
Walk they the while? Oft, when the rafter'd hall
Shook with the jovial laugh of loyalty,
Till each grim ancestor and grandam fair,
That on the smokey canvass smiled for aye,
In multiplied confusion roll'd around,
Would Leonard steal into the quiet air
Of pensive Night, Love's trusty confidante,
To meet his Susan on the silent hill,
And silent sit beneath the silent moon,
His hand laid lightly on his Susan's palm,
While thousand, thousand voices, heard afar,
Were soft as murmurs of the distant ocean—
Solemn and soft—and yet a weary sound
To her, who knew her parent's heart estranged
From him she long'd to call her second sire,
For Susan's father, reckless of her tears,
Of ancient neighbourhood, and deeds of love
Too natural to call for gratitude—
Blind to the pleadings of the meek, sad eyes
Of his child's mother, and his only child—
Had pledged his voice, and purse, and utmost power
To his friend's rival—whether borne away
By the loud torrent of the popular cry,
That universal voucher, for whose truth

No man can vouch—or vex'd by wounded pride
For prudent counsel by his friend refused,
Or by congenial baseness, and the bent
And instinct of an earthy, purblind spirit
That hated honour, as a darkling fiend
Detests the sun, to kindred baseness drawn—
My Muse, unversed in vileness, not reveals

Fearful the perils that beset our youth,
But are there none that lie in wait for age ?
Is not the sight, whose erring faith mistakes
An exhalation for a guiding star,
Better than total blindness ? Good it were
To be a Persian, and adore the sun
At morn and eve—or deem the changeful moon
Imperial arbitress of fickle fate,
To hail the day-dawn as a visible God,
Or, trembling, think the terrible vast sea
A living Godhead in a wrathful mood,
Rather than dwell within the gaol of sense,
To see no God in all the beauteous world—
To feel no God in man ——

     'Twas sad to mark
The passive Susan pace the public way ;
Her meek, obedient head with weight oppress'd
Of gaudy colours, that but ill became
Her pale fair cheek—to hear her soft low voice
Reluctant task'd to warble scurril rhymes,
Set by some ale-bench Pindar to such tunes
As carmen whistle. Worse it was to find
The Nabob and his train of Bacchanals

Establish'd in her home; but worst to see
Her Leonard welcomed with such courtesy
As courtiers use to men they hate and fear.

In vain the eulogists of good old times
Upheld the good old cause. New wealth prevail'd
And Leonard's sire, the lavish contest past,
Found he had fell'd his ancient oaks in vain,
In vain had pawn'd his green, ancestral fields
Bereft his son of just and lineal hopes,
Quench'd the grey vigour of his kindly age
With loyal draughts, and joyless nights of noise
In vain. Indignant he is doom'd to hear
The upstart's triumph clamouring at his doors—
And finds—the sole reward of thousands spent
For Church and King—the prudent world's contempt,
Unspotted honour, and a shatter'd frame,
A broken fortune, and a broken heart

Sad change for Leonard—to no gainful art
Or science bred, untaught to bow his way
Through servile crowds, to fix the flitting eye
Of selfish patronage, or cling secure
To the huge timbers of the rotting state
A battening barnacle, by sloth retain'd,
And nourish'd by decay. His wants, though few,
Were yet refined, and he had known the bliss
Of leisure, which is truest liberty.
And—cruel fate—the time is now fulfill'd,
The year, the month, the long expected day
Of expectation, which had look'd so fair
In the dim brightness of futurity—

The very day prefixed to shake the tower
Of the old ivied church with wedding peals,
When Susan should have trod the church-way path
A blushing bride The weary week past o'er,
And Leonard, in the melancholy hall,
Sat listless, gazing on the naked walls,
And bare, cold floors—for greedy law had stripp'd
The antique mansion of its tapestry,
And Vandal officers had laid their hands
On musty relics of the olden time,
On smokey pedigrees, and antlers vast
Of stags, that fell ere the great Baron fought
At Agincourt; brown bills in rusty ranks,
Primeval guns, of formidable length,
With stubborn matchlocks—all immovable,
Fragments of centuries past, not worth a doit—
But precious ever, and twice precious now,
When all the glory, bounty, wealth, and power
Derived from dark imaginative days,
Was clean departed from the honour'd line—
Say rather, vanish'd from the realm of chance,
To be for aye a thought, a deathless truth
A thing of monumental memory

" 'Tis a fair show a goodly bridal-bower,
Yon grim officials too! attendance meet
To grace a marriage feast " Thus Leonard spake,
And could have laugh'd in downright agony,
But check'd his soul, and almost thought he bore
His grief most patiently; for sorrow seem'd
Reproachful to his father. Mute he sat,
Culling old saws and comfortable texts,

To cheer the old man's desolate heart, and still
Rejecting all, when lo! a message came,
An instant summons from his Susan's sire
Like one lone wandering on a perilous moor,
That hears a voice in darkness, and proceeds,
In desperate haste, to meet or friend or foe,
Regardless whether—Leonard hurried forth
To meet his doom   A little gloomy hope,
Much like despair, was kindled in his eye,
And made his heart beat audible and hard.
The faint alarm had caught his father's view,
As silently he clasp'd his palsied hand;
The old man shook his head with such a smile
As had no comfort in t.

      With louring looks,
And a proud menial's scanted courtesy,
Was Leonard usher'd to the well-known room
Vocal so oft with Susan's melody,
And gladden'd with her smile. 'Tis double woe,
The woe that comes where joy was sweetest found
There sat the parents of his wife betroth'd,
Dear as his own, in happier days, and call'd
By the same filial names   The mother meek,
With sad o'ercharged eyes that dare not weep,
Obey'd the mandate of her husband's hand,
And hastily, without a word, withdrew,
Casting on Leonard one mute pleading glance,
That said—' Remember, he is Susan's father—
Though your's he will not be '—Long pause ensued—
At length the stern man spake · " Young Sir," said he,
" I have an irksome duty to perform,
But 'tis a duty that I owe my child.

Few words are best—my daughter is not for you—
My reasons need no tongue to plead for them—
Urge not my promise—you are not the youth
To whom my word was given—I pledged the girl
To the inheritor of my friend's estate,
Not to the heir of my foe's beggary."
Big-hearted Leonard neither dropt a tear,
Nor spake reproachful word, more grieved to find
A soul so base in form so long revered,
Than for the signet set to his despair—
The coward murder of his dying hope,
And the sweet records of young innocent years
Transform'd to shame-envenom'd agony
Yet long he linger'd at the gate, and raised
To Susan's chamber window a long look
Of resignation deep—a long farewell;
But she was nowhere to be seen; and yet,
He fondly dream'd—what will not lovers dream?—
He heard her sigh, and leant a listening ear
To hear her sigh once more.—Full well he knew,
Though nought distrusting Susan's simple faith,
His claim annull'd—his suit by her forbidden
Not all the sophistry of love, though urged
With eloquence divine, and looks of warmth
To thaw the "chaste and consecrated snow
On Dian's bosom, could induce the maid
To wave obedience, or make head against
The strong religion of her filial fear
So, hopeless—purposeless, he loiter'd home,
If home it could be call'd—begarrison'd
With portly bailiffs, and by duns besieged,
Keen-eyed solicitors, and purple hosts,

And sallow usurers—miscreants, that grow fat,
On general run—bills mis-spelt, as long
As his old father's boasted pedigree
Proud Leonard felt it shame, a burning shame,
To waste a sigh upon his personal grief
Amid the helpless downfall   Nought he told,
His father nought inquired, for all was known
Without the painful index of sad speech.
They talk'd of things long past—of better times,
And seem'd as they were merry. 'Twas the last,
The saddest night beneath the ancient roof—
The next beheld them inmates of a gaol—
And gaol-bird was the word that Susan heard,
Whenever Leonard or his sire was named

 There is no man can love as woman loves,
With such a holy, pure, and patient fire,
Or Susan had gone mad —She pray'd, and wept,
And wept, and pray'd—but never look'd reproach
To him, for whose degenerate soul she pray'd—
And pray d she might not scorn him, might not hate
The author of her being. Though no word—
No brief adieu—had closed the failing eyes
Of her departing hope—for every port
And inlet to her home was closed, and none
Dared name her lover, yet firm faith survived,
The strong assurance of a vow enroll'd
In heaven, and her own wise innocence
Forbade suspicion of her Leonard's truth,
And bade her live, though sure a blessed thing
For her it were to die. What life was hers !
Hard-eyed rebuke, and wrath and ribald scorn,

Solicitation of a mother's tears,
And the perpetual siege of fancies fair
Reflected from old days of happiness,
With Babel dissonance her heart assailing.
Made misery many-faced—a hideous dream—
A monster multiform—a dizzy round
Of aye-revolving aspects—woeful all
Sweet Susan ever was a lowly maid,
Unpractised in the arts of maiden scorn;
Yet she could teach " her sorrow to be proud,"
And walk the earth in virgin majesty,
As one who owed no homage to its rules,
No tribute to its faithless flattery.
She loved her silent, solitary woe,
And thought, poor soul! all nature sympathized
With her lone sorrow Every playful breeze
That dallied with the moonlight on the leaves,
Sung mournful solace to her wounded spirit,
As if it were indeed a mournful sound,
Mournfully kind The gladsome nightingale,
That finds the day too short for half her bliss,
And warbles on, when all the tuneful grove
Is silent as the music of the spheres,
Sounded to her like wakeful melancholy
Dwelling on themes of old departed joy
The nightingale grew dumb—the cuckoo fled—
And broad-eyed Summer glared on hill and plain—
And still no word. Was Leonard dead, or flown
Before the swallow? Doth he dwell forlorn
As the last primrose in the shadowy glade,
That bloom'd too late, and must too soon decline?
The birds are silent, and the shallow brook

Is hardly heard beneath the dark, dark weight
Of over-roofing boughs? And is he gone—
Gone like the riotous waters of the rill,
That smoking, gleaming, whitening on their way,
Display'd an earth-born Iris to the sun,
And in their beauty and their pride exhaled?
Ah no! He lives, in sunless prison pent,
Watching the death-bed of his prison'd sire,
Who, on low pallet stretch'd, in noisome den,
Scarce wider than a captive lion's cage,
Breathes the mephitic and incarcerate fog
That morn not freshens nor still even cools.
His dosing slumbers broke with clank of chains,
And felons' curses, and the horrid mirth
Of reckless misery. Beside him sat
His once gay consort, squalid now, and lost
To self-respect, with grey dishevell'd locks,
All loosely wrapt in rags of silk array
Her aspect, channell'd with impatient tears,
Now sullen mute, now loud in wordy woe,
Chiding the murmurs of her gasping spouse,
And the meek patience of her boy. 'Twas well
The poor old man heard little, nothing mark'd,
For drowsy death lay heavy at the gates
Of outward sense, and the beleaguered brain
Refused its office. Long he lay, and seem'd
A moving, panting corse, without a mind,
By some foul necromancer's horrid charm
In life detain'd. No word to living soul
He spake, and though he sometimes mutter'd prayers,
His understanding pray'd not Leonard pray'd—
But silent as the voiceless intercourse

Of spirits bodiless—whose every thought
Is adoration. Not in Heaven unmark'd
The mute petition   Sudden as the gleam
Of heavenly visitation, a new light,
A glory settled on the pallid face
Of Leonard's sire   The dull unmeaning eye
Of dotage and disease, in rapture fixt,
Glow'd with a saintly fire. The imprison'd soul,
As rushing gladly to its dungeon doors,
Peer'd out, and look'd abroad—one moment—then
Ecstatic flew. " I am going to leave thee, boy—
I thought to leave thee in far other plight—
But that which is, must be   Unseemly 'twere
To see a dying father claim his son's
Forgiveness—else might I implore of thee
To spare thy foolish father's memory—
The world will deal ungently with my name,
But, Leonard, never let thy heart consent
To the blind, coward, malice of the crowd—
And if the prayer of thy father's spirit
Be heard in Paradise, my soul shall pray,
Even at the foot of the Almighty's throne,
For thy best welfare   Good it is that thou
Hast been afflicted in thy lusty youth,
So happier days shall close thine honour'd age—
And, dear my child, I am in haste to Heaven,
My sin is pardon'd, and a mystic robe
Of woof celestial decks my better part
But my poor limbs—far from the reverend dust
Of my dead ancestry—without a chaunt,
Hatchment, or hearse, or green memorial sprigs
Of shiver'd box-wood, and sweet rosemary,

Must soon be earth'd up in a vulgar grave
The hireling shepherd of this wretched fold
Will hurry o'er his ill-paid task of prayer—
And I shall be forgot   But when the smile
Of Fortune shall repay thy honest toil,
Restore thy father's relics to the home
Of thy forefathers' bones.   Thy mother—know
She is thy mother, and thy father's wife.
O God, receive my spirit!"   Thus he spake—
Clasp'd his son's hand—and died without a groan
Did Leonard weep?   Oh, no; he knew too well
The selfish baseness of a private woe—
He shed no tear upon the barren grave,
But cast a long, sad, yearning look to Heaven,
And thought of Susan and his sainted sire
There is a spell in patient filial love,
Can charm the deafest and the hardest heart,
And e'en relax the gripe of hungry law.
So the bleak mercy of a liberal age,
Dismiss'd poor Leonard, and his mother, mark'd
With branded and convicted poverty,
From the ungenial refuge of a gaol
Into the general air.

                'Tis sweet to see
The day-dawn creeping gradual o'er the sky
The silent sun at noon is bright and fair,
And the calm eve is lovely; but 'tis sad
To sink at eve on the dark dewy turf,
And feel that none in all the countless host
Of glimmering stars beholds one little spot,
One humble home of thine.   The vast void sky,

In all its trackless leagues of azure light,
Has not one breath of comfort for the wretch
Whom houseless penury enfranchises,
A brother freeman of the midnight owl,
A sworn acquaintance of the howling winds
And flaggy-pinion'd rain   Now Leonard leaves
The prison gates ;—but whither will he go ?
Must he the high-born, high-soul'd youth, implore
The stinted kindness of offended kin—
Crave pardon for the deadly sin of need
And wrench from shame, not love, a pittance less
Than goes to feed the hounds ?   This he must do
Or eat the bread of loathsome beggary,
For though he did not scorn the honest plough
He knew not how to guide it.   Rustic churls
Bemock'd his threadbare, pale gentility,
And would not grant him leave to toil for hire
Oh, cruel fate !—his spirit stoop'd to beg
A shelter for his mother—'Twas refused.
No matter—There was kindness in the clouds
And son and mother lay secure, beneath
The sylvan roof of charitable boughs
The Lady proudest of the proud, forgot
Her in-bred pride, and wept consoling tears,
And praying—pour'd a blessing on her child

There is more mercy in the merciful God
Than e'er inhabited the pregnant eyes
Of men, who waste unprofitable tears
For all imaginable woes, and leave
The poor uncomforted, to wail their own.
There came a kinsman from a foreign land,

O'erfraught with wealth,—whose British heart, unspoil'd
Had stood the siege of Oriental suns,
And the due sap of all-transmuting gold—
A rich good man —He blamed the tardy winds
Which would not let him flee his old kind coz
From durance vile of helpless poverty;
But still the son survived—the widow'd wife
Still drew her woeful breath—and he had power
To call the orphan to a friendly home—
To bid the widow wear her comely weeds
Beside a plenteous and a smiling board
Few days transpired, and Leonard was again
The heir of thousands—the undoubted lord
Of his paternal acres, all redeem'd
The ancient pictures re-assumed their place
In the old smoky hall—the antique arms
In dusty state resumed their dusk repose.
The blanching trophies, and the furry spoils
Of many an oft-related, endless chace,
Found their due station, while the worn-out steeds,
Repurchased, roam'd the venerable park,
From vilest drudgery freed   The hallow'd bones
Of the late lord, unearth'd, were laid in state
With old, ancestral, lordly rottenness;
And if the pride of earth be known in Heav'n,
Earth's noblest pride—then Leonard's Angel sire
Look'd down exultant on his marble tomb,
And blest his only child

       And shall no drop
Of all this blessing comfort Susan's soul?
Right sorry now, I ween, her sordid sire
For his o'er prudent haste, and breach of faith.—

He saw his daughter's beauty marr'd with tears,
Her soul benumb'd with dull continuous woe,
And a strange wildness in her sad, soft eye,
That rather told of visionary gleams,
And silent commerce with the viewless world,
Than aught which man may love   If e'er she spake,
Her voice was hollow as the moaning wind,
An echo of despair   Yet she would sing
Throughout the long hours of the frosty night
It would have wrung your very heart to hear her—
She sang so like a ghost   " Will the proud youth,"
Thus, measuring other natures by his own,
Her father thought—" Will Leonard love her still?
Will the large-acred heir, whom late I spurn'd,
Accept my child—when all her bloom is fled—
Her eye no longer bright—and her sweet wits
By sorrow crazed? I did him grievous wrong—
And will he sue me for my wither'd rose
And give the glory of his ancient name—
The lusty verdure of his years, and all
His hopes on earth, to a poor moonstruck maid,
The daughter of his father's enemy?"
Base, slanderous fears! For Leonard's love was strong
Beyond the might of mutability.
No rash impatience of the youthful blood,
No sudden liking of enamour'd sense,
His vow had prompted—and no change of hue,
Nor loss of lively cheer, the work of woe,
Could shake his truth   I need not say—how soon
His suit renew'd—nor with what faint excuse
By Susan's sire admitted —Oh, blind haste!—
Of unadvised bliss—that came so late,

And wrought its tyrannous effect so soon—
For sorrow had become the element,
The pulse, the sustenance of Susan's soul,
And sudden joy smote like the fire of Heaven,
That, while it brightens, slays. A hectic flush,
Death's crimson banner, cross'd her marble cheek—
And it was pale again —The strife was past—
She lies, a virgin corse, in Leonard's arms —

He saw her shrouded relics laid to rest
In his ancestral sepulchre. That done,
He was a wanderer long in foreign lands
But when the greenness of his agony
Was sere with age, the hoary man return'd:
And after some few years in virtue spent,
He died.—His bones repose in Susan's grave,
And he is with her, in the land where love,
Immortal and unstain'd, is all in all

ALBUM VERSES

As dark hair straggling o'er a snow-white breast,
Or the light tracks by fairy feet imprest,
Or those which tremulous music would indite
In the pure ether of a summer's night,
If music's course were palpable to sight,—
So fine, in sable tinct and sinuous grace,
The meaning lines which female fingers trace.

Well then may I, whose characters are quaint
As antique legend of a monkish saint,
As hieroglyphic of the wise Egyptian,
Or prentice-posing doctor's learn'd prescription;
As Runic, Coptic, Chaldee, Erse, or Oggham,
Or schoolboy's tasks, for which their masters flog 'em;
As hand of cooks, by love impelled to scrawl,
Or hand of Bishops, which is worst of all,—
Well may I view the argent field with fear,
And all the soft memorials treasured here,
When ask'd by one to whom I can't say nay,
My poor poetic mite of verse to pay,
When bid the melody of song to garble,
Mix hemp with finest flax, and brick with marble
I own I like to see my works in print,—
The page looks knowing, though there's nothing in't,—

But still a thought shews neatest, to my mind,
In well-bound Album penn'd by maiden kind
So smooth each well-turn'd distitch seems to flow,
So bright appears each ardent thought to glow.
So close the epithets in front adhere
To their o'ertopping subjects in the rear,
While, like tall Captains, leading each his column,
As Ensigns spruce, and like Drum-Major's solemn,
In single file the capitals aspire,
Proud of their comely shape and trim attire
We think our thoughts so very fine are grown,
We scarce can think they ever were our own
But how can partial judgment ere be bribed
By halting rhymes in uncouth text inscribed?
Or who'll admire me when, poor barren elf,
I scarce, with all my pains, admire myself?

In eastern tales we read, how, in one night,
A gorgeous palace grew by magic might,
A solid pile of Iris-tinted light.
Whate'er of beautiful or strange, the deep,
Unmoved by winds, and hush'd in endless sleep,
In its abysmal waters held a fee,
Or the dark earth's infernal treasury,
Withheld from mortal touch, and mortal view,
Spontaneous in that wondrous fabric grew
As soft and silent as the falling dew,
It came by strong behest of wizard power,
Nor broke the stillness of the darksome hour
At once mature its radiant domes it rears
'Mid groves of spice and incense, odorous tears
Dropping from hoary trunks, that tell of distant years,

As if a weary age had passed away
In time-forgetting sleep since yesterday
There the dark cypress waved its lofty spire
By walls of ice, and battlements of fire,
And where the mighty banian's "echoing shade"
Spreads far and wide its verdurous colonnade,
The silver portals sent their lucid streams
Adown the umbrageous aisles in lengthen'd beams
The fading hues, so fair, so fleet, alas!
That o'er the cheek of eve like blushes pass
In unabating beauty, here were blended,
Unchanged to last till earth itself were ended
Now, strange to say, this work of mystic art,
The old world's wonder, stored in every part
With every idol of a wanton heart,—
From artist's negligence, or art's defect,
Or some close purpose of the architect,
One window had, unfinish'd, unadorn'd,
An uncouth gap, forgot, or shunn'd, or scorn'd;
A yawning void deform'd the gayest bower
That e'er receiv'd a royal paramour,
And stranger still, not all the flowery groves
That wav'd around, nor all the fair alcoves,
Elaborate pride of oriental loves,
Nor radiant splendours that outshone the skies,
From that unsightly blank could screen the critic eyes.
It grew the talk of all who loved to wonder,
It help'd the crowd to stare, the wise to blunder,—
The magic beauties ne'er perplex'd their soul,
But all were gravell'd with that frightful hole
Wild is the tale, but such in fact we find
The course and current of the general mind.

So fairest things, unnumbered and unnoted,
Pass with the hour while rare defects are quoted—
The timeless frost that in their cradle nips,
The babes of April, or one short eclipse,
One blighting meteor's momentary blaze,
Outlast in fame an age of sunny days

So gentle lady—may I freely call thee
My gentle friend—it happy may befal thee.
When this fair volume. like an honoured face,
Or holy tomb of Saint or Martyr slain,
In Truth's defence, or virgin void of stain,
With gems of verse from many a region brought,
Shall gleam effulgent with untainted thought,
And each soft hand that loves to rest in thine,
With dear memorial decks the beauteous shrine,
Then the wild words, that like bewildered chimes
Limp into tune, and stumble upon rhymes,
And these rude characters, the meet apparel,
Of the strange fancies of my old-world carol,
Shall oft detain the eye that heedless strays,
O'er the smooth page, which calls for nought but praise.
Where all s so good, the critic senses starve all,
But lines like mine will suit them to a marvel.
Nay sometimes many a softer gaze beguile,
And change a winning to a wondering smile,
May light the orbs of darkly-rolling eyes,
With the wide brilliance of a gay surprize,
May prompt some voice in tones acute to ask,
To whom was given, or who usurp'd the task,
To set, 'mid famous Bards' melodious strains,
The product of his own fantastic brains?

What strange acquaintance of a maiden fair,
Could plant a thistle in her prim parterre?
Then may'st thou say—but say whate'er you choose,
Or if you will, confess yourself my muse

AN OLD MAN'S WISH.

I have lived, and I have loved,
　Have lived and loved in vain;
Some joys, and many woes have proved,
　That may not be again;
My heart is cold, my eye is sere.
Joy wins no smile, and grief no tear

Fain would I hope, if hope I could,
　If sure to be deceived,
There's comfort in a thought of good,
　Tho' 'tis not quite believed—
For sweet is hope's wild warbled air,
But—Oh—its echo is despair

THE SABBATH-DAY'S CHILD.

TO ELIZABETH,

INFANT DAUGHTER OF THE REV SIR RICHARD
FLEMING, BART.

PURE, precious drop of dear mortality,
Untainted fount of life's meandering stream,
Whose innocence is like the dewy beam
Of morn, a visible reality,
Holy and quiet as a hermit's dream·
Unconscious witness to the promised birth
Of perfect good, that may not grow on earth,
Nor be computed by the worldly worth
And stated limits of morality,
Fair type and pledge of full redemption given,
Through him that saith " Of such is the kingdom of
    Heaven."—

Sweet infant, whom thy brooding parents love
For what thou art, and what they hope to see thee,
Unhallow'd sprites and earth-born phantoms flee thee,
Thy soft simplicity, a hovering dove,
That still keeps watch, from blight and bane to free thee,

With its weak wings, in peaceful care outspread,
Fanning invisibly thy pillow'd head,
Strikes evil powers with reverential dread,
Beyond the sulphurous bolts of fabled Jove,
Or whatsoe'er of Amulet or charm
Fond Ignorance devised to save poor souls from harm.

To see thee sleeping on thy mother's breast,
It were indeed a lovely sight to see—
Who would believe that restless sin can be
In the same world that holds such sinless rest?
Happy art thou, sweet babe, and happy she
Whose voice alone can still thy baby cries,
Now still itself, Yet pensive smiles, and sighs,
And the mute meanings of a mother's eyes
Declare her thinking, deep felicity
A bliss, my babe, how much unlike to thine,
Mingled with earthly fears, yet cheer'd with hope divine.

Thou breathing image of the life of Nature!
Say rather, image of a happy death—
For the vicissitudes of vital breath,
Of all infirmity the slave and creature,
That by the act of being perisheth,
Are far unlike that slumber's perfect peace
Which seems too absolute and pure to cease,
Or suffer diminution, or increase,
Or change of hue, proportion, shape, or feature,
A calm, it seems, that is not, shall not be,
Save in the silent depths of calm eternity.

A star reflected in a dimpling rill
That moves so slow it hardly moves at all,
The shadow of a white-robed waterfall,
Seen in the lake beneath when all is still,
A wandering cloud, that with its fleecy pall
Whitens the lustre of an autumn moon,
A sudden breeze that cools the cheek of noon,
Not mark'd till miss'd—so soft it fades, and soon—
Whatever else the fond inventive skill
Of Fancy may suggest, can not supply
Fit semblance of the sleeping life of infancy

Calm art thou as the blessed Sabbath eve,
The blessed Sabbath eve when thou wast born;
Yet sprightly as a summer Sabbath morn,
When surely 'twere a thing unmeet to grieve;
When ribbons gay the village maids adorn,
And Sabbath music, on the swelling gales,
Floats to the farthest nooks of winding vales,
And summons all the beauty of the dales
Fit music this a stranger to receive,
And, lovely child, it rung to welcome thee,
Announcing thy approach with gladsome minstrelsy.

So be thy life—a gentle Sabbath, pure
From worthless strivings of the work-day earth
May time make good the omen of thy birth,
Nor worldly care thy growing thoughts immure,
Nor hard-eyed thrift usurp the throne of mirth
On thy smooth brow. And though fast-coming years

Must bring their fated dower of maiden fears,
Of timid blushes, sighs, and fertile tears,
Soft sorrow's sweetest offspring, and her cure ,
May every day of thine be good and holy,
And thy worst woe a pensive sabbath melancholy

MAY, 1832.

Is this the merry May of tale and song ?
Chill breathes the North—the sky looks chilly blue,
The waters wear a cold and iron hue,
Or wrinkle as the crisp wave creeps along,
Much like an ague fit   The starry throng
Of flowrets droop o'erdone with drenching dew,
Or close their leaves at noon, as if they knew,
And felt in helpless wrath, the season's wrong.
Yet in the half-clad woods the busy birds
Chirping with all their might to keep them warm ;
The young hare flitting from her ferney form ;
The vernal lowing of the amorous herds ,
And swelling buds impatient of delay,
Declare it should be, tho' it is not, May.

ISABEL.

Where dwells she now? That life of joy
That seem'd as Time could ne'er destroy,
Nor frail infectious sense alloy,
Its self-derived and self-sufficing gladness?
Abides she in the bounds of space,
Or like a thought, a moment's grace,
Is she escaped from time and place,
The dull arithmetic of prison'd sadness?

May she behold this spot of earth,
This human home, that saw her birth
Her baby tears, her infant mirth,
The first quick stirrings of her human mind?
May she return to watch the flowers
She planted last in fairy bowers?—
They freshen yet with summer showers,
And gambol with the frolic summer wind.

That lovely form, that face so bright,
That changeful image of delight,
May it no more to waking sight,
Or spiritual ken, in very truth appear?
That visible shape, that kind warm glow—
That all that Heaven vouchsafed to shew—
'Tis gone 'Twas all our sense could know,
Of her we loved, whom yet we hold so dear.

The world hath lost the antique faith,
In shade and spectre—warning wraith,
That wander'd forth to blast, and scathe
Poor earth-clogg'd, dark humanity.
No more the mystic craft of hell,
In cavern murk, with impious spell,
Evokes the naked souls that dwell,
In uncreated night's inanity

'Tis well that creed is out of date,
And men have found, at last, though late,
That loathing fear, and fearful hate,
And rankling vengeance, all are cruel liars,
And all the doctrine that they teach
Of ghosts that roam when owlets screetch,
Is but the false, and fatal speech,
Of guilty terrors, or of worse desires

But is there not a charm in love,
To call thy spirit from above ?
Oh—had I pinions like a dove,
Were I like thee, a pure enfranchised soul,
Then might I see thee as thou art,
Receive thee in my inmost heart,
But can it be ? She has no part,
In all she loved beneath the steadfast pole

REPLY

Ah—well it is—since she is gone,
    She can return no more,
To see the face so dim and wan,
    That was so warm before

Familiar things would all seem strange,
    And pleasure past be woe;
A record sad of ceaseless change,
    Is all the world below

The very hills, they are not now,
    The hills which once they were,
They change as we are changed, or how
    Could we the burden bear?

Ye deem the dead are ashy pale,
    Cold denizens of gloom—
But what are ye, who live to wail,
    And weep upon their tomb?

She passed away, like morning dew,
    Before the sun was high,
So brief her time, she scarcely knew.
    The meaning of a sigh

As round the rose its soft perfume,
    Sweet love around her floated,
Admired she grew—while mortal doom
    Crept on, unfear'd, unnoted

Love was her guardian Angel here,
    But love to death resign'd her,
Tho' love was kind, why should we fear,
    But holy death is kinder?

FRAGMENT.

What is the life of man? From first to last,
Its only substance, the unbeing past!
The infant smiling in its sleep must dream
Of something past, before the vexing beam
Of daylight smote the unaccustom'd eye,
Ere the faint mother heard its first faint cry,
Lull'd in its rocking nest, it seeks in vain,
For what has been, and ne'er can be again.
The child, through every maze of wakening lore,
Hunts the huge shadow of what was before,
Sees his old toys in misty phantoms glide,
'Twixt hope and dim oblivion magnified;
As oft on misty hills huge spectres run,
And stalk gigantic from the setting sun—
Still urging onward to the world unseen,
Yet wishing, hoping nought, but what has been
But what *has* been? But *how*, and *when*, and *where*?
Was there a time, when, wandering in the air,
The living spark existed, yet unnam'd,
Unfixt, unqualitied, unlaw'd, unclaim'd,
A drop of being, in the infinite sea,
Whose only duty, essence, was to be?
Or must we seek it, where all things we find,
In the sole purpose of creative mind—

Or did it serve, in form of stone or plant,
Or weaving worm, or the wise politic ant,
Its weary bondage—ere the moment came,
When the weak spark should mount into a flame?

TO ———

I love thee—none may know how well,
And yet—I would not have thee love me,
To thy good heart 'twere very hell,
To love me dear, and not approve me

Whate'er thou lov'st it is not *thine*,
But 'tis *thyself*—then sad it were, love.
If thou for every sin of mine,
Should weep, repent, mayhap, despair—love

Then love me not—thou can'st not scorn;
And mind—I do not bid thee hate me,
And if I die, oh, do not mourn,
But if I live, *do* new *create* me

EXPERTUS LOQUITUR.

" 'TIS SAD EXPERIENCE SPEAKS."

There never was a blessing, or a curse,
So sweet, so cruel, as a knack of verse.
When the smug stripling finds the way to rhyme,
Glad as the wild bee 'mid a bed of thyme.
With dulcet murmuring, all a summer's day,
With many a scrap of many a purposed lay—
Fitful, yet gentle, as a summer wind,
Pleased with himself, and pleased with all mankind,
Sure of the praise which partial friends bestow,
He breathes in bliss, if bliss may be below

Pass some few years—and see where all will end.
The hireling scribe, estranged from every friend,
Or if one friend remain, 'tis one so brave,
He will not quit the wreck he cannot save,
The good man's pity, and the proud man's scorn,
The Muse's vagabond, he roams forlorn—
Thought, wit, invention, tenderness have left him,
All wealth of mind, save empty rhyme, bereft him—
Yet write he must, for still he needs must eat—
Retail fantastic sorrow by the sheet—
Sing in his garret of the flowery grove,
And pinched with hunger, wail the woes of love—
Oh may all Christian souls while yet 'tis time,
Renounce the World, the Flesh, the Devil, and Rhyme

A FAREWELL.

NOT ORIGINALLY WRITTEN IN THE AUTHOR'S
OWN NAME

Sweet vale tho' I must leave
   Thy green hills and thy waters,
Nor sing again at eve,
   To charm thy winsome daughters,
Yet I shall fondly think of thee,
And thy fair maids will think of me,
           When I am far away

I'll think of thee, but not as men
   Who vex their souls with thinking,
With feverish thirst, the reeky fen,
   Of sluggard memory drinking,
Nor shall thy maidens fair and free,
With ought of sadness think of me,
           When I am far away

The fairy lake, tho' still it seems,
   Is evermore a-flowing,
A moment ends the silvery gleams
   That flash as we are rowing
Yet that smooth lake, as smooth shall flow,
And light oars flash, when gay youths' row,
           When I am far away.

So may the tide of virgin life,
   As smooth, as quick, as clear,
If e'er, in momentary strife,
   It dimple with a tear,
As soon regain its sweet repose—
And rest in peace, because it flows,
               For ever on its way

HORACE BOOK I., ODE 38

" Persicos odi, puer, apparatus "

Nay, nay, my boy—'tis not for me,
This studious pomp of eastern luxury·
Give me no various garlands—fine
        With linden twine,
Nor seek, where latest lingering blows
        The solitary rose.
Earnest I beg—add not with toilsome pain,
One far sought blossom to the myrtle plain,
For sure, the fragrant myrtle bough
        Looks seemliest on thy brow;
Nor me mis-seems, while, underneath the vine,
Close interweaved, I quaff the rosy wine.

DEATH

Oh! weep not for the happy dead,
Your tears reproach the Lord ;
To him her virgin soul was wed,
And strong in love, to him she fled
From mother's house, and parent's smiling board.

Alas! we cannot choose but weep,
For we are sore bereaven ,
And all of her that we can keep
Is but an image on the deep,
The deep calm soul, that shews reflected heaven.

If angel spirits aught may know
Of hearts they left behind,
If e er they cast a look below,
The sacrifice of pious woe
May yield a tender joy, even to the angel kind

INANIA MUNERA.

Ah! why should pity wet my bier,
And give my corse her tardy tear?
And the same eye that coldly slew me,
With tears untimely warm bedew me?
Alas! for harm is fleet as wind,
And healing ever lags behind

Perhaps, when life well nigh is spent,
She'll faintly smile a sad consent,—
And, just before she sees me die,
Will leave a kind repentant sigh
For sigh of ruth—Oh, wayward fate!—
Will ever come—and come too late

She cannot undo what is done;
For, if a smile were like the sun,
And sighs more sweet than gales that creep
O'er rosy beds where fairies sleep,
And every tear like summer rain
To thirsty fields—'twere all in vain.

For never sun so bright was seen
Could make a leaf that's sere be green,
Nor spicy gale, nor April shower,
Restore to bloom a faded flower.
Thus sun, and wind, and balmy rain,
And smiles, and sighs, and tears, are vain

TO MY UNKNOWN SISTER-IN-LAW

Mary, our eyes are strangers, but our hearts
Are knit in active sympathy of love
For one, whom love of thee hath sanctified
The lawless wanderings of his youthful thought
For thee he curbed—for thee assumed the yoke
Of humble duty—bade the world farewell
With all its vanities of prose and rhyme—
The secular pride of startling eloquence,
The victory of wordy warfare—all
That charm'd his soul in academic bowers

Not small the struggle and the sacrifice,
When men of many fancies, daring minds,
That for the substance and the form of truth
Delight to fathom their own bottomless deeps,
Submit to authorised creeds and positive laws—
Appointed rites and ceremonial duty—
And he the pastor of a christian flock.
That is no hireling drudging at a task
Ungenial, nor intruder, bold and proud
Unhallow'd, unanointed, self-inspired,
Of all men hath the greatest need of love,
To keep his thoughts, his hopes, his heart at home —
If human speech have aught of holiness,
'Tis all compris'd in three thrice-holy names

Of Father, Husband, Minister of Christ :—
Or if a holier title yet there be,
That name is Mother
                    Dearest sister, I
Am one of whom thou doubtless hast heard much—
Not always well.—My name too oft pronounced
With sighs, despondent sorrow, and reproach,
By lips that fain would praise, and ever bless me
Yet deem not hardly of me   who best know
Most gently censure me,—and who believes
The dark inherent mystery of sin
Doubts not the will and potency of God
To change, invigorate, and purify
The self-condemning heart
                         Good night.—e'en now
Perhaps thou art sleeping by my brother's side,
Or listening gladly to the soft, sweet breath
Of thy dear babe—while I must seek a couch
Lonely, and haunted much by visions strange,
And sore perplexity of roving dreams,
The spectres manifold of murdered hours,—
But yet, good night—good be the night to thee,
And bright the morrow —Once again, good night

P

A MEDLEY

Shall I sing of little rills,
That trickle down the yellow hills
To drive the Fame's water mills?—
Rills, upon whose pebbly brink,
Mountain birds may hop and drink—
Perching with a neck awry—
Darting upwards to the sky—
The artless cunning of their eye—
Then away, away, away—
Up to the clouds that look so grey—
Away away, in the clear blue heaven,
Far o'er the thin mist that beneath is driven—
Now they sink, and now they soar,
Now poised upon the plumy oar—
Do they seek—at brightest noon,
For the light-enveiled moon—
Climbing upwards would they know
Where the stars at morning go—
If I err not—no—no—no—
Soar they high, or skim they low,
Every little bird has still
His heart beside the mountain rill.

What if we have lost the creed,
Which thought the brook a God indeed?

Or a flood of passionate tears,
Inexhaustible by years ?
Or imagined, in the lymph,
The semblance of a virgin nymph,
With panting terror, flying ever,
From hairy Satyr's foul endeavour ?
Hence ! phantoms of a blinded age,
That dream'd of nought but lust and rage,
The echo of a Sabbath bell
Is sweeter in the lonely dell,
Than the quaint fable of the wood-god's lay,
That only warbled to betray.

Ah—never, never may the thought be mine,
Though sung by poets old in song divine,
Which deem'd the pure, and undisturbed sky,
The palace of a tyrant deity—
Which in the thunder, heard a voice of anger,
And ruthless vengeance in the storm's loud clangour,
Which found in every whisper of the woods,
In every moaning of the voiceful floods,
A long record of perishable languish,
Immortal echo of a mortal anguish
  Nay—mine be still,
  The happy, happy faith—
  That in deep silence hymning saith—
  That every little rill,
  And every small bird, trilling joyfully—
Tells a sweet tale of hope, and love, and peace,
  Bidding to cease,
The heart's sharp pangs, aye throbbing woefully

Or shall I sing of happy hours,
Number'd by opening and by closing flowers?
Of smiles, and sighs that give no pain,
And seem as they were heav'd in vain—
Softly heard in leafy bowers,
Blent with the whisper of the vine,
The half-blush of the eglantine,
And the pure sweetness of the jessamine
What is it those sighs confess?
Idle are they, as I guess,
And yet they tell, all is not well —
There is a secret, dim, demurring,
There is a restless spirit stirring,—
Joy itself, the heart o'erloading,
Hath a sense of sad foreboding

Then away to the meadows, where April's swift shadows
 Glide soft o'er the vernal bright patches of green,
Like waves on the ocean, the wheat blades in motion,
 Look blither, and brighter, where sunbeams have been
  So little, little joys on earth,
  Passing gleams of restless mirth—
  Momentary fits of laughter
  Still bequeath a blessing after—
  Flitting by on angel wing—
  And like voices perishing
  At the instant of their birth,
  Never, never, count their worth,
  By the time of their enduring—
  They are gainers in a dearth,
  Pleasant thoughts for age securing—
  Rich deposits, firm ensuring,

Bliss, if bliss below may be,
And a joy for memory

Such themes I sang—and such I fain would sing,
  Oft as the green buds shew the summer near—
But what availeth me to welcome spring,
  When one dull winter is my total year.

When the pure snow-drops couch beneath the snow,
  And storms long tarrying, come too soon at last,
I see the semblance of my private woe,
  And tell it to the dilatory blast.

Yet will I hail the sunbeam as it flies—
  And bid the universal world be glad—
With my brief joy all souls shall sympathise—
  And only I, will all alone be sad

THOUGHTS

Oh, sacred Freedom ! thou that art so fair,
   That all, who once have seen thee, love thee ever—
Thou apparition, that hast been so rare
   That wise men say thou wert embodied never,
And learned sages, doating on their lore,
Say thou hast been, and never shalt be more

When Reason—that whate'er it is, must be—
   Was tangled in the complex web of life,
And Sin, the fruit of that forbidden tree,
   Made human choice an everlasting strife,
Then every Passion, native to the hour,
Claim'd Reason's privilege and Reason's power

Yet some there are, and some that still have been,
   Who feel, and hate, yet cannot cease to feel
The conscious issue of the cause unseen,
   The fate that whirls around the restless wheel—
Some to the stars ascribe the inborn evil,
Some to the Gods, and others to the devil,

To live without a living soul
    To feel the spirit daily pining,
Sinking beneath the base control
    Of mindless chance, itself consigning
To the dull impulse of oppressive time,
To find the guilt without the power of crime.—

Such is the penance, and the meed
    Of thoughts that, boasting to be free,
Spurning the dictates of a practic creed,
    Are tangled with excess of liberty,
Making themselves sole arbiters of right,
Trampling on hallow'd use with proud delight

Perchance they roam in Duty's sacred name,
    Commission'd to erect the world anew—
All worldly ties, all interests they disclaim,
    Sworn votaries of the beautiful and true;
But vainly deem their own device, in sooth,
The very substance of eternal truth

Their duty still is Duty to deny,
    To burst her bonds and cast her cords away·
As some turn rebels for pure loyalty,
    And some, to save the soul, the body slay·
If any law they own, that law decrees,
That sovereign right is born of each man's phantasies

'Twere woe to tell what lamentable wreck
　Such dreams may bring upon the public weal,
If once restraint be broken from the neck
　Of such as grossly think, and fiercely feel,
In whom the noble parts by Nature lent,
Are sway'd and biass'd from their kindly bent.

Thralls of the world, to whom the world affords
　No hope but only this—to toil for food,
And eat that they may toil—vassals of lords
　With slavish minds and tyrant wills endued,
Whose only charity is selfish waste,
Whose brightest honour 'tis, to sin with taste

The master of a slave is never free,
　But still himself the slave of sensual fear —
Woe to mankind—for ever doom'd to be
　The slaves of slaves. The only freedom here
Lives in the spirit that disowns the bands
And dares refuse imperious Fate's commands

From age to age, beneath the base control
　Of servile time, we drudge in sloth or toil;
If hope of freedom fire the indignant soul
　Then follows terror wild, and bloody spoil—
Mad Revolution, like a headlong flood,
O'erwhelms alike the evil and the good

*　　*　　*　　*　　*

ADDRESS

TO CERTAIN GOLD FISHES

Restless forms of living light
Quivering on your lucid wings,
Cheating still the curious sight
With a thousand shadowings,—
Various as the tints of even,
Gorgeous as the hues of heaven,
Reflected on your native streams
In flitting, flashing, billowy gleams!

Harmless warriors, clad in mail
Of silver breastplate, golden scale,—
Mail of Nature's own bestowing,
With peaceful radiance mildly glowing,—
Fleet are ye, as fleetest galley
Or pirate rover sent from Sallee,
Keener than the Tartar's arrow,
Sport ye in your sea so narrow.

Was the sun himself your sire?
Were ye born of vital fire?
Or of the shade of golden flowers,
Such as we fetch from eastern bowers,
To mock this murky clime of ours?

Upwards, downwards, now ye glance,
Weaving many a mazy dance;
Seeming still to grow in size
When ye would elude our eyes—
Pretty creatures! we might deem
Ye were happy as ye seem,—
As gay, as gamesome, and as blithe,
As light, as loving, and as lithe,
As gladly earnest in your play,
As when ye gleam'd in far Cathay,

And yet, since on this hapless earth
There's small sincerity in mirth,
And laughter oft is but an art
To drown the outcry of the heart,
It may be, that your ceaseless gambols,
Your wheelings, dartings, divings, rambles,
Your restless roving round and round
The circuit of your chrystal bound,—
Is but the task of weary pain,
An endless labour, dull and vain,
And while your forms are gaily shining,
Your little lives are inly pining!
Nay—but still I fain would dream
That ye are happy as ye seem,
Deck'd in Oriental pride,
By homely British fire-side.

WHAT I HAVE HEARD.

I've heard the merry voice of spring,
When thousand birds their wild notes fling,
Here and there, and every where,
Stirring the young and lightsome air,—
I've heard the many-sounding seas,
And all their various harmonies —
The tumbling tempest's dismal roar,
On the waste and wreck-strew'd shore—
The howl and the wail of the prison'd waves,
Clamouring in the ancient caves,
Like a stifled pain that asks for pity:—
And I have heard the sea at peace,
When all its fearful noises cease,
Lost in one soft and multitudinous ditty,
Most like the murmur of a far off city:—
Nor less the blither notes I know,
To which the inland waters flow,—
The rush of rocky-bedded rivers,
That madly dash themselves to shivers,
But anon, more prudent growing,
O'er countless pebbles smoothly flowing,
With a dull continuous roar,
Hie they onward, evermore·

To their everlasting tune
When the sun is high at noon,
The little billows, quick and quicker,
Weave their mazes, thick and thicker,
And beneath in dazzling glances,
Labyrinthine lightning dances,
Snaky network intertwining,
With thousand molten colours shining
Mosaic rich with living light,
With rainbow jewels gaily dight—
Such pavement never, well I ween,
Was made, by monarch or magician,
For Arab, or Egyptian queen,
'Tis gorgeous as a prophet's vision,
And I ken the brook, how sweet it tinkles,
As cross the moon-light green it twinkles,
Or heard, not seen, 'mid tangled wood,
Where the soft stock-dove lulls her brood,
With her one note of all most dear—
More soothing to the heart than ear
And well I know the smother'd moan,
Of that low breeze, so small and brief,
It seems a very sigh, whose tone,
Has much of love, but more of grief
I know the sound of distant bells,
Their dying falls and lusty swells,
That music which the wild gale seizes,
And fashions howsoe'er it pleases
And I love the shrill November blast,
That through the brown wood hurries fast,
And strips its old limbs bare at last,
Then whirls the leaves in circling error,

As if instinct with life and terror—
Now bursting out enough to deafen,
The very thunder in the heaven,
Now sinking dolefully and dreary,
Weak as a child with sport a weary.
And after a long night of rain,
When the warm sun comes out again,
I've heard the myriad-voiced rills,
The many tongues, of many hills—
All gushing forth in new-born glory,
Striving each to tell its story—
Yet every little brook is known,
By a voice that is its own,
Each exulting in the glee,
Of its new prosperity

SONNET

All Nature ministers to Hope. The snow
Of sluggard Winter, bedded on the hill,
And the small tinkle of the frozen rill—
The swoln flood's sullen roar, the storms that go
With crash, and howl, and horrid voice of woe,
Making swift passage for their lawless will—
All prophecy of good. The hungry trill
Of the lone birdie, cowering close below
The dripping eaves—it hath a kindly feeling,
And cheers the life that lives for milder hours.
Why, then, since Nature still is busy healing,
And Time, the waster, his own work concealing,
Decks every grave with verdure and with flowers,—
Why should Despair oppress immortal powers?

BY A FRIEND.

I have heard thy sweet voice in the song,
   And listened with delight—
I've seen thee in the glittering throng,
   The fairest mid'st the bright—
I've mark'd thee smile on gallants gay,
   And envied them the lot,
While from the crowd I turn'd away,
   Alone regarded not.

Oh, Lady! it were vain, I own,
   To hope for charms like thine!
The brow that would beseem a crown
   Will frown on love like mine·
That form of light—that heavenly face,
   Those eyes of sweetest hue,
Were form'd some kingly throne to grace,
   And not for me to sue

Yet, though forbidden by despair
   The dream of happier hours—
As once I wreath'd thy sunny hair
   With Summer's brightest flowers—
I'll follow still, with love unseen,
   Thy smile, thy voice's tone,
My heart shall own no other queen,
   But worship thee alone

POIETES APOIETES

No hope have I to live a deathless name,
    A power immortal in the world of mind,
A sun to light with intellectual flame,
    The universal soul of human kind

Not mine the skill in memorable phrase
    The hidden truths of passion to reveal,
To bring to light the intermingling ways,
    By which unconscious motives darkling steal

To show how forms the sentient heart affect,
    How thoughts and feelings mutually combine,
How oft the pure, impassive intellect
    Shares the mischances of his mortal shrine.

Nor can I summons from the dark abyss
    Of time, the spirit of forgotten things,
Bestow unfading life on transient bliss—
    Bid memory live with " healing on its wings "

Oh give a substance to the haunting shades,
    Whose visitation shames the vulgar earth
Before whose light the ray of morning fades,
    And hollow yearning chills the soul of mirth.

I have no charm to renovate the youth
  Of old authentic dictates of the heart,—
To wash the wrinkles from the face of Truth,
  And out of Nature form creative Art

Divinest Poesy!—'tis thine to make
  Age young—youth old—to baffle tyrant Time,
From antique strains the hoary dust to shake,
  And with familiar grace to crown new rhyme

Long have I loved thee—long have loved in vain,
  Yet large the debt my spirit owes to thee,
Thou wreath'd'st my first hours in a rosy chain,
  Rocking the cradle of my infancy.

The lovely images of earth and sky
  From thee I learn'd within my soul to treasure;
And the strong magic of thy minstrelsy
  Charms the world's tempest to a sweet, sad measure

Nor Fortune's spite—nor hopes that once have been—
  Hopes which no power of Fate can give again,—
Not the sad sentence—that my life must wean
  From dear domestic joys—nor all the train

Of pregnant ills—and penitential harms
  That dog the rear of youth unwisely wasted,
Can dim the lustre of thy stainless charms,
  Or sour the sweetness that in thee I tasted.

FROM PETRARCH

Se lamentar augelli, o verdi fronde.

The birds piped mournfully; the dark green leaves
Moved, sweetly trembling, to the summer breeze,—
And deep and low, the lucid rill, that weaves
Its murmuring mazes in the flowery leas,
Warbled along its old monotonies —
Such blended sounds my reckless ear received,
And hearing, heard not.—while my spirit grieved,
Loving its grief and feeding its disease
A mournful strain I conn'd—when she for whom
I vext my soul, because she was conceal'd,
Shone forth on high, to wondering sense reveal'd :—
" Why ever thus," said she, " thy days consume ?
Dying, I live —and when I closed my eyes
They open'd to the light of Paradise. '

REGENERATION.

I NEED a cleansing change within—
My life must once again begin—
New hope I need, and youth renew'd,
And more than human fortitude,—
New faith, new love, and strength to cast
Away the fetters of the past

Ah! why did fabling Poets tell
That Lethe only flows in Hell ?
As if, in truth, there was no river,
Whereby the leper may be clean,
But that which flows, and flows for ever,
And crawls along, unheard, unseen,
Whence brutish spirits, in contagious shoals,
Quaff the dull drench of apathetic souls.

Ah, no ! but Lethe flows aloft
With lulling murmur, kind and soft
As voice which sinners send to heaven
When first they feel their sins forgiven :
Its every drop as bright and clear
As if indeed it were a tear,
Shed by the lovely Magdalen
For him that was despised of men.

It is the only fount of bliss
In all the human wilderness—
It is the true Bethesda—solely
Endued with healing might, and holy —
Not once a year, but evermore—
Not one, but all men to restore

O Fons Blandusiæ, splendidior vitro,
Dulci digne mero, non sine floribus,
Cras donaberis hœdo

— — — — — —

Blandusian spring, more gaily bright,
   In thy never-ceasing birth,
Than gem compact of solar light,
   That, fetter'd long in darksome earth,
Leaps forth to greet a kindred ray—
Thou art worth a Poet's lay

Flowers—them we will not give,—
   Thou hast plenty of thy own,
Little lambkins;—let them live,
   Thou wert loath to hear them moan.
Let them frisk upon thy bourn,
And in thee view the budding horn.

Well I know, an ancient Poet
   Promised thee a kid to-morrow—
I, a Christian Bard, well know it,—
   If he paid it, 'twas thy sorrow —
But he never did the thing
Which he was constrain'd to sing

Poet he, that would have been
   A Christian Poet if he could,—
One that felt far more, I ween,
   Than he ever understood,—
One that only wanted telling
The truth that in his heart was dwelling

Blandusian Fount! I know not thee,
   And learned critics much are troubled,
To find, if yet a stream there be,
   Where, long of yore, thy waters bubbled,
And I could almost wish there were not,
Since all who loved thee dearly are not

The barren rocks are still the same—
   The fertile streams are changing ever,
So, lives, in nature's endless fame,
   The Carthaginian's vain endeavour—
But, Horace, we can only guess
The sweet home of thy happiness

Yet fare thee well, thou lovely spring,
   And never may thy nymphs desert thee,
For while one Bard on earth may sing.
   Not all the powers of earth can hurt thee:
And tho' no lamb to thee we give,
Blest shalt thou be as long as lambkins live

WRITTEN IN JANUARY, 1833

The old year is gone—so uncivil was I,
That I made not a couplet to bid him good bye,
But now that the new year is fairly come in,
Not to bid him a welcome, were surely a sin—
So welcome I bid him, tho' not to myself,
Yet to all who are wealthy in hope or in pelf,
All hearty good fellows to whom life is dear,
I heartily wish you a happy new year
To the man, who is fit to be married, a wife,
And a grave unto him that is tired of life
To my friends, that they may not have much to forgive,
To my foes, that they just may forget that I live,
To my love—that her charms may to her be a blessing,
Tho' to me I confess, they are rather distressing—
For the man of her choice may good fortune await him,
And then—why, I'll try very hard not to hate him.

THE BIRTH-DAY

TO JAMES BRANKER, ESQ

Even as the wise astronomer invents
Zones, colures, cycles, in the trackless sky—
Or as the mariner, whose daring art
Maps out the undistinguishable main
With curious lines, that, to the mind untaught,
Seem all mysterious as a wizard's scheme.
Or the fine traces in a lady's palm,
Interpreted by Egypt's wandering blood,—
So man delights in the wide waste of time,
The tide of moments ebbing as they flow,
To set his land-marks; and recording names,
Pavilions of the pausing memory,
Historic pillars, quaintly sculptured o'er
With hieroglyphics of the heart
      Not least,
In the memorial list of holy times,
Is that permitted epoch of pure mirth—
A good man's birth-day—when the very poor
Pour forth the savings of the stinted meal
To make one hour rejoice in wealth of joy.—
Then long of yore, when duty seem'd to frown,
And love parental wore a brow severe,

And children trembled in their father's eyes,
The sternest sires were not afraid to smile,
And doff'd their honest sage hypocrisy,
Because the birth-day came but once a year.

And those whom fortune, choice, or chance have cast
On the wild billows of the changeful world,
Tho' haply wandering amid Afric sands,
Or wedg'd in thundering straits of "thick-ribb'd ice,"
Or lost in the dark city's wilderness,
Will find their hearts at home, when annual comes
The merry birth-day,—and recall the hours,
The vernal hours, when life itself was bliss,
And every birth-day a new argument
Of hope and pride
      Alas! too oft the day
Remains a hollow cenotaph of Hope,
When Hope is dead and gone. The worst—
The worst of hearts, that hath not ceased to feel,
Grows soft and childish, when the number'd hour
Records the moment of a mother's pain—
When the faint mother lifted first her eyes
To Heaven in thankfulness—then cast them down
Upon her babe in love.—Oh, gracious Heaven!
Thy mighty law—in spite of rebel will,
Spite of all theories of doubting man—
Still rules triumphant through the tribes of life,
Confutes the quirks of calculating pride,
And, o'er the feeblest of all feeble things,
Sheds the strong potency of love divine:
For God is stirring in the mother's heart—
The living God is in her milky breast—

And God's own image, fresh from paradise,
Hallows the helpless form of infancy

   Oh that the God, the same all bounteous Lord
That aids the mother in her agony,
Would save her from the feller pangs, that oft
From love, the sweetest and the holiest love,
Extract all sweetness and all self-esteem,
Making the image of the child beloved
Like a foul phantom, that pollutes the soul,—
A spell, a bondage a continued fear,
A slow consuming fever of the heart,
In sorrow's gloomy creed, almost a sin
Fain would the shame-struck parent tear away
The once glad epoch from the calendar,
The birth-day of the graceless prodigal,
Whose name, forbidden, leaves a blank deform'd
In household records, and familiar feasts.
Breeding sharp envy of that parent's lot
Whose tear was dropp'd upon an infant's grave

   Or if the birth-day bring no thought of shame,
It rarely comes without a drop of woe,
That checks the gay laugh with a sudden sigh
But these are gracious griefs.—For all 'tis good.
Whose taste of goodness is not lost—though sore
May be the thought—to measure back their course
Oft as the birth-day comes
                Wild voyagers.
Launch'd on the perilous sea of human life,
Awhile we paddle by the sunny shores,
The native shores of homely infancy

Young courage, buoyant on the venturous surge,
Taunting the prescience of maternal fear,
Swims light and joyous with the out-bound tide,
That evermore, at stated hour, comes home,
And brings a freight of crimson shells, and weeds,
That mock the things of earth with semblance quaint,
Imperial cradles of purpureal sheen,
And wreathed trumpets, curiously convolved,
Wherein the ocean's mighty harmonies
Serenely murmur in a humming slumber

So childhood passes—but the whistling breeze
Of Time calls shrill, and forth the vessel flies —
The mother, wailing on the wave-kiss'd shore,
Trusts her last counsels to the impatient breeze
That will not hear them—strains her dewy eyes
Till the proud sails diminish to a speck—
That speck to nothing,—questions still the grey
Unfixt horizon, till the setting sun
Sinks sudden in the darkness of the waves,
Then homeward hastening, looks upon the stars,
And knows that *he* beholds them, who no more
Shall look with her upon their household flowers

Where will he go ? To lands of pearl and gold
In search of gain ? or to the fields of Fame,
Where the coarse herb, with honourable blood
Manured and water'd—mail'd with bleaching bones—
Flags rank and noisome o'er promiscuous graves ?
Will he, with petty traffic, slow and sure,
From point to point, along the low flat coast,
Wakeful and cautious cruise ? or launching forth

On the vast main, spread every glittering sail
To catch the winds of chance, and bear away
For frozen continents, or empires dark
With howling woods, or girt with burning sand?
Or will he loiter by the enchanted isles
Of Love, where oft the languid air becalms
The willing bark? or doth he seek in vain
For that lost land, in elder time submerged
Beneath the Atlantic wave?
      But hold—no more.—
Too long we dally with a quaint conceit,
While the swift birth-day wears to jocund night

Thrice happy they, who rest, ere day declines,
Beneath the trees they planted in the morn —
And thou, my friend, whom honourable toil
Hath timely raised to honourable wealth,
And power to diffuse that happiness
Which thou hast earned—may worthily rejoice,
Oft as thy annual natal feast arrives, to see
Thy sire, and hers, whom love to thee hath join'd
In holy bands, beside thy cheerful board,
Placidly smiling in their calm old age,
And blessing Heaven that they can bless the day
When thou wast born.

TO A POSTHUMOUS INFANT

Child of woman, and of Heaven,
Ere thy birth, of sire bereaven,
Offspring of a widow'd dove,
Of half thy heritage of love
Defeated, ere thy little breath
Was drawn from atmosphere of death—
Smiler, that shalt ne'er beguile,
Father's tear with baby smile,
Never laugh on father's knee,
Knows thy father aught of thee?

May the spirit of the Blest,
Look upon its earthly nest?
Breathe upon thine infant slumbers,
The music of angelic numbers,
Glide into the growing soul,
To form, " to kindle, or controul?"
May the sainted parent bless,
His own, the new-born fatherless!

HOMER

Far from all measured space, yet clear and plain
As sun at noon, "a mighty orb of song"
Illumes extremest Heaven. Beyond the throng
Of lesser stars, that rise, and wex, and wane,
The transient rulers of the fickle main,
One steadfast light gleams through the dark, and long,
And narrowing aisle of memory How strong,
How fortified with all the numerous train
Of human truths, Great Poet of thy kind,
Wert thou, whose verse, capacious as the sea.
And various as the voices of the wind,
Swell'd with the gladness of the battle's glee—
And yet could glorify infirmity,
When Priam wept, or shame-struck Helen pined

VALENTINE.

TO A FAIR ARTISTE

Written in 1813

These, if not the first verses that I ever wrote, are the first with which I succeeded in pleasing even myself —in fact, the first in which I was able to express a preconceived thought in metre. I have selected them from a mass of juvenile, or more properly, puerile *poetry*, not as any better, or much worse, than the rest, but from the pleasant associations connected with them. It will do nobody any harm, and to some may be an agreeable remembrancer of old times. The young lady to whom it was addressed is the eldest daughter of the late William Green, an artist of great merit, who possessed a true sense of the beautiful in nature. The lady is now a wife and mother, and probably regards the pictorial skill of her youth, and the compliments it may have gained her, as things that have been.

> O, MISTRESS of that lovely art
> Which can to shadows form impart—
> Can fix those evanescent tints,
> Fainter by far than lovers' hints,
> And bring the scenes we love to mind,
> When we have left them far behind,—
> Thou seest an image in thy glass
> Which does e'en Raphael's art surpass,
> But which Dan Cupid has been able
> To copy in my heart's soft table.

How proud 'twould make a connoisseur
To have so beauteous a picture!
For me, I own, it ill contents me
To have a copy, but torments me,
Unless I might possess, as well,
That copy's fair original

THE FORSAKEN TO THE FAITHLESS

I do not write to bid thee come unto me—
I will not pray thee spare my virgin fame.
Since I am won, 'tis useless now to woo me—
Undone I am, thou canst not more undo me
Boast thy poor triumph o'er an empty name,
When she that shamed it sleeps in silent death,
For what is reputation but a bubble,
Blown up by Vanity's unthinking breath,—
A thing which few, with all their toil and trouble,
Can carry with them to their home, the grave
Since men are fire, and we are as the stubble ·
Men's faults are wink'd at—ours, alas! seen double,
No pardon of the partial world I crave,
That still is Folly's mouth-piece, Custom's slave

Not for my name I mourn—but thou hast ta'en
A dearer jewel—even my precious soul
Nor thou, nor all the world, can give again
What I have thrown away! Tho' Time may roll
His centuries on, when I shall be forgotten,
Thy falsehood mute, and cold thy fickle lust,—
When this polluted body shall be rotten,

And, undistinguished, sleep with virgin dust,—
Tho' all may cease the stars give o'er to shine,
Nor more be witness to that sin of mine,—
Still should I feel my unredeemed loss
And 'mongst the blessed be a thing unblest ;
No power that is can make me what I was—
Oh, might I then not be! Oh vain request!

TO THE MEMORY OF CANNING

EARLY, but not untimely, Heaven recall'd
To perfect bliss, thy pure, enlighten'd mind,
And tho' the new-born freedom of mankind
Is sick of fear to be again enthrall'd,
Since thou art gone, and this fair island, wall'd
With the impregnable, unmaster'd sea,
Mourns with a widow's grief for loss of thee,—
Should we repine, as if thou wert install'd
In Heaven too soon? Nay, I will shed no tear.
Thy work is done. It was enough for thee
To own the glorious might of Liberty,
And cast away the bondage and the fear
Of rotten custom, so the hope, which Fate
Snatch'd from thy life, thy Fame shall consummate.

LIBERTY

Say, What is Freedom? What the right of souls,
Which all who know are bound to keep, or die,
And who knows not, is dead? In vain ye pry
In musty archives, or retentive scrolls,
Charters and statutes, constitutions, rolls,
And remnants of the old world's history:—
These shew what has been, not what ought to be,
Or teach at best how wiser Time controuls
Man's futile purposes. As vain the search
Of restless factions, who, in lawless will,
Fix the foundations of a creedless church—
A lawless rule—an anarchy of ill.
But what is Freedom? Rightly understood,
A universal license to be good.

WHO IS THE POET?

Who is the Poet? Who the man whose lines
Live in the souls of men like household words?
Whose thought, spontaneous as the song of birds,
With eldest truth coeval, still combines
With each day's product, and like morning shines,
Exempt from age? 'Tis he, and only he,
Who knows that Truth is free, and only free,—
That Virtue, acting in the strict confines
Of positive law, instructs the infant spirit
In its best strength, and proves its mere demerit
Rooted in earth, yet tending to the sky,—
With patient hope surveys the narrow bound,
Culls every flower that loves the lowly ground,
And fraught with sweetness, wings her way on high.

THE USE OF A POET.

A thousand thoughts were stirring in my mind,
That strove in vain to fashion utterance meet,
And each the other cross'd—swift as a fleet
Of April clouds, perplexed by gusts of wind,
That veer, and veer, around, before, behind
Now History pointed to the customed beat,
Now Fancy's clue unravelling led their feet
Through mazes manifold, and quaintly twined.
So were they straying—so had ever stray'd;
Had not the wiser poets of the past
The vivid chart of human life display'd,
And taught the laws that regulate the blast,
Wedding wild impulse to calm forms of beauty,
And making peace 'twixt liberty and duty.

YOUNG LOVE

The nimble fancy of all beauteous Greece,
Fabled young Love an everlasting boy,
That held of nature an eternal lease,
Of childhood, beauty, innocence, and joy;
A bow he had, a pretty childish toy,
That would not terrify his mother's sparrows,
And 'twas his favourite play to sport his arrows,
Light as the glances of a wood-nymph coy,
O happy error! Musical conceit,
Of old idolatry, and youthful time!
Fit emanation of a happy clime,
Where but to live, to breathe, to be, was sweet,
And Love, tho' even then a little cheat,
Dream'd not his craft would e'er be call'd a crime.

DEATH-BED REFLECTIONS

OF MICHELANGELO.

Nor that my hand could make of stubborn stone,
Whate'er of Gods the shaping thought conceives,
Not that my skill by pictur'd lines hath shewn,
All terrors that the guilty soul believes—
Not that my art, by blended light and shade,
Express'd the world as it was newly made,
Not that my verse—profoundest truth could teach,
In the soft accents of the lover's speech .
Not that I rear'd a temple for mankind,
To meet and pray in, borne by every wind—
Affords me peace—I count my gain but loss,
For that vast love, that hangs upon the Cross

NOTES.

I

Dedicatory Sonnet, line 3   "Beside my cradle, &c."

Alluding to the poem called "Frost at Midnight," by S. T. Coleridge. The reference is especially to the following lines:

> But thou, my babe! shalt wander like a breeze,
> By lakes and sandy shores, beneath the crags
> Of ancient mountain, and beneath the clouds
> Which image in their bulk both lakes, and shores,
> And mountain crags   so shalt thou see and hear
> The lovely shapes and sounds intelligible
> Of that eternal language, which thy God
> Utters, who from eternity doth teach
> Himself in all, and all things in himself,

As far as regards the *habitats* of my childhood, these lines, written at Nether Stowey, were almost prophetic.   But poets are *not* prophets.

II

Sonnet 1   "To a Friend"

This sonnet, and the two following, my earliest attempts at that form of versification, were addressed to R. S. Jameson, Esq., on occasion of meeting him in London after a separation of some years.   He was the favourite companion of my boyhood, the active friend and sincere counsellor of my youth.   "Though seas between us broad ha' roll'd" since we "travell'd side by side" last, I trust the sight of this little volume will give rise to recollections that will make him ten years younger.   He is now Judge Advocate at Dominica, and husband of Mrs. Jameson, authoress of the "Diary of an Ennuyee," "Loves of the Poets," and other agreeable productions.

III

Sonnet 1, line 3

> *The peace that floated*
> *On the white mist, and dwelt upon the hills*

Love had he found in huts, where poor men lie,
His daily teachers had been woods and rills,
The silence that is in the starry sky,
The peace that sleeps upon the dewy hills
Wordsworth's Song at the feast of Brougham Castle

IV

Sonnet 8, line 9

> *The Fays,*
> *That sweetly nestle in the Fox-glove bells*

Popular fancy has generally conceived a connection between the Fox glove and the *good people* In Ireland, where it is called Lusmore (the great herb) and also Fairy-cap, the bending of its tall stalks is believed to denote the unseen presence of supernatural beings The *Shefro*, or gregarious Fairy, is represented as wearing the corolla of the Fox-glove on his head, and no unbecoming head-dress either See Crofton Croker's "*Fairy Legends of the South of Ireland*," a book to the author of which, unknown as he is to me, I gladly seize this opportunity of returning thanks for huge delight and considerable accession of fairy lore Crofton Croker is evidently a man of genius and poetical feeling Is it not to be wished that he had given more free way to the poetry of his nature? He seems almost afraid lest some one should suspect him of fearing and believing in the good people himself, and consequently *tells* his stories as if he did not believe them, which makes them appear more like great big Irish lies than the genuine educts of superstition Now this may be proper enough in such tales as Daniel O'Rourke's Voyage to the Moon, Ned Sheehy's Excuse, and some others, but still superstition is one thing, and lying another, and though the superstitions are often mendacious or rather destitute of any standard of truth within their minds, and when hard pushed will consciously and conscientiously forge to keep up the credit of their creed, (countless are the falsehoods that have been told as well as believed, for conscience sake,) yet really superstitious persons do not, Falstaff-like, set about of malice propense to raise a laugh by the enormity of their inventions. Many thanks to Crofton for his three delectable little volumes, but I do suspect, that from injudicious emulation of Tam o Shanter, he sometimes " mars a curious tale in telling it." It is his manifest endeavour to be as Irish as possible, but are his Irishmen always genuine Milesians? Are they not too much like the Kilmallocks, and Maetwolters, and Brulgruddenes? all excellent fellows in their way, but not fit company for Fairies. A certain dash of the ludicrous is not amiss in a terrible story, because fear is a ridiculous passion, whether its object be man or goblin, but it should be *naiveté*, or unconscious humour, not irony or sarcasm, far less the slang knowingness of a hoaxer.

Of all the imaginations of Erin, the Banshee is the most affecting, and the best authenticated. There are some narratives of this apparition attested by startling evidence. But perhaps the most beautiful fancy is the Thierna na-Oge, or land of youth, a region of perpetual spring beneath the waters, where there is no decay, no change, no time, but all remains as at the moment of submersion. To this Moore alludes in those lines.—

> On Lough Neagh's bank, as the fisherman strays,
> When the clear, cold eve's declining,
> He sees the round towers of other days,
> In the wave beneath him shining.

To return to the Foxglove. Query. Is not the proper etymology *Folk's*, 1 e Fairie's glove? Surely Renard does not wear gloves in popular tradition.

V

Sonnet 15, last lines.

Of nature's inner shrine thou art the priest,
Where most she works when we perceive her least.

Thou worshippest at the Temple's inner shrine,
God being with thee, when we know it not.

Wordsworth's Sonnets

VI

Sonnet 16, line 5

The patient beauty of the scentless rose

The Chinese, or monthly rose, so frequently seen clustering round the cottage-porch, both in the remotest vales and in the immediate outskirts of busy, smoky towns, is almost destitute of scent. The manner in which this cheerful foreigner perseveres in the habits of a warmer climate, through all vicissitudes of ours, is a remarkable instance of vegetable nationality.

VII

Sonnet 18, line 5

The voiceless flowers ———

In the "Bride's Tragedy," by Thomas Beddoes, of Pembroke College, Oxon, occurs a hypothetical simile which some prose-witted dunce of a reviewer thought proper to assail with great animosity. Something, I forget what, is

Like flower's voices—*if they could but speak.*

Whoever feels the beauty of that line, has a soul for poetry.

VIII

Sonnet 19, line 7

Poor mortality
Begins to mourn before it knows its cause,
Prophetic in its ignorance

Thou know'st, the first time that we smell the air
We waule and cry
When we are born, we cry that we are come
To this great stage of fools.

Shakspeare · King Lear, Act 1

The thought, which is obvious enough indeed, occurs in an older writer than Shakspeare, and might probably be traced to some of the fathers, or to Seneca. Robert Greene reproaches Shakspeare with reading Seneca *done* into English.

IX

Sonnet 19, *line* 10
The hospitalities of earth

Earth fills her lap with pleasures of her own.
Yearnings she hath in her own natural kind,
And even with something of a mother's mind,
    And no unworthy aim,
The homely nurse doth all she can
To make her foster-child, her inmate man,
Forget the glories he hath known,
And that imperial palace whence he came — *Wordsworth*

X

Sonnet 20, *line* 9
Love-sick ether

Purple the sails, and so perfumed, that
The winds were love-sick with them.
    Shakspeare Antony and Cleopatra, Act 2

Imitators and alterers do not often improve upon Shakspeare, but when they do, it is but fair to give them credit for it. Dryden, in his "All for Love," has omitted all the philosophy, and two thirds of the poetry of Shakspeare's play, but he has certainly made a much more compact and consecutive drama, and by putting the description of Cleopatra's "grand aquatic procession" into the mouth of Antony himself, has made it a natural and dramatic portion of the play, whereas, in Shakspeare, it has too much the air of a quotation from an epic or descriptive poem. Neither Shakspeare nor Dryden have done *much* more than versify Plutarch's, or rather Dr. Philemon Holland's prose, and they were wise in not hunting after useless originality but Shakspeare has added some exquisitely poetical touches

At the helm
A seeming mermaid steers, the silken tackles
Swell with the touches of those *flower soft hands*,
That rarely frame their office From the barge
A *strange invisible perfume* hits the sense
Of the adjacent wharfs The city cast

> Her people out upon her, and Antony,
> Enthroned i' the market place, did sit alone
> Whistling to the air, which, but for vacancy,
> *Had gone to gaze on Cleopatra too,*
> And left a gap in nature

If Antony owed to the Egyptian Queen the loss of his empire and life, he is indebted to her for a less hateful renown than would have clung to his name had she never "pursed up his heart on the river of Cydnus." The murderer of Cicero is merged in the lover of Cleopatra.

XI

Sonnet 20, line 10

Middle earth

The phrase occurs in a hymn of the Saxon poet Cædmon, and seems to imply, not the supposed centrality of the earth in the firmament, but the intermediate condition between the poles of good and evil. I have here adapted it to signify, that on earth we only contemplate objects *in transitu*, being unable to trace any process to its origin or its termination.

XII

Sonnet 31, line 11

The full inherency of sin

> This ineradicable taint of sin
> *Childe Harold. Canto IV, 126*

XIII

Sonnet 32

In this and other translations from the Italian, I have not succeeded in preserving the simple purity of the original diction so completely as I could have wished. Italian words are so beautiful, that they are when "unadorned, adorned the most." English, with all its excellencies, is so deficient in euphony, and so large a part of its vocabulary is debased by association, that it always requires strong or deep pathos, beautiful images, profound thought, rapid and striking interest, or much artifice in composition; something, in short, to withdraw the attention from the coarseness of the vehicle. We cannot emulate the simplicity of the Greeks or the Italians. The poet, indeed, who can and dare, may be austere, but austerity and simplicity are different things. Simplicity is never, austerity is always, conscious of itself. The Sunday habit of a modest country girl is simple—the regulation dress of a nunnery is meant to be austere. Simplicity does not seek what it feels no need of—Austerity rejects what it judges unfit.

But neither simplicity nor austerity are necessarily poetical. The simple must be beautiful, the austere must be great, or they have no place in genuine poetry. A daisy is simple, a turnip still simpler, yet the former belongs to the poetry of Nature, the latter to her most utilitarian prose.

XIV
Page 37, line 17

> *The humbler spirit*
> *Hums in the daily round of household things,*
> *A low sweet melody, inaudible*
> *To the gross sense of worldlings*

The still, sad music of humanity
Wordsworth's Tintern Abbey

XV
Page 42, line 5
The choicest terms are now enfeoff'd to folly

Enfeoff'd himself to popularity
Shakspeare, Henry IV Part 1st

XVI
Page 53. Song "'Tis sweet," &c

Among the controversies of the day, not the least important is that respecting the song of the Nightingale. It is debated whether the notes of this bird are of a joyous or a melancholy expression. He who has spoken so decisively of "the merry Nightingale," must forgive my somewhat unfilial inclination toward the elder and more common opinion. No doubt the sensations of the bird while singing are pleasurable, but the question is, What is the feeling which its song, considered as a succession of sounds produced by an instrument, is calculated to carry to a human listener? When we speak of a pathetic strain of music, we do not mean that either the fiddler or his fiddle are unhappy, but that the tones or intervals of the air are such as the mind associates with tearful sympathies. At the same time, I utterly deny that the voice of philomel expresses present pain. I could never have imagined that the pretty creature "sets her breast against a thorn," and could not have perpetrated the diabolical story of Tereus. In fact, nature is very little obliged to the heathen mythology. The constant *anthropomorphism* of the Greek religion sorely perplexed the ancient conceptions of natural beauty. A river is turned into a god, who is still too much of a river to be quite a god. It is a statue of ice in a continual state of liquefaction.

XVII

Page 56

Agony of prayer

I know not who first used this expression, nor at what time it entered into my mind. It occurs where one should hardly expect to find it—in Darwin's Botanic Garden, but I had never read the "Botanic Garden" at the time that I wrote this epitaph. Doubtless I have read the phrase elsewhere. It could not be of Darwin's invention.

XVIII

Page 56, last line

The marriage of pure minds

Let me not to the marriage of pure minds
Admit impediments.

Shakspeare's Sonnets.

XIX

Page 57   To the Nautilus

"There is a kind of Nautilus, called by Linnæus Argonauta, whose shell has but one cell, of this animal Pliny affirms, that having exonerated its shell by throwing out the water, it swims upon the surface, extending a web of wonderful tenuity, and bending back two of its arms, and, rowing with the rest, makes a sail, and at length receiving the water, dives again." *Pliny, IX, 29*

Linnæus adds to his description of this animal, that, like the crab Diogenes or Bernhard, it occupies a house not its own, as it is not connected to its shell, and is therefore foreign to it. Who could have given credit to this if it had not been attested by so many, who have with their own eyes seen this Argonauta in the act of sailing." *Syst Nat p* 1161

"The Nautilus, properly so named by Linnæus, has a shell consisting of many chambers, of which cups are made in the East with beautiful painting and carving on the mother pearl. The animal is said to inhabit only the uppermost or open chamber which is larger than the rest, and that the rest remain empty, except that the siphunculus, which communicates from one to the other of them, is filled with an appendage of the animal like a gut or string. Mr Hook in his Philos. Exper. p 306, imagines this to be a dilatable or compressible tube, like the air bladders of fish, and that by contracting or permitting it to expand, it renders its shell buoyant or the contrary."—*Darwin*

It is not to be supposed that the Nautilus defies the storm. It only sails in fair weather and light breezes, and if the sea become turbulent, or any interruption threaten to cut short its voyage of pleasure, it dives directly. I recollect to have seen, in manuscript, a most beautiful copy of verses, founded on this habit of the Nautilus. Had they been in print, mine should never have appeared. The same may be said of the lines " to certain gold fishes." A *real* poet, among many strains of "higher mood," of which he deems the world unworthy, has an exquisite little piece on those beautiful creatures, in which he has exhibited a more than pictorial power of language. It is saying far too little to say, that he makes you *see* the gold fish—that they flash, in all their effulgence of hue, and complicity of motion, " on that inward eye which is the bliss of solitude.' He makes you feel as if you were a gold fish yourself.

X

It is said, that the gold fish (Cyprinus Auratus of Linnæus) was originally confined to a little lake of China

---

XX

Page 61   Leonard and Susan

This tale, which was first published in Blackwood's Magazine, was intended to form part of a series of narrative and reflective pieces, which should have been intitled "Lucubrations of an Old Bachelor" Leonard was to have been an old man in my, *i e* the Old Bachelor's childhood   This, of course, throws the supposed date of the incidents at least a century back, and may obviate the charge of exaggeration which has been alleged against my description of prison sufferings   A debtor's gaol, however, is still, I suspect, pretty much what it always has been—a place of low dissipation or unprincipled luxury for the dishonest, of ruin, and misery, and debasement to the unfortunate.

Blessed be the memory of that benevolent jurist who struggled so manfully against the barbarism of antichristian ordinances!   May the softest air of Paradise calm and heal the phrenzy which crossed him in an evil hour, and *if* separated spirits have any perception of what passes in the world they have left, may *his spirit* be comforted in seeing the good work which he well begun, perfected to a good end   Our Judges are very fond of asserting that "Christianity is parcel of the law"   it will be more to the purpose when we can truly say that the law is parcel of christianity.

I wish that future ages—on the very improbable supposition that this trifle should exist in a future age—may think the representation of an election a caricature

No reflection is meant upon Nabobs in general   "Wherever the carcase is, there will the *vultures* be gathered together"   Wherever there is a new way opened to riches, there will be a concourse of those who own no God but Mammon, a Fiend compared to whom Juggernaut is merciful, and Cotytto is pure   But there will also be many who seek wealth as the means of doing good, and many such have returned from the shores of Hindostan   Such characters as my Nabob were probably more common when the East first became the scene of British enterprize than at present   India is now visited by men of better education, more refined habits, more philosophic minds, and moreover, the press....Heaven's blessing upon it !---forbids any man to be *very* overtly wicked in any quarter of the globe, who wishes to come back and enjoy his gettings in England

It is hardly worth while to mention that most of the lugubrious love ditties in this volume were conceived in the character of the lovelorn "*old bachelor.*" For what many will deem their silly "mock platonism," and "querulous egotism," I am only *dramatically* answerable *I*, does not always mean myself

---

XXI

Page 74

The chaste and consecrated snow
On Dian's bosom

Thou ever young, fresh, loved, and delicate wooer,
Whose blush doth thaw the consecrated snow
That lies on Dian's lap

Shakspeare's Timon of Athens

XXII

Page 85

And where the mighty Banian's echoing shade

The fig tree, not that kind for fruit renown'd,
But such as at this time to Indians known,
In Malabar or Deccan spreads her arms,
Branching so broad and long, that in the ground
The bended twigs take root, and daughters grow
About the mother tree, a pillar'd shade
High overarched, with *echoing walls between.*

Paradise Lost, b 9.

The palace is Aladdin's It is needless to mention how much my description is indebted to Thalaba The imagination of Southey is as thoroughly Arabesque as that of Moore's is Persian Thalaba, Kehama, and Lalla Rookh, have completely orientalized our imaginations

I love Albums They sometimes procure a sunny look, or a kind word, for some hard-favoured son of the muse, that else might wither in the "shade of cold neglect." Surely there is a moral value in whatever enables a poor man to confer a kindness

---

XXIII

Page 100   *Farewell*

In these "piping times of peace," undergraduates take the place of Ensigns, and the close of the Long Vacation is attended with the same gales of sighs, and showers of tears, as heretofore the sailing of a regiment for actual service. Examinations are as terrible to the fair as battles, and the future first class man, or wrangler is as interesting as the possible hero.

There is something very fascinating about an Undergraduate, he is a rose unblown, and wears "the beauty of promise," he is a member of an ancient establishment, therefore his youth and freshness are at once contrasted and sanctified by beautiful antiquity, he is a spring flower growing on the steeple of a gothic cathedral. He is enough a man to make his notice worth having by a young lady, and yet so much a boy, that ladies *of a certain age* can make a pet of him. He has the reputation of learning without the odium of displaying it, above all, he has a certificate of gentility, which, let his real rank and fortune be what it will, passes unchallenged everywhere but in his own University. There, indeed, he is under the necessity of proving and maintaining his caste, and the stain of a mercantile or agricultural connection can only be washed out with claret. Everywhere else the COLLEGIAN" is *absolute sumptas*, a gentleman. But this enviable distinction belongs to Oxford and Cambridge alone. Edinburgh or Glasgow are no recommendation except to phrenological females, and Trinity College, Dublin, is as alien to English associations as Salamanca or Benares. The London University may have its day, but its day is not yet come. At present it is looked upon as coldly by the *petticoat* as by the *gown*. Should a youth be introduced to a fair partner at a country ball as a collegian, and prove, after all, to be only a member of *Stincomalee*, the lady's delicacy would be as much shocked as if she were to find that the very delightful naval officer with whom she had been dancing under the ambiguous title Captain, was the skipper of a small vessel engaged in the Irish butter trade. It is well the members

of the liberal establishment must be gentlemen, if they desire to be accepted as such

Learning, of itself, confers no rank in England. It does not even give the eclat of a fashionable lion. But, as the passport to learned professions, it enables a man, with good conduct, to overcome any disadvantage of birth, and to achieve a place in the best circles of society. Perhaps this is as it should be.

The peculiar advantage of being an Oxonian or a Cantab is specially felt in the vacation, and in the country. In London they form a pleasant variety indeed, but excite no commotion. They are but as a drop of wine in the ocean. In Liverpool, or Manchester, they are out of place. The academical aristocracy is too strong a discord in the commercial concert. In Bath or Cheltenham they degenerate into mere gentlemen loungers; they partake, but they do not create or authorize, the general dissipation. But in small villages, with a *good neighbourhood* and romantic scenery, they are just what they should be. The custom of reading parties is one of the favourable signs of the times. They read very little; if men want to read, let them take a back-room in Cheapside, or the county gaol. At Ambleside, in Wales, in the Isle of Wight, or the Highlands, what have Euclid or Aristotle to do? But they gladden the waters with their music, and the fair with their gallantry; and what is better still, fill their imagination with beautiful images, and their hearts with kind feelings.

It was on a rusticating (not a rusticated) Cantab that these lines were composed. He was a poet in thought, but either "wanted the accomplishment of verse," or which is more probable, concealed his possession of it. Long will his amiable manners, and green-ribboned guitar, be remembered in Grasmere.

XXIV

Page 119   "*By a Friend*"

I know not whether I am not taking an unwarrantable liberty in giving publicity to these stanzas, but their appearance in my volume is a pleasant record of a valuable friendship, and I trust my friend will not be displeased to see his pretty and tender effusion along with his old acquaintances of mine, some of which owe their preservation to his kind opinion of their merits.

ERRATA.

Page 42, line 16, for *connateral* read connatural
Page 44, last line, for *wing* read wings
Page 68, line 18, for *madning* read madding
Page 87, line 9, for *face* read fane
Page 103, line 10, for *leave* read heave
Page 106, insert notes of interrogation after lines 16 and 18
Page 120, line 21, for *Oh* read Or

LEEDS
PRINTED BY F. E. BINGLEY,
CORN EXCHANGE

Lightning Source UK Ltd.
Milton Keynes UK
UKHW021343010420
361178UK00004B/777

MORAL WRITINGS

BRITISH MORAL PHILOSOPHERS

Essays on Ethics and Method
Henry Sidgwick
Edited by Marcus G. Singer

Moral Writings
H. A. Prichard
Edited by Jim MacAdam

The Right and the Good
David Ross
Edited by Philip Stratton-Lake

MORAL WRITINGS

H. A. Prichard

Edited, with an introduction, by
Jim MacAdam

CLARENDON PRESS · OXFORD

OXFORD
UNIVERSITY PRESS

Great Clarendon Street, Oxford OX2 6DP

Oxford University Press is a department of the University of Oxford.
It furthers the University's objective of excellence in research, scholarship,
and education by publishing worldwide in

Oxford New York

Auckland Bangkok Buenos Aires Cape Town Chennai
Dar es Salaam Delhi Hong Kong Istanbul Karachi Kolkata
Kuala Lumpur Madrid Melbourne Mexico City Mumbai Nairobi
São Paulo Shanghai Singapore Taipei Tokyo Toronto

with an associated company in Berlin

Oxford is a registered trade mark of Oxford University Press
in the UK and in certain other countries

Published in the United States
by Oxford University Press Inc., New York

This edition © Oxford University Press 2002;
introduction and bibliography © Jim MacAdam 2002

The moral rights of the author have been asserted
Database right Oxford University Press (maker)

First published 2002

All rights reserved. No part of this publication may be reproduced,
stored in a retrieval system, or transmitted, in any form or by any means,
without the prior permission in writing of Oxford University Press,
or as expressly permitted by law, or under terms agreed with the appropriate
reprographics rights organizations. Enquiries concerning reproduction
outside the scope of the above should be sent to the Rights Department,
Oxford University Press, at the address above

You must not circulate this book in any other binding or cover
and you must impose this same condition on any acquirer

British Library Cataloguing in Publication Data

Data available

Library of Congress Cataloging in Publication Data

Data available

ISBN 0-19-925018-9
ISBN 0-19-925019-7 (Pbk.)

1 3 5 7 9 10 8 6 4 2

Typeset by Newgen Imaging Systems (P) Ltd, Chennai, India
Printed in Great Britain
on acid-free paper by
Biddles Ltd., Guildford & King's Lynn

For the Love of
my Wife, Elizabeth,
and our Children

Frontispiece: Portrait of Harold Arthur Prichard. Photo from 'Harold Arthur Prichard, 1871–1947' in *Proceedings of the British Academy*, Volume XXXIII, 1947. Published by the British Academy.

Contents

Note to the Original Edition of Moral Obligation *(1949) by W. D. Ross*	ix
Introduction to the Paperback Edition of Moral Obligation and Duty and Interest *(1968) by J. O. Urmson*	x
Editor's Introduction by Jim MacAdam (2002)	xiv
List of Prichard's Writings	xvi
A Note on the Contents	xix
1. What is the Basis of Moral Obligation?*	1
2. Does Moral Philosophy Rest on a Mistake? (1912)	7
3. Duty and Interest (1928)	21
4. Kant's *Fundamental Principles of the Metaphysic of Morals**	50
5. A Conflict of Duties (1928)*	77
6. Duty and Ignorance of Fact (1932)	84
7. The Meaning of ἀγαθόν in the *Ethics* of Aristotle (1935)	102
8. Manuscript on Morals (1928–1945)*	114
9. Moral Obligation (1937)	163
10. Green: Political Obligation (1935–7)	226
11. The Object of a Desire (1940)	253
12. The Obligation to Keep a Promise (c. 1940)	257
13. Exchanging (1940)	266
14. The Time of an Obligation	268
15. The Psychology of Willing	270
16. Acting, Willing, Desiring (1945)	272
17. 'Ought' (1947)	282

CONTENTS

Appendix   *Letter from Cook Wilson to Prichard (1904)***   284
   Letter from Prichard to Ross (1932)*   286

Bibliography   288

Index   295

* Writings not included in the 1949 or 1968 editions and not published previously.
** Writings not included in the 1949 or 1968 editions but subsequently published.

Note to the Original Edition of *Moral Obligation*

It has long been a matter of regret to those who knew Harold Prichard that he published so little of the fruits of his many years of concentrated thought about philosophical problems. On moral philosophy, which was his main subject for the last half of his life, he published no more than two articles and two lectures. But he was known to have written a good deal more, even if his persistent self-criticism had led him to tear up many drafts which he had come to think unsatisfactory. When I was given the opportunity of going through what he had left behind him I found that he had made considerable progress with a book on moral obligation, although he had, apparently, added little to it later than 1937. There were also a certain number of short (in some cases very short) papers dealing with particular ethical questions. Finally, it seemed well to republish the two articles on ethical subjects which had appeared, one in *Mind* for 1912 and one in *Philosophy* for 1935, and his British Academy lecture on 'Duty and Ignorance of Fact'. His inaugural lecture, as White's Professor of Moral Philosophy, on 'Duty and Interest', is not republished, because much of it is used in the long essay on Moral Obligation. The papers have been arranged in their probable chronological order.

An admirable memoir of Prichard by Professor H. H. Price has appeared in the papers of the British Academy, and there is no need to add to this preface a second account of Prichard's views; the essays will speak for themselves. I believe no one can read them without feeling that in him we had one of the finest philosophical minds of the whole generation to which he belonged.

W. D. Ross

3 October 1949

Introduction to the Paperback Edition of *Moral Obligation and Duty and Interest*

This book contains H. A. Prichard's writings on moral philosophy. Some were published in his lifetime, others were selected from his literary remains by W. D. Ross; and they were assembled in the volume *Moral Obligation*, first published in 1949 and here reprinted with the addition of 'Duty and Interest', Prichard's inaugural lecture as White's Professor of Moral Philosophy. Though much of that lecture is incorporated in the long essay entitled 'Moral Obligation', also printed here, its historical importance makes it desirable that it should be readily available in its original form.

Like Ross in his note to the original edition of this book, I draw the attention of readers anxious to know more of the man and his work to H. H. Price's obituary notice of Prichard in Volume XXXIII (1947) of the *Proceedings of the British Academy*. As a member of the very last generation of undergraduates to attend Prichard's lectures and informal instruction, I learnt to admire his patience as a teacher, his philosophical acuity and, above all, his quite exceptional intellectual honesty and independence, before I studied his writings. But some hint of these qualities can be discovered in the writings. I echo the words of Ross: 'I believe no one can read them without feeling that in him we had one of the very finest philosophical minds of the whole generation to which he belonged'.

But, no doubt, if one is sufficiently selective in marshalling facts and arguments, it is not difficult to make a plausible case for the opinion that the philosophical views of Prichard can now be quietly put aside. Certainly it must be conceded that his influence in his lifetime was great, particularly in his own university of Oxford; but this may be counted a misfortune. Did he not constantly overbear his opponents with dogmatic assertion? 'If we reflect, we become forced to admit. . . .', he would say, and further discussion would be fruitless. If his lectures commanded a faithful audience, were they not, dogmatism aside, mainly a destructive criticism of his selected targets? Outside moral philosophy, he was a champion of such lost causes as the synthetic *a priori* truth of Euclidian geometry; within moral philosophy, the intuitionism which he expounded has disappeared, except to be perfunctorily refuted in the first or second chapter of ethical textbooks. For it was an irrational dogmatism—either one saw by inspection the moral truths which Prichard saw or one was morally blind, and nothing more was to be said. Further, what can a generation of philosophers with respect for idiom find of value in a philosopher who perpetrated such barbarisms as

'I shall be oughting to do *a*'? And if we think that philosophy should concern itself with real moral issues, what are we to make of a man whose puzzles are about exchanging a banana for an apple, an obligation to go to bed, or what one should do if a man's life depended on the correct guess of the fall of a die?

This unfavourable judgement of Prichard, while overstated, is not without justice. But it is not merely overstated, it is highly selective. Thus it must be owned that he did maintain his views, once formed, with vehemence, and would brush aside most criticism as shallow and ill-conceived. But these views were arrived at by the most careful and honest thinking, and, outside the dialectical forum, he continually reconsidered them. Views earlier accepted and later abandoned were attacked with the same vigour as those which he had always rejected. Moreover those philosophers whom he attacked most frequently and most vigorously were those he most respected. Thus he dismissed without argument the logical positivism of the thirties as being unworthy of a reply: his sustained attacks on Hume's moral philosophy and Green's political philosophy, on the other hand, were based on careful reading and combined with great respect for his antagonists. When Prichard thought that he had found a fatal flaw in the argument of a Hume, a Green, or a Sidgwick, he concentrated on it and remorselessly exposed it, allowing himself to be sidetracked by no subsidiary issues. But he said of Green in 'Duty and Interest' that 'the more you study any particular sentence, the more you are convinced that every word of it has been weighed and that, whether or not it is true, it expresses exactly what he meant to say'. This is why he thought it worth while to attack Green's views.

Again, it is true that Prichard often employs an odd, or even bizarre, idiom. But he could also employ a powerful and simple prose, and always avoided the facile, thought-saving jargon of philosophy. Still more important, he often showed a very remarkable sensitivity and respect for the features of ordinary language. Anyone who reads 'The Obligation to Keep a Promise' will see that Prichard, at least did not need to be told that a promise was performative, a kind of action, rather than constative. Or, again, Austin's 'Ifs and Cans' is rightly celebrated for its subtle demonstration of the idiosyncratic character of the expression 'I can, if I choose'; he showed differences between this and typical conditional statements which philosophers had to admit that they had overlooked until Austin pointed them out. But the basic point had been seen and made by Prichard in 1932. In 'Duty and Ignorance of Fact', considering the statement 'Well, at least I can do the action, e.g. shout, *if* I choose', he remarks: 'Such a statement, however, as we see when we reflect, is very odd. It cannot be meant literally, and can at best be only an idiom. For while it is sense to say: "If I choose to make a loud noise, I shall in fact make it," it cannot be sense to say: "If I choose to make it, I *can* make it." And no one would maintain that our *ability* to do something, as distinct from our *doing* it, can depend on our choosing to do it.' His own view is that 'I can do X if I choose' is a brachylogical way of saying 'Since I can choose to do X, I can do *X*'; which may or may not be satisfactory. But here again, Prichard's reflection had led him to a degree of clarity denied to his contemporaries.

Much of what is found least acceptable by many in Prichard's philosophy arises from his unwillingness to falsify what seemed to him to be the basic facts. As he makes clear in the penultimate paragraph of 'Duty and Ignorance of Fact', it was clear to him that any philosophical theory must be tested by reference to the less general facts that we know to be the case. To do otherwise is to prefer simplicity to truth. It is from this consideration, not from natural dogmatism, that his intuitionism stems. This intuitionism is the doctrine that there are many distinct obligations, such as truth-telling and promise-keeping, which must be recognized as ultimate and which cannot be argued to or treated as special cases of some more general obligation.

Now it seemed obvious to Prichard that on particular occasions, when explaining why we have a duty to perform some action, we do give such answers as that we had promised to do it, that gratitude required it, that it would be deceitful not to do it, that it would relieve suffering, and the like. Therefore any general ethical theory must make *this* intelligible, not substitute something else for it. Prichard has no objection to our looking for some unifying theory; indeed, he says in the essay 'Moral Obligation' that 'it is almost bound to occur to us that acts of different sorts cannot all be duties unless they possess some common character, the possession of which renders them duties'. But one's zeal for an answer to this inquiry must not be allowed to make one forget or falsify the basic facts to be explained. What Prichard claimed was that a careful examination of attempts to discover such a common characteristic always failed, either by unintelligibility or by falsification of the basic data. If, for example, one claimed that promotion of welfare was the common character of all kinds of duties, Prichard's answer was that, when faced with the performance of an action which one had promised to do, one could not represent the manifest duty of performance as one of promoting welfare without destroying the data one's theory was supposed to explain. If we are tempted by such theories 'the only remedy lies in actually getting into a situation which occasions the obligation, or—if our imagination be strong enough—in imagining ourselves in that situation, and then letting our moral capacities of thinking do their work'.

Whether Prichard succeeded in showing, as he claimed, that all teleological ethical theories must inevitably fail may be doubtful. Many would claim that there are more subtle teleological theories which escape his net. But we do well to heed Prichard's arguments and learn to imitate his scrupulous respect for the facts. It was this, not dogmatism, which led, or misled, him to his celebrated view that moral philosophy, in looking for the common character, rested on a mistake.

Similarly we shall find an unwavering regard for the facts to be the clue to his careful and deflationary examination of the attempts of Green and others to explain the duty of political obedience. On this occasion, perhaps, his views will attract more sympathy from the philosophers of the present day. His lectures on Green's views on political obligations are a model of careful criticism. He ends by asking whether the question about the ground of political obedience has in fact any single correct answer. 'We are apt', he tells us, 'to assume that the questions "Ought an Englishman to obey the Crown and Parliament, an Italian to obey Mussolini, a German to obey Hitler?" are instances of the same question. But is this really so—because the thing called a state may in each case be different, and if there are kinds of state, the duty to obey may depend on the kind?' For candid good sense, expressed in plain and simple English, these lectures have few rivals. When Prichard has compared the question 'Why ought a subject to obey his ruler?' to the question 'Why ought we to read books?', the false assumptions of classical political theory quickly lose their plausibility.

It would be unwise for us, then, to put aside the writings of Prichard. An attentive reader will always learn from them. But no doubt we should read them with the same wary scrutiny that Prichard gave to the works of Green. I myself find Prichard's criticism of Plato and Aristotle surprisingly imperceptive. In 'Does Moral Philosophy Rest on a Mistake?' Prichard speaks of his 'extreme sense of dissatisfaction produced by a close reading of Aristotle's *Ethics*', a work I regard as being still the greatest in its field. When I read his paper 'The meaning of $\dot{\alpha}\gamma\alpha\theta\acute{o}\nu$ in the *Ethics* of Aristotle' I can conclude only that Prichard's dissatisfaction arose from profound misunderstanding. The frequently repeated criticism of Plato also, for trying to found duty on interest, while of great non-historical interest as philosophical argument, seems to lack sympathetic understanding of Plato.

But, though we are all likely to be at times puzzled and repelled by Prichard's views and arguments, a mind so subtle, so candid and so honest as Prichard's, informed by such respect for facts and helped by frequent acuity of ear for linguistic usage, inevitably produced much which we cannot safely ignore. Only the dullest and least teachable of his readers can fail to learn from him.

J. O. Urmson

March 1968

Editor's Introduction (2002)

Harold Arthur Prichard (1871–1947) spent almost his entire adult life at Oxford University. H. H. Price writes in his excellent memoir: 'He was educated at Clifton and New College, Oxford. He came up to New College with a mathematical scholarship in 1890, and had the rare distinction of taking first classes both in Mathematical Moderations and in Literae Humaniores.'[1] His father and grandfather were lawyers, and Prichard himself began to article in London, but returned to Oxford when offered a fellowship at Hertford College. In 1898 he accepted a fellowship at Trinity College where he remained until he resigned in 1923 because of ill health. He was a conscientious tutor, putting in many hours a week, and was always willing to 'find another hour' when needed. His wife, Mabel Ross, later became a councillor of the city of Oxford. They had three children, and lived at 43 Broad Street which later became the site of part of the Bodleian Library, where scholars can now read his unpublished writings. Later the family moved to 6 Linton Road. In 1928 Prichard was elected White's Professor of Moral Philosophy and became a fellow of Corpus Christi College. He was given an honorary degree by the University of Aberdeen. He retired in 1937, but continued to write until his death in 1947.

His methods of isolating small, manageable philosophical problems as exact questions, and insisting upon solutions in clear everyday English influenced his Oxford students. And it may be that Prichard's greatest influence is through the students who attended his lectures and classes. Urmson, Hart, Berlin, Ayer, Hampshire, Nowell-Smith, Raphael, Mabbott, Austin, and Ryle were students when he lectured. Several spoke of him as the personification of philosophy. Hart attended as many as five lecture hours per week. Few agreed with his views, but they held that he portrayed philosophy as important, serious, difficult, and demanding. Urmson remarked that he lectured at dictation speed with a concern for rigorous reasoning. Mabbott, and others, noted that because of his short stature he lectured with a high-backed chair on top of a table, and used the chair 'as a climbing frame'. He sometimes ended his lectures early with the comment 'I am trailing my coat' in the hope of enticing discussion. Philosophy was his

---

[1] 'Harold Arthur Prichard, 1871–1947', *Proceedings of the British Academy*, 33 (1947), 331–50. See also W. D. Ross, 'Harold Arthur Prichard', *Dictionary of National Biography*, (London: Oxford University Press, 1941–50), 697–8.

passion. On vacation at Brighton he sat for hours tossing keys from one hand to the other while he wrestled with a problem. E. F. Carritt, who had Prichard as a tutor, reported that Professor Cook Wilson, who was Prichard's teacher, 'started an informal meeting of some dozen philosophy tutors for tea and the discussion of short papers, with a dinner and longer paper once a term'.[2] When Prichard became Professor, the 'Philosophers' Teas' were held at 6 Linton Road, and if the others lacked a paper to start discussion Prichard 'had one in his pocket'. The subject of the teas frequently spilled over (if you'll allow that description) into discussion through the University's internal mail, by means of which Prichard sent miniature essays to, and received them from, Ross, Paton, Carritt, Laird, Collingwood, and Austin. Prichard says that he continued to discuss philosophy weekly with John Cook Wilson, and Carritt says the same of his later relationship with Prichard.

Cook Wilson was the leader of the group called the Oxford Realists which included Prichard, H. W. B. Joseph, W. D. Ross, E. F. Carritt, and, for a time, R. G. Collingwood. It is questionable whether Cook Wilson's strong influence was beneficial. He was very argumentative, and given too much to destroying the arguments of others. He was also fearful of what he regarded as the deadening effect of publication. Prichard inherited both inclinations. His daughter Marjorie wrote: '[M]y father was always *so* reluctant to publish, never feeling satisfied he had really found the truth about his problems. So much of what he wrote, specially in letters, was an attempt to sort out the ideas in his mind.'[3] Prichard became the leader of a group of moral philosophers, called the Oxford Intuitionists, which included Ross, Joseph, Carritt, and John Laird. Prichard's way of doing philosophy was to discover a problem, work away at it independently of commentaries, being as critical of his own thinking as he was of others', until he reached 'bed rock'. Although nearly all of the philosophers who attended his lectures came to disagree with his rejection of moral theory, he was regarded by some as the ablest philosopher of his generation and representative of what it is to live philosophy as a profession.

[2] 'Professor H. A. Prichard: Personal Recollections', *Mind*, 57 (1948), 146–8.
[3] Personal letter from M.M.L. Prichard to J. MacAdam, 4 Oct. 1981.

List of Prichard's Writings

PUBLISHED WRITINGS

'Appearances and Reality', *Mind*, 15 (1906), 223–9.

'A Criticism of the Psychologists' Treatment of Knowledge', *Mind*, 16 (1907), 27–53.

Kant's Theory of Knowledge (Oxford: Clarendon Press, 1909); reprint available from University Microfilms International, Ann Arbor, Michigan.

'Philosophic Pre-Copernicanism: An Answer', *Mind*, 19 (1910), 541–3.

'Does Moral Philosophy Rest on a Mistake?', *Mind*, 21 (1912), 21–37 [Ch. 2 in this vol.].

'Professor John Cook Wilson', *Mind*, 28 (1919), 297–318.

'Mr. Bertrand Russell's Outline of Philosophy', *Mind*, 37 (1928), 265–82.

'Duty and Interest', Inaugural Lecture, White's Professor of Moral Philosophy, (Oxford: Clarendon Press, 1929) [Ch. 3 in this vol.].

'Duty and Ignorance of fact', Annual Philosophical Lecture, Henriette Hertz Trust, *Proceedings of the British Academy* (1932) [Ch. 6 in this vol.]

'The Meaning of $\dot{\alpha}\gamma\alpha\theta\acute{o}\nu$ in the Ethics of Aristotle' *Philosophy*, 37 (1935), 27–39 [Ch. 7 in this vol.]

'H. W. B. Joseph, 1867–1943', *Mind*, 53 (1944), 189–91.

Moral Obligation: Essays and Lectures, ed. with a note by W. D. Ross (Oxford: Clarendon Press, 1949).

Knowledge and Perception: Essays and Lectures, ed. with a preface by W. D. Ross (Oxford: Clarendon Press, 1950).

Moral Obligation and Duty And Interest: Essays And Lectures, introd. by J. O. Urmson (Oxford: Oxford University Press Paperback, 1968).

UNPUBLISHED WRITINGS

1. Letters of H. A. Prichard, 1924–47, Bodleian Library, University of Oxford, MS English Letters, c 131, c 276, MS Eng. Letters d 116. Three volumes, fifty-one letters. Prichard's scrawls require dedication. Additionally, Geoffrey Warnock allowed me to photocopy an exchange which had belonged to J. L. Austin. The original discussion was between Prichard and H. H. Price. Prichard brought Austin into it. It included J. L. Austin's notes on the issue, and Prichard's two letters to Austin. The issue was whether or not promise statements should be understood as propositions, which are true or false, or actions.

2. Essays of H. A. Prichard, Bodleian Library, University of Oxford, MS English Miscellaneous, d 329, MS Eng. Misc. C 299. Two volumes, of six essays in total.
3. 'Manuscript on Morals', Trinity College Library, University of Oxford, Trinity College Archive, OF 21 Prichard [Ch. 8 in this vol.]. Title is 'Moral Obligation', six chapters, 167 typewritten pages. Two identical typescripts, one contains notes for lectures, the other is left clean and clear. The latter is probably what Prichard refers to in a letter to H. J. Paton in 1928 in which he says 'I am as a matter of fact plugging away on a book of morals and have got a draft of six chapters typed.' Prichard entitles the draft 'Moral Obligation', which is also the title Ross gives to the book of Prichard's papers, the title Prichard uses for chapters, and which Prichard or Ross gave to the long essay which Ross lists as 'Moral Obligation (1937)'. Although the original of the essay is unavailable for comparison, the two writings differ importantly. To lessen the confusion of titles, I entitle the clear typescript of six chapters the 'Manuscript on Morals'. There are other editing problems. In the 'Manuscript', Prichard has a number of footnotes which were supposed to refer to other parts of the work, but are left blank. These footnotes are omitted. Chapters are entitled 'Moral Obligation' and 'Moral Obligation cont'. To lessen that confusion and to emphasize arguments of importance, I have altered the names and divisions of the chapters in the 'Manuscript on Morals'. Prichard repeats arguments in the 'Manuscript on Morals' and the essay 'Moral Obligation'. To minimize repetition where arguments overlap, I omit parts of the typescript 'Manuscript on Morals'. Where these changes are made, titles, omissions, etc. are noted.

    Editing matters aside, the 'Manuscript on Morals' is independently valuable in two ways. First, its arguments are less given to criticism of others, thereby easing interpretation of Prichard's own moral philosophy. Second, he clarifies his differences with Sidgwick, his principal opponent.
4. A copy of a student's notes on Prichard's lectures on Kant's *Critique Of Pure Reason*. Of interest, because the lectures go further into the *Critique* than does Prichard's book. Philosophy Library, 10 Merton Street, Oxford, shelfmark MS Prichard 1; 1907, 1908.
5. A good copy of a student's notes on Prichard's lectures on moral philosophy [Ch. 5 in this vol.]. W. Kneale, himself White's Professor of Moral Philosophy, wrote: 'This is a typescript of lectures which H. A. Prichard gave in 1928 as White's Professor of Moral Philosophy. It was acquired by Messrs. Blackwell in a parcel of books somewhere about 1955 and was given to me by one of the assistants as something which could not be sold but ought nevertheless to be preserved.' Archives, Corpus Christi College, MS CCC 529.
6. A handwritten manuscript entitled 'Republic' of 179 pages, signed 'H. A. Prichard, Trinity College, Oxford'; apparently Prichard's lectures on

Plato's *Republic*, no date, probably given between 1907 and 1923. Interesting for comments on Plato's and early Greek epistemology. Found by Dr W. A. Hart, University of Ulster, Coleraine, County Londonderry, Northern Ireland, BT52 1SA. Dr Hart comments: 'I came across them nicely bound in a second-hand bookshop in Edinburgh some years ago.'

Note on the Contents

The aim of this volume is to provide the definitive edition of the published and previously unpublished moral writings of H. A. Prichard, establishing which are worth preservation. Prichard's writing style is clear and acute enough to make his writings attractive to the general reader and to undergraduates; but the goal is also to establish the scholar's critical edition.

It is appropriate to include all of the writings published in the Oxford paperback edition, which added Prichard's 'Duty and Interest' to the 1949 hardback edition. 'Duty and Interest' was Prichard's Inaugural Lecture as White's Professor of Moral Philosophy. (When Prichard reached the end of the lecture hour, he announced: 'I am not done, not nearly done. If you will leave your name and address on your way out, I'll see that you get a copy.') The paperback edition included also Urmson's valuable introduction. Chapters 11, 13, 15, and 16 in this edition attract readers interested in theory of action. But it is worth considering how important understanding the meaning of 'action' comes to be in Prichard's moral philosophy. At different times he thought that 'acting' meant 'originating causing' and at others 'willing to'. These are different concepts in morally evaluating actions.

In what follows I shall mention only the selections which have been added, and are so identified by the asterisk. Chapter 1 'What is the Basis of Moral Obligation' is among the most interesting and helpful of Prichard's essays. It provides a simple and uncluttered introduction. It is, however, puzzling with regard to moral dilemmas, a philosophical problem that intrigued Prichard. In the concluding paragraph of the Inaugural Lecture (which the attenders would not have heard!), Prichard says that Kant has 'the root of the matter in him'. Chapter 4 is an extensive study of Kant's ethics. In Chapter 2 the response to the problem of moral dilemmas seems rather dismissive. But Chapter 5 shows Prichard's concern once more in revealing difficulties caused by pairing a conflict of duties with 'ought implies can'.

Prichard may give the impression that refutation of the argument of others is a sufficient condition of truth. In Chapter 8, from the 'Manuscript on Morals', Prichard reveals more of his own philosophy than elsewhere. In the first letter in the Appendix, Cook Wilson, in stating bluntly and concisely his denial of theory of knowledge, opens the door to Prichard's rejection of moral theory in 'Mistake'. In the second letter in the Appendix Prichard's letter makes an incisive point in asking whether increasing goodness is of the same moral kind as Ross's other prima-facie duties.

I hope that the publication of these little-known writings, my survey of Prichard's unpublished writings, plus the bibliography of secondary literature, will aid scholars and properly distinguish Prichard's moral intuitionism.

J.I.M

Champlain College
Trent University
31 March, 2002

1. What is the Basis of Moral Obligation?

The thesis which I wish to propound and defend is that the question admits of no general answer, and is, strictly speaking, improper as implying that there is a common reason why all right acts are right. But since in philosophy the truth can only be reached via the ruins of the false, I shall consider first the only plausible answers.

If we waive the appeal to self-interest as not merely inconclusive on its own lines but as obviously irrelevant, we see, I think, that only two answers are possible.

In an action we consciously originate a new state of affairs. In putting on our boots we bring about or produce a state of affairs in which our boots are on our feet. What we originate, however, need not be confined to the state of affairs originated as soon as the action is over, and everything directly or indirectly originated is called, in distinction from the action, an effect or consequence of it. Now it is natural to argue that Kant's mistake lay in refusing to base the rightness of a right action on the nature of its effect. His reason was that otherwise an agent would be moved by *desire*, and desire for *pleasure*. But this consequence can be avoided, if the goodness of the effect be considered the true reason why. For appreciation of the goodness of the effect is different from *desire* for the effect, and will originate not the *desire* but the *sense of obligation* to produce it. Moreover the goodness of the effect is the true reason why. For the goodness of anything involves that, if we can, we ought to bring it into existence. Hence the reason 'why' an action ought to be done lies in the goodness of its effect, and if in a given situation two or more good things cannot all be produced, that action is right which will produce the maximum of good, this maximum being that at which we ought to aim. By accepting this view we retain for morality the required objectivity, i.e. independence of the individual's idiosyncrasies. For while the objects of desire differ for different individuals, the goodness of anything is a fact the recognition of which is the same for all, and so determination of the rightness of an action by reference to the goodness of its effect is as objective as any other process of knowledge.

[This essay, not previously published, appears in the Bodleian Library, University of Oxford, Ms Eng. Misc. c 299.]

This view is, of course, Utilitarianism in the broad sense in which the good to which 'utility' refers is not limited to pleasure. Unfortunately it fails to correspond with our real moral convictions, and any view must satisfy this test. Even the view in question has really to appeal to a direct apprehension that anything good ought, as such, to be produced, and the process of testing it by reference to our moral convictions is only a way of ascertaining by instances whether we have such an apprehension.

On this view the wrongness of a lie would be thought proportional to the badness of the error produced, and the obligation of the widow to give a mite would be thought vastly less than that of a millionaire to give a million. But it most plainly does violence to our moral convictions in respect of the distribution of things good between (*a*) ourselves and others and (*b*) two persons differently related to us. Suppose all the houses and provisions of a village are damaged by a landslide, and suppose every villager but one is hurt. Suppose the circumstances such that the one sound man could only devote himself to providing food and shelter for one person. The acquisition of food and shelter by each would be equally good. Hence on the view there would be an obligation and an equal obligation on the one sound man to find food and shelter for himself, for his parent, and for a stranger. But while it might be contended that he had the right to consider himself as much as any other, (and so that it would be legitimate or not wrong to do so), no one would suppose that he was under a positive obligation to do so. Moreover everyone would hold, contrary to the view, that the obligation to help his father was greater than that to help a stranger. Again, if he happened to be able to help himself *most*, there would, on the view, be a positive obligation on him to neglect the others, and to help them would be wrong. And if he happened to be able to divide his help, it would not matter, on the view considered, whether or not he concentrated on only a few, provided the total good produced were the same, and if he could produce a maximum by concentrating on one sufferer, to do so would be his duty. Yet we all think that, as a matter of *justice*, all the others have claims on him in varying degrees and that he *ought* to *distribute* his help without mere reference to the total result. The fact is that Utilitarianism cannot account for the obligation to act justly. Again allow that for anyone to have mean thoughts is a bad thing in the universe. No one thinks that it is equally an obligation on me to suppress them and to persuade another to suppress them. Their suppression in me is considered as my special business or duty in a way in which their suppression in another is not, and not merely because the latter is more difficult. Again it is thought my duty to make myself, say, courageous in a way in which it is not my duty to make anyone else so, and again not merely because it is more easy.

There does seem, however, an element of truth in the view, viz: that unless the effect of an action were in some way good, there would be no obligation to produce it, i.e., that the goodness of the thing produced is a presupposition of the obligation to produce it. And it may be said truly that Kant ignores this. But this is a long way from saying that this goodness is sufficient to constitute the act an obligation.

If this view fails, there seems only one other to put in its place. This may be put thus. The rightness of a right act must be based on the goodness of *something*. As this goodness cannot be that of the effect, it must be that of the act itself. Certain acts, e.g. acts of courage and generosity, are good in themselves and that is why we ought to do them.

This view is less superficial than the former but, I think, on the whole more wrong. It is quite certain that when we pronounce an act already done intrinsically good or bad, we do so in respect of the motive, i.e. that which led the agent to act as he did. A motive which we recognize as good seems to belong to one of two species. It may be either the sense that the act ought to be done or a desire arising out of some intrinsically good emotion such as sympathy, family affection, shame at being overcome by fear, or some good interest, such as interest in one's family or the public welfare.

It is also, I think, quite certain that the rightness or wrongness of an action is independent of the motive. A man who pays his debts from fear of the consequences does what he ought just as much as the man who does so because he feels that he ought to. No doubt his act is *not* moral, but it *is* right. This is also clear from the fact that the man who is about to act and is considering what he ought to do takes no account of any motive which might lead him to act. In acting we originate something and the agent's problem is simply 'What ought I to originate?' or 'Is some particular thing a thing which I ought to originate, e.g. the pleasure which a sick friend will gain by being read to?'. Though the agent knows that if he acts he will act from a motive, his problem is not in fact 'What is the motive from which I ought to act?' Moreover it cannot be. For if the problem is 'what is the good motive which makes acting on it something which I ought to do?' the good motive must be either the sense that some particular thing ought to be done or some good desire. The former alternative plainly begs the question, for it assumes knowledge of the very thing to be discovered, viz. that some particular thing ought to be done. The latter involves an impossibility. It cannot be true that we ought to act on a certain desire; for at any given moment its existence and degree is out of our power. We either have it, and in the required degree, or we do not. If we have it, we shall act accordingly; if we have not, we shall not.

No doubt a certain act would be *better* if done, say, from sympathy than if done from self-interest, but this fact does not constitute an obligation to do it from sympathy, though it may give rise to an obligation to do acts which will have the effect of making actions from sympathy more possible in the future. In fact the general criticism of the view is that, while it is in our power to act, it is not in our power to act from a certain motive, and there can only be an obligation to do what is in our power.

What then is the truth?

The following considerations are plain:

(1) Obligations are always obligations to do particular things, e.g. to do my work as well as I can, to write home, to conquer my laziness, to pay my taxes, to provide for my family. Correspondingly, our recognition of an obligation is the recognition of a particular obligation.

(2) The question 'Why ought I to do so and so?' is sometimes legitimate and admits of an answer. 'Why ought I to go to Hamlet?'. 'Because it will stimulate a certain higher part of my nature.' 'Why ought I to write to X?'. 'Because he is an old friend and would like news'. 'Why ought I to send Y a cheque for £5?' 'Because I owe him the money'.

(3) Unless trying to defend some theory, we should regard certain answers as sufficient. That is, we should not think of putting the question 'why?' *again*, e.g. 'Why ought I to stimulate that higher part of my nature, viz. my interest in the wider issues of life?', or 'Why ought I to give my old friend the news he would like?'.

(4) If we do put the question again, the answer instead of, as before, stating something *particular* states a *principle*, e.g. 'Because I ought to stimulate *any* higher part of my nature,' or 'Because I ought to do *any* old friend *a* service which I alone can render' or 'because I ought to pay *anything* I owe or have promised to pay.'

(5) Here we come to a stop. We should not ask a reason for the principle, nor, if we did, could we find one. And we should be—inclined to say—truly I think—that anyone must either recognize the truth of the principle directly, i.e. as self-evident, or fail to see it altogether. This implies not only that a further reason is not forthcoming but that it is not needed, the reason lying within the principle itself. Thus it is implied that the fact that I have promised to pay a man so much is the reason why I ought to pay it, i.e. that the connexion between the obligation to pay and my having promised is immediate, i.e. that the one directly necessitates the other, as the straightness of a line necessitates its being the shortest way between its ends. Again it is implied that the very fact that someone is an old friend and that something would be a benefit to him which I alone can render makes the act leading to the benefit one which I ought to do. The connexion being immediate, our apprehension of it must be immediate. It is not that the principle has *no* reason but that it *includes* its reason, the reason becoming explicit when the principle is properly expressed, e.g. my promise to pay someone something, *as such*, (i.e. simply as the promise to pay him) involves that I ought to pay him.

Again (6) analysis of any moral principle will show, I think, that it includes mention of two things, (*a*) a good thing which the action will produce, (*b*) a definite relation in which the agent stands either to another or to himself, this relation forming part of the actual situation in which he has to act. In the case of paying a debt there is (*a*) the creditor's regaining his property and (*b*) the relationship between debtor and creditor constituted by the latter's having previously lent the money on the former's undertaking to repay. In the case of a man's providing for his children there is (*a*) the goodness of the children having the means of subsistence, as a condition of any good life, and (*b*) the relation between the father and his children constituted by his having brought them into existence, necessarily under conditions in which they cannot provide for themselves. In the case of veracity, there is (*a*) the importance of being able to count on the truth from others as a condition of any decent existence in which men live in communication with others, and (*b*) the relationship between one man and another as wanting and asking for the truth. In the case of stimulating our higher nature, there is (*a*) the goodness of actualizing this, and (*b*) the fact that I am in a unique relation towards the possibility of actualizing it, in virtue of which I am responsible for actualizing it in a way in which others are not.

If this be right, moral principles are not deducible from one moral principle, or from anything which is not a moral principle, but each stands on its own footing, i.e. has its own special reason, a reason usually conveyed in the ordinary formulation of it, e.g. a man ought to pay his *debts*, to *provide* for his *family*, to *repay benefits*, to *serve his state*. (cf. The fact that ἀγαθά differ ᾗ ἀγαθά (Eth. I. 6), i.e. that the goodness of different good things lies in what is specific to each.) If, moreover, moral principles *were* all deducible from some one principle, there would be only *one* kind of duty, or *one* moral principle—which is plainly not the case.

To complete this account three facts need to be brought out.

(1) The first concerns the true relation between our apprehension of a particular obligation and that of the corresponding principle. Suppose I ask 'Why ought I to send Y £5 owed?' and get the only answer possible, 'Because you ought to pay *anything* which you owe'—which expresses a *principle*. Clearly I am not really being taken any further. For how can I be brought to see the truth of the principle except in connexion with a particular instance? And for this purpose *any* instance will do. If I cannot see that I ought to pay *this* debt, I shall not be able to see that I ought to pay *a* debt. To see that I ought to pay *a* debt, I must see that I ought to pay some particular debt and then recognize that this obligation does not depend on the action being one of paying, say, £5 to another who would like it—which it is—but simply on its being one of paying to another something which I owe him—which it also is; I then see that similar obligations will hold elsewhere, i.e. that any debt ought to be paid. Hence we do not deduce the particular obligation from a principle apprehended first. We first recognize the particular obligation and then by reflecting on it discover the principle, i.e. formulate to ourselves that general character of the act which renders it, or any act like it, an obligation. The sole value of formulating the principle is that it brings out in black and white, to anyone hesitating to admit the particular obligation, just that feature of the act which constitutes it an obligation.

WHAT IS THE BASIS OF MORAL OBLIGATION?

(2) The second concerns conflicting obligations. How are we to decide what we ought to do when obligations conflict? Here again no general answer seems possible. We can only point out (*a*) that obligations admit of degrees, (*b*) that in a case of conflict the question is simply 'which obligation is the greater?', (*c*) that in the end the question can only be answered by our immediate recognition, when *all* the circumstances have been taken into account, that one is the greater or the greatest, (*d*) that the problem is often one of extreme difficulty, but (*e*) that in any case there is no general criterion for solving it.

(3) Heaven forbid that I should suggest that everyone is aware of their obligations, even when full-grown. Nothing is more obvious than men's differences in this respect and of the blindness of some, especially in regard to their wider obligations, e.g. to the state or to humanity at large. This is largely due to want of thoughtfulness. (Cf. men's attitude to the so-called 'social problem'). And it must be allowed that owing to the complication of human relations, the problem of what one ought to do, from the point of life as a whole, must present itself to any thinking man as one of intense difficulty and, indeed, doubt.

2. Does Moral Philosophy Rest on a Mistake?

Probably to most students of Moral Philosophy there comes a time when they feel a vague sense of dissatisfaction with the whole subject. And the sense of dissatisfaction tends to grow rather than to diminish. It is not so much that the positions, and still more the arguments, of particular thinkers seem unconvincing, though this is true. It is rather that the aim of the subject becomes increasingly obscure. 'What', it is asked, 'are we really going to learn by Moral Philosophy?' 'What are books on Moral Philosophy really trying to show, and when their aim is clear, why are they so unconvincing and artificial?' And again: 'Why is it so difficult to substitute anything better?' Personally, I have been led by growing dissatisfaction of this kind to wonder whether the reason may not be that the subject, at any rate as usually understood, consists in the attempt to answer an improper question. And in this article I shall venture to contend that the existence of the whole subject, as usually understood, rests on a mistake, and on a mistake parallel to that on which rests, as I think, the subject usually called the Theory of Knowledge.

If we reflect on our own mental history or on the history of the subject, we feel no doubt about the nature of the demand which originates the subject. Any one who, stimulated by education, has come to feel the force of the various obligations in life, at some time or other comes to feel the irksomeness of carrying them out, and to recognize the sacrifice of interest involved; and, if thoughtful, he inevitably puts to himself the question: 'Is there really a reason why I should act in the ways in which hitherto I have thought I ought to act? May I not have been all the time under an illusion in so thinking? Should not I really be justified in simply trying to have a good time?' Yet, like Glaucon, feeling that somehow he ought after all to act in these ways, he asks for a *proof* that this feeling is justified. In other words, he asks, '*Why* should I do these things?', and his and other people's moral philosophizing is an attempt to supply the answer, i.e. to supply by a process of reflection a proof of the truth of what he and they have prior to reflection believed immediately or without proof. This frame of mind seems to present a close parallel to the frame of mind which originates the Theory of Knowledge. Just as the recognition that the doing of our duty often

[From *Mind*, 21/81 (Jan. 1912), 21–37.]

vitally interferes with the satisfaction of our inclinations leads us to wonder whether we really ought to do what we usually call our duty, so the recognition that we and others are liable to mistakes in knowledge generally leads us, as it did Descartes, to wonder whether hitherto we may not have been always mistaken. And just as we try to find a proof, based on the general consideration of action and of human life, that we ought to act in the ways usually called moral, so we, like Descartes, propose by a process of reflection on our thinking to find a test of knowledge, i.e. a principle by applying which we can show that a certain condition of mind was really knowledge, a condition which *ex hypothesi* existed independently of the process of reflection.

Now, how has the moral question been answered? So far as I can see, the answers all fall, and fall from the necessities of the case, into one of two species. *Either* they state that we ought to do so and so, because, as we see when we fully apprehend the facts, doing so will be for our good, i.e. really, as I would rather say, for our advantage, or, better still, for our happiness; *or* they state that we ought to do so and so, because something realized either in or by the action is good. In other words, the reason 'why' is stated in terms either of the agent's happiness or of the goodness of something involved in the action.

To see the prevalence of the former species of answer, we have only to consider the history of Moral Philosophy. To take obvious instances, Plato, Butler, Hutcheson, Paley, Mill, each in his own way seeks at bottom to convince the individual that he ought to act in so-called moral ways by showing that to do so will really be for his happiness. Plato is perhaps the most significant instance, because of all philosophers he is the one to whom we are least willing to ascribe a mistake on such matters, and a mistake on his part would be evidence of the deep-rootedness of the tendency to make it. To show that Plato really justifies morality by its profitableness, it is only necessary to point out (1) that the very formulation of the thesis to be met, viz. that justice is $\dot{\alpha}\lambda\lambda\acute{o}\tau\rho\iota o\nu\ \dot{\alpha}\gamma\alpha\theta\acute{o}\nu$, implies that any refutation must consist in showing that justice is $o\dot{\iota}\kappa\epsilon\hat{\iota}o\nu\ \dot{\alpha}\gamma\alpha\theta\acute{o}\nu$, i.e. really, as the context shows, one's own advantage, and (2) that the term $\lambda\upsilon\sigma\iota\tau\epsilon\lambda\epsilon\hat{\iota}\nu$ supplies the key not only to the problem but also to its solution.

The tendency to justify acting on moral rules in this way is natural. For if, as often happens, we put to ourselves the question 'Why should we do so and so?', we are satisfied by being convinced either that the doing so will lead to something which we want (e.g. that taking certain medicine will heal our disease), or that the doing so itself, as we see when we appreciate its nature, is something that we want or should like, e.g. playing golf. The formulation of the question implies a state of unwillingness or indifference towards the action, and we are brought into a condition of willingness by the answer. And this process seems to be precisely what we desire when we ask, e.g., 'Why should we keep our engagements to our own loss?'; for it is just the fact that the keeping of our engagement runs counter to the satisfaction of our desires which produced the question.

The answer is, of course, not an answer, for it fails to convince us that we ought to keep our engagements; even if successful on its own lines, it only makes us *want* to keep them. And Kant was really only pointing out this fact when he distinguished hypothetical and categorical imperatives, even though he obscured the nature of the fact by wrongly describing his so-called 'hypothetical imperatives' as imperatives. But if this answer be no answer, what other can be offered? Only, it seems, an answer which bases the obligation to do something on the *goodness* either of something to which the act leads or of the act itself. Suppose, when wondering whether we really ought to act in the ways usually called moral, we are told as a means of resolving our doubt that those acts are right which produce happiness. We at once ask: 'Whose happiness?' If we are told 'Our own happiness', then, though we shall lose our hesitation to act in these ways, we shall not recover our sense that we ought to do so. But how can this result be avoided? Apparently, only by being told one of two things; *either* that anyone's happiness is a thing good in itself, and that *therefore* we ought to do whatever will produce it, *or* that working for happiness is itself good, and that the intrinsic goodness of such an action is the reason why we ought to do it. The advantage of this appeal to the goodness of something consists in the fact that it avoids reference to desire, and, instead, refers to something impersonal and objective. In this way it seems possible to avoid the resolution of obligation into inclination. But just for this reason it is of the essence of the answer, that to be effective it must neither include nor involve the view that the apprehension of the goodness of anything necessarily arouses the desire for it. Otherwise the answer resolves itself into a form of the former answer by substituting desire or inclination for the sense of obligation, and in this way it loses what seems its special advantage.

Now it seems to me that both forms of this answer break down, though each for a different reason.

Consider the first form. It is what may be called Utilitarianism in the generic sense, in which what is good is not limited to pleasure. It takes its stand upon the distinction between something which is not itself an action, but which can be produced by an action, and the action which will produce it, and contends that if something which is not an action is good, then we *ought* to undertake the action which will, directly or indirectly, originate it.[1]

But this argument, if it is to restore the sense of obligation to act, must presuppose an intermediate link, viz. the further thesis that what is good ought to be.[2] The necessity of this link is obvious. An 'ought,' if it is to be derived at all, can only be derived from another 'ought'. Moreover, this link tacitly presupposes another, viz. that the apprehension that something good which is not an action

---

[1] Cf. Dr Rashdall's *Theory of Good and Evil*, vol. i, p. 138.
[2] Dr Rashdall, if I understand him rightly, supplies this link (cf. ibid. 135–6).

ought to be involves just the feeling of imperativeness or obligation which is to be aroused by the thought of the action which will originate it. Otherwise the argument will not lead us to feel the obligation to produce it by the action. And, surely, both this link and its implication are false.[3] The word 'ought' refers to actions and to actions alone. The proper language is never 'So and so ought to be', but 'I ought to do so and so'. Even if we are sometimes moved to say that the world or something in it is not what it ought to be, what we really mean is that God or some human being has not made something what he ought to have made it. And it is merely stating another side of this fact to urge that we can only feel the imperativeness upon us of something which is in our power; for it is actions and actions alone which, directly at least, are in our power.

Perhaps, however, the best way to see the failure of this view is to see its failure to correspond to our actual moral convictions. Suppose we ask ourselves whether our sense that we ought to pay our debts or to tell the truth arises from our recognition that in doing so we should be originating something good, e.g. material comfort in *A* or true belief in *B*, i.e. suppose we ask ourselves whether it is this aspect of the action which leads to our recognition that we ought to do it. We at once and without hesitation answer 'No'. Again, if we take as our illustration our sense that we ought to act justly as between two parties, we have, if possible, even less hesitation in giving a similar answer; for the balance of resulting good may be, and often is, not on the side of justice.

At best it can only be maintained that there is this element of truth in the Utilitarian view, that unless we recognized that something which an act will originate is good, we should not recognize that we ought to do the action. Unless we thought knowledge a good thing, it may be urged, we should not think that we ought to tell the truth; unless we thought pain a bad thing, we should not think the infliction of it, without special reason, wrong. But this is not to imply that the badness of error is the reason why it is wrong to lie, or the badness of pain the reason why we ought not to inflict it without special cause.[4]

It is, I think, just because this form of the view is so plainly at variance with our moral consciousness that we are driven to adopt the other form of the view, viz. that the act is good in itself and that its intrinsic goodness is the reason why it ought to be done. It is this form which has always made the most serious appeal; for the goodness of the act itself seems more closely related to the obligation to do it than that of its mere consequences or results, and therefore, if obligation is to be based on the goodness of something, it would seem that this goodness

---

[3] When we speak of anything, e.g. of some emotion or of some quality of a human being, as good, we never dream in our ordinary consciousness of going on to say that therefore it ought to be.

[4] It may be noted that if the badness of pain were the reason why we ought not to inflict pain on another, it would equally be a reason why we ought not to inflict pain on ourselves; yet, though we should allow the wanton infliction of pain on ourselves to be foolish, we should not think of describing it as wrong.

should be that of the act itself. Moreover, the view gains plausibility from the fact that moral actions are most conspicuously those to which the term 'intrinsically good' is applicable.

Nevertheless this view, though perhaps less superficial, is equally untenable. For it leads to precisely the dilemma which faces everyone who tries to solve the problem raised by Kant's theory of the good will. To see this, we need only consider the nature of the acts to which we apply the term 'intrinsically good'.

There is, of course, no doubt that we approve and even admire certain actions, and also that we should describe them as good, and as good in themselves. But it is, I think, equally unquestionable that our approval and our use of the term 'good' is always in respect of the motive and refers to actions which have been actually done and of which we think we know the motive. Further, the actions of which we approve and which we should describe as intrinsically good are of two and only two kinds. They are either actions in which the agent did what he did because he thought he ought to do it, or actions of which the motive was a desire prompted by some good emotion, such as gratitude, affection, family feeling, or public spirit, the most prominent of such desires in books on Moral Philosophy being that ascribed to what is vaguely called benevolence. For the sake of simplicity I omit the case of actions done partly from some such desire and partly from a sense of duty; for even if all good actions are done from a combination of these motives, the argument will not be affected. The dilemma is this. If the motive in respect of which we think an action good is the sense of obligation, then so far from the sense that we ought to do it being derived from our apprehension of its goodness, our apprehension of its goodness will presuppose the sense that we ought to do it. In other words, in this case the recognition that the act is good will plainly *presuppose* the recognition that the act is right, whereas the view under consideration is that the recognition of the goodness of the act *gives rise* to the recognition of its rightness. On the other hand, if the motive in respect of which we think an action good is some intrinsically good desire, such as the desire to help a friend, the recognition of the goodness of the act will equally fail to give rise to the sense of obligation to do it. For we cannot feel that we ought to do that the doing of which is *ex hypothesi* prompted solely by the desire to do it.[5]

The fallacy underlying the view is that while to base the rightness of an act upon its intrinsic goodness implies that the goodness in question is that of the motive, in reality the rightness or wrongness of an act has nothing to do with any question of motives at all. For, as any instance will show, the rightness of an action concerns an action not in the fuller sense of the term in which we include the motive in the action, but in the narrower and commoner sense in

---

[5] It is, I think, on this latter horn of the dilemma that Martineau's view falls; cf. *Types of Ethical Theory*, part ii, book i.

which we distinguish an action from its motive and mean by an action merely the conscious origination of something, an origination which on different occasions or in different people may be prompted by different motives. The question 'Ought I to pay my bills?' really means simply 'Ought I to bring about my tradesmen's possession of what by my previous acts I explicitly or implicitly promised them?' There is, and can be, no question of whether I ought to pay my debts from a particular motive. No doubt we know that if we pay our bills we shall pay them with a motive, but in considering whether we ought to pay them we inevitably think of the act in abstraction from the motive. Even if we knew what our motive would be if we did the act, we should not be any nearer an answer to the question.

Moreover, if we eventually pay our bills from fear of the county court, we shall still have done *what* we ought, even though we shall not have done it *as* we ought. The attempt to bring in the motive involves a mistake similar to that involved in supposing that we can will to will. To feel that I ought to pay my bills is to be *moved towards* paying them. But what I can be moved towards must always be an action and not an action in which I am moved in a particular way, i.e., an action from a particular motive; otherwise I should be moved towards being moved, which is impossible. Yet the view under consideration involves this impossibility, for it really resolves the sense that I ought to do so and so, into the sense that I ought to be moved to do it in a particular way.[6]

So far my contentions have been mainly negative, but they form, I think, a useful, if not a necessary, introduction to what I take to be the truth. This I will now endeavour to state, first formulating what, as I think, is the real nature of our apprehension or appreciation of moral obligations, and then applying the result to elucidate the question of the existence of Moral Philosophy.

The sense of obligation to do, or of the rightness of, an action of a particular kind is absolutely underivative or immediate. The rightness of an action consists in its being the origination of something of a certain kind *A* in a situation of a certain kind, a situation consisting in a certain relation *B* of the agent to others or to his own nature. To appreciate its rightness two preliminaries may be necessary. We may have to follow out the consequences of the proposed action more fully than we have hitherto done, in order to realize that in the action we should originate *A*. Thus we may not appreciate the wrongness of telling a certain story until we realize that we should thereby be hurting the feelings of one of our audience. Again, we may have to take into account the relation *B* involved in the situation, which we had hitherto failed to notice. For instance, we may not appreciate the obligation to give *X* a present, until we remember that he has done us an act of kindness. But, given that by a process which is, of course, merely a process of general and not of moral thinking we come to recognize

---

[6] It is of course not denied here that an action done from a particular motive may be *good*; it is only denied that the *rightness* of an action depends on its being done with a particular motive.

that the proposed act is one by which we shall originate *A* in a relation *B*, then we appreciate the obligation immediately or directly, the appreciation being an activity of *moral* thinking. We recognize, for instance, that this performance of a service to *X*, who has done us a service, just in virtue of its being the performance of a service to one who has rendered a service to the would-be agent, ought to be done by us. This apprehension is immediate, in precisely the sense in which a mathematical apprehension is immediate, e.g. the apprehension that this three-sided figure, in virtue of its being, must have three angles. Both apprehensions are immediate in the sense that in both insight into the nature of the subject directly leads us to recognize its possession of the predicate; and it is only stating this fact from the other side to say that in both cases the fact apprehended is self-evident.

The plausibility of the view that obligations are not self-evident but need proof lies in the fact that an act which is referred to as an obligation may be incompletely stated, what I have called the preliminaries to appreciating the obligation being incomplete. If, e.g., we refer to the act of repaying *X* by a present merely as giving *X* a present, it appears, and indeed is, necessary to give a reason. In other words, wherever a moral act is regarded in this incomplete way the question '*Why* should I do it?' is perfectly legitimate. This fact suggests, but suggests wrongly, that even if the nature of the act is completely stated, it is still necessary to give a reason, or, in other words, to supply a proof.

The relations involved in obligations of various kinds are, of course, very different. The relation in certain cases is a relation to others due to a past act of theirs or ours. The obligation to repay a benefit involves a relation due to a past act of the benefactor. The obligation to pay a bill involves a relation due to a past act of ours in which we have either said or implied that we would make a certain return for something which we have asked for and received. On the other hand, the obligation to speak the truth implies no such definite act; it involves a relation consisting in the fact that others are trusting us to speak the truth, a relation the apprehension of which gives rise to the sense that communication of the truth is something owing by us to them. Again, the obligation not to hurt the feelings of another involves no special relation of us to that other, i.e. no relation other than that involved in our both being men, and men in one and the same world. Moreover, it seems that the relation involved in an obligation need not be a relation to another at all. Thus we should admit that there is an obligation to overcome our natural timidity or greediness, and that this involves no relations to others. Still there is a relation involved, viz. a relation to our own disposition. It is simply because we can and because others cannot directly modify our disposition that it is our business to improve it, and that it is not theirs, or, at least, not theirs to the same extent.

The negative side of all this is, of course, that we do not come to appreciate an obligation by an *argument*, i.e. by a process of non-moral thinking, and that, in particular, we do not do so by an argument of which a premiss is the ethical but not moral activity of appreciating the goodness either of the act or of a consequence of the act; i.e. that our sense of the rightness of an act is not a conclusion from our appreciation of the goodness either of it or of anything else.

It will probably be urged that on this view our various obligations form, like Aristotle's categories, an unrelated chaos in which it is impossible to acquiesce. For, according to it, the obligation to repay a benefit, or to pay a debt, or to keep a promise, presupposes a previous act of another; whereas the obligation to speak the truth or not to harm another does not; and, again, the obligation to remove our timidity involves no relations to others at all. Yet, at any rate, an effective *argumentum ad hominem* is at hand in the fact that the various qualities which we recognize as good are equally unrelated; e.g. courage, humility, and interest in knowledge. If, as is plainly the case, ἀγαθά differ ᾗ ἀγαθά, why should not obligations equally differ *qua* their obligatoriness? Moreover, if this were not so there could in the end be only one obligation, which is palpably contrary to fact.[7]

Certain observations will help to make the view clearer.

In the first place, it may seem that the view, being—as it is—avowedly put forward in opposition to the view that what is right is derived from what is good, must itself involve the opposite of this, viz. the Kantian position that what is good is based upon what is right, i.e. that an act, if it be good, is good because it is right. But this is not so. For, on the view put forward, the rightness of a right action lies solely in the origination in which the act consists, whereas the intrinsic goodness of an action lies solely in its motive; and this implies that a morally good action is morally good not simply because it is a right action but because it is a right action done because it is right, i.e. from a sense of obligation. And this implication, it may be remarked incidentally, seems plainly true.

In the second place, the view involves that when, or rather so far as, we act from a sense of obligation, we have no purpose or end. By a 'purpose' or 'end'

---

[7] Two other objections may be anticipated: (1) that obligations cannot be self-evident, since many actions regarded as obligations by some are not so regarded by others, and (2) that if obligations are self-evident, the problem of how we ought to act in the presence of conflicting obligations is insoluble.

To the first I should reply:

(a) That the appreciation of an obligation is, of course, only possible for a developed moral being, and that different degrees of development are possible.

(b) That the failure to recognize some particular obligation is usually due to the fact that, owing to a lack of thoughtfulness, what I have called the preliminaries to this recognition are incomplete.

(c) That the view put forward is consistent with the admission that, owing to a lack of thoughtfulness, even the best men are blind to many of their obligations, and that in the end our obligations are seen to be co-extensive with almost the whole of our life.

To the second objection I should reply that obligation admits of degrees, and that where obligations conflict, the decision of what we ought to do turns not on the question 'Which of the alternative courses of action will originate the greater good?' but on the question 'Which is the greater obligation?'

we really mean something the existence of which we desire, and desire of the existence of which leads us to act. Usually our purpose is something which the act will originate, as when we turn round in order to look at a picture. But it may be the action itself, i.e. the origination of something, as when we hit a golf-ball into a hole or kill someone out of revenge.[8] Now if by a purpose we mean something the existence of which we desire and desire for which leads us to act, then plainly, so far as we act from a sense of obligation, we have no purpose, consisting either in the action or in anything which it will produce. This is so obvious that it scarcely seems worth pointing out. But I do so for two reasons. (1) If we fail to scrutinize the meaning of the terms 'end' and 'purpose', we are apt to assume uncritically that all deliberate action, i.e. action proper, must have a purpose; we then become puzzled both when we look for the purpose of an action done from a sense of obligation, and also when we try to apply to such an action the distinction of means and end, the truth all the time being that since there is no end, there is no means either. (2) The attempt to base the sense of obligation on the recognition of the goodness of something is really an attempt to find a purpose in a moral action in the shape of something good which, as good, we want. And the expectation that the goodness of something underlies an obligation disappears as soon as we cease to look for a purpose.

The thesis, however, that, so far as we act from a sense of obligation, we have no purpose must not be misunderstood. It must not be taken either to mean or to imply that so far as we so act we have no *motive*. No doubt in ordinary speech the words 'motive' and 'purpose' are usually treated as correlatives, 'motive' standing for the desire which induces us to act, and 'purpose' standing for the object of this desire. But this is only because, when we are looking for the motive of the action, say, of some crime, we are usually presupposing that the act in question is prompted by a desire and not by the sense of obligation. At bottom, however, we mean by a motive what moves us to act; a sense of obligation does sometimes move us to act; and in our ordinary consciousness we should not hesitate to allow that the action we were considering might have had as its motive a sense of obligation. Desire and the sense of obligation are co-ordinate forms or species of motive.

In the third place, if the view put forward be right, we must sharply distinguish morality and virtue as independent, though related, species of goodness, neither being an aspect of something of which the other is an aspect, nor again a form or species of the other, nor again something deducible from the other; and we must at the same time allow that it is possible to do the same act either virtuously or morally or in both ways at once. And surely this is true. An act, to be virtuous,

[8] It is no objection to urge that an action cannot be its own purpose, since the purpose of something cannot be the thing itself. For, speaking strictly, the purpose is not the *action's* purpose but *our* purpose, and there is no contradiction in holding that our purpose in acting may be the action.

must, as Aristotle saw, be done willingly or with pleasure; as such it is just not done from a sense of obligation but from some desire which is intrinsically good, as arising from some intrinsically good emotion. Thus, in an act of generosity the motive is the desire to help another arising from sympathy with that other; in an act which is courageous and no more, i.e. in an act which is not at the same time an act of public spirit or family affection or the like, we prevent ourselves from being dominated by a feeling of terror, desiring to do so from a sense of shame at being terrified. The goodness of such an act is different from the goodness of an act to which we apply the term moral in the strict and narrow sense, viz. an act done from a sense of obligation. Its goodness lies in the intrinsic goodness of the emotion and of the consequent desire under which we act, the goodness of this motive being different from the goodness of the moral motive proper, viz. the sense of duty or obligation. Nevertheless, at any rate in certain cases, an act can be done either virtuously or morally or in both ways at once. It is possible to repay a benefit either from desire to repay it, or from the feeling that we ought to do so, or from both motives combined. A doctor may tend his patients either from a desire arising out of interest in his patients or in the exercise of skill, or from a sense of duty, or from a desire and a sense of duty combined. Further, although we recognize that in each case the act possesses an intrinsic goodness, we regard that action as the best in which both motives are combined; in other words, we regard as the really best man the man in whom virtue and morality are united.

It may be objected that the distinction between the two kinds of motive is untenable, on the ground that the *desire* to repay a benefit, for example, is only the manifestation of that which manifests itself as the *sense of obligation* to repay whenever we think of something in the action which is other than the repayment and which we should not like, such as the loss or pain involved. Yet the distinction can, I think, easily be shown to be tenable. For, in the analogous case of revenge, the desire to return the injury and the sense that we ought not to do so, leading, as they do, in opposite directions, are plainly distinct; and the obviousness of the distinction here seems to remove any difficulty in admitting the existence of a parallel distinction between the desire to return a benefit and the sense that we ought to return it.[9]

Further, the view implies that an obligation can no more be based on or derived from a virtue than a virtue can be derived from an obligation, in which latter

[9] This sharp distinction of virtue and morality as co-ordinate and independent forms of goodness will explain a fact which otherwise it is difficult to account for. If we turn from books on Moral Philosophy to any vivid account of human life and action such as we find in Shakespeare, nothing strikes us more than the comparative remoteness of the discussions of Moral Philosophy from the facts of actual life. Is not this largely because, while Moral Philosophy has, quite rightly, concentrated its attention on the fact of obligation, in the case of many of those whom we admire most and whose lives are of the greatest interest, the sense of obligation, though it may be an important, is not a dominating factor in their lives?

case a virtue would consist in carrying out an obligation. And the implication is surely true and important. Take the case of courage. It is untrue to urge that, since courage is a virtue, we ought to act courageously. It is and must be untrue, because, as we see in the end, to feel an obligation to act courageously would involve a contradiction. For, as I have urged before, we can only feel an obligation to *act*; we cannot feel an obligation to *act from a certain desire*, in this case the desire to conquer one's feelings of terror arising from the sense of shame which they arouse. Moreover, if the sense of obligation to act in a particular way leads to an action, the action will be an action done from a sense of obligation, and therefore not, if the above analysis of virtue be right, an act of courage.

The mistake of supposing that there can be an obligation to act courageously seems to arise from two causes. In the first place, there is often an obligation to do that which involves the conquering or controlling of our fear in the doing of it, e.g. the obligation to walk along the side of a precipice to fetch a doctor for a member of our family. Here the acting on the obligation is externally, though only externally, the same as an act of courage proper. In the second place there is an obligation to acquire courage, i.e. to do such things as will enable us afterwards to act courageously, and this may be mistaken for an obligation to act courageously. The same considerations can, of course, be applied, *mutatis mutandis*, to the other virtues.

The fact, if it be a fact, that virtue is no basis for morality will explain what otherwise it is difficult to account for, viz. the extreme sense of dissatisfaction produced by a close reading of Aristotle's *Ethics*. Why is the *Ethics* so disappointing? Not, I think, because it really answers two radically different questions as if they were one: (1) 'What is the happy life?', (2) 'What is the virtuous life?' It is, rather, because Aristotle does not do what we as moral philosophers want him to do, viz. to convince us that we really ought to do what in our non-reflective consciousness we have hitherto believed we ought to do, or if not, to tell us what, if any, are the other things which we really ought to do, and to prove to us that he is right. Now, if what I have just been contending is true, a systematic account of the virtuous character cannot possibly satisfy this demand. At best it can only make clear to us the details of one of our obligations, viz. the obligation to make ourselves better men; but the achievement of this does not help us to discover what we ought to do in life as a whole, and why; to think that it did would be to think that our only business in life was self-improvement. Hence it is not surprising that Aristotle's account of the good man strikes us as almost wholly of academic value, with little relation to our real demand, which is formulated in Plato's words: οὐ γὰρ περὶ τοῦ ἐπιτυχόντος ὁ λόγος, ἀλλὰ περὶ τοῦ ὅντινα τρόπον χρῆ ζῆν.

I am not, of course, *criticizing* Aristotle for failing to satisfy this demand, except so far as here and there he leads us to think that he intends to satisfy it. For my main contention is that the demand cannot be satisfied, and cannot be satisfied because it is illegitimate. Thus we are brought to the question: 'Is there really such a thing as Moral Philosophy, and, if there is, in what sense?'

We should first consider the parallel case—as it appears to be—of the Theory of Knowledge. As I urged before, at some time or other in the history of all of us, if we are thoughtful, the frequency of our own and of others' mistakes is bound to lead to the reflection that possibly we and others have *always* been mistaken in consequence of some radical defect of our faculties. In consequence, certain things which previously we should have said without hesitation that we *knew*, as e.g. that $4 \times 7 = 28$, become subject to doubt; we become able only to say that we thought we knew these things. We inevitably go on to look for some general procedure by which we can ascertain that a given condition of mind is really one of knowledge. And this involves the search for a criterion of knowledge, i.e. for a principle by applying which we can settle that a given state of mind is really knowledge. The search for this criterion and the application of it, when found, is what is called the Theory of Knowledge. The search implies that instead of its being the fact that the knowledge that A is B is obtained directly by consideration of the nature of A and B, the knowledge that A is B, in the full or complete sense, can only be obtained by first knowing that A is B, and then knowing that we knew it by applying a criterion, such as Descartes's principle that what we clearly and distinctly conceive is true.

Now it is easy to show that the doubt whether A is B, based on this speculative or general ground, could, if genuine, never be set at rest. For if, in order really to know that A is B, we must first know that we knew it, then really, to know that we knew it, we must first know that we knew that we knew it. But—what is more important—it is also easy to show that this doubt is not a genuine doubt but rests on a confusion the exposure of which removes the doubt. For when we *say* we doubt whether our previous condition was one of knowledge, what we *mean*, if we mean anything at all, is that we doubt whether our previous *belief* was *true*, a belief which we should express as the *thinking* that A is B. For in order to doubt whether our previous condition was one of knowledge, we have to think of it not as knowledge but as only belief, and our only question can be 'Was this belief true?' But as soon as we see that we are thinking of our previous condition as only one of belief, we see that what we are now doubting is not what we first *said* we were doubting, viz. whether a previous condition of knowledge was really knowledge. Hence, to remove the doubt, it is only necessary to appreciate the real nature of our consciousness in apprehending, e.g. that $7 \times 4 = 28$, and thereby see that it was no mere condition of believing but a condition of knowing, and then to notice that in our subsequent doubt what we are really doubting is not whether this consciousness was really knowledge, but whether a consciousness of another kind, viz. a belief that $7 \times 4 = 28$, was true. We thereby see that though a doubt based on speculative grounds is possible, it is not a doubt concerning what we believed the doubt concerned, and that a doubt concerning this latter is impossible.

Two results follow. In the first place, if, as is usually the case, we mean by the 'Theory of Knowledge' the knowledge which supplies the answer to the question 'Is what we have hitherto thought knowledge really knowledge?', there is and can be no such thing, and the supposition that there can is simply due to a confusion. There can be no answer to an illegitimate question, except that the question is illegitimate. Nevertheless the question is one which we continue to put until we realize the inevitable immediacy of knowledge. And it is positive knowledge that knowledge is immediate and neither can be, nor needs to be, improved or vindicated by the further knowledge that it was knowledge. This positive knowledge sets at rest the inevitable doubt, and, so far as by the 'Theory of Knowledge' is meant this knowledge, then even though this knowledge be the knowledge that there is no Theory of Knowledge in the former sense, to that extent the Theory of Knowledge exists.

In the second place, suppose we come genuinely to doubt whether, e.g., $7 \times 4 = 28$ owing to a genuine doubt whether we were right in believing yesterday that $7 \times 4 = 28$, a doubt which can in fact only arise if we have lost our hold of, i.e. no longer remember, the real nature of our consciousness of yesterday, and so think of it as consisting in believing. Plainly, the only remedy is to do the sum again. Or, to put the matter generally, if we do come to doubt whether it is true that A is B, as we once thought, the remedy lies not in any process of reflection but in such a reconsideration of the nature of A and B as leads to the knowledge that A is B.

With these considerations in mind, consider the parallel which, as it seems to me, is presented—though with certain differences—by Moral Philosophy. The sense that we ought to do certain things arises in our unreflective consciousness, being an activity of moral thinking occasioned by the various situations in which we find ourselves. At this stage our attitude to these obligations is one of unquestioning confidence. But inevitably the appreciation of the degree to which the execution of these obligations is contrary to our interest raises the doubt whether after all these obligations are really obligatory, i.e. whether our sense that we ought not to do certain things is not illusion. We then want to have it *proved* to us that we ought to do so, i.e. to be convinced of this by a process which, as an argument, is different in kind from our original and unreflective appreciation of it. This demand is, as I have argued, illegitimate.

Hence, in the first place, if, as is almost universally the case, by Moral Philosophy is meant the knowledge which would satisfy this demand, there is no such knowledge, and all attempts to attain it are doomed to failure because they rest on a mistake, the mistake of supposing the possibility of proving what can only be apprehended directly by an act of moral thinking. Nevertheless the demand, though illegitimate, is inevitable until we have carried the process of reflection far enough to realize the self-evidence of our obligations, i.e. the immediacy of our apprehension of them. This realization of their self-evidence is positive knowledge, and so far, and so far only, as the term Moral Philosophy is confined to this knowledge and to the knowledge of the parallel immediacy of the apprehension of the goodness of the various virtues and of good dispositions generally, is there such a thing as Moral Philosophy. But since this knowledge may allay doubts which often affect the whole conduct of life, it is, though not extensive, important and even vitally important.

In the second place, suppose we come genuinely to doubt whether we ought, for example, to pay our debts, owing to a genuine doubt whether our previous conviction that we ought to do so is true, a doubt which can, in fact, only arise if we fail to remember the real nature of what we now call our past conviction. The only remedy lies in actually getting into a situation which occasions the obligation, or—if our imagination be strong enough—in imagining ourselves in that situation, and then letting our moral capacities of thinking do their work. Or, to put the matter generally, if we do doubt whether there is really an obligation to originate *A* in a situation *B*, the remedy lies not in any process of general thinking, but in getting face to face with a particular instance of the situation *B*, and then directly appreciating the obligation to originate *A* in that situation.

3. Duty and Interest

You will naturally wish me to begin by giving expression to the regret occasioned by the severance of Professor Stewart's connexion with White's Chair, a connexion which has extended over thirty-one years. He brought to the service of the Chair the mind of a poet, of a mystic, and of a scholar with enthusiasm for learning and especially for the more humane studies. His writings and the variety of the subjects on which he lectured testify to the devotion with which as professor he served the University. Not everyone will go so far with him as to maintain that the real clue to the interpretation of Plato lies in the researches of modern psychologists, and that Plato is at least as important as a prophet or seer as he is as a philosopher; but all will recognize the infectious character of his admiration for Plato and the importance of his insistence that the interpretation of Plato requires a many-sided mind and a penetrating eye for the things which are unseen. Many, too, will think of that mine of information, his *Notes on the Nicomachean Ethics*, with feelings of admiration and personal gratitude. And you will naturally wish to join me in wishing Professor Stewart long continuance of what he has described as the life of practical Platonism.

I cannot refrain from also referring to Wallace and Green. No one, I think, could realize that he was, in a way, standing in their shoes without feeling humbled. To hear Wallace was an impressive experience. You felt that here was a spectator of all time and all existence telling you quietly and dispassionately about what he had seen. His literary skill and, even more, his penetration still strike me as astonishing; and when I have tried to console myself for my inability to follow Hegel's argument, I have found help in the reflection that even Wallace in interpreting him seems unable to do more than repeat what Hegel says in rather different language. Of the weightiness, earnestness, and calibre of Green it would be impertinent for me to speak. But, because it seems seldom recognized, I should like to refer to what has for long struck me as a minor but important merit of his writings. It may be very difficult to make out what Green means, and you may find yourself differing from him in almost every particular; but the more you study any particular sentence, the more you become convinced that every word of it has been weighed, and that, whether or not it be true, it expresses exactly what he meant to say. And this characteristic, I think, renders the study of Green especially valuable at a time like the present, when the most

[Inaugural lecture delivered before the University of Oxford on 29 October 1928.]

obvious feature of current books on philosophy is language so loose that it is usually difficult, and often impossible, to make out what their authors are trying to maintain.

In seeking a subject for an inaugural lecture, I have tried to find one which, without raising too technical issues, is near enough to every one to be of general interest and yet would be considered by philosophers still sufficiently controversial to deserve consideration. This subject I hope I have found in the relation between duty and interest. The topic is, of course, well worn. Nevertheless anyone who considers it closely will find that it has not the simple and straightforward character which at first sight it appears to possess.

A general but not very critical familiarity with the literature of Moral Philosophy might well lead to the remark that much of it is occupied with attempts either to prove that there is a necessary connexion between duty and interest or in certain cases even to exhibit the connexion as something self-evident. And the remark, even if not strictly accurate, plainly has some truth in it. It might be said in support that Plato's treatment of justice in the *Republic* is obviously such an attempt, and that even Aristotle in the *Ethics* tries to do the same thing, disguised and weak though his attempt may be. As modern instances, Butler and Hutcheson might be cited; and to these might be added not only Kant, in whom we should perhaps least expect to find such a proof, but also Green.

When we read the attempts referred to we naturally cannot help in a way wishing them to succeed; and we might express our wish in the form that we should all like to be able to believe that honesty is the best policy. At the same time we also cannot help feeling that somehow they are out of place, so that the real question is not so much whether they are successful, but whether they ought ever to have been made. And my object is to try to justify our feeling of dissatisfaction by considering what these attempts really amount to, and more especially what they amount to in view of the ideas which have prompted them. For this purpose, the views of Plato, Butler, and Green, may, I think, be taken as representative, and I propose to concentrate attention on them.

One preliminary remark is necessary. It must not be assumed that what are thus grouped together as attempts either to prove or to exhibit the self-evidence of a connexion between duty and interest are properly described by this phrase, or even that they are all attempts to do one and the same thing. And in particular I shall try to show that the attempts so described really consist of endeavours, based on mutually inconsistent presuppositions, to do one or another of three different things.

On a casual acquaintance with the *Republic*, we should probably say without hesitation that, apart from its general metaphysics, what it is concerned with is justice and injustice, and that, with regard to justice and injustice, its main argument is an elaborate attempt, continued to the end of the book, to show in detail that if we look below the surface and consider what just actions really consist in and also the nature of the soul, and, to a minor degree, the nature of the world in which we have to act, it will become obvious, in spite of appearance to the contrary, that it is by acting justly that we shall really gain or become happy.

Further, if we were to ask ourselves, 'What are Plato's words for right and wrong?'—and plainly the question is fair—we should have in the end to give as the true answer what at first would strike us as a paradox. We should have to allow that Plato's words for right and wrong are not to be found in such words as χρή or δεῖ and their contraries, as in χρὴ δίκαιον εἶναι or ὅντινα τρόπον χρὴ ζῆν, where the subject is implied by the context to be τὸν μέλλοντα μακάριον ἔσεσθαι, but in δίκαιον and ἄδικον themselves. When he says of some actions that it is δίκαιον, that is his way of saying that it is wrong. And in the sense in which we use the terms 'justice' and 'injustice', it is less accurate to describe what Plato is discussing as justice and injustice than as right and wrong. Our previous statement, therefore, might be put in the form that Plato is mainly occupied in the *Republic* with attempting to show it is by doing our duty, or what we are morally bound to do, that we shall become happy.

This is the account of his object which we are more particularly inclined to give if we chiefly have in mind what Socrates in the fourth Book is made to offer as the solution of the main problem. But this solution is preceded by an elaborate statement of the problem itself, put into the mouth of Glaucon and Adeimantus; and if we consider this statement closely, we find ourselves forced to make a substantial revision of this account of Plato's object. Glaucon and Adeimantus make it quite clear that whatever it is that they are asking Socrates to show about what they refer to as justice, their object in doing so is to obtain a refutation of what may be called the Sophistic theory of morality. Consequently, if we judge by what Glaucon and Adeimantus say, whatever Plato is trying to prove must be something which Plato would consider as affording a refutation of the Sophistic theory. But what is this theory as represented by Plato? It almost goes without saying that in the first instance men's attitude towards matters of right and wrong is an unquestioning one. However they have come to do so, and in particular whether their doing so is due to teaching or not, they think, and think without having any doubts, that certain actions are right and that certain others are wrong. No doubt in special cases, they may be doubtful; but, as regards some actions, they have no doubt at all, though to say this is not the same as to say that they are certain. But there comes a time when men are stirred out of this unquestioning frame of mind; and in particular the Sophists, as Plato represents them, were thus stirred by the reflection that the actions which men in ordinary life thought right, such as paying a debt, helping a friend, obeying the government, however they differed in other respects, at least agreed in bringing directly a definite loss to the agent. This reflection led them to wonder whether men were right in thinking these actions duties, i.e. whether they thought so truly. Then, having failed to find indirect advantages of these actions which would more than compensate for the direct loss, i.e. such advantages as are found in what we call prudent actions, they drew the conclusion that these actions cannot really be duties at all, and that therefore what may roughly be described as the moral convictions which they and others held in ordinary life were one gigantic mistake or illusion. Finally, they clinched this conclusion by offering something which they represented as an account of the origin of justice, but which is really an account of how they and others came to make the mistake of thinking these actions just, i.e. right.

This is the theory which on Plato's own showing he wants to refute. It is a theory about certain actions, and, on his own showing, what he has to maintain is the opposite theory about these same actions. But how, if our language is to be accurate, should these actions be referred to? Should they be referred to as *just*, i.e. right, actions, or should they be referred to as those actions which in ordinary life we *think* just, i.e. right? The difference, though at first it may seem unimportant, is really vital. In the unquestioning attitude of ordinary life we must either be *knowing* that certain actions are right or not knowing that they are right, but doing something else for which '*thinking* them right' is perhaps the least unsatisfactory phrase. There is no possibility of what might be suggested as a third alternative, viz. that our activity is one of thinking, which in instances where we are thinking truly is also one of knowing. For, as Plato realized, to think truly is not to know, and to discover that in some particular case we were thinking truly is not to discover that in doing so we were knowing. Moreover, when we are what is described as reflecting on the activity involved in our unquestioning attitude of mind, we are inevitably thinking of it as having a certain definite character, and, in so thinking of it, we must inevitably be implying either that the activity is one of knowing or that it is not. For we must think of this attitude either as one of thinking, or as one of knowing, and if we think of it as one of thinking, we imply that it is not one of knowing, and *vice versa*. In fact, however we think of the activity, we are committed one way or the other. Now the Sophists clearly implied that this unquestioning attitude is one of thinking and not one of knowing; for it would not have been sense to maintain that those actions which in ordinary life we know to be right are really not right. Their theory, then, must be expressed by saying that those actions which in ordinary life we think, and so do not know, to be right are not really right. Consequently Plato also, since he regards this as the theory to be refuted, is implying that in ordinary life we think, and do not know, that certain actions are right, and that, to this extent, he agrees with the Sophists. And for this reason, if we are to state accurately the problem which he is setting himself, we must represent it as referring not to *just* actions but to those actions which he and others in ordinary life *think* just.

It is clear then that when Plato states through the medium of Glaucon and Adeimantus the problem which he has to solve, he is guilty of an inaccuracy, which, though it may easily escape notice, is important. For Glaucon and Adeimantus persistently refer to the actions of which they ask Socrates to reconsider the profitableness as just and unjust actions, whereas they should have referred to them as the actions which men in ordinary life think just and unjust.

I shall now take it as established that when we judge from Plato's own statement of his problem, worked out as it is by reference to the Sophists, we have to allow that he is presupposing that ordinarily we do not know but think that certain actions are right and that he is thinking of his task as that of having to vindicate the truth of these thoughts against the Sophists' objection. And this is what must be really meant when it is said that Plato's object is to vindicate *morality* against the Sophistic view of it, for here 'morality' can only be a loose phrase for our ordinary moral thoughts or convictions.

Glaucon and Adeimantus, however, do not simply ask Socrates to refute the Sophistic view; they ask him to do so in a particular way, which they imply to be the only way possible, viz. by showing that if we go deeper than the Sophists and consider not merely the gains and losses of which they take account, viz. gains and losses really due to the reputation for doing what men think just and unjust, but also those which these actions directly bring to the man's own soul, it will become obvious that it is by doing what we think just that we shall really gain. And so far as the rest of the *Republic* is an attempt to satisfy this request, this must be what it is an attempt to show.

Now on a first reading of the *Republic*, it is not likely to strike us that there is anything peculiar or unnatural about this part of the request. Just because Plato takes for granted that this is the only way to refute the Sophists, we are apt in reading him to do the same, especially as our attention is likely to be fully taken up by the effort to follow Plato's thought. But if we can manage to consider Plato's endeavour to refute the Sophists with detachment, what strikes us most is not his dissent from their view concerning the comparative profitableness of the actions which men think just and unjust—great, of course, as his dissent is—but the identity of principle underlying the position of both. The Sophists in reaching their conclusion were presupposing that for an action to be really just, it must be advantageous; for it was solely on this ground that they concluded that what we ordinarily think just is not really just. And what in the end most strikes us is that at no stage in the *Republic* does Plato take the line, or even suggest as a possibility, that the very presupposition of the Sophists' arguments is false, and that therefore the question whether some action which men think just will be profitable to the agent has really nothing to do with the question whether it is right, so that Thrasymachus may enlarge as much as he pleases on the losses incurred by doing the actions we think just without getting any nearer to showing that it is a mere mistake to think them just. Plato, on the contrary, instead of urging that the Sophistic contention that men lose by doing what they think just is simply irrelevant to the question whether these actions are just, throughout treats this contention with the utmost seriousness; and he implies that unless the Sophists can be met on their own ground by being shown that, in spite of appearances to the contrary, these actions will really be for the good of the agent, their conclusion that men's moral convictions are mere conventions must be allowed to stand. He therefore, equally with the Sophists, is implying that it is impossible for any action to be really just, i.e. a duty, unless it is for the advantage of the agent.

This presupposition, however, as soon as we consider it, strikes us as a paradox. For though we may find ourselves quite unable to state what it is that does render an action a duty, we ordinarily think that, whatever it is, it is not conduciveness to our advantage; and we also think that though an action which is a duty may be advantageous it need not be so. And while we may not be surprised to find the presupposition in the Sophists, whose moral convictions are represented as at least shallow, we are surprised to find it in Plato, whose moral earnestness is that of a prophet. At first, no doubt, we may try to mitigate our surprise by emphasizing the superior character of the advantages which Plato had in mind. But to do this does not really help. For after all, whatever be meant by the 'superiority' of the advantages of which Plato was thinking, it is simply as advantages that Plato uses them to show that the actions from which they follow are right.

Yet the presupposition cannot simply be dismissed as obviously untrue. For one thing, any view of Plato's is entitled to respect. For another, there appear to be moments in which we find the presupposition in ourselves. There appear to be moments in which, feeling acutely the weight of our responsibilities, we say to ourselves, 'Why *should* I do all these actions, since after all it is others and not I who will gain by doing them?'.

Moreover, there at least seems to be the same presupposition in the mind of those preachers whose method of exhortation consists in appeal to rewards. When, for instance, they commend a certain mode of life on the ground that it will bring about a peace of mind which the pursuit of worldly things cannot yield, they appear to be giving a resulting gain as the reason why we ought to do certain actions, and therefore to be implying that in general it is advantageousness to ourselves which renders an action one which we are bound to do. In fact the only difference between the view of such preachers and that of the Sophists seems to be that the former, in view of their theological beliefs, think that the various actions which we think right will have certain specific rewards the existence of which the Sophists would deny. And the identity of principle underlying their view becomes obvious if the preacher goes on to maintain, as some have done, that if he were to cease to believe in heaven, he would cease to believe in right and wrong. Again, among philosophers, Plato is far from being alone in presupposing that an action, to be right, must be for the good or advantage of the agent. To go no further afield than a commentator on Plato, we may cite Cook Wilson, whose claim to respect no one in Oxford will deny, and who was, to my mind, one of the acutest of thinkers. In lecturing on the *Republic* he used to insist that when men begin to reflect on morality they not only demand, but also have the right to demand, that any action which is right must justify its claim to be right by being shown to be for their own good; and he used to maintain that Plato took the right and only way of justifying our moral convictions, by showing that the actions which we think right are for the good of the society of which we are members, and that at the same time the good of that society *is* our good, as becomes obvious when the nature of our good is properly understood.

Moreover Plato, if he has been rightly interpreted, does not stand alone among the historical philosophers in presupposing the existence of a necessary connexion between duty and interest. At least Butler, whose thoughtfulness is incontestable, is with him. In fact in this matter he seems at first sight only distinguished from Plato by going further. In a well-known passage in the eleventh *Sermon*, after stating that religion always addresses itself to self-love when reason presides in a man, he says: 'Let it be allowed, though virtue or moral rectitude does indeed consist in affection to and pursuit of what is right and good, as such; yet that when we sit down in a cool hour, we can neither justify to ourselves this or any other pursuit, till we are convinced that it will be for our happiness, or at least not contrary to it.'

Here, if we take the phrase 'justify an action to ourselves' in its natural sense of come to know that we ought to do the action by apprehending a reason why we ought to do it, we seem to have to allow that Butler is maintaining that in the last resort there is one, and only one, reason why we ought to do anything whatever, viz. the conduciveness of the action to our happiness or advantage. And if this is right, Butler is not simply presupposing but definitely asserting a necessary connexion between duty and interest, and going further than Plato by maintaining that it is actually conduciveness to the agent's interest which renders an action right.

Nevertheless, when we seriously face the view that unless an action be advantageous, it cannot really be a duty, we are forced both to abandon it and also to allow that even if it were true, it would not enable us to vindicate the truth of our ordinary moral convictions.

It is easy to see that if we persist in maintaining that an action, to be right, must be advantageous, we cannot stop short of maintaining that it is precisely advantageousness and nothing else which renders an action right. It is impossible to rest in the intermediate position that, though it is something other than advantageousness which renders an action right, nevertheless an action cannot really be right unless it be advantageous. For if it be held that an action is rendered a duty by the possession of some other characteristic, then the only chance of showing that a right action must necessarily be advantageous must consist either in showing that actions having this other characteristic must necessarily be advantageous or in showing that the very fact that we are bound to do some action, irrespectively of what renders us bound to do it, necessitates that we shall gain by doing it. But the former alternative is not possible. By 'an action' in this context must be meant an activity by which a man brings certain things about. And if the characteristic of an action which renders it right does not consist in its bringing about an advantage to the agent, which we may symbolize by 'an X', it must consist in bringing about something of a different kind, which we may symbolize by 'a Y', say, for the sake of argument, an advantage to a friend, or an improvement in someone's character. There can, however, be no means of showing that when we bring about something of one kind, e.g. a Y, we must necessarily bring about something of a different kind, e.g. an X. The nature of an action as being the bringing about a Y cannot require, i.e. necessitate, it to be also the bringing about an X, i.e. to have an X as its consequence; and whether bringing about a Y in any particular case will bring about an X will depend not only on the nature of the act as being the bringing about a Y, but also on the nature of the agent and of the special circumstances in which the act is done. It may be objected that we could avoid the necessity of having to admit this on one condition, viz. that we knew the existence of a Divine Being who would intervene, where necessary, with rewards. But this knowledge would give the required conclusion only on one condition, viz. that this knowledge was really the knowledge that the fact of being bound to do some action itself necessitated the existence of such a Being as a consequence. For if it were the knowledge of the existence of such a Being based on other grounds, it would not enable us to know that the very fact that some action was the bringing about a Y *itself* necessitated that it would also be the bringing about an X, i.e. some advantage to the agent. No doubt if we could successfully maintain not only that an action's being the bringing about a Y necessitated its being a duty, but also that an action's being a duty necessitated as a consequence the existence of a Being who would reward it, we could show that an action's being the bringing about a Y necessitated its being rewarded. But to maintain this is really to fall back on the second alternative; and this alternative will, on consideration, turn out no more tenable than the first. It cannot successfully be maintained that the very fact that some action is a duty necessitates, not that the agent will *deserve* to gain—a conclusion which it is of course easy to draw, but that he *will* gain, unless it can be shown that this very fact necessitates, as a consequence, the existence of a being who will, if necessary, reward it. And this obviously cannot be done.

No doubt Kant maintained, and thought it possible to prove, not indeed that the obligation to do *any* action, but that the obligation to do a *certain* action, involves as a consequence that men will gain by carrying out their obligations.[1] In effect he assumed that we know that one of our duties is to endeavour to

---

[1] Kant, *Critique of Practical Reason* (Bk. II, ii. § 5) [Abbott's Translation, pp. 220–9.]

advance the realization of the highest good, viz. a state of affairs in which men both act morally, i.e. do what they think right, purely from the thought that it is right, and at the same time attain the happiness which in consequence they deserve. And he maintained that from this knowledge we can conclude *first* that the realization of the highest good must be possible, i.e. that so far as we succeed in making ourselves and others more moral, we and others will become proportionately happier; and *second* that, therefore, since the realization of this consequence requires, as the cause of the world in which we have to act, a supreme intelligent will which renders the world such as to cause happiness in proportion to morality, there must be such a cause. But his argument, although it has a certain plausibility, involves an inversion. If, as he rightly implied, an action can only be a duty if we *can* do it, and if we can only even in a slight degree advance a state of affairs in which a certain degree of morality is combined with a corresponding degree of happiness, *provided* there be such a supreme cause of nature, it will be impossible to know, as he assumed that we do, that to advance this state of affairs is a duty, *until* we know that there is such a supreme cause. So far, therefore, from the connexion which he thought to exist between right action and happiness being demonstrable from our knowledge of the duty in question, knowledge of the duty, if attainable at all, will itself require independent knowledge of the connexion.

We are therefore forced to allow that in order to maintain that for an action to be right, it must be advantageous, we have to maintain that advantageousness is what renders an action right. But this is obviously something which no one is going to maintain, if he considers it seriously. For he will be involved in maintaining not only that it is a duty to do whatever is for our advantage, but that this is our only duty. And the fatal objection to maintaining this is simply that no one actually thinks it.

Moreover, as it is easy to see, if we were to maintain this, our doing so, so far from helping us, would render it impossible for us, to vindicate the truth of our ordinary moral convictions. For wherever in ordinary life we think of some particular action as a duty, we are not simply thinking of it as right, but also thinking of its rightness as constituted by the possession of some definite characteristic other than that of being advantageous to the agent. For we think of the action as a particular action *of a certain kind*, the nature of which is indicated by general words contained in the phrase by which we refer to the action, e.g. '*fulfilling* the *promise* which we made to X yesterday', or '*looking after* our *parents*'. And we do not think of the action as right *blindly*, i.e. irrespectively of the special character which we think the act to possess; rather we think of it as being right in virtue of possessing a particular characteristic of the kind indicated by the phrase by which we refer to it. Thus in thinking of our keeping our promise to X as a duty, we are thinking of the action as rendered a duty by its being the keeping of our promise. This is obvious because we should never, for instance, think of using as an illustration of an action which we think right, telling X what we think of him, or meeting him in London, even though we thought that if we thought of these actions in certain other aspects we should think them right. Consequently if we were to maintain that conduciveness to the agent's advantage is what renders an action right, we should have to allow that any of our ordinary moral convictions, so far from being capable of vindication, is simply a mistake, as being really the conviction that some particular action is rendered a duty by its possession of some characteristic which is not that of being advantageous.

The general moral is obvious. Certain arguments, which would ordinarily be referred to as arguments designed to prove that doing what is right will be for the good of the agent, turn out to be attempts to prove that the actions which in ordinary life we think right will be for the good of the agent. There is really no need to consider in detail whether these arguments are successful; for even if they are successful, they will do nothing to prove what they are intended to prove, viz. that the moral convictions of our ordinary life are true. Further the attempts arise simply out of a presupposition which on reflection anyone is bound to abandon, viz. that conduciveness to personal advantage is what renders an action a duty. What Plato should have said to the Sophists is: 'You may be right in maintaining that in our ordinary unquestioning frame of mind we do not know but only think, that certain actions are right. These thoughts or convictions may or may not be true. But they cannot be false for the reason which you give. You do nothing whatever to show that they are false by urging that the actions in question are disadvantageous; and I should do nothing to show that they are true, if I were to show that these actions are after all advantageous. Your real mistake lies in presupposing throughout that advantageousness is what renders an action a duty. If you will only reflect you will abandon this presupposition altogether, and then you yourself will withdraw your arguments.'

I next propose to contend that there is also to be found both in Plato and Butler, besides this attempt to show that actions which we *think* right will be for our good, another attempt which neither of them distinguishes from it and which *is* accurately described as an attempt to prove that *right* actions will be for our good. I also propose to ask what is the idea which led them to make the attempt, and to consider whether it is tenable.

When Plato raises the question 'What is justice?' he does not mean by the question 'What do we *mean* by the terms "justice" and "just", or, in our language, "duty" and "right"?', as we might ask 'What do we *mean* by the term "optimism", or again, by the phrase "living thing"?'. And as a matter of fact if he had meant this, he would have been raising what was only verbally, and not really, a question at all, in that any attempt to ask it would have implied that the answer was already known and that therefore there was nothing to ask. He means 'What is the characteristic the possession of which by an action necessitates that the action is just, i.e. an act which it is our duty, or which we ought, to do?' In short he means 'What renders a just or right action, just or right?'

Now this question really means 'What is the characteristic common to particular just acts which renders them just?' And for anyone even to *ask* this question is to imply that he already *knows* what particular actions are just. For even to *ask* 'What is the character common to certain things?' is to imply that we already *know* what the things are of which we are wanting to find the common character. Equally, of course, any attempt to *answer* the question has the same implication. For such an attempt can only consist in considering the particular actions which we know to be just and attempting to discover what is the characteristic common to them all, the vague apprehension of which has led us to apprehend them to be just. Plato therefore, both in representing Socrates as raising with his hearers the question 'What is justice?' and also in representing them all as attempting to answer it, is implying, whether he is aware that he is doing so or not, that they all know what particular acts are, and what particular acts are not, just. If on the contrary what he had presupposed was that the members of the dialogue think, instead of knowing, that certain actions are just, his question—whether he had expressed it thus or not—would really have been, not 'What *is* justice?', but 'What do we *think* that justice is?'; or, more clearly, not 'What renders an act just?' but 'What do we think renders an act just?'. But in that case an answer, whatever its character, would have thrown no light on the question 'What is justice?'; and apart from this, he is plainly not asking 'What do we *think* that justice is?'.

As has been pointed out, however, the view which Plato attributes to the Sophists presupposes that ordinary mankind, which of course includes the members of the dialogue, only thinks and does not know that certain actions are just. Therefore, when Plato introduces this view as requiring refutation and, in doing so, represents the members of the dialogue as not questioning the presupposition, he ought in consistency to have made someone point out that in view of the acceptance of this presupposition Socrates' original question 'What is justice?' required to be amended to the question 'What do we think that justice is?'. But Plato does not do so. In the present context the significant fact is that even after he has introduced the view of the Sophists he still represents the question to be answered as being 'What is justice?', and therefore still implies that the members of the dialogue know what is just in particular. Even in making Glaucon and Adeimantus ask Socrates to refute the Sophists, what he, inconsistently, makes them ask Socrates to exhibit the nature of is not the acts which men think just but just acts. And when Plato in the fourth book goes on to give Socrates' answer, which, of course, is intended to express the truth, he in the same way represents Socrates as offering, and the others as accepting, an account of the nature of *just* acts, viz. that they consist in conferring those benefits on society which a man's nature renders him best suited to confer, and then makes Socrates argue in detail that it is *just* action which will be profitable. In doing so he is of course implying, inconsistently with the implication of his treatment of the Sophists' view, that the members of the dialogue, and therefore also mankind in ordinary life, *know* what is just in particular. For in the end the statement 'Justice is conferring certain benefits on society' can only mean that conferring these benefits is the characteristic the vague apprehension of which in certain actions leads us to know or apprehend them to be just; and the acceptance of this statement by the members of the dialogue must be understood as expressing their recognition that this characteristic is the common character of the particular acts which they already know to be just.

It therefore must be allowed that, although to do so is inconsistent with his view of the way in which the Sophistic theory has to be refuted, Plato is in the fourth book (and of course the same admission must be made about the eighth and ninth) endeavouring to prove that *just*; i.e. *right*, action, will be for the good or advantage of the agent.

Given that this is what Plato wants to prove in the fourth book, the general nature of what he conceives to be the proof is obvious. His idea is that if we start with the knowledge of what right actions consist in, viz., to put it shortly, serving the state, and then consider what the effects of these and other actions will be by taking into account not only the circumstances in which we are placed, but also the various desires of the human soul and the varying amounts of satisfaction to which the realization of these objects will give rise, it will be obvious that it is by doing what is right that, at any rate in the long run, we shall become happy.

Now a particular proof of this kind, such as Plato's, naturally provokes two comments. The first is that there is no need to consider its success in detail, since we know on general grounds that it must fail. For it can only be shown that actions characterized by being the bringing about things of one kind, in this case benefits to society, will always have as their consequence things of another kind, in this case elements of happiness in the agent, provided that we can prove, as Plato makes no attempt to do, the existence of a Being who will intervene to introduce suitable rewards where they are needed. The second is that though the establishment of this conclusion, whether with or without the help of theological arguments, would be of the greatest benefit to us, since we should all be better off if we knew it to be true, yet it differs from the establishment of the corresponding conclusion against the Sophists in that it would throw no light whatever on the question 'What is our duty in detail, and why?'. And this second comment naturally raises the question which seems to be the important one to ask in this connexion, viz. '*Why* did Plato think it important to prove that right action would benefit the agent?'.

The explanation obviously cannot be simply, or even mainly, that the combination in Plato of a desire to do what is right and of a desire to become happy led him to try to satisfy himself that by doing what is right he would be, so to say, having it both ways. The main explanation must lie in a quite different direction. There is no escaping the conclusion that when Plato sets himself to consider not what *should*, but what *actually does* as a matter of fact, lead a man to act, when he is acting deliberately, and not merely in consequence of an impulse, he answers 'The desire for some good to himself and that only'. In other words we have to allow that, according to Plato, a man pursues whatever he pursues simply as a good to himself, i.e. really as something which will give him satisfaction, or, as perhaps we ought to say, as an element in what will render him happy. In the *Republic* this view comes to light in the sixth book. He there speaks of τὸ ἀγαθόν as that which every soul pursues and for the sake of which it does all it does, divining that it is something but being perplexed and unable to grasp adequately what it is; and he goes on to say of things that are good (τὰ ἀγαθά) that while many are ready to do and to obtain and to be what only *seems* just, even if it is not, no one is content with obtaining what *seems* good, but endeavours to obtain what is *really* good. It might be objected that these statements do not bear out the view which is attributed to Plato, since Plato certainly did not mean by an ἀγαθόν a source of satisfaction or happiness to oneself. But to this the answer is that wherever Plato uses the term ἀγαθά (goods) elsewhere in the *Republic* and in other dialogues, such as the *Philebus*, the context always shows that he means by a good a good to oneself, and, this being so, he must really be meaning by an ἀγαθόν, a source of satisfaction, or perhaps, more generally, a source of happiness. The view, however, emerges most clearly in the *Gorgias*, where Plato, in order to show that rhetoricians and tyrants do not do what they really wish to do, maintains that in all actions alike, and even when we kill a man or despoil him of his goods, we do what we do because we think it will be better for us to do so.

Now if we grant, as we must, that Plato thought this, we can find in the admission a natural explanation of Plato's desire to prove that just action will be advantageous. For plainly he passionately wanted men to do what is right, and if he thought that it was only desire of some good to themselves which moved them in all deliberate action, it would be natural, and indeed necessary, for him to think that if men are to be induced to do what is just, the only way to induce them is to convince them that thereby they will gain or become better off.

In Butler also we are driven to find the same attempt to prove that right action will benefit the agent, and to give the same explanation. The proper interpretation of the most important part of the statement quoted from Butler is not very easy to discover. What he says is that when we sit down in a cool hour we can neither justify to ourselves the pursuit of what is *right* and *good*, as such, or any other pursuit, till we are convinced that it will be for our happiness or at least not against it. Here a puzzle arises from the fact that whereas by referring to certain of the actions which we have to justify to ourselves as the pursuit of what is *right*, he inevitably implies that we already *know* them to be right, yet by speaking of our having to justify them to ourselves, i.e. apparently to prove to ourselves that they are right, he seems to imply that we do *not* know them to be right. The interpretation given earlier evaded the puzzle by tacitly assuming that Butler was using the term 'right' loosely for what we think, and so do not know, to be right. But it may well be asked whether the assumption was justified. And if we consider the statement in reference to the *Sermons* generally, we seem bound to conclude that Butler was really maintaining two different, and indeed inconsistent, doctrines without realizing their difference, the one involving that the word 'right' is here used strictly, and the other involving that it is not. When Kant contrasts the two kinds of statement containing the word 'ought' which he designated as Categorical and Hypothetical Imperatives, he implies, although he does not expressly state, that the term 'ought' is being used in the two kinds of statement in radically different senses. In a Categorical Imperative, he implies, 'ought' has the ordinary moral sense in which it is co-extensive with 'duty', and 'morally bound'. In a Hypothetical Imperative it has the purely non-moral sense of proper in respect of being the thing which is conducive to our purpose, whether that purpose be the object of some special desire which is moving us, e.g. as when we wash in order to become clean, or whether it be our happiness, as when we make friends in order to become happy. Corresponding to these two senses of the term 'ought', there will be two senses of 'justifying a certain action', the one moral and the other not. We may mean by the phrase proving to ourselves that it is a duty to do the action, or we may mean proving to ourselves that the act is the proper one to do in respect of its being the act which will lead to the realization of our purpose.

Now if we understand Butler's word 'right' to be a loose phrase for what in ordinary life we *think* to be right, we can understand him to be using 'justify' in the moral sense of 'justify', without having to admit that he is involved in contradiction. We can understand him to be saying that in order to know that some action which we ordinarily think to be right is right, we must first prove to ourselves that it will be for our happiness, or at least not against it; and we shall then be representing him as explicitly maintaining what the Sophists and Plato, in seeking to refute them, presupposed. On the other hand if we understand Butler to be using the term 'right' strictly, we can only avoid attributing to him the self-contradictory view already referred to by understanding him to be using the term 'justify' in the non-moral sense. For while he would be involved in contradiction if he maintained that even where we knew that some action is right, we still need to prove to ourselves that we ought in the moral sense to do it, he would not be so involved, if he maintained instead that what we still need is to prove to ourselves that we ought to do it in the non-moral sense. Now the general drift of what Butler says of conscience, and especially his statement that it carries its own authority with it, implies that he considered that in ordinary life we *know* and do not *think* that certain actions are right; and if we judge by this, we must understand Butler to be here using 'right' strictly, and to be maintaining that even when we know that we morally ought to do something, we still need to know that we ought to do it in the non-moral sense of its being conducive to our purpose, and that therefore, since our happiness is our purpose, we still need to know that it will conduce to our happiness. But if we think that this is what Butler is maintaining, we have to allow that the explanation of his maintaining it can only be the same as that given with regard to Plato. For if we ask 'Why, according to Butler, when we already know that doing some action is a duty, do we still require to know that we ought to do the action in the non-moral sense of "ought"?', the answer can only be 'Because otherwise we shall not do the action'. And the implication will be that when, to use Butler's phrase, we sit down in a cool hour, i.e. when we are not under the influence of impulses, the only thing we desire, and therefore the only purpose we have, is our own happiness, and that therefore we shall do whatever we do only in order that we may become happy. The general drift of his *Sermons*, however, and more especially his statement that it is manifest that nothing can be of consequence to mankind or any creature but happiness shows that Butler actually thought this. We have therefore to attribute to Butler side by side with the view already attributed to him, and undistinguished from it, a view which is inconsistent with it, and is really the second view already attributed to Plato, viz. that even though we know certain actions to be right, we must have it proved to us that they will be for our good or happiness, since otherwise, as we act only from desire of our own happiness, we shall not do them.

I propose now to take it as established (1) that both Plato and Butler in a certain vein of thought are really endeavouring to prove that right actions, in the strict sense of 'right actions', will be for the agent's advantage; (2) that their reason for doing so lies in the conviction that even where we know some action to be right, we shall not do it unless we think that it will be for our advantage; and (3) that behind this conviction lies the conviction of which it is really a corollary, viz. the conviction that desire for some good to oneself is the only motive of deliberate action.

But are these convictions true? For if it can be shown that they are not, then at least Plato and Butler's reason for trying to prove the advantageousness of right action will have disappeared.

The conviction that even where we know some action to be right, we shall not do it unless we think we shall be the better off for doing it, of course, strikes us as a paradox. At first no doubt we are apt to mis-state the paradox. We are apt to say that the conviction, implying as it does that we only act out of self-interest, really implies that it is impossible for us to do anything which we ought to do at all, since if we did some action out of self-interest we could not have done anything which was a duty. But to say this is to make the mistake of thinking that the motive with which we do an action can possibly have something to do with its rightness or wrongness. To be morally bound is to be morally bound to *do* something, i.e. to bring something about; and even if it be only from the lowest of motives that we have brought about something which we ought to have brought about, we have still done something which we ought to have done. The fact that I have given *A* credit in order to spite his rival *B*, or again, in order to secure future favours from *A*, has, as we see when we reflect, no bearing whatever on the question whether I ought to have given *A* credit. The real paradox inherent in the conviction lies in its implication that there is no such thing as moral goodness. If I gave *A* credit solely to obtain future favours, and even if I gave him credit either thinking or knowing that I ought to do so, but in no way directly or indirectly influenced by my either so thinking or knowing, then even though it has to be allowed that I did something which I was morally bound to do, it has to be admitted that there was no moral goodness whatever about my action. And the conviction in question is really what is ordinarily called the doctrine that morality needs a sanction, i.e. really the doctrine that, to stimulate a man into doing some action, it is not merely insufficient but even useless to convince him that he is morally bound to do it, and that, instead, we have to appeal to his desire to become better off.

Now we are apt to smile in a superior way when in reading Mill we find him taking for granted that morality needs a sanction, but we cannot afford to do so when we find Butler, and still more when we find Plato, really doing the same thing. Moreover when Plato and Butler maintain the doctrine that lies at the back of this conviction, viz. the doctrine that we always aim at, i.e. act from the desire of, some good to ourselves, they are in the best of company. Aristotle is practically only repeating the statement quoted from the sixth book of the *Republic* when he says in the first sentence of the *Ethics*, that every deliberate action seems to aim at something good, and that therefore the good has rightly been declared to be that at which all things aim. For this to become obvious it is only necessary to consider what meaning must be attributed to the term ἀγαθόν in the early chapters of the *Ethics*. Again, to take a modern instance, Green says: 'The motive in every imputable act for which the agent is conscious on reflection that he is answerable, is a desire for personal good in some form or other. . . . It is superfluous to add good to *himself*, for anything conceived as good in such a way that the agent acts for the sake of it, must be conceived as *his own* good, though he may conceive it as his own good only on account of his interest in others, and in spite of any amount of suffering on his own part incidental to its attainment.'[2] Moreover the doctrine seems plausible enough, if we ask ourselves in a purely general way 'How are we to be led into doing something?'. For the natural answer is: 'Only by thinking of some state of affairs which it is in my power to bring about and by which I shall become better off than I am now'; and

---

[2] *Prolegomena to Ethics*, §§ 91–2.

the answer implies that only in this way shall we come to desire to do an action, and that, unless we desire to do it, we shall not do it.

Nevertheless it seems difficult, and indeed in the end impossible, to think that the doctrine will stand the test of instances. It seems impossible to allow that in what would usually be called disinterested actions, whether they be good or bad, there is not at least some element of disinterestedness. It strikes us as absurd to think that in what would be called a benevolent action, we are not moved at least in part by the desire that someone else shall be better off and also by the desire to *make* him better off, even though we may also necessarily have, and be influenced by, the desire to have the satisfaction of thinking that he is better off and that we have made him so. It seems equally absurd to maintain that where we are said to treat someone maliciously, we are not moved in part by the desire of his unhappiness and also partly by the desire to *make* him unhappy. Again when we are said to be pursuing scientific studies without a practical aim, it seems mere distortion of the facts to say that we are moved solely by the desire to have the satisfaction of knowing some particular thing and not, at least in part, by the desire to know it. And we seem driven to make a similar admission when we consider actions in which we are said to have acted conscientiously.

In this connexion it should be noted that the doctrine under consideration, viz. that our motive in doing any action is desire for some good to ourselves to which we think the action will lead, has two negative implications. The first is that the thought, or, alternatively, the knowledge, that some action is right has no influence on us in acting, i.e. that the thought, or the knowledge, that an action is a duty can neither be our motive nor even an element in our motive. The existence of this implication is obvious, since if our motive is held to be the desire for a certain good to ourselves, it is implied that the thought that the action is a duty, though present, is neither what moves us, nor an element in what moves us, to do the action. The second implication is that there is no such thing as a *desire* to do what is right, or more fully, a desire to do some action in virtue of its being a duty. The existence of this second implication is also obvious, since if such a desire were allowed to exist, there would be no reason for maintaining that when we do some action which we think to be a duty, our motive is necessarily the desire for a certain good to ourselves. The truth of the doctrine could therefore be contested in one of two alternative ways. We might either deny the truth of the former implication; or, again, we might deny the truth of the latter. The former is, of course, the line taken by Kant, at any rate in a qualified form. He maintained in effect that the mere thought that an action is a duty, apart from a desire to do what we ought to do—a desire the existence of which he refused to admit—is at any rate in certain instances the motive, or at least an element in the motive, of an action. No doubt he insisted that the existence of this fact gave rise to a problem, and a problem which only vindication of freedom of the will could resolve; but he maintained that the problem was soluble, and that therefore he was entitled to insist on this fact. Now this method of refutation has adherents and at first sight it is attractive. For it seems mere wild paradox to maintain that in no case in which we do what we think of as right, do we ever in any degree do it *because* we think it right; and to say that we do some action *because* we think it right seems to imply that the thought that it is right is our motive. Again the statement seems natural that where we are said to have acted thus, we obviously did not want to do what we did but acted against our desires or inclinations. Nevertheless we are, I think, on further reflection bound to abandon this view. For one reason, to appeal to a consideration of which the full elucidation and vindication would take too long, the view involves that where we are said to have done some action because we thought it right, though we had a motive for what we did, we had no purpose in doing it. For we really mean by our purpose in doing some action that the *desire* of which for its own sake leads us to do the action. Again, if we face the purely general question 'Can we really do anything whatever unless in some respect or other we desire to do it?' we have to answer 'No'. But if we allow this, then we have to allow that the obvious way to endeavour to meet Plato's view is to maintain the existence of a desire to do what is right. And it does not seem difficult to do so with success. For we obviously are referring to a fact when we speak of someone as possessing a sense of duty and, again, a strong sense of duty. And if we consider what we are thinking of in these individuals whom we think of as possessing it, we find we cannot exclude from it a desire to do what is a duty, as such, or for its own sake, or, more simply, a desire to do what is a duty. In fact it is hard to resist the conclusion that Kant himself would have taken this line instead of the extreme line which he did, had he not had the fixed idea that all desire is for enjoyment. But if we think this—as it seems we must—we, of course, have no need to admit the truth of Plato's reason for trying to prove that right actions must be advantageous. For if we admit the existence of a desire to do what is right, there is no longer any reason for maintaining as a general thesis that in any case in which a man knows some action to be right, he must, if he is to be led to do it, be convinced that he will gain by doing it. For we shall be able to maintain that his desire to do what is right, if strong enough, will lead him to do the action in spite of any aversion from doing it which he may feel on account of its disadvantages.

It may be objected that if we maintain the existence of a desire to do what is right, we shall become involved in an insoluble difficulty. For we shall also have to allow that we have a desire to become well off or happy, and that therefore men have two radically different desires, i.e. desires the object of which are completely incommensurable. We shall therefore be implying that in those instances—which of course must exist—in which a man has either to do what is right or to do what is for his happiness he can have no means of choosing which he shall do, since there can be no comparable characteristic of the two alternative actions which will enable him to choose to do the one rather than, or in preference to, the other.

But to this objection there is an answer which, even if it be at first paradoxical, is in the end irresistible, viz. that in connexion with such instances it is wholly inappropriate to speak of a *choice*. A choice is, no doubt, necessarily a choice between comparable alternatives, e.g. between an afternoon's enjoyment on the river and an afternoon's enjoyment at the cinema. But it is purely arbitrary to maintain that wherever we have two alternative courses of action before us we have necessarily to *choose* between them. Thus a man contemplating retirement may be offered a new post. He may, on thinking it over, be unable to resist the conclusion that it is a duty on his part to accept it and equally convinced that if he accepts it, he will lose in happiness. He will either accept from his desire to do what is right in spite of his aversion from doing what will bring himself a loss of happiness, or he will refuse from his desire of happiness, in spite of his aversion from doing what is wrong. But whichever he does, though he will have *decided* to do what he does, he will not have *chosen* to do it, i.e. chosen to do it in preference to doing the alternative action.

For the reasons given I shall treat it as established that, though there is to be found in Plato and Butler what is really an attempt to prove that right action is advantageous, the question of its success or failure can be ignored, since the attempt is based on a fundamental mistake about actual human nature.

I next and last propose to consider what I shall contend to be an instance of the third of what I referred to as three different endeavours which would ordinarily be described as attempts either to prove or to exhibit the self-evidence of a connexion between duty and interest. This consists in what must be allowed to be Green's attempt to make out that the very idea that a certain action is a duty involves the idea that it will be for our interest.

Green holds, for a reason which will have to be considered, that he is bound to give an account of the origin of the moral ideal, i.e. really, to explain how men's thought that certain actions are duties has arisen out of a prior state in which they had no thought of duties at all. At the root of his explanation lies his analysis of deliberate action. Of this analysis an outline is given in a sentence already quoted: 'The motive in every imputable act for which the agent is conscious on reflection that he is answerable is a desire for personal good in some form or other.' He draws a sharp distinction between instinctive action, the capacity for which men share with animals, and deliberate action, which is distinctive of human beings. And when he speaks of an action to which praise or blame can be imputed, or of a moral action, in the sense of an act of a kind which is either morally good or morally bad, what he is thinking of is a deliberate action, i.e. an action in which we have a purpose. He expresses the fact that in such an action we have a purpose by saying that in it we have a motive, and he maintains that a motive is always a desire. At first he represents a desire for some particular thing as a good to, i.e. as something which will give satisfaction to, the agent. But later his account of a desire becomes more complicated. He represents it as implying in the agent the thought of himself as a being who is distinct from his various wants and impulses, which may be of animal origin, who may become completely satisfied by having his wants satisfied, and for whom there is in given circumstances a greatest good possible, i.e. a state in which the nearest approximation to his being completely satisfied will be attained. And he represents a desire as a desire of some particular thing as that which will be in the circumstances his greatest good, i.e. will render himself as completely satisfied as possible in the circumstances. And, in accordance with this, he represents Esau's motive in selling his birthright for a mess of pottage as being the desire of the pleasure of eating the pottage as under the circumstances his greatest good.

He is emphatic in insisting that this account of deliberate action is an account of *all* deliberate action, whether morally good or morally bad, and that therefore it raises the question 'What are the distinguishing marks of morally good and morally bad deliberate action, i.e. of virtue and vice?'. To this question his real answer is that as everyone in acting always does what he thinks will be productive of his greatest good, the distinguishing characteristic of a morally bad, i.e. vicious, action, lies in an error made by the agent about what will be for his greatest good. At first, no doubt, this interpretation seems obviously wrong. For it is glaringly inconsistent with his general descriptions of a morally good action, as when he speaks of having taken the moral ideal to be a devotion of character and life in some form or other to the perfecting of man,[3] and again of having found that the highest moral goodness was an attribute of character, in so far as it issued in acts done for the sake of their goodness.[4] Moreover he seems expressly repudiating this interpretation when he shows anxiety to remove what he describes as the impression to which his account of conduct, whether virtuous or vicious, is likely to give rise, viz. that this account, if true, would take away the only intelligible foundation of Ethics by reducing virtuous and vicious action to the same motive.[5] Nevertheless, this is the interpretation required by his account of deliberate action, an account to which he always adheres. And later on we find what amounts to an explicit statement of the doctrine. Speaking of a man's thought of himself, and of his thought of himself as a being capable of being satisfied, he says: 'Hence arises the impulse which becomes the source, according to the direction it takes, both of vice and virtue. It is the source of vicious self-seeking and self-assertion, so far as the spirit which is in man seeks to satisfy itself or to realize its capabilities in modes in which, according to the law which its divine origin imposes on it, and which is equally the law of the universe and of human society, its self-satisfaction or self-realization is not to be found. Such, for instance—so self-defeating—is the quest for self-satisfaction in the life of the voluptuary. So it is again with the man who seeks to assert himself,

---

[3] Ibid., § 310.   [4] *Lectures on the Principles of Political Obligation*, § 2.
[5] *Prolegomena*, § 115.

to realize himself, to show what he has in him to be, in achievements which may make the world wonder, but which in their social effects are such that the human spirit, according to the law of its being which is a law of development in society, is not advanced but hindered by them in the realization of its capabilities. He is living for ends of which the divine principle that forms his self alone renders him capable, but those ends, because in their attainment one is exalted by the depression of others, are not in the direction in which that principle can really fulfill the promise and potency which it contains.'[6]

Here Green is plainly contending that what renders the voluptuary or the ambitious man vicious is that, though equally with the virtuous man he is seeking the complete, or at least the completest possible, satisfaction of himself, he is seeking it in a way in which in view of man's actual nature, and in particular in view of man's actual wants, it is not to be found. This account of how there come to be such things as virtuous and vicious action is, of course, not an account of how men come to have the idea that certain actions are duties. But it at least makes clear that Green really holds the view which eventually turns out to underlie his account of this, viz. the view that in all deliberate action whatever, bad as well as good, what the agent is wanting is the good or the satisfaction of himself.

We are now in a position to follow Green's account of the origin of what he describes as the moral ideal, i.e. really, of the idea that certain actions are duties. This is given in a later chapter entitled *The Origin and Development of the Moral Ideal*. Its essence is contained in a short paragraph. Having pointed out that a human being obviously has a disinterested interest in the good of others, he goes on to say: 'The conception of a moral law, in its strict philosophical form, is no doubt an analogical adaptation of the notion of law in the more primary sense—the notion of it as a command enforced by a political superior, or by some power to which obedience is habitually rendered by those to whom the command is addressed. But there is an idea which equally underlies the conception both of moral duty and legal right; which is prior, so to speak, to the distinction between them; which must have been at work in the minds of men before they could be capable of recognizing any kind of action as one that *ought* to be done, whether because it is enjoined by law or authoritative custom, or because, though not thus enjoined, a man owes it to himself or to his neighbour or to God. This is the idea of an absolute and a common good; a good common to the person conceiving it with others, and good for him and them, whether at any moment it answers their likings or no. As affected by such an idea, a man's attitude to his likes and dislikes will be one of which, in his inward converse, the "Thou shalt" or "Thou must" of command is the natural expression, though of law, in the sense either of the command of a political superior or of a self-imposed rule of

---

[6] Ibid., § 176; cf. 'The true good we shall understand in the same way. It is an end in which the effort of a moral agent can really find rest' (§ 171).

life, he may as yet have no definite conception.'[7] An adequate consideration of the meaning of this passage would require much comment. More especially we should have to ask 'What is meant by "a common good"?', and even whether the phrase does not really involve a contradiction in terms. But without going into details it is possible to say that Green at least means that if a man is to think of some action as a duty, he must think of it as conducive to the realization of something which is at once the good of a society of which he is a member and his own good. It is, he implies, neither enough to think of that to which the act is conducive as the good of the whole body, nor enough to think of it as his own good. He must think of it as at once both. And if we allow, as we must, that this is what Green means, the real nature of his thought becomes obvious. He sees perfectly well that no one will come to think of some action as a duty by simply thinking of it as conducive to his own personal interest. He considers, whether rightly or wrongly, that on the contrary we shall not think of an action as a duty unless we think of it as part of a plan of action devised for members of a society as conducive to the good of the whole body. But also thinking that we only desire anything as being for our own good, and that in consequence we only think of an action as one which we ought to do, in virtue of thinking that it will be conducive to our own good, he holds that, in order to think of some action as a duty, we must not only think of it as conducive to the good of the whole but must also think of that good as our good. In other words, by holding that underlying any thought of some action as a duty there is the thought of the good of the whole as our good, he thinks himself able to reconcile two apparently inconsistent positions (1) that in coming to think of some action as a duty we are determined solely by the consideration of what will be for the public good; and (2) that, nevertheless, we must be thinking of the action as for our own good, since otherwise we should not be thinking of it as a duty. And he really implies that while we arrive at the character in detail of the acts which we think duties by thinking of these actions as conducive to the public good, we arrive at their character as duties by thinking of them as for our good, or, more accurately, as for our greatest good.

His view, therefore, implies that we cannot even raise the question whether a right action will be for the advantage of the agent, since the connexion is really self-evident. For according to him it is only if we think of some action as for our own good that we shall think of it as a duty at all. We may of course question whether some particular action is a duty by questioning whether it will really be for our good, but once we imply that some action is a duty, as we do by referring to it as a duty, we imply that we have already thought of it as for our good.

Here it may be pointed out that this doctrine of Green's is very different from that of Plato in the fourth book of the *Republic*, at any rate if Plato has been

[7] Ibid., § 202.

rightly interpreted. They have no doubt an important implication in common, viz. that in all deliberate action we are moved by the desire of our own good. But there the identity ends. For while Green is maintaining that the very thought that some action is right involves the thought that it will be for our good, with the implication that the rightness of a right act depends on its advantageousness and that this dependence is self-evident, Plato is allowing that even if a right act be advantageous, its rightness is independent of its advantageousness, so that its advantageousness, if it be advantageous, requires to be proved.

But if we allow, as we must, that Green has been rightly interpreted, it is not difficult to see that his view is fundamentally mistaken. He is in effect offering as the explanation of our having come to think certain actions duties, the real or supposed facts (1) that we think of these actions as conducive to the good of the society of which we are members, and (2) that we think of the good of that whole as our good. And he implies that the thought to be explained and the thoughts which explain it are related as conclusion and premises. According to him, the thinking that a certain action is a duty is really the concluding that it is a duty in virtue of its being, as we think, for the good of the whole and of that good's being, as we think, our greatest good, and therefore the thinking that the action is a duty requires as its explanation the prior existence of the thoughts which form the premises of the argument. And the view really amounts to resolving the idea of duty into the idea of conduciveness to our advantage, or, in other words, resolving the moral 'ought' into the non-moral 'ought' in the sense in which it means conducive to our purpose, on the supposition that our purpose is always our greatest good or advantage. For it is only if the 'ought' in the conclusion that we ought to do these actions is understood in the non-moral sense that the conclusion can be plausibly represented as following from the premise.

If, however, we allow this, we ought to go on to ask how Green was led to make such a fundamental mistake.

Although in the *Prolegomena* he freely uses the terms 'Ethics' and 'Moral Theory', and although he obviously regards the *Prolegomena* as including an exposition, at any rate in outline, of his own moral theory, it is difficult to make out what he means by these phrases. Probably, if asked, he would have said that by 'a moral theory' he meant an account of what in the last resort renders an action a duty. Probably he would have also said that the principal object of the *Prolegomena* was to advance a moral theory.

But the Introduction makes it clear that Green considers that before he can even begin to advance a moral theory, he has to execute a preliminary task. He feels that he has first to vindicate the very existence of the subject-matter with which he proposes to deal. It is of course only possible to propound a theory of duty, or, more fully, a theory of the basis of duty, to someone who admits that there are such things as duties. For anyone who denies this will inevitably go on to contend that there is nothing about which to form a theory. And Green finds himself confronted by a school of contemporary thinkers, who, influenced by the growth of physical science, contend that for a *theory* of ethics there should be substituted a *science* of ethics. Ostensibly the contention is that whereas up to the present a special method of treatment of the subject of duty, designated 'philosophical', has been considered appropriate, the proper method is to treat duty as a fact belonging to the physical world and therefore by the same method as that by which we study other physical facts. But if we look below the surface, we find that the contention is quite different. To limit the contention to what is necessary for our purpose, it is really the contention that the fact to be considered and explained, i.e. have the reason for it exhibited, is not the fact that it is our duty to do certain actions but the fact that we have come to think so. This fact, it is implied, requires explanation, because obviously at an earlier stage of our lives we had no such thought at all; and in any case we are in the last resort descended from men who had no such idea, and, ultimately, from animals. And the only kind of explanation possible must be scientific, i.e. physical. We have to show how the original nature of ourselves or our ancestors taken in conjunction with our environment results in, and so accounts for, our having this conviction, just as the present state of the earth and of the stars has to be shown by science to result from, and to be accounted for, by their state at an earlier time. Further it is really implied that our present thought that certain actions are duties is false, since any suggested physical explanation, say by reference to sympathy as an element in man's original nature, would only explain at best how we come to make the mistake of thinking these actions duties. It is implied, therefore, that if Ethics is to be the name for a real subject it must have as its subject-matter not duties, since there are no such things, but our false convictions that there are duties; and that its business must be to give a scientific explanation of our coming to have them, and so to state the origin of the *idea* of duty. And Green, finding this view pervading the atmosphere round him, naturally thinks that he must first demolish this view of the 'scientific' moralists before he can proceed to develop a moral theory, i.e. a theory about duty, at all.

Now there are two fundamentally different ways in which anyone who wanted to destroy this view might proceed. He might agree with the 'scientific' moralists that our possession of moral convictions requires accounting for by some prior state or activity, either of ourselves or of certain other things or beings, but insist that that prior state or activity must be non-physical. Or, alternatively, he might go further by denying that our possession of moral convictions, along with our possession of certain other things such as the ideas of space, of time, and of cause, can be accounted for by any preceding state or activity whether physical or not, and maintaining that it requires for its explanation the pre-existence in us of the capacity for having or forming these convictions, a capacity of the existence of which our previous states or activities afford no indication whatever. And if he took the latter line, he could go on to add, that in the case of any state or activity which can only be accounted for in this way, i.e. by allowing its existence to require a pre-existing corresponding capacity, the process through which the subject of the state has gone can only be understood by, so to say, reading it backwards, and not, as the scientist would like to read it, forwards. For he could say that where this kind of explanation is necessary, it is only possible to discover all that existed in the earlier stage by the help of our knowledge of the states and activities at the later stage, since the existence of the corresponding capacities at the earlier stage could be discovered only at the later stage through our knowledge of the states and activities then attained.

Of these two possible ways of meeting the 'scientific' moralists it is obvious that Green adopts the former and less drastic. In this respect his attitude towards his opponents resembles that of Plato towards the Sophists in that he agrees with them in principle but differs on a matter, though no doubt an important matter, of detail. And so far as the *Prolegomena to Ethics* is what it is called, viz. *prolegomena* to Ethics and not an ethics, it is an endeavour to meet the 'scientific' moralists on their own ground by allowing that our moral convictions must have as their explanation some prior state or activity, but trying to show that this prior state or activity must be non-physical in character.

Green's own explanation really falls into two parts, of which one has already been stated. He offers as the proximate explanation of our conviction that some action is a duty our possession of the thought that the action will be for the good of the whole, together with that of the thought that the good of the whole is our good. But he contends in effect that this latter thought presupposes the thought of ourselves as beings capable of having a good or being satisfied, and that in turn the existence of this thought in ourselves requires explanation. Consequently he implies that the complete explanation of our moral convictions requires the explanation of the existence of this thought. And, in its barest outline his explanation of the latter is as follows: What would ordinarily be described as a man's possession of animal wants and impulses, such as the want of food and hunger, may, and perhaps does, admit of a physical explanation. But no such explanation is possible of a man's thought of himself as capable of a good, a thought which is implied not merely in any moral conviction but also in any deliberate action. The existence of this thought in a man implies that he is a self-conscious being, who in virtue of his self-consciousness is able to distinguish himself from his various wants, and think of himself as a being who may become satisfied and whose satisfaction is distinct from the satisfaction of any particular want. And, this being so, the presence of this thought can be explained only by supposing that the eternal self-conscious subject of the world has reproduced itself in man, i.e. really has caused man to have the nature of a self. Consequently its presence in man cannot possibly be the result of any physical process in the world of nature, but, on the contrary, implies the operation of a non-physical cause working *ab extra*.

Now there is really no need for us to consider whether this explanation of the thought of ourselves as capable of a good is successful. For it is only introduced in order to supply part of the basis of his proximate explanation of our moral convictions, and if this proximate explanation is not in fact successful, it does not matter whether the proffered explanation of part of its basis is successful. If our conviction that we ought to do a certain action does not in fact arise from our thought that the action will conduce to the good of society which is also our good, then of course it does not matter whether Green succeeds in explaining something implied by this thought, viz. the thought of ourselves as beings capable of a good. For in that case even a successful explanation of the latter will not help him to explain the former. There is, however, no way of escaping the admission that what I have called Green's *proximate* explanation, i.e. account of the origin, of our moral convictions fails. It must in the end be allowed that in offering this explanation Green is really substituting for his opponents' physical explanation, which, it is hardly necessary to point out, is absurd on the face of it, what may in contrast be called in a very restricted and special sense a 'rational' explanation. If this explanation did explain our moral convictions then, of course, he would have explained them; but it does not, and, as I propose to contend, no 'rational' explanation, in the special sense intended, is possible.

These statements, of course, require both elucidation and vindication. When in ordinary life we ask 'What is the origin, or what is the explanation, of a man X's having a certain idea, say the idea that Y is unscrupulous?', and again when we ask what is in fact the same question, viz. 'How did X get the idea?', we are presupposing that the idea for the origin of which we are seeking was acquired by a process of reasoning, and are really asking what were the thoughts from which as premises X obtained the idea as a conclusion. We think, and think rightly, of X's having the idea as requiring explanation by reference to his past because we are thinking of the idea as one at which he has arrived, as we say, by an inference; and the explanation for which we are looking can in a special sense be called rational, because we think it consists in the prior existence of certain *thoughts* together with the exercise of the capacity of *reasoning* on the part of X. And when Green is looking for the origin of our idea that certain actions are duties, what he must really be doing, though of course without realizing it, is looking for the thoughts from which as premises we conclude that these actions are duties; and for that reason he can be said to be looking for a rational explanation of them in the sense explained. And if only it had been true, that we do sometimes think of the good of some society as our good, and that, when we think so and also think that some action will be for the good of that society, we conclude that the action is one which we are morally bound to do, Green's account of the origin of our moral convictions would have been successful. But unfortunately it is not true.

The broad fact is that on the one hand Green is really trying to show that we deduce the idea that some action is a duty from ideas which do not involve the idea of duty, and that on the other hand any such attempt must from its very nature fail. There is, of course, no difficulty in allowing that if we already think some *given* action a duty, we may go on to think in consequence that some other given action is a duty. If we think that we ought to do our day's work, then if we realize that the work cannot be done without getting up early, we shall think it a duty to get up early. There is, again, no difficulty in allowing that if we think that a given *kind* of action is a duty, we may in consequence go on to think of some given action as a duty. If we think it a duty to abstain from hurting people's feelings, then if we think that telling a man what we think of him would be hurting his feelings, we shall think we ought to abstain from telling him. But what cannot be done is to conclude that some action is a duty from thoughts *neither of which* is the thought that some action or kind of action is a duty. Aristotle was right on a fundamental matter when he pointed out the impossibility of a $\mu\epsilon\tau\acute{\alpha}\beta\alpha\sigma\iota\varsigma$ $\epsilon\grave{\iota}\varsigma$ $\mathring{\alpha}\lambda\lambda o$ $\gamma\acute{\epsilon}\nu o\varsigma$, and not the least important case of this impossibility is to be found in the impossibility of deducing a conclusion which contains the term 'duty', from premises which do not. It is not merely that Green fails to give a successful rational explanation, in the sense explained, of our idea that certain actions are duties. Any one must fail. For he will be attempting to find the premises from which we arrive at a thought which is in fact not arrived at by an argument at all. And I would suggest as a prominent instance of the fallacy involved the attempt which is often made nowadays (as e.g. I think it is by Professor Moore and Professor Laird) to maintain a view which implies that we deduce the rightness of certain actions from our knowledge of what is *good* taken in conjunction with our knowledge of our powers of action and of existing circumstances.

The question, of course, arises. 'What line ought Green to have taken against his opponents?'. The answer is surely that he ought to have abandoned any attempt to offer a rational explanation of our moral convictions, in the sense of 'rational' explained, i.e. to represent them as attained by some process of reasoning; and that, instead, he ought to have taken the more drastic line of opposition by maintaining that they imply for their explanation the prior existence of the corresponding capacity on our part, which only becomes actualized given the appropriate stimulus. As a clue to explaining what is meant, it is worth pointing out that it may well be questioned whether in any case whatever in which we do come to have a thought by way of inference, the thoughts which we must already have in order to draw the conclusion do *by themselves* explain our coming to have the thought. For to come to have the thought, besides having to have the thoughts which are to be its premises, we must, as we say, draw the conclusion from them; and this drawing the inference, i.e. this activity of inferring, implies the prior existence in us of something not actual, and therefore not discoverable by any activity of self-consciousness, viz. the capacity of reasoning, or, in other words, intelligence. Therefore it may rightly be said that even to account for our having a thought which we are said to acquire inferentially, we have to presuppose the pre-existence in us of a certain capacity, and therefore to allow that the explanation of the thought does not lie solely in any preceding state or activity. In an analogous way, it may, I think, rightly be contended that what Green ought to have maintained is that our possession of moral convictions cannot be explained in terms of any past state or activity of ours in which we had no such convictions, but requires us to presuppose the prior existence in ourselves of a certain capacity, viz. the capacity of having them. Two not unimportant additions may be made. First it may be said that Green himself takes a similar view with regard to our thought of ourselves as capable of a good. For he urges in effect that, to account for this thought, we have to allow that prior to having it we were selves, i.e. beings capable of self-consciousness, though he spoils the effect of this contention by going on to imply that this capacity can, and indeed must, be generated in us *ab extra*. The second addition is more important. It may fairly be said that if Green had maintained that what is required to explain our moral convictions is the prior existence of the corresponding capacity on our part, he would have maintained an explanation of them, which, unlike that offered by the 'scientific' moralists, in no way implied them to be false. For, on this view, the nature of the pre-existing capacity which we think presupposed by our possession of moral convictions will depend entirely on what we think the intrinsic nature of what are here called our moral convictions. As Plato saw, we can only discover what our capacities are through our apprehension of their actualizations. And if as the result of considering our so-called moral convictions in themselves, we consider them to be really the *knowledge* that certain actions are right, we shall have to maintain the existence in us of the capacity of *knowing* what is right. If on the other hand we consider them to be really the *thought* or *conviction* that the actions are right, then we shall have to maintain the existence in us of the capacity of *thinking* or *being convinced* that they are right, which as such may be either true or false. Consequently if Green had taken this line, he could have gone on to maintain that the need to account for our so-called convictions in no way implies them to be false, and that if anyone is anxious to discover whether they are true, he will find no light whatever thrown on this question by considering the question which the 'scientific' moralists think all-important, viz. 'What is required to account for them?'.

I am only too conscious of the length of my argument. My sole defence is that it is impossible to consider one issue without considering others. But I think it possible to sum up most of what I have been contending for by a reference to Kant. His moral philosophy is of course open to many obvious criticisms. Nevertheless he always strikes me as having, far more than any other philosopher, the root of the matter in him. More especially, he seems to me to steer completely clear of those views which I have been maintaining to be errors, and indeed to insist that they are errors. He will have nothing to do either with the idea that the rightness of action depends on its being for our own good, or with the idea that we think of it as so depending, or with the idea that desire for our own good is our only motive. And it is, I think, for this reason that in spite of his obvious mistakes he retains so close a hold on his readers.

4. Kant's *Fundamental Principles of the Metaphysic of Morals**

The aim of the *Metaphysic of Morals* is, broadly speaking, twofold, (1) to elucidate the nature of Morality, i.e. what is meant by a morally good act, (2) to discover the basis of moral obligation, i.e. to show the reason why we ought to do those acts usually called right, and so to prove that moral rules are really binding on us. (2) presupposes that there *is* a common reason why (a presupposition which Kant never thinks of questioning), and involves, according to Kant, such a proof as is possible of the freedom of the will.

As to the *method* of finding this reason, Kant starts from the conviction that the ordinary moral rules, if binding at all, must be binding on all *rational* beings and not merely on all *human* beings. Hence his method is to deduce the obligation to act on these rules from the nature of rationality as such (i.e. assuming that there are ways in which a rational being ought to act, he is to discover what those ways are from the very nature of a rational agent, and thence to conclude that these are the ways in which *we* ought to act).

Kant's famous opening sentence strikes the keynote of his position. It forms practically a text on which the rest of the book is to be a commentary.

What immediately follows is an elucidation not of the nature of this will to which the first sentence supplies no clue—but of the unique nature of its goodness. It is the only thing good in its own right i.e. independently of what exists along with it, and its coexistence is a condition of the goodness of any other mental quality or of any state of happiness.

The notion of something only conditionally good strikes us as strange. We naturally think of resolution or courage, e.g. as, if good at all, good anyhow— (e.g. courage of Iago). But we hesitate to maintain this in connection with *one* of the things which Kant mentions, viz. happiness. That it is good to be happy only if we are *worthy* of happiness strikes us as by no means odd.

Kant goes on to point out that the goodness of happiness is *intrinsic* and not the goodness of *utility* i.e. of *usefulness* in respect of its *results*. And he enforces this

[From MS. Eng. Misc. C 299, Bodleian Library, University of Oxford.]

* [In the original manuscript, Prichard provides three titles: (1) 'The Metaphysic of Morals', crossed out; (2) 'Grundlegung', crossed out; (3) 'Kant's Grundlegung zur metaphysik der Sitten', handwritten and left in place. Having confirmed that Prichard used T. K. Abbott's translation (London: Longmans, Green, no date given), I changed the title to Abbott's title: 'Kant's Fundamental Principles of the Metaphysic of Morals'. Ed.]

by a teleological argument. Given that nature has given us our faculties with a purpose i.e. to enable us to realize something which nature intends us to realize and which therefore is the proper thing for us to realize, this purpose of nature cannot be our happiness. For in that case our power of acting intelligently or in virtue of our reason must have been given us simply to discover and execute the means to happiness. But the process of calculation is so difficult that instinct would have enabled us to achieve happiness much better. Hence if we had been designed to achieve happiness, we should have been given instinct and not the power of acting intelligently; and we must have been given the power of acting intelligently, not to be exercised as a mere means to happiness but as something the exercise of which is good in itself.

To elucidate the nature of a good will, Kant proceeds to analyze the nature of a moral or dutiful action—this being, according to him, the form which a good will must take in a human being. He lays down three propositions:

(1) A moral action must be one in which we do what we do purely from a sense of duty and not from *inclination*. (N.B. Kant specially urges that a moral action is not the only action in which we may act *against inclination*; it may be an act of prudence, in which we act for our advantage, i.e. happiness. This is important in connection with hypothetical imperatives.)

(2) The second proposition Kant formulates thus: 'An action done from duty derives its moral worth, *not from the purpose* which is to be attained by it, but from the maxim by which it is determined, and therefore does not depend on the realization of the object of the action, but merely on the *principle of volition* by which the action has taken place, without regard to any object of desire.'

This is difficult. (*a*) What is meant by the maxim or principle of volition; and (*b*) what is the contrast to which Kant is calling attention? For Kant opposes his view that the moral worth of an act depends on the maxim to the view that it depends on the *effect* of the act *and* the view that it depends on its *purpose*. The effect should be ignored. For he connects purpose with desire, implying that by the purpose of an act is meant *that the desire of existence of which* leads us to act: he is plainly thinking *in the main* not of the *actual production* of certain effects but of the *desire* of them as influencing our action, whether they are produced or not; and his main contrast is between a principle of volition and a desire, a principle here—as other passages show—meaning our recognition of the fact that we ought to do such and such a thing. Hence his real point cannot be that moral value of an act lies in its principle as opposed to its actual effect nor even, as his *words* would suggest, that it lies in the principle as opposed to the purpose or object of the desire which actuates us—a moral act implying *both* a principle and a purpose. It must be that the moral value of an act lies in its being actuated not by a desire at all but by the recognition that we ought to do an act of this kind. If so, proposition (2) is only (1) in another form.

(3) 'Duty is the necessity of acting from respect for the law'. This is also difficult. Though said to follow from (1) and (2), it is really new. 'Necessity' should be omitted. The proposition really means 'Doing our duty consists in doing an act prescribed by a moral law simply from respect for that law as a moral law.' It introduces two new features in Kant's view of a moral act:

(*a*) that our attitude to a moral principle is one of respect and not of inclination.

This is, I think, a mistake. Respect is felt only for persons. Kant here is really resolving the sense of obligation into respect. Kant usually ignores this respect and we can do the same.

(*b*) that moral principles are of the nature of laws, in the legal sense. (This of course common in moral philosophers. Cf. e.g. Plato and Butler.)

The term 'law' applied to a moral principle is, of course, a metaphor. The use of a metaphor need not be erroneous: it may express a fact. Yet the metaphorical character of a metaphor must be kept in mind; otherwise we may be taken in, by treating a metaphorical description of a thing as a literal description. Hence in using a metaphor we must keep before ourselves the fact of which the metaphor is the metaphorical expression, and be ready to replace the metaphorical expression by a literal expression of it.

Kant is led to speak of moral principles as laws for three connected reasons:

(1) A ruler in imposing a law does not appeal to the wishes or inclinations of his subjects; he does not recommend certain actions because they will *like* to do them. He issues the laws as *commands*. His mood is the imperative.

Similarly, Kant thinks our attitude to an act which we ought to do is not that of liking to do it but of feeling commanded to do it. In other words our sense of obligation to do so and so is the sense of being commanded to do it, thus being opposed to feeling inclined to do it.

(2) The commands of a ruler expressed in laws ought to be obeyed by *all* his subjects irrespectively of their inclinations which differ in different subjects. So Kant thinks a moral principle ought to be acted on by *all rational* beings indifferently, whatever their individual inclinations. 'One ought to pay one's debts' applies not only to certain individuals but to all men and, in fact, to all rational beings.

There is, however, this important difference. In the case of a law, there is a distinction between the being commanded and the being under an obligation to obey it, the one being the basis of the other. 'The subject ought to obey the ruler's command *because* it is his command.' He ought, e.g., not to cycle on a footpath because he is ordered not to. But in the case of a moral principle there is no such distinction. We cannot say 'we ought to pay our debts because we are commanded to do so'—the sense that we ought to *is* the recognition that we are commanded to. The term command is just the metaphorical expression of the obligation and so when Kant is talking 'moral', we are always justified in replacing an imperative formula by the expression of an obligation. 'Pay your debts' may, and indeed should, be taken to mean 'you ought to pay your debts'.

(3) A ruler does not *find* or *discover* laws: he *makes* or *invents* them. Similarly, Kant thinks, moral principles are not facts which we discover; we make them for ourselves. This view is of course, implied on speaking of them as laws but Kant also holds it explicitly.

The imperative character of moral obligation is made explicit in chapter 2, where Kant distinguishes *categorical* and *hypothetical imperatives*.

'All imperatives command either *hypothetically* or *categorically*. The former represent the practical necessity of (i.e. the obligation to do) 'a possible action as means to something else' which is or might be willed (Kant should have said 'desired'). The categorical imperative would be that which represented an action as necessary (i.e. as one which we ought to do) of itself and without reference to another end.' (Kant should have said 'any object of desire').

Kant also expresses the distinction by the help of the term 'good'. His language implies that a hypothetical imperative is one representing that some action is good only as a means to something else, viz. some actual or possible purpose, and that a categorical imperative is one representing that some action is good in itself.

The former is the right formula. For Kant by 'an imperative' means to express an obligation and any statement of an obligation requires the word 'ought'. 'Good' will not do as a substitute; for even if paying one's debts is good in itself, this is not *identical with* the obligation to pay them.

Kant then divides hypothetical imperatives into two classes:

(1) *Problematical*, where that to which the prescribed action is a means is only a *possible* object of desire. E.g. 'Be industrious in youth (*if* you want comfort in old age)'; 'use plenty of soap (if you want to become more clean)'.

(2) *Assertorial*, where the object to which the prescribed action is a means is actually desired. E.g. 'get up early (*since* you want health)'.

He assumes one desire to be common to every one, viz. the desire for happiness. Hence any imperative prescribing a means to happiness is assertorial; e.g. 'Make yourself heathy (*since* you want happiness)'.

Comments on the Distinction between Categorical and Hypothetical Imperatives

(1) *A difficulty relating to moral imperatives*.

Kant's imperatives are meant to express obligations and are in fact a metaphorical formulation of them. Hence Kant's hypothetical imperatives, if really imperatives, must be replaceable by propositions (in the indicative) expressing obligations; e.g. 'Use plenty of soap' by 'you ought to use plenty of soap'. And Kant apparently considers that actions so commanded are really obligations;

e.g. that if you wish to become clean, there is really an obligation upon you to use soap.

Now this implies that the obligation has a reason, viz. the object of the desire to which the action commanded is a means, and therefore suggests that a *categorical* imperative must also have a reason. Yet when we look for the reason we cannot find it, since here *ex hypothesi* there is no object of desire to form the reason; and we are even led to wonder whether in the case of categorical imperatives there is really an obligation at all. Hence to Kant moral obligation comes to present a paradox. There must be a reason why we ought to do actions usually called right and yet it can't be found where on general grounds we should expect to find it, viz., in some desired effect. And the problem becomes that of finding a reason why an action ought to be done which is independent of desire and therefore of any effect of the action.

(2) Kant's hypothetical and categorical imperatives are not really distinguished as hypothetical and categorical. According to Kant, a hypothetical imperative is binding on an individual only *if* he wants the end to which the prescribed action is a means. It is binding only on some individuals, whereas a categorical imperative is binding on every one.

But (*a*) an imperative prescribing means to happiness, which Kant regards as hypothetical is really not hypothetical at all, since here everyone desires the end, and there is no 'if'. Kant himself implicitly admits this in calling such an imperative assertorial.

(*b*) Only a hypothetical imperative of the other kind, viz. a problematic imperative, is really hypothetical. But even this is absolutely and not hypothetically binding on those who desire the end. Hence the term hypothetical distinguishes the imperative to which it is applicable not in respect of the nature of the obligation but in respect of the persons under the obligation; i.e. it implies simply that an imperative which is so called applies only to certain individuals, whereas a categorical imperative applies to all. It is not that there are two sorts of obligation, the one hypothetical and the other categorical; it is that certain obligations apply to some and others apply to all.

(*c*) What really distinguishes the two species of hypothetical imperatives from categorical imperatives is that in the former the obligation depends on desire, while in the latter it does not.

(3) Hence Kant's so-called hypothetical imperatives are not really imperatives. There are not two species of imperative, the one moral and the other non-moral: there is simply an imperative, or more strictly a feeling commanded, and, opposed to it, a desire. According to Kant, a man who desires to become clean will feel that he *ought* to use plenty of soap. But in fact, the only attitude to using soap which can be originated by the desire to become clean is that of desire. A desire for X can originate only the desire, and not the sense of obligation, to take the means to X.

Hence Kant has no right to speak of hypothetical *imperatives* at all, since he uses the term 'imperative' to express an obligation. Moreover Kant's general view agrees with this criticism. For what Kant really contrasts with acting from a sense of obligation is acting from desire, and acting from desire is taking the means to an object of desire in consequence of that desire. Hence the real contrast in Kant's mind is not that between a moral and a non-moral imperative, but that between the appreciation of an imperative, i.e. a sense of obligation to do something and the desire to do something because it will lead to something which we desire for its own sake. In other words, according to Kant, there are two possible attitudes to an action, the moral attitude of feeling that we ought, or are commanded, to do it and the non-moral attitude of desiring to do it as a means to something which we desire for itself.

Hence Kant's account of the distinction between categorical and hypothetical imperatives only adds to the account of moral action in the first chapter, that the sense of obligation is a feeling of the *imperativeness* of acting in a certain way.

The Holy Will

So far we have only considered Kant's account of the good will in the imperfect form in which it exists in man, a being only partially rational since he is affected by desires which are, as such, non-rational. From this form Kant distinguishes the perfect form, the holy or completely rational will, which being without desire always does what it ought. The main distinction which Kant draws out is that for the holy will there is no such thing as obligation, since a sense of obligation can only arise in opposition to inclinations which may thwart it.

Now this idea of a holy will is untenable. The issue is important, since it is often held that the sense of obligation is a mark of imperfection and that in a perfectly moral being it would not exist. Kant represents the purely rational will as a will which is always determined to act by the thought of a moral law. But how is a moral law here to be formulated? Not in terms of good; e.g. it cannot be held that the holy will is determined to act by the recognition that paying debts is good. For 'paying debts is good', though possibly expressing a fact, does not express a direction to act. A moral principle can only be expressed in terms of an 'ought', and the apprehension of a moral principle involves a certain emotion, viz. the sense of obligation. Hence even a perfectly moral being cannot be exempt from the sense of obligation, and Kant's holy will, as a will moved neither by desire nor by a sense of obligation, must be an impossibility.

We cannot amend Kant here by maintaining that the perfectly moral will would act from a desire but a desire of a special kind, viz. a good desire. For though it is possible to perform duties from some good motive other than a sense of obligation, e.g. a desire arising from affection or public spirit, and though such an act will manifest goodness, the goodness manifested will not be moral goodness.

Kant's Criterion of the Rightness of a Right Action

Kant, having formulated the spirit in which a moral being will act, viz. the sense of obligation, rightly goes on to ask 'what in particular will a moral being do?' And this involves the question 'what is it in an action which makes it such that it ought, or ought not, to be done?' Kant expresses this question in the form 'What law (i.e. principle) can that be the conception of which must determine the will without regard to any effect expected from it, in order that this will may be called good absolutely?' Kant's answer is in effect this. The idea of obligation implies that if *I* ought to perform an action of a certain kind, then *everyone* ought to perform it. This in turn implies that an action of this kind must be possible for everyone. Hence we have a criterion at hand; an action of a certain kind will be one which we ought to perform, if it can be such that everyone can perform it. Kant expresses this criterion thus: 'I am never to act otherwise than so that I could also will that my maxim should be a universal law.' His view is that that act and that act alone ought to be done which can be thought of without contradiction as being universally done; and he is driven to this paradox because no other alternative seems open. Since the obligation to do something cannot depend on the nature of the effect produced, particular moral principles must be derived from their mere form as *principles*, i.e. as he thinks, from their capacity of being acted on universally. Further he tests his criterion by a series of examples which seem to him to show that its application leads to just those principles which we recognize in our unreflective consciousness.

Kant subsequently adds a second and a third criterion of moral principles. The second is based on the idea that man's rational nature gives an absolute value to his personality i.e. a goodness which is not that of being a means or instrument to something else but which is intrinsic and constitutes the man, in Kant's language, an end in himself. This fact, according to Kant, justifies the principle 'So act as to treat humanity whether in thine own person, or in that of any other, in every case as an end, and never as a means only', and by examples Kant seeks to show that application of this principle leads to the ordinarily recognized moral rules.

On this principle it is only necessary to remark that it cannot serve as a criterion of morality. Consider first that part of it which concerns the treatment of others. What is really meant by 'We ought to treat others always as ends and never as means'? The meaning of the positive half is difficult, for neither a person nor even his rational nature can strictly be an end i.e. the effect of an action desire for which leads to the action. The clue lies in the fact that this half expresses the positive side of the fact of which the second half expresses the negative side. 'Treating another merely as a means' plainly means 'treating him simply as a tool or instrument for the achievement of our own ends.' Now what do we have in mind when we say 'we ought not treat another merely as a 'means'? We are thinking that another man, as a man, or as a friend, or as a servant etc.—which a mere physical *thing* cannot be—has certain claims on us, i.e. rights against us, which we ought to respect, in virtue of which we ought to act towards him in certain ways, whether it suits us or not. If so, the positive implication of 'we ought not to treat another simply as a means' is that we ought to perform our obligations to that other, and this must be the meaning of 'we ought to treat another always as an end'. But if so, the principle, so far from being a principle from which particular duties can be *derived*, will *presuppose* them. For it will be 'we ought to do to another the particular things which we ought, and not merely treat him as a convenience': and, to apply this, we must already *know* what in particular we ought to do to that other.

Similarly, 'we ought to treat ourselves as ends, and not merely as means' will mean, to take a particular instance, 'we ought not simply to use our capacity to compose music in the way which will bring the largest income, but we should limit this use to the extent required to satisfy the obligation which we, as possessing this capacity, are under to use it in a way which will produce the best music'. And if so, the same criticism applies, viz. that we cannot by applying it *discover* particular duties but that on the contrary any application of it *presupposes* an independent knowledge of them.

(3) The third criterion is based on the idea that a moral principle is something which a man in virtue of his rational nature *imposes on himself and all other men*, i.e. in Kant's words, the idea that the will of every rational being is a universally legislative will (i.e. a will which gives the law to itself and all other rational wills).

This idea gives rise: (*a*) to the idea that moral beings form a *kingdom of ends*, i.e. a democracy of rational beings who impose on themselves and others, as subjects, a common system of law; (*b*) to the principle 'so act that the will can regard itself as *giving* in its maxims universal laws to itself'.

This criterion only differs from the first by the addition of the notion that moral principles are imposed on ourselves *by ourselves*. This addition is important, for it leads Kant to speak of our will, so far as we act from a sense of obligation, as *autonomous*, and of our will, so far as we act from desire, as *heteronomous*. The underlying idea is, of course, that, since our rational nature is our real nature, in acting from desire we are not acting freely or 'of ourselves' but are, so to say, constrained from outside; and that it is only when acting morally, i.e. from principles due to our own rational nature, that we act freely.

The view, however, that we impose moral principles on ourselves is mistaken. For though, no doubt, it is *we* who *recognize* moral principles, and though the recognition is *our* act and an act of our own rational nature, we do not *invent* the principles, as the legislator invents laws. We *find* them. This is perhaps the fundamental mistake involved in speaking of moral *laws*. While a law is always the invention, though not the arbitrary invention, of a human being, a moral principle is not invented at all. There seems only one respect in which the analogy of law helps to elucidate the nature of morality, viz. that a law is binding on *all* the subjects of the legislator.

The success of this third criterion as a criterion need not be considered, for the addition which it makes to the first, viz. that moral principles are given to ourselves by *ourselves*, makes the first no better for the discovery of particular moral principles. To complete Kant's account of moral action, two points remain to be brought out:

(1) Kant's first criterion of moral principles is, clearly, the important one, being that which naturally belongs to his view taken as a whole, whereas the second is an artificial addition, and the third is only an unfortunate variant on the first. Now it is important to see—what apparently Kant does not—that this criterion expresses what, on Kant's view, is really the reason why we ought to do the actions which we ought to do. According to him, what distinguishes keeping a promise as an action which we ought to do from breaking a promise where it suits us as an action which we ought not to do is the fact that only the former can be universally carried out. This involves that the sole characteristic of an action which makes it such that we ought to do it consists in the possibility of its being carried out by everyone; i.e. that the reason why we should keep a promise is simply that it is possible for every one to keep promises. In other words, if any one asks '*why* ought I to do an action of one of the kinds usually called moral?' the answer is simply 'Because such an action is possible for all'.

(2) A passage in the *Critique of Practical Reason* makes his general view clearer. 'The conception of good and evil must not be determined before the moral law (of which it seems as if it must be the foundation), but only after it and by means of it.'

What Kant means is this. We can't derive the fact that a certain action ought to be done or is right, from the previously recognized goodness of anything. For this would involve that the good thing in question is some good which the action will bring about or achieve, and the goodness of this will consist in its conduciveness to the agent's pleasure. Hence what is right is not a consequence of what is good. On the contrary as the only unconditional good is the good will, i.e. the moral will or the will which acts from a sense of obligation, the thought of what is moral is prior to the thought of what is good and is presupposed by it.

Examination of Kant's View of Morality

We have to consider (1) any criticisms which Kant's view naturally suggests, (2) if these criticisms prove justified, how Kant's view should be amended or by what it should be replaced.

The view provokes two main criticisms. We distinguish, quite rightly, between what we ought to do and the spirit in which or the motive with which we do it; and these are independent in the sense that it is possible to do the same act with different motives. In the same circumstances I may kill a man out of revenge, or in self-defence, or in defence of my country. In the same circumstances, I may help a friend to further my advantage, or from sympathy with my friend, or to gain praise. In particular I may do what I ought either because I ought, i.e. from a sense of obligation, or from some desire; e.g. I may pay a debt, either because I ought, or to maintain my credit or from the desire that my creditor shall regain his money. This implies (1) that it is possible to do a right action from an indifferent and even a bad motive and therefore (2) that the questions 'what makes an action right or such that I ought to do it?' and 'what is the proper or good motive which makes a right action good?' are different and independent. For if a right action can be done with a bad motive, it is clear that its rightness cannot lie in the motive.

Now it is natural to urge that Kant answers both these questions wrongly; for it cannot be true (1) that what makes an act of a certain kind right is that it can be done by every one, or (2) that the only good motive is the sense of duty. In fact it will be said with respect to (2) that the truth lies in the precise contrary and was expressed by Aristotle when he contended that an act to be done virtuously must be done with pleasure, and therefore, presumably, not from a sense of obligation. Kant, it will be said, makes his ideal man cold, hard, and repulsive, a man divested of all sympathy and interest in others, and we rightly shrink from such a person. It will probably be added that Kant is only led to this mistake because he insists wrongly that if we are influenced by desire, the desire is always at bottom desire for our own pleasure.

The first criticism is irrefutable. No one could suppose that the reason why an act ought to be done consists in the fact that every one could do it. Even Kant could not have supposed this. The difficulty simply escaped him because it didn't occur to him that his criterion of moral rules must express what, on his view, is their reason.

Moreover it is easy to see that this 'reason' couldn't give rise to a code of principles of action at all, whether the code did or did not coincide with the code ordinarily recognized.

(1) A preliminary point. From Kant's point of view, the test should have been more than a test or criterion, i.e. something by which we can decide whether an act *otherwise suggested* is moral. It should have been something from which by itself we could have developed the system of moral rules. For if the rules have to be otherwise suggested, the application of the test involves an appeal to experience, which he doesn't allow, viz. to the experience of men's actual desires and the circumstances in which they live.

(2) Plainly *any* course of action can be universally acted on: for if it be possible for one man, contradiction cannot arise from supposing any number of men so acting; e.g. every one could kill his enemy or commit suicide. Kant denies this. He urges that to suppose every one making promises with the intention of breaking them is self-contradictory. But it is not. Of course, if every one makes deceitful promises, no one will be deceived, and so making false promises will be *unsuccessful*; but the action consists in *saying* that we shall do what we mean not to do. Even Kant hedges. What he really urges is not that making deceitful promises if it became universal, would become *impossible*, but that it, if it became universal, would become seen to be *useless*, since no one would be deceived, and so would be no longer attempted. (N.B. His words 'if they believed me over-hastily, they would pay me back in their own coin' expressly allow the *possibility*.)

Of course we can think of an action in its *own nature* self-contradictory e.g. jumping 20 feet high, or squaring the circle. But then such an action is impossible for *any* one. It may be urged that not every one could act on the rule 'We ought to heal the sick', since there would not be enough sick to go round. But this principle *presupposes* the existence of sick to be healed, and would be maintained by no one, unless he thought there were sick. The supposition of a state of affairs in which every one healed the sick is not *self*-contradictory, *self*-inconsistent, but only inconsistent with our knowledge that the number of sick is limited. Similarly the inconsistency involved in supposing that every one made deceitful promises is not internal but is its inconsistency with our knowledge that in a society men rely on the profession of others.

It may be urged that there must be some truth in Kant's criterion, since we often try to convince men of the wrongness of certain actions by asking them to imagine what would happen if everyone so acted; e.g. if everyone was unpunctual, or used either side of the road. And, it will be said, though the supposition involves no contradiction, it does imply such bad consequences that no one would accept them, or at least think the action legitimate. But this procedure is adopted only to make the bad consequences of single actions of the kind more obvious, by increasing the scale.

It is usually only adopted in cases—which do exist—where the badness of the consequences may increase more than in proportion to the number of offenders. Thirty per cent of unpunctual people may cause more than three times the inconvenience caused by ten per cent. But even then a single action must have a bad consequence, if several of the same kind are to have consequences worse in proportion.

Even Kant is unable to apply his criterion successfully. He expressly admits that some actions which are contrary to morality (viz. those contrary to the duties of so-called imperfect obligation e.g. that of relieving the distressed or of improving our faculties) *can* be universally performed. In these cases Kant tries to meet the difficulty by contending that at any rate we cannot *will* the universal practice of these actions. But even so there is no self-contradiction in such willing. The willing that everyone in distress be neglected is only inconsistent with something else, viz. our own desire for help when in distress.

This vindication of the immorality of a rule is expressly based upon the existence of a desire—and a purely selfish desire. Kant considers four cases. In only one does he even try to apply his criterion, viz. that of making deceitful promises (Abbott, p. 40, yet on p. 19 he really abandons this case). In one case, that of relieving the distressed, he retains the criterion, but falls back on the contradiction between the willing the universal performance of an action and the individual's own desire.

In the other cases he abandons the criterion altogether. In contending for the wrongness of *suicide*, he assumes that suicide is prompted by self-love, and that self-love involves the desire for the continuance of our existence, and thence concludes that to commit suicide would be self-contradictory. But the inconsistency lies in the inconsistent nature which Kant here gives to self-love; there is no pretence of considering more than the action of a *single* individual.

The only reason which he gives for the obligation to *improve our faculties* is since the faculties of a rational being serve for all sorts of purposes, a rational being must will that they be developed.

Now return to the second criticism. Reflection will, I think, easily shew it to be an over-statement. Compare two doctors at work in a hospital. Suppose the one so much absorbed in the health of his patients, or caring so much for the exercise of his skill that, though tired and unwell, he hardly hesitates to continue all day at his work. Suppose the other to have these interests only in a slight degree but to be carried through his work by a sense of duty arising from his recognition of his position as doctor of the hospital. On Kant's view, only the actions of the latter are intrinsically good. On Aristotle's view, the actions of the former alone are good or at least they are better. But surely *both* are in part right, each stating a half of the whole truth. Both men exhibit goodness, the latter exhibiting moral goodness, the former the goodness of what in distinction from morality should be called virtue. The former acts on desires which spring from intrinsically good interests, and which, as such, have goodness of virtue; but this goodness doesn't preclude the existence of goodness of another kind, that of morality. It can't, I think, even be said that the goodness of virtue is greater than moral goodness, though perhaps the reverse is true. What is, I think, plainly true is that we think the really best man to be the man in whom both forms of goodness are combined. Thus we think that there is something lacking in the first man, if the sense of obligation is not present, as well as his interest in his patients; and in the second, in that his interest in his patients is defective.

Kant's only mistake is that he takes moral goodness to be the only form of goodness. And it is not the proper correction of this mistake to go to the other extreme and to maintain that virtue is the only form of goodness.

Further, paradoxical as it may seem, Kant is, I think *not far* wrong in holding that actions from desire are actions from desire for pleasure. This view, I think, only needs qualifying by restricting the acts in question to reflective acts. Suppose I see a friend fall on his head in the street. Sympathizing with him, I at once run and pick him up, actuated by the desire for the cessation of his pain. But suppose instead that I hear a friend at a distance has been damaged, that I know that I can help him if I go to him, but that going to him will be irksome, it being wet and dark; suppose also that I feel no obligation to help him, or rather, since this is probably impossible, abstract from any sense of obligation that I may feel. The knowledge of the irksomeness of going leads me to hesitate and reflect. I say to myself 'Shall I go?' Now suppose eventually I decide to go and go, what leads to my decision? Surely the fact that, when I reflect, I find that I would rather go and help him in spite of the discomfort involved than stay at home comfortably reading a novel, i.e. my interest in my friend being what it is, I shall like better, i.e. enjoy more or be less pained by, going out than staying in feeling I am doing nothing to help my friend.

If that be the correct analysis, what moves me to go is the desire for pleasure. We are reluctant to admit this only because we are inclined to think that any action due to desire for pleasure is selfish. But at any rate in this case it is not. For the pleasure which I expect to get, or the pain which I hope to avoid, is due to my unselfish interest in my friend. (N.B. Selfishness is difficult to analyze.)

(For a discussion of the true answer to the question 'Why are actions of certain kind such that they ought to be done'? see article in *Mind* (January 1912), entitled 'Does Moral Philosophy Rest on a Mistake?').*

Kant's Approximation to the Truth

If the contentions of the article in *Mind* are true, Kant is much more nearly right than is usually supposed.

(A) Kant's answer to the question 'What makes an action such that it ought to be done?'

No doubt Kant does not successfully answer this question, and, no doubt, his mistaken answer is partly due to the common mistake of supposing a *general* answer to be possible.

(B) In effect he will have nothing to do with the view common among moral philosophers that having discovered that an action is right we still have to find

* [See ch. 2 in this vol. Ed.]

a reason for doing it—i.e. a reason why we should do it in the shape of some personal advantage. This is probably the cause of the hold which Kant's moral philosophy has gained on many in spite of the unworkableness of its detail.

(C) Though Kant's view is wrong that those acts *ought* to be done which *can* be done by *every* one, the conviction which suggested it is true and important; viz. that any particular right action involves a principle binding on every one always.

Our obligations are, no doubt, always *particular*, e.g. to pay a certain debt to X; and what we directly recognize is always a *particular* obligation. But in recognizing it we imply the truth of a *principle*. For, e.g., in recognizing that we ought to pay 5 pounds to X, what in the act makes us feel that we ought to do the act—which consists in writing a cheque and posting it to X—is not that the act is one in doing which we should giving a postman extra labour, or adding twopence to the revenue, or giving another man a chance of buying something—though it is all of these—but simply that it is one in doing which we should be repaying some one something promised. In other words, we recognize that we ought to do that act in virtue of its being the repayment of something promised and not in virtue of its being anything else which it would be. We thereby *imply* the *principle* that we, and indeed anyone, ought to repay what we have, or he has, promised to repay.

Our recognition of the particular obligation implies our acceptance of the principle, in the sense that if on reflection we refused to accept the principle we should have to allow that our recognition of the particular obligation was an illusion. Moral obligations, though particular, involve principles or they are illusions. (A particular obligation, however, must not be regarded as *deduced* from a principle, in the sense that we first apprehend the principle and then infer the particular obligation from it. For the discovery of moral principles is only attained by reflecting on the particular obligations which we recognize. Hence it is a mistake to suppose that we discover what we ought to do in particular circumstances by *applying* the general rules. (Cf. our procedure in geometry.))

Kant's insight into this fact carried him to the length of maintaining that there are no circumstances in which we ought not to tell the truth, keep our promises, etc.

This view is usually met by the contention that no moral rule is universally applicable, since situations can always be imagined in which we think we ought to act against, rather than on, the rule. But this view, if pressed, becomes the view that there are *no* moral rules, and then obligations become thought of as chaotic, and, in the end illusory. And, though Kant went too far (as can be seen from the fact that if he were right, there could only be *one* moral rule, since if there were two or more, circumstances can always be imagined in which only one could be acted on), his view is only the expression in too extreme a form of the true conviction that any moral rule is universally binding. The difficulty, of course, is to reconcile the truth of this conviction with the admitted fact that circumstances can always be imagined in which we ought to act against any given moral rule. But this reconciliation is possible. For the circumstances imagined are always those in which there are conflicting obligations, and the conflict of an obligation of one kind with that of another kind implies not that in that case one of them is *unreal* but that in that case it is *over-ridden* by the other, as the less by the greater. There is always an obligation to tell the truth in a law court, even though under certain circumstances there may be a greater obligation to say in court something untrue which will prevent a gross miscarriage of justice. And it is a sign of the fact that, whenever we feel a conflict of duties, neither is rendered illusory by the other. In such cases, whatever we decide to do, we feel uncomfortable.

Freedom of the Will

In the *Metaphysic of Morals* Kant's main object is apparently to bring us to recognize that we really ought to act in the ways usually called moral, and he apparently considers that this recognition is attained through the consciousness of freedom. (In the *Critique of Practical Reason* he thinks of the relation in the reverse way, i.e. he thinks that the thought of the moral law leads us to the consciousness of freedom (as the presupposition of obligation).

The *Critique of Pure Reason* (Dialectic, Book 2, chapter 9, section 3) takes the problem of freedom as far as the speculative reason can take it. The outline of the argument is as follows:

'Only two kinds of causality are thinkable, that of nature and that of freedom. The former depends on temporal conditions; in it one state of affairs (the cause) originates another (the effect) as its necessary consequent, but only because it has itself been originated by a preceding state (e.g. hot water's standing in a cold glass causes the glass to become cracked, but only because it is itself the outcome of the hot water's previously resting in an inverted can above the glass). The latter is not dependent on temporal conditions; in it something originates a state of affairs *spontaneously*, i.e. without its origination depending on a preceding state of affairs. Now the phenomenal world contains instances only of the former causality, for the states of objects in nature are throughout determined by preceding states in a necessary succession. Still reason leads us to form the idea of a free (or spontaneous) causality, for the search for causes in nature leads only to causes which, as themselves caused, have to be in turn accounted for and the endeavour to account for them leads to an infinite regress. Hence, to render the course of nature intelligible to our reason, we are led to think of a cause which begins to act of itself. This, however, *ex hypothesi* cannot be found in nature.'

'On the other hand man's freedom or freedom of the will, *if* it exists, implies a causality of the second kind. For it is what we imply when we blame a past action, saying that something else *ought* to have been done, though it was not done. Here we imply that the agent, though led by his desires to act wrongly, need not have been so led; i.e. that the agent was free, in the sense of able to originate something independently of, or free from, the coercion of his desires, which, as such, form part of the temporal order of nature.'

'To vindicate the existence of this freedom, we must, as a *sine qua non*, show it to be compatible with the universality of the first kind of causality in nature, for the necessity of the succession of events in nature is absolute. This can be done. The key lies in the fact that man is a member of two worlds. As a being with faculties of perception, imagination, and desire, he belongs to the world of sense, or nature, of the phenomenal world; but, as possessed of reason, which cannot be object of the external or the internal sense, he belongs to the intelligible world, or world of things in themselves, which is the object not of perception but of thought. Now grant that man's reason is causally related to phenomena, i.e. that through his reason a man can originate changes in nature by presenting to himself, and acting on the thought of, the moral law (which, unlike the objects of a desire is non-sensuous). Then, though a man thus originates a phenomenal effect which is the first member of a necessary series of causes and effects, his action is not itself determined by a preceding member of the series of events in nature. For the thought of the moral law which determines his action being the thought of something non-sensuous is not, like a desire, an event in the sensible world and so is not the result of previous events. (N.B. This does not follow.) It is a condition of a series of events itself empirically unconditioned. Reason, then, in action acts spontaneously and not in virtue of something itself due to prior events. *On the other hand* man, as a member of the sensible world, has an empirical character, manifested in his desires; and from this standpoint, his actions are not spontaneous but the outcome of his desires and so part of the temporal nexus of the phenomenal world. So much so that "if we could investigate all the phenomena of human volition to their lowest foundation in the mind, there would be no action which we could not anticipate with certainty and recognize to be absolutely necessary from its preceding conditions. So far as relates to this empirical character there can be no freedom." These positions are not inconsistent, since they imply different standpoints from which a man's actions are regarded. Hence, *on the supposition* that man can originate actions through his reason, freedom can be reconciled with the necessity of nature. The speculative reason cannot *justify* this supposition but it can clear the way for the practical reason, i.e. reason in its capacity for action, by showing that freedom is not on speculative grounds *impossible*. To show that man's reason can originate action, the practical reason has to be brought in.'

This account needs close consideration. Bear in mind (1) that Kant's object is to meet the difficulty that if all actions are necessary, moral obligation is illusory, for to say 'X ought to have done so and so' is to imply that he really could have done it, though he did not; (2) that his removal of the apparent inconsistency between necessity and freedom is to rest on (*a*) the distinction between free and natural causation, (*b*) a certain distinction of standpoints from which any action can be regarded.

The key to understanding Kant's doctrine (and perhaps the problem of freedom) seems to lie in seeing that Kant mis-draws the distinction between the causality of freedom and that of nature, in consequence of substituting a false for a true doctrine, viz. that between things in themselves and phenomena for that between minds and bodies (or the mental and the physical).

It is a presupposition of such of our actions as directly relate to the physical world that in them we, who are minds, *originate* a change of state of some body or bodies. Thus, if we thought that when, as we say, we move our limbs, the motion of our limbs was really due to the action of some other body, we should cease to say that we *acted* or that we *moved* our limbs. With such action we contrast physical action, such as the production of motion in one billiard ball by another which hits it.

If asked to distinguish the two kinds of causation or origination, we should probably reply (1) that *our* action is conscious or deliberate, involving, though not being the same as, an act of will or decision; (2) that, while one *body* does not act on another of itself, but is *made* to act on the other by the prior action of a third body on it, e.g. a billiard cue, *we* act of *ourselves* or *spontaneously*, and are not forced or constrained to act by anything else. For, though in acting we may be influenced by desire or by the sense of obligation, this influence is not a *compulsion* exerted on us by some *other* thing.

We thereby imply a distinction between two kinds of origination or causation, the one intelligent and the other physical. And we might call the former *free* causation, to indicate that in it the agent is not *forced*, the freedom being the negative side of voluntariness; and we might call the latter *natural* causation, as being the causation belonging to a thing in *nature*. And if we describe *ourselves* as free or as free agents, we should mean that we are able to originate *voluntarily*, i.e. to act, an action which was not free, in the sense of *constrained*, being a contradiction in terms.

Now the very existence of one of these kinds of causation, viz. free causation—if it exists—raises a problem. For it implies that physical events are not always due to physical causes, and therefore that nature is not 'uniform' in the sense in which the term is usually understood. In other words, freedom and physical necessity cannot be reconciled. Kant seems to have this fact often before him in an unconscious way.

The reality, however, of 'free' or intelligent action—so defined—does *not* involve a hiatus in what—for lack of a better phrase—may be called *mental necessity*. Doubtless an act of human origination of a state of something physical presupposes a decision to act on the part of the agent; but the reality of the origination does not imply either that the decision is, or that it is not, necessary in consequence of the agent's state of desire. In other words, the reality of human action does not imply freedom of the *will*, in the proper sense of the term, viz. that of a power of choosing or deciding to act independently of the agent's condition of desire. On the other hand, even the determinist has to face the problem which is still presented by the hiatus in physical necessity involved by the existence of human action, even if the decision of which it is the outcome be itself thought to be necessary.

If we now look for the presupposition of moral obligation, we see, I think, that we get a problem and a solution of it to some extent on Kant's lines. To say that I ought to repay a benefit to X is to presuppose and to presuppose simply that I *can* do it, i.e. that the physical change which is asserted that I *ought* to originate *can* be originated by me, i.e. that I have the power to produce it. It would be absurd to say that I ought to jump a ditch 25 feet wide to fetch a doctor for a friend, simply because I could not do it. An obligation, however, is independent of the agent's character. I ought equally to repay a benefit, whether I am selfish and self-centred or not. Nothing, therefore, is presupposed by the obligation as to whether I have it in me to *choose* to do the act in question, i.e. as to whether or not my selfishness makes it impossible to do the act.

Hence, supposing that I do not repay the benefit, then even if it be allowed that, my character being what it is, a decision to repay the benefit, and therefore, repayment, was impossible, it will still be true that I ought to have repaid the benefit.

If this be right then:

(1) Obligation presupposes freedom of agent in the sense already explained, of the ability of the subject of the obligation to originate freely or voluntarily.

(2) Obligation does not presuppose freedom of *will*, i.e. ability to choose independently of the agent's character manifested in his desires and in his sense of obligation.

(3) It becomes possible to appeal to a difference of standpoint to remove the apparent inconsistency between freedom and necessity. It can be urged that it can be said truly of a man who has not done what he ought *both* that he could have done it *and* that he could not. For in asserting that he *could* have done it, it may be said, we are thinking only of the presupposition of the obligation, viz. that he had the power to act thus, and are abstracting from whatever may condition the exercise of this power in respect of the decision involved; whereas in asserting that he *could not* have done the action, we are taking a wider standpoint and, in considering the possibility of the action, are also taking into account his character, as affecting his decision to act, and therefore, his action.

(4) The real problem raised by obligation is common to the libertarian and the determinist alike, viz. that of showing that in spite of the apparent dependence

of all physical changes on physical causes, we really can *act* i.e. produce changes in the physical world involved.

We should now return to Kant's view and see how the distinction between free and natural causation works out there.

(1) For the distinction between minds and bodies—two different realities—Kant substitutes the distinction between two ways of considering any reality (*a*) as it is in itself, (*b*) as it appears to us. (This comes from his general theory of knowledge.) Both minds and realities independent of the mind have an existence in themselves; so considered, they are described as members of the world of things in themselves or the intelligible world. Both also appear to us in a different way to that in which they exist in themselves; and, so considered, they are described as members of the phenomenal or natural or physical world.

(2) Kant, in dealing with freedom, considers the application of this distinction to minds only. What characterizes us as we really are and so makes us members of the intelligible world is our rationality. The activity of reason and, in particular, the thought of the moral law manifest our real nature. On the other hand, desires, not being rational, belong to us only as we appear to ourselves, i.e. to ourselves as members of the world of phenomena or appearances; they are foreign to us, i.e. alien to our real nature.

(3) Kant substitutes for action 'willing' or 'choosing', conceiving of willing as if it were itself the origination in which action consists. Hence, an obligation, instead of being an obligation to *do*, becomes an obligation to *choose*.

Consequently the distinction between free and natural causation is no longer that between intelligent agency, free in the sense that it is not due to the constraint upon the agent exercised by another thing, and physical agency, in which one body is constrained to act on another by a third. It is, instead, the distinction between (*a*) a volition (which = an origination), considered as a volition of ourselves as members of the intelligible world, and, therefore, as brought about *not* by the influence of something other than ourselves, viz. a desire, *but* by the thought of the moral law and (*b*) the same volition, considered as a volition of ourselves as members of the phenomenal world and, therefore, as brought about by the influence of a desire, which, as such, is part of the necessary order of the world.

And the terms free and natural are used to indicate that a volition considered in the former way, is free from the constraint of desire and is spontaneous as a manifestation of the agent's own nature, and that a volition, considered in the latter way, is due to the constraint of desire, in the way in which the action of everything in the world of *nature* is due to constraint upon it of something else.

Consequently the problem is different. Instead of its being to sustain the view that we do originate states of things in nature, in face of the apparent origination of all physical states by physical causes, it is to sustain the view that our acts of will are independent of desire, in face of the fact that as events in the phenomenal world they must be due to the constraint of desire.

In the *Critique of Pure Reason* Kant carries the solution of this problem to the point of contending that this view is at least *not inconsistent with* this fact. His contention is that since the agent who wills can be considered not only as a member of the phenomenal world but also as a member of the intelligible world, it is not inconsistent to hold that his volitions both are and are not determined by desire; for the two assertions are made from different standpoints and so, instead of clashing, miss one another. Hence, he contends, there is at least no contradiction involved in maintaining that a man *ought* to have done (i.e. willed) so and so, though in fact he *could* not have done so; for given different standpoints it is possible to say both that he could have done it and that he could not have done it.

The view on the face of it presents two difficulties:

(1) How can any distinction of standpoints reconcile the statements that one and the same volition was and that it was not determined, i.e. caused, by a desire? It would seem that at best it could only be contended that of two *different* volitions the one was and the other was not caused by desire.

(2) (More important.) In calling a volition free Kant means in the first instance that it is not due to desire. Now this freedom has *alternative* implications, viz. (*a*) that the volition is not due to anything at all; (*b*) that the volition, though not due to desire, is due to something, this something having to be the thought of the moral law (= the sense of obligation). Correspondingly, 'freedom of the *will*' (i.e. of the *faculty* of volition) will mean either the capacity of choosing, independently of desire *and* of the sense of obligation, i.e. independently of a motive or something which determines or leads us to choose; or the capacity of being determined to choose by the thought of the moral law. And prima facie it is freedom in the first sense which is implied by obligation, *if* the formula of obligation is 'you ought to have *chosen* X' (not *done* X). For this formula carries with it not only the implication which Kant sees but another which he does not. It implies not only that 'you *might* have chosen X, though you did not, and, therefore, somehow your actual choice was not *determined* by your desire' but also that 'as you did not choose X, your choice was not *determined* by the thought of the moral law, for you had this thought and yet you did not act accordingly'. In other words, it implies that a man's choice might have been otherwise, and that this is because his choice was not determined *at all*, i.e. neither by desire nor by the thought of the moral law. That is, it implies freedom of will in the ordinary sense of the ability to choose independently of whatever may move or stir us to choose, an ability implying the real possibility of choosing otherwise than we do.

Now Kant never speaks of freedom in this sense. His free volition is a volition determined by, i.e. due to, the thought of the moral law. This implies that the thought of the moral law, like a desire, leads us to act. And his free will is the capacity in virtue of which this thought leads us to will. (His *spontaneity* of free causation is not an uncaused causation but a causation uncaused by anything outside ourselves.) This implies that if, as is the case, we have the thought of the moral law, we shall act accordingly.

Hence (1) Kant appears to prove too much. For in contending that from one standpoint our choice is not due to desire, he implies that from this standpoint it is due to the thought of the moral law. He implies, therefore, that with respect to all acts due to desire in which the agent does not do what he ought, it is possible to say from another standpoint that the agent's act is due to the thought of the moral law and therefore is what it ought to have been: hence he implies that *all* acts are in one aspect moral. Conversely, he implies that all acts in which the agent does what he ought have a non-moral side on which they are due to desire, and therefore that *all* acts are in one aspect non-moral.

(2) His vindication of moral judgements seems to vanish. For according to him, the implication of 'you ought to have chosen *X*' is that 'though you did not, you could have chosen *X*', and this implication is not vindicated by the contention that 'though from one standpoint you did not choose *X*, from another you actually did'.

The moral is (1) that *if* obligation relates to choice, the freedom implied is freedom in the ordinary sense, viz. freedom to choose, independently both of desire and of the sense of obligation, and (2) that the freedom of will for which Kant is contending is inconsistent with this freedom and therefore, on this hypothesis, with the validity of obligation.

Now there are plainly difficulties in accepting freedom of the will in the ordinary sense. The most obvious are (1) that we normally think that a choice must be motivated, i.e. that we must be moved to choose, either by a desire or by a sense of obligation, and that otherwise our choice would be a matter of chance, and (2) that, if the will be free in this sense, our choice will be independent of our character and responsibility for our actions will be excluded. (Responsibility has, of course, also been held to *require* freedom in this sense.)

But (1) it may be urged that what raises the demand for freedom in this sense is the view that an obligation is an obligation not to *do* but to *choose*, and that this view is untenable. For (*a*) it is inconsistent with the ordinary linguistic expression of our obligations; e.g. we ought to *tell* the truth, to *pay* our debts, etc. (*b*) If the sense of obligation is to affect our decision, the term 'ought' must relate to one of the things between which in making up our minds we think we have to choose, and between which we eventually choose. These will be *actions* and not *choices*; otherwise we shall be choosing to choose. We choose to do; we do not choose to choose. Hence an obligation is an obligation not to *choose* but to *do*.

(2) We have seen reason for thinking that what obligation presupposes is not freedom of will in the ordinary sense but freedom of the agent in the sense of ability to originate 'freely' or 'voluntarily', i.e. to act.

(3) It may be said that if obligation is obligation to do, Kant's problem, though not the right problem, is nearly the right problem,. For his aim is to square the reality of obligation with a natural necessity apparently inconsistent with it, and his mistake is simply that he takes this necessity to be the necessitation of all choice by desire instead of taking it as the necessitation of all physical changes by all physical causes; this being due (1) to his treating 'willing' as if it were identical with 'acting' (2) to his substituting for the distinction between minds and bodies that between things considered in themselves and things considered as phenomena.

Kant's Treatment of Freedom in the *Metaphysic of Morals*

Kant begins by defining freedom of will, in conformity with his account of it in the *Critique of Pure Reason*. (Abbott, pp. 65–6 top. N.B. in line 3, p. 65, as the context shows 'can be' should have been 'is'.)

His account amounts to this. 'The will being a capacity of a rational being by which it originates in virtue of its rationality, its freedom is in the first instance something *negative*, consisting in the fact that its exercise is not itself originated or caused by the influence on the agent of something foreign to the agent (viz. a desire). But all causes act according to a law. Hence a free will is not a will which acts anyhow. Its activity must itself be caused in a definite way. Hence the negative side of its freedom involves a positive, viz. that its activity is determined by something belonging to the agent's own nature. This must be the thought of the moral law. Hence a free will has a *positive* character, consisting in the fact that its origination is an origination due to the thought of the moral law. A free will, then, and a moral will, in the sense of a will which always acts morally, are one and the same.'

(Notice an important equivocation. 'The conception of causality involves that of laws, according to which, by something which we call cause, something else which we call effect, is produced' uses 'a law' in the *scientific* sense of a general mode of behaviour of a thing. 'Freedom is a property of the will to be a law to itself' uses 'a law' in the *legal* sense of a command of a ruler. The use of the term law in a scientific context involves an unfortunate antithesis, viz. that while a 'legal' law is not always obeyed, a scientific law is always obeyed. The antithesis is improper (1) because obedience is out of place in science and (2) because 'a legal law is not always obeyed' means 'to the *execution of a command* there are exceptions', and 'a scientific law is always obeyed' means 'to a *certain mode of activity* of a thing there are no exceptions'.

Kant's transition from the statement that a free will is subject to law in the scientific sense to the statement that it is subject to law in the legal sense is important for this reason. His main object is to show that man is subject to moral laws in the sense that he *ought* to obey certain quasi-commands. To prove this he thinks it is necessary to prove that man's will is free. Now if he so defines a free will as to make it a will which is always determined to act by the thought of the moral law and which therefore always acts morally then in showing that man's will is free, he is showing that man is subject to moral laws only in the scientific sense of a moral law as a way in which man always *actually* behaves. Kant is, I think, in ch. 3, constantly affected by this equivocation; i.e. in proving that man is subject to moral laws, while he *thinks* that man *ought* to obey them (in a legal sense) he is *actually* proving that man always does obey them (in a scientific sense).

Kant's Proof of Freedom

The proof is described as practically or from a practical point of view, though not theoretically, conclusive. The phrase looks like, and strictly speaking is, a contradiction in terms. A proof is either theoretically conclusive or not conclusive at all, 'theoretically' adding nothing to 'conclusive'. Plainly Kant's idea is to show that all action presupposes the idea of freedom, i.e. the belief that we are free, and thence to conclude that this belief is true. This really implies not that the argument is *practical* rather than *theoretical* but that it is *hypothetical*, i.e. that it is designed to show that the belief in freedom must be true, *if* our belief that we can act, involved in all action, is not an illusion. Coupled with this argument we have Kant's conviction that the belief that we can act is not an illusion—a conviction which he makes no attempt to justify. This attempt he should have made, since from his own point of view it is the absence of this which makes the proof of freedom *theoretically* inconclusive.

Further if this analysis of '*a practical* proof of freedom' be right, 'a theoretically conclusive proof' must be one not based on the *hypothesis* that the belief that we can act, involved in action, is not illusory.

Now what is naturally meant by 'We cannot act except under the idea of freedom'? Simply, I think, that in making up our minds to act we must think of the things between which we are trying to decide as *possible actions*, i.e. as things which we can do. In other words, it means that action implies belief in our freedom, in the sense of our ability to originate, of course voluntarily or freely, certain physical changes. And the significance of the implication would be that it runs counter to the apparent independence of physical nature from outside interference. The argument would be that whether we can or cannot show on its own merits that physical necessity is not thoroughgoing, we at least know that unless our belief that we can act, and therefore our belief in moral obligations, are illusions, this necessity cannot be thoroughgoing. And the *practical* proof of freedom would be this proof of freedom in the sense just stated, based on the hypothesis underlying all *action* (hence the term *practical*), and, therefore, very difficult to abandon, that we can act.

But examination of the passage shows (1) that this is not the freedom which Kant is trying to establish, and (2) that, paradoxically enough, his actual argument is not based on the *idea* of freedom involved in action. On the contrary, his argument is theoretical, being based simply on analysis on the nature of a rational agent. It is that 'in a rational being we conceive a reason that is practical, i.e. has causality in reference to its objects'. In other words, a rational agent is, as such, an agent who in willing is determined to originate (or will) not from outside but from inside, viz. by the thought of the moral law; hence freedom of will being the capacity to originate in this way, a rational agent is, from the nature of the case, free. And the freedom so established is not the ability to originate but the ability to originate in virtue of the thought of the moral law; i.e. what is proved is that rational agents, and we, as rational, are determined to will by the thought of the moral law, and therefore always act morally (for otherwise the acts would not be rational and therefore the agent would not really be acting).

If this be right, Kant just misses making the right point. Though he has the important notion that action is only possible under the idea of freedom, he makes no use of it, and partly in consequence, does not establish the freedom which we want.

In connection with this an important consideration should be noticed. He repeatedly raises the question 'How is freedom possible?' His reply is that it is impossible to *understand* how freedom is possible but nevertheless we can defend the *fact* of freedom. Now it is, I think, easy to see that Kant is putting the difficulty in the wrong place and why he is led to do so. To be free, according to Kant, is to be determined in action by the thought of the moral law. Hence the question 'How is freedom possible?' means 'How can the thought of the moral law move us to act?' And this question for Kant resolves itself into the question 'How can a mere *thought*, which, as such, is not a desire, move us to act?' This to Kant is the central difficulty involved in freedom. The difficulty, however, seems to arise from a mis-statement of the problem. There is no such thing as the *mere thought* of the moral law; what exists is the *sense* of obligation. In other words, our recognition that an act of a certain kind ought to be done involves of its very nature *emotion*. (Hence the phrase *sense* of obligation.) It is not that the recognition is an act of intelligence and the emotion a non-rational feeling joined to it. The emotion is through and through rational, and the recognition and the emotion, though distinguishable, are inseparable. (Cf. the appreciation, or sense, of beauty.) And it is no more difficult to understand how the sense of obligation can move us to act than how a desire can do so; for the one *stirs* as much as the other.

But if this be right, what is the real problem expressed by the question 'How is freedom possible?' It is, I think, the problem already often referred to, viz. 'How is it possible for a mind to originate something in the world of nature?' The difficulty is (1), as before, that of reconciling such origination with the apparent self-completeness of the physical system, (2) that of understanding such origination in itself. With respect to (2) one remark may be made. It is commonly assumed that the difficulty is confined to *our* origination and that there is no difficulty in understanding how a physical change in a body is produced by *another body*. Yet it is quite certain that at present we no more understand the latter than the former.

Kant's Final Problem

Kant's object in discussing freedom is to show through the reality of freedom that moral rules are really binding upon us. What is his argument?

Kant's main problem is expressed in chapters 2 and 3 in the form 'How are categorical imperatives possible?' The meaning of the question can be seen from his treatment of the parallel question 'How are hypothetical imperatives possible?' This latter question, he says, presents no difficulty; a hypothetical imperative prescribes an action as a means to some possible object of desire, and he who wills the end necessarily wills the means. Now Kant certainly thinks—though wrongly—that a hypothetical imperative expresses an obligation, e.g. you *ought* to get up early, (if you want health). Hence, when he says that a hypothetical imperative presents no difficulty, what he means is that, e.g., given that you want health, you will necessarily feel that you ought to get up early, this being the means to health. And, approaching categorical imperatives from *this* standpoint, he naturally finds difficulty in them. 'How', he asks himself, 'can we feel we ought, e.g. to pay our debts when *ex hypothesi* there must be no desire of any result of paying them to originate the sense that we ought to pay them?'

How does Kant meet the difficulty? By the help of two connected distinctions (a) between a holy or rational and a human or imperfectly rational will, and (b) between the intelligible and the phenomenal world. The main difficulty in stating his argument lies in the impossibility of thinking of Kant's holy will as a will from which the sense of obligation is absent. To make sense of Kant's holy will, we must think of it as a will which feels that it ought to act in the ways we call moral and which always acts from that feeling. Given this, we can distinguish a holy and a human will as a will which recognizes that it ought to do certain things and always does them and a will which recognizes that it ought to do certain things but which, owing to the presence of desires, sometimes does and sometimes does not do them.

Bearing this distinction in mind, consider the critical passage. 'What makes categorical imperatives possible is that the idea of freedom makes me a member of an intelligible world, in consequence of which if I were nothing else, all my actions *would* always conform to the autonomy of the will; but as I at the same time perceive myself as a member of the world of sense, they ought so to conform.'

The sense requires correction of 'idea of freedom' into 'freedom'. Given this, the first part means, 'My being free makes me one of a world of beings whose actions are determined by the thought of the moral law, in consequence of which, if I were nothing else, my actions would always be moral'. How then should Kant have gone on? Surely thus: 'But as, in virtue of my desires, I am (*not* 'perceive myself as') *also* a member of the world of sense, my actions are not only always moral but also always non-moral in the sense of determined by desire'. This conclusion is doubly removed from Kant's actual conclusion. (1) If we disregard the fact that obligation has somehow to be brought in, we see that the conclusion wanted is, at least, not that my actions are always moral *and* non-moral but that they sometimes are and sometimes are not moral. This is needed to conform (*a*) to the facts, (*b*) to Kant's conviction that 'I ought to do so and so' implies that I may not do it. But the premiss needed for this is not that I am a member of both worlds but that I am in part a member of one world and in part a member of the other.

(2) Kant's actual conclusion that my actions *ought* to be those which are moral is simply a non-sequitur. It follows in no way whatever from his premisses. This seems to be one of the cases where an apparently carefully thought out argument breaks down altogether and cannot even be stated. In such cases nothing can be done but to point out where the argument breaks down, and then leave it.

In conclusion it may be pointed out that if—as is the case—the holy will must be thought of as feeling a sense of obligation, the argument must be a petitio principii. If I am to be convinced that I ought to act in certain ways by the argument, I must first apprehend its premisses. I must therefore apprehend that I am a member of both worlds. But if so, I must be a member of both worlds and therefore, as a member of the intelligible world, I must already have the sense of obligation. This is only one of many signs that the sense of obligation is immediate and underivative.

Kant's Proof of Immortality and the Existence of God
(Critique of Practical Reason, Book 2, Chapter 2, §§ 4, 5)

The argument is as follows. 'The aim of a being subject to the moral law is the realisation of the summum bonum, viz. the union of virtue—the condition deserving happiness—and happiness.' (This is inconsistent with the *Metaphysic of Morals*.) Any presupposition of the moral law must be true; otherwise the moral law would be an illusion. And this fact enables us to establish certain things beyond the reach of speculative reason on the basis of practical reason.

In particular (1) Perfect virtue, i.e. perfect holiness of will, is impossible to a rational being who, as part of the sensible world, has desires. But indefinite progress towards that ideal is possible to such a being, and is therefore the aim of his moral will. Hence there must be immortality, as the presupposition of the possibility of its realization.

(2) In this world virtue does not necessarily lead to happiness. For the attainment of happiness rests not on moral but physical laws, and there is nothing to justify the connexion between the morality and the happiness of a being who lives in a world of which the laws are physical and not moral. It rains equally on the just and on the unjust. But our moral aim, being virtue together with the happiness which it deserves, presupposes a connexion between virtue and happiness. This connexion presupposes a cause of all nature which will bring about the connexion. This cause must be an intelligent being having a causality of will corresponding to moral character, i.e. God. Therefore God exists.

5. A Conflict of Duties

If certain moral judgements, or acts of moral thought, have been rightly analysed, and if they may be regarded as typical, we can give the following general account of our moral thought. In order to think some action right, we must believe or imagine ourselves in certain given circumstances—for instance, while walking we meet a damaged young cyclist, in plus-fours, lying in a ditch. If we do this, we think that certain of the given circumstances render us bound to do a certain action, for instance, the cyclist's being damaged and helpless as distinct from being young and in plus-fours, renders us bound to help him.

In thus judging we imply a general condition, which we have only to reflect on to formulate. For though the actions and the circumstances which we think render the action a duty, are particular, for instance, meeting a given helpless cyclist, it is only because we think of the circumstances and the action as a particular kind that we think the particular circumstances render the particular action a duty. The precise formulation of the general conviction which we imply may be difficult, but in the present context is not important. But it is of importance in the present context to recognize that certain of our particular judgements imply different general convictions, not reducible to one another, and that these different general convictions find expression in current moral rules or lists of commands. This shows that there is no single characteristic which leads us to think right those acts which we do think right.

But if this account of our moral thinking is true, we are confronted with an obvious difficulty if we wish to maintain that what we have called our moral thinking is knowing, or at least is true. Whatever two general convictions we consider, we shall have to allow that circumstances may be such that we cannot act on both of the two particular judgements which respectively imply them. Yet no act, it would seem, can be a duty unless we can do it. Hence it would seem that at least one of the two particular judgements and the general conviction which it implies, is false, and as we can have no means of discovering which pair is true, we have no reason for thinking either of the pair true. Hence it would seem we have no reason for thinking any particular judgement or any general judgement or conviction true. The difficulty is general and does not apply specially to any particular set of moral rules. Even an ideal list of

[From lecture notes of Prichard's lectures in 1928 by an unknown student. MSSCCC529, The Archives, Corpus Christi College, Bodleian Library, University of Oxford.]

commandments would be exposed to the difficulty, for so long as more than one general conviction is implied by our moral judgement, then conflicting particular judgements will be possible. And in particular, the difficulty cannot be got round by maintaining that the general convictions which are really implied in our particular judgements are much more concrete than those expressed by the moral precepts usually offered, and that the difficulty only arises from a too general formulation of the convictions. For, however much for instance we may hedge round with conditions, what we call the duty to tell the truth, such as that the person addressed must be sane and well disposed to us, we still imply that the rule offered expresses a general conviction that, under such and such circumstances we are bound to tell the truth, with the implication that it doesn't in the least matter what in a particular case the other circumstances are.

At best, therefore, we are left with two very concrete but nevertheless general rules, and a conflict of particular judgements will therefore always be possible. Further it seems doubtful whether, if there were only one general conviction implied in our moral judgements it could be true, since its truth would require the possibility of doing both of two acts only one or the other of which is in fact possible. It may be impossible for me to speak the truth both to A and B or to keep a promise to one or the other. In fact the difficulty looks solvable only if we could, as we can't, make out that 'ought to be done' means proper to be done in respect of being conducive to our purpose. For if we could do this, we could lay down the single principle that we ought to do whatever it is will conduce to our purpose, and this would give rise to no conflict.

There being this obstacle to our maintaining that our particular moral judgements are true, is it possible to remove it? It may occur to us at first that we ought simply to cut the Gordian knot by maintaining that after all a conflict of duties is possible and that where it exists the truth is that we ought to do that act which is more of a duty than the other. This suggestion, which of course, implies that being under an obligation admits of differences of degree, has obviously something to be said for it. For:-

(i) We often speak quite naturally of a man having more obligations than he can fulfill, especially when he has brought them upon himself say by making rash promises.

(ii) We might say that a man confronted by a so-called conflict of duties realizes, for instance, that he has either to disobey the state or do an injustice, and actually thinks that whatever he does he will be doing a wrong to someone, and that afterwards he will consequently feel regret whatever he does on the ground that he will have done wrong.

(iii) It does not seem absurd to talk of degrees of obligation and wrongness, for instance to say that it is more of a duty to push someone out of the way of a motor than to pick up his hat, and more wrong to kill a man than to hurt his feelings.

Yet the view will not really stand scrutiny. To maintain that we ought to do that of two actions which we ought to do more is to be involved in a contradiction, because it is to imply both that while the one act is a duty the other is not, and that the latter is a duty though to a less degree than the former. Putting this otherwise, if we think that of two acts there is a greater obligation to do one of them, we cannot go on to think that we ought to do that action without implying that there is no obligation to do the other in any degree whatever. Consequently we gain nothing by maintaining the existence of degrees of obligation. The plain fact is that in the end we get driven to conclude that nothing will help us out of the difficulty short of allowing that, speaking strictly, a conflict of moral duties must be impossible, that there are no kinds of act which are right or wrong, and that a so-called statement of moral principle, to be really defensible, must be understood as stating, not that some kind of action is a duty, but that it is something else. If we then ask ourselves what this something else is, we seem driven to say that, though there is not a phrase really appropriate for it, it is best described as there being a claim on us to do the action, and to say for instance that that to which our having promised to do something gives rise is, strictly speaking, not a duty but a claim on us to carry it out. We can then go on to add that what is called a conflict of duties is really a conflict of claims on us to act in different ways, arising out of various circumstances of the whole situation in which we are placed. Further we find no difficulty whatever in allowing that what we call claims on us may differ in degree, or that where there are two claims on us so differing, the act which there is the greatest claim on us to do is duty. Hence, provided we allow, as we seem driven to do, that what are usually thought of as and are called 'duties', are really claims on us to do certain actions, then we are driven to the following general conclusion. 'In any situation we are morally bound to do that act of those which various different circumstances severally give rise to a claim on us to do, the claim on us to do which is the greatest.'

In order to ascertain that some action is a duty, the reason why we have to ascertain all the circumstances is that certain circumstances by themselves can only give rise to a claim on us to do the action, and therefore we have to ascertain whether the rest of the circumstances do not include others which give rise to a greater claim. At the same time, the apprehension that of two claims, a given one is the greater, can be attained only, if at all, immediately, i.e., by a direct comparison of them and not by a process of calculating the amount of something which will be produced by the two actions which there is a claim on us to do, or the amounts of anything else. But if we allow this conclusion, we have to allow that unless our ordinary moral judgements or convictions have been incorrectly described, they are all mistaken in one fundamental respect, and so need correction. For if any given set of circumstances can by themselves give rise only to a claim and not a duty, then I was mistaken in thinking for instance, that the cyclist's being in an undeserved difficulty rendered it a duty to help him. We are therefore led to consider whether after all, in imagining ourselves meeting the cyclist, we did in fact do what we were represented as doing, namely, think that his distress rendered us bound to help, or whether we only thought that his distress gave rise to a claim on us, and then afterwards came to think it a duty to help by considering whether there were other claims at least as great, and coming to think that there were not. And if we face this issue we seem to have to allow that the original account was right and that in fact we came afterwards to correct our original judgement.

When it has also occurred to us in a similar way that some other set of circumstances may likewise give rise to a different duty, we are driven to think that what at first we thought of as giving rise to a duty, really can only have given rise to a claim, and that therefore in this respect, my first thought was mistaken.

But if we accept this conclusion, we find ourselves bound to decide between two alternative doctrines, each difficult to accept. It should however be noticed that there is an analogous difficulty to be found in any other attempt to formulate what renders an action a duty. The problem becomes obvious as soon as we recognize that we have in fact to act in ignorance of many things which, it would seem, if the conclusion is right, we must first know before we can know what is a duty. The formula expressing the conclusion is one which makes no reference to our state in respect of knowledge or ignorance. It is, that an act is rendered a duty by being that act, of all those which various different circumstances severally give rise to a claim on us to do, the claim on us to do which is the greatest. And if we try to apply this formula in some actual situation, it becomes obvious that we may be prevented by lack of knowledge of things of one of at least three kinds.

(i) The acts referred to are similar to those expressed in the Commandments, for instance, helping some man out of his difficulty, speaking truthfully, etc. But with the best of will, and using all the evidence available to us, we may only be able, in a given situation, to reach the opinion that some one, of all the possible actions of which we are capable will be an act of any given one of these kinds, e.g., helping our neighbour, etc.

(ii) Usually we don't know, and at best can only believe that certain of the actual circumstances *are* of the kind which give rise to a given claim, for instance that X has been a great benefactor to us that X is really in a great difficulty and not shamming, or that Z had understood that we had promised something.

(iii) We are often uncertain of the relative strength of two claims on us. For instance to do the work for which we are paid, or to help someone who is ill, or to obey the state and commit an injustice.

Once we recognize these limitations on what we can know, we begin to wonder whether we can adhere to the formula. For we shall have to allow that, if it be right, then usually, at least, we cannot possibly discover what we ought to do, and it seems a paradox to maintain that in a given situation there is some action which we are really bound to do, though it is not in our power to discover what it is. And in this way we come to wonder whether we should not so alter the formula, as to represent what we ought to do as discoverable, by representing what we ought to do as depending on what, after doing our best, we come to believe about certain things. And, if we work out the required alternatives, we find that the formula has then to be this:

> 'An act is rendered a duty by being that act of all those which, on the available evidence, we believe to be that most likely to produce certain results, and which, what we believe to be the special nature of various different circumstances severally give rise to a claim on us to do, the claim on us to do which we believe to be the greatest.'

If we amend the formula thus, we do succeed in maintaining that we can discover what we ought to do in any given circumstances, but we do this at the cost of having to allow that what is right or wrong depends, not on the circumstances, but on what we can come to believe about them, and so differs from man to man. And it should be noticed that the difference is apt to escape our notice when we consider what we ought to do in imagined circumstances. For in imagining ourselves in certain circumstances, we are imagining ourselves as at least knowing that certain of the circumstances are as imagined. Consider a simple instance. Suppose that a man believes that, with leisure, he could make useful scientific discoveries, but knows that to get the leisure, he would have to scamp educating his family, and that he believes that the claim on him to educate his family is the greater. And suppose we know that the claim on him to make scientific discoveries was the greater, especially as he was capable of doing so, then if we accept the original formula, we have to allow that what we ought to do was to investigate, and if we accept the second formula, we have to allow that his duty is to educate his family properly. But if we accept the first, we have to allow that it is his duty to investigate in spite of its being impossible for him to know that it is, and therefore, also in spite of the fact that if he does investigate, he necessarily does the duty accidentally, in the sense of doing it without knowing it to be his duty. If we accept the second alternative, we have to allow that though his duty, namely, to educate his family, is something he can discover, yet the fact of the educative duty depends not on the actual circumstances but simply on what he can come to think about them, so that another man's duty in similar circumstances might differ if his means of information differed.

Notice here that even in the second alternative, a man's duty is something objective in the sense that there really is an action which is his duty, and so the rightness of a right action does not depend on what the agent thinks right but its rightness only depends on what the agent thinks about certain other things. It might be suggested that there may be a third alternative, but this suggestion can be negated straight away, because plainly what is a man's duty must depend, or not, on what he can know.

We cannot for instance maintain that both alternatives are true on the grounds that there are two senses of the term 'duty', in one of which the term is applied solely with reference to the circumstances, and in the other of which, in applying it, we take account of the agent's lack of knowledge. There are not two senses of the term duty, and plainly, a given action is either a duty or it is not. Which then is the true alternative? Either is difficult to accept, the first because it seems in conflict with our conviction that an act can only be a duty if we can do it, and on the first alternative we can only do what is a duty accidentally, the second because it seems to make our duty in a way a subjective affair. When thus puzzled there is one reflection which seems decisive. When we are in circumstances like those stated, where we are at best uncertain of some of them, if we ask ourselves, do we or can we know what we ought to do? the answer which expresses what we really think, is that we neither do nor can. This seems decisive, because, in thinking this we are implying that there is some act which is really a duty in spite of our having no means of discovering which one it is, and also that its being a duty depends on the nature of the actual circumstances whether or not we have the opportunity of knowing it. And here we have to be on our guard. We are apt to say to ourselves that owing to our ignorance of the circumstances, we are obviously often unable to advance beyond believing some act to be a duty. Where this occurs what ought we to do? In other words, what is our duty in the special case where we can only believe some act to be a duty? Then we are tempted to answer that in that special case our duty is to do what we believe to be our duty. But if we say this we deceive ourselves, for the very question is by its terms unanswerable. By the terms of the question we are made to ask ourselves, what ought we to do in the circumstances in which, *ex hypothesi*, it is impossible to find out what we ought to do? And yet by the terms of the question we are implied to be able to answer it. The only answer possible is that the question is one which it is impossible to answer. To this it may be rightly added that where we are thus ignorant, our desire to do what is right cannot lead us to do anything but what we believe to be right and that as far as we are actuated by this desire, we do not afterwards blame ourselves for what we did on the ground that what we believed was not true.

I propose now to assume that for the reasons given, the original formula is right and that we have to accept it as true on the ground that it expresses the principle, the knowledge of which is implied in the actual process by which we come to know or even to believe that some action is a duty. The formula is of course an answer to the only question of the original five which has not been disposed of, i.e., What renders a right action right? In accepting the formula we are therefore implying that the question is legitimate, but we shall have to allow that as this question is first asked, it is asked under a mistake, namely, that of thinking of the various actions which there are claims on us to do as duties, and in consequence of the mistake, we are originally asking what is the common character of these actions which renders them duties, and if we correct this mistake we have to transform the question into the question, What is the common character which renders these actions actions which there is a claim on us to do? We have then got to allow that if our analysis of our ordinary moral convictions is right, this question also is fallacious, since there is no such common characteristic, and what we think gives rise to a claim is not always of the same kind, this being the fact which underlies the existence of a plurality of commandments wherever a statement of what we ought to do is formulated.

6. Duty and Ignorance of Fact

The question which I propose to consider is essentially dull and tiresome; it worries us little, if at all, in practical life; and it is apt to be ignored or, at least, only casually treated by those whose business is theory. Nevertheless, at any rate for theory, it is important.

As it first presents itself the question is: If a man has an obligation, i.e. a duty, to do some action, does the obligation depend on certain characteristics of the situation in which he is, or on certain characteristics of his thought about the situation?' The question is vague because of the vagueness of the term 'thought', but at the outset this does not matter. Consideration of it, however, will force us to consider another question, viz.: 'Can an obligation really be an obligation to do some *action*, and, if not, what should be substituted for the term "action"?' And, should a substitute prove necessary, the main question will have to be modified accordingly.

To appreciate the importance, and even the meaning, of the question, we have first to see how it arises.

We have all from time to time thought that we ought, and again that we ought not, to do certain actions. And, if we were asked to give a general account of these actions, we should be inclined to say that, though not all of one sort, yet they all fall under one or other of a limited number of kinds of action which are set out in current moral rules, i.e. current general statements each stating that a man ought or ought not to do an action of a certain kind. Further, at any rate until certain difficulties have occurred to us, we think these rules true. We think, for instance, that a man ought to speak the truth, to carry out the orders of his government, not to steal, and not to hurt the feelings of another. And this is not surprising, since these rules are simply the result of an attempt to formulate those various general characteristics of the particular acts we have thought duties, which have led us to think them duties.

Elucidation, however, is needed of the general character of the meaning of a moral rule, and therefore also of the thought which it is used to express.

It is, no doubt, not easy to say what we mean by 'an action' or by 'doing something'. Yet we have in the end to allow that we mean by it originating, causing, or bringing about the existence of something, viz. some new state of an existing thing or substance, or, more shortly, causing a change of state of

[Annual Philosophical Lecture, Henriette Hertz Trust, British Academy, 1932.]

some existing thing. This is shown by the meaning of our phrases for various particular actions. For by 'moving our hand' we mean causing a change of place of our hand; by 'posting a letter' we mean bringing about that a letter is in a pillar-box; and so on. We may be tempted to go farther, and say that we mean by 'an action' the *conscious* origination of something, i.e. the originating something knowing that we are doing so. But this will not do; for no one, for instance, thinks himself to be denying that he has hurt a man's feelings when he says that he did not know that he was hurting them and, indeed, thought he was not. Correspondingly, we mean by 'doing an action of a certain kind' bringing about something of a certain kind, viz. a state of a certain kind, of a thing of a certain kind. Consequently the meaning of a moral rule can be stated in the form: 'A man ought, or ought not, to bring about a thing of a certain kind.' Thus by 'A man ought to honour his parents' we mean: 'A man ought to bring about in his parents the knowledge that he holds them in honour.'

But this is not all. We ordinarily think that in doing certain actions we bring about the things which we do directly, while in doing certain others we do so indirectly, i.e. by directly bringing about other things which in turn cause them. Thus we think that in moving our head we bring about a change of place of our head directly, whereas in giving a friend the family news we bring about his receipt of the news indirectly, i.e. by bringing about directly certain other changes which in turn cause it. No doubt on reflection we may find it difficult to defend the thought that, e.g., in moving our head we directly cause our head to change its place; and we may be reduced to thinking that, in moving our head, what we bring about directly is some new state of certain cells of our brain of which we are wholly unaware in doing the action. But such a reflection does not conflict with our thought that we bring about certain things indirectly. Nor does it lead us to deny the distinction between bringing something about directly and bringing something about indirectly, since, so long as we think that we bring about certain things indirectly, we inevitably imply that there are certain things which we bring about directly, even if we do not know what they are. It is as impossible for all bringing about to be indirect as for all knowledge to be indirect. And, if we now turn to the phrase for the act of a certain kind referred to in some moral rule, we find that in every case it stands for bringing about something of a certain kind indirectly. We mean, for instance, by 'honouring a parent' causing a parent to find himself held in honour by causing something else to cause it; we mean by 'speaking the truth' causing another to know our thought by causing certain sounds which cause him to have this knowledge; and so on. We can therefore say generally that the meaning of a moral rule has the form: 'A man ought, or ought not, to bring about a thing of a certain kind indirectly.'

To bring about something indirectly is, however, to bring it about in a less strict sense than that of bringing it about directly. For, where we bring about something by causing something to cause it, the result is not wholly due to us.

And, where we bring about something X indirectly, what we bring about in the strict sense is the thing which causes X. Correspondingly, we use the term 'action' both in a strict sense in which it means bringing about something directly, and also in a looser sense in which it means bringing about something whether directly or indirectly. And where, e.g., some action of ours is referred to as giving some relation the family news, we must allow that our action in the strict sense is some such act as transferring certain ink to certain places on a piece of paper; and in support of this admission we might point out that, in the strict sense of 'action', our action must cease with the cessation of our activity. We have, therefore, to allow that if a moral rule is stated in terms of 'doing something' and of 'bringing about something' in the strict sense, its meaning will be of the form: 'A man ought to do such an act or acts, i.e. bring about such a thing or things, as will cause a thing of the kind A to assume a state of the kind X.'

Further, in stating some moral rule, we are plainly in two respects speaking elliptically. Thus, in asserting that a man ought to support his indigent parents, we clearly do not mean that a man ought at *any* time to support his indigent parents. We are thinking, and expect to be understood as asserting, that the duty exists only when two conditions are satisfied. The first is, of course, that the man has parents who are indigent and willing to receive the means of support; and the second is that he is able to support them. For we never think that an action can be a man's duty unless he is able to do it. But since to support parents is to bring about something indirectly, the realization of the second condition involves the existence of a certain combination of things capable of having certain changes of state effected in them, such that, on the one hand, the man can produce the changes directly, and also such that, on the other hand, if these changes are produced, they will result in the parents' having the means of support. In asserting a moral rule, however, we take for granted that a man has permanently the capacity of bringing about certain things directly, and therefore we think of the realization of the second condition as consisting simply in the fact that the situation in which the man is such that some one, or some group, of the things which he can bring about directly would, if produced, effect his parents' possession of the means of subsistence. Consequently, to generalize, we can say that any moral rule, when modified to express fully the thought which it is used to express, will be of the following form: 'When the situation in which a man is contains a thing of the kind A capable of having a state of the kind X effected in it, and when also it is such that some state or combination of states Y which the man can bring about directly would, if brought about, cause a state of the kind X in A, the man ought to bring about that state or combination of states.'

Again, once the thought is expressed in this form, it becomes obvious that, in having the thought, we are implying that when a man has an obligation to do some act in the strict sense, corresponding to the rule, what renders him bound to do the action is the special character of the situation in which he is, in the two respects just indicated, this being what gives rise to the fact that, if he were to do the action, he would indirectly be causing a state of the kind in question. Plainly, therefore, if we were to put forward a particular set of rules as exhaustive, we should be implying that the question whether we are bound to do some particular action, in the strict sense, will turn on whether the existing situation contains any of the various pairs of conditions which would bring the act under one or other of the rules. Clearly also, even if we did not think such rules as we could offer exhaustive, we should still think that the question could only be settled in the same kind of way, although we could not settle it.

Now when we reflect on this general idea or thought underlying our assertion of a set of moral rules, viz. that where we have an obligation to do some action in the strict sense, it depends on certain characteristics of the situation, we find it in two related respects very attractive. For, first, being the thought that any obligation depends solely on certain characteristics of the situation, it is on its negative side the thought that the obligation is wholly independent of our knowledge and thought about the situation. And we welcome this negative side, since we do not like to think that the question whether some action is a duty turns not on the nature of the situation but on that of our attitude towards it in respect of knowledge and thought. Moreover, the thought seems implied in much of our procedure in actual life. For frequently when in doubt, as we often are, whether some action in the narrow sense is a duty, our doubt seems to arise from doubt about the actual facts. Thus when I see someone who shows symptoms of having fainted and it occurs to me that, if I shouted, I might revive him, I may doubt whether I am bound to shout; and, when I do, my doubt sometimes seems to arise partly from doubt whether he has really fainted, and partly from doubt whether shouting would revive him. And if I try to resolve my doubt about the duty by resolving my doubt about the facts, I at least seem to be implying that the question whether I am bound to shout turns on what the facts really are. Second, the thought implies that if some action is a duty, it would bring about some state referred to in a moral rule, such as the recovery of a sick man, and would not be merely an act which we think would be likely to do so; and we welcome this implication because we should like to think that, if we have done some duty, we have achieved some change to which a moral rule refers, e.g. that we have helped a man out of trouble, and not merely done something which we thought would do this but which possibly has in fact damaged a man who was in no trouble at all.

Yet there is no denying that if we try to defend this thought we become involved in very awkward consequences. There are various admissions which we shall have to make which we thoroughly dislike when we come to reflect on them.

The most awkward of these emerges as soon as we ask: 'How am I to *know* that some moral rule is applicable to me here and now?' The rule being of the form recently stated, the question becomes: 'How am I to *know* that the situation satisfies the two conditions necessary for the application of the rule, viz. first, that it contains a particular thing of the kind *A* capable of having a state of the kind *X* effected in it, and, second, that it is such that some act or acts which I can do would cause this *A* to assume a state of the kind *X*?' And as regards the first condition, we shall have to admit that the situation may often satisfy it, without my knowing, or even being able to discover, that it does so. We may perhaps insist that sometimes I know that there is someone to whom I have made a promise, or again that I have parents who are in difficulties; but we cannot deny that sometimes I am uncertain whether there is someone to whom I have made a promise, or whether my parents are in difficulties, or again whether a man whom I meet is ill, at any rate with an illness which anything I can do would be likely to diminish. And we shall have to allow that in most of these latter cases I have no means of resolving my doubt. We shall therefore have to admit that for this reason alone I may often have a duty without knowing, or even being able to discover, that I have. Again, as regards the second condition, there are, undeniably, absolutely no occasions on which, where some particular state *Y* which I can bring about directly would cause an effect of the kind *X*, I either *know*, or can even come to *know*, that it would, although of course I may have a strong opinion about the matter. For plainly I never either do or can *know* that any particular action which I can do in the narrow sense would have a certain effect. Thus, unquestionably, I neither do nor can know that giving a man a certain drug would cause his recovery; and if in fact I give him the drug, and afterwards find that he has recovered, even then I cannot *know* that I have cured him, though I may think it very likely. Again, I never *know* that by uttering certain sounds I shall cause a man to know what I think; and I know that however much I may try to speak the truth, I may fail. Consideration, then, of the second condition forces us to admit that there is absolutely no occasion on which a moral rule applies to me on which I can know that I have the duty in question. In fact, reflection on these conditions compels us to admit that no moral rule can express knowledge, and that, to express knowledge, we must substitute a hypothetical statement in which we replace the word 'when' of a moral rule by 'if'. To express knowledge, its form will have to be: '*If* the situation in which a man is contains a thing of the kind *A* capable of having a state of the kind *X* produced in it, and *if* also it be such that one of the things which he can bring about directly will, if he brings it about, cause *A* to assume such a state, then he ought to bring about that thing.' The need of this substitution is obvious, since for the reasons given an individual is sometimes uncertain whether the first, and always uncertain whether the second, condition is realized. Indeed, on this view that an obligation, if there be one, depends on certain features of the situation, we are driven to the extreme conclusion that, although we may have duties, we cannot know but can only believe that we have; and therefore we are even rendered uncertain whether we, or anyone else, has ever had, or will ever have, a duty.

Here we may note the answer which this view requires us to give to a question which is often raised. Obviously at different times opposite views have been taken of the rightness or wrongness of certain kinds of action, in consequence of different views concerning matters of fact. Thus while some men must in the past have been sincerely convinced that it was a duty to torture heretics, most men are now equally convinced that a man ought not to do so; and the explanation obviously lies in a difference of opinion about the effects of torture. And the question is often asked: 'Where there is such a difference of view concerning the rightness or wrongness of a certain kind of action, which party is right?' To this question, on the view we are considering, the answer can only be: 'We do not know; no one knows; and no one ever will know. Even those, e.g., who considered it a duty to torture heretics may have been right.'

That we can never know that we have a duty is not, however, the only conclusion to which we are driven on this view. There are others related to it. One is that, though we may have duties, we can never, strictly speaking, do a duty, if we have one, *because* it is a duty, i.e. really in consequence of *knowing* it to be a duty. And the reason is, of course, simply that we can never have the knowledge. At best, if we have a duty, we may do it because we think without question, or else believe, or again think it possible, that the act is a duty. Another conclusion is that some past act of mine may have been a duty although in doing it I believed that the act was one which I ought not to do. Thus my shouting on seeing a man may have been in fact a duty, because he was faint and shouting would revive him, and yet I may have shouted to satisfy a grudge, believing that he was asleep and that my shouting would disturb him. A third is that I may do some act which is in fact a duty, although in doing it I do not even suspect that it will have the effect which renders it a duty. This would happen, e.g., if I shouted simply to attract the attention of the passers-by and without noticing the man's condition at all. Similar conclusions, too, have to be drawn with regard to acts of the kinds which we think we ought not to do.

These conclusions being all unwelcome, we naturally want to discover what modifications of the form of a moral rule would enable us to escape them, and then to consider how we fare if we accept it. Now what the conclusions all followed from was the thought underlying the assertion of a set of moral rules, that if some particular action is a duty, the obligation depends on certain facts of the situation. And to this thought there is only one alternative, viz. the thought that the obligation depends on our being in a certain attitude of mind towards the situation in respect of knowledge, thought, or opinion. This thought can be described as the subjective view of the basis of an obligation, not in the sense that no acts are really right or really wrong, but in the sense of the view that the ground of an obligation lies in some state of the man's own mind. And in contrast the opposed view can be designated the objective view.

The question, therefore, at once arises: 'What have we to represent this state or attitude as being, if we are to render this alternative view at least plausible?' The most obvious suggestion is, of course, to represent it as our thinking certain things likely or probable, and to represent the alternative view as being that if, e.g., I am bound to shout, it is because I think it likely that the man in front of me has fainted and that, if he has fainted shouting would cure him, i.e. have his revival as an effect. But, when we come to consider this view, we find that we do not like it either.

It seems to have, no doubt, at least one definite advantage over the view which it is to replace. It seems not to preclude us from thinking that it is possible to *discover* our duties, since, when we think something likely, we either know, or at least by reflecting can discover, that we do. The question whether I am thinking something likely is no more one about which I can be mistaken than is the question whether I have a certain pain. Consequently, also, the view does not preclude us from thinking that it is sometimes possible for us to do some action, knowing that we ought to do it. For the same reason it saves us from having to allow that we are, and must always remain, uncertain whether we have or shall ever have a duty.

On the other hand, it of course inevitably implies that any obligation I may have depends not on the fact that the action would have a certain character, if I were to do it—that of producing a certain effect—but on my thinking it likely that it would. It implies, e.g., that where I am bound to shout, my obligation depends not on the fact that if I were to shout I should be reviving a man who has fainted, but on my thinking it likely that I should. And a paradox involved comes to light if we imagine ourselves omniscient beings, who in consequence knew the circumstances. For if we were such beings, the analogous view would be that, if we were bound to shout, what would render us bound to shout would not be the fact that shouting would cure the man, but our knowing that it would; and it would therefore imply that this knowledge, so far from being the knowledge of the ground of the obligation, was itself the ground of the obligation, and that our knowledge of the ground of the obligation consisted in our knowing that we knew that shouting would cure the man.

Again, to defend the view, we shall have to modify it at least to the extent of maintaining that if, for instance, I am bound to shout, what renders me so bound is not simply my thinking it likely but my thinking it at least in a certain degree likely that shouting would cure the man. For no one would maintain that I am bound to shout if I think the likelihood remote beyond a certain degree. But then we are faced by the question: 'What degree is necessary?' And we have to answer that we can formulate it only within certain limits which differ in different cases according to the degree of benefit to the other man which I think likely to accrue from my shouting. We shall, therefore, also have to allow that I shall not always be able to discover whether I ought to shout, since there will be borderline cases in which I shall be unable to discover whether the degree to which I think the act likely to confer a certain benefit is sufficient to render it a duty. And therefore we shall have to allow that even on this view I may have a duty without being able to discover that I have it.

Again, the view, at any rate unless further modified, implies not only that in similar circumstances it may be one man's duty but not another's to do some action, owing to some difference in their thought about the facts, but also that the same thing is true of a single individual at different moments. For I may at first think it just, but only just, possible that shouting would cure a man, and then on further consideration think that there is a very good chance that it will; and, if so, while at first I shall not be bound to shout, afterwards I shall. And, again, the converse may happen.

Also, we have to distinguish from 'thinking likely' what for lack of a better phrase we may call 'thinking without question'. For on seeing a man who has fainted, instead of thinking it likely, I may from lack of reflection think without question that shouting would cure him, not being uncertain that it would, and therefore not 'thinking it likely', but at the same time not being certain. And on the view in question, unless it be modified, we shall have to hold that when this happens I am not bound to shout, in spite of thinking without question that shouting would cure him, since I am not thinking it likely.

It will, however, probably occur to us that these last two difficulties can be met by a further modification. This is to maintain (1) that I am bound to shout only if I think it likely that shouting would effect a cure, *after* having considered the circumstances fully, i.e. after having considered as fully as I can whether he is ill and whether shouting would cure him if he is, and so having obtained the best opinion I can about the circumstances, and (2) that whenever I have not done this I am bound to do something else, viz. to consider the circumstances fully.

This modification, it must be allowed, does remove the difficulties. Nevertheless, the idea that, where we have not done so, we ought to consider the circumstances fully, is itself not free from difficulty. This becomes obvious as soon as we ask: '*Why*, for instance, when it first strikes me that shouting might cure the man, am I bound to consider fully whether it would?' For the answer which we are first inclined to give is: 'Because, if I were to consider the matter fully, I might come to think shouting in a certain degree likely to cure him, and, if I did, I should then be bound to shout.' And yet this answer cannot be right. For plainly the duty of doing one action cannot possibly depend on the possibility of the duty of doing another the duty of doing which cannot arise unless the former action has actually been done. Moreover, if the answer were right, I could always escape a duty to shout merely by abstaining from considering the circumstances, and yet no one thinks this possible. The truth is that our having a duty to consider the circumstances cannot be based on the possibility of our having a future duty of another kind if we were to consider them. Rather, to vindicate such a duty, we must represent the two so-called duties as respectively an element and a possible element in a *single* duty, viz. to consider the circumstances, and then *if*, but only if, as a result, we reach a certain opinion, to do a certain future action. And if we do this we can explain the need of this complicated and partially hypothetical phrase for what is, after all, a single duty by the fact that the duty is one of the full nature of which we are at the time inevitably ignorant owing to our ignorance of the facts.

Again, if the view is to correspond with what we ordinarily think, still further modifications may seem necessary for various reasons, of which one is that we ordinarily think, for instance, that before it can be a duty for me to shout I must also have considered what is likely to be the effect of shouting on anyone else who may be within range.

But, in order to consider the main issue, we need not inquire what, if any, further modifications are needed. For, even if they are needed, the fundamental issue will remain the same, viz.: 'If I have an obligation, does it depend on the existence of certain facts of the situation or on my having certain thoughts about certain facts of the situation?'

Here it may be noted that the issue is not avoided by those who would deny the truth of any set of moral rules on the ground that, if we think them true, we are involved in the absurdity of admitting that we may at any moment have conflicting duties, i.e. two or more duties only one of which we can carry out. For, in order to avoid this admission, they have to maintain that where some action is a duty it is because it would possess some such character as that of producing something good in a greater degree than any other of the acts which the man is able to do. And, in maintaining this, they will be faced with the same question in a slightly different form, viz.: 'Does the obligation depend on the fact that the action would possess this character in a greater degree than any other, or does it depend on the fact that the man, after full consideration, thinks it likely that it would?'

The issue, then, being as stated, the first thing to do appears to consist in ascertaining which of the alternative views better corresponds with the thought of our ordinary life.

There are two ways in which this thought appears to imply the objective view. First, we frequently think without question both that the situation contains some thing in a certain state, and also that some action which we could do would produce a change in it of a certain kind, and then think without question that we ought to do the action. Thus, when we do not reflect, we frequently think without question that a man whom we meet has some malady and that giving him some drug would relieve it, and, where we do, we think without question that we ought to give the drug. And here we seem to imply that what renders us bound to do the act is just the fact that the situation is of a certain sort, together with the fact that the act would have a certain effect in that situation. Secondly, we often seek to change the mind of someone else about a duty by trying to convince him that he is mistaken about the facts; and, in doing so, we seem to imply that the question whether he has the duty depends on the nature of the facts. Thus, where A thinks he ought to vote for X rather than Y, B may try to convince A that he ought to vote for Y by arguing that X and Y will, if elected, act otherwise than A expects. Again, we may argue with a friend that he ought to send his child to school M rather than school N, which he considers the better, on the ground that M is really the better. And if someone were to maintain that he ought to torture a certain heretic, as the only way of saving his soul, we should presumably try to convince him that he was mistaken by convincing him that torture would not have this effect.

On the other hand, at any rate a large portion of our ordinary thought is in direct conflict with the objective view. Consider, e.g., our attitude to the question: 'Ought we to stop, or at least slow down, in a car, before entering a main road?' If the objective view be right, (1) there will be a duty to slow down only if in fact there is traffic; (2) we shall be entitled only to think it likely—in varying degrees on different occasions—that we are bound to slow down; and (3) if afterwards we find no traffic, we ought to conclude that our opinion that we were bound to slow down was mistaken. Yet, provided that after consideration we think that there is even a small chance of traffic, we, in fact, think that there is definitely a duty to slow down, and that the subsequent discovery that there was no traffic would not prove us mistaken. Again, imagine that we are watching a car approaching along a road which we know forks, and of which one fork has, we know, just suffered a landslide, and that we have no idea which road the driver is intending to take, or whether he knows about the landslide.[1] The objective view would require us to think that there is a duty to stop the car only if it is going to destruction, so that, if we are anxious to do what we ought, we can only insure ourselves against the possibility of failure to do what we ought by stopping the car, knowing that, after all, we may be doing something we are not bound to do. Yet plainly we in fact think without any doubt whatever that we are bound to stop the car, unless we have reason for being quite confident that the car is about to take the safe fork. Again, no nurse thinks that she is bound to light a fire in her patient's room only if in fact there will be a frost next morning. She thinks she is bound to do so, unless she thinks there is practically no chance of a frost. Indeed, the objective view is in direct conflict with all the numerous cases in which we think without question that we ought to do something we are thinking of as of the nature of *an insurance* in the interest of someone else.

[1] I owe the illustration to Mr R. G. Collingwood.

Moreover, the extent to which our ordinary thought involves the subjective view is usually obscured for us by our tendency to think that the terms 'likely' and 'probable' refer to facts in nature. For we are apt, for instance, to express our thought that someone has probably fainted, and that shouting would probably revive him, by the statements 'He has probably fainted' and 'Shouting would probably revive him'. We are then apt to think that these statements state the existence of certain facts in nature called probabilities, in the spirit which leads some physicists to regard electron-waves as waves of probability;[2] and we are then apt to think that an obligation to shout arises from these probabilities. It needs, however, but little reflection to realize that there are no such things as probabilities in nature. There cannot, e.g., be such a thing as the probability that someone has fainted, since either he has fainted or he has not. No doubt it is extremely difficult to formulate the precise nature of the fact which we express, for instance, by the statement: 'X has probably fainted.' But at least we must allow that, whatever its precise nature may be, the fact must consist in our mind's being in a certain state or condition. And, once this is realized, it becomes obvious that most of our ordinary thought involves the subjective view.

Again, even when we try to change someone else's mind about a duty, we do not really imply the objective view. This is shown by our thinking that when our attempt to change his opinion about the facts is over, then, whether we have or have not succeeded, the question whether he is bound to do the action will turn on the nature of *his opinion* about the facts. Thus we think that, provided the would-be torturer remained, in spite of all we have said, in a very high degree confident that torturing, and torturing only, would save the heretic, he would be bound to inflict the torture. No doubt we also think that we should take steps to prevent him; but here there is no inconsistency. And, in fact, we not infrequently think ourselves bound to do some action which will prevent someone else doing something which he is bound to do. Indeed, if this were not so, few would fight conscientiously for their country.

Undoubtedly, then, the subjective view better corresponds with our ordinary thought. Yet, as should now be obvious, it is exposed to various difficulties. Of these the chief are two. The first is that on this view knowledge of the existence of borderline cases precludes us from thinking that we can always discover our duties. Still in this respect it is more satisfactory than the objective view, since the latter implies that we can never discover a duty. The second and more fundamental difficulty is that it represents the duty of doing some action as depending not on the fact that the action would have a certain character if we were to do it, but on our thinking it likely that it would. And to maintain this seems impossible.

---

[2] Cf. *The Mysterious Universe*, p. 122 (Sir James Jeans).

We thus seem to have reached an impasse. For both the alternative views lead to fundamental difficulties, and yet there is no third course.

Before, however, we consider the matter further, we ought to consider a difficulty which is common to both views, and which, if it proves well founded, will force us to modify both.

In considering the problem, we have throughout been taking for granted that an obligation is necessarily an obligation to do some *action*, and, strictly speaking, an action in the strict sense. But we ought at least to ask ourselves whether this assumption, obvious though it seems, is true.

Unquestionably an obligation must be an obligation to perform some *activity*. An obligation can be an obligation only to be *active*, and not to be *affected*, in a particular way. And to say that an obligation is always an obligation to do some *action*, in the strict sense, e.g. to move my arms, is really to say that the activity which an obligation is an obligation to perform consists in *doing* something, as distinct from an activity of some other kind, such as thinking or imagining. But, as was said earlier, by 'doing something' in the strict sense, we mean bringing about something directly, i.e. bringing about something in the strict sense. Therefore to assert that an obligation is an obligation to do something is really to assert that the activity of the kind which an obligation is an obligation to perform consists in bringing about something. And in making this assertion we are implying that there is a special *kind* of activity, and indeed a special kind of *mental* activity, for which the proper phrase is 'bringing about something'. For if we thought that what we call 'bringing about X' really consists in performing an activity of some other kind of which X will be an effect, we should have to allow that what we call the obligation to bring about X is really the obligation to perform some particular activity of this other kind of which X would be an effect, and that, therefore, an obligation, so far from being an obligation to do something, is always an obligation to perform an activity of this other kind. In asserting, then, that an obligation is an obligation to *do* something, we are implying that there is a special kind of activity consisting in doing something, i.e. bringing about something.

On reflection, however, we become forced to admit that, though on certain occasions we do bring certain things about, yet there is no kind of activity consisting in bringing about something. We can realize this in the following way. It will, of course, be allowed that where we think of some past action of ours as one in which we indirectly brought about some particular thing, as where we think of ourselves as having cured someone's illness, we think it fair to ask: '*How* did we do the action?' We take the question to have the intelligible meaning: 'What was that by the direct production of which we indirectly produced what we did?'; and we can give some sort of answer. But we can also ask a question verbally similar, where we think of some past action as one in which we directly brought about something. Where, e.g., I think of myself as having moved my hand, I can ask: '*How* did I move it?' In such a case, of course, the question cannot be of the same kind, because *ex hypothesi* I am not thinking of the action as one in which I caused some particular thing by causing something else, and so I cannot be asking: 'By directly causing what, did I cause what I did?' The legitimate question is: 'What was the activity by performing which I caused my hand to move?', and an answer would be 'Willing the existence of the movement'. And in so answering I should be implying that what I called moving my hand really consisted in setting myself to move it, and that I referred to this activity as moving my hand because I thought that this activity had a change of place of my hand as an effect. Again, in another case my answer might be: 'By setting myself to move my other hand,' the case being one in which I set myself to move one hand and in fact moved the other. And here also I should be implying that what I called 'moving my hand' really consisted in a particular activity of another sort of which the change of place of my hand was an effect. The general moral can be stated thus: In no case whatever, where we think of ourselves as having brought about something directly, do we think that our activity was that of bringing about that something. On the contrary, we think of the activity as having been of another sort, and mean, by saying that we brought about directly what we did, that this activity of another sort had the change in question as a direct effect.

The same conclusion can be reached by considering what we really mean by saying, 'I can do so and so', when we use 'do' in the strict sense. It may first be noticed that if in ordinary life we are asked whether we can do some action in the strict sense, we cannot always give a definite answer. No doubt if we were asked: 'Can we make a noise identical in pitch with the highest C of the piano?' we should unhesitatingly answer 'No'; and if we were asked: 'Can we make a loud noise?' we should unhesitatingly answer 'Yes.' But if we were asked: 'Can we make a noise similar in pitch to the middle C of the piano?' we should have to answer 'I don't know', though we might possibly add 'But I *think* I can.' It may next be noticed that even where we unhesitatingly answer 'Yes' we are, if pressed, inclined to hedge to the extent of saying: 'Well, at least I can do the action, e.g. shout, *if* I choose.' Such a statement, however, as we see when we reflect, is very odd. It cannot be meant literally, and can at best be only an idiom. For while it is sense to say: 'If I choose to make a loud noise, I shall in fact make it,' it cannot be sense to say: 'If I choose to make it, I *can* make it.' And no one would maintain that our *ability* to do something, as distinct from our *doing* it, can depend on our choosing to do it. Indeed, the statement really presupposes the thought that I *can* choose to make a loud noise, and is in fact only a brachylogical way of saying: 'Since I can choose to make a loud noise, and since choosing to make it would in fact have a loud noise as an effect, I can make it.' At the same time 'choose' cannot be an accurate phrase for what we mean, since 'choose' means choose between alternatives, and in fact we have no alternatives in mind. 'Will', the verb corresponding to 'volition', might perhaps be suggested as the proper substitute; but the term would be merely artificial. What seems wanted is one or other of the two phrases which have already been used, viz. 'setting myself to', or 'exerting myself to', so that 'choosing to make a loud noise' becomes 'setting or exerting myself to make a loud noise'. And, if this is right, what is in our minds when we say 'I can make a loud noise' is not the thought that there is a special kind of activity of which I am capable consisting in bringing about a loud noise, but rather the thought that a special kind of activity of which I am capable, consisting in setting myself to bring about a loud noise, would have a loud noise as an effect.

Two conclusions are at once obvious. (1) The first is that the true answer to any question of the form 'Can I do so and so?' must be 'I don't know.' This is, of course, clear in certain cases. Plainly we never *know* that if we were to set ourselves to thread a needle, we should thread it; or that if we were to set ourselves to draw a line through a point on a piece of paper, we should succeed. But in the last resort this is the only answer ever possible, since we never *know* that we have not become paralysed. Even in the case of moving our arms or making a noise we do not *know* that, if we were to set ourselves to do it, we should do anything, though, of course, we may think it very likely both that we should do something, and also that we should move our arms, or make a noise, in particular. (2) The second conclusion is that whatever we are setting ourselves to do, we never in so setting ourselves *know* that we shall be doing what we are setting ourselves to do, bringing about what we are setting ourselves to bring about, or indeed that we are doing anything at all. In other words, it follows that where we are setting ourselves to do something, we never *know* what we shall be doing, and at best can only find out afterwards what we have done. And for this reason alone we cannot sustain the view to which reference was made earlier that 'doing something' means not simply bringing about something, but bringing about something knowing that we are doing so. For, apart from other objections, if it did, we in using the phrase should be implying that there is a special kind of activity consisting in bringing about something, of the special nature of which we are aware in performing the activity; and we do not think this. At the same time, the view has an underlying element of truth; for though bringing about something is *not*, setting ourselves to bring about something *is*, a special kind of activity of the special nature of which we are aware in performing it; and therefore the idea underlying the view is sound, though misapplied.

As regards an obligation, the moral is obvious. It is simply that, contrary to the implication of ordinary language and of moral rules in particular, an obligation must be an obligation, not to *do* something, but to perform an activity of a totally different kind, that of setting or exerting ourselves to do something, i.e. to bring something about.

It may be objected that, if an obligation were an obligation to perform a mental activity of a special kind other than that of bringing something about, the nature of that activity would have to be describable by itself, and not solely by reference to something else, as it is implied to be if we describe it as setting ourselves to bring something about. But to this two replies can be given. The first is that we find no difficulty in allowing the appropriateness of this procedure in analogous cases. Thus we have no difficulty in allowing the existence of such a kind of thing as desire, although we are perfectly aware that to desire is necessarily to desire something, e.g. the eating of an apple or the prosperity of our country, so that no desire can be described simply in terms of a certain state of mind. Again, we readily allow that there is such a thing as a state of wondering, or, again, of being angry, although we are quite aware that to wonder is to wonder, for instance, whether rain is coming, and to be angry is to be angry with someone for what he has done. The second reply is simply that if we try to describe the nature of the activity which we perform when we think we are bringing about something, without reference to bringing about something, we find that we totally fail.

If, however, we allow, as we now must, that an obligation must be an obligation not to do something but to set ourselves to do something, we have to modify accordingly not only the original question but also both the alternative views of the basis of an obligation.

The effect, however, as regards the relation between the alternatives is simply to intensify their difference. For, given the modification, on either view an obligation will be an obligation not to bring about something directly but to set ourselves to do so. And if there be an obligation to set ourselves to bring about some particular thing Y directly, then, on the objective view, the obligation will depend on an additional fact the existence of which we shall be unable to discover, viz. that setting ourselves to bring about Y would bring it about directly, while on the subjective view it will depend in part on an additional thinking something likely, viz. our thinking that setting ourselves to bring about Y would be likely to bring it about.

The question therefore arises whether this modification renders it any easier to decide between the alternatives. And the answer appears to be that in one respect it does. For once it has become common ground that the kind of activity which an obligation is an obligation to perform is one which may bring about nothing at all, viz. setting ourselves to bring about something, we are less inclined to think that, for there to be an obligation to perform some particular activity, it must have a certain indirect effect. To this extent the modification diminishes the force of the objective view without in any way impairing that of its rival. Yet undoubtedly it does nothing to remove what is, after all, the outstanding difficulty of the subjective view—a difficulty compared with which the others are only difficulties of detail, i.e. difficulties concerning its precise nature. This difficulty of the view in its original form lies in its representing the obligation to do some action as depending not on the fact that the action would have a certain character, if we were to do it, but on our thinking it likely that it would. This dependence seems impossible. For an obligation to do some action seems to be a character of the action; and therefore, it would seem, it must depend on the fact that the action would have a certain characteristic, if it were done, and not on our thinking it likely that it would. And if here we substitute for 'do some action' 'set ourselves to do some action', there is a difficulty of precisely the same kind.

It is, however, worth considering whether, after all, this difficulty is insuperable, and whether it may not simply arise from a mistake. We are apt to think of an obligation to do some action as if it were, like its goodness or badness, a sort of quality or character of the action. Just as we think that when we say of some action which we could do that it would be good, or, again, bad, we are stating that, in a wide sense of the term 'character', it would have a certain character, so we are apt to think that when we say of it that we are bound, or bound not, to do it, we are stating that it would have a certain character, for which the proper term would be 'ought-to-be-doneness' or 'ought-not-to-be-doneness'. And this tendency is fostered by our habit of using the terms 'right' and 'wrong' as equivalents for 'ought' and 'ought not'. For when we express our thought that we ought, or ought not, to do some action by saying that the act would be right, or wrong, our language inevitably implies that the obligation or disobligation is a certain character which the act would have if we were to do it, a character for which the only existing words are 'rightness' in the one case and 'wrongness' in the other. And when we think this, we inevitably go on to think that the obligation or disobligation must depend on some character which the act would have. But, as we recognize when we reflect, there are no such characteristics of an action as ought-to-be-doneness and ought-not-to-be-doneness. This is obvious; for, since the existence of an obligation to do some action cannot possibly depend on actual performance of the action, the obligation cannot itself be a property which the action would have, if it were done. What does exist is the fact that you, or that I, ought, or ought not, to do a certain action, or rather to set ourselves to do a certain action. And when we make an assertion containing the term 'ought' or 'ought not', that to which we are attributing a certain character is not a certain activity but a certain man. If our being bound to set ourselves to do some action were a character which the activity would have, its existence would, no doubt, have to depend on the fact that the activity would have a certain character, and it could not depend on our thinking that it would. Yet since, in fact, it is a character of ourselves, there is nothing to prevent its existence depending on our having certain thoughts about the situation and, therefore, about the nature of the activity in respect of its effects. Indeed, for this reason, its existence must depend on some fact about ourselves. And while the truth could not be expressed by saying: '*My setting myself to do so-and-so* would *be* right, because *I think* that it would have a certain effect'—a statement which would be as vicious in principle as the statement '*Doing so-and-so* would *be* right because *I think* it would be right'—there is nothing to prevent its being expressible in the form 'I ought to set myself to do so-and-so, because I think that it would have a certain effect'. We are therefore now in a position to say that the fundamental difficulty presented by the subjective view is simply the result of a mistake.

This being so, there remains only one thing to do. This is to consider, in some instance where we have considered the circumstances as fully as we can, whether we ought to perform some particular activity, and then ask: 'Does the answer to this question turn on the nature of our *thought* about the situation, and therefore about the effect of the activity, or on the nature of the *situation* and therefore on that of the effect of the activity?' This must be our remaining task, once general difficulties have been cleared away. For there is no way of discovering whether some general doctrine is true except by discovering the general fact to which the problem relates; and there is no way of discovering some general fact except by apprehending particular instances of it. And here there is little that need be said. For we have only to carry out this procedure to find not that we are *inclined to think*, or even that we are of the opinion that, but that we are *certain*, i.e. *know*, that the answer turns not on the nature of the situation but on that of our thought about it. This certainty is attainable most readily if the instance taken is similar to those already considered in which our doubts about the nature of the situation are considerable. But it is attainable in any instance, provided that we really face the question.

We therefore cannot but allow that the subjective view is true, in spite of what at first seems its paradoxical character, and that, therefore, in order to defend any moral rule whatever, we must first modify its form accordingly.*

P. 95, para. 4. The argument appears fallacious. For to say that an obligation is an obligation to do *some action* is consistent with holding that it is an obligation, e.g., to perform a particular activity of a certain sort which will have a certain particular effect. And we are only implying that there is a kind of activity which in certain cases has effects.

The concluding part seems to contain two mistakes:

(1) pp. 96–100. It looks as though 'willing *X*' at any rate as used technically is a synonym for what I have called 'setting ourselves to bring about *X*'. This, however, does not affect the general argument. But the other mistake does;

(2) pp. 97–98. The difficulty put up for consideration is that the obligation to do some action must depend on some character that the action would have, and not on our thinking that it would have some character. And it is said to remain if we substitute for 'some action' (i.e. bringing about *X*) 'setting ourselves to do some action' (i.e. willing the existence of *X*). And it is resolved by denying that 'duty' is a property of an *action* as distinct from a person.

This resolution, except indirectly, does not affect the difficulty—which is that if we ought e.g. to will something *X*, it must be in virtue of a character which willing *X* would have and not in virtue of our thinking it would have it.

* [This is the end of the Hertz Trust Lecture as published by the British Academy. Presumably Prichard added the notes that follow for the publication of *Moral Obligation* (1949). Ed.]

DUTY AND IGNORANCE OF FACT

The proper resolution is to point out that if 'willing X' be substituted for 'bringing about X', then our thinking X likely to effect something else Y does enter in the character of the *activity* to which the 'ought' refers. For to will X, thinking it likely to produce Y, is one willing, and to will X, thinking it unlikely to produce Y, or to will X, not thinking of Y at all, is another. In other words, the *thinking* enters into the character of the *willing*.

P. 97, para. 3. The moral should be that if an obligation is to *do* some particular action, i.e. to will a change the willing of which would cause a certain change, we can never know that we ought to do a certain action.

P. 97, para. 2, sentence beginning 'And for this reason'. Fallacious, because this reason can't prevent our meaning this by 'doing something', but only shows that if we mean this by 'doing something' we are mistaken in thinking there is such a thing.

In the next sentence the 'if it did' statement is untrue.

H.A.P.

7. The Meaning of ἀγαθόν in the *Ethics* of Aristotle

I have for some time found it increasingly difficult to resist a conclusion so heretical that the mere acceptance of it may seem a proof of lunacy. Yet the failure of a recent attempt to resist it has led me to want to confess the heresy. And at any rate a statement of my reasons may provoke a refutation.

The heresy, in brief, is that Aristotle (in the *Nicomachean Ethics*, except in the two discussions of pleasure—where ἀγαθόν is opposed to φαῦλον and μοχθηρόν) really meant by ἀγαθόν conducive to our happiness, and maintained that when a man does an action deliberately, as distinct from impulsively, he does it simply in order to, i.e. from the desire to, become happy, this being so even when he does what is virtuous or speculates. Of this heresy a corollary is the view that Aristotle, being anxious to persuade men first and foremost to practise speculation and secondarily to do what is virtuous, conceived that, to succeed, what he had to prove was that this was the action necessary to make a man happy. This corollary, however, which may seem only a further heresy, I propose to ignore. The heresy, in my opinion, is equally attributable to Plato, and for much the same reasons. But for simplicity's sake I propose to confine consideration to Aristotle, with, however, the suggestion that the same argument can be applied to Plato.

In attributing this view to Aristotle I do not mean to imply that he does not repeatedly make statements inconsistent with it. Nor do I mean to imply that the question of the consistency of these statements with the view simply escapes him; it seems to me that it does not, but that owing to a mistake he thought they were consistent with it. Nor do I mean to imply that his acceptance of this view appears on the surface; but rather that it becomes evident once we lay bare certain misleading elements in his account of the motive of deliberate action.

The first two chapters of the *Ethics*, and especially its opening sentence, are undoubtedly puzzling. Aristotle begins by saying: πᾶσα τέχνη καὶ πᾶσα μέθοδος, ὁμοίως δὲ πρᾶξίς τε καὶ προαίρεσις, ἀγαθοῦ τινὸς ἐφίεσθαι δοκεῖ· διὸ καλῶς ἀπεφήναντο τἀγαθόν οὗ πάντ' ἐφιέται. 'Every art and every inquiry, and similarly every action and purpose, is thought to aim at some good; and for this reason the good has rightly been declared to be that at which all things aim.' Then after pointing out that certain aims or ends are subordinate to others, he

[From *Philosophy*, 10/37 (Jan. 1935).]

contends that there must be one final end to which all others are subordinate, and that this will be τἀγαθόν, the good, and that, consequently, knowledge of this final end will have great influence on our lives, since if we have it, we shall have a definite mark or goal to aim at. And he goes on to say that, this being so, his object in the *Ethics* is to discover what this final end is.

Here, as the rest of the first book shows, Aristotle, in his first sentence, is not simply stating a common opinion, but stating it with approval and on the assumption that it is an opinion which his hearers will accept and so which can be used as a basis for his subsequent argument. And, so regarded, it is very sweeping.

Even if he had said that in every deliberate action we have an aim or are aiming at something, we should have regarded the statement, put forward as expressing a fact obvious to everyone, and so as needing neither elucidation nor discussion, as sufficiently sweeping. But what he does say is more sweeping. In effect, taking for granted that there is always something at which we are aiming, he commits himself to a general statement about its nature, stating that it is always ἀγαθόν τι, or, as we may translate the phrase, a good.

But besides being sweeping it is obscure. Even if Aristotle had said that in all action we are aiming at something, we should have felt that the statement needed elucidation. But saying as he does that we are aiming at something good, we have an additional puzzle. If, instead, he had said that we are always aiming at a pleasure, or at an honour, or at doing some good action, then we should have at least suspected we knew what he meant, whether or not we agreed. But the meaning of ἀγαθόν is not clear.

Consequently to discover his meaning we have to find out not only what he means when he speaks of us in a deliberate action as aiming at something (ἐφίεσθαί τινος) or as having a τέλος or end, but also what he means by ἀγαθόν. And of these tasks, plainly the former has to be accomplished first.

The idea, which of course underlies the *Ethics*, that in all deliberate action we have an end or aim, is one the truth of which we are all likely to maintain when we first consider action, 'action' being a term which, for shortness' sake, I propose to use for deliberate action. The idea goes back to Plato; and Mill expresses it when he says that all action is for the sake of an end. We take for granted that in doing some action there must be some desire leading or moving us to do the action, i.e. forming what we call our motive, since, as we should say, otherwise we should not be doing the action; or, for this is only to express the same idea in other words, we take for granted that in doing the action we have a purpose, i.e. something the desire of which moves us to do the action. And, taking this for granted, we are apt to maintain that our purpose in doing the action always consists in something, other than the action, which we think the action likely to cause, directly or indirectly, such as an improvement in our health which we expect from taking a dose of medicine.

Further, taking this view of the motive of action, we are apt to express it metaphorically by saying that in any action we have an aim or that there is something at which we are aiming. For when we consider, e.g., taking a drug from the desire to become healthy, we are apt to think of the thing desired, viz. our health, as that by reference to which we have devised the action as what is likely to cause it, and so as similar to the target by reference to the position of which a shooter arranges his weapon before shooting. We are also apt to speak of our purpose metaphorically as our end, as being something which we think will come into existence at the end of the action. In either case, however, it is to be noticed that the terms 'end' and 'aim' are merely metaphorical expressions for our purpose, i.e. for that the desire of which is moving us to act. No doubt further consideration may afterwards lead us to abandon this view. For certain actions and notably acts of gratitude or revenge seem prompted by the desire to do the action we at least hope we are doing, such as the desire to inflict an injury on another equal to that to which he has done us. Yet we may not reflect sufficiently to notice this, or even if we do we may fail to notice that such actions require us to modify the view, or may even think, as Aristotle did, that the doctrine may be made to apply to them.

Plato, it may be noticed, expressly formulates this view in the *Gorgias*. In trying to show that orators and tyrants have the least power in States, he lays down generally[1] that a man in doing what he does wishes not for the action but for that for the sake of which he does it, this being implied to be some result of the action. And in support he urges that a man who takes a drug wishes not for taking the drug but for health, and that a man who takes a voyage wishes not for the sailing and the incurring of dangers but for the wealth for the sake of which he takes the voyage. He is, however, here obviously going too far in asserting that the man does not want to do the action itself, for if the man did not want to do the action, he would not be doing it. What Plato should have said and what would express the view accurately is this:

A man undoubtedly wants to do what he does, and this desire is moving him. But the desire is always derivative or dependent. His having it depends on his having another desire, viz. the desire of something to which he thinks the action will lead, and that is why this latter desire should be represented as what is moving him, since it is in consequence of having this latter desire that he has the desire to do the action.

The view, therefore, implies the idea that the desire to do some action is always a dependent desire, depending on the desire of something to which we think the action will lead. But, as we soon notice, this latter desire must either be itself an independent desire, i.e. a desire which does not depend on any other, or else imply such a desire, since otherwise, as Aristotle put it, desire would be empty and vain. We are therefore led to draw a distinction between an independent

[1] *Gorgias*, p. 467.

desire and a desire depending on a desire of something which we think the thing desired will cause. Aristotle, of course, recognized and even emphasized the distinction, but unfortunately he formulated it with a certain inaccuracy. He implies that it should be expressed as that between τὸ βούλεσθαί τι δι' αὐτό, or καθ' αὑτό, and τὸ βούλεσθαί τι δι' ἕτερον. But the latter phrase must be short for τὸ βούλεσθαί τι διὰ τὸ βούλεσθαι ἕτερόν τι, and, this being so, the former phrase must be short for τὸ βούλεσθαί τι διὰ τὸ βούλεσθαι αὐτό, which, meaning wishing for something in consequence of wishing for itself, is not sense. The distinction should have been expressed as that between τὸ βούλεσθαί τι μὴ διὰ τὸ βούλεσθαι ἕτερόν τι and τὸ βούλεσθαί τι διὰ τὸ βούλεσθαι ἕτερόν τι or, to be more accurate, between desiring something not in consequence of desiring something else, and desiring something in consequence of desiring something else to which we think it will lead. And in this connexion it should be noticed that the English phrase for an independent desire, viz. the desire of something for its own sake, which is the equivalent of Aristotle's βούλεσθαί τι δι' αὐτό, has really only the negative meaning of a desire which is not dependent on any other desire.

Further, having reached this distinction, we are soon led, as of course Aristotle was, to hold that in every action we must have some ultimate or final aim, consisting of the object of some independent desire, and to distinguish from this aims which we have but which are not ultimate.

Having drawn this distinction we do not ask: 'Of what sort or sorts are our non-ultimate aims?' since obviously anything may be such an aim. But we do raise the question: 'Of what sort or sorts is our ultimate aim in various actions?'

To this question Aristotle's answer is ἀγαθόν τι, since his opening statement covers ultimate as well as non-ultimate aims. And the most obvious way to ascertain what Aristotle considers our ultimate aim is, of course, simply to find out what he means by ἀγαθόν. But, as should now be obvious, there is also another way. Like ourselves, he must really mean by our ultimate or final aim that the independent desire of which, or, as he would put it, that the desire of which καθ' αὑτό, is moving us to act. Consequently, if he says of certain things that we desire and pursue, i.e. aim at, them καθ' αὑτά, we are entitled to conclude that he considers that in certain instances they are our ultimate aim. Now in Chapter 6 of Book I he maintains that there are certain kinds of things, viz. τιμή, φρόνησις, and ἡδονή, which are διωκόμενα καὶ ἀγαπώμενα καθ' αὑτά; and to these he adds in Chapter 7, § 5, νοῦς and πᾶσα ἀρετή, of which, together with τιμή and ἡδονή, he says that though we choose them for the sake of happiness, we also choose them δι' αὑτά, i.e. as being what they severally are, since we should choose them even if nothing resulted from them. And to say this is only to say in other words that in some instances our ultimate end is an honour, in others it is a pleasure, in others our being φρόνιμος, and so on. Consequently, if we hold him to this, the only possible conclusion for us to draw is that he considers (1) that in such cases our ultimate end is not ἀγαθόν τι, whatever he means by ἀγαθόν, and also (2) that our ultimate end is not always of the same sort, so that no single term could describe it. We thus reach the astonishing conclusion that Aristotle, in insisting as he does that we pursue these things for their own sake, is really ruling out the possibility of maintaining that our end is always ἀγαθόν τι, or indeed anything else, so that we are in a position to maintain that he has no right to assert that our ultimate end is always an ἀγαθόν, even before we have attempted to elucidate what he means by ἀγαθόν.

Further, if we next endeavour, as we obviously should, to do this, we get another surprise. Aristotle's nearest approach to an elucidation is to be found in Chapter 6, §§ 7–11, and Chapter 7, §§ 1–5. There he speaks of τὰ καθ' αὑτὰ διωκόμενα καὶ ἀγαπώμενα as called ἀγαθά in one sense, and gives as illustrations τιμή, φρόνησις, and ἡδονή; and he speaks of τὰ ποιητικὰ τούτων ἢ φυλακτικά πως as called ἀγαθά in another sense, and he implies that these latter are διωκτὰ καὶ αἱρετὰ δι' ἕτερον[2] and that πλοῦτος is an illustration.[3] Further, he appears to consider that the difference of meaning is elucidated by referring to the former as ἀγαθὰ καθ' αὑτά and to the latter as ἀγαθὰ διὰ ταῦτα, i.e. ἀγαθὰ διὰ ἀγαθὰ καθ' αὑτά. But this unfortunately is no elucidation, since to state a difference of reason for calling two things ἀγαθόν is not to state a difference of meaning of ἀγαθόν, and indeed is to imply that the meaning in both cases is the same. Nevertheless, these statements seem intended as an elucidation of the meaning of ἀγαθόν. And the cause for surprise lies in this, that if they are taken seriously as an elucidation, the conclusion can only be that ἀγαθόν includes 'being desired' in its meaning, and indeed simply means τέλος or end. For if they are so understood, Aristotle must be intending to say (1) that when we say of something that it is ἀγαθὸν καθ' αὑτό what we *mean* is that it is διωκόμενον καὶ ἀγαπώμενον καθ' αὑτό, i.e. simply that it is an ultimate end, and (2) that when we say of something that it is ἀγαθὸν δι' ἕτερον, what we mean is that it is διωκόμενον καὶ ἀγαπώμενον δι' ἕτερον, i.e. simply that it is a non-ultimate end. In other words, if here he is interpreted strictly, he is explaining that ἀγαθόν means τέλος, and by the distinction between an ἀγαθὸν καθ' αὑτό and an ἀγαθὸν δι' ἕτερον he means merely the distinction between an ultimate and a non-ultimate end. Yet if anything is certain, it is that when Aristotle says of something, e.g. πλοῦτος, that it is an ἀγαθόν he does not mean that it is a τέλος, i.e. that it is something at which someone is aiming, and that when he says of something, e.g. τιμή or φρόνησις, that it is an ἀγαθὸν καθ' αὑτό, he does not mean that it is someone's ultimate end, i.e. what he speaks of in Book VI, 9, § 7 as τὸ τέλος τὸ ἁπλῶς. Apart from other considerations, if he did, then for him to say, as he in effect does, that we always aim at ἀγαθόν τι would be to say

[2] *Ethics*, i. 7. 4. [3] Ibid. i. 5. 8.

nothing, and for him to speak, as he does, of the object of βούλησις as τἀγαθόν would be absurd.

But this being so, what *does* Aristotle mean by ἀγαθόν? Here there is at least one statement which can be made with certainty. Aristotle unquestionably would have said that where we are pursuing something of a certain kind, say, an honour, καθ' αὑτό, we are pursuing it ὡς ἀγαθόν, i.e. as a good. Otherwise there would not even have been verbal consistency between his statements, that we pursue, i.e. aim at, things of certain stated kinds, and that we always aim at ἀγαθόν τι. Again, unless we allow that he would have said this, we cannot make head or tail either of his puzzling statement in Book I, Chapter 2 that since, as there must be, there is some end which we desire for its own sake, this end must be τἀγαθόν, or, again, of its sequel in Chapter 7, where he proceeds to consider what that is to which the term τἀγαθόν is applicable by considering which of our various ends is a final end. For we are entitled to ask: 'Why does Aristotle think that if we discover something to be desired and pursued for its own sake, we shall be entitled to say that it is τἀγαθόν?' And no answer is possible unless we allow that he thought that in desiring and pursuing something for its own sake we are desiring and pursuing it ὡς ἀγαθόν.

But Aristotle in saying, as he would have said, that in pursuing, e.g., an honour, we are pursuing it ὡς ἀγαθόν could only have meant that we are pursuing it in virtue of thinking that it would possess a certain character to which he refers by the term ἀγαθόν, so that by ἀγαθόν he must mean to indicate some character which certain things would have. Further, this being so, in implying as he does that in pursuing things of certain different kinds καθ' αὑτά we are pursuing them ὡς ἀγαθά, he must be implying that these things of different kinds have, nevertheless, a common character, viz. that indicated by the term ἀγαθόν. It will, of course, be objected that he expressly denies that they have a common character. For he says: τιμῆς δὲ καὶ φρονήσεως καὶ ἡδονῆς ἕτεροι καὶ διαφέροντες οἱ λόγοι ταύτῃ ᾗ ἀγαθά.[4] But the answer is simple; viz. that this is merely an inconsistency into which he is driven by his inability to find in these things the common character which his theory requires him to find, and that if he is to succeed in maintaining that we pursue these things of various kinds ὡς ἀγαθά, he *has* to maintain that in spite of appearances to the contrary they have a common character.

Nevertheless, though we have to insist that Aristotle in fact holds that in pursuing any of these things καθ' αὑτό, i.e., as we should say, for its own sake, we are pursuing it ὡς ἀγαθόν, we cannot escape the admission that in doing so he is being inconsistent. For to maintain that in pursuing, e.g., an honour, we are pursuing it καθ' αὑτό, or, as we should say, for its own sake, is really to maintain that the desire of an honour moving us is an independent desire,

[4] Ibid. i. 6. 11.

i.e. a desire depending on no other. And, on the other hand, to maintain that in pursuing an honour, we are pursuing it ὡς ἀγαθόν, or as a good, is really to maintain that the desire of an honour moving us is a dependent desire, viz. a desire depending on the desire of something which will possess the character indicated by the word ἀγαθόν, i.e. that we desire an honour only in consequence of desiring something which will possess that character and of thinking that an honour will possess it. It is, in fact, really to maintain that in pursuing an honour, our ultimate aim, i.e. that the independent desire of which is moving us, or what Aristotle would call that which we are pursuing καθ' αὐτό, is not an honour but a good, i.e. something having the character, whatever it may be, which is indicated by the word ἀγαθόν, i.e. that we desire an honour only in consequence of desiring a good. The principle involved will become clearer, if we take a different illustration. In Chapter 6 Aristotle speaks of ὁρᾶν as one of the things which are pursued for their own sake; and if he had said that we pursue ὁρᾶν ὡς αἰσθάνεσθαι he would in consistency have had to maintain that what we are pursuing καθ' αὐτό is not ὁρᾶν but αἰσθάνεσθαι, and that the desire of ὁρᾶν moving us is only a dependent desire depending on our desiring something else which we think ὁρᾶν will be.

It will be objected that there is really no inconsistency, since Aristotle conceives the characteristic referred to by ἀγαθόν as a characteristic of an honour and of anything else which he would say we pursue καθ' αὐτό, and that to speak of us as desiring something in respect of some character which it would have is not to represent our desire of it as dependent. In illustration it may be urged that to speak of us as, in desiring to do a courageous action, desiring it as a worthy or virtuous action is not to represent our desire to do a courageous action as dependent. But the objection cannot be sustained. For if we desire to do a courageous action, as something which would be a virtuous action, i.e., really, a something which we think would be a virtuous action, although our desire does not depend on a desire of something which we think a courageous action would *cause*, it does depend on the desire of something which we think it would *be*. And as a proof of this dependence we can point to the fact that if, while having this desire, we were to do a good action of another sort, e.g. a generous action, the desire would disappear.

What is in the end plain is that Aristotle cannot succeed in maintaining that our ultimate end is always ἀγαθόν τι without abandoning his view that we pursue such things as τιμή and ἀρετή καθ' αὐτά, or, as we should say, for their own sake, and maintaining instead that we pursue them as things which we think will have the character to which the term ἀγαθόν refers. Nevertheless, in spite of having to allow that we are thereby attributing inconsistency to Aristotle, we have to admit that he, in fact, holds that in desiring and pursuing certain things for their own sakes we are desiring and pursuing them in respect of their having a certain character, viz. whatever it be to which he refers by the term ἀγαθόν.

So far the only clue reached to the meaning of ἀγαθόν is the idea that Aristotle used it to refer to a certain character possessed by certain things, the thought of the possession of which arouses desire for them, and indeed is the only thing which arouses desire for anything, except where our desire depends on another desire.

We have now to try to get to closer quarters with the question of its meaning. The question is really: 'What is the character which Aristotle considered we must think would be possessed by something if we are to desire it, independently of desiring something else to which we think it will lead, that character being what Aristotle used the word ἀγαθόν to refer to?'

Here it seems hardly necessary to point out that the answer cannot be 'goodness'. To rule out this answer it is only necessary to point out two things. First, if Aristotle had meant by ἀγαθόν good, he would have had to represent us as desiring for its own sake any good activity, whether ours or another's, whereas he always implies that a good activity which we desire is an activity of our own, and in addition he would have had to drop, as he never does, the idea of a connexion between a good activity and *our own* happiness. And second, Aristotle's term ἀγαθόν is always ἀγαθὸν τινί, as appears most obviously in the phrase ἀνθρώπινον ἀγαθόν and in the statement in Book IX, 8, § 8–9, where he says that reason always chooses what is best for itself—πᾶς γὰρ νοῦς αἱρεῖται τὸ βέλτιστον ἑαυτῷ—and goes on to add that the man who gives wealth to a friend assigns the greater good, the having done what is noble (τὸ κάλον), to himself. Once, however, we regard this answer as having to be excluded once for all, there seems to be no alternative to attributing to Aristotle a familiar turn of thought to which we are all very prone and which is exemplified in Mill and T. H. Green.

When we consider what we desire we soon come to the conclusion, as of course Aristotle did, that there are things of certain kinds which we desire, not in consequence of thinking that they will have an effect which we desire, but for themselves, such as seeing a beautiful landscape, being in a position of power, helping another, and doing a good action. We then are apt to ask, 'What is the condition of our desiring such things?' and if we do, we are apt to answer—and the tendency is almost irresistible—'It is impossible for us to desire any such thing unless we think of it as something which we should like, since, if we do not think of it thus, we remain simply indifferent to its realization.' Then, if asked what we mean by its being something we should like, we reply: 'Something which would give us enjoyment, or, alternatively, gratification, or, to use a term which will cover either, pleasure.' The tendency is one to which Mill gives expression when he says that desiring a thing and finding it pleasant are two parts of the same phenomenon; and Green exhibits it when he maintains, as in effect he does, that we can desire something only if we think of it as something which will give us satisfaction, i.e. gratification. In maintaining this we are really maintaining that the thing which we at first thought we desired for its own sake, such as seeing a beautiful landscape, or doing a good action, is really only being desired for the sake of a feeling of enjoyment or gratification, or, to put it generally, pleasure, which we think it will cause in us. And correspondingly, where we think of the desire as moving us to act, we are really maintaining that what we at first thought our ultimate end is really only our penultimate end or the proximate means, and that our ultimate end is really a pleasure which we think this will cause. We are, however, apt to think of a thing's giving us enjoyment, or alternatively gratification, as if it were a quality of the thing, just as we think of the loudness of a noise as a quality of the noise. And our tendency to do this is strengthened by the fact that the ordinary way of stating the fact that something X excites a feeling of pleasure, or of gratification, is to say that X is pleasant or gratifying, a way of speaking which suggests that what is in fact a property possessed by X of causing a certain feeling is a quality of X. The tendency is mistaken, since, as anyone must allow in the end, something's giving us enjoyment is *not* a quality of it, and when we say that something *is* pleasant, we are not attributing to it a certain quality but stating that it has a certain effect. Nevertheless, the tendency exists. And when it is operative in us, we state our original contention by saying that in desiring to see a beautiful landscape for its own sake, we desire it as something which will be pleasant, and that when we are acting on the desire, our ultimate end is the seeing a beautiful landscape as something which will be pleasant, thereby representing what on our view is really the proximate means to our end as our end.

This being the line of thought to which I referred, it remains for me to try to show that it was taken by Aristotle. Before we consider details we can find two general considerations which are in favour of thinking that he took it. In the first place, if we assume it to be indisputable that he thought that there are things of a certain sort which we desire for their own sake, but that in desiring them we desire them in respect of having a certain character to which he refers by the term ἀγαθόν, and then ask 'What can be the character of which he is thinking?' the only possible answer seems to be: 'That of exciting either enjoyment or gratification.' And in particular two things are in favour of this answer. First, it is easy, from lack of consideration, to think of exciting pleasure as a quality of the thing desired—as indeed Aristotle appears to do when he speaks of virtuous actions (αἱ κατ' ἀρετὴν πράξεις) as φύσει ἡδέα and as ἡδεῖαι καθ' αὐτάς,[5] i.e. as pleasant in virtue of their own nature; and second, the perplexity in which he finds himself in Chapter 6 when trying to elucidate the meaning of ἀγαθόν would be accounted for if what he was referring to was something which is not in fact a character common to the various things said to be ἀγαθά, although he tended to think of it as if it was. In the second place he applies the term ἀγαθόν

---

[5] Ibid. i. 8. 11.

not only to the things which we desire for themselves, but also to the things which produce or preserve them, and it is difficult to see how he can apply the term to the latter unless ἀγαθόν means productive of pleasure, whether directly or not. In fact, only given this meaning is it possible to understand how Aristotle can speak not merely of τιμή but also of πλοῦτος as an ἀγαθόν.

To pass, however, to special considerations, we seem to find evidence, and decisive evidence, in a quarter in which we at first should least expect it. At the beginning of Chapter 4 he directs his hearers' attention to the question: τί ⟨ἐστι⟩ τὸ πάντων ἀκρότατον τῶν πρακτῶν ἀγαθῶν, i.e. 'What is it that is the greatest of all achievable goods?' and he proceeds to say that while there is general agreement about the name for it, since both the many and the educated say that it is happiness, yet they differ about what happiness is, the many considering it something the nature of which is clear and obvious, such as pleasure, wealth, or honour, whereas, he implies, the educated consider it something else of which the nature is not obvious. Then in the next chapter he proceeds to state what, to judge from the three most prominent types of life, that of enjoyment, the political life, and that of contemplation, various men consider that the good or happiness is, viz. enjoyment, honour, and contemplation. And later he gives his own view, contending, with the help of an argument based on the idea that man has a function, that happiness is ψυχῆς ἐνέργειά τις κατ' ἀρετὴν τελείαν.[6]

Here it has to be admitted that Aristotle is expressing himself in a misleading way. His question 'What is the greatest of goods?' can be treated as if it had been the question 'What is a man's ultimate end?' i.e. τὸ τέλος τὸ ἁπλῶς. For as Book I, 2, § 1 and Book I, 7 show, he considers that to find what is the greatest good, or the good, we must find a man's final end, i.e. that which he desires and aims at for its own sake, and in Book I, 5 he judges what men consider the good from what their lives show to be their ultimate aim. And his answer to this question, if taken as it stands, is undeniably absurd. For, so understood, it is to the effect that, though all men, when asked 'What is the ultimate end?', answer by using the same word, viz. εὐδαιμονία, yet, as they differ about what εὐδαιμονία is, i.e., really, about the thing for which they are using the word εὐδαιμονία to stand, some using it to designate pleasure, others wealth, and so on, they are in substance giving different answers, some meaning by the word εὐδαιμονία pleasure, others wealth, and so on. But of course this is not what Aristotle meant. He certainly did not think that anyone ever meant by εὐδαιμονία either τιμή or πλοῦτος; and he certainly did not himself mean by it ψυχῆς ἐνέργειά τις κατ' ἀρετὴν τελείαν. What he undoubtedly meant and thought others meant by the word εὐδαιμονία is happiness. Plainly, too, what he thought men differed about was not the nature of happiness but the conditions of its realization, and when he says that εὐδαιμονία is ψυχῆς ἐνέργειά τις κατ'

---

[6] Ibid. i. 13. 1.

ἀρετὴν τελείαν, what he really means is that the latter is what is required for the realization of happiness. Consideration of the *Ethics* by itself should be enough to convince us of this, but if it is not, we need only take into account his elucidation of the meaning of the question 'τί ἐστιν;' to be sure that when he asks 'τί ἐστι ἡ εὐδαιμονία;' his meaning is similar to that of the man who, when he asks 'What is colour?' or 'What is sound?' really means 'What are the conditions necessary for its realization?' We must therefore understand Aristotle in Chapter 4 to be in effect contending that while it is universally admitted that our ultimate aim is happiness, there is great divergence of view about the conditions, or, more precisely, the proximate conditions, of its realization.

But, this conclusion reached, we can plainly take one step farther and conclude that Aristotle himself is in agreement with the view that our ultimate end is happiness, and that, taking its truth for granted, his *Ethics* is concerned first to prove that it is by virtuous action that it will be realized, and then to work out in detail the character of virtuous action, so that we shall be better able to obtain our aim. In other words, we can conclude that his real answer to the question, 'What is τὸ τέλος τὸ ἁπλῶς, i.e. our ultimate aim?' is not, as we may at first think, ψυχῆς ἐνέργειά τις κατ' ἀρετὴν τελείαν but εὐδαιμονία, i.e. happiness. Putting this otherwise, we can say that the accurate statement of his own view is to be found in I. 12, where he gives as a reason why εὐδαιμονία is τίμιον, whereas ἀρετή is merely ἐπαινετόν, that it is for the sake of εὐδαιμονία that we all do everything.[7]

Now, if by thus going behind Aristotle's terminology we are driven to conclude that Aristotle really considered our ultimate end to be always our happiness, or alternatively some particular state of happiness on our part—for sometimes he seems to imply the one view and sometimes the other—we are also driven to conclude that, though he at times makes statements to the contrary, he also holds that where we are said to have as our ultimate end τιμή or ἐνέργειά τις κατ' ἀρετήν or anything else of a kind which we consider a condition of happiness, the thing in question is really according to him only our penultimate end, and the desire of it is only a derivative desire depending on our desire of happiness. And then it becomes obvious that when he implies, as he always does, that in desiring one of these things we desire it as an ἀγαθόν, what he means by ἀγαθόν is 'productive of a state, or rather a feeling, of happiness', i.e., as I think we may say in this context, a feeling of pleasure. Further, this being so, we have to allow that he fundamentally misrepresents his own problem. Assuming that we all always have either a single ultimate aim, or at least, alternatively, an aim of one sort, what he ostensibly maintains is that we are uncertain about its nature, and that therefore he has to discover its nature in order to help us to achieve it. But, as we must now conclude, what he is really maintaining is that though the nature

---

[7] [ταύτης (i.e. εὐδαιμονίας) γὰρ χάριν τὰ λοιπὰ πάντα πάντες πράττομεν, Ibid. i. 12. 8.]

of our ultimate aim, happiness, is known to us, for we all know the nature of that for which the word 'happiness' stands, we are doubtful about the proximate means to it, and that consequently he has to discover the proximate means. In other words, in maintaining ψυχῆς ἐνέργειά τις κατ' ἀρετὴν τελείαν to be our ultimate end of the nature of which we are uncertain, he is putting what on his view is really the proximate means to our end in the place of what on his view is really our end. And if we ask 'How can he have come to misrepresent his own view so fundamentally?', then, if the contentions already advanced are true, we have at hand a satisfactory answer. We can reply that the misrepresentation is due to his making two mistakes to which we are all prone: first, that of thinking of the property of causing happiness as a quality of what causes it, and secondly, that of thinking that where we are aiming at something of a certain kind for its own sake, and so having it as our ultimate end, we are nevertheless aiming at it in respect of its having a certain character.

By way of conclusion it may be well to refer to an objection which will inevitably be raised, viz. that I have been, in effect, representing Aristotle as a psychological hedonist, and that to do this is absurd. I admit the charge, but do not consider the representation absurd. It seems not only possible, but common, to hold that there are a number of things other than pleasure which we desire for their own sake, and then when the question is raised, 'How is it that we desire these things?', to reply: 'Only because we think they will give us pleasure.' In my opinion, the reply is mistaken, and is made only because we are apt to think of the gratification necessarily consequent on the thought that something which we have desired is realized as that the thought of which excites the desire. But the mistake is a very insidious one, as, if I am right, is shown by the fact that Green, in spite of all the trouble he takes to point out that Mill falls into it, falls into it himself.

8. Manuscript on Morals

I. The Main Questions about Duty

The study of books on Moral Philosophy is apt to produce an acute sense of dissatisfaction. It is not merely that the conclusions, and still more the arguments, of particular thinkers are unconvincing. There is an air of artificiality about the whole subject; and in particular we find it difficult to say precisely what the main problems are which the various writers consider it their business to solve. It would probably be agreed that the central subject is that of duty or moral obligation; even when we read Plato and Aristotle, who have no obvious word for it, our chief aim is to find out what they have to say about duty. Yet we find it difficult to state exactly what the various writers are trying to establish or even to discover about it. We may perhaps suggest vague phrases for their object, saying, for example, that it is to vindicate morality, or to find the basis or ground of moral obligation, or to discover the sort of life we ought to lead, or to find the relation between duty and goodness, or, again, to find the relation between duty and happiness. But such phrases are too vague to be satisfying, and they fail to account for the artificiality with which the subject seems invested. The prevailing impression produced is that, although when men begin to reflect about what may be called their moral notions, they find themselves faced by important and difficult questions, it is not easy even to say precisely what the questions are.

Assuming that we are thus dissatisfied and perplexed, the first step towards the discovery of the truth would seem to consist in an endeavour to clear the ground by formulating clearly and unambiguously the main questions about duty to which we really want the answer, and, in doing so, to gain what assistance we can from what may be called the ordinary literature of the subject.

If we propose to ourselves this task, it will probably occur to us that there is one question which should take precedence of all others, whether as a matter of history it has been raised first or not. This is the simple question 'What *is* moral obligation?' When we say that we *ought*, or that it is our *duty*, or that we are *morally bound* to do some action e.g., to pay some debt, it is plain that we *mean* something by 'ought', or 'duty', or 'morally bound'. Consequently the first question to be answered may seem to be the question 'What do we mean by this

[The chapters have been edited to eliminate direct overlap with 'Moral Obligation' and some titles (II, III, and IV) changed by the editor. Some references in the notes have also been completed and appear in square brackets. Ed.]

term?', or, what comes to the same thing, 'What is *the being morally bound* to do so and so?' In other words, if we are to consider the subject of duty, our first task, it may seem, is to obtain a *definition* of duty or moral obligation. And it would be only to state this in other terms, if we were to say that our first task must consist in *analysing the idea or notion of duty*; for here by 'the idea or notion of duty' we should only mean the nature of duty in general, and we should mean by 'analysing the nature of duty' the making clear to ourselves what an action's being a duty or what the being morally bound to do some action is.

It will, however, be clear on reflection that the question 'What is moral obligation?' is not a real question. We have only to consider its nature to be able to dismiss it as unreal. Moral obligation, i.e., that for which the phrase 'moral obligation', or the word 'duty', stands, is something of which the nature is simple and therefore *sui generis*; consequently its nature, although apprehended by us, is indefinable, i.e. incapable of being expressed in terms of the nature of other things. It is what Locke would have described as a simple idea, and in that respect it resembles space, time, red, i.e. a red colour, pleasure, identity and difference, and—to take instances which might be considered controversial—knowledge, and continuity. To be definable, a thing must be complex,[1] its definition consisting in a statement of the elements of which its nature consists. Selfishness, for instance, is definable, although no doubt difficult to define, but that is only because we mean by 'selfishness' something the nature of which is complex. Thus if we contended that selfishness consists in caring much for what is advantageous to ourselves and caring little for what is advantageous to others, the contention, whether true or false, would bring out the complexity which we think inherent in selfishness.

The unreality of the question 'What is moral obligation?' will most easily become clear if we first appreciate the unreality of a parallel question, such as the question 'What is space?' If the question 'What is space?' is to be a real question, i.e. not a mere form of words but a form of words to which there corresponds on our part a questioning attitude of mind, then in order to be able to put the question to ourselves we must already be apprehending the nature of that for which the word 'space' stands, since otherwise we shall not understand the meaning of the question, and we must also be ignorant of its nature, since otherwise the question could not be to us a question. And that we do apprehend its nature and therefore cannot put the question to ourselves is shown by the fact that in ordinary life we never fail to distinguish what we should call a particular space from what we should call, e.g. a particular time, or a particular body which occupies the particular space, or in general, from what we might call a particular anything else. And we may put the reason why the question is unreal

---

[1] For the meaning here of 'complex' and 'simple', cf. J. Cook Wilson, *Statement and Inference*, ed. Farquharson, A., II, sections 276–8, pp. 498–504 [Oxford: University Press, 1926, repr. 1969 Ed.].

in a paradoxical form by saying that it is by its very nature a question to which we must already know the answer in order to be able to ask it. It may be objected that the question cannot be unreal, because there are contexts in which it is both significant and appropriate to state that space is *space*, and this statement can be considered as an answer to the question 'What *is* space?'. But plainly when we have occasion to state that space is space, our object is just not to state what space is but on the contrary to point out that space, in virtue of its special nature, is just different and therefore to be distinguished from everything else, and that it is therefore just not something the nature of which can be expressed in terms of other things.

Mutatis mutandis, exactly the same statements can be made about the question 'What is moral obligation?'. The mere fact that we are proposing to ourselves to ascertain the main questions which can be raised about duty, presupposes that we know what it is to be morally bound to do so and so; and if we did not know this, no one could help us to acquire the knowledge by attempting to formulate the nature of moral obligation in terms of the nature of other things that we know. It is, no doubt, true that owing to lack of consideration of the nature of the question 'What is moral obligation?', moral philosophers have made statements which either are or imply a definition of moral obligation. Thus when Herbert Spencer maintains that the sense of duty or of moral obligation is transitory and will diminish as fast as moralization increases,[2] he is really implying, as the context shows, that to be morally obliged is to be obliged, i.e. coerced, by the fear of political, divine and social penalties. Again when Hutcheson says 'When we say one is obliged to do an action, we either mean (1) that the action is necessary to obtain happiness to the agent, or to avoid misery; or (2) that every spectator, or he himself upon reflection must approve his action . . .',[3] he is really implying that the being morally obliged to do a certain action *is* our being under the necessity of approving the action in virtue of our moral sense. Again when Kant refers to moral principles as moral *laws*, he is implying that the nature of moral obligation, if not definable in terms of legal obligation, is at least to some extent capable of elucidation by the analogy of legal obligation. But all such statements covertly resolve moral obligation into something else which is not moral obligation. And against such statements, the apparent tautology 'moral obligation is moral obligation' is a useful reminder of the fact that the nature of moral obligation, like that of certain other things, is *sui generis*.

Although, however, we cannot ask, and therefore cannot answer, the question 'What is the being morally bound to do so and so?' or the corresponding question 'What is the being morally bound *not* to do so and so?', and so cannot answer

---

[2] H. Spencer, *The Data of Ethics* (New York: A. L. Burt, 1879), section 46, 151.
[3] F. Hutcheson, *An Essay on the Nature and Conduct of the Passions and Affections, With Illustrations on the Moral Sense* (3rd edn., 1742), Scholars, Facsimiles Reprints (Gainesville, 1969), 232.

the equivalent questions 'What is rightness?' or 'What is wrongness?' there is something else which we can do, and can usefully do, instead. We can recognize the ultimate nature of the difference between the things which are thus referred to and certain other things from which moral philosophers have sometimes failed to distinguish them, such as goodness and badness, advantageousness and disadvantageousness. And in particular it is in certain contexts important to recognize that the statement that some act is right or ought to be done, or that it is wrong or ought not to be done, and the statement that some act is good or that it is bad, are statements of quite different kinds, even though their meanings may be related.

It will probably next occur to us that though we cannot ask 'What *is* rightness, or moral obligation?, this so-called question is only a mistaken version of another question which forms the real question to be answered. This is the question, 'What characteristic must an action have, if it is to be right?' i.e. 'What renders or constitutes a right action right?', or, more shortly, though less accurately, 'What constitutes an action right?'[4] There are various actions which are right or duties; they can only be right, it would seem, in virtue of having a common characteristic, and consequently this common characteristic has to be found. The question will carry with it the corresponding question 'What constitutes a wrong action wrong?'; and it will be parallel to, if not identical with, the question in the *Republic* 'What is justice?', where those who put the question are not asking 'What does the term "just" mean?' but are looking for the common character, to be expressed in some general formula, which constitutes just acts just. Further the question will be similar to certain others, such as 'What is beauty?' or 'What is courage?', where what is being looked for is really not the meaning of the terms 'beautiful' or 'courageous'—but the common character which things or acts must possess if they are to be beautiful or courageous, i.e. that which *constitutes* beautiful things beautiful or courageous acts courageous.

The question, it should be noticed, has two presuppositions which are apt to pass unnoticed. In the first place, if we ask it we imply, as has been suggested, that there *is* a single common characteristic uniting the various acts that are duties. For if two right acts are right in virtue of different characteristics, it will be a mere mistake to ask the *general* question 'What constitutes right actions right?', for the truth must then be that there is a plurality of characteristics which render an action right, and so no single common characteristic at all. The question is at least in this respect precisely parallel to the questions 'What is goodness?', 'What is beauty?', and 'What is courage?', i.e. really to the questions 'What constitutes things which are good, beautiful or courageous, good, beautiful or courageous

---

[4] The question in this latter form, though less accurate, is not likely to mislead us, since though in putting the question we refer to an action, the form of the question implies that it is being asked only about a right action.

respectively?' For should there turn out to be no *common* constitutive characteristic, these questions too will prove merely to involve a mistake. Moreover the difficulty of answering a question of this form even about courage, where it is at least hard to deny that there is some such common characteristic, suggests that the answer to the question 'What constitutes right actions right?'—should there be one—may be difficult to find.

In the second place, if we put the question, we are implying that in ordinary life we already know, or at least can discover when we wish, what actions in particular are right. For we are asking, not 'What renders *any* action right?', which would be nonsense, but 'What renders *certain* actions, viz. *those which are right*, right?'; and therefore we are implying that we already know, or can at will discover, what actions are right. More precisely, we are implying that we have already apprehended certain acts to be right or duties in virtue of some vague apprehension of that character which renders them duties, and that what we want to gain is a clear apprehension of that character which can be expressed in some general phrase. And here again there is a precise parallel in the case of the analogous questions 'What is courage?', 'What is beauty?' and 'What is goodness?'. For in asking, for example, 'What is courage?' we are implying that we have recognized or can recognize directly that certain acts are courageous in particular and are trying to apprehend clearly the common character which has led or may lead us to recognize them to be courageous. Further it may be noted that just because to ask 'What constitutes right actions right?' is to imply that we know what acts in particular are right, if we do ask the question, we cannot expect the answer to be of use in practice. For should we come to doubt whether in thinking some particular action to be right, we think so truly, the doubt would equally extend to the truth of any thought as to what constitutes right actions right, since the truth of this latter thought would wholly depend on the truth of our thoughts that this and certain other acts are right.

It should also be noticed that if as the result of reflection we cease to imply that in our so-called unreflective state of ordinary life we *know* what is right in particular, and if, instead, we think that in this state we simply *think; whether truly or falsely*, that certain actions are right, the question 'What constitutes right actions right?' becomes transformed. It becomes the question 'What is the common character which leads us to think certain actions right, whether truly or falsely?', or more exactly, 'What is the precise nature of that characteristic the vague apprehension of which in certain actions leads us in ordinary life to *think* them right?'. This question, also, seems a question which we really can ask, though of course not at the same time as the preceding question, since we cannot ask at the same time two questions, one of which implies that we know and the other of which implies that we do not know what is right in particular. Nevertheless it should be noticed that this question relates not to right actions but solely to what will have to be called our moral thoughts or convictions, i.e. our thoughts that certain actions are right, and an answer to it will throw no light whatever on the question 'What constitutes a right action right?'.

There remains to be noticed a question about moral obligation which when stated nakedly looks so ridiculous that it seems a waste of time even to refer to it. This is the question, 'Why are we bound, or why ought we, to do what is right?'. The question not only looks but is ridiculous. For to refer to a certain group of actions as right actions is to imply that we already know that they are right, and therefore, since 'right' is after all only a synonym for 'ought to be done', that we already know that we ought to do them. Yet to ask 'why ought we to do them?' is to imply that we have still to be convinced, and therefore *a fortiori* do not as yet know that we ought to do them. We cannot ask a question, the very terms of which imply that we know what also by the terms of the question we do not. Yet the question has, at any rate as a matter of words, been asked, and we shall find it necessary to refer to it later.

Of the three questions already referred to only one has so far survived as legitimate, viz. the question 'What constitutes right actions right?'. This question can strictly be said to be a question about moral obligation, as its formulation implies; and it presupposes, as has been pointed out, that we know what actions are right in particular.

If, however, we think of the history of Moral Philosophy we see that the question which has been raised first in connection with moral obligation is one which implies that we do not know what is right in particular, and which, though it may lead to questions about moral obligation, is strictly speaking a question about the truth of what may be called our moral convictions. We cannot, of course, ask ourselves questions about duty any more than about anything else *in vacuo*. A questioning frame of mind presupposes and arises out of an unquestioning frame of mind. Indeed we can only put a question to ourselves if, as we may say, we think certain things without question or unquestioningly. If we ask ourselves 'How did that man get on to that rock?', we are thinking without question that he is on the rock, and that it is difficult for a man to get there. And in particular we can only ask ourselves what may roughly be called questions about duty because we already have what may for the present be called moral 'convictions', or 'convictions' that we ought to do certain actions. The attitude of mind implied, for which the term 'conviction', though inaccurate, since it implies uncertainty, is the least inaccurate, is both unreflective and unquestioning. It can fairly be said to be *unreflective* because, although in having these 'convictions' we must as self-conscious beings be aware that we are having them, we are not interested in this fact and do not make it the object of consideration, i.e. we do not reflect upon this fact. It can fairly be said to be *unquestioning* because, although in this attitude we may, when the circumstances are unusual, be doubtful whether a certain action is a duty, yet normally we are not. In ordinary circumstances it no more occurs to us that we may be mistaken in thinking certain actions duties than it does when, for instance, looking at something near the horizon we think it to be a tree.

Now plainly the history of Moral Philosophy shows that the considerations which have first led men to ask themselves what may roughly be called questions about moral obligation have led them to wonder whether in thinking in their ordinary unreflective state that certain actions were right, they were thinking truly. The first question, therefore, which men have asked themselves implies that so far from *knowing* what is right, they have only various thoughts about it, the truth of which has still to be determined.

The considerations are two. Of these the first, together with the line of thought which it has provoked, might be stated thus:

'The Greek Sophists laid stress on the fact, which early comes home to individuals of an enquiring turn of mind, that the various particular actions which we think duties, although they fall into a variety of kinds, such as keeping a promise or obeying the government, agree in being disadvantageous to the agent, although advantageous to someone else. The Sophists, taking for granted that right action must be advantageous to the agent, concluded that these actions were not really right and even went so far as to offer an explanation of how men came to make the mistake of thinking them right. Others, however, whose moral convictions were stronger thought otherwise. Plato, for example, shared the presupposition of the Sophists and consequently thought that the obvious disadvantages of doing these actions at least constituted an objection to the truth of our conviction that they are duties. But he felt that the objection was capable of being met, and indeed met in the only way possible, that of showing that in some other and less obvious way these actions were advantageous, and advantageous to an extent which outweighed their disadvantageousness. And in the *Republic* he put forward Glaucon and Adeimantus to represent this frame of mind. In particular he made Glaucon in effect ask Socrates: "What is it which renders the actions which we think right really beneficial to the agent, in spite of the obvious disadvantage of doing them?"; and he represented Glaucon as wanting an answer in order to convince himself that in thinking certain actions right or duties, he and others were not mistaken. In fact the main task which Plato set himself in the *Republic* was to answer this question. Plato may thus be said to hold that, as soon as we realize a certain disadvantageousness in doing the actions which in our unquestioning and unreflective state of mind we think right, we find ourselves, if our moral convictions are strong, faced with the problem which we must solve unless we are to be forced to allow that these convictions are a mere mistake. We have, according to Plato, to vindicate to ourselves the truth of our ordinary moral convictions, and to do so by answering the question, "What is the real gain to ourselves of doing the actions which we and others think right?"'

Certain reflections might be added. 'At any rate,' it might be said, 'at a certain stage in the history of our own minds we share Plato's difficulty. Moreover Plato, in feeling the difficulty, and we, in sharing it with him, are right. For when we think it out we have to allow that, although the characteristic which has in fact led us to think some action right is never its advantageousness, yet it cannot really be right unless it is advantageous; so that if complete investigation showed it not be advantageous to the agent, we should have to allow that we were mistaken in thinking it right. Again it has been one of the main objects of many of those whom we call moral philosophers to remove the difficulty, and thereby to vindicate morality, i.e. really, the truth of our ordinary moral convictions. Of these writers Butler is a conspicuous modern instance. For one of the chief aims of his *Sermons* is to show that acting on the dictates of our conscience will really prove to our advantage, at any rate if the facts of theology are taken into account; and he seems to be urging that the vindication of our moral convictions requires such proof when he says "Let it be allowed, though virtue or moral rectitude does indeed consist in affection to and pursuit of what is right and good, as such; yet, that when we sit down in a cool hour, we can neither justify to ourselves this or any other pursuit, till we are convinced that it will be for our happiness, or at least not contrary to it."[5]

Here, even if we do not assume that Plato and Butler have been rightly interpreted, we have at least two questions which we can say have been asked, and possibly been asked by ourselves. The questions, however, are only loosely speaking questions about duty or right actions. Strictly speaking, the one is a question about our ordinary moral convictions, viz. 'are these convictions that certain actions are duties true, in view of the obvious disadvantages of doing these actions?'; and the other is a question about the actions which we thus think are duties, viz. 'What renders these actions nevertheless really advantageous to the agent?' And the relation between the questions consists in the fact that an affirmative answer to the first question requires an answer to the second.

Now we need only consider the nature of our moral convictions and also that of the assumption implied in asking these questions to be able to dispose of these questions once for all, and to maintain that if Plato and Butler have here been rightly interpreted, they were on a completely wrong track.

First, as regards our moral convictions, in thinking in ordinary life that certain actions are a duty or right, we are in every case not simply thinking that the action in question is right but thinking of its rightness as constituted by the possession of a certain characteristic other than that of being advantageous to the agent. For each of these actions is, and is thought of by us as being, a particular action of a certain kind which is indicated by certain general words contained in the phrase by which we refer to the action, e.g. *'fulfilling* the *promise* which we made to X yesterday', or *'looking after* our *parents'*. And we do not think these actions

---

[5] [J. Butler, *Fifteen Sermons*, Sermon XI, in D. D. Raphael (ed.), *British Moralists*, 1650–1800, I, s. 423, 373 (Oxford, 1969). Ed.]

right *blindly*, i.e. irrespectively of the special character which we think of them as possessing; we think of each of them as right in virtue of its possessing a particular characteristic of the kind which is indicated by the phrase by which we refer to it. Thus in thinking that keeping our promise to X is right we are thinking of its rightness as constituted by its being the *keeping of our promise* to X. This is obvious because we should never, for instance, think of giving as an illustration of an act which we think right telling X what we think of him, or meeting him in London, even though we may think that if we apprehended these actions in certain other aspects we should think them right. Consequently in ordinary life we are thinking of the rightness of the various actions which we think right as in each case constituted by the possession of the characteristic which is indicated by the phrase by which we refer to the action and which is therefore something other than that of being advantageous to the agent.

If now we return to consider the first presupposition, we see that if we are in earnest with the view that an action to be right must be advantageous to the agent, we cannot stop short of maintaining that it is precisely advantageousness and nothing else which constitutes an action right. For if we were to allow that the rightness of an action is constituted by the possession of some other characteristic, we should have to allow that we could never come to know whether a right action must be advantageous or whether it need not without first knowing what this characteristic is, and then ascertaining—much as Butler tried to do—whether the nature of human beings and of the world in which they have to act is such as to necessitate that actions possessing this characteristic are advantageous. We should therefore have to allow that even if it be true that right actions are advantageous, we could not possibly come to know this fact unless we already knew that actions possessing a certain characteristic are right, and right, whether advantageous or not, and that therefore it could not possibly be a condition of an action's being right that it should be advantageous.

From this consideration of our moral convictions and of the initial assumption it follows that in the state of mind which gives rise to the two questions under consideration we are exposed to a fatal dilemma. If we persist in maintaining that an act to be right must be advantageous, we shall have to allow that our unreflective moral convictions were simply a mistake, and are therefore incapable of vindication, since our unreflective conviction, e.g. that we ought to keep our promise to X, is really the conviction that we ought to do this as being the keeping of our promise to X, and not as being advantageous to ourselves. We shall also have to allow that when we really *think*, we in fact only think of that or of any other action as right, if we think of it as advantageous, and that we in fact only think of it as right *in virtue* of its advantageousness. We shall also have to allow not merely that it is a duty to do whatever is advantageous to ourselves but also that this is our only duty. If, on the other hand, in order to avoid these consequences we still insist that our ordinary convictions are true, we shall have to allow that as in that case what leads us in having these convictions to think certain actions right must in fact be what renders them right, advantageousness to the agent does not render them right, and that therefore our initial assumption that an act to be right must be advantageous was a mistake. In other words any reconciliation of our ordinary moral convictions with our initial assumption is impossible. Either the one or the other has to be abandoned.

The fact is that when we are in the state of doubt in question what we really have to do is to put to ourselves the definite question 'Is or is not the rightness of a right act constituted by advantageousness to the agent?'. And once the issue is thus squarely presented, there can be no doubt about the answer. For no one, when he puts the issue clearly before himself really thinks that the fact that a certain action would be advantageous or beneficial to himself constitutes the action a duty on his part. And if we consider any case in which we do in fact think that some action which will be advantageous is a duty we shall have to allow that what in fact has led us to think the action a duty is some characteristic which, whatever it is, is not that of being advantageous.

The fact is that when we reflect we have simply to abandon the very presupposition which has given rise to the attempt to vindicate the truth of our moral convictions, viz. the presupposition that an action to be right must be advantageous. And if we seek to explain how we have come to take this advantageousness for granted, we seem driven to find the explanation in one or both of two possibilities. We may have failed to distinguish the view that the man who has done something which he ought will *in fact* gain from the view that he *deserves* to gain. And we may have failed to distinguish two radically different senses of the word 'ought' which shortly will have to be considered.

We may therefore omit all consideration in detail of the attempts made by moral philosophers and others to vindicate the truth of our moral conviction by showing that acting on these convictions will really be to our advantage. And in particular we need not consider whether these attempts are facilitated by the contention of Plato and others that the advantages which accrue from doing the actions which we think right are of a superior kind to those which accrue from doing those which we think wrong. Any such attempt is doomed to failure from the beginning, and, as soon as we realize the mistake involved, we shall cease to make the attempt.

II. Why Ought I to Do My Duty? Two Different Senses of the Word 'Ought'

There is however a quite different line of reflection which has led men to question or doubt the truth of their unreflective moral convictions, and which has led to a further question in the endeavour to answer it. It of course soon occurs to us that men's moral convictions exhibit great differences. It strikes us not merely that the convictions of our maturity differ substantially from those of our youth, but still more that the convictions of men of different races and still more of different stages of civilization are very varied. And we reflect that since there are these differences, at best only some of the convictions can be true. This reflection, coupled with the idea that in childhood we have acquired our convictions by being *taught* that certain acts are right and certain others wrong, and so have at best gained our convictions at second hand, leads us to doubt the truth of all men's unreflective moral convictions. For there being no means of deciding which among these convictions is true, it seems possible that all of them are false. We are thus led, as Descartes was led with regard to his convictions on all matters, to ask which of these moral convictions are true and which are false, and to attempt to answer this question, by endeavouring to answer *de novo* another question, viz. 'What ought we, or what really ought we, to do in life?'. This question in turn leads to another, viz. 'What characteristic must an action have, if it is to be right or a duty?' Undoubtedly too the state is not uncommon in which men, having come in this way to distrust all their moral convictions, set themselves the task of trying to find out *de novo* or, as they would say, from first principles, what they ought to do in life generally, with a view to applying the knowledge thus gained in practice and to testing the truth of their existing moral convictions. And we find Sidgwick, for example, actually assigning this task to Ethics when he defines ethics, as he in effect does, as the endeavour to answer the question 'What ought I to do or aim at?'[6] and says 'the aim of Ethics is to systematize and free from error the apparent cognitions which most men have of the rightness or reasonableness of conduct'.[7]

Two features of this state of doubt should be emphasized. In the first place it differs from the state of doubt just discussed in one important respect. When we doubt the truth of our ordinary moral convictions on the ground that the various actions which we are convinced we ought to do are disadvantageous, since the ground of our doubt is a characteristic common to all those actions alike, we think that any process, if there be one, which will resolve the doubt in the case of one of these convictions will equally resolve it in the case of any other. Consequently we think that the final result of any attempt to resolve the doubt will have to be either that all our moral convictions will be left standing, or that all will disappear, as being false, and will disappear without having the possibility of a substitute. On the other hand when we doubt the truth of these convictions on the ground that they are inconsistent with our previous convictions or with the convictions of others, we are asking '*Which* if any, among all these convictions is true?'.

---

[6] [H. Sidgwick, *The Methods of Ethics* (7th edn., London, 1962), 1–2. Ed.]   [7] Ibid., 77.

In the second place the fact that in this, as in the former, state of doubt we are doubting the truth of *all* our moral convictions needs emphasis. For it shows that, strictly speaking, the question to which the doubt gives rise is the question 'What, *if anything*, ought we to do in life?' and that, strictly speaking, the question to which this in turn gives rise is the question 'What is the characteristic, *if there be one*, the possession of which will constitute an action right?' And it also shows that if we are to succeed in answering the former question we shall have to satisfy three conditions. First, we must not at any stage make use of any of our ordinary moral convictions by appealing to the fact that in ordinary life we think certain actions right. Otherwise we shall only be begging the question. Second, our procedure must be different from the procedure, whatever it be, by which we have attained our ordinary convictions; otherwise our answer will be exposed to a similar doubt. Third, our procedures must take the form of a *proof* that we ought to do certain actions. For if we were to maintain that we have the power to apprehend *directly* certain actions to be right, and that we can answer the general question by the exercise of this power, we should be exposed to the fatal objection that if so, our ordinary moral convictions could truly be said to be the result of the exercise of this power and so would really be knowledge and therefore in no need of vindication or criticism, and further that in that case, the divergence of men's ordinary convictions would be left unaccounted for. . . .

We should now return to the question 'why should I do my duty?', or, more fully, 'why ought I to do what it is my duty to do?'. For, though, as has been pointed out, the question taken as it stands is absurd, as implying that we do not know what by the terms of the question we do know, yet, as a matter of words, it has actually been asked and discussed; and we may even find that we are asking the question ourselves. Suppose some one is trying to persuade me to do something which I am very unwilling to do. He may succeed in persuading me that it is a duty on my part to do the action. At a certain phase of my experience, I may find myself saying, 'Well, I grant that the act is a duty, but even so, why should or why ought I to do it?'. Again it looks as though Butler was insisting that this question has to be answered in his well-known dictum already quoted to the effect that we can neither justify the pursuit of what is right or of anything else, till we are convinced that it will be for our happiness. For in referring here to the pursuit of what is *right*, he is implying that we *know* certain actions to be right, and consequently his reference to *justifying* the pursuit of what is right seems to imply that even where we *know* certain actions to be right, we still need to discover a reason why we ought to do them.

Plato again can plausibly be represented as trying in the *Republic* to show why we *should* do what is right.

The explanation of the fact that the question has been, and is still, put can only be that, as actually asked, its meaning is other than what the words in which it is expressed naturally suggest. The clue to its meaning lies in an ambiguity of the term 'ought', which will be found to have two radically different senses, the one of moral and the other not. The difference between these senses, which Kant brought to light when he distinguished categorical and hypothetical imperatives, is so radical that in the interest of clearness it is worth dwelling on even at the risk of covering familiar ground.

A statement of the form 'you ought to do so and so' may have either of two totally different kinds of meaning, the one moral and the other not,—the particular kind of meaning being usually indicated by the context. Suppose I say to X 'you ought to use plenty of soap'. If I say this in a normal context, as where e.g. I am watching X washing himself without much success, I am presupposing that X is wanting and endeavouring to become clean, i.e. that he is acting with the purpose of becoming clean; and what I am asserting is that putting plenty of soap on his hands is the proper step to take, or the act which he *should* or *ought* to do, as being the act which will lead to the realization of his purpose. Here 'should' or 'ought' has no moral sense whatever. I could in the same sense say to a poisoner 'you ought to give a larger dose'. But the term has an appropriateness which comes to light when we speak of the action as the *proper* step for X to take. This appropriateness implies, and indeed depends on the fact, that X has a certain purpose, i.e. a certain something the desire of which for its own sake is leading him to act. In fact 'should be done' or 'ought to be done' in such a context *means* 'proper for realizing the agent's purpose'. On the other hand suppose that in a normal context I say to X 'you ought to keep your promise to Y'. Here I am not presupposing that X has a certain purpose, or indeed any purpose at all, and what I am asserting is that it is X's *duty* to keep his promise, 'ought' here meaning *morally* ought. And I am thinking of the truth or falsity of my statement as wholly independent of what X's purpose is and even of whether he has a purpose.

Kant does not expressly point out that the two meanings are quite different. On the contrary his language implies that they are not, since he designates statements of both kinds by the same term, viz. 'imperatives'. But his whole account of the meanings of these statements and especially his insistence that statements of the second kind involve no reference to a purpose shows that he thought of these two meanings as quite different, and in fact one of his most important contributions to moral philosophy may be said to consist in his insistence on this radical difference. His phrases, however, for the two kinds, viz. '*hypothetical* imperatives' and '*categorical* imperatives' are unfortunate. He implies that a statement of the first kind can be called hypothetical on the ground that in it we really only state, e.g., that X ought to use plenty of soap, *if* his purpose is to become clean. But, as Kant himself sees, we only make the statement 'You ought to use plenty of soap.'; to some one who, we think, actually has the becoming clean as his purpose—otherwise we should not think it true; and the statement, being thus addressed, implies no 'if' whatever. Moreover even Kant himself to some extent goes back on his own terminology. For he distinguishes one special kind of hypothetical imperative, which he calls a counsel of prudence, from all others, which in contrast he calls precepts of skill. This special kind is that where the purpose presupposed is one which Kant thinks common to everyone, viz. the becoming happy; it might be illustrated by 'You ought to make friends.', or even by 'You ought to keep your promises.', if stated with the implication that the agent's aim is to become happy. And to this kind of hypothetical imperative Kant applies the term 'assertorial', thereby, of course, implying that here the term 'hypothetical' is out of place.

If we refer to the distinction as that between moral and non-moral imperatives, we at least get rid of the mistake implied by the use of the terms 'categorical' and 'hypothetical'. But even the term 'imperative' is open to criticism. Kant of course chooses it because he thinks that moral principles present themselves to us as the commands of a ruler or legislator and this choice is connected with his doctrine that moral principles are of the nature of moral *laws*. But since the phrase 'moral law' is at best only a misleading metaphor which does nothing to elucidate the nature of moral principles, and since to refer to a statement containing the term 'ought' as an imperative is to imply that what we call the fact that a certain act ought to be done really consists in our being commanded to do it, it is better to drop the term 'imperative' altogether. Unfortunately there is no appropriate substitute, and for lack of a better phrase it seems best to refer to the two kinds of statement as statements of a moral 'ought' and of a non-moral 'ought' respectively.

It may, however, seem to be going too far to maintain that the statement of a non-moral 'ought' presupposes the thought of some *actual* purpose. For, first, when we are asking how to achieve a certain purpose, as when wanting to be at a certain place with the least trouble we ask which turning we should take, it would seem that the purpose cannot as yet be ours, since *ex hypothesi* we do not as yet know what steps to take and therefore cannot be taking steps to achieve it. But here the answer of course is that acquisition of the necessary knowledge is the first step required and that in endeavouring to acquire it we already have the purpose in question. Again in the second place it may be contended that we may continue to state a non-moral ought even when we think a man has ceased to have the purpose which it presupposes. Thus a dentist, it may be said, may infer from my visit to him that my purpose is to suffer as little toothache as possible and may in consequence say 'you ought to let me take out a certain tooth'; but if he finds that out of fear I hesitate and in fact become wholly undecided—so that my purpose has for the time being disappeared—he may still repeat the statement. This contention, however, can be met by a simple denial. The dentist will not repeat the statement. He will at best only introduce an 'if' and say 'should you once more come to have the minimum of toothache as your aim, the proper step for you to take will be to let me extract the tooth'. But, it will be rejoined, there is still something else which the dentist may do. He may point out that the more distant relief will more than compensate for the more violent pain of extraction, so that by submitting to him I shall suffer less pain altogether; and if he does so he will imply, even if he does not go so far as to say, that I ought to aim at suffering the minimum of pain altogether rather than at the absence of immediate acute pain. It is obvious, however, that in this last statement, the term 'ought', if appropriate at all, has a *moral* sense; and again that the form of the statement, viz. that I ought to *aim at*, as distinct from *do*, so and so, differs from that of any normal statement of an 'ought', whether moral or non-moral, and raises the question which will have to be considered later whether it can possibly be true that there is something which we ought to aim at, as distinct from something which we ought to *do*.

In the light of the two different senses of the word 'ought', it will become obvious that the phrase, 'justifying an action', i.e. justifying the statement or conviction that we ought to perform it, has two corresponding senses. It may mean *either* proving that, or giving a reason why, the action will be the proper action for achieving our purpose, *or* proving that, or giving a reason why, we are morally bound to do it. It will also become obvious that the double ambiguity will be a source of confusion, if we apply the term 'ought' in one sense to some action and at the same time speak of justifying the action in the sense of 'justify' appropriate to the other sense of 'ought'. And this is what we are really doing when we say, 'I grant that such and such an action is a duty, but nevertheless I want to have the doing it justified to me, i.e. to know why I ought to do it'. We are not asking the unreal question, 'Why am I morally bound to do this action, which I know to be a duty?', but, presupposing that our aim is to become better off, we are asking 'What shall I gain by doing this right action?'. This question is, of course, a real question which we can and often do put to ourselves. And it is really being answered in a general form by anyone who is contending that honesty is the best policy. But it is not a moral question, in the sense that it is not a question why we are morally bound to do certain actions; and once the ambiguity of the term 'ought' is exposed no one thinks of it as a moral question. . . .

It should be noticed that the view that a man will only be induced to do what he morally ought to do by consideration of personal advantage is not a doctrine concerning how a man *should* act, or what he *should* aim at. It is simply a doctrine concerning how a man *will* act; in other words, it is simply a doctrine about actual human nature. It should also be noticed that it implies on its negative side that no one ever does an action *because* he apprehends it to be right or ever refrains from doing an action *because* he apprehends it to be wrong, so that knowledge of what is right and wrong is implied to be at best of merely theoretical interest, and to have no influence whatever on action. And the paradox of this implication is so great, that the question naturally arises, 'What, if any, correction of this view of human nature is required?' An answer which would frequently be given is one which goes back to Kant. It would be said that the mere *knowledge* or that the mere *thought* that a certain action ought to be done tends to lead on to cause us to do the action and in some cases actually leads or causes us to do it, so that it is not true that an impulse and a desire—whether a desire is always desire of personal advantage or not—are the only things which can move or lead us to act; and that, consequently, inducements are not *necessary* if we are to do what we know or think to be right. This answer seems borne out by the fact that we frequently say of some action which we thought we ought to do and which we did, that we did it without in the least wanting to do it, and in fact contrary to all our inclinations. It also seems borne out by our knowledge of the effort needed to do certain actions which we think we ought to do. Nevertheless we are forced to abandon this answer. For when we really face the questions (1) 'Impulses apart, could we do any action whatever unless we desired to do it in some respect or other?' and (2) 'Could the thought of a certain action as right possibly make any difference to what we actually do, if it left us entirely cold or unmoved and, in fact, did not in some way arouse a desire to do this action?', we are obliged in both cases to answer 'No'.

The truth appears to be simply that the very thought or knowledge[8] that we ought to do a certain action necessarily arouses in some degree the desire to do it, just in respect of its being a duty or an act which we ought to do,[9] and that the mistake of Plato and Butler and of those who follow them lies in failure to see that the desire to do what we ought *may* be a motive of our actions. The view at first sight seems a paradox, because we think of the doing a right act as often laborious, disagreeable, or painful, and we are apt to think of pleasure and pain as the only things the thought of which necessarily excites desire and aversion. But, as Butler insisted, we desire many things without thinking of them as things which we shall enjoy, such as ascertaining the result of a race, our children's welfare after our death, and revenge on an enemy. Moreover we often speak quite naturally of someone's desire to do his duty, and even the equally natural phrase 'a strong sense of duty' seems to stand for something which includes such a desire. Further, if it be said that at best the thought of some act as right does not *as such* arouse the desire to do it but does so only in those who are constituted in a particular way,—just as only some people have curiosity on a given matter—it can be replied that everyone will allow that at least the thought of enjoyment as such arouses a desire and that therefore there is no difficulty of principle in allowing that certain other things, including rightness, *may* do the same.

Further, if this view be right, it will have to be allowed that Kant went too far. In pointing out that our recognition of a hypothetical imperative presupposes,

---

[8] For the purpose of the argument, it does not matter here which is the right term.
[9] Cf. Ch. I, pp. 121–2.

and is relative to, a desire, he was pointing out what is true and important. But he went too far when he insisted that in a morally good act we are moved not by a desire of any kind, but simply by the thought, which aroused reverence but not desire, that we are morally bound to do what we are doing. Kant himself evidently felt a certain uneasiness about this position, since he considered it a violent paradox, and a paradox which only the vindication of freedom could resolve. But he could have elucidated the nature of moral goodness without the paradox, if he had insisted that what distinguished a categorical from a hypothetical imperative was that instead of *presupposing* it *gave rise* to a desire.

The net result of the preceding discussion is that assuming Plato and Butler to have been rightly interpreted, there is no need to consider in detail the success or failure of the attempts which they and others have made to show that doing what is right will be to the advantage of the agent, or indeed the success or failure of any attempt to formulate the so-called sanction of morality. For first, all such attempts are based on a mistake, viz. the mistake of thinking that as a matter of actual human nature men are moved—impulses apart—solely by the desire of personal advantage. And second, although we can ask whether right action pays and although in doing so we shall be asking for a reason why we *should* do what is right, the 'should' will be the non-moral 'should', and an answer will throw no light either on the nature of what constitutes rightness of action or, if what have been called our ordinary moral convictions are only convictions, and not knowledge, on their truth or falsity.

III. What Ought I to Aim at? Reply to Sidgwick

The two questions about moral obligation which ... have so far survived for consideration are the questions (1) 'What, if anything, ought we to do in life?' with the question which it in turn raises, 'What, if anything, constitutes an act a duty?' or, in other words, 'What, if there are right actions, constitutes a right action right?' and (2) 'What constitutes a right action right?'. Of these it would seem that the former should be considered first. For since when we first reflect on what we call our ordinary unreflective moral convictions, we doubt whether these so-called 'convictions' are true, we are not really in a position even to raise the second question, which, as has been seen, implies that in our ordinary unreflective states of mind we *know* certain actions to be right, unless and until the former question which implies the doubt has been not only considered but shown to be erroneous.

As a way of approaching the first question, consideration of Henry Sidgwick's treatment of it will have a certain advantage. It will force us to clear our minds on certain matters and in particular to face the apparently innocent and simple but really difficult question 'What *is* Utilitarianism?'. For this reason this procedure will be adopted.

It may be objected on the score of accuracy that the question which Sidgwick actually proposes to himself for discussion is not the qualified question 'What, *if anything*, ought I to do?' but simply 'What ought I to do?'. But for our purpose this difference may be ignored. For the reason why Sidgwick does not introduce the qualification is simply that he does not see that in maintaining that his own aim and that of other moral philosophers is 'to systematize and free from error the apparent cognition that most men have of the rightness or reasonableness of conduct', he has no right to assume—as he is doing—that there are really actions which we ought to do. Hence we can ignore the qualification provided we remember, should the occasion arise, that its introduction is really required, if the question is to represent accurately the state of mind of the man who is seeking to discover the truth or falsity of his ordinary moral convictions.

The main feature of Sidgwick's treatment of the question which renders consideration of it valuable to us is his view that the question should at once be split up into two alternative questions.

Sidgwick begins by explaining that he means by 'a Method of Ethics' 'any rational procedure by which we determine what individual human beings "ought"—or what is "right" for them—to do, or to seek to realize by voluntary action',[10]—i.e. any rational procedure by which we answer the question 'What ought I to do or aim at?'.[11] And he adds that he cannot avoid thus taking account of two different forms in which the fundamental problem of Ethics is stated because 'Ethics is sometimes considered as an investigation of the true Moral laws or rational precepts of Conduct; sometimes as an inquiry into the nature of the Ultimate End of reasonable human action—the Good or "True Good" of man—and the method of attaining it.'[12]

Here Sidgwick is evidently maintaining that a certain question, the endeavour to answer which constitutes Ethics, has to be considered as assuming one of two alternative forms; viz. either 'What ought I to do?' or 'What ought I to aim at?'. And, as Sidgwick realizes, this view needs defence since a single subject must have a single main or principal problem. Unfortunately Sidgwick's own defence is useless; since merely to point out, as he does, that attempts to answer both questions have received the same name Ethics does not show what it is his business to show, viz. that they are entitled to the same name, as really forming one, or parts of one, enquiry.

---

[10] H. Sidgwick, *Methods of Ethics*, 1.   [11] Ibid., 2.

[12] Ibid., 3. It is clear that, according to Sidgwick, 'an Ethics' stands for an articulated view of what we ought to do in particular and 'the method of a particular Ethics' for the rational procedure, i.e. the process of argument, by which a particular articulated view is arrived at; and as the process of argument involved in a particular Ethics will imply certain special premises, a particular Ethics will, on his view, involve certain special premises.

The real defence must be that those who have considered the single problem 'What ought I to do?' fall into two groups, distinguished by a difference of view concerning the method of solution. It must lie in the contention that while the one group think a solution obtainable directly, viz. by first ascertaining, and then applying to particular actions 'the true moral laws or rational precepts of conduct' (i.e. the principles which define the kinds of action which we ought to do), the other group consider a solution obtainable only indirectly, i.e. by answering a question about something else first, viz. the question 'What is that at which I ought to aim?', and then discovering what particular actions will lead to the realization of this something. And this is undoubtedly how Sidgwick thinks of the two groups of enquirers as distinguished. For, according to him, the one group, whom he designates as taking the 'Intuitional view of Morality', holds conduct to be right 'when conformed to certain precepts or principles of Duty, intuitively known to be unconditionally binding',[13] and the other group, whom we may by contrast designate as taking the Non-Intuitional view of Morality,[14] and among whom Sidgwick includes himself, seek 'knowledge of the end' ('the end' here being equivalent to 'the ultimate end of reasonable human action' and to 'what I ought to aim at') 'in order to ascertain what actions are the right means to its attainment'.[15]

It should, however, be added that although Sidgwick thus represents these two accounts of the way in which the right actions are discovered as exhaustive, he shortly afterwards introduces a third and totally different account, and even states it to be legitimate. This resembles the second in maintaining that we ascertain certain actions to be right by finding them to be the means to a certain something, but differs by maintaining that the something is not that at which we *ought to aim* but that at which we *are aiming*, so that to ascertain what we ought to do what we have first to discover is what that is at which we *are* aiming. Sidgwick throughout presupposes a sharp distinction between what he calls ultimate ends (e.g. fame) and what he calls rational ultimate ends. And the third view emerges when he says: 'At the same time, it is not necessary, in the methodological investigation of right conduct, considered relatively to the end either of private or of general happiness, to assume that the end itself is determined or prescribed by reason: we only require to assume, in reasoning to cogent practical conclusions, that it is adopted as ultimate and paramount. For if a man accepts any end as ultimate and paramount, he accepts implicitly as his "method of ethics" whatever process of reasoning enables him to determine the action most conducive to this end.'[16] The view appears again where he says 'The applicability of a method for determining right conduct relatively to an ultimate end—whether Happiness or Perfection—does not necessarily depend

---

[13] Ibid., 3. [14] Sidgwick himself has no name for this view. [15] Ibid. [16] Ibid., 8.

on the acceptance of the end as prescribed by reason; it only requires that it should be in some way adopted as ultimate and paramount.'[17] ...

We have now to consider ... where [Sidgwick's] main mistake lies. The problem, however, is complicated by the fact that it has never occurred to him that a statement of the form 'we ought to aim at X' could possibly give rise to a difficulty of principle, and that in consequence he thinks we have only to ascertain whether there is something in particular at which we ought to aim.

In addressing himself to this task Sidgwick considers, as most people would, that the first step is to ascertain what answers have commonly been given to the question 'What ought I to aim at?' whether by 'common sense' or 'common moral opinion', i.e. by ourselves in our ordinary unreflective state of mind, or by more or less professed moral philosophers. It will then be possible, he implies, to consider which of these answers is right. The result of his survey is that three, or, more accurately, four, answers have been commonly given. Four things, he holds, have been widely considered to be things at which we ought to aim: (1) our own happiness, (2) the general happiness, (3) the perfection or excellence of our own nature, (4) the general perfection or excellence of human nature. The first two he assigns to the view of common sense, and, apparently, the last two to more or less professed moral philosophers, and we find Sidgwick himself in the end agreeing with the views which he attributes to common sense[18] and disagreeing with the others.

So far as this step is concerned, of course the only question which arises is not whether he succeeds in showing that these views are true but whether he succeeds in showing that they are widely held. For our purposes, however, this question can be narrowed down to the question whether he is successful in showing that the first two views are held by common sense; since for a reason which will appear later, the question whether the last two views are widely held by moral philosophers is not really of any importance.

The most important passage to be considered is one in which he contends that according to common opinion we ought to aim at our own happiness. The passage runs thus: 'What then are these different methods? What are the different practical principles which the common sense of mankind is *prima facie* prepared to accept as ultimate?' Some care is needed in answering this question, because we frequently prescribe that this or that 'ought' to be done or aimed at without any express reference to an ulterior end, while yet such an end is tacitly presupposed. It is obvious that such prescriptions are merely, what Kant calls

---

[17] Ibid., 77 n.
[18] It does not occur to Sidgwick that the question 'What ought I to aim at?', if legitimate at all, can admit of only one answer, and though he subsequently has to allow that the conviction that we ought to aim both at our own and at the general happiness involves a contradiction, he still maintains both that we hold it and that we are right in holding it.

them, Hypothetical Imperatives; they are not addressed to anyone who has not first accepted the end.

'For instance: a teacher of any art assumes that his pupil wants to produce the product of the art, or to produce it excellent in quality; he tells him that he *ought* to hold the awl, the hammer, the brush differently. A physician assumes that his patient wants health: he tells him that he *ought* to rise early, to live plainly, to take hard exercise. If the patient deliberately prefers ease and good living to health, the physician's precepts fall to the ground: they are no longer addressed to him. So, again, a man of the world assumes that his hearers wish to get on in society, when he lays down rules of dress, manner, conversation, habits of life. A similar view may be plausibly taken of many rules prescribing what are sometimes called "duties to oneself": it may be said that they are given on the assumption that a man regards his own Happiness as an ultimate end: that if anyone should be so exceptional as to disregard it, he does not come within their scope: in short, that the *"ought"* in such formulae is still implicitly relative to an *optional* end.'

'It does not, however, seem to me that this account of the matter is exhaustive. We do not all look with simple indifference on a man who declines to take the right means to attain his own happiness, on no other ground than that he does not care about happiness. Most men would regard such a refusal as irrational, with a certain disapprobation; they would thus implicitly assent to Butler's statement[19] that "interest, one's own happiness, is a manifest obligation". In other words, they would think that a man *ought* to care for his own happiness. The word "ought" thus used is no longer relative: happiness now appears as an ultimate end, the pursuit of which—at least within the limits imposed by other duties—appears to be prescribed by reason "categorically", as Kant would say, i.e. without any tacit assumption of a still ulterior end. And it has been widely held by even orthodox moralists that all morality rests ultimately on the basis of "reasonable self-love"[20]; i.e. that its rules are ultimately binding on any individual only so far as it is his interest on the whole to observe them.'[21]

Here the position which Sidgwick appears to be endeavouring to put forward is as follows:

'In our ordinary unreflective state of mind, when we offer to X a precept of skill, e.g. "You ought to rise early", on the ground that the action referred to is necessary for the realization of some state of affairs which is not X's happiness, e.g. X's health, we imply that X has that state of affairs as his purpose, and we think that otherwise the precept would be false. It is plausible to contend in a similar way that when—once more to use a phrase of Kant's—we offer to X a counsel of prudence, e.g. "You ought to make friends" or "You ought to rise

---

[19] See the Preface to Butler's *Sermons on Human Nature*'. [J. Butler, *Fifteen Sermons* in D. Raphael (ed.), *British Moralists 1650–1800*, I, preface, 331 (Oxford, 1969). Ed.]
[20] The phrase is Butler's.   [21] Sidgwick, *Methods of Ethics*, 6–7.

early", on the ground that doing so is necessary for X's happiness, we equally imply that X has his happiness as his purpose, and think that otherwise the counsel would be false. But this is not really the case. In ordinary life we should in fact think the counsel of prudence true, even if we thought X did not have his happiness as his purpose, and we should think so, because we think that X ought to aim at his happiness, i.e. have his happiness as his purpose. Here then is a clear case where in ordinary life we hold that we *ought* to have a certain something as our aim.'

Now this position, whether it be the position which Sidgwick actually puts forward or not—and the formulation of it represents an endeavour to make the best of what he says—will not stand examination. For we do not in fact think it a *duty* on our part to aim at—i.e. to act from the desire of—our happiness; nor do we even in fact think that it is a duty to do what may be represented as the closest possible approximation to aiming at our happiness, viz. to do those acts which we think will lead to our happiness. Thus, if we think that getting up now is necessary for our happiness but are nevertheless wholly irresolute or undecided owing to laziness or distaste for the chilly and tedious process of dressing, we do *not* think that getting up a *duty* to get up on the ground that it is necessary for our happiness, though of course we may think it a duty on other grounds. In the state of irresolution we may, of course, think that it will pay us to get up; we may also think that it is *weak* to be thus in a state of hesitation, or, again, that it would be *weak* to stay on in bed, or even that we shall be ashamed of ourselves if we do; but we shall not think it a duty to get up unless there supervenes some consideration other than that of conduciveness to our happiness.

Further the position attributes to us a purely artificial or 'paper' line of thought, which has no counterpart in fact. This is a line of thought which Sidgwick himself later on maintains to be legitimate when he says: 'It can hardly be denied that the recognition of an end as ultimately reasonable, [i.e. the recognition of something as a something which we ought to have as our end] involves the recognition of an obligation to do such acts as most conduce to the end'.[22] At first sight no doubt it is plausible to say that *if* we grant that we ought to have something X, e.g. our own happiness, as our end, we have to allow as a corollary that we ought to do those acts which most conduce to X. But, apart from the difficulty of allowing that it can be true that we ought to have X as our end or purpose, it is obvious that as the 'ought' in the statement 'we ought to do these acts which most conduce to X' can only be the non-moral 'ought', it has no force for us whatever, unless X actually *is* our purpose.

But it is not merely that the position is untenable. When we consider his actual words, we find that he does not get even so far as to put it forward. For whereas it is his business to contend that men think they ought to have their own happiness

[22] Ibid., 35.

as their end, all he actually goes so far as to assert is (1) that men *disapprove* the refusal to take the means to it, and (2) that men think a man ought to *care for* his own happiness; and plainly to *disapprove* is not the same as to *think wrong*, and to *care* for happiness is not the same as to have it as our *purpose*.

He then proceeds to vindicate his attribution to common sense of the *second* of the two views, viz. that we ought to aim at the general happiness. After contending that common moral opinion recognizes other fundamental rules, besides the duty of prudence (i.e. of aiming at our own happiness), e.g. those of justice, good faith and veracity, and is inclined to treat them as binding without qualification and without regard to ulterior consequence, he continues thus: 'On the other hand it is contended by many Utilitarians that all the rules of conduct which men prescribe to one another as moral rules are really—though in part unconsciously—prescribed as means to the general happiness of mankind, or of the whole aggregate of sentient beings; and it is still more widely held by Utilitarian thinkers that such rules, however they may originate, are only valid so far as their observance is conducive to the general happiness. This contention I shall hereafter examine with due care. Here I wish only to point out that, if the duty of aiming at the general happiness is thus taken to include all other duties, as subordinate applications of it, we seem to be again led to the notion of Happiness as an ultimate end categorically prescribed,—only it is now General Happiness and not the private happiness of any individual. And this is the view that I myself take of the Utilitarian principle.'[23]

Here the failure of this vindication is obvious. We need only notice (1) that men in thinking, e.g. that they ought to tell the truth do not in fact do so *on the ground that* telling the truth will be for the general happiness, (2) that if they did, the principle which they would formulate would be the principle not that they ought to tell the truth but that they ought to bring about the general happiness, (3) that no one in fact really thinks that he ought to bring about the *general* happiness, as distinct from the happiness of *others*, and (4) that even if men did think that they ought *to bring about* the general happiness, to think this would not be to think that they ought to *aim at*, to have as their purpose, the general happiness.

The fact is, of course, that Sidgwick has never set himself to consider what is meant by 'aiming at something' and therefore never has had occasion to face the difficulty of principle involved in maintaining a statement of the form 'I ought to aim at X'. But just for this reason a defender of Sidgwick might urge that the preceding criticism really misses its mark. 'Sidgwick is quite right' he may say, 'in attributing certain views to common sense. What mistake he makes consists merely in expressing these views in the inappropriate phraseology of "aiming at something". If, as we should, in order to state his real meaning, we remove this

[23] Ibid., 8.

form of expression, we find that he is attributing to common sense two views which can be expressed in either of two forms, viz. that we ought to *bring about* our own, or, in the other case, the general happiness or that we ought to do *whatever will lead to* this.'

There seems force in this contention. It seems impossible that Sidgwick should have meant precisely what he said and would have refused to modify his phraseology if it had been pressed against him. Moreover the view thus attributed to him is plausible, at any rate where the happiness referred to is the general happiness. For it is plausible to say that we think it our duty, so far as we can see, to make mankind, including ourselves, happy, and that we think of this duty as summing up, or at least as being the basis of, all our so-called other duties. Nevertheless this interpretation, promising as it seems, is at once open to the objection that, if it be right, Sidgwick appears to be attributing to common sense an *intuitional* view of morality, viz. that we intuitively, i.e. directly, apprehend that actions of a certain kind, viz. making people happy, are right. For if he had been asked 'how according to common sense do we come to apprehend that such actions are right?', he could only have answered that, according to common sense, we do so directly. Yet he would certainly not have called the view of morality which he was attributing to common sense intuitional.

IV. Intuitionism and Consequences

We are therefore forced to consider more closely than we have done what Sidgwick really meant by an intuitional view, as a condition of determining what he meant by the opposed type of view. What Sidgwick means by 'An Intuitional view of Morality' can be gathered from the following statements:

(1) 'According to the[24] intuitional view of morality, "conduct" is held to be right when conformed to certain precepts or principles of duty, intuitively known to be unconditionally binding.'[25]

(2) 'Writers who maintain that we have "intuitive knowledge" of the rightness of actions usually mean that this rightness is ascertained by simply "looking at" the actions themselves, without considering their ulterior consequences.'[26]

(3) 'In such maxims as that duty should be done "*advienne qui pourra*", that truth should be spoken without regard to consequences, that justice should be done "though the sky should fall", it is implied that we have the power of seeing clearly that certain kinds of actions are right and reasonable in themselves, apart from their consequences;—or rather with a merely partial consideration

---

[24] Accuracy would require the substitution of 'an' for 'the'.   [25] Ibid., 3.   [26] Ibid., 96.

of consequences, from which other consequences admitted to be possibly good or bad are definitely excluded.'[27]

From these statements it may be gathered that by 'An Intuitional view of Morality' Sidgwick means a view according to which we intuitively, i.e., directly, apprehend actions of certain kinds, e.g. speaking the truth, or educating our children, to be right *in themselves* and *independently of their consequences*, and that we come to apprehend some given particular action, e.g. my answering 'No' to X's question, to be right by coming to apprehend it to be an act of one of these kinds, e.g. speaking the truth. And though such a view, as the name for it implies, is primarily a view concerning *our apprehension* of morality as distinct from *morality* itself, to use Sidgwick's phrase, yet it *implies* a view concerning morality, i.e. concerning what constitutes a right action right.

The view concerning morality is that actions of certain kinds, e.g. actions of helping a neighbour out of a difficulty, are right *in themselves*, i.e. in virtue of being acts of these kinds, and therefore *independently of their consequences*, and it implies that certain specified particular actions, e.g. my helping my neighbour out of his present difficulty, are right in themselves, i.e. as being the particular cases which they are of acts of one of these kinds, and therefore *independently of their consequences*.

Such a view therefore seems to imply that in order to discover what actions and kinds of action are right we need never consider consequences. Yet a man who thought that helping a neighbour was in itself right might think giving his neighbour a shilling right, and right just because his neighbour's being benefited would be a consequence; and a man who thought hurting another's feelings wrong might think making personal remarks wrong, and wrong just because it would have damage to another's feelings as a consequence. Thus there seems to be consideration of consequences even on an intuitional view.

The obscurity can best be cleared up by considering two objections which Sidgwick himself thinks beset the contention that according to those who maintain that we have 'intuitive knowledge' of the rightness of actions, we disregard consequences.[28] The first objection is that on *every* view of morality we consider ulterior[29] consequences to some extent; and the second is that it is difficult to draw the line between an act and its consequences, since the effects which follow each of our volitions form a continuous series stretching to infinity.

As regards the second objection, it will be found always possible, and never difficult, to distinguish, and so to draw the line between, an act and its consequences. In respect of an action of a given kind, e.g. giving a man a shilling, this is obvious. By 'an action of a given kind' we mean the bringing about

---

[27] Ibid., 200.   [28] Ibid., 96–7.

[29] Ulterior rests on a confusion and should be ignored. We can distinguish (*a*) an act from (*b*) its consequences and we can distinguish (*c*) the nearer from (*d*) the ulterior consequences of an act. But to distinguish (*a*) from (*d*) is to confuse the two distinctions.

a state of affairs of a certain kind S which is indicated by the phrase by which we refer to such an action, e.g. another man's being in possession of a shilling.

By 'a consequence of an act of a given kind' we mean a state of affairs of another kind S_1 to which the existence of a state of affairs of the kind S necessarily leads, e.g. the recipient's being pleased. Hence, though we may think that when we do an action of a given kind we shall be bringing about a plurality of states of affairs of definite kinds, the line between (*a*) that state of affairs of the kind S the bringing about which constitutes an act of the given kind an act of that kind and (*b*) the states of affairs of the kinds $S_1, S_2, \ldots$ which are its consequences is clear and definite, and indeed fixed by the phrase by which we refer to an act of that kind, e.g. 'giving a neighbour a shilling'. Again, to consider the case of given particular actions, we can only refer to a given particular action by using some definite phrase for it. This phrase will indicate that the act consists in bringing about a certain particular thing X, as when I refer to some act of mine as my having given my neighbour a certain shilling, and thereby imply that my act consisted in bringing my neighbour into possession of that shilling. By 'a consequence of the act', when the act is thus referred to, we mean a particular something Y caused by X, and so brought about by the agent indirectly, e.g. my neighbour's being able to get out of his difficulty. And the bringing about X and anything Y brought about indirectly by bringing about X are necessarily different and therefore distinguishable. But it is also true—and it constitutes a truth underlying Sidgwick's difficulty—that since in bringing about X, we are also indirectly bringing about Y, my action can *also* be thought of and referred to as my bringing about Y, and that, so thought of and regarded, Y is not a consequence of my action but something which in doing it I bring about or originate. Thus I can also refer to my giving my neighbour a shilling as my helping my neighbour out of a certain difficulty, and my neighbour's ability to get out of the difficulty will not be a consequence of my action, so referred to. In general, therefore, it is possible to regard anything which a particular action brings about either as a consequence of the action or as that in the origination of which the action consists, and therefore as something which is not a consequence of the action,—which we do depending on how we regard the action. Nevertheless, for clearness' sake, it should be noticed that there is a limit to this possibility. For in the case of any action whatever there must be something which we originate absolutely directly, and there can be no way of regarding the action which will enable us to regard this something as a consequence of the action, since *ex hypothesi* we originate it directly, and therefore not by originating something else of which it is the consequence. Thus if it were true that in doing a certain action we originated certain noises directly, there would be no way of regarding our action which would involve that the noises were a consequence of the action. And the mere fact that in actual conduct we are unable to say what it is that we originate directly does not disprove the necessity of there being such a something.³⁰

As regards Sidgwick's first objection, it appears to come to this, that both in the case of actions of given kinds and of given particular actions, which we think right or think wrong, every one in order to think of them as right or as wrong has at least in certain cases first to think of certain consequences of doing them, so that if 'intuitionism' stands for a view according to which right actions are, and are apprehended to be, right independently of their consequences, it stands for a view which no one has ever held.

Here again there is a difficulty, but at the same time a difficulty which can be met. We may consider first the case of actions of given kinds.

When we are said to apprehend that carrying out a promise is in itself right, the statement, whether true or not, undoubtedly means that we apprehend that what constitutes such an act right is just that it is the carrying out a promise. It therefore undoubtedly implies that in coming to apprehend the carrying out a promise to be right, we are disregarding the consequences of doing so. Now no one who maintained that we apprehend that keeping a promise is in itself right, would maintain that we apprehend e.g. that rising early is *in itself* right or that making personal remarks is *in itself* wrong; yet he might maintain that we apprehend early rising to be right and making personal remarks to be wrong, and if he did, he would have to allow that in doing so we are taking into account certain consequences of such actions, e.g. the having enough time in which to earn a living for one's family, or pain to other's people's feelings. And this constitutes a truth underlying Sidgwick's first difficulty. But the intuitionist could go on to say that we only think early rising a duty as being e.g., really the initial portion of the day's work of earning a living for one's family, which we apprehend to be in itself a duty, and that we only think making personal remarks wrong as being a particular species of an action of a kind which is in itself wrong, viz. hurting the feelings of others. He could add that our apprehension, for example, that making personal remarks is wrong is essentially derivative or inferential, being a conclusion from our apprehension that making a personal remark has a certain consequence, viz. pain to another's feelings, and our apprehension that hurting the feelings of another is in itself wrong. The intuitionist could therefore maintain that the apprehension in question, though not itself the apprehension that an act of a certain kind is in itself wrong, implies such an apprehension, and that in the apprehension which is thus implied we ignore consequences, since though, for instance, pain to another's feelings is a consequence of making

---

³⁰ For the reasons given above it will be obvious that when Rashdall says [H. Rashdall, *The Theory of Good and Evil* (Oxford: Oxford University Press, 1924), i. 87, Ed.]: 'Indeed, you cannot really distinguish an act from its present or foreseeable consequences. The consequences, in so far as they can be foreseen, are actually part of the act', he goes too far, although it is possible to see why he has been led to go too far.

a personal remark, it is not a consequence of hurting another's feelings but that which in hurting another's feelings we originate. He could therefore fairly say that, though a man, in apprehending the making of a personal remark to be wrong is taking into account a certain consequence of doing so, the consequence is not a consequence of the action in that aspect of the action in which it is apprehended to be in itself wrong. And he could add that in all cases where we apprehend an act of a certain kind to be right or to be wrong, we apprehend an act of a certain kind—which may or may not be the same as the former—to be right or to be wrong in itself and apart from its consequences.

Next we may consider the case of given particular actions. To revert to the instance of giving my neighbour a certain shilling, no one would say that we apprehend this action to be right in itself, and apart from its consequences. On the contrary even an intuitionist would have to allow that we could not apprehend the action to be right unless we considered its consequences, e.g. our neighbour's ability to get out of his difficulty, and a certain consequence which renders the act an act of one of these kinds which are right in themselves, e.g. helping a neighbour out of a difficulty. Thus we have to allow that even on the intuitionist view, in order to apprehend the act of giving our neighbour the shilling to be right, we have to consider its consequences. This is true and constitutes a truth underlying Sidgwick's difficulty. But the intuitionist could fairly go on to contend that we can only apprehend the act to be right if we regard it—as *ex hypothesi* we can regard it—as our helping our neighbour out of a certain difficulty, and that our neighbour's ability to get out of his difficulty is not a consequence of the action so regarded; so that in apprehending the action to be right, what we are taking account of is not a consequence of the action regarded as we are regarding it in apprehending it to be right. Further it could be fairly contended that on the intuitional view the particular action, if regarded in the way in which it has to be regarded, in order to be apprehended as right, viz. as getting my neighbour out of his difficulty, and if correspondingly referred to, is, and is apprehended to be, right *in itself*, i.e. as being the getting my neighbour out of his difficulty, this being simply a given case of helping a neighbour out of a difficulty.

The general conclusion, therefore, that may be drawn is that what Sidgwick refers to as an intuitional view of morality is a view according to which a kind of action, or an action, which is right either is, or is apprehended to be, right in itself, and independently of its consequences, or else it implies that some other kind of action or some other action is so, and that therefore it is consistent with holding that the rightness of some kinds of action and of some actions depends on their having certain consequences. And the various particular views of this type will differ from one another by the differences in the particular kinds of action which are maintained to be in themselves right.

As soon, however, as we reach this conclusion, we begin to wonder whether there can be a type of view which is opposed to this type. For it must at least negatively be one according to which no actions or kinds of action whatever are right in themselves; and if the preceding argument is conclusive, it is impossible to maintain that certain actions and kinds of action are right in virtue of having certain consequences without implying that the actions considered in some other way and also certain other kinds of action are right in themselves. . . .

V. What is Utilitarianism?

Now if we consider Sidgwick's two versions of the non-intuitional type of view of morality, i.e. of what constitutes rightness,* we see that they can fairly be contrasted as an artificial or 'paper' version and as natural or real version. For if we consider them in respect of plausibility, we find that there is not the slightest plausibility in maintaining that we ought to do a certain action *on the ground* that it will lead to a certain state of affairs, unless the term 'ought' is understood in the non-moral sense of conducive to our purpose, i.e. to our actual purpose. If we grant that 'ought' should be understood thus, we shall admit the truth of the statement at once; if we do not, we shall find that it has no plausibility whatever. To use a phrase which John Grote used in another connection,[31] it sounds well to say, 'I ought to aim at X; this action A will lead to X; and therefore I ought to do A'; but though it may sound well that is all. The statement sounds well in exactly the way in which the statement of a syllogistic argument in terms of the class theory of propositions sounds well; and it is just as artificial—as we realize when we try to attach a definite meaning to the statement 'I ought to aim at X'. Hence we expect to find, as later we shall find, that when Sidgwick endeavours to vindicate the truth of certain non-intuitional views, although he may try to do so in terms of his 'paper' version of the non-intuitional type of view, the thought which underlies what he says really implies the other version.

As soon as we admit, as we must, that only the second version of the non-intuitional type of view has any plausibility, we are led to a general conclusion which cannot but at first strike us as surprising, but which at the same time helps us to understand why we find it difficult and elusive to answer the apparently elementary and simple question 'What is Utilitarianism?'. The general conclusion, which later we shall see to be verified in the case of Sidgwick himself, is that whereas we are apt to think that what a non-intuitionist is doing is to put forward a view, though possibly a peculiar and possibly a false view, of what constitutes

---

* [viz what 'ought' to be our end or 'is' our end. Ed.]

[31] J. Grote, *A Treatise On Moral Ideals* (London, Deighton, Bell and Co., 1876), 200.

right actions right and wrong actions wrong, what in fact he is doing is denying by implication that there really are such things as right actions and wrong actions at all in the moral sense of these terms, and maintaining that all that exists instead is right actions and wrong actions in the purely non-moral sense of actions which are, and of actions which are not, conducive to our purpose. When a non-intuitionist lays down that actions are right so far as they lead to a certain consequence X, he is tacitly presupposing, whether he realizes it or not, that X is our purpose, and what he is really maintaining is that having X as a consequence constitutes an action right, in the non-moral sense of proper in respect of being conducive to our purpose. And what distinguishes one non-intuitional view from another is simply a difference of view concerning what our actual purpose is,—according as it is considered, for instance, to be our own happiness, the general happiness, or the perfection of character, either of ourselves or of human nature generally.

As soon as we reach this conclusion, we see that the explanation of the difficulty which we find in formulating the nature of Utilitarianism, and indeed of any other non-intuitional view of morality, lies in our failure to recognize the difference, or at least the radical nature of the difference, between the moral and the non-moral senses of the word 'ought', together with the ambiguity of statements of the form 'we ought to do the acts which will lead to X'. Utilitarianism is often defined as the doctrine that we ought to do the actions which will lead to the general happiness. Again J. S. Mill states that his creed 'holds that actions are right in proportion as they tend to promote happiness, wrong as they tend to produce the reverse of happiness'. Now either statement, if taken by itself, is naturally understood to mean that, in the moral sense of 'ought', we ought, so far as we can, to bring about the general happiness. In fact Mill's statement seems inevitably to imply this sense of 'ought', since it refers to *right* and *wrong*, and Mill himself in thus stating his creed refers to it as accepting Utility as the foundation of *morals*. In consequence we become puzzled. For it is hard to see why, if this be the doctrine, it is not a particular intuitional view of morality, viz. the view that the bringing about the general happiness is in itself right, or that what constitutes an action right is its bringing about the general happiness. Yet we feel that the doctrine is somehow very different from an intuitional doctrine and that Mill himself would be the first to insist on the difference. The truth is, however, that the real nature of Mill's view, and therefore the real meaning of his own formula for his creed, does not appear until he goes on to speak, as shortly afterwards he does, of the theory of life on which this theory of morality is grounded, viz. that pleasure and freedom from pain are the only things desirable (i.e. really, as appears later, desired) as ends. This statement shows that his real view is quite different from what his initial statement of it, if interpreted by itself, suggests that it is, and that it is in fact the view that while no acts whatever are *right* and while no acts whatever are *wrong*, there are nevertheless certain acts which ought to be done in the sense of being conducive to our purpose and certain acts which ought not to be done in the sense of not being conducive to our purpose, viz. those acts which do and those which do not lead to the realization of what is our purpose in acting, viz. pleasure or freedom from pain.[32] Mill's own statement, therefore, in order to be understood as a true statement of his creed, has to be taken to imply that happiness is our purpose and to mean that actions, so far as they lead to happiness are right, in the sense of conducive to our purpose, and actions so far as they are the reverse, are wrong, in the sense of not conducive to our purpose. Similarly the statement that we ought to do whatever will lead to the general happiness, if meant as a statement of Utilitarianism, has to be understood to imply that the general happiness is our purpose and to have a corresponding meaning.

Further, as soon as we see that this interpretation is right, we see that such a view has lost its appearance of being intuitional. For, to put the matter generally, suppose it be held that X is our purpose, and that an action which consists in bringing about Y will have X as its consequence. The view will be that the bringing about Y will be right, in the non-moral sense of 'right', in virtue of its leading to X. But on this view, although the bringing about Y will be the bringing about X, and although the bringing about Y will be right, we shall not be required to hold that the bringing about X will be right, and right in itself, since 'right' will only mean proper in respect of being conducive to our purpose. And, in particular, the statement that we ought to do whatever will lead to the general happiness, if meant as a statement of Utilitarianism, can neither be transformed into the statement, nor can be held to imply, that bringing about the general happiness is right.

Similar conclusions can be drawn with regard to other non-intuitional views. Thus if anyone were to maintain, as Green really sometimes maintains in his *Principles of Political Obligation*, that the real reason why acts which are duties are duties lies in their being the means to moral perfection—whether the moral perfection meant be that of ourselves or that of human beings generally—he would similarly, in spite of his reference to *moral* perfection, be in reality substituting a non-moral for the moral 'ought', and the justice of this criticism would be unaffected by the fact that what he would be presupposing as our purpose was not happiness but moral perfection. And in general it may be laid down that anyone who maintains that the actions which should be done should be done on the ground that they will be the means to a certain something is really—whatever the something may be—substituting the non-moral for the moral 'ought', and by implication denying the existence of moral obligation altogether. The plain

---

[32] This must be his view whether the pleasure or happiness to which he is really referring be the agent's happiness or whether it be the general happiness, for his position implies that the happiness to which actions should lead and the happiness which is our purpose are the same.

fact is that in any discussion of what is required to render an action a duty there is no place for the language of means and end at all.

The general conclusion which can be drawn is, of course, that any view of morality of the type which Sidgwick opposes to the intuitional type and which we have designated non-intuitional can be ruled out on the general ground that it substitutes the non-moral for the moral 'ought', and is therefore not a view of morality at all.

As has been pointed out, according to Sidgwick's 'paper' or ostensible version, a non-intuitional view of morality is one according to which right actions are, and are apprehended to be, right as leading to a certain something at which we ought to aim. Now Sidgwick from time to time gains a certain plausibility for such a view by maintaining in effect that it is inseparable from a doctrine which he himself considers true, viz. that we as rational beings ought to aim at what is good, i.e. really the view that if X be that at which we ought to aim, the reason why we as rational beings ought to aim at it is that X is good. This view first emerges clearly when Sidgwick says 'Nothing that I have [just] said is inconsistent with the view that Truthspeaking is only valuable as a means to the preservation of society; only if it be admitted that it *is* valuable on this ground I should say that it is implied that the preservation of society—or some further end to which this preservation, again, is a means—must be valuable *per se*, and therefore something at which a rational being, as such, ought to aim'.[33] He also expresses it when he says 'It is evident to me that as a rational being I am bound to aim at good generally . . . and not merely at a particular part of it.'[34]

Given that Sidgwick thus connects a non-intuitional view, or his paper version of it, with the doctrine that we ought as rational beings to aim at what is good, it is evident that he conceives that on a non-intuitional view our recognition that X is something at which we ought to aim, or is a *rational* end, is not ultimate but depends on our recognition that X is good. And it is plain that the nature and success of this doctrine has to be considered, especially as he afterwards maintains that two particular non-intuitional views of morality which imply it together constitute the truth—although in the end he has to allow that they are mutually inconsistent.

If we are to find any plausibility in this doctrine we have to amend it in an important particular. Even if it be conceded to Sidgwick that it may be true to speak of something at which we ought to aim, it must be insisted that it is absurd for him to speak of something at which a *rational being* ought to aim, and that the absurdity is only emphasized when he speaks of something at which a rational being, *as such*, ought to aim. Plainly he thinks of rationality as something which is actualized not only in thinking but sometimes also in acting or doing

---

[33] Sidgwick, *Methods of Ethics*, 35–6. A not dissimilar statement at the end of section 2 of page 4 is ambiguous. [34] Ibid., 382.

something. Equally plainly he would have to allow that a rational being, i.e. really, a purely rational being, would be actualizing his rational nature in *all* his actions. He would therefore have to allow that while it may be true to speak of something which *is* aimed at by a rational being, it cannot be true to speak of something which *ought* to be aimed at by a rational being. For *ex hypothesi* a rational being will always in acting aim at that which his rational nature necessitates that he will aim at; and consequently there cannot be something at which he ought to aim although in fact he may not do so. For the same reason, while Sidgwick is entitled to hold that it may be true to speak of what we, as rational beings,—i.e. *so far as* we are rational beings—*do* aim at, he is not entitled to hold that it may be true to speak of what we, *as rational beings*, *ought* to aim at. Hence the doctrine, if it is to be given a chance of being true, has to be amended to the doctrine that rational beings, as such, and we, so far as we are rational, *aim at* what is good.

Given this amendment, a non-intuitional type of view, when represented as connected with this doctrine, will be one according to which, since rational beings and we, so far as we are rational, have as our purpose or aim the existence of what is good, we ought to do those acts which will lead to the existence of what is good. And it will imply (1) that what we ought to do in a moral sense will be what an agent whose purpose is the existence of what is good ought to do in a non-moral sense, and (2) that it can be deduced from the nature of what is good, considered in conjunction with the nature of the situation in which a man is and of his powers of bringing things about. Further, it will imply that particular non-intuitional views differ from one another solely by differences of view concerning what kinds of things are good.

Such a view has a certain plausibility. We naturally think of the being here meant by 'a rational being' as a perfect being, and it is plausible to maintain that a perfect being will be moved solely by the desire that whatever is good shall come to exist, and that he will consider, and rightly consider, that the actions which he ought to do will be those which lead to the existence of what is good. It is then plausible to add that, though we, being only imperfect, do not always have the existence of what is good as our purpose, yet we can only find out what in a moral sense we ought to do by working out what would be the actions we ought to do in the non-moral sense, if the existence of what is good were our purpose. . . .

We have now to consider the meaning of the second and more important paragraph of the passage, . . . that in which he offers what he considers to be a proof of the principle of rational benevolence, i.e. the principle that each one is morally bound to regard the good of any other individual as much as his own. In this proof the idea is prominent that the process by which we come to apprehend one of its premisses as something self-evident is parallel to the process by which we come to apprehend as self-evident the principle that we ought to aim at our good on the whole. Sidgwick appears to be arguing thus:

'If I begin, as I can, with the thought of certain particular goods to me, $a, \beta, \gamma \ldots$ I can go on to form the idea that there is such a thing as my good on the whole[35] by thinking of $a, \beta, \gamma \ldots$ as forming a certain totality, this totality being what I call my good on the whole; and then when I have done so, it will be self-evident to me that $a, \beta, \gamma \ldots$ are equally parts of my good on the whole irrespectively of when they occur. In a similar way, if I begin, as I can, with the idea of the good of myself A thus formed and with the idea of B's good, the idea of C's good, etc., similarly formed, I can go on to form the idea that there is such a thing as Universal Good by thinking of my good, B's good, C's good... as forming a certain totality, this totality being what I call Universal Good; and then when I have done so, it will be self-evident to me that my good, B's good, C's good... are equally parts of Universal Good, irrespectively of whose good they are. Consequently, as it is also self-evident to me that as a rational being I am bound to aim at good generally [i.e. presumably, bound to do whatever will lead to the existence of what is good] it will be self-evident to me that, as a consequence, I am morally bound to do that action which will lead to the greatest amount of good to individuals, irrespectively of who the individuals are.'

The argument, so stated, is plausible and presents the appearance of proving a *moral* principle. Yet when we consider the passage more closely we find that the real thought underlying Sidgwick's language is quite different. In the process considered to afford a parallel it is obviously a condition of my coming to think of $a, \beta, \gamma \ldots$ as forming a certain whole called my good on the whole that I should think of $a, \beta, \gamma \ldots$ as each a good *to myself*. I could not, for instance, think of a good to myself and a good to B as forming a whole at all. And in the process considered parallel there must likewise be a condition of my thinking of my good, B's good, C's good... as forming a certain whole called Universal Good. Sidgwick by his use of the phrase 'Universal Good' implies that the condition is that I think of my good, of B's good, of C's good... as each good, my thinking of them thus enabling me to think of them as together constituting the totality of things which are good. But that this is not really the condition implied will be seen if we consider the implication of Sidgwick's statement 'And here again . . . I obtain the self-evident principle that the good of any one individual is *of no more importance*, from *the point of view* (if I may say so) of the Universe, than the good of any other.'[36] This statement is plainly of crucial importance for understanding Sidgwick, since without it he could not go on to maintain, as he does, that each of us is bound to regard the good of any other individual as much as his own.

---

[35] Sidgwick appears to be—without justification—treating my good and my good on the whole as identical.
[36] The italics are mine.

The statement, therefore, together with its implications, should be pressed. Now a point of view is somebody's point of view, and to be of importance is to be of importance to somebody. Hence if the statement is to be regarded as sense, 'the Universe' must be understood as an inaccurate phrase for the author of the Universe, or, at least, for a spectator of it. Further, to say in this context that something X is of importance to someone A is to imply that X is a good to A, in the sense of something which pleases A, or at least of something which is a source of satisfaction to A. Hence Sidgwick in making this statement is tacitly implying—whether he realizes it or not—that the author or the supposed spectator of the universe is a benevolent being to whom my good, B's good, C's good... are goods in virtue of his benevolence, i.e. his disinterested interest in these goods. For if the author or spectator were malevolent, it would be—to coin a phrase—the bad of myself, the bad of B, the bad of C... which were of importance to him, and if he were neither benevolent nor malevolent, neither the good nor the bad of any individual would be of any importance to him. Again the author or spectator is implied to be *purely* or *simply* benevolent, i.e. to be without any personal wants or tastes of his own, for it is implied that the good of myself, the good of B, the good of C... together and without anything else make up or constitute the good of the author or the spectator. Again Sidgwick's argument implies that if *we* are to recognize that we are bound to regard the good of any other individual as much as our own, *we* must be purely benevolent beings; otherwise our own good, B's good, C's good... will not be of equal importance to us and the only things of importance to us. Also it has to be added that the argument needs correction if, as we may assume, it is to have at least some plausibility. For, strictly speaking, and as Sidgwick himself would allow, to a purely benevolent spectator, it is not my good, B's good, C's good... but the thought of my good, the thought of B's good, the thought of C's good... that are goods, and it is not the former but the latter which, as a totality, constitute the good of the spectator, or of myself, if I were a purely benevolent being.

Hence the real thought underlying the passage requires 'Universal Good' to mean not what the phrase suggests, viz. the totality of things which are good, but the totality of the things which make up or constitute the good either (*a*) of a purely benevolent spectator of the universe or (*b*) of ourselves, with the implication that we are purely benevolent beings; and it implies that this totality consists in the thought of my good, the thought of B's good, the thought of C's good etc. Consequently Sidgwick's so-called proof that we are morally bound to regard the good of others as much as our own reduces to a contention which implies that we are purely benevolent beings; viz. that it is self-evident to us that since we are purely benevolent, and since therefore (1) the thoughts of the good of various individuals are all equally goods to ourselves, and (2) no other things are goods to ourselves, we ought in a given situation to do that which will lead to our good on the whole by bringing about the greatest amount of good to individuals irrespectively of who they are. Moreover the contention implies that we have, and know that we have, our own good, or more accurately our good on the whole, as our actual purpose. For if we are to think of the principle as self-evident, we have to think of ourselves as desiring, and acting from the desire of, our good on the whole, although at the same time affected by our knowledge that we are purely benevolent beings in determining what action will be for our good on the whole. . . .

There is an element of irony about his position. While he thinks that he is proving that our own good and the good of another enter on the same footing into what an action must be conducive to, if it is to be right, his proof really implies that in considering what we ought to do our own good cannot come into view at all. For we cannot possibly be benevolently disposed to *ourselves*, i.e. *disinterestedly* interested in our *own* happiness or good, and consequently our own good cannot form part of the totality of the various persons' goods which make up our good on the whole. Hence while Sidgwick has a show of a case for the non-moral principle that 'In considering whether we are to produce happiness in A or in B we should ignore the question who they are and consider only the amount of happiness which we can produce in each', he has not even a show of a case for a similar principle when the question is whether we are to produce happiness in *ourselves* or in *another*.

We can now understand how it is that Sidgwick later on comes to find that the position which he has advanced in the passage under discussion gives rise to two difficulties which he is unable to resolve and of which one leads him to conclude in effect that our apparent intuitions of what is reasonable [i.e. right] in conduct exhibit an ultimate and fundamental contradiction and therefore must be illusory,[37] or that, as he puts it elsewhere, morality is not completely rational.[38]

What Sidgwick considers that he has shown is the self-evidence of two principles, (1) that we ought—in the moral sense of 'ought'—to aim at our good on the whole, or, as we may say, our happiness on the whole, and (2) that we ought—again in a moral sense of 'ought'—to aim at the good of others and of ourselves indifferently, or, as we may say, to aim at the general happiness. The first difficulty which he afterwards finds this position to involve is really that there is no way of convincing a man in respect of whom the first principle is self-evident that the second principle is true, since in his case the second principle is really not only not self-evident but self-evidently false. The second difficulty is that the two principles must be allowed to be inconsistent, unless it can be shown, as it cannot, that the actions which are conducive to the general happiness will also always be those conducive to the agent's happiness on the whole. And it is in view of this second difficulty that Sidgwick, assuming for the time being that

---

[37] Cf. Sidgwick, *Methods of Ethics*, 508.   [38] Ibid., 498.

both principles are self-evident, concludes that our apparent intuitions of what is right exhibit a fundamental contradiction, and consequently must be illusory.

Sidgwick states the first difficulty thus: 'If the Egoist strictly confines himself to stating his conviction that he ought to take his own happiness or pleasure as his ultimate end, there seems no opening for any line of reasoning to lead him to Universalistic Hedonism as a first principle; it cannot be proved that the difference between his own happiness and another's happiness is not *for him* all important.' Shortly afterwards, however, Sidgwick goes on to add what appears to be a qualification. 'When, however, the Egoist puts forward, implicitly or explicitly, the proposition that his happiness or pleasure is Good, not only *for him* but from the point of view of the Universe—as (e.g.) by saying that "nature designed him to seek his own happiness"—it then becomes relevant to point out to him that *his* happiness cannot be a more important part of Good, taken universally, than the equal happiness of any other person. And thus, starting with his own principle, he may be brought to accept Universal happiness or pleasure as that which is absolutely and without qualification Good or Desirable; as an end, therefore, to which the action of a reasonable agent as such ought to be directed.'

Now when we bear in mind that both principles of which he has established the self-evidence are really non-moral and that each presupposes a certain character on the part of the man in respect of whom it is self-evident, it is easy to see why it is that in the case of man with regard to whom the first principle is self-evident, the second principle is not merely not self-evident but self-evidently false. For when Sidgwick says that it cannot be proved that the difference between the Egoist's own happiness and the happiness of another is not *for the Egoist* all important, he is implying that he himself knows, and therefore that it is true, that to an Egoist his own happiness is all important and the happiness of another is of no importance. Hence Sidgwick here obviously means by an Egoist a man who not only desires, and acts from the desire of, the greatest happiness of himself but to whom also, since he is totally devoid of benevolence, the things which are goods do not include the thoughts of the happiness of others, and who therefore will recognize as something self-evident, that in considering what actions will lead to his own greatest happiness he ought to take *no* account of the effect of any suggested action on the happiness of anyone else. It follows, of course, that the difficulty which Sidgwick thus propounds to his own view is insoluble. Again it is easy to see that his own attempt in the sequel to solve the difficulty—an attempt which he himself recognizes to be inadequate—is useless. In effect he first assumes that an egoist has somehow been transformed into a purely benevolent being, and then contends that by this transformation the egoist has become committed to the view that he ought to aim at the general happiness. But to do this is useless. For in the first place it implies that an egoist has ceased to be an egoist and so a being in regard to whom the first principle is self-evident; and in the second place it implies that the principle to which the man thus transformed is committed is not that he should do the acts which lead to the general happiness *as such*, but only that he should do those acts in virtue of the fact that, since he is purely benevolent, they will lead to his own greatest happiness.

Of the second difficulty little need be said. It is not surprising that Sidgwick should find inconsistency between the two principles which he has maintained to be self-evident, viz. (1) that we ought to do what will lead to our own greatest happiness and (2) that we ought to do what will lead to the general happiness. For if 'ought' here has a moral sense, they are obviously inconsistent, since actions conducive to one thing are not necessarily conducive to another; and if—as is really true—'ought' has the non-moral sense of conducive to our purpose, then though the same purpose is really implied by both principles, viz. the agent's greatest happiness, the agent is implied by the one principle to be devoid of benevolence and by the other to be purely benevolent, and this difference is bound to give rise to a difference in the actions which will be conducive to the agent's happiness. It need only be added that when Sidgwick goes on to conclude that our apparent intuitions of what is right exhibit a fundamental contradiction and must therefore be illusory, he is taking a radically false step, and that instead he should have reconsidered his view that both principles are self-evident.

VI. Right and Good

As has been pointed out, Sidgwick divides the answers to what is really the question 'What, if there are right actions, constitutes a right action right?' into two types according to the kind of argument by which we are conceived to discover some given particular action to be right; we may be conceived to do this either by apprehending the act to be a case of an act of some definite kind which we directly apprehend to be right or by apprehending it to lead to something which Sidgwick sometimes represents as our actual aim or purpose and sometimes as what ought to be our aim or purpose.

We have, however, to notice the existence of, and to consider, a third type of answer, which Sidgwick either does not notice or at least does not distinguish from the types which he recognizes. According to this third type, in order to discover a certain given particular action to be right, we have first to ascertain what things are good. And the type of view will admit of two varieties according as what we are considered to apprehend constitutes the action right is (*a*) its leading to the existence of something good, or more accurately of the maximum of things which are good, or (*b*) the action's being itself good, or more accurately the best possible. This third type of view resembles Sidgwick's non-intuitional type of view in representing our knowledge of what is right as depending on our knowledge of something different in kind, but differs from it in representing this latter knowledge not as the knowledge of what our *purpose* either is or ought to be, but as the knowledge of what is good.

Of this third type of view we may consider first the variety according to which those acts are right which *lead to* the existence of what is good. This variety is plausible, since it is plausible to maintain that where an action will be productive of something good it follows immediately from this fact that it is a duty to do the action. It is a view which is put forward in a particular form by Professor Moore,[39] and we may begin by considering this form.

Professor Moore's view, when worked out consistently, appears to be as follows:

'When we act we cause something to exist. In order to answer the question "What action ought we to do?" we have to answer two other questions first; viz. (1) "What things are good in themselves?", and (2) "What will be the effect of the various actions of which we are capable?". When we have answered the latter questions we shall be in a position to say of certain actions of which we are capable that they will cause a good something, and to say this is to say that these actions are right, for "right" does and can mean nothing but cause of a good result.[40] But we must distinguish between right and absolutely right. For among the alternative actions of which we are capable there may be more than one which will cause a good result, and if there is, while each of these actions will be right—for each will cause a good result—only one of them will be *absolutely* right, or our *absolute* duty; i.e. that act which will cause the maximum of what is good, or, more shortly, of good.'

Professor Moore, however, also holds that an action besides causing something good, may have a goodness of its own, and he unfortunately holds that in consequence, in order to estimate what action will be productive of most good, we have also to take into account the goodness which various actions may have in themselves.[41] To maintain this, however, is to be inconsistent since if 'to be right' means to cause a good result, the intrinsic goodness of a good action not being the goodness of something which it causes cannot affect its rightness. Hence this part of Professor Moore's view is best ignored. ...

Unfortunately also Professor Moore obscures the nature of his view by mistakenly connecting the meaning of the term 'good' with the distinction of means and end, and thereby really implying that the view can be expressed in terms of this distinction. He contends that we use the term 'good' in two senses, (1) that of 'good as a means', i.e. 'A means to good', and (2) that of 'good as an end',

---

[39] (G. Moore, *Principia Ethica*, sections 88–91 and sections 15–17; cf. sections 58–62 (Cambridge: Cambridge University Press, 1980). [40] Ibid., section 89.

[41] Ibid., section 17. Rashdall holds a similar view. Cf. Rashdall, *The Theory of Good and Evil*, i. 135–8 with i. 96–7.

which is equivalent to 'good in itself'.[42] This contention implies that his doctrine that our absolute duty is to do that act which will cause the maximum of good can be stated in the form that it is to do that act which will be *the means* to the maximum of good. And Professor Moore himself expressly goes on to maintain that because 'right' means cause of a good result, and is consequently identical in meaning with 'useful', the end always justifies the means.[43] The use of this terminology, however, is unfortunate. For when we use the terms 'means' and 'end' in describing some action, we are really referring to the desire which moves us in doing it, and to refer to the action which is to be absolutely right as the means to the maximum of what is good is to imply that it is one in which we shall be moved by the desire of the maximum of what is good; yet evidently on the view which Professor Moore is propounding the nature of the desire which will move us in doing a right action has nothing whatever to do with its rightness. Hence in considering his view we should also ignore any formulation of it which makes use of the terms 'means' and 'end'.

As soon, however, as we have realized the necessity of excluding from Professor Moore's account of his view both the inconsistent addition that the intrinsic goodness of an action may contribute to its rightness and any use of the terms 'means' and 'end', we are forced to allow that it is mistaken. For when we state of some suggested action, e.g. our keeping our engagement with X, that we ought, or that it is a duty on our part, it is plain that whatever we *do* mean by the statement, and whether the statement is true or not, we do *not mean* by it that the act will cause a good result. This is so obvious that when we consider an instance our only difficulty is to understand how Professor Moore can have come to persuade himself that 'right' *means* cause of a good result. . . .

We have next to consider the other variety of the third type of view, viz. that according to which we apprehend certain actions to be themselves instances of what is good. This variety is much more attractive. It really represents the things that are good by reference to which we apprehend right actions to be right as being the actualizations in action of a certain good capacity, or of certain good capacities, of human nature, and as it inevitably represents these actualizations as the motives of right actions, it represents the rightness of a right act as constituted by the goodness of its motive.

This view, which may be called the 'good will' view of what constitutes rightness, is, of course, prominent in the history of Moral Philosophy. We find it most prominently in Kant, although in Kant it appears along with a rival view. It is also prominent in those who have been influenced by Kant; Green, for instance, finds the highest moral goodness to be an attribute of character, in so

---

[42] *Principia Ethica*, section 17.   [43] Ibid., section 89.

far as it issues in acts done for the sake of their goodness.[44] We also find the view in Hutcheson, in Butler, and, to take another modern instance, in Martineau.[45] Indeed, it is apt to appear anywhere outside the ranks of Utilitarians.

It is, of course, obvious, as is constantly being pointed out by moral philosophers, that in ordinary life we approve and even admire some action actually done, and consequently think it good, in virtue of the spirit in which, or, more precisely, the motive from which it has been done and independently of the goodness of any results to which it has led. This approval is implied, for instance, when we refer to the self-sacrifice or disregard of self, or again to the generosity, shown in certain actions. These actions, we say, exhibit a certain goodness of character and a goodness which we are apt to call moral goodness. And we are apt to go on to maintain that this moral goodness constitutes these acts which ought to have been done, and that consequently, in order to find out what we ought to do in the future we have only to ascertain (1) the quality or qualities which constitute moral goodness, and (2) the acts in which this quality or these qualities will be actualized.

Of this view it is necessary from the beginning to distinguish two varieties, according as the motive constituting an act morally good is considered to be (a) the thought that the act is a duty, or, if not this thought, the desire to do the action as being a duty, or (b) some good desire other than the desire to do what is a duty. And it will be found conducive to clearness to consider first the former variety of the view, and to consider this in the form in which it is presented by Kant, its classical exponent.

If we endeavour to give a systematic account of Kant's *Fundamental Principles of the Metaphysic of Morals* we find ourselves confronted at the outset by an unexpected difficulty. A study of the preface suggests that Kant's object is, to use his own phrase, to discover the *basis* of moral obligation, i.e. really, to discover what constitutes those actions, whatever they may be, which are duties duties; and this suggestion is borne out by a comparison of the end of the first chapter with the beginning of the second. Consequently we are led to think that Kant's proper course is to begin by considering *duties*, i.e. really, the various actions which we think to be duties, with a view to ascertaining what constitutes these acts, if they are duties, and any other acts which may be duties, duties. And then we become puzzled because we find that Kant actually begins by doing something quite different, viz. by first laying down that the one thing which is good, independently of the existence of special conditions, is a good will, and then proceeding to analyse the nature of *a good will*, i.e., of a morally good will. The explanation, of course, is that Kant thinks that moral goodness somehow

---

[44] (T. H. Green, *Lectures on the Principles of Political Obligation*, section 2 (London: Longmans, Green and Co., 1921).

[45] (J. Martineau, *Types of Ethical Theory*, II, Part II, Book I (Cf. esp. Ch. I, section 1, 1, Ch. V, section 4, Ch. VI, section 15) (Oxford: Clarendon Press, 1885).

forms the basis of duty or moral obligation, i.e. that the reason why acts which are duties are duties is to be found in the moral goodness actualized in doing them. His view, which, whether it be tenable or not, can at least be expressed shortly, may be stated thus:

'Analysis of moral goodness shows that it is constituted by the fact that the agent in doing a morally good act is actuated solely by the conviction that the act is a duty. Now what constitutes the acts which are duties duties is moral goodness. Consequently our duty consists in acting solely from the conviction that what we are doing is a duty.'

Unfortunately we have only to render the nature of this view fully explicit to discover that it is inherently untenable. In order to bring to light its real nature it will be best to begin by noticing two senses, a narrower and a wider, in which we use the term 'action'.

The phrase 'an action'—together with the corresponding phrase 'doing something'—is ambiguous.[46] Ordinarily it stands simply for the origination or bringing something about, as when we speak of the action of poking a fire or of annoying a neighbour. And in this sense of 'action' an action of one kind is distinguished from an action of another kind by the special kind of thing brought about, e.g. a certain arrangement of the materials of a fire or a pain suffered by a neighbour. Sometimes, however, 'an action' is used with a wider or more inclusive meaning to stand for the bringing something about from a motive, as when we speak of an act of benevolence or of revenge. And in this wider sense of 'action' an action of one kind is distinguished from an action of another kind by the kind of motive—as when we speak of benevolent acts, acts of gratitude, and so on. These two usages, however, though different, are essentially related. For when we refer to some action already done by a phrase which implies that we are using the word 'action' in the narrower sense, as when we speak of X's action of poking his fire, we know that the agent had a motive in doing the action, although we may have no opinion as to what his motive was, and although, even if we have an opinion as to what his motive was, we are considering his action in abstraction from what we think his motive was. Again when we refer to some action already done by a phrase which implies that we are using the word 'action' or 'act' in the wider sense, as when we speak of X's act of revenge on Y, we imply that the agent in being actuated by a certain motive was actuated to do something in particular, in the narrower sense of 'doing something',—i.e. to bring about something—though the phrase by which we refer to the action may do little or even nothing to indicate what, in this sense of 'do', he did. Further it is to be observed that while when we speak of some action as good or as bad in itself, we are using 'action' in the wider sense,—for the goodness or badness of

---

[46] 'An action' here is to be understood in the restricted sense of a deliberate action, the only sense required for the consideration of Kant's view.

which we are speaking is the goodness or badness of the motive, yet when we speak of some action as right or as wrong, we are using 'action' in the narrower sense. For when *before* acting we are considering whether some suggested action is a duty, we cannot know what our motive would be if we were to do the action and—what is, of course, more important—we should not think the knowledge, even if we possessed it, relevant.

This distinction between the two senses of the word 'action' will become clearer if we consider the question whether it is possible to do two actions identical in character from different motives. In ordinary life we find no difficulty in allowing this to be possible. Suppose that someone in the position of a Lord Mayor, considering whether to initiate a relief fund for the victims of an earthquake, foresees that, if he does, not only will the victims obtain relief but also he himself will gain *kudos*, and that he thinks that there is a certain duty incumbent on him as Lord Mayor to help the victims. X in a position of that kind may start a fund animated mainly by the desire to help the victims as a duty; Y may do so animated mainly by the desire of *kudos*. Here we should ordinarily find no difficulty in allowing that if they act thus, then although their motives were mainly different, their actions were of precisely the same kind, since what they brought about was of precisely the same kind. Yet to this admission there seems, on reflection, to be an objection of principle; viz. that since their motives were different, their actions must have been different. It may, however, be answered that while, in the wider sense of 'action', their actions were different, in the narrower sense they were not, since what X brought about and what Y brought about were identical in character. It may, perhaps, still be objected that this cannot really be so, since in similar circumstances a difference of motive must give rise to a difference in what men do—in the narrower sense of 'do'. But to this it can be replied that it *is* really possible to do from *different* motives actions which will lead, directly and indirectly, to states of affairs of precisely the same kind, and which, consequently, are actions—in the narrower sense of 'actions'—of precisely the same kind.

In the light of those considerations we may now endeavour to make clear to ourselves the real nature of Kant's view of what constitutes an action a duty. For this purpose we have first to make clear the nature of Kant's view of moral goodness, considered apart from the use which he makes of it in order to represent moral goodness as the basis of obligation.

Unquestionably when Kant speaks of a morally good action, he is using 'action' in the wider sense; for he thinks of its moral goodness as consisting in the fact that the agent in doing the action is being actuated by a certain motive. But also unquestionably Kant must be implying that the agent in being thus actuated is being actuated to do some action in the *narrower* sense of bringing something about; e.g. to pay a certain debt, or to torture a certain heretic. For he must be implying that in *any* action in the wider sense, whether it be morally good or not, the agent is being actuated to do some action in the narrower sense of 'action'.

Again in order to state Kant's view of the motive of a morally good action we must unquestionably describe the motive as the thought or the conviction that the action is a duty. But to make sense of this description, the term 'action' here has to be understood in the narrower sense. It is intelligible to speak of a man who does some action, in the narrower sense of 'action', e.g. of a man who tortures some heretic, as animated by the conviction that he ought to do that action in the narrower sense of 'action' and it is then intelligible to go on to say that the fact that the man is thus animated renders his action, in the wider sense of 'action', morally good. But it is not intelligible to speak of a man who does some action, in the *narrower* sense of 'action', as animated by the conviction that he ought to do a certain action, in the *wider* sense of 'action'—the sense required by 'morally good'. For to speak thus would be to imply that the man was animated, not by the conviction that he ought to do what he does in the narrower sense, e.g. torture the heretic, but by the conviction that he ought to do it from a certain motive; and then if we were asked what this motive is, we could only reply that it is the conviction that he ought to do this action from another certain motive, and thus we should become involved in an infinite process. Moreover it is quite clear that when Kant is actually analysing moral goodness, and not attempting to use his analysis in order to draw conclusions concerning our duty, his view is that a morally good act is one in which the agent does what he does, in the narrower sense of 'do', purely from the thought that he ought to do this something, in the narrower sense.

Now this view of moral goodness considered in itself is at the very least plausible, if not true. Anyone would at least have to allow that it contains elements of truth. But, it has to be admitted that Kant's attempt to use it in order to represent moral goodness as the basis of duty, i.e. as what constitutes duties, is wholly untenable, and involves an inversion.

According to Kant, the moral goodness of an action, in the wider sense, consists in the fact that the agent in doing the action which, in acting thus, he does, in the narrower sense, is actuated solely by the conviction that he ought to do this action, in the narrower sense. Consequently, according to him, the answer to the question whether some particular action, in the wider sense, is morally good is wholly independent of what in doing this action the agent does, in the narrower sense; i.e. it is wholly independent of what the agent brings about; it depends solely on the way or manner in which he does it, i.e. on his motive. In fact moral goodness is implied to consist not in a man's doing certain actions—in the narrower sense—in particular, but in his doing in a particular way whatever it is that, in the narrower sense, he is doing, viz. from the conviction that he ought to do it. Consequently on Kant's view that what constitutes actions duties is moral goodness, our duty consists, not in doing certain actions, as distinct from certain others, in the narrower sense, since *no* actions in this sense are duties, but in doing some action, whatever the action may be, in the narrower sense, from the conviction that we ought to do it. Thus, according to him, it is not a duty to pay a certain debt or to torture some heretic or indeed to do anything else whatever but if, for instance, I have the conviction that I ought to pay the debt, then it will be a duty on my part to do so from the conviction that I ought, and what will render the acting thus a duty is not the fact that in doing so I shall be paying the debt but the fact that in doing so I shall be actuated by this conviction. Again if instead of being convinced that I ought to torture the heretic, I am convinced that I ought to load him with kindness, then, according to Kant, it will be a duty on my part to load him with kindness from this conviction.

As should now be obvious, this account of what constitutes an action a duty really involves a contradiction. The contradiction is that while it is intended to be an answer to the question 'What characteristic of an action—in the narrower sense of "action"—constitutes it right?', it implies that there is no such characteristic, since rightness is constituted, not by some character possessed by certain actions, in the narrower sense, but solely by the way in which we do whatever actions we do, in this sense. In fact from this point of view the defect of Kant's doctrine is not that it gives no clue to what it is that we ought to do—though it actually gives no clue; the defect lies in its implication that there is *nothing* which we ought to do. Further the doctrine, when made explicit, has plainly another fatal defect. For it implies that a morally good action requires on the part of the agent a conviction which is inconsistent with the view and therefore false,—viz. the conviction that the doing a certain action, in the narrower sense, and therefore the mere doing it irrespectively of how it is done, is a duty. Hence the view implies that both the existence of moral goodness, and also the reality of such moral obligation as there is, viz. to act from the conviction that we ought to do what we are doing, presuppose the existence of a fundamental mistake or illusion on the part of the agent. For without the existence of a conviction of this kind, which on the view is fundamentally mistaken, neither could exist. Further as soon as this implication is realized, the view ceases to have any plausibility. For while there is some plausibility in maintaining that we ought to do, from the conviction that we ought, any action which we are convinced that we ought to do, *provided* it be allowed that such a conviction may be true, there is no plausibility whatever in maintaining this, if at the same time it be maintained that any such conviction must be false. Consequently, as soon as this implication is brought to light, Kant has really lost all prospect of persuading anyone that he ought to do what is morally good.

The fact is that Kant is simply inverting the relation between the thought that a certain action is right and the thought that a certain action is morally good. Whereas in fact the thought that a certain action is morally good presupposes the existence in the agent of the thought that it is right, and right on grounds which are independent of moral goodness,—so that this latter thought is independent of any thought of moral goodness—Kant is representing the thought that a certain act is right as presupposing, and indeed derived from, the thought that it is morally good.

It need hardly be said that Kant failed to realize the absurdities in which his position is involved. Plainly he had not fully thought the position out. Moreover the absurdities are doubtless in part concealed from him by the fact that side by side with this view of the basis of obligation there runs another which does not involve these absurdities. This other view emerges where Kant, asking himself 'What actions are categorically prescribed to us?', is struck with the idea that as their nature, in contrast with that of actions hypothetically prescribed, cannot be deduced from any purpose which we may have, it only remains for it to be deduced from the bare nature of a moral or categorical principle as such, i.e. as a principle or law binding on everyone. Realizing of course that only an act of a kind which can be done by everyone can be binding on everyone, he is led to conclude that any kind of action capable of being done by everyone is, as such, a duty.[47] This view, though, of course, open to the objection that it represents the fact that everyone *can* do an act of a certain kind as constituting a reason why it *ought* to be done, is free from the absurdities in question.

At this point it may be objected that though the preceding criticisms are unanswerable, yet the failure of Kant's attempt to represent moral goodness as the basis of rightness is really due to a mistake about the nature of moral goodness, and that the criticisms cease to apply if we substitute the truth, viz. that a morally good act is one actuated not by the *thought* that the act is a duty but by a desire which involves this thought, viz. the *desire* to do the right act in question. It will, however, be found that if we make this substitution, the criticisms are still applicable, and also that the view will then be liable to the additional objection of implying that our duty is to *act from a certain desire*, viz. the desire to do our duty, and so *to aim* at a certain something.

It should, however, be observed that none of the preceding criticisms shows or even suggests that Kant is mistaken in his analysis of moral goodness. They only show that Kant is mistaken in representing moral goodness as the basis of rightness. And if we consider the analysis itself we are bound to allow that in the main it is right. Kant is of course sometimes criticized for representing moral goodness as something cold and heartless; and it is urged that we think much better of a man who has done certain actions out of, say, kindness or pity, than of a man who has done similar actions from what we usually call a sense of duty.

---

[47] Although Kant expresses his conclusion in the form 'Act only on that maxim whereby thou *canst* at the same time *will that it should become* a universal law', and although in discussing particular maxims he usually refers to it in this form, the contrast which he draws between categorical and hypothetical imperatives shows that his view in its strict form should be expressed by the statement 'Act only on that maxim which can *become* a universal law'. And he expressly points out that maxims which violate strict, as distinct from meritorious duties, not only cannot be willed to be, but also cannot even be conceived to be, universal laws.

But this criticism involves a certain ambiguity and is, at best, an overstatement. For plainly we approve both an act prompted by a sense of duty, even though we may think the agent mistaken in thinking the particular act which he does, e.g. torturing some heretic, a duty, and also, an act prompted by what we should call kindness of heart or gratitude or the like; and our recognition that an act of the latter kind has a goodness of its own in no way precludes our recognizing that an act of the former kind has a goodness, and a different goodness, of its own. And the question 'Which kind of action is better entitled to the term "morally good"?' is really a question concerning the usage of the term 'moral goodness'. If we use the term 'moral goodness' in a broad sense, as equivalent in meaning to 'goodness of character', we shall have to allow that actions of *both* kinds are morally good. It is, however, more in accordance with ordinary usage to use 'moral goodness' as standing for that form of goodness which is actualized when, or rather, so far as, a man acts, as we say, from a sense of duty. And, given this usage, if we ignore the question whether strictly speaking, where a man is said to do some action from a sense of duty, his motive is the *thought* that the act is a duty or the *desire* to do the action, as being a duty, we shall have to allow that Kant's analysis of moral goodness is right. . . . But, otherwise, the only criticism to which he is justly liable is that he is mistaken in thinking moral goodness, in the narrower sense of 'moral goodness', the only form of goodness of character. And the only positive contention which his critics are entitled to advance is that there are other, and perhaps better, forms of goodness of character. If, however, they go on to maintain that these other forms are the only forms of goodness of character, they are merely repeating Kant's mistake in another form by going to the opposite extreme.

We may now consider the other variety of what may be called the 'good will' view of what constitutes rightness, the variety according to which the motive which constitutes an act morally good, in the wider sense in which 'moral goodness' is equivalent to 'goodness of character', is some good desire other than the desire to do what is a duty. If we look for a word for the kind of goodness on which the critics of Kant's account of moral goodness lay stress, we find the least inappropriate to be 'virtuousness'. And if we adopt this terminology, we can express the contrast between this variety of the 'good will' view and the Kantian variety by saying that, while, according to Kant, our duty consists in acting solely from the conviction that what we are doing is a duty, according to this variety our duty consists in acting solely from some virtuous desire.

This variety of the view is to be found in Butler.[48] It is also well represented by Hutcheson. Hutcheson was impressed by our disinterested approval of certain actions, an approval which he sometimes refers to as our perception of their

---

[48] It is most prominent in his *Dissertation on the Nature of Virtue*. [J. Butler, *The Analogy of Religion* (including *Dissertation of the Nature of Virtue*) (London, 1736). Ed.]

moral goodness. He considered that on examination the acts which we thus approve turn out to be acts prompted by benevolence. And he drew the conclusion that what we ought to do is to act benevolently, i.e. really to act from the desire to help others. Hume, also, thought that the actions which we think, and which are, right are those which we praise and think meritorious, and that we think them meritorious in respect of their having a virtuous motive, such as arises from parental affection or gratitude; and on this basis he developed a well-known argument which is at least conclusive in showing that *if* this view be true, it is impossible for the motive of any right action to be what Hume called the sense of its morality, i.e. the thought that the action is right, or if not this, the desire to do that action as right. The argument is as follows:

It appears, therefore, that all virtuous actions derive their merit only from virtuous motives, and are consider'd merely as signs of those motives. From this principle I conclude that the first virtuous motive, which bestows a merit on any action, can never be a regard to the virtue of that action, but must be some other natural motive or principle. To suppose that the mere regard to the virtue of the action, may be the first motive, which produc'd the action, and render'd it virtuous, is to reason in a circle. Before we can have such a regard the action must be really virtuous; and this virtue must be deriv'd from some virtuous motive; and consequently the virtuous motive must be different from the regard to the virtue of the action. A virtuous motive is requisite to render an action virtuous. An action must be virtuous, before we can have a regard to its virtue. Some virtuous motive, therefore, must be antecedent to that regard.

Nor is this merely a metaphysical subtlety; but enters into all our reasonings in common life, tho' perhaps we may not be able to place it in such distinct philosophical terms. We blame a father for neglecting his child. Why? Because it shows a want of natural affection, which is the duty of every parent. Were not natural affection a duty, the care of children cou'd not be a duty; and twere impossible we cou'd have the duty in our eye in the attention we give to our offspring. In this case, therefore, all men suppose a motive to the action distinct from a sense of duty. . . .

In short, it may be establish'd as an undoubted maxim, *that no action can be virtuous, or morally good, unless there be in human nature some motive to produce it, distinct from the sense of its morality.*[49]

Here Hume plainly means by 'a regard to the virtue of the action' what he afterwards refers to as a sense of duty; and what he establishes is that if, as he thinks, right action consists in virtuous action, then, since the virtuousness of a virtuous action consists in the virtuousness of its motive, such as a desire arising out of parental affection, in doing a right action our motive can *never*[50] be a sense

[49] (David Hume, *A Treatise of Human Nature*, Book III, Part II, section 1, 478–9 (Oxford, 1941).

[50] Hume himself only concludes that the sense of duty can never be the *first* motive, but his premises justify the conclusion that it can never be a motive at all. It may be noted that Martineau in denying that conscience is 'a spring of action' is really maintaining a similar view, viz. that the thought that what we are doing is right can never by our motive. [J. Martineau, *Types of Ethical Theory*, P. II, Bk. I, Ch. V, section 4. Ed.]

of duty, i.e. the thought that this act is a duty, or, if not this, the desire to do the right act in question. The net result is that Hume's view resembles Hutcheson's, being the view that, for example, what would ordinarily be called the duty of looking after our children is really the duty of acting from parental affection, and that the one thing which can never be the motive of a right action is the sense of duty.

When the nature of this variety of the 'good will' view of right action is thus made clear, it becomes obviously exposed to one main fatal objection. It amounts to maintaining what we ought to do is to aim at, i.e. have as our purpose, the object of one of our virtuous desires. It is therefore only a special form of what in Chapter III we found to be the fundamentally erroneous view that we ought to *aim at* a certain something or certain somethings. It is moreover significant of the inherent weakness of this variety of the 'good will' view that neither Hutcheson nor Hume is able to adhere to it consistently. When Hutcheson comes to consider what acts are right in particular his conclusion is in effect that we ought to do those actions which will be productive of the greatest amount of happiness in all rational agents whom our influence can reach.[51] Again in order to reach this conclusion, he asserts—obviously both inconsistently with his general view and also untruly—that we judge the degree of *virtue* of an action to be in proportion to the number of persons made happy and to the degree in which they are made happy. Yet in regard to both contentions he need only have remembered the widow's mite to have convinced himself that, on his own view that what we approve in an action is its benevolence, the doctrine that our approval depends on the amount of happiness produced must be false. Again Hume has to allow that the sense of duty *may* produce an action without any other motive; and he endeavours to show this admission is consistent with his general view thus:

'When any virtuous motive or principle is common in human nature, a person, who feels his heart devoid of that motive, may hate himself upon that account, and may perform the action without the motive, from a certain sense of duty, in order to acquire by practice, that virtuous principle, or at least, to disguise from himself, as much as possible, his want of it. A man that really feels no gratitude in his temper, is still pleas'd to perform grateful actions, and thinks he has, by that means, fulfill'd his duty.'[52] Yet in saying this he is obviously implying, *contrary* to his general view, that under certain conditions we actually think right certain actions which *ex hypothesi* can have no virtuous motive, viz. those which will eventually enable us to acquire, and so to act from, a virtuous motive, or at least those which will conceal from us our lack of a virtuous motive.

---

[51] F. Hutcheson, *An Inquiry Into the Original of our Ideas of Beauty and Virtue* (4th edn., 1738), section 3, subsections VIII–X [(London, republished by Gregg International Publishers, 1969), 180–6, Ed.].

[52] D. Hume, *Treatise*, Book III, Part II, section 1, 479 (Oxford: Clarendon Press, 1941).

9. Moral Obligation

I. The Main Questions about Moral Obligation

The object of this inquiry is first to consider, with the help of the treatment they have received, the chief questions which have been raised about moral obligation, and then to examine certain questions which arise as the result of this consideration. To many it will come as a surprise that there are questions to be raised about moral obligation. For although a normal person, once he has reached a certain age, plainly has the idea of moral obligation, since he thinks of himself as morally bound to do certain actions and as morally bound not to do certain others, and although he will have asked himself on various occasions whether he ought or ought not to do certain actions, he is not thereby necessarily led to ask any general question about moral obligation, such as: What character must an act have for us to be morally bound to do it? Yet the existence of such questions is shown by the existence of what are called books on moral philosophy, in whose subject duty undeniably occupies an important if not the central place.

To ascertain the chief questions raised it would seem necessary only to refer to the chief writers. Yet the attempt to do this is apt to be bewildering. For it will be found difficult to find a single set of questions which each writer in his own way is trying to answer. And in some cases, as in that of Butler or, to take a modern instance, that of Bradley, it is even difficult to be sure about the questions which they are trying to answer. Even if we find a formula such as the question: What is the basis of moral obligation?, it may be vague and in need of clearing up.

Nevertheless, consideration seems to show that four chief questions have been raised, though not necessarily by the same thinkers.

First, there is the question which Plato raises in the Republic: 'Will a man be better off for doing his duty?'—a question which he puts in the form: 'Is just action profitable?'

Second, there is the question, the answer to which Plato considered to turn on the answer to the first question: viz. 'Should or ought a man to do his duty (or, as Plato put it, do what is just)?' In putting this question it is of course implied that 'should' or 'ought' is being used in some sense other than that in which to say that I ought to do so and so is only another way of saying that I am morally bound to do so and so. And the sense implied must be one in which we use it in connexion with any action which we do not think of as a duty, as when we ask: 'Should I take the first turn to the left?'

Third, there is the question which almost inevitably arises as soon as we recognize that the various acts which we think duties fall into groups of different sorts, such as speaking the truth, obeying the government, keeping a promise. For, this once noticed, it is almost bound to occur to us that acts of different sorts cannot all be duties unless they possess some common character, the possession of which renders them duties. And if this does occur we are led to ask: What is the character which an act must have for us to be bound to do it, and the possession of which by our action is the reason why we ought to do it? The question is sometimes put in the form: What is the criterion of a duty? And by 'a theory of moral obligation' seems to be meant an answer to this question.

Fourth, there is the question: What is moral obligation? i.e. what is it for someone to be morally bound to do some action?, along with which goes the corresponding question: What is it to be morally bound *not* to do some action?, where plainly 'morally bound not to do some action' does not mean 'not morally bound to do some action' but stands for something positive.

These questions are, of course, not necessarily independent. Thus it would at least seem impossible to answer the question whether we shall be better off for doing our duty without first ascertaining the character common to the acts which form our duties. And for this reason it will not be easy to settle which question should be considered first. Moreover, though they are few they may none the less be difficult to answer, possibly partly because to get an answer to them we may have first to find the answer to other and difficult questions, such as, e.g., 'What is doing something?'; and when we have found an answer, we may find ourselves still faced by other and difficult questions.

Of these questions, the last will be considered first, because although it is not the first which anyone is likely to raise, the answer to it bears on the answers to the others. Then the first and the second will be considered together, as being the questions which most men raise first. And then the ground will be cleared for consideration of the third, which will be found to need much more discussion.

II. The Question 'What is Moral Obligation?'

As has already been implied, we, in our ordinary unreflective state of mind, regard statements of the form, 'X ought to do so and so', 'X has the duty of doing so and so', and 'X is morally bound to do so and so', as equivalent in meaning. And Hume is only expressing the necessity of answering the question 'What is moral obligation?' in the phraseology of 'ought' when he says:

I cannot forbear adding to these reasonings an observation, which may, perhaps, be found of some importance. In every system of morality, which I have hitherto met with, I have always remark'd, that the author proceeds for some time in the ordinary way of reasoning, and establishes the being of a God, or makes observations concerning human affairs; when of a sudden I am surpriz'd to find, that instead of the usual copulations of propositions, *is*, and *is not*, I meet with no proposition that is not connected with an *ought*, or an *ought not*. This change is imperceptible; but is, however, of the last consequence. For as this *ought*, or *ought not*, expresses some new relation or affirmation, 'tis necessary that it shou'd be observ'd and explain'd; and at the same time that a reason shou'd be given, for what seems altogether inconceivable, how this new relation can be a deduction from others, which are entirely different from it. But as authors do not commonly use this precaution, I shall presume to recommend it to the readers; and am persuaded, that this small attention wou'd subvert all the vulgar systems of morality, and let us see, that the distinction of vice and virtue is not founded merely on the relations of objects, nor is perceiv'd by reason.[1]

For the context shows that he is here thinking of the terms 'ought' and 'ought not' as terms used in connexion with actions, and from other passages it is clear that he would accept the statement, 'X is under a moral obligation to educate Y' as equivalent in meaning to 'X ought to educate Y'. Indeed, as Hume is putting the question, it is in effect the question 'What distinguishes a statement of the form, "X *ought* to do so and so", from a statement of the form, "X *is* doing so and so"?' And it will refer to something which we should have in mind if we said to someone, as we might: 'I am not considering the question whether X is doing (or was doing, or is going to do) a certain action, but the quite different question whether X is (or was, or will be) morally bound to do it.' We substitute 'is morally bound' for 'ought' only because 'ought' does not admit of difference of tense. And the question is in the first instance best considered in Hume's formulation of it, because the form 'X ought to do so and so' is the more usual, and the other, if used in preference, seems intended as an elucidation of it. To make sure, however, of not misunderstanding the question when thus formulated, it is necessary to apprehend clearly that the sense in which 'ought' is being used here is quite different from that to which Kant refers when he speaks of hypothetical imperatives. Kant designates all statements of the form 'I ought to do so and so' imperatives, choosing this term because he considers that they express commands. And he divides them into two kinds which he calls respectively hypothetical and categorical according as the idea on which the statement is based is (*a*) the idea that the doing of the act is necessary for the realization of something which I am or possibly might be willing, i.e. which is or might be my purpose in action, or (*b*) the idea that the act is one which I ought to do of itself, i.e. independently of its being necessary for the realization of some actual or possible purpose of mine. Instances of the former would be 'I ought to get up early', when asserted on the ground that my purpose in acting is the maintenance of my health and that my early rising is necessary for this; and, again, 'I ought to make friends', when asserted on the ground that my happiness is my purpose and that its attainment requires the making of friends. Further,

---

[1] D. Hume, *A Treatise of Human Nature* (ed. Selby-Bigge), pp. 469–70.

he subdivides what he calls hypothetical imperatives into two kinds which he calls respectively counsels of prudence and rules of skill according as the purpose implied is or is not our happiness.

Kant, here, in drawing his main distinction, viz. that between categorical and hypothetical imperatives, does not say that the term 'ought' has a different meaning in each of the two kinds of statement. Indeed, what he says suggests the contrary, for he uses the same term 'imperative' for both, and represents the difference as consisting solely in the difference of the grounds on which they are asserted—grounds which can only be ascertained from the context; so that when told, e.g., that we ought never to drive a hard bargain, we cannot tell whether the imperative is 'categorical' or 'hypothetical' unless we know whether the speaker is or is not attributing to us some purpose, such as increase of our business. Yet plainly Kant thinks that there is a difference of meaning, for he goes on to speak of categorical imperatives as *moral* imperatives, or imperatives of *morality*. And, in fact, there is a difference and indeed a total difference of meaning. This difference becomes obvious if we consider instances. Thus, to borrow from Kant an instance of a hypothetical imperative, we say to a would-be poisoner: 'You ought to give a second dose'; the thought which we wish to convey is that if he does not, his purpose, viz. the death of his would-be victim, will not be realized. Indeed, this is what we really mean by our statement. At first, no doubt, the statement, 'If you do not give a second dose, your purpose will not be realized', seems to state our reason for our assertion, 'You ought to give a second dose', rather than what we mean by it. But this cannot be so, for if it were, we should in making the assertion be implying the idea that whenever a man has a certain purpose, no matter what the purpose be, he ought to do whatever is necessary for its realization, and no one has such an idea. Hence, to put the matter generally, whenever we use the term 'ought' thus, what we really mean by the categorical statement 'I ought to do so and so' has to be expressed by the hypothetical statement: 'If I do not do so and so, my purpose will not be realized.'

It may be noticed that this is the real justification for Kant's designating as hypothetical the imperatives which he distinguishes from imperatives of morality. On the other hand, if we say to a man 'You ought to tell the truth' and mean by it what Kant evidently understood it to mean in calling it a categorical imperative, we do so, as Kant saw, without any reference to some purpose we may think he has, and if we are asked what we mean, we should, ordinarily at least, only answer by using what we considered a verbal equivalent such as 'should' or 'duty' or 'morally bound'. Indeed, as we cannot fail to allow on reflection, the difference in meaning is complete. And for this reason the distinction which Kant is formulating is really not, as he represents it as being, one between two statements containing the word 'ought' made on different grounds, but one between two statements in which 'ought' has a completely different meaning. Consequently the two kinds of statement should be referred to not by Kant's phrases 'categorical' and 'hypothetical imperatives' but rather by phrases indicating the difference in meaning borne by 'ought' in each. And for this purpose the least unsatisfactory phrases seem to be moral and non-moral imperatives. But if this be done, 'moral' must be understood not in its ordinary sense of morally good, but as simply the equivalent of 'duty' or 'morally bound'.

Hume's question then, stated unambiguously, is: 'What distinguishes our assertion, e.g., that X *ought* to be educating his son Y—where "ought" is being used in the moral sense—from our assertion, e.g., that X *is* educating his son Y'?

To this question one answer can be ruled out at once. This is the answer implied by Hume when he speaks of 'ought' and 'ought not' as expressing some new relation, i.e. some relation different from that implied by 'is' and 'is not'. For to speak thus is to imply that what distinguishes the former assertion from the latter is that instead of asserting that a certain subject of attributes, viz. X, stands in the relation to a certain attribute, viz. that of educating Y, of being something which *does* possess it, it asserts that the subject stands to the attribute in the relation of being something which *ought* to possess it, the problem being to ascertain what this relationship is. And there can neither be nor be thought to be any such relationship. For as we recognize when we reflect, the only relations in which a given subject of attributes can possibly stand to a given attribute are those of possessing and not possessing it, no third alternative being possible. And consequently, when we assert that X ought to be educating Y, we cannot possibly be asserting that X stands to the act of educating Y in a relation indicated by the word 'ought' which is neither that of possessing it nor that of not possessing it. As Kant pointed out when considering the term 'sollen', the very question: 'What ought to be the properties of a mile?', as distinct from: 'What are the properties of a mile?', is absurd.

This being so, what seems to distinguish the second assertion from the first is that in it we are attributing to the same subject of attributes X, i.e. asserting him to possess, an attribute of a different kind, viz. that of being under an obligation to educate Y, as distinct from that of educating Y, so that Hume's question becomes: 'What is the *being under an obligation to do some action?*', as distinct from doing some action. And if this be right, the nature of the thought which we express by a statement of the form 'X ought to do so and so' is more clearly expressed by substituting a statement of the form 'X is under an obligation to do so and so'.

It might, however, be maintained that if we consider the nature of the thought which the assertion that X ought to be educating Y expresses, we find that (1) although in making the assertion we are attributing an attribute to a subject of attributes, yet in this case the subject of attributes to which we are attributing an attribute is not X, as it is when we assert that X is educating Y, but the action, viz. educating Y; and that (2) we use the term 'ought' to indicate the nature of the attribute which we are attributing to the action. But if this contention be advanced, the question will have to be answered: 'If so, what is the attribute indicated by the term "ought"?', and the only possible answer will be: 'That of being something which ought to exist.' Consequently the view will be that in asserting, e.g., that X ought to be educating Y, what we are really asserting is that X's educating Y is something which ought to exist. And if it be objected that the phrase 'ought to exist' is artificial, it can be replied that at any rate we are prepared to apply it to things which we think to be good.

Nevertheless, this way of interpreting what we mean by 'X ought to educate Y' is open to a fatal objection. For we can no more either think or assert of something which we think does not exist that it ought to exist than we can think or assert anything else about it. Of what we think does not exist we can think and assert nothing at all. Yet unquestionably, in asserting that X ought to be educating Y, we need not be thinking of X's educating Y as existing, since we think the truth of our assertion independent of whether X is educating Y. Consequently we cannot be asserting that X's educating Y is something which ought to exist. Consequently anyone who begins by offering this interpretation can be forced into modifying it to the extent of allowing that 'X ought to be educating Y' is really hypothetical in meaning, and that if the thought which it is used to express is expressed accurately, it must be expressed in the form: 'If X is, or will be, educating Y, his educating Y is, or will be, something which ought to exist.' And if this interpretation be right, there will be no such thing as the attribute of being under a moral obligation to do some action, but only that of being something which ought to exist, this being attributable only to acts which we think were, are being, or will be done, and the very phrase 'being under an obligation to do so and so' will be misleading, as standing for something which can have no existence.

There seems, therefore, to be no way of avoiding the admission that an assertion of the form: 'X ought to do so and so', when 'ought' is being used in a moral sense, has to be interpreted in one or other of two ways. We have either to maintain that it means 'X is under a moral obligation to do so and so', being under a moral obligation to do some action being implied to be a special kind of attribute of a man; or else to maintain that it means: If X does so and so, his doing so and so ought to exist.

We at once find the second interpretation very difficult to accept, partly because the phrase 'ought to exist' strikes us as artificial, but still more because we find it hard to convince ourselves that such a statement is not in meaning as well as in grammatical form categorical. And it does not seem possible to find any thinker who has explicitly offered this interpretation. Nevertheless, as will appear later, there are many who when they raise the question, 'Why is a man bound to do a certain action?' give answers which imply this interpretation. And it should be noticed that this interpretation cannot be ruled out on the general ground that any assertion which is grammatically categorical cannot be hypothetical in meaning, for we have to allow that at any rate a non-moral imperative though categorical in form is hypothetical in meaning.

Nevertheless, when we consider the matter thoroughly we find ourselves forced to admit that when we assert, e.g., that X *ought* to be educating Y, we *are* attributing a certain attribute to X, and therefore are implying the existence of such an attribute as the being under an obligation to do some action.

This being so we must allow that Hume's question really reduces to the question: 'What is the kind of attribute to which we refer when we say, e.g., that X is under a moral obligation to educate his son Y?'

If we consider this question in connexion with instances, we soon become forced to admit that the kind of attribute is *sui generis*, i.e. unique, and therefore incapable of having its nature expressed in terms of the nature of anything else. To bring the necessity of making this admission home to ourselves, we need only consider various definitions which have been offered and which fail either because they treat 'ought' in the moral sense as if it were the same as 'ought' in the non-moral sense, or because they imply that the statement 'I ought to do so and so' is really hypothetical in meaning. Hobbes, e.g., is implying such a definition when he implies that to be morally bound to do some action is to be coerced, i.e. constrained to do it, by the fear of the sovereign's penalties; and so is Paley when he maintains that it is to be urged by a violent motive resulting from the command of another. So, also, is Hutcheson when he says that by a man's being obliged we mean that every spectator or he himself upon reflection must (i.e. really does) approve his action. So again is Joseph[2] when he says that being obliged is being moved by the thought, being moved by which makes the act which a man does right. For we have only to consider these alleged definitions to become certain that what we refer to as our being morally bound to do some action is none of the things which it is being asserted to be. Thus it is plain that even though when we think ourselves bound to do some action we do feel ourselves constrained to do it, we do not mean by our being bound our feeling constrained, but something else; and again, that even if, when we do the action, we do approve it, we do not mean that we approve it. Recognition of the failure of these supposed definitions is no proof of the unique and therefore indefinable character of the thing meant by 'our being morally bound to do some action', but it does help us to recognize its unique character by forcing us to recognize its difference from other things with which it has been confused. Further, it should be noted that the summary attempt to elucidate the nature of moral obligation by the analogy of law, an attempt illustrated by Kant's phrase 'categorical *imperative*' and by the reference to a principle of duty as a moral *law*, is only mischievous, because it represents our being morally bound to do some action as if it were our being commanded to do it.

[2] *Some Problems in Ethics*, p. 54.

III. The Relation between Moral Obligation and the Agent's Happiness

The next question to be considered is: Does a man's performance of his duty necessarily render him happier? It will, however, be found in the course of considering it that a stage is reached at which it will be appropriate to consider the second of the questions enumerated, viz. Ought a man to do his duty?

The treatment of this question has differed, and necessarily differed, radically according as those who have considered it have or have not distinguished 'ought' in the moral from 'ought' in the non-moral sense. And I propose first to consider its treatment by the latter. For these the attempt to give an affirmative answer has to take one or other of two forms. It must *either* contend that it is a condition of our being bound to do some action that doing it would make for our happiness, *or* else contend that though this is not so, yet the performance of our duty by its own nature must bring us happiness. As an instance of the former class I propose to consider Butler, and as instances of the latter, Plato and Aristotle.

Butler at least seems to be declaring himself a member of the former class when he says, in a well-known passage:

> Let it be allowed, though virtue or moral rectitude does indeed consist in affection to and pursuit of what is right and good, as such; yet, that when we sit down in a cool hour, we can neither justify to ourselves this or any other pursuit, till we are convinced that it will be for our happiness, or at least not contrary to it.
>
> Common reason and humanity will have some influence upon mankind, whatever becomes of speculations; but, so far as the interests of virtue depend upon the theory of it being secured from open scorn, so far its very being in the world depends upon its appearing to have no contrariety to private interest and self-love.[3]

This interpretation is sometimes disputed on the ground that here he is only arguing *ad hominem*, contending that even if conduciveness to our happiness were a condition of our having an obligation to do some action, as some think it is but as he does not, we should really be bound to do the acts which we ordinarily think we are bound to do, viz. virtuous actions, since they will be for our happiness. But that he himself considers conduciveness to happiness to be the condition of a duty seems conclusively shown by two earlier passages. In leading up to the statement quoted, he says:

> And to all these things may be added, that religion, from whence arises our strongest obligation to benevolence, is so far from disowning the principle of self-love, that it often addresses itself to that very principle, and always to the mind in that state when reason presides; and there can no access be had to the understanding, but by convincing men, that the course of life we would persuade them to is not contrary to their interest. It may be allowed, without any prejudice to the cause of virtue and religion, that our ideas of

[3] Selby-Bigge, *British Moralists*, i, p. 240.

happiness and misery are of all our ideas the nearest and most important to us; that they will, nay, if you please, that they ought to prevail over those of order, and beauty, and harmony, and proportion, if there should ever be, as it is impossible there ever should be, any inconsistence between them: though these last too, as expressing the fitness of actions, are real as truth itself.[4]

Again, in his Preface to the *Sermons*, he asserts that interest, one's own happiness, is a manifest obligation, and (considering as he does that vicious action constitutes what we ought not to do) meets the objection that in a case where a vicious action is for our interest there would be an obligation to do the vicious act, only by saying that it is always uncertain whether some vicious action *is* for our interest, thereby implying that if it is, as it may be, for our interest, there is an obligation to do what is vicious. There seems to be no doubt then but that Butler considered that no act can possibly be really a duty unless it will be for our happiness.

If we now go on to consider whether he is right it takes only little consideration to satisfy ourselves that he is not. To do this we need only imagine ourselves unwilling to do some action, e.g. to get up early in the morning, and then thinking of some substantial gain which it would bring us which we consider would more than outweigh the loss of comfort. For we then find that though the thought might make us less unwilling to do it, it would do nothing to make us think that it was a *duty* on our part to do it. And by doing this we can come to recognize that conduciveness to our advantage is simply irrelevant to the question whether it is a duty to do some action. In fact, this seems so obvious when we consider the matter that we then find it difficult to see how Butler and others who follow him can have come to think what they have. Light, however, on this question seems to be thrown by a passage in Butler's *Dissertation of the Nature of Virtue*. He says:

> It deserves to be considered, whether men are more at liberty, in point of morals, to make themselves miserable without reason, than to make other people so; or dissolutely to neglect their own greater good, for the sake of a present lesser gratification, than they are to neglect the good of others, whom nature has committed to their care. It should seem, that a due concern about our own interest or happiness, and a reasonable endeavour to secure and promote it, which is, I think, very much the meaning of the word prudence in our language; it should seem that this is virtue, and the contrary behaviour faulty and blameable; since, in the calmest way of reflection, we approve of the first, and condemn the other conduct, both in ourselves and others.[5]

This suggests as the explanation that our admitted approval of some act of prudence, i.e. an act in doing which a man with a view to his own welfare overcomes a disinclination to do it, is regarded as either identical with or, if not, as at least carrying with it, the thought that it is a duty on his part to do it.

[4] Ibid. 239–40.   [5] Ibid. 249–50.

We have now to consider the other form of the attempt to connect happiness with the performance of a duty, viz. that of trying to show that the latter by its very nature carries happiness with it. Of this form Plato's is undoubtedly the best to consider, partly because he puts with unrivalled force the difficulties to be overcome, and partly because he realizes better than others a condition essential to success.

In attributing this attempt to Plato two assumptions have been made. The first is that in the *Republic* what Plato means by just and unjust actions is the various actions which we ought, in the moral sense, to do and not to do respectively. And the second is that his object in dealing with just and unjust actions is to show that it is by doing what is just, i.e. what we ought, rather than what is unjust, i.e. what we ought not, that we shall become happy. But both assumptions can be justified. There is no obvious word in Plato for 'ought' in the moral sense, duty or obligation; and in the *Republic* χρῆ or δεῖ, as in χρῆ δίκαιον εἶναι, except in one passage, are shown by their context to mean 'must do' if the happiness which a man is seeking is to be attained. And we are driven to think, especially when we take into account the wide sense in which Plato is obviously using δίκαιον, that when he says of an action that it is δίκαιον (just), that is his way of saying that we ought to do it. Again, as regards the second assumption, Plato usually puts the conclusion he wants to draw in the form 'just action is profitable' (λυσιτελεῖ), and, in the wide sense in which he is using 'profitable', we may fairly say that he means that it makes for one's happiness.

To follow his argument, however, we have to elucidate what he means by two terms by the help of which he expresses it, viz. ἀγαθόν and κακόν, which would ordinarily be translated 'a good' and 'an evil'. And to do this with success we need first to notice that in English there are two usages of the word 'good' and that in these there is a complete difference of meaning. The term 'good' is used both as an adjective, as in the statement 'courage is good', and also as a part of a substantival phrase, as in the statement 'having friends is a great good' or 'the goods of life are numerous'.[6]

When we use the term 'good' as an adjective, as when we make the statement 'Courage is good' or 'That man is good in respect of his courage', we can be said—provided that we use the terms 'character' and 'quality' in a very wide sense—to be attributing to what we state to be good a certain character or quality which it possesses in itself, i.e. independently of its relatedness to other

---

[6] Cf. the distinction between the adjectives ἀγαθός and ἀγαθόν, and the substantival phrases ἀγαθόν τι and ἀγαθά. It may be noted that 'bad', the contrary of 'good', is only used adjectivally, and that the corresponding substantival phrase is 'an evil', as in the statement 'The loss of reputation is an evil'. It may also be noted that when someone considers the question 'What is the origin of evil?' he does not always stop to ask himself whether the question to which he is addressing himself is the question 'What is the origin of what is bad?' or the very different question 'What is the origin of evils?'

things. The character or quality meant seems coextensive, though of course not identical, with that of being something the thought of which excites approval. It is not, however, a quality of the ordinary kind of which it is true to say that one quality exists side by side with others. We can say, e.g., of a certain plate that it is round and hard; and if, having said that it is round, we go on to say that it is hard, we are thinking of its hardness as something separate from its roundness. Similarly we can say of a certain man that he is generous and courageous; and if, having said that he is generous, we go on to say that he is courageous, we are thinking of his courage as something separate from his generosity. But if we then go on to say that a man is in these respects good, we are not thinking of his goodness as something separate from his courage and his generosity; on the contrary we think that, in being generous, although he is not being courageous, he is being good, and similarly that in being courageous, although he is not being generous, he is being good. The quality, however, to which we refer by the term 'good' plainly cannot be defined. Although we mean to attribute a certain character to, e.g., a courageous disposition when we state that it is good, just as we do when we state that some body is red, that a line is continuous, or that the soul is not extended, we can no more state the nature of this character in other terms than we can in the case of 'red', 'continuous', or 'extended'.

As regards the application of the term 'good', it may be observed that we apply it most naturally either (1) to certain capacities or dispositions, or to the actualizations of certain dispositions, of human or sentient beings—the word 'disposition' being used here in a wide sense—or (2) to human or sentient beings in respect of these dispositions or of their actualizations. Indeed, it even looks as though we apply the term exclusively thus. For if we are asked 'Is pleasure good?'—though at first we may be inclined to answer 'Yes', yet if we reflect, we are likely to answer: 'It all depends on the disposition of which it is an actualization; the pleasure, for instance, excited by the thought of the ill fortune of someone we hate being bad, and the pleasure excited by the thought of a friend's good fortune or, indeed, the pain excited by the thought of his ill fortune, being good.'

When, however, we use the word 'good' as part of a substantival phrase, as in speaking of having friends as a good, we are *not* stating that that to which we apply the phrase 'a good' has a certain quality in itself. In using the phrase thus we are no more doing this than we are when we state that something, e.g. the possession of power or pleasure, is an object of desire. We mean by 'a good', 'a good *to someone*'. Thus when we speak of the having of friends as a good, we mean that it is a good to the man who has the friends. And where this addition is not stated it is always implied.[7] In the same way by 'an evil' we mean an evil to someone. What, however, precisely we mean by 'a good to someone' and by 'an evil to someone' is not easy to elucidate. As the first step it seems

---

[7] ἀγαθόν has similar implication.

necessary to recognize that in ordinary speech we apply these phrases with a certain looseness. We should, for instance, as a matter of ordinary language say that to most mean a son's having done something disgraceful was a great evil. Yet if we were asked whether X's son's having done something disgraceful would have been an evil to X if X had not learned of the action, we should have to say 'No'; and then, if pressed, we should have to say that what, as a matter of accuracy, we should have stated to be evil to X was the *thought* that his son had done the disgraceful action. Similarly we might without artificiality say of a certain man who, having one ticket for the theatre, is considering whether to use it himself or to send a friend that, though his seeing the play himself would be a good to him, his friend's seeing the play would be a greater good to him; yet, if pressed, we should have to allow that what we vaguely had had in mind, and ought to have spoken of, as a greater good to him was *the thought* that his friend was seeing the play. As a result of recognizing the need for this correction we should probably at first go on to say that what we really mean by 'a good to us' is something which gives us, i.e. excites in us, satisfaction, i.e. a feeling of satisfaction, and similarly what we really mean by 'an evil to us' is something which gives us dissatisfaction. But these statements would be inaccurate. For a feeling of satisfaction implies the prior existence of a desire, viz. a desire of that the thought of the realization of which excites the satisfaction; and we should also apply the phrase 'a good to us' to what we call enjoyments, such as that of seeing a beautiful landscape, which do not imply a preceding desire. This being so, we seem forced to allow that we mean by 'a good to us' something which *pleases*, i.e. excites pleasure in us, pleasure being something which admits of two forms, viz. satisfaction (or gratification) and enjoyment; and similarly that by 'an evil to us' we mean something which excites pain, pain admitting of two forms, viz. dissatisfaction and something for which we have no word but 'pain'.

It has, however, to be added that if this account is to stand, 'to excite pleasure' or 'to excite pain' must be understood as meaning to excite it whether *directly or indirectly*. For we do not restrict the phrase 'a good to us' (to consider that only) to things such as seeing a beautiful landscape, of which we should say that they are *in themselves* a good, i.e. which create pleasure directly, but apply it also to things such as our being healthy or rich, of which we should say that they are a good though not in themselves, meaning that though they do not directly excite pleasure yet they indirectly excite pleasure by causing other things which directly excite pleasure.

If then, as seems clear, we mean by 'a good to us' something which directly or indirectly excites pleasure in us, the difference in meaning between it and the term 'good' must be radical, in spite of the occurrence of the word 'good' in both. Indeed, in the end we have to allow that statements of the forms 'X is good' and 'X is a good to us' are *totally* different in meaning, so that the meaning of neither is capable of being stated in terms of, or even derivable from, the meaning of the other.[8] The difference, however, is one which we have no difficulty in admitting in particular cases. Thus we readily allow that although a certain act of revenge was bad, it was a good to the agent, though, no doubt, we should add that so far as he felt compunction, it was also an evil to him. Again we readily allow that to a given man, A, the thought that he is courageous himself, or, again, the thought that his friend, B, is courageous, is a good, although this could not be so unless A thought courage a good quality, whether in himself or in another. And examples like these last are important in two ways. First, they illustrate a use of the term 'good' as part of a substantival phrase which *presupposes* its use as an adjective. Second, consideration of them shows us that where that which is a good to us is a thought, that thought has what may be called a personal reference which is absent in the thought that something is good. Where, e.g., to one man, A, the thought that another man, B, is good (say in respect of being courageous) is a good, this is only because he is thinking of B as in some special relation to himself, as being, e.g., a friend, or a fellow countryman or a man of whom he is fond, and if he were to abstract from any such relationship the thought of B as good would cease to excite satisfaction, whereas, of course, in thinking of B as good in respect of his courage, he is abstracting from any such relationship. And just for this reason A's thought of his own goodness and his thought of his friend B's goodness are goods to himself of different kinds; for the one implies the desire to be himself good and the other the desire for his friend to be good—and these desires are different, for the former is the desire for himself as being himself, and not as just being someone, to be good, and similarly the latter is the desire for his friend to be good, as being his friend and not just as being someone.

Kant, it may be observed, emphasizes the difference in meaning between 'good' and 'a good to us'. He speaks of the ambiguity of the terms *bonum* and *malum* and says that German has fortunately two expressions which prevent the difference from being overlooked. 'For *bonum*', he says, 'it has *das Gute* (good) and *das Wohl* (well), for *malum*, *das Böse* (bad) and *das Übel* (ill, evil).' He adds later that '*das Wohl oder Übel*' (well or ill) implies only a reference to our condition of pleasure or pain; and concludes that we make two quite different judgements when we consider the goodness or badness of an action and when we consider its relation to our *Wohl oder Weh* (good or evil).

It is also to be observed that connected with the phrase 'a good to ourselves' we have the phrases 'our good' and 'our own good', and that by this we mean either our happiness or else the totality of the things which render us happy.

---

[8] 'To be valuable' and 'to be of value', except where they mean being capable of being exchanged for money, appear to mean 'to be valuable or of value to someone', and to be identical in meaning with 'to be a good to someone'. Hence it seems impossible to allow that there can be such things as judgements of value except in the sense of estimates of the extent to which various things will excite pleasure in individuals; and it seems merely the result of confusion to describe a judgement that such and such an act or character is good as a judgement of value.

And for this reason we have to distinguish sharply between the meanings of 'my good' and 'your good' on the one hand and those of 'my goodness' and 'your goodness', i.e. the goodness of me and that of you, on the other. Consequently, when Professor Moore[9] criticizes the doctrine that a man ought to aim at his own good as self-contradictory, the basis of his argument, viz. the contention that the goodness of anything good is independent of what or whom it is the goodness of, must be admitted to be irrelevant. For what the doctrine criticized represents as what a man ought to aim at is not his own goodness, i.e. the goodness of himself as opposed to the goodness of another, but his own happiness as opposed to the happiness of another; and Professor Moore seems here to be treating the phrase 'a man's good' as if it meant 'a man's own goodness'.

We are now in a position to consider Plato's treatment of justice, i.e. of the acts which form our duties, in the *Republic*. In Plato, corresponding to 'good' and 'a good to us', there is the use of ἀγαθός (good) as an adjective and of its neuter ἀγαθόν as a substantival phrase. By the adjective ἀγαθός he, of course, means good, as when he speaks of a man or a city as good, and maintains that there is a better and a worse element in the soul. And by the substantival phrase ἀγαθόν he must be admitted to mean not something good but what we mean by 'a good to us', i.e. something which excites pleasure in us whether directly or indirectly. The admission is inevitable for various reasons; but two considerations may be mentioned as decisive. The first is that in Plato ἀγαθόν means ἀγαθόν τινι, a good to *someone*, as in the statement put into the mouth of Thrasymachus that just action is ἀλλότριον ἀγαθὸν τῷ ὄντι, τοῦ κρείττονός τε καὶ ἄρχοντος συμφέρον, οἰκεία δὲ τοῦ πειθομένου τε καὶ ὑπηρετοῦντος βλάβη,[10] i.e. is a good to another, being advantageous to the stronger and the ruler but being loss to the agent.

The second consideration concerns what is ostensibly a division of ἀγαθά (goods) but is really a division of objects of desire, at the beginning of the second Book. There he divides the things which we desire into three classes:

1. things which we desire for themselves and not for the sake of their consequences, such as rejoicing and harmless pleasures,
2. things which we desire both for themselves and for the sake of their consequences, such as intelligent activity, seeing, and being healthy,
3. things which we desire only for the sake of their consequences, such as gymnastic training, receiving medical treatment, and practising medicine.

These he represents respectively as (1) goods in themselves, (2) goods both in themselves and on account of their consequences, and (3) goods on account of their consequences. And since in referring to these as ἀγαθά, i.e. as goods, he cannot possibly be meaning that they are objects of desire, and so just stating

---

[9] *Principia Ethica*, §§ 58–62.   [10] *Rep.* 343 c.

in other words that we desire them, the only meaning which it is possible to attach to ἀγαθά is that of 'goods to us', i.e. things which directly or indirectly excite pleasure in us, these being divided into three kinds according as they excite pleasure directly, indirectly, or in both ways. No doubt this interpretation requires us to allow that Plato is involved in holding that we only desire anything so far as we think it will excite pleasure directly or indirectly. But this cannot be helped.

It is now possible to state Plato's treatment of justice. His first task is to state as strongly as possible the case against thinking that it is just rather than unjust action which is profitable. He represents the Sophists as presenting the case in two forms, in both of which just action is held—with, of course, some plausibility—to consist in carrying out the laws of the state, i.e. obeying the orders of the government. In its *more* superficial form, put into the mouth of Thrasymachus, the government is held to consist of a ruler who has successfully devised the laws in his own interest, so that it is the ruler who gains by just action, and the agent suffers whatever evil is incurred by conferring the benefit in question on the ruler. And Socrates is made to refute this view by an argument which even on its own lines, although showing that 'the ruler does not gain', does nothing to disprove what *prima facie* is the truth, viz. that by obeying the law, e.g. by refraining from stealing, it is not the agent but another subject who gains. In its *less* superficial form, put into the mouth of Glaucon, the case put forward is more complicated. According to Glaucon, men originally pursued their own interest regardless of that of others. But they found that they lost more by others acting regardless of any interest other than their own, than they gained by acting thus themselves. In consequence they mutually agreed to abstain from gaining at the expense of others, and to set up a government to order and enforce this abstinence. And a government having been thus set up, justice consists in refraining from gaining at the expense of others in a state thus set up, and so a state where this abstinence is ordered and enforced. Hence for most men it is not a good, but only a lesser evil than unjust action—being a lesser evil because the loss incurred by doing what is just is a lesser evil than suffering the penalty for doing what is unjust; but for those men—and there are such—who are either strong enough or skilful enough to avoid the penalties, just action is an evil, and unjust action a good.

In addition, Glaucon is made to strengthen the case in the following way. He is made to say that if Socrates is to show that the man who does what is just is necessarily happier than he who does what is unjust, he must succeed in taking into account both the case of the completely successful unjust man, who by his skill manages to obtain the advantages of a reputation for complete justice as well as those of his injustice, and also that of the completely just man, who in spite of his justice has the reputation for the greatest injustice, and so not only fails to gain the advantages of his justice but also suffers the penalties which attach to injustice. And though the reason for this which Glaucon is made to offer is irrelevant, viz. that otherwise the just man may be considered to be doing what is just for the sake of its rewards, he should have been made to offer a good reason, viz. that such a case is possible.

Finally, Glaucon is made to state what, in view of the case to be met, is the only possible method of meeting it, if it can be met. According to him, since all the rewards normally open to a just man are equally open to an unjust man, and since a just man may suffer all the penalties which normally go to unjust action, just action can only be shown to bring happiness by ignoring rewards altogether, and by showing that just action is *in itself* a good so great as to outweigh any possible combination of resulting evils.

Plato certainly did not underrate his task. Indeed, in reading his statement of it, we wonder how he ever came to think that he could execute it.

To carry it out he naturally thinks that he has first to get the right answer to the question 'What is justice?', i.e. 'What is the character common to the acts which are just or those which it is our duty to do?' And ostensibly he proceeds thus: He first considers what he represents as only an analogy to the just action in individual men, viz. the just action of members of an ideal community, and finds it to consist in each of what he finds to be the three parts of the community (the rulers, their subordinates, and the artisans) contributing that service to the community for which the special nature of each is best suited. Then, turning to the individual man, he finds that he also has three parts, viz. the intellectual, the spirited, and the concupiscent, and that his just action, and so justice proper, consists in each part doing in the interest of the individual that for which its special nature is best suited. And finally he urges that once we have realized this it becomes ludicrous even to ask whether a man gains by just action.

Yet this can only ostensibly be his procedure. For, in spite of what he says, he must be implying that his 'justice in the state' is identical with and not only analogous to his 'justice in the individual', and he must be going too far when he asserts that justice must really concern the internal and not the external performance of a man's proper work.[11] For the just actions, the profitableness of which his speakers are considering, are certain acts of a man to others, and unless he holds that the activity within the soul, which he maintains that just action consists in, shows itself outwardly in these acts, his argument is broken-backed. For otherwise there is nothing to connect the activity of which he is maintaining the profitableness with that whose profitableness the various speakers are considering. Moreover, Plato himself maintains this connexion when he makes Thrasymachus say that the just soul, i.e. the man whose parts work properly, will keep the ordinarily recognized commandments. And plainly Plato's own answer to the question which Thrasymachus answered by saying that justice is

[11] Ibid. iv. 443 *b*.

promoting the interest of the ruler is: 'Doing that in the service of the community for which our nature is best suited.'

What then is Plato's argument to show that the just man, i.e. the man who carries out his duty by serving the state, necessarily gains thereby? To answer this question we have to bear in mind that Plato's three parts of the soul are really certain capacities of desiring. This must be so, even though Plato introduces the rational part as reasoning, and afterwards speaks of it as exercising forethought on behalf of the whole soul. For his test for a difference of parts of the soul is the existence of a mental conflict, and the only things which can conflict are desires. Hence Plato must mean by the rational part of the soul the capacity for a desire of a special kind entitled to be called rational. In addition, the objects of this desiring part must be held to include the doing of what is just, i.e. serving the community. For he represents the just individual as one in whom the rational part is dominant, and so requires the doing of what is just, although the other parts prompt him to act otherwise. Plato must, therefore, be attributing to the just man a desire to do his duty of serving the State, and maintaining it to be stronger in him than any other desire.

This being so, we can, of course, understand how Plato came to maintain that just action is in itself a good. For where we desire something, the thought that it is being or has been realized necessarily excites satisfaction, and if we desire to serve the State, either as serving the State, or as a duty, then serving the State, or (to speak accurately) the thought involved in doing it that we are serving the State, will necessarily itself excite satisfaction and so be a good to us, and we can distinguish its being thus in itself a good from the action's causing something which will be a good to us. But even so, strictly speaking what will be a good will not be serving the State, as Plato implies, but the thought that we are serving the State. And we can now see what he means when he says in effect that when we understand the nature of the just soul it is ludicrous even to ask whether the just man gains by his justice; viz. that just action will in itself excite in him a satisfaction so great as to outweigh any possible evils in the way of consequences. In fairness to Plato, however, two things should be noted. First, he seeks in Book IX to supplement the argument of Books I–IV by trying to show in detail that the pleasures obtained from satisfying the rational part of the soul are more permanent and less bound up with pain than those of the other parts. Second, at the end of the fourth Book he makes it clear that he does not go so far as to contend that any given man will *at once* gain in happiness by doing what is just, but is only contending that he will gain in the long run, first by a course of just action developing the just disposition (i.e. really the desire to do what is just), and then, though not before, by attaining a satisfaction, by doing what is just, which will outweigh all possible evils.

This being Plato's argument, what comments does it suggest? It has at least one outstanding merit. It does proceed on the only plan which has any hope of success, that of trying to make out that doing our duty is in itself a good so great as to outweigh any combination of resulting evils. For whatever be the kinds of action held to be our duty, since *ex hypothesi* they cannot be that of making ourselves happy (for if they were, there would be nothing to be proved), they must consist of acts causing things of another sort or sorts, and an act consisting of causing something of one kind cannot possibly be shown necessarily to cause something of another kind. Hence no consideration of the results of the acts held to be our duty can succeed in showing that we shall necessarily be the happier for doing them. And in this respect Plato's argument is only a special form of the endeavour to show that obedience to conscience is itself a reward sufficient even to outweigh any resulting evils.

Nevertheless, there is no denying that it is open to two fatal objections. The first is that even if for one whose desire to serve the state, or, alternatively, to do his duty, is at the maximum possible for any human being, the satisfaction excited by the thought that the object of this desire is realized would outweigh all possible resulting evils, yet any given individual may be incapable of having this desire developed to that extent, and so may not even in the long run become happier by doing what is just. Indeed, it is more plausible to say that the actions conducive to a given man's happiness will depend on his nature and that, e.g., if he is initially ambitious and little anxious to serve the state, he will gain most happiness by first developing and then gratifying his ambition rather than his desire to serve the state. And though Plato in Books VIII and IX does much to mitigate the force of this objection, what he says can only be a mitigation; and even Plato himself insists that those who, after contemplating the good, return to the cave to take their share of ruling and in doing so do what is just are making a sacrifice of happiness. And the second objection is that even for the man whose desire to do what is just is at the maximum possible for anyone, there must come a point at which, if the evils resulting from doing what is just continue to be piled up, they will outweigh the good to the man of knowing that he is doing what is just.

Here it may be noted that these objections are independent of Plato's view of what a man's duty consists in, viz. serving the state, so that if any other be substituted they still hold; and for that reason, in considering the success of Plato's argument, there is no need to consider whether he is right in thinking that what justice consists in is serving the state. The plain truth is, of course, that apart from theological reasons for thinking that the results of doing what we ought and doing what we ought not are specially adjusted by rewards and penalties, no general answer either way is possible to the question: 'Will doing our duty be for our happiness?' The only possible answer must be: 'It all depends; in some instances it may be and in others it may not.'

Aristotle, it may be noted, appears to follow Plato in offering a proof that it is by doing our duty that we shall become happy, but in his case the argument is curiously crude. In contrast to Plato he appears to hold that our duty consists in exercising the various virtues, and his argument appears to be this.[12] A man, to be a special craftsman such as a flute-player or a shoemaker, has a function, i.e. is an instrument, and indeed is a human instrument. Now in the case of an instrument of a given sort, e.g. a flute, there is a difference between its performing its function, i.e. exercising the activity the capacity for which renders it an instrument of the sort it is, and performing its function well, i.e. exercising that activity well. And in the case of a human instrument, its happiness arises from its performing its function well. Therefore, to find what will render a man happy, we must find what the function of a man is and then find what performing that function will consist in. But to find the function of a man, as of any instrument, we have to find the capacity for activity special to a man. This consists in the capacity for rational activity; and to exercise this function well is to exercise good rational activity, i.e. to exercise the various virtues. And, therefore, it is by the exercise of the various virtues, the exercise of which is our duty, that we shall be happy.

The argument, however, is really only verbal. For (1) a man is not an instrument, nor does Aristotle refer to any special skill possessed by a man, which would justify his implying that man is an instrument. (2) There is no distinction other than one of degree between an instrument's performing an activity and its performing that action well. Unless the activity included in its nature something of what is meant by 'well', it would not be the activity of the instrument. We could not, e.g., distinguish a knife's cutting from its tearing a piece of paper, or playing the flute from making a noise on the flute, unless we meant by 'cutting' something only different in degree from cutting well, and by 'playing the flute' making in some degree beautiful sounds, i.e. playing the flute well. (3) Consequently Aristotle cannot reach his conclusion that it is *virtuous* activity that is required for a man to perform his function well from consideration of what the function of a man is; and in fact he only speaks of virtuous activity because, independently of an idea of man's having a function, he thinks of it as the best activity of which a man is capable. All we are left with, therefore, is a bare *assertion* on Aristotle's part that it is by doing the best actions of which we are capable that we shall become happy.

IV. Do We Always Seek Our Own Happiness?

In considering Plato's treatment of the connexion between duty and happiness, an underlying idea with which he approached the question has, for clearness' sake, been ignored. The idea lies in the background, and it may even escape notice. Yet it is undeniably there, and its presence explains the intensity of Plato's

[12] *Eth. Nic.* i. 7. 9–15.

desire to prove that justice leads to happiness. Moreover, as the idea has not only been not infrequently shared by others, but may also affect either the questions asked about obligation or the answers given, its truth ought to be considered. The idea is one which concerns not how men ought to act but how they do act, and at first at least it strikes us as having little plausibility. It is that whenever we act deliberately, and not on an impulse, and so have a purpose, our final purpose, i.e. that the desire of which for its own sake leads us to do what we are doing and so forms our motive, is always the realization of our own good, i.e. of what will make us happy, or, more accurately, of our own happiness. The idea is one which Plato had formulated in the *Gorgias*,[13] where after contending that men do all that they do for the sake of the good (τὸ ἀγαθόν), i.e. as the context shows, of what is a good to themselves, he says of anyone who kills or exiles a man or despoils him of his wealth that he does it because he thinks it will be better for himself. In the *Republic* the idea first emerges in a rather disguised form at the beginning of Book II. There Glaucon is made to contend that men in fact only do what is just, i.e. their duty, ὡς ἀναγκαῖον, i.e. as an evil which has to be endured only to avoid a greater evil, and to urge in support that no one, like Gyges, able to do what is unjust with impunity would in fact do what is just. And that Plato himself here accepts this contention is shown by his representing Socrates, the mouthpiece of the truth, as having to show not that Glaucon's contention is mistaken, but that men in acting thus are mistaken in thinking just action the incurring the lesser of two evils. Later, however, in Book VI[14] the idea is explicitly stated, though in a way which may be misunderstood. There, in introducing the subject of the Idea of good, Socrates says that, while we are willing to put up with things which *seem* just and beautiful, it does not suffice us to obtain things which seem a good (τὰ δοκοῦντα ἀγαθά), but we seek things which are really a good (τὰ ὄντα ἀγαθά). And he goes on to speak of the good (τὸ ἀγαθόν) as that which every soul pursues and for the sake of which it does everything that it does, divining its existence, but perplexed about it and unable adequately to grasp its nature, and so misses such benefit as it might have got from other things. This statement, especially when taken in connexion with the earlier books, must be taken to mean that in all action what we are striving to bring into existence is—not what is good but—what is really good for us, or for our own good.

If we allow, as we must, that this interpretation is right, then we can, of course, understand the intensity of Plato's desire to prove to us that we shall gain by doing our duty. For plainly he was passionately anxious for men to do what is just, and if he considered that men always seek their own good, he must have thought that men could only be persuaded to do what is just by being persuaded that it was the course of action by which they would gain. Also, we can then understand his

[13] 468 b.   [14] 505 d–e.

contention that the ultimate question under consideration, for the sake of which he is considering whether justice is profitable, is: 'Should or *ought* we to do what is just, i.e. our duty?' For this question will have the intelligible meaning of: 'Ought we to do our duty', in the non-moral sense of 'ought', i.e. is doing it necessary for the realization of our purpose in all action? And in view of what has been said, we may take it that this is the ultimate question to which Plato is addressing himself. We are, therefore, brought to the conclusion that the ultimate question which Plato is considering is: 'Should or ought we, in the non-moral sense, do our duty?' and that it is forced on him by his idea that men always pursue their own good. Further, *if* we share this idea, then for the reasons already given we shall have to conclude that the true answer is:

No general answer is possible; on some occasions it may be that we ought to do our duty, and on others it may not, but as we never know all the consequences to ourselves of an action, we never *know* whether we ought, in the non-moral sense, to do any particular action, whether a duty or not, though sometimes we may be able to have a fairly good opinion about it.

The idea that we always seek, i.e. act for the sake of, our own good is one which has not infrequently been held. Aristotle shared this idea with Plato, and it was in effect held by Hobbes, Bentham, Mill, and T. H. Green. And we ought to consider whether it is true, if only because our conclusion may affect the question: Should or ought we to do our duty? For if we think our purpose in acting is not always the realization of our own good, the question will have disappeared as one admitting of a general answer, since the answer on any particular occasion will depend on what our purpose happens to be. And if, further, we think that sometimes our purpose is the doing of our duty, the question will have disappeared as a general question, since if our purpose on a given occasion is the doing of our duty, we cannot even ask 'Should we do our duty?' since it will mean: Is the doing our duty necessary for the realization of what it is *ex hypothesi* itself? Doing our duty cannot be necessary for the realization of our purpose, unless our purpose is something other than doing our duty.

There is, however, a much more important reason for considering whether the idea is true. This is that if we accept the idea, we shall be involved in very awkward consequences. For we shall then be forced to allow (1) that there is really no such thing as a conscientious action or a benevolent or a malevolent action, and also (2) that there is really no difference of motive between the acts of a so-called good man and those of a so-called bad man.

The idea is, of course, limited to deliberate actions, i.e. to actions in doing which we should be said to have a purpose. No one would maintain that a man who acts on an impulse is seeking his own good, or indeed *seeking* anything. Yet even though the idea is thus limited, it by no means seems even plausible to anyone to whom it is presented for the first time. And it appears to be one of those to which men are only driven by a course of reflection, the process in this case being started by raising the general question: What is required, for a man to be led to act? In dealing with this question we take for granted, and (it seems) truly, that for us to do some action deliberately, there must be something which we think of as non-existent and the existence of which we desire, the desire of this being what we call our motive, i.e. what leads us to do the act if we do it. In other words, we take for granted that in all action we must have a purpose, since we mean, by our purpose in doing an action, that the desire of which leads us to do the action, i.e. that the desire of which is our motive. And the idea in question appears to arise by our taking three steps. First, having asked what our purpose is, we think of it as always something, other than an action, which we think an action likely to cause, directly or indirectly, such as the disappearance of a headache which we think taking some drug will effect. Mill expresses this idea when he says that all action is for the sake of an end. And Plato in the *Gorgias*[15] expressly states this idea. In trying to show that orators and tyrants have the least power in states, he lays down generally that what a man wishes for in doing some action is not the action but the result for the sake of which he does it, the man who takes a drug, e.g., wishing not for this but for health, and the man who takes a voyage wishing not for the sailing and the incurring of dangers but for the resulting wealth. Here, however, Plato is plainly going too far in asserting that a man does not want to do the action: what he meant and should have said is rather that though he desires to do the action this desire depends on the desire of a certain result, this latter desire being more properly said to be what is moving him, as being what gives rise to the desire to do the action. Further, it is worth observing that it is because we are apt to think of our purpose in action as being always something, other than our action, which we think our action will cause, that we have come to use as we often do two metaphorical expressions for our purpose. First, we are apt to refer to our purpose as our aim, or as what we are aiming at. And the justification of the metaphor is that if, e.g., our health is our purpose, it is that by reference to which we have devised what we are doing, e.g. taking some drug, as being what we think most likely to cause it, just as a target is that by reference to the position of which a shooter arranges his weapon before shooting. And, second, we are apt to refer to our purpose as our end, as being that which will be realized only at the end of the action. It should, however, be borne in mind that the terms 'aim' and 'end' thus used are only metaphorical expressions for our purpose, and that they are appropriate only if our purpose is something, other than our action, to which we think it will lead.

Having thus come to think that our purpose is always some expected result X, we are led to take the second of the three steps referred to. This is to insist that the action requires the desire of something for its own sake. For we recognize that it

---

[15] 467 c.

is impossible to desire everything for the sake of something else; since otherwise, as Aristotle said, all desire would be empty and vain; and that in particular in desiring X we must either be desiring X for its own sake or else desiring it for the sake of something else which we are desiring for its own sake. In this way we are led not only to distinguish the desire of a thing for its own sake and the desire of a thing for the sake of something else, as respectively independent and dependent desires, but also to distinguish our ultimate purpose in doing some action from some non-ultimate purpose, and to insist that in all action we must have some ultimate purpose, i.e. something the desire of which for its own sake is what is independently moving us, our other desire being dependent on this. Finally we are led to take the third step referred to. We ask: What is that in our various actions desire of which for its own sake moves us to do them and so forms our ultimate purpose? And our first answer is likely to be: 'This is of different sorts in different instances; we desire things of very varied kinds for their own sake.' And Aristotle in effect gave this answer.

V. Teleological Theories of Obligation

There remains for consideration the third of the main questions which were said to have been raised about moral obligation, viz. the question: 'What is the character which an act must possess for it to be one which we are morally bound to do?' or, as it is sometimes expressed, 'What is the criterion of duty?' To put the question is to imply the idea that we can only be morally bound to do the various acts which from time to time we are morally bound to do, in virtue of some common character, their possession of this character being what renders us bound to do them; this being what we call the *basis* of our obligation to do them. And the idea is at least very plausible, for unless it be true, it would seem that, to use Joseph's phrase, 'our obligations will be an unconnected heap',[16] and there will be no connexion between the nature of an act which we are bound to do and our obligation to do it. And given that we have the idea—and the idea is certainly shared by most thinkers—we think of the question as one to which we are still without the answer, since if we survey the acts of these various kinds into which we ordinarily think duties fall, such as telling the truth, sparing the feelings of others, and so on, it is not even obvious that they have a common character. And even for practical purposes we seem to need the answer, since, unless we can find it, it would seem that we never can be sure that any of the acts which we ordinarily think duties are duties.

In considering the question, it seems best to begin by considering the various answers it has received—these answers being what is usually meant by theories

---

[16] *Some Problems in Ethics*, 67.

of obligation. And the great divergences between these theories suggest that the endeavour to find the right answer is a long and laborious process. Of these I propose to consider first the theories which have been called by Paulsen and Muirhead teleological, my reason being that once we have grasped their real nature, they are the easiest to make up our minds about once for all. Early in his *Methods of Ethics*, Sidgwick says:

> It is not necessary, in the methodical investigation of right conduct, considered relatively to the end either of private or of general happiness, to assume that the end itself is determined or prescribed by reason: we only require to assume, in reasoning to cogent practical conclusions, that it is adopted as ultimate and paramount. For if a man accepts any end as ultimate and paramount, he accepts implicitly as his 'method of ethics' whatever process of reasoning enables him to determine the actions most conducive to this end.[17]

Unfortunately, although Sidgwick constantly makes use of the term 'end', he does little to explain what he means by it. But his use of the term seems to show that he uses it as a synonym for purpose, and this interpretation is borne out by his statement[18] that all he means by 'end' is 'an object of rational aim—whether attained in successive parts or not—which is not sought as a means to the attainment of any ulterior object, but for itself'. And if, as we seem to have to allow, this interpretation is right, by 'accepting X as an ultimate end' he must mean 'having X as our ultimate purpose'. This being so, Sidgwick is here laying down that to discover what he ought to do a man has only to discover what his end is and then discover what actions will most contribute to it. He is, therefore, implying the idea that, at any rate where we have something X as our purpose, the character which an act must have, to be what we ought to do, is that of contributing more than any other in our power to the realization of X. Now Sidgwick in making the statement quoted is not implying that we always have one and the same purpose or even that we always have a purpose. But some who have taken the same view about the connexion between our purpose, where we have one, and our duty, have held that we always have a purpose and that that purpose is always the same, and consequently according to them the task of discovering what we ought to do consists in ascertaining first what that purpose or end of ours is and then what the acts are on various occasions which would do most to effect its realization, the character required for an act to be what we ought to do being that of contributing most to its realization. And such a theory appears to be what Muirhead means by a 'teleological theory of duty'. For in *Rule and End in Morals*, although his language is vague, he refers to the theory which he thus designates as one which takes its start from the idea of benefits to

---

[17] H. Sidgwick, *Methods of Ethics*, p. 8; cf. p. 77n.   [18] Ibid. 134.

oneself and others to be obtained, ends to be gained by the conduct in question, and deduces that of duty (i.e. deduces the duty of doing the action) from it.[19]

Further, Professor Muirhead makes a sweeping division of all theories of duty into two species, of which teleological theories form one, and of which the other consists of those in which the idea of an end is replaced by that of rules according to which men should direct their conduct; and he calls the latter deontological to mark their difference from the former. And among exponents of a teleological theory he includes both Plato and Aristotle, and of English thinkers Bentham and Mill, and, in recent times, Green and Bosanquet, and he seems to regard Kant as the most prominent exponent of the opposite theory.[20]

Now of teleological theories of duty there are really only two forms. For if we try to make out that we always have a single final end in action, there are only two things which it is at all plausible for us to represent as this end. These are (1) the realization of a life of enjoyment on our part, and (2) the realization of our own good, i.e. really the realization of the totality of things which will give us a life of satisfaction. On the one hand, we may, as Mill was, be struck by the idea that what we want for its own sake is always something we shall enjoy, and thence conclude that as we think of our life as going to continue, our purpose is always the realization of the things which will give us most enjoyment in life generally. On the other hand, we may be struck by the idea, as Plato, Aristotle, and Green undoubtedly were, that what we want for its own sake is always something which will give us satisfaction, and thence conclude that as we think of our life as going to continue, our purpose is always the realization of the totality of those things which will render us satisfied in life generally, those being what we call our own good. There is no third idea which has any plausibility whatever.

Further, between these two ideas there is no distinction of importance, as becomes obvious when we realize that each requires a certain correction. For the enjoyment of something which we enjoy, e.g. the enjoyment of seeing a beautiful landscape, is related to the thing we enjoy, not as a quality but as an effect, being something excited by the thing we enjoy, so that if it be said that we desire some enjoyment for its own sake, the correct statement must be that we desire the experience, e.g. the seeing some beautiful landscape, for the sake of the feeling of enjoyment which we think it will cause, this feeling being really what we are desiring for its own sake. And for an exactly similar reason, when it is said that we desire for its own sake something which will gratify us, e.g. the thought that some friend is prosperous, the correct statement must be that what we are desiring for its own sake is the feeling of gratification, and that we are desiring the thought only for the sake of the feeling of gratification which we think it will cause. Hence, given the necessary correction, the one view will be that our final aim is our being constantly in the state of feeling enjoyment, and

---

[19] J. H. Muirhead, *Rule and End in Morals*, p. 3.   [20] Ibid. 6–8.

the other will be that it is our being constantly in the state of feeling gratified. And since it must be allowed that enjoyment and gratification are species of pleasure, the views only differ in that the one implies the idea that enjoyment is the only form of pleasure, and the other the idea that gratification is the only form of pleasure. Further, as there seems to be no denying that by being happy we mean being pleased, whether the being pleased takes the form of enjoying ourselves or of being gratified or, for that matter, of both at once, as obviously may happen, both views seem only different forms of the view that our final end or purpose is always our happiness.

It does not, however, take much consideration to discover that a teleological theory, whichever form it takes, is open to a fatal objection of principle. This is not that it represents as what renders some act a duty something which we know does not do so. This is undoubtedly an objection, and a fatal one. For we have only to ask ourselves whether some act's being that which would do most to make us happy would render it what we are bound to do, to *know* that it would not. The fatal objection of principle is that it resolves the moral 'ought' into the non-moral 'ought', representing our being morally bound to do some action as if it were the same thing as the action's being one which we must do if our purpose is to become realized. And in consequence, strictly speaking the theory is not a theory of *obligation*, or *duty*, at all, but, if anything, is a theory that what are called our obligations or duties are really something else.

An attempt to meet this criticism may be made in the way indicated by Muirhead, who himself accepts the teleological theory. Attributing the theory to Plato, he represents Plato as, while agreeing with the extreme Sophists that all men are moved by desire of profit to themselves, meeting them by so deepening the meaning of profit as to make it scarcely recognizable under that name. And he represents Plato's argument thus: 'Man sought his profit or advantage in all that he did. But there was all the difference in the world between the things in which he sought his profit: whether, for instance, he sought it in what satisfied the desires of the body which he appeared to be or those of the soul which he really was; in material possessions which are at best mere means, or in the possession of qualities which are good in themselves wholly independent of anything they bring.' And Muirhead then meets the objection that nevertheless Plato and the Sophists are agreed in principle by saying: 'If the meaning they respectively attach to profitableness does not constitute a difference of principle, what would? As well say that there is no difference of principle involved in a famous question as to the exchange value of the world as against one's soul.'[21] Here the argument is, of course, that Plato in differing from the Sophists as to what the actions are which are necessary for a man's attainment of his purpose, viz. happiness, and so are profitable to him, was altering the meaning of the term 'profit', and that,

---

[21] The references are to *Rule and End in Morals*, pp. 24–5.

consequently, when he maintained that a man ought to satisfy his better desires, he was using the term 'ought' in a different sense from that in which the Sophists maintained that a man ought to satisfy his worst desires.

But unfortunately the argument fails. For (1) though, of course, there can be different views as to what is profitable, there are not two 'senses' of 'profitable', and even to differ from another as to what is profitable is to imply that there is only one sense. And (2) as Muirhead interprets Plato, Plato is differing from the Sophists about what a man ought to do, and, if so, he must be using 'ought' in the same sense as that in which the Sophists were using it, viz. the non-moral sense. Otherwise there need not be any quarrel between them. And the alleged difference of opinion, so far from implying that what they meant is different, implies that it is the same. Moreover, even Professor Muirhead's own language implies a tacit admission that a teleological theory is treating the moral 'ought' as having a non-moral sense. For he describes any opposed theory as *deontological*, and this amounts to saying that any opposed theory is one which represents duty as really duty and not as something else, and therefore implies that a teleological theory does represent duty as something else. It should, however, be added as a matter of caution that it must not be assumed that this division of theories into teleological and deontological is correct, since if a thinker does not resolve the 'ought' of duty into the 'ought' of 'necessary for one's purpose', he may nevertheless be resolving it into another 'ought', and so not be deontologist; and, as will be seen later,[22] this has been done.

It has to be admitted then that any teleological theory of duty can be rejected, even without considering its details, on the ground that it represents the moral 'ought' as if it were the non-moral 'ought', and so is not a theory of moral obligation at all.

It may be objected that, this being so, there cannot really have been any adherents of a teleological theory, since the difference of meaning of 'ought' in the two senses is so obvious that no one can have failed to be aware of it. To this, however, the reply can be made that there have been instances, and prominent instances, of this failure. The failure can, of course, take place in either of two ways. Someone may ask himself whether when we say that we are morally bound to do some action we mean the same thing as we do when, thinking of some action as necessary for some purpose, we say we ought to do it, and he may answer that we do. Or again, he may simply fail to notice the difference in meaning, i.e. fail to distinguish the things meant.

Now unquestionably Bentham did the former.

Nature [he says[23]] has placed mankind under the governance of two sovereign masters, *pain* and *pleasure*. It is for them alone to point out what we ought to do, as well as to determine what we shall do. On the one hand the standard of right and wrong, on the

[22] See Chapter vi.   [23] Selby-Bigge, *British Moralists*, i, pp. 339–42.

other the chain of causes and effects, are fastened to their throne. ... The *principle of utility* recognises the subjection. ... By the principle of utility is meant that principle which approves or disapproves of every action whatsoever, according to the tendency which it appears to have to augment or diminish the happiness of the party whose interest is in question: or, what is the same thing in other words, to promote or to oppose that happiness. ... Of an action that is conformable to the principle of utility, one may always say either that it is one that ought to be done, or at least that it is not one that ought not to be done. ... *When thus interpreted, the words ought, and right and wrong, and others of that stamp, have a meaning: when otherwise, they have none.*[24]

This passage is, of course, sufficient to show that Bentham explicitly maintained that the so-called moral 'ought' is the non-moral 'ought', and the explicitness of his contention renders further comment superfluous. And the mistake is so obvious that it is not often made. But a failure to distinguish the two senses is common, and of this failure Mill and T. H. Green may be taken as instances illustrating the two forms which the teleological theory may take.

Mill so often uses the terms 'moral obligation', 'right' and 'wrong', and 'conscience' that at first we are very unwilling to allow that he is really failing to distinguish the moral from the non-moral 'ought'. And we are thrown off our guard by his initial statement of his doctrine, viz. that actions are right in proportion as they tend to promote happiness, wrong as they tend to promote unhappiness.[25] But we get a rude awakening when we find him saying on the next page that the basis of this doctrine is the theory that pleasure is the only thing which is desirable as an end, and then find later that he means by 'desirable as an end' desired for its own sake. And we have to conclude that his view is quite different when we take his statement of the basis of his doctrine along with (1) his statement:[26] 'All action is for the sake of some end, and rules of action, it seems natural to suppose, must take their whole character and colour from the end to which they are subservient', and (2) his idea that the proof of his view consists in showing that pleasure is the only thing which we want for its own sake.[27] It then becomes clear that his view is simply that what we ought to do is whatever would be most conductive to our pleasure or happiness, just because our pleasure or happiness is always our purpose. And the only comment needed is that this implies that 'ought' in the moral sense really only means necessary for the realization of our purpose, and so is not a theory of obligation at all.

Green, in the *Prolegomena to Ethics*, introduces his theory of obligation by giving an account of the motive of all deliberate action which is rather like Aristotle's. He contrasts what he calls moral actions in the sense of actions which may be good or bad, i.e. actions which would be called deliberate actions, with instinctive actions. And he maintains that what distinguishes a moral, i.e. a deliberate, action from an instinctive action is that what determines it is not an

---

[24] The italics are mine. [25] Mill, *Utilitarianism*, p. 8.
[26] Ibid. 2. [27] See ibid., Chapter iv.

impulse but what he calls a motive, consisting of a desire for personal good in some form or other; meaning by an instinctive action one not determined by a conception, on the part of the agent, of any good to be gained or evil to be avoided by the agent. It is superfluous, he continues, to add good *to himself*, for anything conceived as good in such a way that the agent acts for the sake of it must be conceived as *his own* good (i.e. as a good to himself), though he may conceive it as his own good only on account of his interest in others, and in spite of any amount of incidental suffering on his own part.[28] A little later, however,[29] when he takes into account the fact that an agent thinks of himself as having a future and as having various desires to be satisfied, he substantially modifies this account and represents the desire which forms the motive of every moral action, virtuous or vicious, as the desire of some possible state or achievement of his own as being for the time his greatest good—Esau's motive, e.g., in selling his birthright, being the desire of the satisfaction of his hunger, as that which for the time he conceives as his greatest good. And, as the sequel shows, this is his more considered doctrine.

Here Green is plainly intending to state what he considers to be our *final* purpose when acting deliberately; and, as he explains later[30] that he means by 'good' such as will satisfy desire, and as his usual use of the phrase 'a good' is in conformity with this explanation, his general statement must be an inaccurate statement of the view which he is expressing. For something which excites satisfaction, e.g. the thought of some friend's success, is related to the satisfaction as cause to effect, and therefore to desire something as a good, i.e. as something which excites satisfaction, is to desire it not for itself but for the sake of the satisfaction which it will excite. And, therefore, to express his view accurately he should have said that our motive is always the desire of a life of satisfaction, and that in desiring what we consider our greatest good, we are desiring this only as a means to our final end, viz. the continued realization of a state of satisfaction. It, therefore, may be noticed incidentally that although he regards Mill, a psychological hedonist, as his chief opponent, the line dividing himself from Mill is very thin; Mill considers the only form of happiness to be enjoyment, while Green considers it to be satisfaction.

Now the contention that in *all* deliberate action our motive is desire of a continued state of satisfaction has, of course, an awkward implication. For we ordinarily regard a good act as distinguished from a bad one by its motive, and yet if in all actions our motive is the same, this idea must be false, and it will only be possible to hold that what really distinguishes the acts which we ordinarily regard as good and as bad is a difference of opinion as to how a continued state of satisfaction is to be attained. The contention therefore implies the view that our ordinary idea of what distinguishes good from bad acts is mistaken. But the

---

[28] *Prolegomena to Ethics*, §§ 91–2.   [29] Ibid., §§ 95–9; cf. § 128.   [30] Ibid., § 171.s.

contention does not *by itself* involve a teleological theory of obligation. Acceptance of it, no doubt, involves us in holding that what we ought to do in the non-moral sense is whatever would cause us most satisfaction. But such acceptance does not preclude us from thinking, as I have contended Plato thought,[31] that there are such things as *moral* obligations, distinct from obligations in the non-moral sense, although if we do, we shall have to allow that we shall carry out our moral obligations only so far as, and because, we think that doing so will be what would give us most satisfaction. So far, then, Green has said nothing which commits him to a teleological theory of duty.

But in Book III he does. For after reiterating that his account of moral actions, which he now calls acts of will, is formal, i.e. is an account of all acts of will whether good or bad, he lays down that the distinction between the good will and the bad will must be at the root of any system of ethics. And to do this is to imply that he has the idea that he, like others, has to find the character of an act, required to render the doing of it a duty, in its goodness. And as, according to Green, the motive of all deliberate acts whether good or bad is the same, viz. the desire of continued satisfaction, what Green must be considering as that whose goodness renders an action a duty is its contributing most to the continued satisfaction which is the agent's purpose—since there is no other alternative open to him. He must therefore be thinking of the moral 'ought' as if it were the same thing as the non-moral 'ought', i.e. representing our duty of doing some action as being its contributing most to the realization of our purpose. Consequently it is not surprising to find that later[32] he expresses this view almost in so many words. Apparently speaking of a man's desire to satisfy himself as the impulse which becomes the source, according to the direction it takes, both of vice and of virtue, he speaks of this impulse thus:

> It is the source of vicious self-seeking and self-assertion, so far as the spirit which is in man seeks to satisfy itself or to realize its capabilities in modes in which, according to the law which its divine origin imposes on it and which is equally the law of the universe and of human society, its self-satisfaction or self-realisation is not to be found. ... So it is again with the man who seeks to assert himself, to realise himself, to show what he has in him to be, in achievements which may make the world wonder, but which in their social effects are such that the human spirit, according to the law of its being, which is a law of development in society, is not advanced but hindered by them in the realisation of its capabilities. He is living for ends of which the divine principle that forms his self alone renders him capable, but these ends, because in their attainment one is exalted by the depression of others, are not in the direction in which that principle can really fulfil the promise and potency which it contains.[33]

It seems clear, then, that Green must be holding that what renders an act good and so what we ought to do is its contributing most to our purpose, viz. our

---

[31] pp. 176–82. [32] *Prolegomena*, § 171. [33] Ibid., § 176.

continued satisfaction, and must therefore equally with Mill be resolving the moral into the non-moral 'ought'.

Yet it may be objected to this interpretation (1) that Green constantly insists that we have and are influenced by disinterested desires for the welfare of others, and so cannot be holding that at bottom all our actions are selfish; and (2) that in him the idea of duty is plainly so vivid that he, least of all men, can have resolved the 'moral' into the 'non-moral' 'ought'. These objections need consideration, especially as no reference so far has been made to an idea which is prominent in his exposition of this theory of obligation, viz. the idea that the existence of obligations among a group of men implies that of what he calls 'a common good'.

In his lectures on Political Obligation, where, though he is primarily occupied with a question about a particular obligation, viz. 'Why is a subject bound to obey his ruler?', he has also to state a general theory of obligation, Green insists that there are no such things as natural obligations in the sense of obligations independent of what he calls a society. And as a close examination of his use of the phrase 'a society' will show, he really means by 'a society' not a society in any ordinary sense but a group of persons which satisfies what he considers the two conditions necessary for the existence of a system of obligations. These are (1) that each of the members has as his own good, and so as his purpose in action, the totality consisting of the various goods of each member, this totality being referred to by Green as the public good,[34] or as the 'general interest' or 'general well-being' of the members;[35] and (2) that there are rules devised by a regulating body, the observance of which is required for the realization of this public good. And it is implied that a man's obligations consist in obeying the rules of a group to which he belongs, and that the reason why he ought to obey these rules is that obedience is necessary for the attainment of his purpose, viz. his own good, it, however, happening that his purpose is identical with that of the other members of the group, since the good of each is the same, viz. the respective goods of all the members of the group.

In consequence Green is able to make it appear as though in his view (1) a man in carrying out his duties is actuated by public spirit and not by self-interest, and (2) the acts which are a man's duties at least correspond to the acts we ordinarily think duties, since it is at least plausible to say that the latter are for the public interest; and this correspondence at any rate helps to disguise Green's resolution of the moral into the non-moral 'ought'.

The question, however, at once arises: Can Green justify his contention that what he calls the public good, i.e. the totality consisting of the good of each member, is the good of each member, so that they have a *common* good, two members, A and B, e.g., having as their own good one and the same thing? For prima facie, at least, the existence of such a thing as what Green calls 'a common

---

[34] T. H. Green, *Lectures*, § 108. [35] Ibid., § 151.

good' is impossible. By 'a good to a man A' he means a something which excites, i.e. directly excites, satisfaction in A, and by 'A's good' the totality of the things which excite satisfaction in A. And the only thing which can excite satisfaction in A is a state or activity of his own, such as the thought that another man B is satisfied. Consequently nothing can be a good to A and also to another man B, unless in reality B is not a person other than but actually identical with A, so that what we should call B's thought, e.g. that B is satisfied, is really A's thought. No doubt in certain instances the satisfaction which each has implies a common *object of desire*. Thus the satisfaction which each gets from thinking that B is satisfied implies a *desire* by each for the satisfaction of B. But it is not the satisfaction of B which gives them satisfaction but their thought that B is satisfied, as is obvious from the fact that even where B is satisfied A and B could get no satisfaction unless they either knew or believed that B was satisfied. Consequently it cannot be maintained that A and B can have a good in common or, again, their good in common, unless it be maintained that A and B are really the same individual.[36]

Strangely enough, although it is not obvious on the surface, this is just what Green does maintain. Though he insists that we always seek our own satisfaction, there is nothing which he emphasizes more than our possession of *disinterested* interests, of which the most obvious are benevolence, i.e. a disinterested interest in the welfare of others, and interests in the welfare of other members of our family or of our country.[37] 'These', he says,[38] 'are not merely interests dependent on other persons for the means to their gratification, but interests in the good of those other persons, interests which cannot be satisfied without the consciousness that those other persons are satisfied.' And by way of emphasizing their disinterestedness he ridicules[39] the idea that the man who looks forward to the well-being of his family after he is dead is desiring the satisfaction of seeing it well off. Further, he evidently considers that often we act on the desires involved in such interests, and so have the satisfaction of certain others as our end. Consequently he has to reconcile this conviction with his idea of the nature of all deliberate action, with which it at least seems utterly inconsistent. To do this, it would, of course, be useless for him to contend that when the desire moving us seems to be the desire of something which would excite satisfaction in another for its own sake, it is really the desire of this as a means to something which would excite satisfaction in ourselves. For to do this would be to deny the disinterestedness of the desire. Nor does he do so. Anxious to maintain the disinterestedness at all costs, he tries to effect the reconciliation by what is really the only method open to him, viz. that of contending that where one man A has a disinterested interest in another, B, B is identical with A.

---

[36] It may be noted that for the same reason there cannot be such a thing as a *goodness* common to two people unless they are one and the same. [37] *Prolegomena*, § 167.
[38] Ibid., § 199.   [39] Ibid.

The first hint of this view is given in paragraph 200 of the *Prolegomena*. There, apropos of the interest in other persons, or, as he also calls it, a distinctively social interest, he speaks of the feeling of pleasure or pain which arises in response to manifested pleasure or pain on the part of another sentient being, and he says that this feeling does not contain the germ of such an interest unless the subject of it is conscious of the agent occasioning the feeling as an 'alter ego'. And later on (paragraphs 229–32), the view is stated, though we may fail to notice this from reluctance to think that he intends his statements to be taken literally.

He speaks (paragraph 229) of a man who reflects on the transitoriness of the pleasures by the imagination of which his desires are from hour to hour excited, and asks himself what can satisfy the self which abides throughout and survives those desires. And he says of such a man that his mind becomes possessed by the thought of the well-being of a family, with which he identifies himself, and of which the continuity is as his own (i.e. with whose members he thinks of himself as identical and whose continuity therefore he thinks of as his own continuity). He also speaks of him as looking forward to the well-being of his family, even though he may expect to be laid in the grave before it is realized, and as in doing so thinking of himself as still living in this welfare when dead, thus immortalizing himself (i.e. thinking of himself as immortal). Again later (paragraph 231) he says: 'At a stage of intellectual development when any theories of immortality would be unmeaning to them, men have already, in the thought of a society of which the life is their own life but which survives them, a medium in which they carry themselves forward beyond the limits of animal existence.' Lastly, in paragraph 232, he speaks of a man's thought of himself as permanent as inseparable from an identification of himself with others in whose continued life he contemplates himself as living, and he draws the general conclusion that the distinction commonly supposed to exist between considerate benevolence and reasonable self-love, as co-ordinate principles on which moral approbation is founded, is a fiction of philosophers.[40]

The underlying thought is obvious. Assuming it to be undeniable that in certain instances a man A has a disinterested desire for something which will satisfy another, B, he is contending that the disinterestedness of the desire implies that B is really identical with A and so not another at all. Again, assuming it to be undeniable that A in having this desire is thinking of B's satisfaction as being his own satisfaction in being B's, he is contending that this thought implies that A is thinking of B as being himself. The doctrine indeed is that foreshadowed by Plato where he says of the just city-state that it is one in which the largest number apply the terms 'mine' and 'non-mine' to the same things in the same respects, and implies that the application applies *inter alia* to pleasures and pains.[41]

---

[40] Cf. § 233 end, where he speaks of the *identity* as distinct from the *co-ordination* of these principles.
[41] *Republic*, p. 462.

The net result is that, according to Green, where the members of a group of two or more persons are disinterestedly interested in one another's welfare they are really only one person, and not more than one at all—a state of B, e.g., being related to a state of A in exactly the same way that some other state of A is related to that state of A, the states being all states of one and only one self. Consequently Green, in thinking as he does of the duties of the members of the group as consisting in carrying out rules devised for the greatest satisfaction possible of the group, is thinking of the carrying out of their duties as a sort of enlarged prudence, i.e. a prudence enlarged by taking into account the fact that the self to be made happy is the so-called plurality of selves taken together. And thereby Green seems able to represent a man who does his duty as at once acting *both* disinterestedly *and interestedly*, thus seeming to be able to have it both ways.[42]

Comment on Green's view that a duty implies the existence of a common good is, of course, almost superfluous once it is realized that a common good requires the identity of the persons to whom the good is common. For whatever be the paradox which the exigencies of a theory may tempt us to maintain, there is in the end no denying that two individuals, however disinterestedly interested in the welfare of each other, are two persons and not one, and indeed that for an interest in another to be *disinterested* that other has to be *another*, since otherwise it would not be *disinterested*. Three minor comments, however, may perhaps be usefully made. (1) Green, instead of trying to make his theory fit the facts, is trying to make the facts fit his theory. Starting with the idea that a man can only desire his own satisfaction, when he comes to consider disinterested desires, instead of abandoning his idea, as he should have done, he represents them as really interested. (2) By doing this, he resolves benevolence into self-love and so abolishes it, thereby rendering himself open to a criticism which he passes on the Hedonists. (3) Even on its own lines Green's doctrine is exposed to two very awkward objections. For (*a*) plainly in fact a man A may have a disinterested interest in B without B's having a disinterested interest in A, and in such a case Green would have to allow that A was identical with B, without B's being identical with A. And (*b*) plainly malevolence, i.e. a disinterested interest in the unhappiness of another, is, as he himself admits,[43] as much a fact as is benevolence. He would, therefore, have to allow that malevolence equally with benevolence implies the identity of the persons concerned, and therefore also that where A desires the unhappiness of B, he is in doing so desiring his own unhappiness.

---

[42] Cf. *Prolegomena*, § 203.   [43] Ibid., § 161.

VI. Quasi-teleological Theories of Obligation

Teleological theories of obligation are based on two general ideas, first, that in all deliberate action we have a single final aim or purpose, and second, that an act is rendered what we ought to do by being that which conduces most to the realization of this aim, so that to discover what we ought to do we have first to discover what this aim is, and then to discover the act which would most conduce to its realization. And, as has been contended, these theories break down because we have no single final aim and because, if we had, these theories would resolve the moral into the non-moral 'ought'. Nevertheless, it may be contended that they are on the right track in making use of the idea that in action we have an aim or purpose, and that given a certain, though no doubt a radical, alteration in the first general idea, a tenable theory can be found. This consists in substituting for the idea that there is a single something at which we *are aiming*, the idea that there is a single something at which we *ought* to aim, and thereby representing an act as rendered what we ought to do by being the most conducive to whatever it be that we ought to aim at—as distinct from our actually aiming at it.

Theories which involve this idea may, for lack of a better term, be called quasi-teleological, and Sidgwick goes so far as to maintain that they form one of the two main kinds into which all theories of obligation fall, their underlying ideas being held by all except those who consider that there are kinds of action which in their nature are duties, and whose views he calls intuitional.[44] And in view of their at least seeming to have an affinity with teleological theories they seem to be those which next need consideration.

Such theories will, of course, differ from one another by the particular view taken of what we ought to aim at. And according to Sidgwick[45] there are four which deserve serious consideration, viz. those which represent what we ought to aim at as respectively (1) our own happiness, (2) the general happiness, (3) our own perfection, and (4) the perfection of human beings generally. And strangely enough, he maintains, inconsistently, that *two* of these theories are true, viz. the first and the second, as though there could be two things which are what we ought to aim at.

The two general ideas underlying such views are of course very attractive. For when we reflect we are apt to think (1) that there must be some one thing at which we ought to aim in acting, however difficult its discovery seems to be. And if we think this, we are also apt to think (2) that the character of what we ought to do must be determined by the character of what we ought to aim at, what we ought to do having to be what would be most conducive to what we ought to aim at, so that the initial task has to be that of discovering what we ought to aim at.

---

[44] *Methods of Ethics*[7], pp. 1–3. Inconsistently with this, however, p. 8 and p. 77 (note) he admits teleological theories of a third kind.   [45] Ibid. 9.

Nevertheless, when we consider the first of these underlying ideas we find it exposed to an objection so formidable that it is advisable to consider it before considering any particular theory or what Sidgwick has to say in favour of the first and the second.

The objection can be stated thus: In ordinary speech a statement containing the term 'ought' in the moral sense is always of the form: 'I ought to do so and so', i.e. I ought to effect a certain change, or else, if this elucidation of 'doing something' be not accepted, to make an effort to effect a certain change, and so, on either alternative, to perform a certain activity. But by 'aiming at something X', or 'having something X as our aim', we mean having X as our purpose, and by 'having X as our purpose' we mean having the desire of X as our motive, i.e. being moved to act by the desire of X, so that the statement 'I ought to aim at X' will mean: 'I ought to be moved to act by the desire of X.' The question therefore arises: Can a statement of this form be true if the term 'ought' be used in the moral sense? And the answer seems to have to be 'No', on the ground that a moral obligation is by its very nature a moral obligation to perform some activity, and that therefore there cannot be such a thing as a moral obligation to be moved by a certain desire, since whatever our being so moved may be, it is not an activity. To this reason can be added another, viz. that we can only be bound to do what it is in our power to do, and while it is in our power to perform certain activities, it is not in our power to desire something, still less to desire it enough to enable us to overcome some aversion, and still less again to be moved to act solely by the desire.

No doubt we think that we can often do something to excite or to strengthen a desire of which we already have the capacity. Thus we may think that by making ourselves dwell more upon the advantages of some piece of hard work we can bring ourselves to desire it more, and that we can stimulate, or strengthen, the desire to relieve A's suffering by imagining his suffering, or by imagining it more fully. But to think that we ought to stimulate or to strengthen a certain desire is one thing, and to think that we ought to act from that desire is another. To think the former is really to think that we ought to *do* a certain action, viz. that act which will stimulate or strengthen the desire; and though that act may render it more likely that we shall act from that desire, it is different from acting from that desire.

These reasons receive confirmation in two ways. For, first, if we ask of some particular desire, e.g. the desire to help our friend A, 'Is it a *duty* on our part to be moved by it to act?' we answer 'No', although we may wish to be moved by it on account of its goodness, and may think it a duty to do some act to which the desire prompts us. And, second, if we consider any instance of what we do in fact think a duty we find that it always consists simply in doing a certain action, e.g. paying a certain debt, and not in doing it from a certain motive, e.g. paying the debt from desire to help the creditor, and that, therefore, we do not in fact think of the duty as including the having a certain motive. In addition we find that when we consider whether some past act is one which the agent ought to have done, we think the question independent of the question of what his motive was in doing it; we think, e.g., that the question whether X ought to have paid the bill he paid is independent of whether he paid it, e.g., to retain his neighbour's goodwill or to spite a third party, although of course we think the latter question bears on the *goodness* or *badness* of his action.

Underlying this objection is the idea that an act has a character of its own which is independent of that of its motive, so that it is possible to do the same act from different motives. And anyone trying to meet the objection can do so only in one or other of two ways. For he must either accept this underlying idea or else attempt to reject it. If he accepts it, his attempt has to take the form of contending that in spite of the difference between doing some action and being moved to do it by a desire, the term 'ought' in the moral sense is applicable to some things of the latter kind as well as to some things of the former kind; and this view is, in fact, taken by Sidgwick when he speaks of acts as capable of two kinds of rightness, which he calls objective and subjective rightness, the former being the rightness of the act and the latter the rightness of the motive. Such an attempt, however, must be admitted to fail, on the ground that it is really self-evident that an obligation is necessarily an obligation to perform a certain action, and not to have a certain motive. He may, however, attempt to reject the idea on the ground that an act has no character which is independent of that of its motive, and if he succeeds in establishing the dependence of the character of the act on that of its motive, he will then have an effective way of meeting the objection. For he can then argue thus: It is admitted by everyone, including the objector, that an obligation is necessarily an obligation to do some action, i.e. some particular action. But the character of a particular action being dependent on, and so inseparable from, that of its motive, to assert that there is an obligation to do some particular action is really to assert that there is an obligation to do an action having a certain motive, and so is to assert that there is an obligation to have that motive. And, therefore, the ground is cut from under the objector's feet, since the very thing which he contends there is an obligation to do is, as is obvious when its nature is apprehended, an action having a certain motive—and, therefore, it must be true that there is something at which a man ought to aim.

Now Joseph in *Some Problems in Ethics*[46] takes this course. He allows that an obligation is always an obligation to do some *action*. But he distinguishes two senses of 'action', viz. (1) that in which we speak of an automatic action, e.g. locking a desk from force of habit, as an action (he calls this an act of behaviour), and (2) that in which we speak of a deliberate action as an action; and he maintains that 'ought' and 'ought not' are applicable only to actions in the second sense. He then insists that actions in this sense include a motive. 'I submit then', he says, 'that there is no action in which we must not include a motive: at least none

---

[46] H. W. B. Joseph, *Some Problems in Ethics*, Chaps. iv and v.

that concerns Ethics.'[47] And he states the reason thus: 'No act exists except in the doing of it, and in the doing of it there is a motive; and you cannot separate the doing of it from the motive without substituting for action in the moral sense action in the physical, mere movements of bodies.' And a little later[48] he adds:

> What is left, if you take away the motive, is conscious behaviour like that of animals. . . . Whether there be not, in some animals, the germ of action proper, I do not discuss: but if there be, the instances of it are not behaviour and something besides, an undeveloped motive: the behaviour is no longer itself just the same. And so an act proper is not analysable into behaviour and motive; it is indivisible. You cannot conceive that the motive might be taken away, and the behaviour left really the same.

Further, in accordance with this he denies that it is possible for the same act to be done from different motives, contending that, e.g., eating a plateful of oysters is different when done (a) by someone who is fond of oysters and eats them for the sake of their flavour, (b) by someone who loathes them but eats them to avoid hurting his host's feelings, and (c) by someone who loathes or is indifferent to them but eats them to prevent his neighbour's getting a second helping.[49] To the objection that it is not in our power to act from some particular desire, he replies as follows: When I do have a certain desire, it may be my duty to act on it. Thus if I am prompted by affection to do some act of kindness but hesitate from desire to amuse myself, I ought to do the act of kindness, and ought to do it because it would be prompted by affection. On the other hand, when I do not have a certain desire it may be my duty to do the act to which the desire would have prompted me from another motive, viz. the idea that I ought to do the act as one which would realize a certain goodness,[50] this being different from the idea of duty in general, and in that case the act will be a duty because it would have this motive.[51] And as regards this second contention, Joseph is alive to the objection that an act cannot be rendered a duty by being one which if a man were to do it he would do because he thought it a duty. But he considers that he escapes it because the motive which he is attributing to himself in the instance taken is not the idea of duty in general (i.e., really, the idea that he ought to do the act as being one of a system of duties), but the idea that he ought to do the act as being one which would realize a certain goodness. Here, however, it must be allowed that he is mistaken; for he *is* representing as the reason why he ought to do the act the fact that it would have as its motive the thought that he ought to do it, and to represent the agent as having as his special reason for this thought that the act would have a certain goodness makes no difference whatever.

We have now to consider this view. It should first be noticed that Joseph cannot here be stating his doctrine accurately. When he uses the phrase 'separating an

---

[47] Ibid., 43.   [48] Ibid. 45–6.   [49] Ibid. 45.
[50] This seems the only way of understanding an obscure passage, ibid. 46–7.
[51] Ibid. 47–8.

action from its motive' he is undoubtedly thinking of an act of abstraction, and means by it abstracting an act from its motive, i.e. considering an action in abstraction from, i.e. without taking into account, its motive. Hence when he says 'you cannot separate the doing of an action from its motive without substituting for action in the moral sense mere movements of bodies' (i.e. acts of behaviour), he cannot be intending to say exactly what he does. For if he were he would be implying that the abstracting is possible, and that when we perform it, i.e. consider an act in the moral sense in abstraction from its motive, we find that it is an act of behaviour. And that it is an act of behaviour is just what he is denying. What he must really be meaning, i.e. intending to say, is that to abstract an act in the moral sense from its motive, i.e. to consider it in abstraction from its motive, is *impossible*; and he must be implying as the reason for this that an action in the moral sense has no *character* of its own, i.e. one which is independent of that of its motive. And what he says about substituting for an act in the moral sense an act of behaviour must be regarded as offering a *reductio ad absurdum* to show the impossibility of the abstraction, the argument really being that if you try to perform the abstraction, you will find yourself trying to think of a moral action as an act of behaviour, which you know it is not.

Certain parallels will make the doctrine clearer. If we try to think of some universal, e.g. greenness, in abstraction from some instance, i.e. some particular colour, we find that we cannot, the reason being that a universal has no nature which is independent of its relation to instances of it. And the difficulties which we find in admitting the reality of universals arise from our trying to think of them as things having a nature which is independent of their relation to instances of them. Again, while we can consider the movement of a piece of lead in abstraction from its being the movement of *a piece of lead*, as we do when we consider it as the movement of a body, we cannot consider it in abstraction from its being the movement of *a body*, just because a movement has no nature, apart from its being the movement of a body. For a similar reason, though we can consider the pitch of a particular sound in abstraction from its being the pitch of *that sound*, we cannot consider it in abstraction from its being the pitch of *a sound*, and if we try we shall find ourselves ceasing to think of anything at all. In the same way Joseph is really contending that no moral action can be considered apart from its motive because it has *no* nature independently of its motive; and this view is implied when he maintains that to do the same action from different motives is impossible.

It has, however, to be admitted that when the nature of Joseph's view is thus made clear it is on the face of it untenable. For if an action in the moral sense has no character independently of that of its motive, there is no action for a motive to be the motive of, and therefore no motive either. Indeed, on this view what is called doing a certain action from a certain motive cannot even be illustrated. And even Joseph in giving illustrations of motives is forced to use language which implies, contrary to his theory, that the acts of which they are the motives have a nature which is independent of their motives, referring to the act, e.g., as one of eating a plateful of oysters, where *ex hypothesi* the act to which he is referring is not an act of mere behaviour. And no escape from this procedure is possible, because otherwise he cannot state what the motive of which he is thinking is the motive of. It should, moreover, be added that Joseph in trying to show that acts are done from different motives does not choose his instances quite fairly. For the acts of his three oyster-eaters are, on his own description of them, acts which will have different effects and so are really different actions irrespective of their motive. And if, as it seems clear that he could and should have done, he had taken as instances acts of which the effects would have been the same, it would not have been possible for him to deny that the acts were the same in spite of the differences of motive.

Yet this criticism may provoke a retort. 'The preceding argument', it may be said, 'is undeniably hard to refute. But there must be a mistake somewhere. For at any rate when we are considering actions already done we distinguish them as good or bad or neither according to their motive, thereby implying the idea that acts differ on account of a difference of motive, and that even where these effects are the same, but the motives are different, the acts are different.'

To speak thus, however, is to imply the idea that an action is something which includes a motive, and though, no doubt, we often think of an act thus, the idea cannot be right. An act, no doubt, must have a motive. But one thing may be necessary to another without being part of it. We cannot, e.g., think without mental imagining; but though mental imagining is necessary to a process of argument, it is not part of it. Again, we cannot hit something unless there is something to hit, or know something unless there is something to be known, yet the thing to be hit is not *part* of the hitting it and the thing to be known is not a *part* or a *constituent*, to adopt a phrase sometimes used, of the knowing it. And similarly a motive, though necessary to an action, is not a part of it. By the term 'action' we mean an activity of a certain kind, though of what kind we may find it difficult to say. But the being moved by some desire to perform an activity of a certain kind is not an *activity*. And should anyone be inclined to persist in maintaining that an action includes a motive, he should ask: 'If so, what is that part of an action which is not a motive?' The answer will have to be 'an action', since that is that to which a motive moves us; and then an action will be represented as being part of itself, which is, of course, impossible. And this being so it must be allowed that when we speak of actions as good or bad in respect of their motives, we should, to be accurate, restrict the application of the terms 'good' and 'bad' to their motives, and refuse to apply them to the actions. In conclusion it may be noted that if Joseph were right the question which we frequently put to ourselves: 'Ought we to do so and so?' must be an improper question. For in asking this we mean by 'doing so and so' such things as going to bed, or knocking someone down, or, if not, at least making an effort which we think likely to have a certain effect, and according to Joseph, such a question is as improper as the question: 'Is a noise greedy?'

The general conclusion reached is, of course, that there cannot be anything at which we ought to aim in action, the ground for this conclusion being that to aim at something is to have the desire of it as our motive and there cannot be an obligation to have a certain motive. And, incidentally, the conclusion has been reached that where there is an obligation to do some action it is independent of what our motive would be if we were to do it, so that if we were to do the action we should carry out the obligation, whatever our motive in doing so was.

This conclusion is, of course, the conclusion that the first of the two ideas underlying quasi-teleological theories of obligation is mistaken. But when we consider the second, viz. the idea that what we ought to do is whatever would most conduce to what we ought to aim at, we find that it also must be mistaken. For it can only be true if there be something at which we ought to aim, and there is not. But even if we thought that there were something at which we ought to aim, we could not vindicate the second idea. No doubt there is plausibility in Sidgwick's assertion that it can hardly be denied that the recognition of an end as ultimately reasonable (i.e. as something which we ought to have as our ultimate aim) involves the recognition of an obligation to do such acts as most conduce to the end.[52] But this is not really so. For even if we were bound to have something X as our final end, we should not *in consequence* be bound to do what would most conduce to X, nor would it be self-evident that we ought to do what would most conduce to X as being what we ought to aim at, and so irrespectively of whether we are aiming at it.

Quasi-teleological theories then can be rejected on general grounds, and so irrespectively of the special character which distinguishes one from another. Therefore, strictly speaking, there is no need to consider them. Nevertheless, Sidgwick is so emphatic in maintaining the truth of two of them, viz. that we ought to aim at, respectively, our own happiness and the general happiness, that it seems worth while to consider what he has to say on their behalf.

He prepares the ground for his vindication of these theories by urging that they are widely accepted either by men in ordinary life or by theorists. As regards acceptance of the idea that we ought to aim at our own happiness he argues as follows: The teacher of an art who advances an imperative of skill assumes that a man wants that to which the imperative relates, e.g. a physician in telling a man that he ought to take hard exercise assumes that he wants health. And it is sometimes maintained that someone who advances a prudential imperative, e.g. that you ought to make friends,[53] assumes that the man to whom it is addressed

---

[52] *Methods of Ethics*, p. 35.   [53] The instance is mine.

wants that to which the imperative relates, viz. his own happiness, and that if he does not, the imperative is untrue. But this contention is false. For

We do not all look with simple indifference on a man who declines to take the right means to attain his own happiness, on no other ground than that he does not care about happiness. Most men would regard such a refusal as irrational, with a certain disapprobation; they would thus implicitly assent to Butler's statement that 'interest, one's own happiness, is a manifest obligation,' though the phrase might strike them as unusual. In other words, they would think that he *ought* to care for his own happiness. The word 'ought' thus used is no longer relative: happiness now appears as an ultimate end prescribed by reason.[54]

Here it need only be noted (1) that the argument is curiously weak, since while the conclusion drawn is that most men think that a man ought to be moved by the desire of his own happiness, he only urges in support of it that most men *disapprove* a man's *refusal* to do what his happiness requires on the ground that he does not want happiness—which is quite different, and (2) that the conclusion is palpably false since no man thinks it a *duty* to be moved by the desire of his happiness.

As regards acceptance of the idea that we ought to aim at the general happiness, he contends (1) that the moral rules prescribed to one another are really—though in part unconsciously—prescribed as means to the general happiness, and (2) that Utilitarians even more widely think that such rules are only valid so far as they conduce to the general happiness. And about these contentions it need only be remarked that neither does anything towards showing that any men think that they ought to *aim at* the general happiness.

Having thus prepared the ground, Sidgwick offers his vindication of the two theories in an obscure passage of Chapter XIII in Book III of his *Methods of Ethics*, in which he is looking about for principles of obligation which are really self-evident.

> The principle just discussed, which seems to be more or less clearly implied in the common notion of 'fairness' or 'equity', is obtained by considering the similarity of the individuals that make up a Logical Whole or Genus. There are others, no less important, which emerge in the consideration of the similar parts of a Mathematical or Quantitative Whole. Such a Whole is presented in the common notion of the Good—or, as is sometimes said, 'good on the whole'—of any individual human being. The proposition 'that one ought to aim at one's own good' is sometimes given as the maxim of Rational Self-love or Prudence: but as so stated it does not clearly avoid tautology; since we may define 'good' as 'what one ought to aim at'. If, however, we say 'one's good on the whole', the addition suggests a principle which, when explicitly stated, is, at any rate, not tautological. I have already referred to this principle[55] as that 'of impartial concern for all parts of our conscious life': we might express it concisely by saying 'that Hereafter *as such* is to be regarded neither less nor more than Now'. It is not, of course, meant that

[54] *Methods of Ethics*, p. 7. [55] Cf. ibid. 124 n.

the good of the present may not reasonably be preferred to that of the future on account of its greater certainty: or again, that a week ten years hence may not be more important to us than a week now, through an increase in our means or capacities of happiness. All that the principle affirms is that the mere difference of priority and posteriority in time is not a reasonable ground for having more regard to the consciousness of one moment than to that of another. The form in which it practically presents itself to most men is 'that a smaller present good is not to be preferred to a greater future good' (allowing for difference of certainty): since Prudence is generally exercised in restraining a present desire (the object or satisfaction of which we commonly regard as *pro tanto* 'a good'), on account of the remoter consequences of gratifying it. The commonest view of the principle would no doubt be that the present *pleasure* or *happiness* is reasonably to be foregone with the view of obtaining greater pleasure or happiness hereafter: but the principle need not be restricted to a hedonistic application; it is equally applicable to any other interpretation of 'one's own good', in which good is conceived as a mathematical whole, of which the integrant parts are realized in different parts or moments of a lifetime. And therefore it is perhaps better to distinguish it here from the principle 'that Pleasure is the sole Ultimate Good', which does not seem to have any logical connexion with it.

So far we have only been considering the 'Good on the Whole' of a single individual: but just as this notion is constructed by comparison and integration of the different 'goods' that succeed one another in the series of our conscious states, so we have formed the notion of Universal Good by comparison and integration of the goods of all individual human—or sentient—existences. And here again, just as in the former case, by considering the relation of the integrant parts to the whole and to each other, I obtain the self-evident principle that the good of any one individual is of no more importance, from the point of view (if I may say so) of the Universe, than the good of any other; unless, that is, there are special grounds for believing that more good is likely to be realised in the one case than in the other. And it is evident to me that as a rational being I am bound to aim at good generally,—so far as it is attainable by my efforts,—not merely at a particular part of it.

From these two rational intuitions we may deduce, as a necessary inference, the maxim of Benevolence in an abstract form: viz. that each one is morally bound to regard the good of any other individual as much as his own, except in so far as he judges it to be less, when impartially viewed, or less certainly knowable or attainable by him.[56]

The passage is evidently intended to convince us of the self-evidence of two principles which he calls the principles of Prudence and Rational Benevolence. Unfortunately it is obscure owing to its use of vague phrases such as 'impartial concern for', 'reasonably to be preferred to', and 'of importance to'; but there seem to be three main clues to its interpretation, viz. (1) the designation of the principles as those of *Prudence* and *Rational Benevolence*, which implies that the principles concern a man's motive, (2) his idea that the self-evidence of each is connected with the necessary relation which must hold between a certain whole and its parts, and (3) his idea that the procedure by which the second principle

[56] Ibid. 380–2.

becomes self-evident to us is similar to that by which the first becomes self-evident. Further, by 'a good' Sidgwick here appears to mean something directly exciting satisfaction, and by 'our good on the whole' what would more accurately be called our whole good, viz. the totality of the states and activities which, if they occurred during the various parts of our life, would excite satisfaction during those parts; and though our good and our happiness can be dissociated, his use of the terms 'Prudence' and 'Benevolence' to designate his principles seems to show that he is implying that satisfaction is identical with happiness.

On this basis the argument of the first part seems to be as follows: In the first instance we think of various states or activities of ourselves as things which if they occurred during various parts of our life would be good to us, and so desire them. And when we reflect we come to form the idea of these as forming one whole, which we may call our whole good; and then we come to desire this totality. But besides desiring this totality we on some occasions specially desire one of these particular goods, possibly because we think it will come soon; and then the desire of our whole good and the desire of some particular good prompt us to do different actions. And when this happens it is self-evident that we ought to aim at, i.e. be moved to act by the desire of, our whole good, rather than aim at, i.e. be moved to act by our desire of, the particular good.

On this part of the argument the only comment needed is that it is self-evident that there is no such duty.

The second part of the argument looks as if it were meant to be a demonstration that we ought to be benevolent, and the consideration of it is plainly more important. It appears to start thus: In the preceding process of thought we started with the idea of particular goods to ourselves, and thence formed the idea of a whole which they make up, viz. our whole good. This done we can now start afresh and, having formed ideas of the whole good of other persons similar to that of our own, we can then form the idea of a second whole which these make up, viz. the totality of the whole good of everyone. To this whole or totality Sidgwick then without any justification whatever gives the name 'universal good', by which he means the totality of things which are good. And then he continues:

> Here again, just as in the former case, by considering the relation of the integrant parts to the whole and to each other, I obtain the self-evident principle that the good of any one individual is of no more importance, from the point of view (if I may say so) of the Universe, than the good of any other.[57]

Now being of importance, as he here implies, is being of importance to someone, and he appears to mean by it 'being something for which someone has concern', i.e. being wanted by someone. He is therefore implying (1) that the Universe is a *person*, a *benevolent* person, and indeed *simply* a benevolent

[57] Ibid. 382.

person, i.e. a person who desires only and equally the good of all the inhabitants of the Universe, and also, since the argument is to apply to us, (2) that we are benevolent and simply benevolent persons, i.e. beings who desire only and indeed equally the good of all the inhabitants of the Universe. Consequently, if he had proceeded on the lines of his first argument, what he would have concluded to be self-evident is that we, being simply benevolent beings, ought to aim at, i.e. be moved to act by the desire of, the totality of the whole goods of all others, rather than by that of the whole good of any single person, whether ourselves or another. And had he proceeded thus his failure would have been obvious. For plainly (1) we are not purely benevolent beings, (2) the desire of *our own* whole good cannot be included, along with the desire of the whole goods of others, in benevolence, since the desire of our own good cannot be disinterested, and (3) even if we had been purely benevolent beings, there would not have been a *duty* to be moved by the desire of the good of all others.

But his actual procedure is an even worse failure. For at this point there is a complete break in his argument. He substitutes for the totality of the whole goods of all individuals something quite different, viz. what he calls universal good, i.e. the totality of all the things which are good—and then asserts it to be self-evident that he as a rational being is bound to aim at good generally, i.e. the totality of things that are good, and not at a particular part of this totality, thereby treating being someone's whole good, i.e. being what renders someone satisfied throughout life, as if it were the same thing as being good. And of the various confusions to be found in the *Methods of Ethics* perhaps the most fundamental and the most prevailing is the treatment of 'being a good to someone' and 'being good' as identical.[58]

The inconsistency of his two conclusions, that we ought to aim at our own happiness and also at the general happiness, which has already been pointed out,[59] comes home to Sidgwick himself later.[60] For on p. 420 he has to allow that an egoist, by which he means a man who thinks that he ought to aim at his own happiness, cannot be argued into thinking that he ought to aim at the general happiness, since to such a man his own happiness is the only thing of

---

[58] Some case can be made out for holding that Sidgwick does not mean by 'aiming at X' 'having X as our purpose', but doing what is most conducive to X. Thus on p. 412 he treats the statement, 'Each ought to seek the happiness of all', as identical with the statement, 'That act is right which will produce the greatest amount of happiness.' And if this interpretation is adopted it can be urged that his fundamental idea is that where something would be good this fact involves that we ought to do what would most conduce to it, the notion of 'end' or 'purpose' having nothing to do with obligation. To this interpretation there are various objections into which it seems unnecessary to enter. If it be right, then Sidgwick's theory of obligation will be subject to the criticism advanced on pp. 216–17, 221–5. What seems most likely is that he failed to distinguish the two doctrines which it is possible to attribute to him, and that there are streaks of both to be found in him, that which I have attributed to him preponderating.   [59] p. 197.

[60] See *Methods of Ethics*, p. 420, and the concluding chapter.

importance, i.e. the only thing which he wants. Driven to this admission, he tries to mitigate its force by maintaining that an egoist *can* be thus persuaded if he can be made to allow, as he need not, that his own happiness cannot be a more important part of good than that of any other person. But the attempt is futile. For it treats being of importance to someone, i.e. being wanted by someone, as if it were the same thing as being good. And if this mistake is removed Sidgwick is only saying that if he can convert a man who wants only his own happiness into a purely benevolent being, such a man will have to admit that the happiness of all others is what he ought to aim at, because he has ceased to want his own.

VII. Goodness and Obligation

Teleological and quasi-teleological theories of obligation having been examined, there remains to be considered a group of three theories which between them include most of those which have been advanced. Indeed, it is plausible to represent them as forming an exhaustive division of theories of obligation. For it is plausible to argue thus: 'It is an idea common to everyone that no act can be a duty unless there is something good connected with the action, so that if the act be done, something good will come to exist which otherwise will not. It is therefore only possible to differ about what the good thing is. The only things, however, connected with an action which it is possible to represent as good are (*a*) some effect and (*b*) the action itself. Hence what has to be represented as the thing the goodness of which is necessary, for an act to be a duty, must be either (1) some effect, or (2) the action itself, or (3) either some effect or the action.' And in fact each of these views has been taken, and so there are three and only three possible views. These are that the character which an act must have, to be a duty, is respectively (1) that of *causing* something good, (2) that of *being* good, and (3) either that of *causing* something good or that of *being* good.

The three theories just referred to are those to be now considered. They have certainly been held. The first, for instance, has been held by those called Ethical Hedonists who *inter alia* maintain that only the results of actions can be good. Again, the second is to be found in Kant, who considers that only actions are good, and in those who, like Bentham, Hutcheson, Butler, and Price, are greatly impressed with the goodness of certain actions. And, as will appear shortly, the third is to be found in certain modern writers, of whom Rashdall and Professor Moore are notable examples.

It should be noted, however, that each of these theories is apt to be modified if it occurs to a supporter that the doing of one action is incompatible with doing various others. For then the question 'What is required to render an act a duty?' is apt to be transformed into the question 'What is required to render an act, out of all those any one of which I can do, the act which I ought to do?'; and given this alteration the answers become respectively: the act's being (1) that which would cause *most good*, (2) that which itself is the *best*, and (3) that by doing which *most good* would come to exist, whether in the act or as a result.

The three theories, although they at least seem to have a common idea, nevertheless are very different. For while, according to the first, to discover whether there is an obligation to do some action we must consider only the goodness which its results would have and ignore any goodness which it would have itself, according to the second we must do the opposite, and according to the third we must consider both. And these differences will be more obvious if we allow, as we must, that with one exception, which will be considered later,[61] those who speak of the goodness of certain actions themselves really mean by it the goodness of their motives; for, plainly, to consider the goodness of a result is one thing and to consider the goodness of the motive is another. The third, too, seems to have an element of queerness about it which distinguishes it from the other two in a special way. For the question being: 'What is the character which an act must have for us to be bound to do it?' its answer is: '*Either* that of causing something good *or* that of being good', and thereby it implies, as the others do not, that there is no such single character, and that two quite different characters are somehow equivalent. The difference between the theories seems to become more marked if we ask whether they all share what Joseph calls the idea that good is the fundamental notion of Ethics.[62] By this, it appears, he means the idea not that while goodness is *sui generis* obligation is not, but that while obligation equally with goodness is fundamental in this sense, it is dependent on goodness in the sense that an obligation to do some action depends on the goodness of something connected with the action, so that unless something connected with an action was good, there could be no such thing as an obligation. For while the third view plainly does imply this idea, the other two seem not to do so. For what the first view appears to represent an obligation as dependent on is not the goodness of *anything* good connected with the action but the goodness of some *result*, since it seems to be implied that for there to be an obligation a result of the act has to be good, whether or not the act is itself good. Indeed, it looks as though the first view could be expressed by saying that the fundamental notion of Ethics is not that of goodness but that of the goodness of certain *results* of action. Similarly, what the second view appears to represent an obligation as dependent on is the goodness of certain actions, and it appears capable of being expressed by saying that the fundamental notion of Ethics is that of the goodness of certain *actions*.

Nevertheless, it will have to be considered later whether the three views are really as different as they seem, and whether the third is as queer as it looks.

---

[61] See p. 215. [62] *Some Problems in Ethics*, p. 75.

The truth respectively of these three theories is to be found insisted on in recent writings.

Thus Rashdall is insisting on the truth of the first view when he says:

> All Kant's difficulties arose from the attempt to give a meaning to, and to find a context for, the idea of 'right' without appealing to the idea of 'good'. In our view the idea of 'good' or 'value' is logically the primary conception. ... That action is right which tends to bring about the good. There is no attempt here to get rid of the ultimate unanalysable 'ought'. The good is that which 'ought to be'.[63] ... Our moral judgements are ultimately judgements of Value. The fundamental idea in Morality is the idea of Value, in which the idea of 'ought' is implicitly contained. ... The idea of 'good' and the idea of 'right' are, as it seems to me, correlative terms. It is implied in the idea of 'good' that it ought to be promoted: the idea of 'right' is meaningless apart from a 'good' which right actions tend to promote.[64]

Again, Professor Moore is insisting on the truth of the first view when he says that it is demonstrably certain that the assertion 'I am morally bound to perform this action' is identical with the assertion 'This action will produce the greatest possible amount of good in the Universe'.[65]

Again, Laird, in his *Study in Moral Theory*, asserts the truth of the second view very emphatically.[66] He speaks of an inescapable question set by the fact of action, viz. 'Is any given action what it ought to be?' and he refers to moral theories, i.e. to attempts to answer the question, as concerned with reasons which justify or else condemn actions. And he goes on to say:

> It is plain that the only consideration relevant to the justification or condemnation of an action is its value or lack of value, its goodness or badness. ... Accordingly, we are bound to maintain that the only reason which can justify or condemn is a reason based upon worth or its opposite.[67]

Later he adds:

> When we say, for short, that duty is the adoption of the best, ... we are asserting a necessary and a fundamental connection between value and obligation, excellence and authority, worth and duty. In the language of philosophers this connection is a *synthetic* connection, a union of things significantly different. ... We are saying, indeed, that the character of excellence implies a command, that excellent things, just because of their excellence, ought to be sought and achieved.[68]

Again, Joseph expresses his adherence to the third view by saying that he believes good to be the fundamental notion of Ethics,[69] and he expresses this

---

[63] H. Rashdall, *Theory of Good and Evil*, i. p. 135.   [64] Ibid. 137–8.

[65] *Principia Ethica*, § 89. For the justification of this interpretation see pp. 211–12, below.

[66] In his later *Enquiry into Moral Notions*, p. 10, he says that he wants to renounce his past *in toto* and to make no attempt to defend any opinion formerly held. I only refer to the doctrine of his earlier *Study* as a typical view.

[67] *Study in Moral Theory*, pp. 17–18.   [68] Ibid. 21–2.   [69] *Some Problems in Ethics*, p. 75.

belief in an earlier passage, thus:

> A right act, some say, is not to be defined as one causally related to what is good; and it may have no value in itself; nevertheless, I ought to do it. In spite of the arguments by which this position has been defended, it seems to me absurd. Why ought I to do that, the doing which has no value (though my being moved to do it by the consciousness that I ought, has), and which being done causes nothing to be which has value? Is not duty in such a case irrational?[70]

When, however, we come to consider the various statements made by the four writers just referred to, we find to our surprise that not one of them is content with only one view and that each, while beginning with one of the three, ends with another.

Professor Moore says: 'All moral laws, I wish to shew, are merely statements that certain kinds of action will have good effects.... What I wish first to point out is that "right" does and can mean nothing but "cause of a good result", and is thus identical with "useful".'[71] He adds that it is demonstrably certain that the assertion, 'I am morally bound to perform this action', is identical with the assertion, 'This action will produce the greatest possible amount of good in the universe'. And a little later he says: 'Our "duty", therefore, can only be defined as that action, which will cause more good to exist in the Universe than any possible alternative.'

Here the context shows that Professor Moore is using 'right' as the equivalent of 'ought' or 'duty'. Hence, in the sentence just quoted he is in effect asserting that the statement, 'I ought to do an act of a certain kind', e.g. help my neighbour, *means*: 'An act of a certain kind will cause something good', and consequently he is here offering a *definition* of the terms 'ought' and 'duty', viz. causing something good. And this interpretation is confirmed by his repeatedly contending that in Ethics, i.e. in the inquiry into what we ought to do, the goodness of something is the one thing which is simple and therefore incapable of definition.

Yet, if anything is certain, it is that by 'I ought to do so and so' we do not *mean* 'doing so and so will cause something good'. Hence, if we are to attribute to Professor Moore a view which has at least some plausibility, we must interpret him as if he had said: We always *base* the assertion, 'I ought to do an act of a certain kind' on the assertion, 'Such an act will cause something good', thereby implying that what renders such an action a duty is that it will cause something good. For this interpretation there is the additional justification that in his later *Ethics* he in effect makes this modification himself by saying:

> It is indeed quite plain, I think, that the meaning of the two words[72] is *not* the same: for if it were then it would be a mere tautology to say that it is always a duty to do what will have the best possible consequences. Our theory does not, therefore, do away with the

---

[70] Ibid. 26.   [71] *Principia Ethica*, § 89.
[72] Sc. 'right' and 'expedient', i.e. useful, or causing something good.

distinction between the *meaning* of the words 'duty' and 'expediency'; it only maintains that both will always apply to the same actions.[73]

The interpretation is also borne out by his refutation of Egoistic Hedonism, which can be shortly stated thus: Either the agent's happiness is good or it is not. If it is not, there can be no reason why the agent ought to aim at (i.e. cause) it. If it is, another's happiness is also good, and there is equally a reason why the agent ought to aim at (i.e. cause) that.

Further, Professor Moore, in stating his theory, constantly distinguishes between 'right' and 'absolutely right', thus implying a distinction between a duty and an absolute duty, and he confines the term 'absolutely right' to the act which will cause most good in the universe. This being so, the doctrine stated in the sentences quoted must be this: 'Any act in our power is rendered a duty by being one which will cause something good. But since at any moment there is a variety of acts which will cause something good, only one of which we can do, one of these acts is rendered our absolute duty by being that which will cause more good than will any of the others.'

The doctrine so interpreted, however, is open to the charge of inconsistency. For the term 'absolute' applied to 'duty' can only add emphasis. There cannot be two kinds of duty, the one absolute and the other not. Either we are bound to do some action or we are not; we cannot be bound to do something but not absolutely. Consequently one act cannot be rendered a duty by causing something good, while another is rendered an absolute duty by causing the most good. And it seems only fair to represent Professor Moore as originally adopting the first of the three views in its modified form, viz. that causing something good renders an act a duty, and then on consideration substituting the modified form, viz. that causing most good renders an act a duty, as his more considered view.

This, however, is not the whole story. For Professor Moore frequently implies not only that an act may cause something good but also that it may itself have intrinsic value, i.e. *be* good. And when he has goodness of this kind in mind, he maintains[74] that in considering what action is our absolute duty we must take into account the goodness of various actions as well as that of their effects. Moreover, in one passage he states almost in so many words the third of the three views under consideration, in its modified form. 'In short', he says, 'to assert that a certain line of conduct is, at a given time, absolutely right or obligatory, is obviously to assert that more good or less evil will exist in the world, if it be adopted, than if anything else be done instead.'[75] It is, then, plain that there are to be found in Professor Moore two inconsistent views, viz. the first and the third of those under consideration, each in its modified form, and also that of these

[73] *Ethics*, p. 173.   [74] See e.g. *Principia Ethics*, §§ 17 and 89.   [75] Ibid., § 17.

the third (which of course implies the third of the three underlying ideas[76]) is his more considered view, and that by which he would stand if forced to choose.

In Rashdall also we find the same transition from the first to the third view. For while we find such statements as 'That action is right which tends to bring about the good'[77] and 'The right action is always that which (so far as the agent has the means of knowing) will produce the greatest amount of good upon the whole',[78] we find that when he has in mind the goodness which certain actions themselves have, he insists as emphatically as does Professor Moore that the goodness of various acts, as well as that of their effects, has to be taken into account in estimating their rightness.[79]

In Laird also we find a transition, but a different transition, viz. that from the second view to the third. For although in the passage quoted[80] he speaks of the only consideration which can justify an action as being its goodness, he also speaks of things which because of their excellence ought to be *sought and achieved*,[81] and when he considers the application of moral rules, he holds that goodness of results should be taken into account.

Joseph, however, differs markedly from the others by first proclaiming himself an adherent of the *third* of the three views, and then afterwards substituting for it the second in a modified form. Early in *Some Problems in Ethics* he says: 'Let me state here by way of anticipation what I propose to argue for. An act may be right because productive of good results. ... An act may also be right not because productive of good results; but if so, it must have intrinsic goodness, which goodness must involve the agent's motive.'[82] In a later chapter, however, entitled 'An ambiguity in the word *right*', he puts forward a quite different doctrine. He allows that we often mean by calling an act right that we ought to do it, but he asserts that we also use the term to mean some character in the act, because of which we ought to do it.[83] And he maintains that this character must be a sort of goodness, although it is difficult to state what it is. And as, of course, to *cause* something good is not to *be* good, he is here abandoning his original contention that an act can be a duty because productive of good results, and limiting the reason to the goodness of the act itself. Afterwards he devotes himself to the problem of ascertaining what this goodness is which is common to all right acts, although he is ultimately forced to allow that he can find no account of it which is wholly satisfying.[84] He is, however, driven to deny that it can be the goodness of the motive, on the ground that at least in one instance we think we ought to do

---

[76] See p. 209, above.   [77] *Theory of Good and Evil*, i, p. 135.   [78] Ibid. 184.
[79] Ibid. 97.   [80] See p. 210 above.   [81] See p. 210 above. The italics are mine.
[82] *Some Problems in Ethics*, p. 28; cf. the statement quoted on p. 210 above.
[83] Ibid. 59. The statement is hard to understand unless it means that we also mean by calling an act right that it has a certain character—the character being in fact that character which we think renders an act a duty, although its so rendering it is not part of the meaning of 'right'.
[84] Ibid. 83.

one act rather than another although the motive of each would be the same and so equally good, viz. the thought that we ought to do the action.[85] The instance is that of our thinking that we ought to give to another the means for a much-needed holiday rather than to use it for a much-needed holiday for ourselves. Here, he holds, the superior goodness which we are thinking of as involved in the former action cannot be that of the other's having a needed holiday, since this cannot be better than our having such a holiday; but neither can it be that of the motive, since *ex hypothesi* we are asking what we ought to do, so that, whichever we do, we shall be moved by the thought of the rightness of (i.e. a certain goodness in) the action, and therefore the motive in each case will be the same.[86] And he becomes driven to find it in the goodness which the act would have if it were the manifestation of a rule of action such that if all the members of a community acted on it, their actions in acting on it would as a system be good.[87]

Unfortunately, however, this conclusion is undeniably exposed to two fatal objections. For, first, on Joseph's own showing, the goodness which he attributes to giving another a needed holiday is one the act usually would *not* have, since the goodness is one which the act would only have as one of a system of similar acts done by all, and at least in most cases, if not in all, not all the others would act similarly. Secondly, there cannot be any such goodness. For avowedly the goodness which he is attributing to the act is one which it has only as a part of a system of such acts, and to attribute a character to the parts of a system only as parts of that system is really to attribute the character to the system and to deny it to the parts. Thus, to assert that the parts of a picture are beautiful only as parts of the picture is really to attribute beauty to the whole picture and to deny it to its parts. And, for the same reason, to maintain that the goodness of which he is thinking belongs to the act *only* as part of a system of acts is in effect to deny that the act has any goodness of its own.

At this point it may be noted that a survey as a whole of the writers under consideration suggests two comments. The first is that there is a tendency in them all to treat causing something good as if it were a special way of being good—a treatment encouraged by the misleading phrase 'instrumentally good'—for without such a tendency they could not have failed to notice their transition from one view to another. The second is that, if we except Joseph, who is driven into what must be allowed to be an untenable view of the goodness of an action required

---

[85] Ibid. 96–7. Here, it may be noted, Joseph *is* admitting, contrary to his general account of 'moral' actions, that a moral action has a character which is independent of the character of its motive (see pp. 200–1, above). [86] Ibid. 96.

[87] This seems to be the only interpretation possible of an obscure passage which runs thus: 'We must look beyond the particular action not to its effects but to the rule of action of which it is a manifestation. This, however, is not enough. We must look to the whole form of life in some community, to which all the actions manifesting this rule would belong, and ask whether it, or some other form of life is better, which would be lived by the community instead, if this rule were not helping to determine it.' Ibid. 98.

to render it a duty, there is a tendency to begin with one or other of the first two views and to end with the third, and this tendency raises the question whether after all the first two views are not arbitrarily restricted versions of the third.[88]

At this point, also, it may fairly be objected that so far no instance of the expression of the second view has been given, since though Joseph's more considered doctrine finds the goodness required, for an act to be a duty, in the goodness of the action, the goodness is one which the act cannot have. The truth, however, appears to be that, with the exception of Joseph, those who place the goodness necessary, for an act to be a duty, within the action itself are thinking of the goodness of its motive, and are thinking of the act as something which includes its motive. And this being so, to give instances is easy. Kant, e.g., is expressing the second view when he says:

> Since every practical law represents a possible action as good and *on this account*,[89] for a subject who is practically determinable by reason, necessary,[90] all imperatives are formulae determining an action which is necessary according to the principle of a will good in some respects. ... If now the action ... is conceived as good *in itself* and *consequently*[91] as being necessarily the principle of a will which of itself conforms to reason, then it is *categorical*.[92]

The second theory, again is to be found in Hutcheson when he insists on our disinterested approval of certain acts—an approval which he sometimes describes as our perception of their moral goodness—and subsequently finds that the acts which he approves are those prompted by benevolence, and concludes that what we ought to do is acts prompted by benevolence.[93] Martineau, too, propounds the same theory in a more elaborate form. For he holds that our various desires form a sort of hierarchy in the scale of goodness and that our duty consists in following, i.e. in acting on, the higher of two desires, whenever they conflict.

The theory, however, perhaps finds most explicit expression in Richard Price:

> *Morally good and evil* [he says], *reasonable* and *unreasonable*, are epithets also commonly applied to actions, evidently meaning the same with *right* and *wrong, fit* and *unfit*.
>
> *Approving* an action is the same with discerning it to be *right*; as *assenting* to a proposition is the same with discerning it to be *true*.
>
> But *Obligation* is the term most necessary to be here considered; and to the explication of it, the best part of this chapter shall be devoted.
>
> *Obligation* to action, and *rightness* of action, are plainly coincident and identical; so far so, that we cannot form a notion of the one, without taking in the other. This may appear to any one upon considering, whether he can point out any difference between what is

---

[88] See p. 209 above. [89] The italics are mine. [90] i.e. an act which he ought to do.
[91] The italics are mine.
[92] *Fundamental Principles of the Metaphysics of Morals* (Abbott's trans.), 37.
[93] It is, however, significant that he is unable to keep to this view, and when he comes to consider the details of what we ought to do, represents as the most virtuous act that which tends most to the general happiness, thus tacitly dropping the motive as the ground of obligation.

right, *meet* or *fit* to be done, and what *ought* to be done. It is not indeed plainer, that figure implies something figured, solidity resistance, or an effect a cause, than it is that *rightness* implies *oughtness* (if I may be allowed this word) or *obligatoriness*. And as easily can we conceive of figure without extension, or motion without a change of place, as that it can be *fit* for us to do an action, and yet that it may not be what we *should* do, what it is our *duty* to do, or what we are under an obligation to do.—Right, fit, ought, should, duty, obligation, convey, then, ideas necessarily including one another. From hence it follows,

First, that virtue, *as such*, has a real obligatory power antecedently to all positive laws, and independently of all will: for obligation, we see, is involved in the very nature of it.[94]

It should be noted, however, that the second view has taken one or other of two very different forms. As Hume insisted, when we praise some action and consider it good, we do so on account of its motive. But among the motives which we think good, in addition to certain desires which we ordinarily group together as virtuous, such as the desire to repay a benefit and the desire to overcome our fear, there is one which is very different from the rest. This is what we sometimes vaguely call the sense of duty, and either consider to be the thought that the act is a duty or else consider to be the desire to do it as being a duty. And some theorists, and notably Kant, have singled out this either as the only motive which is good, or else as a motive which is pre-eminently good, and have in consequence represented what we call moral goodness, i.e. conscientiousness, as the basis of duty,[95] their view being that the character required for an act to be a duty is that of being morally good. Others, however, have concentrated attention on the other good motives, and consequently have represented virtue as the basis of duty, their view being that the character required is that of being virtuous. Of this latter view Hutcheson is a prominent exponent, and also Butler, who always takes for granted that what we ought to do is virtuous actions. And in modern times a more elaborate form of the same view is to be found in Martineau.

VIII. Goodness and Obligation (continued)

In considering the truth of the three theories set out in the preceding chapter, it seems best to consider first the difficulties which arise out of the special nature of each, and then those which are common to them all.

To the truth of the first of the three it must be allowed that there is one outstanding and indeed insuperable objection. This is simply that it fails to stand the test of instances. If we are to become convinced that what renders some act a duty is its causing something good, then when we consider some act which would cause something good, we must think not only that the act is a duty but that it is rendered a duty by its causing something good, or more accurately by

---

[94] R. Price, *Review of the Principal Questions in Morals*, ed. D. D. Raphael, pp. 104–5.

[95] It should be noted, however, that another view is also to be found in Kant: see pp. 219–20 below.

the fact that it would if done cause something good. But we do not. To realize this, we must consider an instance of an act which would cause something which is indubitably good, such as an increase in that disposition which we call patience. And such an instance would be found in some act of self-restraint which we thought of as one which to some slight extent would render us more patient, and, again, in the making of some remark to another which we thought of as an act which would render him more patient. According to the theory we should not only think that we ought to do the action, but also think that what renders us bound to do it is that in doing it we should be causing something to become better. But though we shall think in the one case that we ought to perform the act of self-restraint and in the other that we ought to make the remark, we shall not in so thinking be abstracting in the one case from the fact that we shall be making *ourselves* better and in the other from the fact that we shall be making *another* better, and so shall not be thinking of the act as one in which we shall be making someone or something better. We shall be thinking of the acts as duties of different sorts just because the one will be making *ourselves* better and the other making *someone else* better; and we shall be thinking of the act of self-restraint as being a duty just because it would be one of making not someone but ourselves better, and of the making the remark as being a duty just because it would be the making another better. And in a similar way, when we consider whether we ought to help to make some child better, we do not think the question irrelevant whether the child is ours or the child of some relation, or the child of a stranger, or, again, an orphan without relations. Yet we should think this question irrelevant if we thought that what mattered was our making someone better. The truth indeed appears to be that in order to think of some change as one which *we* ought to cause, we must think of the change as in some special way related to ourselves, even if that way consists in its affecting someone other than ourselves. Consequently, it may be noted, we need only to consider our thought about particular instances to be able to reject Professor Moore's refutation of Egoism, viz. his contention that if a man's happiness is not good, he is not justified in pursuing it, i.e. bringing it about, and if it is, everyone else has an equal reason to pursue it.[96]

To the truth of the second of the three theories it must also be allowed that there is an insuperable objection, although of quite a different sort. This is, to put it shortly, that the theory (*a*) on its positive side implies an idea which we have already seen to be false,[97] viz. that our duty is to have a certain motive in action, and (*b*) on its negative side implies another idea which cannot be true, viz. that there cannot be any *action* which we ought to do.

The theory, in representing as it does the ground of an obligation to do some action as lying in its goodness, and its goodness as lying in the goodness of its

[96] *Principia Ethica*, § 64.   [97] See pp. 197–203 above.

motive, is implying the idea that the motive of an action is part of it. But, as has been pointed out earlier, the motive of an action, though necessary to it, is not part of it. And once the necessary correction has been introduced into the theory, it becomes the theory not that we ought to do a certain action because it would be good (since no action would be good) but that we ought to be moved by a certain desire or a certain thought, because that desire or thought would be good, it therefore being implied that there is no action which we ought to do. No doubt, then, according to the theory, if we are moved to act by the good desire or thought, we shall do some action, viz. the action which the desire or the thought moves us to do, but our duty will consist in being moved by the desire or thought, and is irrespective of what it would move us to do, so that, to put it rather loosely, our duty does not concern what we do but only our manner or way of doing what we do.

This conclusion, it should be noticed, would have to be admitted even if we were to allow that the motive of an action is part of it. For anyone who maintains this would have to allow that in doing so he was using the term 'action' in the more inclusive sense in which we speak, for instance, of some action as generous, and not in the narrower sense in which we speak, for instance, of killing someone as an action; and he would then have to distinguish from an action in the more inclusive sense an action in the less inclusive sense, viz. that of effecting, or at least making an effort to effect, some change, since otherwise he would have nothing for the motive to be the motive of. He would then have to allow that according to the theory only acts in the more inclusive sense can be duties, so that acts in the less inclusive sense cannot.

The theory therefore substitutes for the obligation to effect something, or, alternatively, to make an effort to effect something, the obligation to be moved by some thought or desire to effect or make an effort to effect something, and thereby it leaves us with nothing which we ought to do.

We can bring home to ourselves the nature of this conclusion by noticing the forms which it takes according as the goodness of certain actions, on which the duty of doing them is represented as depending, is (*a*) that of virtuousness or (*b*) that of moral goodness. According to the former view, to have a duty we must have some virtuous desire, such as the desire to help another out of trouble, and if we have such a desire, our duty will be to be moved by this desire to act, no matter what the act be to which the desire prompts us, and whatever we do, it will not have been our duty to do it. Again, according to the latter view, to have a duty we must have the idea that there is a certain act which we ought to do, e.g. to torture a certain heretic, or alternatively to load him with kindness, and given that we have this desire, our duty will be to be moved to act by this idea, or alternatively, by the desire to do this as being an act we think a duty, and whether we do this or anything else, it will not have been our duty to do it.

The latter form of the view, moreover, involves the paradoxical, and indeed untenable, idea that the existence of moral goodness depends on the existence of an illusion. To see this we need only consider the special form which this view assumes in Kant, for *mutatis mutandis* the same consideration will apply to basing duty on moral goodness, while at the same time considering a morally good action to be that prompted by the *desire* to do the action as one the agent thinks to be a duty. According to Kant, a morally good action requires the idea that there is a duty to do it, and indeed is an action prompted solely by this idea. But also, according to Kant, this idea is false, since there are no acts which we ought to do, and our duty is only to have a certain idea as our motive. Now if it be allowed that a man in doing some action has been wholly or in part influenced by the idea that he ought to do it, to assert that his idea is mistaken is no ground for refusing to attribute complete or some moral goodness to his action, provided it be held that there is some act which it is his duty to do, and therefore that he is only mistaken about what his duty is. And, in fact, we think that the question whether some act was morally good is quite independent of whether he was right in thinking he ought to do what he did. Again, provided we think, for instance, that an inquisitor was acting conscientiously, we think his action morally good however misguided we think his idea of his duty. But it is quite a different matter to try to attribute moral goodness to an act if it be held, as it really was by Kant, that the very idea that there can be a duty to *do* something, i.e. to effect something, as distinct from a duty to have a certain motive, is a mistake. And we certainly should not continue to believe that there is such a thing as moral goodness, if we thought it a mistake to think that there is a duty to do anything whatever. Indeed, in this respect Kant is killing the goose which is to lay his golden eggs. For he is trying to convince us that we have a duty, viz. to act morally, while telling us that if we so act we shall be acting on a mistake; and to do this is impossible. Indeed, if he succeeds in persuading us that our idea that there can be actions which we ought to do is false, he will render it impossible for us to act morally, for we cannot be led to act on an idea which we know to be false, and therefore no longer have.

It will naturally be asked, 'How, if this be so, did the objection fail to escape Kant's notice?' The answer, however, does not seem hard to find. For there is in him, besides this representation of moral goodness as the basis of duty, a totally different view according to which our thoughts that particular actions of certain sorts, e.g. acts of telling the truth, are duties *are* true, and consequently he fails to see that according to him to do a morally good action is to act on an illusion. This view arises when, ceasing to be preoccupied with the goodness of conscientious action, he asks himself, 'What acts in particular ought we to do?' He is then struck with the idea that, since the character required for an act to be a duty, unlike that of an act hypothetically prescribed, cannot be deduced from that of a purpose, the only thing left for it to be deducible from is the nature of a principle of duty, which is necessarily binding on all; and realizing that only the doing of an act capable of being done by all can be binding on all, he is led to conclude that the character required for an act to be a duty is that of being capable of being done by all;[98] and he considers that the acts which we ordinarily think duties have this character. What, however, he fails to see is that *both* accounts of the basis of duty cannot be true, and therefore also that in accepting moral goodness as the basis, he is tacitly rejecting the other account of the basis according to which our thoughts that certain actions are duties are true.

It should, however, be noticed that Kant's main mistake does not lie in his account of moral goodness. Anyone would at least have to allow that this, if not true as it stands, contains an element of truth, and would be true if modified to the extent of substituting for the *thought* of the duty of doing some action the *desire* to do it as an act we think a duty. His main mistake lies in representing moral goodness as the basis of duty. The truth is that here Kant is guilty of an inversion. Whereas, in fact, to arrive at the idea that certain acts are morally good, we must already, and so independently, have the idea that there are acts which are duties, Kant is maintaining that to arrive at the latter idea we must already, and so independently, have the former.

There remains, however, to be pointed out a further objection to the second of the three theories under consideration, viz. that if it be true, there cannot be such a thing as conscientious action, whether by 'conscientious action' be understood action prompted by the thought that we ought to do the action, or action prompted by the desire to do the act as being a duty. The objection is one of which Hume had a glimpse in connexion with the second of the two forms which it assumes,[99] without, however, appreciating its full force. Hume brings forward an argument which at least proves that if we ought to do what is virtuous, our motive in doing our duty can never be what he calls the sense of duty.[100] The argument, though well known, does not seem to have been given the weight it deserves. Hume himself states it obscurely and indeed inaccurately,[101] but properly stated it is this: 'What we ought to do is virtuous actions. But the virtue of a virtuous action is that of its motive, i.e. the goodness of some desire forming its motive, such as the desire of a parent to help his child, arising from parental affection. Hence, what we ought to do is actions of which the motive would be some virtuous desire, and therefore in doing something which we ought our motive cannot be the thought that we ought to do it, for if it were, the act would not be virtuous and so not a duty.' Hume, however, in presenting the argument only states the conclusion thus: 'In short, it may be established as an undoubted maxim, *that no action can be virtuous, or morally good, unless there be in human nature some motive to produce it, distinct from the sense of its morality*', thereby implying

---

[98] It need hardly be pointed out that this conclusion is untrue.
[99] See p. 216, above.
[100] For Hume's use of the phrase, see his *Treatise*, Book III. 2, § 5.
[101] Ibid., § 1.

only that the motive cannot *always* be the thought that we ought to do it but must sometimes be a virtuous desire. And this is unfortunate because if the premisses prove anything they prove that the motive can *never* be the sense of duty; and in a later passage[102] he himself gives this as the conclusion. His half-heartedness is due to his conviction that sometimes we really do do an action from the sense of duty.[103] But he fails to notice that in admitting this he is abandoning his view that we only think an act a duty if we think it would be virtuous.

Hume's argument, of course, only applies to the form of the second theory which represents virtue as the basis of obligation. But a similar argument applies to the form which bases obligation on moral goodness. For this form really implies the idea that there are two forms of the sense of duty, viz. (1) the mistaken thought that we ought to do so and so, and (2) the true thought that we ought to have this thought as our motive, in virtue of the goodness of being so moved. And an argument similar to Hume's will establish that our motive in doing what we ought must always be the false, and can never be the true, sense of duty.

Hence on either form of the view, though we have duties and know that we have, we cannot do a duty from the sense of duty. And in this connexion it is significant that Martineau is driven to admit this when he is forced to allow that the sense of duty cannot be a spring of action.

Of special difficulties presented by the third of the three theories hardly anything need be said. For according to this view what is required for an act to be a duty is either that it would cause something good or that it would be good. For the objections to considering (*a*) that causing something good, and (*b*) that being good, can render an act a duty have already been considered, and whatever objection there may be to representing these as alternative grounds of an obligation will turn out if examined, as will appear presently,[104] to be bound up with an objection which is common to them all.

IX. Goodness and Obligation (continued)

It now remains to be considered whether there are any objections to the three theories under consideration which are common to them all. And here, to anticipate matters, it will have to be allowed that we get a surprise—the surprise of finding that they involve a mistake which is far more radical than any which we should even be inclined to suspect beforehand. The mistake is analogous to that underlying teleological theories in that it consists in resolving obligation into something else; and in particular it consists in resolving it into what has to be called ought-to-existness.

---

[102] Ibid., § 5.   [103] Ibid., § 1.   [104] See pp. 221–5.

We shall be more ready to admit the existence of the mistake if we notice a certain implication, which so far has not been referred to, of the question to which these theories are intended to be the answer. As has already been pointed out,[105] the question is: 'What is the character which an act must possess for us to be morally bound to do it?', and to ask it is to imply the idea that all the acts which we are bound to do have in common a character their possession of which renders us bound to do them, and so is in effect to ask: 'What is this common character?' But, as is clear when we reflect, the only thing which it is possible to think that an act's possession of a certain character can give rise to is its possession of some other character. Therefore, to ask: 'What is the common character the possession of which renders us bound to do the various acts which we are bound to do?' is to imply the idea that what we call our being bound to do these various acts is their possession of a certain character. It is, therefore, to imply the idea that that to which we are referring when we say of ourselves that we ought, or that we are morally bound, to do a certain action is not even in the widest sense of the term a characteristic of ourselves, as the statement suggests that it is, but a characteristic of the action. Anyone, therefore, who puts the question is implying the idea that that to which the term 'ought' refers is really a character of some action, and he is therefore resolving what is really someone's obligation to do some action into something which it is not, viz. some character of the action, i.e. thinking of it as being something which it is not.

Joseph would have denied this. For while agreeing that there is no such thing as the obligatoriness of an action, he does hold that an act's having a certain character gives rise to something which is not its having some other character, viz. our obligation to do it; and thereby he implies that it is possible to think of an act's having a certain character as giving rise to something which is not its having some other character.

Obligatoriness [he says] is not a character of actions. There is no ought-to-be-doneness, or ought-to-be-forborne-ness. To say that an act is obligatory means that the doing it is obligatory on me. An obligatory act is like a well-remembered face; the face no doubt has characters because of which it is well remembered, but it is called well-remembered to signify not those characters, but that others remember it well. And an act is called obligatory because of some character which it has, but to signify not that character, but that we ought to do it because thereof.[106]

This position, however, must on reflection be admitted to be untenable. It is impossible to maintain that what is called my being bound to do a certain action arises from that action's having a certain character, without being committed to holding that what is so called is the action's having a certain character. And the parallel case of a well-remembered face only serves to bring this impossibility home. For it cannot be maintained that what renders a face well remembered is

---

[105] See p. 185, above.   [106] *Some Problems in Ethics*, pp. 61–2.

its having certain distinctive features, as distinct from our having noticed that it has them, without implying that what is called its being well remembered is a certain character of the face.

Since then anyone who puts the question to which what we called theories of obligation are intended to be the answer, is implying the idea that what is called an obligation to do some action is really the act's possession of a certain character, we must ask, in the case of any given individual who asks the question, what in particular is the character into the possession of which he is resolving obligation. At any rate we can say that it cannot be that the appropriate term for which would be that coined from the term 'obligation', viz. obligatoriness. For anyone who speaks of some action as obligatory on X would allow, as Joseph would admit, that in speaking thus he was only stating in a misleading way that X ought to do the action. No one thinks that there is such a thing as obligatoriness. And this being so, it at least seems likely that what anyone who puts the question is resolving obligation into is that for which we have to coin the term 'ought-to-existness', simply because it is difficult, if not impossible, to think of anything else into which it can be resolved.

Given this preparation, it will become easy to recognize that at any rate the three theories under consideration are resolving obligation into what for lack of a better term has been called ought-to-existness. For it is now clear (1) that in common with other theories they are resolving it into some character of an action; (2) that this character is not what if it existed would have to be called obligatoriness; and (3) that they agree in holding that for there to be an obligation to do an action, something related to the action must be good. This being so, it becomes clear that the only character which they can be resolving it into is that ought-to-existness which at least some think is possessed by anything good. To see this we need only consider what defence of these views their respective supporters could offer. A supporter of the second view, if asked: 'Why does an action's being good render us bound to do it?', could only answer: 'Because it is involved in the very nature of goodness that whatever is good should or ought to exist.' A supporter of the first, if asked: 'Why does an act's causing something good render us bound to do it?', could only answer: 'Because causing something good, though not itself good, and therefore not for that reason something which ought to exist, yet is something which ought to exist, as being something which causes something which is itself good and therefore ought to exist. And a supporter of the third view would have to defend it by applying these arguments respectively to acts themselves good and acts causing something good.

Confirmation of the conclusion that these theories involve the reduction of obligation to 'ought-to-exist' is to be found in statements of some of the writers referred to, in which when trying to state what is fundamental they express themselves in terms of 'ought-to-exist'. Thus Rashdall, in a passage already quoted,[107] says: 'There is no attempt here to get rid of the ultimate unanalysable "ought". The good is that which "ought to be"', and in effect he repeats this statement a little later[108] by saying: 'The fundamental idea in Morality is the idea of Value' (i.e. goodness), 'in which the idea of "ought" is implicitly contained.' Other instances are to be found in Laird. In an article in *Mind*[109] I had in effect contended that to be able to conclude from our knowledge that a certain thing would be good that we ought to do some action which would produce it, we need in addition the knowledge that what is good ought to exist, on the ground that an 'ought', if it is to be deduced, can be deduced only from another 'ought'. Laird, commenting on this contention, admits the need of this additional knowledge that what is good ought to exist, as a link between the premiss and the conclusion, and says that this link is peculiarly obvious and that he is only concerned to state it firmly and with precision.[110] Also, speaking of the question which moral inquiry has to consider, he says: 'This question is whether any given action is what it *ought to be*. In other words, moral theory is concerned with the reasons that *justify* action.'[111] Again, the language of Professor Moore's *Principia Ethica* is even more explicit. For in it we find (*a*) statements which imply the idea that the fact that something X ought to exist, if not actually identical with its goodness, is at least necessitated by it; and (*b*) others which imply the idea that the statement 'I ought to do this' is only a way of saying 'This act ought to exist'. As an instance of the former we may take: 'Whenever he [i.e. someone] thinks of "intrinsic value" or "intrinsic worth", or says that a thing "ought to exist", he has before his mind the unique object—the unique property of things—which I mean by "good"',[112] and he also speaks of the question: 'What *sort of* things are good, what are the things which, whether they *are* real or not, ought to be real?'[113] As instances of the latter we may cite his speaking[114] of the question: 'What ought we to do?' or 'What ought to exist now?' and of 'the reason why a thing ought to be done or to exist now'. In addition he makes statements which imply both ideas. Thus he says:[115] 'It is plain that when we assert that a certain action is our absolute duty, we are asserting that the performance of that action at that time is unique in respect of value.' And again,[116] he implies that a thing ought to be done or to exist now only if it itself has intrinsic value or else causes something which has. Again,[117] he speaks of almost all ethical writers as having failed to distinguish whether the reason why a thing ought to be done or to exist now, is that it is itself possessed of intrinsic value, or that it is a means to what has intrinsic value. It is, therefore, abundantly clear that at least in the minds of Rashdall, Laird, and Professor Moore the 'ought' of duty is reducible to, i.e. is really, the 'ought' of 'ought-to-exist' which some at least think inseparable from whatever is good.

---

[107] See p. 210 above.   [108] *Theory of Good and Evil*, i, p. 135.   [109] See p. 9, above.
[110] *Study in Moral Theory*, p. 25 n.   [111] Ibid. The italics are mine.
[112] *Principia Ethica*, § 13.   [113] Ibid., § 70.   [114] Ibid., § 104.   [115] Ibid., § 89.
[116] Ibid., § 104.   [117] Ibid.

And even in the case of Joseph, who does not use the language of 'ought-to-exist', it is difficult to see what answer he could give to the question: '*Why* does the goodness of an act give rise to the obligation to do it?', except that whatever is good should or ought to exist.

Further, since it is now clear that the three theories involve the reduction of the 'ought' of duty to the 'ought' of 'ought-to-exist' involved in the goodness of anything good, it is also clear that they are at bottom the same, in spite of what at first seem their differences,[118] and differ only about the kinds of thing which can be good. For the same reason, the appearance of queerness presented by the third theory as laying down alternative grounds of an obligation disappears, since anyone who considers the goodness of an action as a reason why it ought to exist will have to allow that its causing something good is equally a reason, as being the causing of something which ought to exist, and anyone who considers causing something good as a reason will have to allow that being good is also a reason. In addition we can now understand, as we could not otherwise, how a supporter of the first or of the second view comes to pass so easily to the third, all that is needed being that he should take into account the goodness in the one case of an action and the goodness in the other of a result, which hitherto he had ignored.

Now that the nature of the three theories is thus clear, it might seem that no comment on them is needed beyond that of pointing out that the 'ought' of obligation is not that of 'ought-to-exist', and that therefore they are resolving obligation into something which it is not. There is, however, another which may usefully be made, in case it should be thought that after all these theories are right in representing what we at least call our obligation to do some action as being the action's being something which should or ought to exist. This is simply that if this idea were true, there could be no such thing as an obligation to do some action, until the act is already done, whereas from its very nature there can only be an obligation to do an action so long as it is not done. This must be so, because, though it may at first escape our notice, only something which is can be something which ought, or ought not, to exist. To say, e.g., that a feeling of generosity which I am not having 'ought' to exist is to say nothing, just because *ex hypothesi* there is nothing here for 'being something which ought to exist' to be attributed to.

---

[118] See pp. 208–16, above.

10. Green: Political Obligation

I

Green's lectures on the Principles of Political Obligation are in the main an attempt to answer two related questions. The first of these is the question: *Why* is it the duty of a subject to obey his ruler or sovereign or government? This question of course takes for granted, as in ordinary circumstances we all do, that there is such a duty, i.e. that the mere fact of a sovereign's ordering us to do some action gives rise to a duty on our part to carry it out. And the question arises naturally out of this idea, for after all the mere receipt of an order backed up by a threat seems, if anything, to give rise to the duty of resisting rather than of obeying, and so we naturally ask, why is this otherwise in the special case where the order comes from a ruler?

The question, it should be noted, is similar to questions about acts of other kinds which we ordinarily think duties, such as, *why* ought we to speak truthfully or to consider the feelings of others? Hence an answer is really only part of a theory of Moral Obligation in general, viz. that part which concerns one special obligation, and unless we recognize this we are apt to go astray in looking for the answer.

Green puts this question in the form: What is the true ground or justification of obedience to law? At the same time his answer, as will appear later, has a peculiarity. This is that by its very nature it is at the same time a theory of Moral Obligation in general, i.e. an answer to the question, *why* ought we to do any of the actions which are duties? And indeed his lectures will be better understood if they are regarded as a theory of Moral Obligation generally rather than a theory of Political Obligation in particular, though they are both.

The second question is one the answer to which in Green's mind is bound up with the answer to the first. It is the question put by a *ruler*: What is the principle which should guide me in making laws, i.e. in ordering and enforcing various actions?

Green's treatment of these questions exerts a peculiar fascination. It gives the impression of propounding a profound truth, the ignoring of which has led his predecessors astray, and the discovery of which at last renders it possible to give the right answer.

At the same time the lectures are undeniably very obscure. And the impression of their obscurity is apt to grow rather than to diminish with further acquaintance. Indeed we more and more find ourselves asking not so much: Is the doctrine true? but: What *is* the doctrine?

Once the reader has realized the obscurity, what he would like to see offered in the first instance is a clear statement, kept clear of all commentary, of what the doctrine is. And he would prefer any comments to be reserved till afterwards.

Now I flatter myself that I could offer such an outline. But if I did, you would only call it a caricature. For it would differ so widely from Green's own statements that it would strike you as mere misrepresentation, and you would object that I have simply misunderstood him. To avoid this objection, it would be necessary simply to construct an outline by piecing together in as connected a way as is possible the statements to which Green seems to attach most importance. But you would find the result just as obscure as the lectures. It would, in fact, only present the obscurity in a tabloid form, and it would be no help towards discovering what the doctrine really is.

The chief reason of this lies in a fact which only becomes clear as the result of considering very closely what Green says. Underlying the lectures is a peculiar theory of Moral Obligation which is totally inconsistent with our ordinary moral ideas and therefore also with ordinary language, which is after all only the expression of our ordinary ideas. Unfortunately, however, Green does not realize this; and in consequence, when stating what he considers to be the truth, he retains ordinary language, thereby speaking as though our ordinary ideas were true, although it is really his object to make out that they are not. Thereby he conceals both from himself and from his readers the real nature of his view, and in fact fundamentally misrepresents it. And in consequence, to represent his doctrine accurately, radical restatement becomes necessary. Incidentally, it may be added, Green by expressing his view in ordinary language gives it a plausibility which it does not deserve, by making it seem consistent with our ordinary ideas although in fact it is not.

This being so, the only useful plan is to take the statements to which Green would seem to attach most importance, and ascertain what he is really implying in making them, and then to formulate his doctrine in accordance with these implications, regardless of whether or not the formulation agrees with his ordinary method of expressing himself.

And this is the procedure which I propose to adopt. It unfortunately, of course, involves a good deal of discussion of matters of interpretation. But this has to be regarded as inevitable.

At the same time, to do this with success some preparation is necessary. As any consideration of Green will show, he is on certain matters confused, and on these things we must first get ourselves clear.

1. It is important to bear in mind that to have a Legal Obligation and to have a Moral Obligation to do some act are facts of quite different sorts. The former consists in the fact that we have been ordered to do it and are subject to

coercion if we do not, while the latter consists in our having the duty of doing the action.

2. Consider the meaning of the phrase 'a moral right'. As instances will show, we use 'having a moral right' in two senses according as that to which we are said to have a right is (*a*) our doing something, e.g. taking a holiday or killing someone in self-defence, or (*b*) another's doing something, e.g. our son's maintaining us in old age, or our government's protecting us from violence. In the former case we mean simply that our act would not be wrong, i.e. that we are not under a disobligation to do it. In the latter case, we are referring to the other's obligation to do the action, his obligation being from our point of view our right.

3. Consider a favourite phrase of Green's, viz.: 'a system of rights and obligations enforced by law'. Here the rights and obligations meant must be *moral* rights and obligations. For since our having a legal right or obligation is something which includes an enforcing, it cannot be enforced, since it is impossible to enforce an enforcing. Further, strictly speaking, what is implied to be enforced is not the rights and obligations but the acts to the doing of which there is a right or an obligation. In addition, when we speak of the ruler as enforcing a right of *mine*, we really mean his enforcing on another the doing of an act to his doing of which I have a right and he has an obligation, e.g. the ruler's enforcing on another the refraining from interfering with my body, to which refraining I have a right. Correspondingly, when we speak of the ruler as enforcing an obligation of mine, we mean his enforcing on me an act to the doing of which I have an obligation and someone else has a right. Hence the phrase 'rights and obligations enforced by law' is really the equivalent of the obligations of others to a man and his obligations to them enforced by law, i.e. the system of mutual obligations enforced by law—so that the thing meant can be referred to in terms only of obligation.

4. Green always speaks of a right as being a *power* to do some action, i.e. really a power to do it in consequence of someone else's action. This cannot be true of a right in either the legal or the moral sense. At best such a power can only be something *to* which we have a right in either sense. And the only truth underlying Green's way of speaking is that where we have a legal right to do some action, i.e. where the government orders and enforces on others actions which will give us the power to do it, we shall to some extent have the power in consequence of the government's coercion. Where, however, we have a moral right to a power due to the nature of the action in question, we need not have the power.

We can now turn to Green. It is, of course, a prominent feature of the lectures that they are largely taken up with a criticism of previous theories of Political Obligation, and notably of the Social Contract theory, and in effect he regards this theory as enemy number one, and indeed as a theory to be demolished before it is possible to attain the true theory. And the ground of his objection to this theory lies in his denial of the existence of any such thing as a system of natural rights and obligations, as the phrase 'natural rights and obligations' is usually understood.

The first thing to do for any one who is trying to elucidate Green's theory is to ascertain what precisely he is maintaining in making this denial. For this denial is an essential part of the negative side of his doctrine, and the positive part has to be consistent with it. Whatever his positive doctrine is, it has to be one which is consistent with this denial.

The first question, therefore, to be answered is: What does Green mean when he denies the existence of natural rights and obligations, as the phrase is usually understood?

This denial first appears in § 9. He says:

> There has been much objection to the admission of *natural* rights and obligations. At any rate the phrase is liable to misinterpretation. It may be taken to imply that rights and obligations can exist in a 'state of nature'—a state in which every individual is free to do as he likes; that legal rights and obligations derive their authority from a voluntary act by which individuals contracted themselves out of this state, and that the individual retains from the state of nature certain rights with which no legal obligations ought to conflict. Such a doctrine (he adds—and obviously with approval) is generally admitted to be untenable.

And he endorses the truth of this admission by implying that no such system ever did or could exist independently of force exercised by society over individuals. Then later, in § 20, he says: 'a law is not good [i.e. really is not one which the legislator ought to make] because it enforces "natural rights", but because it contributes to the realisation of a certain end'. And, as the context shows, he implies that the reason why a law cannot be good because it enforces natural rights is that there are no such things as natural rights.

Here, of course, he is referring to the social contract theory. And in § 22 he, in effect, represents this theory thus: Men originally existed in a state of nature, i.e. in a community *not* united by subjection to a government. In this state men had various rights against and obligations to one another. Then at some time with a view to the general interest men *agreed* to, and did, set up a government, i.e. a body which would order and enforce various actions which individuals were under an obligation to do, and also others the doing of which generally would be in the general interest. This done, if the question was raised 'Why is an individual bound to obey his government?', the answer in some instances would be 'Because there is an obligation to do the action, natural in the sense of being independent of the government's order', and in others, 'Because, though there is no natural obligation to do the action, yet there is a natural obligation to carry out the original promise or agreement to obey the government', so that in every case the duty to obey rests on a natural obligation.

The implication is that here by 'a system of natural rights and obligations' is meant a system of rights and obligations which existed before there was a government, and which therefore, being independent of any order, still exists after there has come to be a government.

Therefore what Green is denying is the existence of natural rights and obligations in this sense, i.e. in the sense of rights and obligations independent of a government's order.

This denial is, of course, very drastic, though until we consider closely what Green must be meaning by 'natural' we do not realize how drastic it is. He is here denying that you or I who are members of a state have any moral rights or obligations, apart from a law (i.e. a ruler's action of ordering and enforcing the acts in question). And this denial is in two respects totally at variance with our ordinary convictions. (1) As regards our obligations to other members of the state to do certain actions, or their right to our doing them *we* think that, while some depend on the ruler's order, e.g. our obligation to keep to the left of the road, or to give our shop assistant a half-holiday on Thursdays, others do not, e.g. our obligation to educate our children, or to refrain, except in self-defence, from killing another. In fact we should sharply divide our moral obligations to other members of our state into two kinds in this respect. (2) We do not regard our obligations to others as limited to obligations to other members of our state. We should regard it as absurd to maintain that an Englishman, e.g., can have no obligations to, say, a Frenchman or a German. And we regard Locke as right when he replies to the objection that there never has been a state of nature by urging that the rulers of two independent states, and again an Indian and a Swiss in the backwoods of America, are even now in relation to one another in a state of nature, and have certain obligations to one another arising out of that state, the obligations, e.g., to keep faith with one another, belonging to men *as men*, and independently of belonging to one and the same community.

And Green here, in denying the existence of natural obligations in the ordinary sense, is maintaining that in both respects we are mistaken.

In addition there is one special obligation to be considered which makes it look as though Green here is cutting the ground from under his own feet. His primary object plainly is to discover why we ought *to obey our government*, a task, of course, which implies that in fact we are so bound. But from the very nature of the case, if there be a duty to obey our sovereign, this particular duty cannot depend on the order of any *body* whatever. For, if it did, (1) it would depend on the order of a body other than our so-called sovereign, and that so-called sovereign would only be a *subordinate* body like, e.g., a County Council deriving its authority from the order of another body, and so not a sovereign body at all; and (2) the obligation to obey the other body would have in turn to depend on the order of a third body, and so on.

Hence it at least looks as if Green by denying the existence of natural obligations in the ordinary sense is rendering it impossible for himself to answer his own chief question. And to this objection it will in the end have to be admitted that there is no answer.

Here it should be noted that the social contract doctrine, however weak it may be in other ways, is free from this objection, because, asked why we are bound to obey our ruler, it has a natural obligation to fall back on, viz. the natural obligation to keep a promise.

What Green would have replied to these objections is shown by § 9. He would have said that he had expressly only denied the existence of natural rights and obligations in the ordinary sense, and expressly asserted their existence in another and an important sense, and that this assertion meets the objections. This other sense he explains by saying: 'There is a system of rights and obligations which *should be* maintained by law, whether it is so or not, and which may properly be called "natural", because necessary to the end which it is the vocation of human society to realise.' But this statement raises the question: 'What is this different sense of "natural"?'

The statement makes use of a phraseology frequently to be found in Green, viz. that in which he speaks of law, i.e. really the government, as maintaining and again as enforcing rights and obligations. Here, of course, 'rights and obligations' means moral rights and obligations, because a government cannot enforce its own enforcing, and what must be meant is that the government secures or enforces the doing by a subject *A* of those actions which he is under a moral obligation to do, and to the doing of which another subject *B* has a right. Now the use of this language, of course, implies the idea that the moral rights and obligations enforced exist independently of the enforcement, for otherwise there is nothing to enforce; and the language *is* appropriate for those who believe in natural rights and obligations in the sense to which he objects, i.e. rights and obligations independent of an order and enforcement. But for Green it is not, because according to him there are no independent rights and obligations to be enforced. What he should from the point of view of his own doctrine have spoken of the law or the government as doing is *creating* rights and obligations, thereby making it clear that it is only by the government's action that there came to be moral rights and obligations. And his constantly speaking of the law as maintaining or enforcing rights and obligations is very unfortunate because it inevitably implies that, contrary to his own theory, there are moral rights and obligations which are independent of law. Hence, by using this language he misrepresents his own doctrine, giving both his readers and himself the false impression that some moral rights and obligations have an independence of law which he is really denying to them. And just for this reason his own statement of his view requires to be re-written, if it is to be made accurate.

If we bear this in mind we can answer the question: In what sense of 'natural' is he maintaining the existence of natural rights and obligations? His statement is: There is a system of rights and obligations which should be maintained by law whether it is or not, which may properly be called natural. Now if the word 'maintained' is kept, this must mean that there are rights and obligations which are natural in the very sense in which he objects to this, viz. existing independently of law. And this cannot possibly be right. If, however, we substitute as we should for 'maintained' 'created', Green is making the intrinsically untenable assertion that there is a system of rights and obligations which the law should create whether it does so or not, as though things which if they are to exist require to be created exist equally, whether or not they have been created. And once this becomes clear, it also becomes clear that what Green is really asserting the existence of in nature is the fact that the law should create certain rights and obligations whether it does or not. What, in fact, he is doing is denying the existence of natural rights and obligations in any sense whatever and representing the existing fact that the government should make certain laws, and thereby create certain rights and obligations, as the proper substitute for natural rights and obligations. In other words, he is saying: Where people assert that there are moral rights and obligations independent of law they are wrong, and the nearest fact corresponding to such supposed natural rights and obligations is the fact that a government *should and ought to* make certain laws and thereby create certain moral rights and obligations.

The main conclusion is, of course, that Green has completely failed to state a sense in which there really are natural rights and obligations, and substitutes for it the existence in nature of something quite different.

II

We have, however, not yet done with considering Green's treatment of the doctrine of natural rights and obligations. The view which has been attributed to Green has been based on statements taken from the first 20 paragraphs of Chapter A.

The later part of A, however, and subsequent chapters, and especially G, H, and I, appear to offer a different doctrine and one according to which it is possible for a ruler to *maintain* rights and obligations. Thus in § 138 he speaks of the sovereign, and also of the State, as *presupposing* rights, and as an institution for their maintenance. And in § 148 he speaks of those rights which do not come into being with the State, and implies that they may exist where a State is not, it being the first, though not the only, office of the State to maintain these rights.

These statements, of course, directly contradict the view implied in the first part of Chapter A (that the member of a State has no rights and obligations independently of the sovereign's order, the sovereign creating his rights and obligations). And they agree with the Social Contract view to the extent of representing the sovereign's activity as mainly consisting in maintaining or enforcing already existing rights and obligations.

Green, however, when making such statements is usually careful to add that the rights (and he could always have added 'obligations') which the State maintains belong to a man only as a member of a society. Thus in § 134, e.g., he says: 'A state presupposes other forms of community, with the rights that arise out of them, and only exists as sustaining, securing, and completing them.' (N.B. 'completing' is difficult.) And he adds that in order to make a State there must have been families of which the members recognized rights in each other, and also tribes grown out of families, of which each similarly recognized rights in each other. Again in § 138 he insists that the rights which the State maintains belong to individuals only as members of a Society (cf. also § 148).

Indeed this insistence is the basis of his main criticism of the Social Contract theorists given in the later chapters.

By conflating §§ 113 (beginning of G) and 137–8 (beginning of H), we can state his criticism thus:

Their fundamental mistake (and also that of Spinoza) was that they misunderstood the very question: 'Why ought subjects to obey their ruler?' They took 'subjects' to refer to men who apart from being subjects were a mere aggregate as distinct from members of a society, and doing this committed them to giving a false answer. For it exposed them to a fatal dilemma. They had either to assert or to deny that this aggregate had rights and obligations apart from the ruler's action. If with the Social Contract theorists they did the former, they had, to answer the question, to represent individuals as having consented to being ruled. And this can only be done so long as the ruler rules in accordance with their several wishes (N.B. this is quite untrue) and as to some extent this is impossible, this answer is bound to fail. If, however, they did the latter, they were representing all rights and obligations as derived from the sovereign, and therefore were reduced to treating 'having an obligation' as meaning being *forced*, i.e. forced by the ruler—and this is untrue. To get a true answer we must think of 'subjects' as referring to men who are not an aggregate but members of a society.

Hence Green's correction of the Social Contract theorists seems to consist in substituting for their 'men in a state of nature' 'men in a society'. While seeming to agree with them that the sovereign *maintains* already existing rights and obligations, he represents these as possessed by the subjects not as men but as members of a society.

This doctrine, of course, requires the admission of 'natural' rights and obligations, as the phrase is used in §§ 1–20, i.e. in the sense of rights and obligations independent of a ruler's order. It therefore involves an abandonment of the view given in §§ 1–20 and is to that extent more plausible, because it leaves to the sovereign rights and obligations to enforce.

Unfortunately, however, there is reason to doubt whether the statements quoted, and therefore also this account of Green's view which is based on them, are accurate expressions of his view. The doubt arises as soon as we ask: When Green says 'The rights and obligations which the sovereign maintains imply membership of a society', what does he mean by 'a society'? This question is difficult and I propose to defer adequate consideration of it. But without this we can give an answer sufficient to decide whether these statements express his real view.

In § 116 Green makes a statement which, though surprising, is one by which he would evidently stand. Apropos of Rousseau's view that the social pact is the foundation not merely of civil government but of morality, Green says in support of Rousseau: 'It remains true that only through a recognition by certain men of a common interest, and through the expression of that recognition in certain regulations of their dealings with other, could morality originate, or any meaning be found for such terms as "ought" and "right" and their equivalents.'

This and similar statements imply that Green thinks that there are no such things as rights and obligations apart from *regulations*, or as he calls them just afterwards (§ 117) rules, i.e. really that there can be no obligation to do an action unless there is a regulation enjoining the doing it. A regulation, however, implies the existence of a body which imposes and enforces the rule, which therefore is in fact at least the analogue of a ruler. And the underlying idea must be that where someone is under an obligation to do some action, and so also where another has a right to his doing it, the obligation and the right have been *created* by a regulating body's enjoining the action. Hence when Green maintains that the rights and obligations which the sovereign maintains are rights and obligations which the subjects have only as members of a society, he must at least mean by 'a society' a group of men who are subject to a regulating body which by its regulations has created the rights and obligations they have. Hence just as before, in the first chapter, Green implied that the rights and obligations of the members of a State are the creation of its sovereign, so now he is implying that the rights and obligations of the members of a society have been the creation of its regulating body.

But, this being so, Green would have had, if pressed, to withdraw as inaccurate his statement that the sovereign *maintains*, i.e., really, enforces, rights and obligations which the subjects have as members of a society. What he is thinking of is a supposed change in which men who were members of a society become members of a State. And he is exposed to a dilemma. He has either to maintain that the society survives the change and continues to exist along with the State, or else to maintain that it disappears and is in fact superseded by the State. If he does the former, he has to allow that the sovereign is only doing over again what the ruling body of the society is still doing, viz. creating the rights and obligations. On the other hand, if he does the latter, he is really maintaining that the sovereign is now re-creating, i.e. creating anew, those rights and obligations which the ruling body of the society created, until it was superseded and so disappeared. Consequently on neither alternative is Green justified in speaking of the sovereign as maintaining, as distinct from creating, rights and obligations. As a matter of fact, of the alternatives Green would obviously have accepted the second. For apart from its greater plausibility, he expressly says (§ 139): 'The state is a form which society takes in order to maintain them': and this implies not only that a State is a species of society, but that where a society which is not a State is followed by a State, it *becomes* that State. And this being so, instead of speaking of the State as maintaining the rights and obligations which its members have as members of a society, Green ought to have expressed his view by speaking of the State as re-creating the rights and obligations which its members formerly had as members of a society, and which were then the creation of the regulating body of that society.

The broad fact is, as should now be obvious, that in spite of the language in which Green expresses it, Green's second view is really only a more general form of his first, being the view that there are no *natural* rights and obligations, in the sense of rights and obligations independent of the action of a regulating body, whether that body be a government or not.

It is really the view that, there being societies or communities other than states, i.e. groups of individuals united by being under a regulating body other than a government, the rights and obligations of any individual whatever are created by the regulating body of a society to which he belongs, it merely happening that the rights and obligations of the members of a State are created by its government, as a particular case.

We therefore find that Green's second view is really just as paradoxical as the first, being the view that no one has any right or obligation independently of some order or quasi-order of a ruler or quasi-ruler of a society to which he belongs. It is, in fact, a complete denial of natural rights and obligations, not indeed in the first sense of rights and obligations independent of membership of a State, but in the second sense of rights and obligations independent of membership of a society whether a State or not, i.e. independent of some order or quasi-order.

Further, it should be noticed, in its application to the State the paradox of this latter view is disguised by his use of inappropriate language, and even by his speaking of rights and obligations, i.e. the rights and obligations which men have as members of a society, as *maintained* by the sovereign. This disguise is exactly parallel to that found in expressing his earlier view in the first chapter. But this time the disguise is more effective because it passes unnoticed until we ask: What does Green mean by 'a society'?

There is, too, something else to be noticed. Green's denial of natural rights and obligations even in the second sense exposes him to the criticism that he himself holds a view to which he expressly objects, viz. that all right in a State is derived from the sovereign. For this is precisely his own doctrine, in spite of his denial of this view in § 138. The nature of his view is only disguised by his use of inappropriate language. Consequently he is himself exposed to the charge which he makes against Hobbes of identifying 'I ought to do so and so' with 'I am forced to do so and so' (§ 137). And it is significant that even Green himself (§ 132) is driven to allow that there is a sense in which all rights are derived from the sovereign.

So far we have only succeeded in formulating the negative part of Green's political theory—viz. his denial that we can answer the question 'Why ought we to obey our government?' by maintaining the existence of any obligation independent of our government's order, this denial being as much really implied in what I have called his second view as in his first.

III

We now have to look for the positive part of Green's doctrine. Some clue is to be found in § 23. There he states a difference of principle dividing him from the Social Contract theorists. And he does this by expressing agreement in one respect with the Utilitarians. Of them he says—with approval—'They do not seek the ground of actual rights in a prior natural right, but in an end to which the maintenance of the right contributes.' This statement needs elucidation. It must mean: The Utilitarians consider that the reason why I, a subject, ought to do the various acts, to my doing of which others have a legal right, i.e. those acts which make up my duties, lies not in a prior natural right of others to my doing them, i.e. a natural obligation of mine to do them, but in the acts contributing to the realization of an end. Further, by 'end' must be meant 'purpose', and since it is I that am bound, 'an end' here must be a loose phrase for 'my purpose'.

The difference of principle meant, therefore, is that while the Social Contract theorist represents as what renders obedience a duty its being the carrying out of some natural duty, he represents as the reason its contributing to the realization of the subject's purpose. And these reasons are, of course, of quite different sorts.

Further, Green must be tacitly attributing to the ruler in issuing and enforcing his orders the same purpose, and therefore also attributing to the various subjects a common purpose.

But what according to Green is this common purpose?

To this question we unfortunately get two different answers. The first is that implied by §§ 1–20—viz. the doing by the subjects of morally good actions, i.e. actions of which the motives are good. And in giving this answer Green takes the opportunity to urge that as the ruler can only exercise coercion, he can only achieve his purpose indirectly by producing conditions favourable to the doing of morally good actions. Then later we find substituted for morally good actions 'the public good' or 'public interest' (§ 108), or the general interest (§ 99), or the general well-being of the members of the society (§ 151), and this we may take to mean that state of affairs which would render all the subjects well off or happy. And this is unquestionably his *dominant* answer, the earlier answer afterwards simply dropping out.

Correspondingly as regards societies generally, of which states are implied to be a species, the common end attributed to the regulating body of a society and to its members must be the well-being of its members, and the ground of obligation is in both cases implied to be the conduciveness of the doing of the action to this purpose.

The view, of course, differs radically from the Social Contract theory. It is not merely that one asserts and the other denies the existence of *natural* rights and obligations. There is also a greater difference. We see this as soon as we consider what Green's doctrine implies as regards what is meant by the term 'ought'. The Social Contract theorist may be mistaken, but he does at least consider that by 'ought' what is meant is what we may call the 'ought' of moral obligation or duty. But Green really does not. This will be obvious to anyone who has considered the distinction which Kant draws between categorical and hypothetical imperatives. For unless we are prepared to maintain, as no one really will, that we consider it a duty to do whatever will contribute to the realization of our purpose, whatever the purpose may be, we shall have to allow that when we say of some man who has something β as his purpose, that he *ought* to do an act a because doing a will contribute to the realization of β, we only mean by 'he *ought* to do it' that a is an act he *must* do, if his purpose is to be realized. Consequently Green must be maintaining that what we call the 'ought' of duty is really resolved into 'ought' in this sense. Correspondingly, Green is at any rate not entitled to use the phrase 'a right' in the ordinary sense of the term. For suppose the act a enforced on X is one to his doing of which Y has a right, e.g. X's refraining from interfering with Y's body. Then if we ask: What in Green's view can be meant by 'Y has a right to X's doing a'? we have to answer: It can only mean that X's doing a is necessary for the realization of Y's end or purpose, viz. the happiness of the whole state—so that, oddly enough, for Green 'a right' comes to have the same meaning as an obligation.

Further, two characteristics of Green's answer need emphasis.

1. To make it successful even on its own lines, Green must succeed in showing that both the ruler and his subjects have the purpose he ascribes to them. (Since otherwise they will not be bound—in Green's sense—to do the actions he considers they are bound to do.)

Yet when we consider human nature we should at least hesitate to allow this.

2. There is a characteristic which when noticed looks very strange. There must be some actions such as refraining from playing a gramophone late at night in

a town, which on balance would contribute to the happiness of the subjects as a whole, *even when not ordered*. Yet, according to Green, such actions are not duties, unless ordered. And not only do we think such actions duties, but Green on his own principles should have maintained that they are, because they contribute to the agent's purpose.

Similarly according to Green, in societies which are not states, such acts are not duties unless prescribed by a regulation: 'It remains true that only through a recognition by certain men of a common interest and through the expression of that recognition in certain *regulations* of their dealings with each other, could morality originate, or any *meaning*[1] be found for such terms as "ought" and "right" and their equivalents.' And he adds, 'Morality (i.e. man's duty), in the first instance, is the observance of such regulations.'[2] Yet such acts would be contributing to the agent's purpose.

The fact is that even from his own point of view, Green's idea that for an act to be a duty it must have been ordered, either by a ruler or by the analogue of a ruler in anything we can call a society, is an arbitrary importation. This of course raises the question: What led Green to import it? And the only possible answer seems to be: His having somehow acquired a sort of fixed idea that there can be no such thing as a natural obligation.

IV

The account of Green's theory, however, is still incomplete. (A rather complicated story cannot be told all at once.)

The account itself suggests this. For to attribute to rulers and subjects as their common purpose the realization of what he calls the public interest seems contrary to fact—or at least to involve exaggeration. And therefore we expect Green to consider it an essential part of his position to show that here he is right. And indeed, for a reason which will appear shortly, from Green's point of view it is specially important to do this.

Moreover, consideration of passages purporting to state the ground of political obligation suggests that a vital part has been omitted. For what they *emphasize* is not so much that the common purpose is the realization of the public interest as that this is, and presents itself to the subjects as, a common good; and so far this idea has not been referred to. As instances of this emphasis we may take the following statements. (Unfortunately they are vague.) 'No one can have a right' (and he could have added 'or an obligation') 'except as a member of a society ... in which some common good is recognised by the members of the society as their own ideal good.'[3] In § 98 he says: 'An interest in common good

---

[1] The italics are mine. [2] § 117. [3] § 25.

is the ground of political society, in the sense that without it no body of people would recognise any authority as having a claim on their common obedience.' Again in § 117 he speaks of primitive morality as consisting in rules established for the common good. And in § 139 he speaks of the possession of a claim (i.e. really a right) as implying a 'consciousness of having an object', i.e., a purpose, 'in common with others, a well-being which is consciously his in being theirs and theirs in being his'.

These passages show that Green considers (1) that a subject *cannot* have the realization of the general interest as his purpose unless he conceives it as his own good, and (2) that he cannot really be bound to obey unless the general interest is his own good, in which case the subjects will have a common good.

To understand how Green came to have these ideas we have to go to the *Prolegomena*. There in § 91 he maintains that the motive of every deliberate action is desire for personal good in some form or other. And he adds in the next paragraph: 'By an instinctive action we mean one *not* determined by a conception ... of any good to be gained.... It is superfluous to add, good *to himself*; for anything conceived as good in such a way that the agent acts for the sake of it, must be conceived as *his own* good, though he may conceive it as his own good only on account of his interest in others, and in spite of any amount of suffering on his own part incidental to its attainment. Again, in § 96 he represents Esau as selling his birthright because at the time he thinks of satisfaction of his hunger as his greatest good.

Here Green is advancing a view about all deliberate action. This he first represents as being that in such action what a man has as his purpose is always *some* good to himself, and afterwards as being that this is always his own good, i.e. his own greatest good—the latter account expressing his more considered view. Thinking this as he does, when he comes to consider Political Obligation he is inevitably driven to two conclusions. The first is that to vindicate his contention that in a state men have the realization of the public interest as their purpose, he must show that they conceive the public's interest as their own good. The second is that to prove that men ought to obey the ruler's orders—orders which he assumes to be devised in the public interest—he must show that the public interest really is their own good.

For the reader, therefore, the question at once arises: 'Can this be shown?' And this question should be considered before considering Green's attempt, because by doing so we shall better see the nature of the task which Green has set himself.

To answer this question, we have first to ascertain what Green means by (1) 'a good', and (2) 'your good', 'my good', &c.

In § 171 of the *Prolegomena* (where he is distinguishing himself from a Hedonist), he explains that in his view the common characteristic of the good is that it satisfies some desire, and he uses the phrase 'good, i.e., such as will satisfy desire'. This is really to say that he means by 'a good' a something which produces, i.e. directly produces, satisfaction of a desire, i.e. really gratification. And his use of the phrase bears out this statement. Also from this it follows that he must mean by 'my good' that which renders me completely satisfied, i.e. having the gratification consisting in the satisfaction of all my desires.

Once, however, we realize this, we become forced to deny that, except on one hypothesis to which we shall have to refer later, the realization of the public interest can be *conceived* by members of a state as, or *be*, their own good.

The reason lies in a consideration which, though apt to escape our notice, is conclusive.

A feeling of satisfaction or gratification can be excited only by a state or activity of ourselves. If, e.g., I desire a member of my family to get some post, and if I learn that he has got it, or even think that he has, or will, get it, I shall necessarily have a feeling of satisfaction or gratification. But what excites the gratification is the knowledge or belief that the thing I desire is or will be realized, and not the *realization* of the thing desired—so that, shortly speaking, the thing which I desired and the thing which gratifies me cannot be the same, and Green is mistaken in speaking of the realization of some object of desire as necessarily exciting satisfaction. And since by 'a good' Green means something which excites satisfaction, there cannot be such a thing as a good common to two different persons, unless the two so-called different persons are really one and the same, and so not different persons.

For even if X and I want the same thing, and so have a common object of desire, as where X and I both want X to get a certain post, we can have *a* common good, i.e. a common source of satisfaction connected with these desires, since the sources will be respectively *his* thought that he has the post and *my* thought that he has, and his thought cannot be mine and vice versa, unless he and I are really the same individual. And for the same reason my good, i.e. that state which renders me *completely* satisfied, cannot be identical with his, unless we are the same. For the same reason, too, what Green calls the public interest, by which here must be meant those states of all the individuals which render each completely satisfied, taken together, cannot be that of a single individual, unless he is identical with all the others, nor again can a single individual *conceive* the public interest as being identical with his own, unless he *conceives* the other as identical with himself.

Now though it is not very apparent on the surface, yet strangely enough the existence of this identity and of the thought of this identity is exactly what Green does maintain.

In spite of his conviction that in deliberate action men have always one and the same motive, viz. desire of what will excite satisfaction in themselves, there is nothing which he emphasizes more than our possession of disinterested interests, of which the most obvious are an interest in the welfare of others, commonly called benevolence, and an interest in the welfare of certain others, such as other members of our family, or of a society to which we belong, or of our country. These interests in other persons, he says (§ 199),[4] are not merely interests dependent on other persons for the means to their gratification, but interests in the good of those other persons, interests which cannot be satisfied without the consciousness that those other persons are satisfied. And he obviously considers that we not only have the desire of others' welfare which is involved in this interest, but often act upon it, thus acting disinterestedly, i.e., as we should say, without regard to our own interest or happiness. Green has therefore to reconcile this latter conviction, which of course most of us share, with the former. For they at least seem violently inconsistent. For just so far as we are being moved by the disinterested desire of what would satisfy another, i.e. the desire of this for its own sake, the desire moving us, it would seem, cannot be the desire of what would satisfy ourselves; and even the thought of something which would give us satisfaction may be absent.

How then does Green seek to remove the appearance of inconsistency? It would, of course, be useless for him to contend that what is called the desire of what would satisfy another for its own sake is really only the desire of this as *a means* to what would satisfy ourselves. For to do this would be just to deny the disinterestedness. Nor does he. He is anxious to maintain the reality of the disinterestedness at all costs. Instead he adopts the only method open to him, viz. to maintain that where one man A has a disinterested interest in the welfare of another B, B and A are really identical.

Given this view it, of course, becomes justifiable for him to speak of a common good, i.e. a common source of satisfaction, since if B is A, what would excite satisfaction in B would excite satisfaction in A; and also to speak of B's good as identical with and also as thought of as identical with A's. But it is not justifiable otherwise. This should be emphasized, since to understand Green's doctrine that obligation implies the existence of a common good it has to be realized that it implies the idea that the persons to whom it is common are identical.

Here it is worth while for a moment to pass from elucidation to commentary.

The underlying thought is obvious. Green is taking his stand on the idea that in certain instances a man A disinterestedly, i.e. for its own sake, desires the welfare of (or as Green should rather say, what would satisfy) another man B. And he is contending that A's possession of this desire shows that A is thinking of B as a being who is really identical with A, and not another being at all, since a man can only desire what would satisfy himself. He is further thinking that A in thinking this is right, i.e. that in this case B is identical with A. (The doctrine is one foreshadowed in *Republic* V (462), in which Plato says that the just state

---

[4] Cf. *Prolegomena*, §§ 161, 200.

is one in which the largest number of citizens apply the terms 'mine' and 'not mine' to the same things in the same respects, and implies that this applies *inter alia* to pleasures and pains.)

The net result is that according to Green, where a group of, say, five persons are disinterestedly interested in one another, they are really not five persons but one, a state of A being related to a state of another, B, just as it is related to another state of A—these states being states of one self.

The first and most important comment is that when Green comes to consider the nature of disinterested action, instead of revising his previous account of the general nature of deliberate action, in such a way as to include disinterested action—as he should—he freely adapts his account of the latter to fit his general theory, and that by doing so he really abolishes its disinterestedness. Having laid down that in all deliberate action a man's motive is desire of what would satisfy himself, he nevertheless, when he comes to consider disinterested acts, at first thinks of them as moved by the desire of what would satisfy another. Then to square the two ideas he untruly represents the disinterested agent A, in desiring what would satisfy B, as really thinking of B as a being who is *not* another than himself, and if he were right here, A's desire would have lost any appearance of disinterestedness, since then, e.g., there would be no difference in kind between desiring, say, an honour for himself, and desiring an honour for B, i.e. disinterestedness would be resolved into interestedness.

The fact, of course, is that a disinterested desire is not a desire of a good to oneself at all.

In addition two minor facts should be noticed:

1. Green is undoubtedly implying that, whenever A has a disinterested interest in the satisfaction of B, B similarly has a disinterested interest in the satisfaction of A, as is normally the case with members of a family. For otherwise he cannot, as he does, represent the satisfactions of A and B together as identical with the satisfaction of each. But this need not be so, and where it is not, B's satisfaction cannot be represented as identical with those of both together. And the curious conclusion emerges that if Green were forced, as he could be, into allowing that the disinterested interest need not be reciprocal, he would have to allow that where B did not reciprocate, B was identical with A without A's being identical with B.
2. Malevolence is just as much a fact as benevolence, i.e. what we can have a disinterested interest in is just as much the unhappiness (or dissatisfaction) of another as the happiness (or satisfaction) of another. And Green admits this in § 161. Hence he ought to have maintained that malevolence of A towards B equally with benevolence of A towards B implies the identity of B with A, and therefore also that in desiring B's unhappiness A is desiring his own.

V

We are now in a position to give a complete statement of Green's theory. His proof of the duty to obey the government is one which tacitly assumes that our being bound to do some action *is* the act's being one which we must do if our purpose is to be realized, i.e. its contributing to our purpose; and it may be stated thus: Our purpose is necessarily our own good. But we being disinterestedly interested in the good of other members of our State, the other members are necessarily identical with ourselves, and therefore the public interest, i.e. the various things which are the good of each subject taken together, is necessarily identical with our own good. But obedience to the ruler is contributory to the public interest, and therefore to our own good, and this being our purpose obedience is necessarily a duty. To this account, however, it ought to be added that he also maintains that only acts ordered are duties, a contention which is only consistent with the rest of the theory if it be also held that no act unless ordered will be for the public interest. This addition really has no connexion with the rest of the theory.

An analogous statement can, of course, be made for members of a society which is not a State.

The theory is, of course, a general theory of Moral Obligation which takes the form of a political theory in the case of members of a State.

It now becomes fairly easy to answer the question: What does Green mean by 'a society'? The question is one which we find ourselves constantly asking when reading the lectures, especially when trying to understand such statements as 'a man has rights only as a member of a society'.

He cannot be using the phrase in its ordinary sense of a voluntary association such as an essay society. For he speaks of a State as a society, and yet he certainly does not think it a voluntary association. Still he probably would have called a voluntary association a society. And 'a community'—a phrase he sometimes uses—would better express what he means. On the other hand, he cannot be using it so widely as to include any group of men related in some special way, e.g. as friends or as united by a promise. Unfortunately he never offers a definition though he uses phrases which are really though not ostensibly partial definitions, as when (§ 26) he speaks of 'a society [i.e. a group of men] in which some common good is recognized as their own good'. The proper clue lies in the reflection that he would have applied and only applied the term to groups of men who satisfy the conditions which he considers necessary for the existence of rights and obligations among them. For, this being so, he must really mean by a society a group satisfying these conditions. Now plainly these conditions are (1) that the members of the group have a common good, and (2) that they are subject to regulation of their dealings with each other for this common good.

Hence Green must really mean by 'a society' men, i.e. a group of men, having a common good and subject to regulations for this good.

A regulation or rule, however, implies an imponent. How then does Green think of this imponent? Certainly not as necessarily a definite body, such as a government or a committee. For in the case of a society which is not a state he is wont to speak of it as custom, or authoritative custom, or the law of opinion (§ 4). But if his idea of a society is to be plausible, this part has simply to be discarded, as putty used to fill up a gap. For we can only rightly speak, as Green always does, of a man's community as securing to him certain powers, if we think of it as doing so through an agent. To substitute something called custom or the law of opinion is useless, for the phrase can only be a veiled term for the thoughts held by individuals that certain acts are duties, and though these thoughts may help to secure the doing of the actions, it cannot be said that the community acts through them. Moreover—and this is decisive—according to Green there cannot be such thoughts apart from regulations, and therefore on his view they cannot be considered a substitute.

Hence, if Green's idea of a society is to escape absurdity, his society must include the analogue of a ruler in the shape of a regulating body.

If this be granted there is one thing which becomes obvious. His statement, 'Men have rights and obligations only as members of a society', is not one in which 'society' is being used in some ordinary sense, and which in consequence, if accepted, can be used as a *premiss* to justify his theory. It is simply a *statement* of the theory which he has to justify, being the statement that men only have rights and obligations where they have a common good and are subject to a regulating body.

Reverting to the consideration of Green's general theory, we should next consider what are the main comments it suggests. (And here it may, I think, be fairly asserted that it is one of those theories about which, when its nature is grasped, little need be said, the main difficulty being to discover it.)

If we survey the theory, the main contentions appear to be these:

1. The duty of doing an action *is* its contributing to the realization of our purpose (this contention being implied and *not stated*).
2. We always (except when moved by an impulse) act for our own good.
3. In view of our disinterested interests in others they are identical with us.
4. There is no duty without an order, or at least a quasi-order.

Of these, the fourth contention seems to stand apart from the rest—having, it would seem, no connexion with it. And of the rest, the second seems the one deserving the most attention, as the explanation of why Green puts forward the first and the third.

Consider the fourth first. Unfortunately it will not stand the test of instances. For we do think with Locke that one individual has certain obligations to and rights against another without their being members of the same state or community—and we do think again that we have certain obligations to certain animals, i.e. that they have certain rights against us. (Green denies that animals have rights, but the denial seems due to the exigencies of his theory.) Again, to take an instance specially unfortunate for Green, we think we ought to obey our ruler, and here the obligation *ex hypothesi* cannot depend on *orders* to obey.

In this connexion it is worth while to refer to the so-called eighteenth-century Rationalists, Cudworth and Samuel Clarke. They have been, to my mind, far too much neglected, for their main burden is just to insist against Hobbes, not only that there are such things as natural obligations, in the first sense, that of obligations independent of an order, but also that it is impossible for *all* obligations to be non-natural, since by its very nature the existence of a non-natural obligation implies the thought of a natural obligation. And, if I am right, they performed an outstanding service in doing this, but a service which would have been much more effective if subsequent writers had paid more attention to them.

Cudworth really comes first, for though his *Treatise* was not published till 1731, some sixteen years after Samuel Clarke's *Discourse on Natural Religion*, he died in 1688.

This is what Cudworth says:

Now the necessary Consequence of that which we have hitherto said is this, That it is so far from being true, that all Moral Good and Evil, Just and Unjust are mere Arbitrary and Factitious things, that are created wholly by Will; that (if we would speak properly) we must needs say that nothing is Morally Good or Evil, Just or Unjust by mere Will without Nature, because every thing is what it is by Nature, and not by Will. For though it will be objected here, that when God, or Civil Powers Command a Thing to be done, that was not before obligatory or unlawful, the thing Willed or Commanded doth forthwith become Obligatory, that which ought to be done by Creatures and Subjects respectively; in which the Nature of Moral Good or Evil is commonly Conceived to consist. And therefore if all Good and Evil, Just and Unjust be not the Creatures of mere Will (as many assert) yet at least Positive things must needs owe all their Morality, their Good and Evil to mere Will without Nature: Yet notwithstanding, if we well Consider it, we shall find that even in Positive Commands themselves, mere Will doth not make the thing commanded Just or Obligatory, or beget and create any Obligation to Obedience; but that it is Natural Justice or Equity, which gives to one the Right or Authority of Commanding, and begets in another Duty and Obligation to Obedience. Therefore it is observable, that Laws and Commands do not run thus, to Will that this or that thing shall become Just or Unjust, Obligatory or Unlawful; or that Men shall be obliged or bound to obey; but only to require that something be done or not done, or otherwise to menace Punishment to the Transgressors thereof. For it was never heard of, that any one founded all his Authority of Commanding others, and other Obligation or Duty to Obey his Commands, in a Law of his own making, that men should be Required, Obliged, or Bound to Obey him. Wherefore since the thing willed in all Laws is not that men should be Bound or Obliged to Obey; this thing cannot be the product of the mere Will of the Commander, but it must proceed from something else; namely, the Right or Authority of the Commander, which is founded in natural Justice and Equity, and an antecedent Obligation to Obedience in the Subjects; which things are not Made by Laws, but pre-supposed before all Laws to make them valid: And if it should be imagined, that any one should make a positive Law to require that others should be Obliged, or Bound to Obey him, every one would think such a Law ridiculous and absurd; for if they were Obliged before, then this Law would be in vain, and to no Purpose; and if they were not before Obliged, then they could not be Obliged by any Positive Law, because they were not previously Bound to Obey such a Person's Commands: So that Obligation to Obey all Positive Laws is Older than all Laws, and Previous or Antecedent to them.[5]

This is what Clarke says:

The true State therefore of this Case, is plainly this. Some things are in their own nature Good and Reasonable and Fit to be done, such as keeping Faith, and performing equitable Compacts, and the like; And these receive not their obligatory power, from any Law or Authority, but are only declared, confirmed and enforced by penalties, upon such as would not perhaps be governed by right Reason only. Other things are in their own nature absolutely Evil, such as breaking Faith, refusing to perform equitable Compacts, cruelly destroying those who have neither directly nor indirectly given any occasion for any such treatment, and the like; And these cannot by any Law or Authority whatsoever, be made fit and reasonable, or excusable to be practised. Lastly, other things are in their own Nature Indifferent; that is, (not absolutely and strictly so; as such trivial Actions, which have no way any tendency at all either to the publick welfare or damage; For concerning such things, it would be childish and trifling to suppose any Laws to be made at all; But they are) such things, whose tendency to the publick benefit or disadvantage, is either so small or so remote, or so obscure and involved, that the generality of People are not able of themselves to discern on which side they ought to act: And these things are made obligatory by the Authority of Laws; Though perhaps every one cannot distinctly perceive the reason and fitness of their being injoined: Of which sort are many particular penal Laws, in several Countries and Nations.[6]

Then later, after pointing out that Hobbes was forced to suppose some particular things obligatory, originally, and in their own nature, he says:

If the Rules of Right and Wrong, Just and Unjust, have none of them any obligatory force in the State of Nature, antecedent to positive Compact, then, for the same Reason, neither will they be of any force after the Compact, so as to afford men any certain and real security; . . . For if there be no Obligation of Just and Right antecedent to the Compact, then Whence arises the Obligation of the Compact itself, on which he supposes all other Obligations to be founded? If, before any Compact was made, it was no Injustice for a man to take away the Life of his Neighbour, not for his own Preservation, but merely to satisfy an arbitrary humour or pleasure, and without any reason or provocation at all, how comes it to be an Injustice, after he has made a Compact, to break and neglect it?[7]

[5] Selby-Bigge, *British Moralists*, ii, pp. 249–50.   [6] Ibid. 9.   [7] Ibid. 45.

Further, here it is worth noting that on Green's own showing his theory is beginning to break down. For

1. In chapter i, §§ 148–51, he is forced to single out certain rights, viz. to liberty, life, and property (viz. those which we think of as natural rights), as forming a special class which do not come into being with the state and can be treated without reference to the form of the society which concedes them. And in § 154 he is reduced to admitting that the right to free life on the part of every man as man implies the conception of men as forming one society, and adds that if a claim is made on behalf of any and every human being, it must be a claim on human society as a whole. And as he obviously thinks there is such a right, he implies thereby that he considers mankind one large society, which it obviously is not, either in his or even in any other sense of 'society'.
2. He attributes rights to individuals who plainly are not members of a society in his sense, viz. to (*a*) members of a family; (*b*) a group of slaves (§ 140); (*c*) a group of persons consisting of a slave and the family of his owner (§ 140); (*d*) certain citizens and certain slaves. And he even emphasizes the existence of the rights possessed by certain slaves by insisting that though the state may refuse them rights it cannot extinguish them. (Here, of course, his moral convictions are, so to say, bursting through the theory.)

If all this be allowed, it becomes worth asking, Where does the root of Green's mistake lie? The answer is, it seems to me, obvious. It lies in his second contention, viz. that we always act for the sake of our own good. We are therefore brought to the consideration of this.

The contention is one which any one must in the end admit to be false. To convince ourselves of this we need only allow, as in the end we must, that some deliberate actions have at least shown some element of disinterestedness, whether this has taken the form of benevolence or malevolence, and others again some element of conscientiousness. And the contention seems only to arise from the idea, which, though plausible, is mistaken, that we can only be led to desire to do some action by coming to think of it as one which will be, or else cause, something which we shall like, i.e. give us either enjoyment or satisfaction.

I shall therefore take for granted that it is false. But once we realize that Green has this idea it becomes easy to see how most of the rest of his position follows. For if every one necessarily has his own good as his purpose, it becomes idle to maintain that there can be anything which it is his duty to do, and the only thing left for the term 'ought' to refer to is an act's being necessary for the realization of the agent's purpose, and then what we ought to do necessarily becomes those actions which are necessary for the realization of the thing which is our purpose, viz. our own good.

Green being driven to hold this, we have the paradoxical consequence that on fundamentals Green is in agreement with Hobbes, his chief enemy. For in maintaining that we always act for our own good, and therefore ought to do what is necessary for its realization, he is at bottom only repeating Hobbes's view, and his difference from Hobbes lies merely in a matter, though no doubt an important matter, of detail. He is in effect saying to Hobbes: 'I entirely agree with your general contention, but I differ completely as to what acts are necessary for the realization of our own good. You, ignoring our possession of disinterested interests, fail to see that, owing to this, it is just by contributing to the public good that we shall contribute to our own.'

And, of course, just because Green thinks this, we should all like to think that here he is right, for even though we do not think that the duty of obedience to the state arises from the fact that obedience contributes to our own good, we should all like to think that obedience is contributing to it.

There is, however, another comment which is important because it shows that Green's view will not work even on its own lines.

Green is really insisting that to maintain, as he does, that two subjects of a ruler, A and B, have a common purpose, he must show that B is identical with A, and thus that B's satisfaction is A's. Hence he is implying that when A considers how to get most satisfaction, he will consider it indifferent whether some satisfaction which an act would cause would arise in B or in himself.

Hence A's problem will be simply to ascertain what action would produce the greatest amount of satisfaction in A and B together, irrespectively of how the satisfaction will be distributed. And as Green considers the ruler's purpose identical with that of A and B, the ruler's problem in devising rules will be the same. Suppose then, e.g., the ruler found A and B each fetching his own newspaper before breakfast and realized that fetching two papers would be very little more trouble than fetching one. He would think he should issue an order as the result of which on any given occasion one of them fetched both papers, thereby diminishing the aggregate dissatisfaction. But he could only decide by tossing up who was to be ordered to do the fetching, i.e. whether it was to be A always, or B always, or A and B alternately, and so on—because any arrangement would be *equally* effective in diminishing dissatisfaction. Yet Green obviously thinks that the ruler would in fact order A and B to divide the fetching equally. And for this idea, for the reason just given, he has on his own theory *no* justification. To notice this is important. For (1) it shows that Green's theory is unable to take into account the idea of fairness, on which actual rules are based. And (2) it brings out the fact that the idea of fairness, which underlies actual rules, so far from implying that individuals have identical satisfactions, implies that individuals have satisfactions which are not only different but such that the conditions of their realization are incompatible. The fact is that, if a ruler's rules are to come out anything like what we ordinarily think of as rules, he must be implying that individuals' goods so far from being identical are inconsistent, i.e. that their interests so far from being the same are conflicting. And if Green, to meet this objection, were to allow that the rules should take account of fairness, he would in doing so both be allowing a natural obligation and going back on his view that the subjects have a common good.

VI

The drastic nature of the criticisms just made naturally provokes the question: Is there not after all some important truth to be found in Green's lectures?

To this question the answer seems to be Yes. The doctrine of Green's which seems closest to the facts is that epitomized in the title of Chapter A: 'Will, not force, is the basis of the state.' In this chapter he discards the question: 'Why *ought* a subject to obey his ruler?' for the very different question: 'Why *does* a subject obey?', i.e. what is the motive of his obedience? And here negatively his aim is to refute the view of Hobbes and certain others that the state rests simply on force or compulsion, i.e. that what gets a government obeyed is simply desire to escape its penalties. He is, of course, not denying that this desire is an essential factor, and with some individuals the only factor; he is only maintaining that if this were the only factor *no* government would in the long run get itself obeyed. And in consequence he thinks it fallacious to regard a state—as he thought Hobbes did—as an aggregation of individuals under a sovereign body able to compel their obedience (for the phrase see § 137)—by 'individuals' here being meant men who will be led to obey only by fear of penalties. Here Green seems perfectly right. Even with our experience of modern dictatorships—an experience, of course, denied to Green—it seems impossible to hold that over a long period *any* government could get itself obeyed if its subjects obeyed only so far as they thought the existence of penalties rendered obedience advantageous.

What, however, is Green's positive contention, i.e. what does he consider the other fact necessary for obedience? The answer is: The desire of the public welfare, as being their own welfare, which the subjects have in consequence of recognizing that the other members of the public, being individuals in whom they are disinterestedly interested, are identical with themselves, the desire being accompanied by the conviction that obedience will be conducive to the public welfare.

This answer is, of course, less satisfactory. For it really just as much represents the additional factor as the outcome of selfishness. For the desire for what will give me satisfaction is the same in kind as the desire for what will cause me dissatisfaction. Yet after all Green is insisting on men's possession of disinterested desires, and if only he had dropped the representation of these as *interested* (by representing others as identical with ourselves), he would have been contending that the additional factor necessary to secure obedience is the subject's unselfish interest in the welfare of other members of the community; and then he would have been on very strong ground. For anyone would have to allow that this interest is a large factor in what gets the government obeyed—not because it is appreciable in those least likely to obey but because its existence in others makes practicable the task of enforcing laws on the reluctant minority. What, however, would have been *most* appropriate for Green to point out as the other factor is simply the thought itself that it is a duty to obey, combined of course with the desire to do what we ought. And he could have done this without entering into the question *why* individuals thought they ought to obey.

The Ground of Political Obligation

In conclusion I propose to make some general remarks about the question which Green is discussing, viz. why ought a subject to obey his ruler?

Two things may be noticed at the outset:

1. *We* are apt to assume that the question admits of a single answer, i.e. that whoever be the ruler, the answer will be the same.
2. Green assumes that the answer must take one or other of two mutually exclusive forms—basing the obligation either on a certain origin of the government, and indeed on some form of contract, or on the fact that obedience will help to bring certain things about.

These alternatives are of course poles apart. For on the latter alternative the mode of origin of a government is simply irrelevant—(since so long as obedience will achieve certain things, it does not matter how the government achieved its position, i.e. whether by violence or otherwise)—while on the former it is all-important.

Further, both Green's alternatives are to be found in actual political controversy. Thus on the one hand, before the Irish Free State existed, the Southern Irish denied that they owed any allegiance to the British Crown and Parliament, on the ground that it was a mere coercive body, i.e. a body which had just imposed its power on them, and was acting without their consent and even against it. The extremists in India make similar statements about the Government of India. Similarly members of subordinate communities speak of their right to self-determination, i.e. really to be self-governed, i.e. governed by a government of their own appointment or creation.

On the other hand, it is often said by way of retort: 'That may be so; nevertheless the government in question is doing its work, i.e. the work of a government, with great efficiency; it is giving and enforcing on you subjects the laws which you need, and doing this much more effectively than would any government you could set up.'

And here what is chiefly noteworthy is the complete lack of common ground. Each simply ignores the contention of the other and substitutes his own. And in consequence they never get to grips—and completely fail to convince each other.

Now this makes one think. For it suggests that possibly the deadlock is due to the idea common to both that there can only be *one* ground of the duty of obedience, and that if we can satisfy ourselves that the idea is mistaken, we can get rid of the deadlock. In this connexion the doctrine of the *Crito* is suggestive. There Socrates is made to explain why he considers himself bound not to disobey the state by escaping from prison and so avoiding being put to death. And what is suggestive is that his answer gives *more than one* reason. He states three ideas, first that the state or the laws or the government is his father, second that it is his benefactor, to whom he owes his upbringing and education, and third that, as on growing up the laws had left him free to go elsewhere if he did not like them, he, by staying, had entered into a tacit agreement with the laws, i.e. the government, to do what the government commanded. φαμέν τοῦτον ὡμολογηκέναι ἔργῳ ἡμῖν ἃ ἂν ἡμεῖς κελεύωμεν ποιήσειν ταῦτα.[8] And though he represents the three grounds of the obligation as concurrent, he says nothing which excludes the idea that any one by itself would be sufficient.

This leads us to ask whether there need be only one ground, the same in all cases, rather than different grounds in different cases, with the possibility of concurrent different grounds in any given case. If there need not, both contending views may contain an element of truth, each only making the mistake of putting forward as *the* ground what is *a* ground of political obligation. The question can be put in another form thus: We are apt to assume that the questions 'Ought an Englishman to obey the Crown and Parliament, an Italian to obey Mussolini, a German to obey Hitler?' are instances of the same question. But is this really so—because the thing called a state may in each case be different, and if there are kinds of state, the ground of the duty to obey may depend on the kind?

And our attitude, e.g. to the controversialists about India, suggests that on considering instances we may find the doubt justified. For we think there is something in which each party says—viz. in the one case, that in view of the greater efficiency of such a government, it ought to be obeyed in the interest of the other subjects, and in the other case, that if a government in some way appointed by the inhabitants of India had been in its place, the subjects would have been bound to obey by that fact alone, irrespectively of the effect of obedience—and that in any case such an appointment forms an additional ground for the duty to obey. How prevalent the latter idea is shown by the attempts which most revolutionary governments make to get what at least looks like some form of election, however farcical it really is.

---

[8] *Crito*, 51 e.

(N.B. What they really want is something which looks not like the legal right but the moral right to sovereignty. For the very phrase 'a legal right to sovereignty' involves contradiction, for, a law being the order of a sovereign, the act of creating a sovereign cannot be an act of law. And if we allow, as it seems we can, that there is some truth in this idea, we must allow that there is some truth in the social contract theory. For what we call appointing, or accepting, or consenting to a government, is some kind of agreeing.)

If, however, we allow, as it seems we must, that there are different grounds of political obligation, then we have to admit that strictly speaking the very question 'Why ought a subject to obey his ruler?' is fallacious, and is therefore bound to ensure a false answer—just because there are sorts of rulers, and the sort makes a difference, and that the question ought to be split up into the questions 'Why ought the subjects of certain specified *sorts* of government to obey them?' If so, the question is like the question: 'Why ought we to read books?'; for here obviously there is no proper question, so long as we are considering books generally, as distinct from books of a particular sort.

In addition, even if we ignore this, we have to allow that in another way the question requires modification and that unless we modify it, we only get into confusion.

As it stands, the question Why ought a subject to obey his ruler? is parallel to similar questions about other moral rules, e.g. Why ought a man to speak the truth? or Why ought a man to educate his family? Now consideration of instances of what seem conflicting duties is enough to show that no kind of action whatever can, strictly speaking, be a duty, if only for the reason that if it were, there might be occasions on which we were bound to do two actions, although we could only do one or other of them. This reflection forces us to allow that what we at first think of as a duty must really be something else, for which, in my opinion, the least unsatisfactory phrase is 'a claim', and that the proper question with regard to some moral rule is of the form: 'Why is there a claim on us to do such and such an action?' For this reason the proper form of the question: 'Why ought a subject to obey his ruler?' must at least be: 'Why is there a *claim* on the subject to obey his ruler?' And unless we put the question in this form, we shall only find ourselves in a state of confusion when considering whether we ought to obey in instances where obedience involves the failure to satisfy certain other claims—the question then really being: 'Does the claim to obey outweigh the other claims?'

11. The Object of a Desire

If in considering what it is we desire we confine attention to such desiring as is involved in action, it is plausible to speak of a desire as necessarily a desire for the existence of something not existing. For whether we think of the thing desired as being the action or as being something which we think the act will effect, the thing desired seems essentially something not yet existing, and the existence of which must be in the future. And Cook Wilson, in an unpublished essay on *Means and End*, speaks of a desire as the desire for the existence of something not existing. Mitchell,[1] too, implies this view when he says: 'The point is that we do not desire what we already have; to use the word [sc. desire] in this sense is confusing, for we mean simply that we like it, and that is only emotion.'

This way of speaking, of course, requires an obvious correction. We need instead to say: 'A desire is necessarily a desire for the existence of something which we either know or think, i.e. think without question, to be not existing, i.e. not now existing.' (By 'think without question' here is meant Cook Wilson's 'being under the impression that', and by 'think' here will always be meant 'thinking without question', this referring to a condition in which we are not uncertain.)

This amended statement is undoubtedly plausible. It has two implications, viz. that we cannot desire something unless we know or think it (1) not to be existing, and (2) not to be existing now.

If someone who accepts it is asked: 'Existing *when* do we desire it?' he has to answer 'at once', i.e. in the immediate future—with the implication that we shall go on desiring it until we know or think it is existing. Further, if the statement is true, we cannot desire something to exist at a later moment than the present—say, in ten minutes' time—or for a period of time beginning at a later moment, e.g. we cannot desire ourselves, or another, X, to be at a certain place, or to be free from pain, ten minutes hence, or to be free from pain during tomorrow, or our family to have the means of subsistence next year or after our death. Therefore, if the statement is true, where we are said to have these desires the desire we have must really be different, must be, e.g., the desire for the state of things to be at once such as will involve that our family will be well off after our death. And in support of this it may be urged that when we come to think the state of things to be such, owing to our thought of what we or others have done,

---

[1] *Structure and Growth of the Mind*, p. 34.

the desire we had has gone, we are merely pleased by the thought that things are such that our family will be well off.

To this position it may be objected (*a*) that there really is such a desire as, e.g., our desire for our family to be well off after our death, and (*b*) that there really is such a desire even when we think things to be such that it will be well off, so that implication (1) of the amended statement is untrue.

Whether, however, statements (*a*) and (*b*) are true or not, there are other objections which are fatal.

The first is that 'not existing now' means not existing at this moment, and 'existing at once', or in the immediate future, will have to mean 'at the next moment'. But there is no such thing as the next moment. There is, of course, such a thing as the next portion of time, which is next to the last portion, the common limit of both being the present, but there is no moment next to the present moment. Consequently the 'desiring something to exist at once' (desiring, e.g., to be free from pain at once) part of the formula will not do.

The second is that the desire connected with the thought of something as not existing now, if there be one, will really have to be the desire of its existing now. And it seems impossible to deny that there is such a thing, though we usually call it a wish, e.g. my wish, when I have a toothache, that I were free from pain—though of course this desire is not one which can lead to action. But this desire is not the desire for the thing thought not to exist now to exist later.

The third is that even anyone who holds that we cannot desire something to exist at some future time, or for a time beginning at some moment in the future, will have to allow that we desire certain things which involve a certain duration, though he would say, and would have to say, that we desire them to exist at once, e.g. that we desire to turn our head or to hear 'God save the King'. But such a thing, since it has a duration, can neither exist now, i.e. at the present moment, nor can it exist at any moment in the future. To meet this objection, the view will have to be amended to: 'A desire is necessarily a desire for the existence in the immediate future of a process which we know or think has not yet existed.' But this statement will not hold because, if the process in the immediate future does take place, it will not be the process which did not take place before, for my turning my head, e.g., beginning at 12 o'clock will not be my previous turning my head. Strictly speaking, the desire for the thing which I think did not happen will be the wish that it had happened, as when I wish I had turned my head; and this will be different from the desire for its going to happen. The statement, therefore, requires a further amendment to: 'A desire is a desire for myself or another, X, to go through a certain process similar to one which I know or think he or I have not gone through.' But then the statement is open to the fatal objection that the desire to go through a certain process in the immediate future does *not* require the thought that I have not been through a similar process in the past. I can, e.g., desire X to be free from pain for the next five seconds, without thinking that he has been in pain for the last five seconds or for any time, as is implied where I give X a drug which I think will prevent a pain starting in him now, instead of giving him a drug which I think will cause him at once to become free from a pain which he already has been having. To meet this objection, the statement has to become: 'A desire is necessarily the desire of the existence in the immediate future of a process which I know or think will not exist in the immediate future.' This alteration is plainly a great alteration. And if it be allowed that some desires are desires for the existence in the immediate future of processes which we know or think will not exist in the immediate future, all objection seems gone to allowing the existence of desires for the existence of processes in the *not* immediate future, which we know or think will not then exist, such as the desire for our family's welfare after our death.

Implication (2) at p. 253 therefore has to go, and the formula will at least have to be: 'A desire is necessarily a desire for the existence during some time in the future of a process which we know or think will not exist during that time (the future here including the immediate future as a special case).'

Then, however, it is easy, without causing objection, to widen this formula to one which will take into account (1) desires which concern the past and the present as well as the future, and (2) desires concerning momentary states, e.g. my being at place A at 4 o'clock. We can say: 'A desire is necessarily a desire for the existence of some process during some portion of time in the past or in the future, as the case may be, or of the existence of some state at some moment in the past or in the future or at the present moment, the process or state being known or thought of as not going to exist during that time or at the moment in question, as the case may be.'

This statement retains implication (1) on p. 253 that what we desire is something which we know or think of as not existing, though we have ceased to understand not existing as not existing now.

The question, however, still remains: Is *know or think of* as not existing *at* or *during* a certain time right? And here, once more, an amendment seems required. For what, on reflection, we become forced to admit to be required if we are to desire X to have existed, to exist, or to be going to exist, is not that we know or think it not to have existed, to exist, or to be going to exist, but that we are uncertain about its existence. We therefore have to substitute for 'something which we know or think of as not having existed, not existing, or not going to exist', 'something of the existence of which in the past, the present, or the future, as the case may be, we are uncertain'.

Here, however, we seem to have reached bedrock, i.e. a position which is unquestionably true. And this seems to be the truth which underlies Cook Wilson's account of desiring as the desiring the existence of what does not exist, and of Mitchell's statement that we cannot desire what we already have—it being the truth, so to say, after which Cook Wilson and Mitchell are feeling or for which they are groping. In other words, to put the thing shortly, what they should have said is that we can only desire the existence of that of the existence of which in the past, present, or future, as the case may be, we are uncertain. No doubt the alteration is considerable, but it does leave a sort of core of truth in what they say.

Further, if this be allowed, then it cannot be true that we can desire, e.g., our family to be well off after our death, when we think without question that it *will* be well off, or, analogously, desire X to be now happy or at a place A when we think he *is* happy or at a place A, or desire X to have had a good holiday when we think he *has* had a good holiday.

In the preceding 'desiring something X' has throughout been represented as the desiring the existence of X, and the problems that have arisen have been concerned with the question 'existence when?' and the question 'Does it involve the thought or knowledge of X as existing?' But the question may be asked: 'Is this representation not misleading, if only because it is artificial to speak of thinking or apprehending something X as not existing—or even as existing?' For to think of anything as something or as not something, or to apprehend it as something or as not something, we must be thinking of it or apprehending it as something, i.e. something existing. The alternative account seems to be to represent a desire as a desire for something which I apprehend or else think of as having existed, existing, or going to exist, to have been, be, or be going to be of a certain sort, or, to put this otherwise, to have had, have, or be going to have a certain character, e.g. to represent (*a*) my desire to turn my head, as the desire for the process which I think of as that which I am going to go through, to be going to be one of turning my head, and (*b*) my desire for my family's being well off after my death, as the desire for what I think of as my family's state after my death, to be going to be one of being well off. Stated thus, a desire is not a desire for the existence of something but a desire for something *to be* (or, more fully, to have been, to be, or to be going to be, as the case may be) *so and so*. This seems a better answer, as soon as we take into account the thought (here using the word in a very wide sense) which is involved in a desire.

12. The Obligation to Keep a Promise

In promising, agreeing, or undertaking to do some action we seem to be creating or bringing into existence the obligation to do it, so much so that promising seems just to *be* binding ourselves, i.e. making ourselves bound, to do it, and the statement 'I ought to keep a promise', like 'I ought not to steal', seems a mere pleonasm. Once call some act a promise and all question of whether there is an obligation to do it seems to have vanished. In fact, the difference between doing something and promising to do it seems just to be that while in the one case we bring something into existence, in the other we bring into existence the obligation to bring it into existence.

Yet an obligation seems a fact of a kind which it is impossible to create or bring into existence. There are, no doubt, certain facts which we do seem able to create. If, e.g., I make someone angry, I appear to bring into existence the fact that he is angry. But the fact that I am bound to do some action seems no more one of these than does the fact that the square of three is odd.

The paradox is one which promising shares with giving and exchanging something. For, to take the case of giving only, what we call my giving X something seems to consist in substituting for an obligation on other people's part to refrain from doing anything which would prevent my having the power to use some material thing, a similar obligation on the part of me and everyone else except X to refrain from doing anything which would prevent X having the power to use it—so that it seems to consist in destroying one obligation and creating another. And for this reason giving and exchanging are just as paradoxical.

I propose to assume that we shall all allow on reflection that an obligation is a fact of a kind which it really is impossible to create or bring into existence directly. On this assumption we shall have to allow that the only way to resolve, i.e. to get rid of, the paradox is to succeed in making out that in what we call promising to do some action what we create or bring about is not really, as the term 'promising' suggests, the obligation to do the act promised but something else, our creation of which renders us bound to do the action promised. In other words, I shall assume that on reflection we shall all have to agree that what we call 'promising' to do so and so cannot really be what the term 'promising' suggests it is, viz. creating an obligation to do the action, but must be the creating something else, the creation of which gives rise to the obligation to do it, and that the problem is to find out what that something is. If we can find out what this is we shall, of course, remove the appearance of impossibility which promising presents. And in doing so we should, it may be noticed, be assimilating promising to acts of certain other kinds, our having done which we think leads to an obligation to do something else. Instances would be (1) hurting the feelings of another, which we think renders us bound to assuage them so far as we can; (2) misleading another, which we think leads to the obligation to correct the misconception; and (3) becoming the father of a family, which we think gives rise to the obligation to feed and educate it. The assimilation, however, it would seem, cannot be complete, since our immediate object in what we call promising to do some action seems to be to create, even though indirectly, the obligation to do some action, as it is not, e.g., in hurting the feelings of another.

We get into difficulties, however, as soon as we try to state what that is in what we call making a promise the production of which renders us bound to do the action which we are said to promise to do.

We never do what we should describe as promising a man X to do some action unless we have in some degree the expectation that if we do we shall produce in X the expectation that we shall do the action. Hence, the suggestion which is first likely to occur to us is that the thing for which we are looking is the expectation in the person promised that we shall do the action. But, of course, this suggestion is at least too wide. Otherwise, when, hoping to stave off the interruptions of a neighbour, I drive past him in a taxi loaded with luggage, I should be said to be promising to go away. At least the expectation, as is otherwise obvious, must be an expectation produced in a particular way, viz. by the use of language. But even so the suggestion is too wide. Otherwise an employer who, on learning that his men hesitated to put their backs into their work for fear that if they did their time rates of pay would be reduced, *argued* them into believing that he would not be such a fool as to do this, would be said to be promising not to do it. Nor—and this is more important—is the suggestion right, if it be further limited by the condition that the language used is the expression of the thought of a resolve. If, instead, the employer said, 'I have no intention of reducing the rates', i.e. really 'I have *resolved* not to', he still would not be *promising* not to reduce them, even if his men expected that he would not change his mind and so would not, in fact, reduce the rates. And anyone in the employer's position would recognize that in saying this he was not promising. For suppose, having said this, he found he had not convinced the men, he might then, in the hope of convincing them, say: 'Well, I *promise* not to change the rates if you speed up.' And in saying this he would be aware that he was now doing something different. Moreover, if in promising we were stating that we had made a resolve, a promise would be true or false, yet while everyone would allow that a promise may be made either in good or in bad faith, no one would allow that it could be either true or false. Rather, they would insist that promising resembles asking a question or issuing an order, in that it consists not in making a statement but in doing something, in the sense in which we oppose doing to mere talking.

Further, consideration of the contrast between the employer's expressing the resolve to maintain the wage rates and his promising to do so brings to light a more important fact. The expectation, so far as it is produced, will in each case be based on quite different beliefs. In the one case it will be based on the beliefs (1) that the employer was speaking truthfully, and (2) that he is not likely to change his mind on such a matter. In the other it will be based at least in part on the belief that the employer thinks that he has bound himself simply by promising, whether he produces the expectation or not, together with the belief that since he is a comparatively moral, i.e. conscientious, being he is likely to do whatever he thinks he is bound to do. And once we realize that such expectation as is produced by a promise is of this character, we shall have to allow that any attempt to base the obligation to keep a promise on promising's being the creating of an expectation is doomed to failure. For what we have to do is to state what it is that I bring about in what is called my promising X to do some action, the thought of my bringing which about leads me or X or anyone else to think that I am bound to do the action. And this cannot be represented as the expectation in X that I shall do the action, if the expectation be one resting on the belief that I believe that, by what is called my promising, I become bound to do the action irrespectively of whether I produce the expectation that I shall do the action. For on this hypothesis X will be thinking what it is impossible for him to think, viz. that I have a certain thought which neither he nor anyone else can have.

To this we may simply add that, in fact, where I do what is called making a promise, I do not think that my obligation to do the action promised arises from my producing the expectation.

Hence, we cannot resolve the paradox by representing promising as producing an expectation. Nor do we fare better if we represent it as expressing a resolve, for even if, when we make a promise in good faith, we necessarily have resolved to do the action promised, no one on close consideration would allow that the promise is just the expression of our resolve.

What, then, are we to do? One thing is obvious. Promising requires the actual use of the word 'promise' or else of some equivalent, such as 'undertake', 'agree', 'give you my word', or 'will' in 'I *will*'. This being so, we can at least say that when I promise X to do some action, I am causing X to hear a certain noise, which has a definite meaning both to X and to me, together with the term ordinarily used for the action, in such a way that X believes that the sounds proceed from me. But then the question at once arises: 'How can my doing this give rise to an obligation to do the action?' And the answer seems to have to be: 'Only because I have already promised not to cause a noise of that kind in connexion with the phrase for some action, without going on to do the action.' And if this answer is right, what we call promising to do some action appears to be causing someone to hear in connexion with the term for the action a noise of a kind which I have promised never to use in this kind of way without going on to do the action; and, again, the reason why, when I say to X 'I promise to do so and so', I am bound to do the action is that I have previously made him a certain general promise.

Now this account of what promising is is, of course, rather odd. For 'promising' as ordinarily used means 'binding oneself', i.e. rendering oneself bound, and if the account is right, what is usually called, say, my promising to meet X in London, is, strictly speaking, not *promising* to meet him but making certain noises in virtue of which I become bound to meet him in consequence of my having previously made a certain general promise, and the real promise lies in this previous act.

Further, the most obvious objections to this account are two:

1. It seems merely fanciful to maintain that we can trace in our own mental history this general promise.
2. Even if we can make out that we have made this general promise, then, though we shall have removed the paradox of its seeming to create an obligation from what is usually called making some particular promise, we shall only have transferred the paradox to the general promise, for we shall have to allow that in making the general promise not to use a certain noise in a certain way without going on to do some action, we are *creating* the obligation not to do so; so that we are really no better off.

Here, however, two remarks may be made:

1. Even if it be true that the problem has only been transferred from one thing to another, it may still be true that the problem has to be so transferred. It may be *true* that a so-called particular promise implies a prior general promise, and if so we have to transfer the problem to get at it in its proper form. It is therefore of importance to ascertain whether what we call a particular promise really *does* imply a prior general promise.
2. The account is *not* open to what at first seems a fatal objection, viz. that it bases the obligation to keep an agreement (a promise) on a general agreement to keep agreements, and on that ground involves us in an infinite regress. For, strictly speaking, according to this account, an agreement to do a particular action is *not* an agreement, and the general agreement is not an agreement to keep our agreements, but an agreement to do what is ordinarily called keeping our agreements, i.e. not to make a certain noise in connexion with the phrase for some action without going on to do the action.

Before considering, however, whether this account can be defended, it will be well first to do something else. It is, no doubt, puzzling to be told that where we have used the language of promising, what we call the obligation to keep a promise depends on our having made a previous general promise. But, nevertheless, as things are now, we all in fact think that by using this language in connexion with the phrase for some action we do become bound to do the action.

It is, however, possible to imagine ourselves at a stage at which we do not think that by using this or any other special form of language we become so bound. And if we do this, we can ask: (1) Should we at this stage come to want at least to be *able* by using some special form of language to become bound, and (2) if we did, is there any step which we could take, by taking which we should become able?

These assertions, however, need some elucidation and defence before we can try to act on them.

Two things at least seem clear. One is that keeping some promise cannot be the first act which a man thinks himself bound to do. For if he is even to think of such a thing as promising, or to know the meaning of the term 'promising' or a synonym for it, he must already have the thought of obligation, and therefore must have already thought of other acts as duties. The second is that promises can only be made between members of a group of men—which need not consist of more than two—each of whom believes, and in acting to some extent relies on the belief, that the others are beings who not only think they have certain obligations but are likely to do what they think themselves bound to do. For promising seems to require a certain reliance by others on the belief that the man who promises is to some degree likely to carry out what he thinks he is bound to do, and others can only acquire this belief by finding that he has frequently carried out other acts he thought duties because he thought them duties. For promising, then, to be possible, there must be a group of men who think they have certain obligations to others, natural in the sense of independent of any promise, and who are, and are thought, likely to carry out what they think obligations. Instances of what they might think to be such obligations might be to refrain from affecting or dealing with the body of another and to refrain from affecting those material things with which a man has 'mixed his labour'.

It is, therefore, not nonsense to speak of the existence of such a group, and we can imagine ourselves as forming such a group, i.e. a group of men who as yet have no idea that there can be such a thing as promising, but who think they have certain duties to the others and are, and are thought, likely to act on the thought. Now imagine ourselves such a group. It is obvious that if we formed such a group, we should each soon come to realize that the success of any efforts to achieve a welfare of our own would depend not merely on the fact that the others would act, and refrain from acting, in certain ways which they thought a duty, but also on our being able to rely on the belief that they would. Otherwise we could not hope with success even to make plans for seeking our welfare, except in a very minor degree. But it would soon also become obvious to us that to devise even moderately hopeful plans we should need more. To realize that more is needed we should only have to notice that nearly all action which is of importance for our own welfare requires the co-operation of someone else, and then to consider what is required for the co-operation to be possible.

Where two people co-operate, they have either the same or different ends, but the realization of their end or ends requires the realization of a common means which has in part to be brought about by the one and in part by the other, as where two walkers by their joint efforts manage to remove from their path an obstructing log, which neither could move separately. And their co-operation requires the use of language, in a wide sense of the term, whereby each comes to have some expectation that the other will do a certain action if he himself does a certain other action. Further, to a limited extent co-operation is possible if the communication between them consists in the expression of an intention, i.e., really, of a resolve. For let A and B stand for the men whose way is blocked by a log, and assume that A is a sensible or rational person, and also that A thinks B a sensible or rational person. For A to start shifting one end of the log it is enough for him to come to think, on the strength of some communication from B, not, of course, necessarily in words, that B has resolved to start shifting the other end, if he sees A starting to shift the former end. For A will then think that B, being a sensible person, is unlikely to change his mind either before A starts lifting or half-way through. But the possibility of the co-operation which depends on the expression of a resolve is very limited in range because everyone knows men's liability to change their minds. And what each of us would soon realize is that, for co-operation to be possible for us on any important scale, we should have to get into a position in which, if some other member of our group were to use certain language with reference to some action he might take, we could rely on the belief that he would, in fact, go on to do the action in consequence of having used the language, even in cases where he would have been likely to change his mind but for having used the language.

We should then begin to consider how it would be possible to get into such a position, as a condition necessary for the successful pursuit of our own welfare to a reasonable extent.

It would, of course, occur to us that some outside party could get us into the position if he could devise and set up the means of enforcing a system of penalties for using some given symbol in connexion with the term for some action without going on to do the action. For the position would then be one in which someone else by, e.g., signing a legal document, would be bringing on himself the prospect of such a heavy loss if he did not do a certain action that we could rely on his being too little of a fool not to carry out the action, even if apart from the prospect of a penalty he was anxious to avoid doing it.

Again—and I mention this to introduce what Hume has in mind[1]—it would occur to us that provided that in some unexplained way we had all acquired the belief that others would do an action with reference to which they had used certain language, we might come to think the advantage to ourselves of

---

[1] *A Treatise of Human Nature*, Bk. III, § 5.

others continuing to think this about ourselves in particular so great that for that reason we should as sensible or rational beings always carry out such an action in consequence—to quote Hume's phrase[2]—of having subjected ourselves 'to the penalty of never being trusted again'. In this way (we should realize) we should produce the position desired for ourselves, though the possibility of our doing it would seem to be barred by what would seem the impossibility of acquiring the initial belief.

But, of course, we should realize that if the position were arrived at in either of these ways, we should not, when we had reached it, in the least be led to think that we were bound to do any action with reference to which we had used the language. We should only think doing the action wise or sensible.

We should next come to think that as we were all fairly conscientious we could attain the position if we could all somehow manage to come to think that if we used certain language in connexion with some action we thereby became bound to do the action, since then also each of us could rely on the belief that another would do the action. We should then wish we all did think this. But, unfortunately, being neither lunatics nor pragmatists, we should recognize that any attempt to attain the position in this way would fail, since our knowledge that if we all had this belief our having it would be extremely useful to ourselves would not in the least lead us to have it. And we should abandon any attempt to carry out this plan, merely regretfully wishing we had the belief, and perhaps envying any who had it.

As regards what we should, in fact, do next there seems to be little doubt, even if afterwards we could not defend our procedure from the charge of absurdity. We should say to one another: 'Obviously we all want this position to arise: let us attain it by first fixing on a certain noise or mark on paper which could be made in connexion with using the term for an action, and then agreeing or promising not to make this noise or mark in connexion with using the term for some action without going on to do the action. If we do this the trick will be done, because then, by making the noise or mark thus, we shall be bringing into existence the obligation to do the action in virtue of our general agreement or promise.' And we should, in fact, come to agree to do this because we should recognize that we should have much to gain by agreeing and nothing which we should necessarily lose, since there is no hardship in abstaining from making a certain noise, and we could keep our agreement by never making the noise.

Now it is, of course, easy to retort that to talk thus is simply to talk nonsense. In particular it is easy to urge (1) that the supposed general agreement could itself only be made by the use of special language, and that to account for our thinking we were bound by it we should have to allow that we thought we had already made another agreement which formed the reason why, when using

---

[2] Ibid. 522 (see Selby-Bigge).

this language in making the general agreement, we were bound to keep it, and that this thought would in turn require another similar thought, and so on; and (2) that in imagining that we in the circumstances supposed should make the general agreement, we are tacitly taking for granted that we are the beings we are now, who already think ourselves bound by any agreement.

Nevertheless, it is not clear that even if the idea stated is nonsense, it is such nonsense as all that, and that there may not after all be something in it. We all think that by what we call promising to do some action we do render ourselves bound to do it, so much so that if we are asked what we mean by 'promising', we are apt to answer that it is just binding ourselves to do it. But obviously it is impossible by any action whatever simply to create an obligation, i.e. to create it and nothing else. If we are to create an obligation, we can do it only by creating or bringing into existence something else. And, in the case of what we call promising to do some action, that by creating which we think we are creating the obligation to do the action is, strictly speaking, certain noises. Consequently we have got to account for the fact that we do think that by making certain noises we render ourselves bound to do a certain action; and consequently we must admit the reality of any thought which we must have, if we are to have, as we do have, this thought. And if we can make out that it would be simply impossible to think that the production of the noises would give rise to an obligation, unless we thought that we had already made some promise about our making such noises, then we have got to allow that in some way or other we have this thought, and that therefore there must have been some such promise, though from the nature of the case we must have made it somehow without language. And here, to emphasize the difficulty of avoiding giving this answer, it is worth while to notice two answers which certainly will not do.

First, it is of course obvious that if I merely cause the hearing of the noise 'promise' in the mind of another along with the noise ordinarily used as a symbol for some action, without my knowing, or without his knowing, what (as we should say) the noise means, I am not making a promise, nor do we think that I thereby become bound to do the action. Where I make a promise, not only must I make the noise 'promise' but I must know and the other man must know what the word means. Realizing this, we are apt to try to maintain, as a way of getting an easier solution, that the very act of using the term 'promise' in its ordinary sense in connexion with the phrase for some particular action, to someone who understands this sense, involves as something inseparable from itself an act of promising not to make such a noise in connexion with the term for any action without going on to do the action. This answer would have the advantage of saving us from having to admit the existence of a *prior* promise. But unfortunately it will not do. For the problem is to understand how it is that we think that if we make the noise 'promise' in connexion with the phrase for some action we shall thereby become bound to do the action. And to account for this thought we shall have to represent ourselves, not as thinking that by doing the action we should be making the general promise, but as thinking that we have already made it. To put this otherwise, to account for our using the term 'promise' in the ordinary sense, we must think of ourselves as thinking we have already made the general promise, and not as thinking that, in using it, we shall be, or are, making it.

Then, second, as an alternative way of easing the difficulty we may try to maintain that where we are said to promise someone that we shall do some action, we are inevitably representing ourselves to him as a being who *thinks* that by making the noise 'promise' in connexion with the term for some action he becomes bound to do the action, and that by so representing ourselves we become as much bound to do such an action as we should be if making the noise really did render us bound to do it. But if this answer were right we could not do what is called making a promise without lying, for in doing this we should inevitably be representing ourselves as thinking that by making the noise we became bound, although in fact we thought we were not.

The general conclusion which I wish to suggest, but only with the greatest hesitation, is that promising to do this or that action, in the ordinary sense of promising, can only exist among individuals between whom there has already been something which looks at first like an agreement to keep agreements, but is really an agreement not to use certain noises except in a certain way, the agreement nevertheless being one which, unlike ordinary agreements, does not require the use of language. But, of course, it would be more accurate to say that what I am suggesting is not a conclusion but rather a problem for consideration; viz. what is that something implied in the existence of agreements which looks very much like an agreement and yet, strictly speaking, cannot be an agreement?

13. Exchanging

Even exchanging one thing for another seems to involve promising. Suppose I have a spare banana, and X has a spare apple, and we meet. I realize that I should gain if it happened that I lost control of the banana and also gained control of the apple. But I want not to lose control of the banana unless somehow I do it by an act which will give me control of the apple. I may, e.g., resolve to hand over the banana, if I can be assured that if I do I shall in consequence receive the apple. But I shall not hand over the banana unless I have some confidence that if I do I shall in consequence get the apple. How am I to acquire this confidence?

In actual life I should say to X, 'I will give you this banana if you will give me that apple', and X might say to me, 'All right; if you hand over the banana I will hand you the apple'—and then I, hearing X, would be likely to hand over the banana, expecting that when I have done so X will hand over the apple.

Can we express these statements in terms of expressing a resolve?

The first will have to be: I have resolved to hand over to you this banana, if I hear you say, 'I have resolved to hand over this apple, if I find you hand over the banana.'

This implies that it is possible for me to think that it is possible for X to have resolved to hand over the apple, *if* he finds that I have handed over the banana. But though it is possible for X to resolve to hand over the apple anyhow, he cannot resolve to do it if, i.e. *only if*, I have handed over the banana. For *ex hypothesi* if X had not resolved to hand it over before, the knowledge that I have handed over the banana would not get him any nearer resolving to hand over the apple. And, again, for this reason, X cannot truthfully say 'I have resolved to hand you over the apple if I find you have handed over the banana'.

This is parallel to Hume's case, where my corn is ripe to-morrow and X's corn is ripe to-day. X cannot resolve to cut my corn to-morrow if he finds I have cut his to-day. And so I cannot say, 'I will cut your corn to-day, if you have resolved that if I do you will cut mine to-morrow.' I do not think such a resolve on X's part is possible.

I must mean: 'I bind myself to hand over the banana, provided you bind yourself, on seeing me hand it over, to hand over the apple.' And X must mean: 'Since you have bound yourself to hand over the banana provided that I bind myself to hand over the apple provided that I see you hand over the banana, I bind myself to hand over the apple provided that I see you hand over the banana.'

The difference between my act and his is that I bind myself to do some act α, provided that X binds himself to do some other act β, if he finds I do the action α, whereas X binds himself to do something β provided he finds that I do something α.

I, in binding myself thus, think that if he binds himself to do a certain action if he finds a certain condition fulfilled, he will do it if he finds the condition fulfilled.

X, in binding himself thus, thinks that as I have bound myself to do a certain action if a certain condition is fulfilled, I shall in consequence do it.

In the above cases my action comes first (handing over the banana; reaping X's corn), and X binds himself to do his action, if he finds that I have done mine.

But what about the cases where my action need not come first, and X's obligation is not conditional on knowing that I have done it? Such a case would be: 'I will fetch water for you if you will fetch bananas for me.' I make the proposal and say: 'I bind myself to fetch water for you, provided you bind yourself to fetch bananas for me.' X must mean: 'Since you have bound yourself to fetch water for me provided I bind myself to fetch bananas for you, I bind myself to fetch bananas for you.'

I in promising think that if X binds himself he *will* fetch bananas for me.

X in binding himself thinks that as I have bound myself to fetch him water if he binds himself to fetch bananas for me, if he binds himself I shall in consequence think myself bound to fetch his water, and shall in consequence fetch it.

14. The Time of an Obligation

1. To express the thought that I ought to do a certain action a in the *is* form, in order to make an understandable contrast with 'I am doing a', we have to substitute either 'I am oughting to do a' or else 'I am under an obligation to do a', in both statements 'am' seeming to have the sense of the present tense.

2. It would ordinarily be said that it is a condition of my oughting or being under a moral obligation to do a, that I have not done a and that it may be that I shall not. The alternative view is that this is not true, the truth being that it is not a condition either that I shall or that I shall not, my obligation being independent of whether I shall or whether I shall not do it, and (it seems also) that it is impossible that I should have done what I am under an obligation to do.

3. The proper contrasts are between:

 (a) 'I shall do a'
    and 'I shall be oughting to do a'.
 (b) 'I am doing a'
    and 'I am oughting to do a'.
 (c) 'I was doing a'
    and 'I was oughting to do a'.

An action takes time. And it would be natural to say: 'I shall to-morrow from ten to eleven be under an obligation to lecture from ten to eleven,' and also: 'I was yesterday from ten to eleven under an obligation to lecture yesterday from ten to eleven,' the truth of the first statement being independent of whether I shall, and that of the second independent of whether I did—so that it may be the case that I was from ten to eleven both oughting to do a from ten to eleven and also from ten to eleven doing a from ten to eleven; and the truth of the first half of the statement being compatible with that of the second, and not requiring that I *did not* lecture from ten to eleven.

What about the contrast between, e.g. 'I am going to bed' and 'I should be going, or am *oughting* to go, to bed'?

'I am going to bed' really refers to an action, part of which is just over and part of which is to come. And with this contrasts 'I ought to go to bed, or am under an obligation to go to bed', a statement referring partly to a just past being under an obligation to go to bed during that past time, and a just future obligation to go to bed during that future time—I *am* oughting to go to bed not having the force of a present.

Alternatively, however, 'I am going to bed' may mean 'I am starting to go to bed', i.e. *beginning* a certain process, and with this contrasts 'I am under an obligation to begin the process of going to bed'; this statement being independent of whether I *am* going to bed.

The corresponding independence in the former case is the non-dependence of a past obligation to do part of the process of going to bed on my having done this, and that of a future obligation on my coming to do it.

4. The moral is that 'I am oughting, or under an obligation, to go to bed' refers to the future, meaning 'from now on I shall be under an obligation to go to bed', the obligation coinciding in time with the act, and has as its contrast 'from now on I shall be going to bed'; and that it does not require that I shall not do the action; and also, that it does not require that I have not done the action.

15. The Psychology of Willing

There are many occasions on which if I were to do a certain action, although my doing it would cause a certain evil to me, it would cause a benefit to me greater than the pain. Instances would be (1) putting a drug on my tooth which would kill a nerve, and so permanently getting rid of the pain, (2) asking a dentist to take out a certain tooth. There are also occasions on which, although doing the action would cause a certain gain to me, it would bring me a greater evil later, e.g. (1) taking an extra glass of wine, or an extra helping of a certain food, (2) when I have gout, taking a drug which would stop the pain for the moment, but would make the gout worse.

In any of these cases, I may do what we should describe as considering doing it. When this happens, what will happen? No general answer is possible.

Consider the drugging the tooth case (killing the nerve). A dentist may have told me that though the pain will be sharp it will not be more than sharp, and will not last, and I may believe him and be confident that the toothache will go on if I do not put on the drug. It may happen that I shall decide without difficulty to put it on, i.e. it may not take much, if any, effort to decide. And having decided to put it on, I put it on. (This implies a distinction between deciding to put it on and putting it on.) And it might afterwards happen that, having put it on, I found the pain so very much worse than I had been led to expect, that I should say afterwards 'Putting it on was not worth it', and that if the situation were to repeat itself with another tooth, I should decide not to put the nerve-killing stuff on. And I might add that my decision would be correct or the right decision. (E.g. 'It would be the right decision not to take the pain-killing stuff in the next case, when I had on a former occasion taken the drug, thinking that I should thereby gain more than I should lose.') Suppose the situation repeated itself about the nerve-killer. I should at once conclude that to put on the nerve-killer would not bring me gain, and I should have an instinctive aversion to putting the nerve-killer on. Would there be a decision not to put the stuff on? It looks as if there would, and a decision at once. Suppose, however, that I had once put on the nerve-killer (or that someone else had for me) and afterwards I thought it had been worth while, and now thought that the situation repeated itself in the case of another tooth, and thought that if I put the stuff on, I should on balance gain. Suppose, too, that I desired to put the stuff on.

I want the iodine to be on my gum. I know that if it is to come to be on my gum, I must cause it to go from the end of a brush in my hand to my gum.

I ask: 'How am I to cause it to go through this movement?' I answer: 'I must cause my hand which is holding the brush to go from where it is to a spot A. How am I to cause this?' The question is mistaken, involving an infinite process. But I may think that if I were to will this movement, my willing it would cause my hand to go from where it is to A.

Suppose I say: If I am to will this movement to exist, I must cause the willing to exist', and suppose I then ask: 'How am I to cause the willing of that movement?' I might answer: 'Well, to cause this to exist, I must will the willing of that movement, thinking this willing the willing which would cause it to exist'; and this seems impossible.

I say to myself: 'How is the willing of that movement to come to exist?' (not 'How am I to cause it?'). Only by my desiring to will it, and desiring to will it more than I am averse to willing it.

I then say to myself: 'Desiring to will it, I in consequence desire to come to desire more to will it, and desiring to desire more to will it, I in consequence desire to think more of what I should gain if I should will that movement'—thinking that if I thought more of what I should gain if I willed that movement, I should in consequence come to desire more to will that movement, in the hope that in consequence I should desire to will it to a degree sufficient to make me will that movement. (Here I am presupposing that, if I come to desire to a sufficient degree to will it, I shall will that movement.)

I am then presupposing that if I *do* come to will that movement, that in consequence of which I shall come to will it is my coming to desire to a sufficient degree to will that movement; so that if I do come to will that movement, I come to will it not by doing something but by desiring something, i.e. desiring to a sufficient degree to will it. For this to happen I must will the thinking, more than I *am* thinking, of what I should gain if I willed that movement more.

Desiring to desire more the willing the change, I desire to come to think more of what would happen if I willed that movement, since I think that if I do I shall strengthen my desire to will that movement; and thinking thus I shall think more fully of what I shall gain if I do come to will this change—thinking that if I do I shall increase my desire to will the change—so that it comes about that I will the thinking of what I shall gain if I do will that movement; this really, of course, being an act of will. If, then, I do come to will the change X, there has been beforehand my willing to think more of what I shall gain if I will it, this causing an increase of my desire to will that change. There will then have been two acts of will: first, a willing to think more of what I shall gain if I will X—this due to the desire to will X—and second, a willing the change X.

16. Acting, Willing, Desiring

The question 'What is acting or doing something?' seems at first unreal, i.e. a question to which we already know the answer. For it looks as though everyone knows what doing something is and would be ready to offer instances. No one, for instance, would hesitate to say to another 'You ought to go to bed', on the ground that neither he nor the other knows the kind of thing meant by 'going to bed'. Yet, when we consider instances that would be offered, we do not find it easy to state the common character which we think they had which led us to call them actions.

If, as a preliminary, we look for help to the psychologists, from whom we naturally expect to get it, we find we fail. We find plenty of talk about reflex actions, ideo-motor actions, instinctive actions, and so on, but no discussion of what actions are. Instead, they seem to take for granted that our actions are physical processes taking place within our body, which they certainly are not.

We should at first say that to do something is to originate or to bring into existence, i.e., really, to cause, some not yet existing state either of ourselves or of someone else, or, again, of some body. But, for clearness' sake, we should go on to distinguish those actions in doing which we originated some new state directly from those in which we did this only indirectly, i.e. by originating directly some other state, by originating which we indirectly originated the final state. As instances of the former we might give moving or turning our head, and as instances of the latter, curing our toothache by swallowing aspirin, and killing another by pressing a switch which exploded a charge underneath him. If challenged, however, we should have to allow that even in instances of the former kind we did not originate directly what the instances suggest that we did, since what we did originate directly must have been some new state or states of our nerve-cells, of the nature of which we are ignorant. We should, however, insist that in doing any action we must have originated *something* directly, since otherwise we could not originate anything indirectly.

The view that to act is to originate something was maintained by Cook Wilson in a paper on *Means and End*. In the course of this paper he also maintained (1) that an action required the desire to do it, and (2) that it is important to avoid the mistake of thinking that the origination of something X is the willing of X, apparently on the ground that if it were, X would exist as soon as we willed it, and yet it usually does not. He also appeared to hold that the origination of X, though not identical with willing the origination, required it, so that when

I originated a movement of my hand, this required as an antecedent my willing this origination, and this willing in turn required the desiring to originate the movement.

According to Cook Wilson, then, in considering an action we have to distinguish three things: first, the action itself, the originating something; second, the required willing to originate this; and third, the required desire to originate this. And according to him what we will and what we desire are the same, viz. the action.

Professor Macmurray, in a Symposium[1] on 'What is action?', takes substantially the same view of what an action is. He says: 'An action is not the concomitance of an intention in the mind and an occurrence in the physical world: it is the *producing* of the occurrence by the Self, the *making* of a change in the external world, the *doing* of a deed. No process which terminates in the mind, such as forming an intention, deciding to act, or willing, is either an action or a component of action.' But he goes on to add: 'In certain circumstances such a mental event or process may be followed *necessarily* by action.'

Now, so far as I can see, this account of what an action is, though plausible and having as a truth underlying it that usually in acting we do cause something, is not tenable.

Unquestionably the thing meant by 'an action' is an activity. This is so whether we speak of a man's action in moving his hand, or of a body's action such as that of the heart in pumping the blood, or that of one electron in repelling another. But though we think that some man in moving his hand, or that the sun in attracting the earth, causes a certain movement, we do not think that the man's or the sun's activity *is* or *consists in* causing the movement. And if we ask ourselves: 'Is there such an activity as originating or causing a change in something else?', we have to answer that there is not. To say this, of course, is not to say that there is no such thing as causing something, but only to say that though the causing a change may require an activity, it is not itself an activity. If we then ask: 'What is the kind of activity required when one body causes another to move?', we have to answer that we do not know, and that when we speak of a force of attraction or of repulsion we are only expressing our knowledge that there is some activity at work, while being ignorant of what the kind of activity is. In the case, however, of a man, i.e., really, of a man's mind, the matter is different. When, e.g., we think of ourselves as having moved our hand, we are thinking of ourselves as having performed an activity of a certain kind, and, it almost goes without saying, a *mental* activity of a certain kind, an activity of whose nature we were dimly aware in doing the action and of which we can become more clearly aware by reflecting on it. And that we are aware of its special nature is shown by our unhesitatingly distinguishing it from other special mental activities such as

---

[1] Aristotelian Society, Supplementary Volume XVII (1938).

thinking, wondering, and imagining. If we ask 'What is the word used for this special kind of activity?' the answer, it seems, has to be 'willing'. (I now think I was mistaken in suggesting that the phrase in use for it is 'setting oneself to cause'.) We also have to admit that while we know the general character of that to which we refer when we use the word 'willing', this character is *sui generis* and so incapable of being defined, i.e. of having its nature expressed in terms of the nature of other things. Even Hume virtually admits this when he says: 'By the will, I mean nothing but *the internal impression we feel and are conscious of, when we knowingly give rise to any new motion of our body or new perception of our mind*',[2] and then goes on to add that the impression is impossible to define. Though, however, the activity of willing is indefinable, we can distinguish it from a number of things which it is not. Thus obviously, as Locke insisted, willing is different from desiring, and again, willing is not, as some psychologists would have it, a species of something called conation of which desiring is another species. There is no such genus. Again, it is not, as Green in one passage[3] implies, a species of desiring which is desiring in another sense than that ordinary sense in which we are said to desire while hesitating to act.

In addition, plainly, willing is not resolving, nor attending to a difficult object, as James holds, nor for that matter attending to anything, nor, again, consenting to the reality of what is attended to, as James also maintains, nor, indeed, consenting to anything, nor, once more, identifying ourself with some object of desire, as Green asserts in another passage.[4]

Consequently, there seems to be no resisting the conclusion that where we think of ourselves or of another as having done a certain action, the kind of activity of which we are thinking is that of willing (though we should have to add that we are thinking of our particular act of willing as having been the doing of the action in question, only because we think it caused a certain change), and that when we refer to some instance of this activity, such as our having moved our finger or given some friend a headache, we refer to it thus not because we think it was, or consisted in, the causing our finger to move or our friend's head to ache, but because we think it had a certain change of state as an effect.

If, as it seems we must, we accept this conclusion, that to act is really to will something, we then become faced by the question: 'What sort of thing is it that we will?'

Those who, like Cook Wilson, distinguish between acting and willing, answer that what we will is an action, which according to him is the originating some change. Thus Green says: 'To will an event' (i.e. presumably some change) 'as distinguished from an act is a contradiction.' And by this he seems to mean that, for instance, in the case which he takes of our paying a debt, what we will is the paying of our debt and not our creditor's coming into possession of

---

[2] Hume, *Treatise* (Selby-Bigge, p. 399).   [3] *Prolegomena*, §§ 140–2.   [4] Ibid. § 146.

what we owe him. Again, James and Stout, though they do not consider the question, show by their instances that they take for granted that what we will is an action. Thus James says: 'I will to write, and the act follows. I will to sneeze and it does not.'[5] And Stout illustrates a volition by a man's willing to produce an explosion by applying a lighted match to gunpowder.[6] But, unfortunately, James speaks of what he has referred to as, the act of writing which I will, as certain physiological movements, and similarly Stout speaks of, the production of an explosion which I will, as certain bodily movements. And, of course, the bodily movements to which they are referring are not actions, though they may be the effects of actions. Plainly, then, both are only doing lip-service to the idea that what we will is an action. And James, at least, drops doing even this. For immediately after making the statement just quoted, viz. 'I will to write, and the act follows. I will to sneeze and it does not', he adds: 'I will that the distant table slide over the floor towards me; it also does not.' Yet no one would say that the sliding of the table, as distinct from my sliding it, was an action.

In this connexion it is well for clearness' sake to bear two things in mind. The first is that some transitive verbs used for particular actions are also used intransitively. Thus one not only speaks of turning one's head but also says that one's head turned. And the second is that, while the phrase 'turning one's head' stands for an action and so for an activity of one's mind, yet when I say 'my head turned' I am speaking simply of a movement of my head which is a change of place and not an action. The difference is made clear by considering what is plainly a mistake made by Professor Macmurray. He says that the term 'action' is ambiguous. He says: 'It may refer either to what is done or to the doing of it. It may mean either "doing" or "deed". When we talk of "an action" we are normally referring to what is done. ... To act is to effect a change in the external world. The deed is the change so effected.' And he emphasizes what he considers the ambiguity in order to indicate that it is doings and not deeds that he is considering. Obviously, however, there is no ambiguity whatever. When I move my hand, the movement of my hand, though an effect of my action, is not itself an action, and no one who considered the matter would say it was, any more than he would say that the death of Caesar, as distinct from his murder, was an action or even part of an action.

This difference between, e.g., my moving my hand and a movement of my hand, is one which James and Stout seem to ignore, as becomes obvious when James speaks of the sliding of a table as, like writing, an action. We find the same thing, too, in Locke. For though, e.g., he says that 'we find by experience, that, barely by willing it, we can move the parts of our bodies',[7] yet in contrasting a human with a physical action he implies that what we will is a movement of

---

[5] James, *Psychology*, ii. p. 560.   [6] Stout, *Manual of Psychology*, iv, p. 641.
[7] Locke, *Essay*, ii. 21, § 4.

our body. Probably, if pressed, he would have said that, strictly speaking, what we will is a movement and so not an action. In addition, James and Stout seem to treat the distinction between an act of willing, or, as they prefer to call it, a volition, and what is willed, as if it were the same as the distinction between an act of willing and its effect, although they are totally different.

It should be clear from what I have just said that those who hold that what we will is an action must, to be successful, mean by an action something which really is an action. They may, of course, maintain that what we will is a physical process, such as a movement of my hand, but if they do they are really denying that what we will is an action.

It should also now be clear that if we face the question 'What sort of thing do we will?', we have only two answers to consider: (1) that it is some change of state of some thing or person; and (2) that it is an action. If, however, we are forced to conclude, as we have been, that doing something is an act of willing, we seem forced to exclude the second answer, simply on the ground that if it were true, then whenever we think of ourselves as having done some action, we must be thinking of ourselves as having willed some action, i.e. as having willed the willing of some change X; and to think this seems impossible. By the very nature of willing, it seems, what we will must be something other than willing, so that to will the willing of a change X must be an impossibility. And if we even try to deny this, we find ourselves forced to admit that the willing of X, which (we are contending) is what we will, must in turn really be the willing the willing of something else, and so on, and thus become involved in an infinite regress. It is true that Cook Wilson, in a long unpublished discussion, tried to vindicate the analogous idea that in certain limiting cases, viz. those in which the desire moving us is not the desire of some change but the desire to cause it ourselves, as happens in playing golf or patience, what we originate is identical with our origination of something. But he never seems to me to succeed in meeting the objection that this identity must be impossible. Similarly, it seems to me, it is impossible for there to be a case in which the willing the willing of X is identical with willing X.

We are thus left with the conclusion that where we think we have done some action, e.g. have raised our arm or written a word, what we willed was some change, e.g. some movement of our arm or some movement of ink to a certain place on a piece of paper in front of us. But we have to bear in mind that the change which we willed may not have been the same as the change we think we effected. Thus, where I willed some movement of my second finger, I may at least afterwards think that the change I effected was a movement of my first finger, and, only too often, where I willed the existence of a certain word on a piece of paper, I afterwards find that what I caused was a different word. Again, in two cases of the act we call trying to thread a needle, what I willed may have been the same, though the changes I afterwards think I effected were very different, being in the one case the thread's going through the needle and in the other its passing well outside it.

Suppose now that it be allowed that so far I have been right. Then the following admissions must be made:

1. An action, i.e. a human action, instead of being the originating or causing of some change, is an activity of willing some change, this usually causing some change, and in some cases a physical change, its doing or not doing this depending on the physical conditions of which the agent is largely ignorant.
2. Sometimes, however, we have performed such an activity without, at any rate so far as we know, having caused any physical change. This has happened when, e.g., we willed a movement of our hand, at a time when it was either paralysed or numb with cold, whether we knew this or not. No doubt in such cases our activity would not ordinarily be called an action, but it is of the same sort as what we ordinarily call and think of as an action.
3. There is no reason to limit the change which it is possible to will to a movement of some part of our body, since, as James says in effect, we can just as much will the sliding of a table towards us as a movement of our hand towards our head. Indeed, we may, in fact, will this in order to convince ourselves or someone else that by doing so we shall not cause the table to slide. And it looks as though we sometimes will such things in ordinary life, as when in watching a football match we want some player's speed to increase, and will it to increase.
4. Where we have willed some movement of our body and think we have caused it, we cannot have directly caused it. For what we directly caused, if anything, must have been some change in our brain.
5. Where we think that by willing some change we effected some change in the physical world, we are implying the idea that in doing so, we are butting into, or interfering with, the physical system, just as we think of an approaching comet as effecting a breach in the order of the solar system, so long as we do not regard the comet as part of the system. This idea is, of course, inconsistent with our belief in the uniformity of nature unless we include in nature minds as well as bodies; and in any case it is inconsistent with our belief in the conservation of energy. But so long as we think, as we do, that at any rate on some occasions we really effect something in the physical world, we must admit this. And if we knew that such effecting was impossible, we should give up acting.

We have now to face another question, viz. 'Does acting require a desire, and if it does, the desire of what?'

It is at least very difficult to avoid Aristotle's conclusion that acting requires a desire, if only for the reason he gives, viz. that διάνοια αὐτὴ οὐθὲν κινεῖ. It seems that, as Locke maintained, if we never desired something we should never do anything. But what is the desire required?

Here only one or other of two answers seems possible, viz. (1) that it is a desire of the change X which we will, and (2) that it is a desire of the willing of X. And when we try, we do not find it easy to decide between them. For on the one hand, the desire required seems to have to be the desire of X, on the ground that, if we are to will X, we must desire X. And on the other hand, it seems that it must be the desire to will X, since unless we *desired* to will X we could not will X. Indeed, just for this reason Plato seems to have gone too far in the *Gorgias* when he maintained that in acting we never desire to do what we do, but only that for the sake of which we do it. For, if acting is willing, it seems that the desire required must be a desire of the willing, even though the desire be a dependent desire, i.e. a desire depending on the desire of something else for its own sake, viz. that for the sake of which we do the action. And Plato's mistake seems to have been that of restricting desiring to desiring something for its own sake.

The two answers are, of course, radically different. For if the desire required is the desire of X, the thing desired and the thing willed will be the same, as indeed Green implies that they are when he maintains that willing is desiring in a special sense of 'desiring'. But if so, while the willing of X will require what for want of a better term we seem to have to call the thought of X, as being something involved in the desire of X, it will not require either the desire of the willing of X or, for that reason, even the thought of willing X. On the other hand, if the desire required is the desire to will X, the thing desired and the thing willed will necessarily be different, and while the willing of X will require the desire of willing X and so also the thought of willing X, it will not require the desire of X, though it will require the thought of X, as being something involved in the thought of willing X. It should, however, be noted that in the case of the latter alternative, the desire of X may in some cases be required indirectly as a condition of our desiring the willing of X.

To repeat here for clearness' sake what is central—if the desire required is the desire of X, the willing of X will not require either the desire of the willing of X or even the thought of willing X, while, if the desire required is the desire of willing X, the willing of X will not require the desire of X, though it will require the thought of X.

On consideration, however, we have to reject the idea that the desire required is the desire of X, on three grounds. First, if it were true, we should always will any change which we desired to happen, such as the sliding of the table, whether or not we thought that if we were to will it to happen we should thereby cause it to happen; and obviously we do not. Second, we occasionally will a change to happen without any desire for it to happen. This must occur, e.g., if a man ever does an act moved solely by the desire for revenge, willing, say, the movement of a switch which he is confident will result in the death of another, not from any desire for his death but solely from the desire to cause it by willing the movement. And even if there are no acts animated solely by the desire for revenge, there are certainly actions approximating to this. At all events, in the case of playing a game the desire at work must be not the desire of some change but the desire to cause it. A putter at golf, e.g., has no desire for the ball to fall into the hole; he only desires to cause it to fall in. This contention is, I think, not met by maintaining, as Cook Wilson in fact does, that the player desires the falling into the hole as caused by his action, and so desires the falling as part of, or an element in, his action. Its falling is neither a part of, nor an element in, his action; at best it is only an effect of it. And the player could only be said to desire the falling if, as he does not, he desired it to happen irrespectively of what would cause it to happen. And in this connexion it may be added that if the desire required were the desire of X, it would be impossible to do any act as one which we think would or might fulfil some obligation, since *ex hypothesi* the desire required will be a desire for a change X and not a desire to *will* a change X. Then, third, there is a consideration which comes to light if we consider more closely what it is that we will in certain cases, and more especially in those in which we describe an action as one of trying to do so and so. Suppose, e.g., I have done what we describe as having tried to jump a ditch, and so imply that beforehand I was doubtful of success. Obviously I did not will a movement of my body which I was sure would land me, say, two clear yards on the other side, since if I had thought of willing this I should have realized that willing this would not result in my getting across. I willed that movement the willing of which, if I were to will it, I thought the most likely of all the willings of movements in my power to result in my landing on the farther bank. And in this connexion it seems worth nothing that what we call trying to do something is as much doing something as what we ordinarily call doing something, although the word 'trying' suggests that it is not. It is the willing a change described in the way in which I have just described what I willed in trying to jump a ditch.

It therefore seems that the desire required must be the desire of the willing of a certain change X. Yet this conclusion is exposed to two objections. The first is that if it were true, it would be impossible to will something X for the first time. For in this context we mean by a desire to will X a desire we can only have in consequence of thinking that if we were to will X, our doing so would be likely to cause something else, and ultimately something which we desire for its own sake. But we cannot desire to will something X, unless we at least have a conjecture that if we were to will X, our willing X might cause some change which we desire for its own sake. And this conjecture requires the thought that on some previous occasion we have willed X and thence concluded from what we think followed this willing of X that it may have caused something else Y. Yet *ex hypothesi* we cannot have willed X on this previous occasion from the desire to will X, since then we had no idea of what willing X might cause. James expresses what is really this objection, though in a misleading way, when he says: 'If, in voluntary action properly so-called' (i.e. in what is really an action), 'the act must be foreseen, it follows that no creature not endowed with divinatory power can perform an act voluntarily for the first time.'[8] The statement as it stands is, of course, absurd, because no one before acting *knows* what his act will be, or even that he will act. But it can be taken as an inaccurate way of expressing the thought that an act of will requires an idea of something which we may cause if we perform the act.

To this objection I have to confess that I cannot see an answer. Yet I think that there must be an answer, since, however it has come about, for us as we are now an act of will does seem to require the desire of it, and so some idea of something which it might effect. I need hardly add that it is no answer to maintain that the desire immediately required by willing something X is in some cases the desire of X, and in others the desire of willing X.

The second objection is one which seems to me, though insidious, an objection which can be met. It can be stated thus: 'It is all very well to say that the desire immediately presupposed by willing X is the desire to will X. But to say this is not enough. For we often desire to will X, and yet do not, as when we hesitate to get out of bed or out of a warm bath, and when this is so, obviously something else is required, and this something can only be the willing to will X, so that after all there must be such a thing as willing to will.' But to this the reply seems clear. Though it is possible to desire to desire, as when I desire to desire the welfare of my country more than I do, it is impossible to will to will, for the reason already given. And where we hesitate to will X, what is required is not the willing to will X but either a certain increase in our desire to will X or a decrease in our aversion to doing so. Certainly, too, we often act on this idea, hoping, e.g., that by making ourselves think of the coldness of our breakfast if we stay in bed we shall reach a state of desire in which we shall will certain movements of our body. And sometimes we succeed, and when we do, we sometimes, as James puts it, suddenly find that we have got up, the explanation of our surprise apparently being that we, having been absorbed in the process of trying to stimulate our desire to get up, have not reflected on our state of desire and so have not noticed its increase.

There is also to be noticed in this connexion a mistake into which we are apt to fall which leads us to think that there must be such a thing as willing to will. We of course frequently want certain changes to happen and also want to will certain changes. But we are apt not to notice that the objects of these desires differ in respect of the conditions of their realization, and in consequence to carry the account of the process of deliberation described by Aristotle one step too far—as Aristotle did not. According to him, when we want the happening of

[8] James, *Psychology*, ii, p. 487.

something Z which is not an action of ours and which we think we cannot cause directly, we often look for something else Y from the happening of which the happening of Z would result, and then if necessary for something else X from the happening of which Y would result, until we come to think of something A from the happening of which X, Y, and Z would in turn result, and which we also think it in our power to cause by a certain act a. And when we have found A the process stops. We, however, are apt to carry the process one step farther, and apply to the act a, i.e. the willing of something β, the willing of which we think likely to cause A, the same process that we applied to Z, Y, X, and A, thus treating the willing of β as if it were not the willing of something (which it is), but a change which some act of willing might cause. As a result of doing this we ask 'From what act of willing would the willing of β result?', and the answer has to be 'The willing the willing of β'. But the very question is mistaken, because the willing of β is not a change like Z, Y, X, and A. The only proper question at this stage must be not 'From what *willing* would the willing of β result?' but 'From what *something* would the willing of β result?' And the proper answer must be: 'From a certain increase in our desire to will β.'

17. 'Ought'

Suppose 'I ought to will a' means 'my willing a ought to exist'. Then the only true statement would have to be: 'If I were to will a certain change a, my willing a would be something that ought to exist.'

For this statement to be true, it would have to be true either that if I were to will a my willing a would itself be something good, or that if I were to will a my willing a would be something which would cause something good and would therefore be something which ought to exist.

If, therefore, I were to *know* that if I were to will a, my willing a would be something which ought to exist, I should have to know either (1) that willing a would be itself good, and that what would be good would be something which ought to exist, or (2) that willing a would be something which would cause a thing β, that β would be itself good and therefore ought to exist, and that what would cause something which ought to exist would itself be something which ought to exist.

Accept alternative (2). And suppose that I know that if I willed a, my willing a would be something which ought to exist as causing something β which ought to exist. Suppose that then I ask myself 'How is it to come about that I will a?', i.e. 'What would have to happen from the happening of which it would follow that I willed a?' What is the answer? 'My desiring the willing of a as being something which ought to exist.'

But why is not the answer 'My desiring the willing of a, for *any* reason', and so desiring a even if I did not know that willing a would be something which should exist? Of course, if the thought that willing a certain thing a would be something which should exist necessarily aroused the desire to will a, and if the desire to will a certain something necessarily led to my willing it, then knowing that I knew that willing a ought to exist would enable me to know that I shall in fact will a, since I should know that if I am to will a, all that is required is a desire to will a, and that I shall have this desire.

Substitute for *knowing* that if I were to will a, my willing a would cause something which should exist, *thinking* the same thing, i.e. that if I were to will a, my willing a would cause β and so would cause something which should exist, then I could only *think* that if I were to will a, my willing a would be something which should exist.

Suppose, then, it were true that if I were to will a change a, my willing it would cause the change β, then willing a would be something which ought to exist. And in that case I should know that if I were to will a certain unknown change, my willing would be something that should exist, but that I could not know what this change was, and it might happen that I came to will a change a, the willing of which caused β and so did cause something which should exist, though in willing it I should think it very unlikely that I should cause β.

Substitute for 'If I were to will a, my willing a would be something which would cause something good, and so be something which should exist' 'If I were to will a, a would be something which would cause something good, and so be something which should exist'. Then, as before, I cannot know that if I were to will a, a would be something which should exist, because I cannot know that it would cause something which would be good.

Then, as a substitute, try 'If I were to will a, a would be something which I think would be likely to be something which would cause β, and so be something which should exist'.

Thus, if I am thinking that if a were to exist, a would be something which should exist, I could will a, and could will a thinking a would be something which should exist.

Then there is the same objection as before, viz. that I cannot know that if I were to will a, my willing a would be something which ought to exist; I should only know that if I were to will a I should be willing something which I *thought* should exist.

Appendix

Letter from Cook Wilson to Prichard

My Dear Prichard, 6 Jan. 1904

Your letter is very welcome, for though I am not at all in a fit condition to answer it, it accords with a strong feeling I have had for some little time that I ought to get into shape something on the pure 'theory of knowledge' in distinction from my Logic lecture. . . . But tho' so unfitted, I will say something on one question, and that may be some help for the moment, though I hope when more free to address myself to it in the precise form in which you put it.

. . . If we think of knowing as an activity, as doing something, then, as if we had to do with relations of objects, . . . we think that the knowing subject must, in knowing, do something to the object it knows and [that] that object must suffer something. Or if we don't envisage this to ourselves as clearly as you seem to do—for to put it so clearly is, I suppose, half the answer, we tend to think on this principle. Now we must know something about knowledge, and we know when we reflect that the very idea of it is incompatible with any such *action* upon, or *suffering* in, the object known. You can no more act upon the object by knowing it than you can 'please the Dean and Chapter by stroking the dome of St Paul's'. . . . Obviously if we 'do anything to' anything in knowing, it is not done to the object known, to what we know, for that simply contradicts the presuppositions of the act of knowledge itself. . . .

Now representation is only another form of the same fallacy. We want to explain knowing an object and we explain it solely in terms of the object known, and that by giving the mind not the object but some idea of it which is said to be like it—an image (however the fact may be disguised). The chief fallacy of this is not so much the impossibility of knowing such image is like the object, or that there is any object at all, but that it assumes the very thing it is intended to explain. The image itself has still to be *apprehended* and the difficulty is only repeated. We still distinguish the image and the knowing, or perceiving, or apprehending it. The theory which is to explain subjective apprehension of the object cannot, as one could predict, do anything but presuppose the absolute ultimate fact of apprehension of an object, and so explain apprehension of the object (unconsciously) as apprehending another object like it. . . . Perhaps most fallacies in the theory of knowledge are reduced to the primary one of trying to *explain* the nature of knowing or apprehending. We cannot *construct knowing*—the act of apprehending—out of any elements. I remember quite early in my philosophic reflection having an instinctive aversion to the very expression '*theory* of knowledge'. I felt the words themselves suggested a fallacy—an utterly fallacious inquiry, though I was

[Taken from J. Cook Wilson, *Statement and Inference*, ed. A. S. L. Farquharson (Oxford: Oxford University Press repr. 1969), V. II, § 541, pp. 801–8.]

not anxious to proclaim [it]. I felt that if we don't [know] what knowledge is, we know nothing; and there could be no help for us. I feel sure many most respectable theories commit the fallacy of supposing the presupposition of all explanation can be explained. What on earth is gained by 'construction' or 'reconstruction' over 'representation'? ... It's no good—knowledge and apprehension can only be described in terms which already mean knowledge and apprehension. ...

Now let us consider what we mean by our 'idea of a thing', or 'conception of a thing'. Suppose an object of perception—Cologne cathedral. If asked what was my idea of it, I should at once state certain judgements of mine that the church (a reality) had certain real attributes when I saw it. Such judgements are accompanied by a mental image, but that is not my conception or idea *of* the church, nor do I say it is. On the contrary I think the image is more or less inadequate, and I say the church was something like the image I am forming. The judgement is obviously not the image and can be reduced to no kind of terms of images. The image is as distinct from the judgement as the object (the church) of which I say I have an idea. In the judgement about an object not present to perception, what is the fact before me? It is not the church but the fact that the church looked so and so when I saw [it]; it is a fact *now* that this was so in the past. It is the fact which is before me, the fact, i.e. which I apprehend in the judgement now. There is nothing between me and it, no intervening image. I may forget details but I remember a general character, such as two spires, very much crocketed. And this which I do not forget, viz. that I apprehended then the general character, is what I now apprehend. Besides this there is an uncertainty about details not certainly remembered; this is not an image, it is a state of my thinking consciousness which can be expressed in no terms except its unique self, uncertainty. ...

The judgement of knowledge is apprehension of reality or fact, it is not the fact, it is not the reality; but neither is it any image of the reality nor the apprehension of any such image. Nor is it mere apprehension as a subjective state—mere apprehension is impossible—it is (1) apprehension (2) of the reality.

The ideal element we are looking for, and always (all of us) tend to misrepresent as an image of the reality, is the apprehending side as our act: the fact that we apprehend the reality. It is not here the least necessary to say *how* we come to be able to apprehend reality; the whole point is that the very conception of knowledge as such must necessitate this and nothing short of that will do. ...

You have really done me a great service. It is one of the most useful things possible to me that I have the good fortune to know a number of earnest thinkers ... who will put difficult questions to me and not let me off. The cleverest man in the world gets into his own grooves of thinking, and that can only be cured by the independent activity of other people's minds, and I consider myself specially fortunate in having so much access to it. ...

I went to the Watts Exhibition on Saturday (this letter has flowed over to the Sunday). It is splendid and probably a unique opportunity.

Yours,
J.C.W.

APPENDIX

Letter from Prichard to Ross

My dear Ross, 6 LR .O 14.7.32

I hope you will forgive my taking a sort of pot shot at something in your book. But I have got it on my chest.

On p. 27 you reduce the 6 or rather 7 prima facie duties enumerated on pp. 21 to 4, viz: your original (1) *a*, (1) *b* & (2) & the prima facie duty of producing as much good as possible* ... And I have for long wondered that you should feel comfortable in co-ordinating the last with (1) *a*, (1) *b* and (2), e.g. the prima facie duty of keeping a promise.

But I have never till now seen clearly what has been puzzling me about this procedure—though I have always felt it was queer. The queerness I think lies in this—that whereas e.g. to describe an act as one of keeping a promise or as one of making reparation is to describe it in respect of a character it has in itself, to describe [an act] as producing as much good as possible, is only to do this *verbally*; it is really to describe it as having a character which it possesses only in relation to all the other acts the man can do—the character of producing good in a degree greater than that produced by any of the others.

This difference seems to me vital. The last does not seem to me the character of an action in the way in which the first 3 are. And the difference seems to me one which is paralleled in your distinction between some prima facie duty of a man and his duty *sans phrase*, and, also to be out of place in a list of prima facie duties. Whether the phrase 'prima facie duty' is appropriate for the thing you refer to in your doctrine or not, the thing referred to is some character which an action of a certain kind possesses *in itself* i.e. as an instance of a certain kind and apart from its relatedness to the actions of other kinds possible to a man—a character e.g., due to an act being one of keeping a promise.

And I take your view about duty to be that in a given situation *the* action which it is my duty to do is that out of all the actions which I can, there is the greatest *prima facie duty* to do—so that where some action is what you call 'my duty'—or as I would rather put it *the act* which I am bound to do, or *what* I ought to do, it is so in virtue of having more prima facie obligatoriness than any of the other acts I can do—and so in virtue of a character which the act possesses only in relation to all the others. (cf. Pickard-Cambridge, note 3, p. 150, *Mind*, April, 1932.)

Hence while the basis of a prima facie duty is a character which the action has in itself, i.e. apart from its relation to the others, the basis of a particular act's being 'my' duty is not.

Hence, also, it seems to me, *given* your distinction between *a* prima facie duty of mine and *my* duty, the so-called character of producing as much good as possible, i.e. really the character of producing more good than any other possible action, while it might possibly be maintained to be the basis of some actions being *my* duty, can't be held to be a base of an action being a prima facie duty.

[H. A. Prichard, 'Letter to W. D. Ross', Bodleian Library, University of Oxford, MS Eng. Lett. d. 116 fos. 99 ff.]

[* W. D. Ross, *The Right and the Good*, (Oxford, 1930; repr. 1961, 21. The four are (1) *a* promising (1) *b* reparation, (2) gratitude, (4) beneficence. Ed.]

But, further, strictly speaking I don't see how it can be maintained even to be the basis of the thing called an action being my duty,—i.e. your 'an action being my duty sans phrase'. For to produce more good than any other possible action is to have a certain character in *a greater degree* than certain other actions, and this cannot give rise to anything but a greater degree of something else; yet on your view to say of some act that it is a *prima facie duty* and to say of it that it is *my duty* are to make *qualitatively* different statements.

The truth is that the more I consider it the less I can make sense out of '*the* act which I am bound to do'—as distinct from '*an* act which I ought to do'—and the more I get to think that the only fact corresponding to the phrase 'is the act which I ought to do more than I ought to do any other', and that your 'a prima facie' duty is really a duty, your 'my duty sans phrase' is, really that of a man's duties which he most ought to do, i.e. that so far as these phrases can be made to stand for facts these must be the facts.

I expect the thing to bore you hopelessly. For personally I find that once I have got a thing down in print, the issue ceases to interest me unless I have to re-write it.

May I have this back some time? But *don't* bother to answer unless you feel inclined. My main object has been to get my idea down in black and white.

yrs ever
HAP

Bibliography

REVIEWS OF PRICHARD'S BOOKS

Broad, C. D., 'Critical Notice, H. A. Prichard, *Moral Obligation: Essays and Lectures*', *Mind*, 59 (1950), 555–66.

Dawes Hicks, G., 'Recent Criticism of Kant's Theory of Knowledge' (reviews Sidgwick's *Lectures on the Philosophy of Kant* and Prichard's *Kant's Theory of Knowledge*), *Mind*, 22 (1913), 331–43.

Findlay, J. N., 'Kant and Anglo-Saxon Criticism', in *Kant's Theory of Knowledge*, ed. Beck (Dordrecht: Reidel, 1974).

Hardie, W. F. R., 'H. A. Prichard, *Moral Obligation: Essays and Lectures*', *Philosophy*, 26 (1951), 159–61.

Hawkins, D. J. B., 'The Ethics of H. A. Prichard', *Philosophical Quarterly*, 1 (1950–1), 242–7.

Marvin, W. T., 'Review of H. A. Prichard's *Kant's Theory of Knowledge*', *Philosophical Review*, 18 (1909), 653–8.

Price, H. H., 'Review of H. A. Prichard: *Knowledge and Perception: Essays and Lectures*', *Mind*, 60 (1951), 103–21.

Richardson, E. E., 'Review of H. A. Prichard's *Kant's Theory of Knowledge*', *Journal of Philosophy*, 7 (1910), 359–61.

Walsh, W. H., 'Kant's Critique of Pure Reason, Commentators in English, 1875–1945', *Journal of the History of Ideas*, 42 (1981), 723–37.

Whitely, C. H., 'H. A. Prichard, *Knowledge and Perception, Essays and Lectures*', *Philosophy*, 25 (1950), 358–60.

Woozley, A. D., 'H. A. Prichard, *Knowledge and Perception, Essays and Lectures*', *Philosophical Quarterly*, 1 (1950–1), 172–3.

OBITUARIES

Carritt, E. F., 'Professor H. A. Prichard Personal Recollections: A Memorial', *Mind*, 57 (1948), 146–8.

Price, H. H., 'Harold Arthur Prichard, 1871–1947', *Proceedings of the British Academy*, 33 (1947), 331–50.

Ross, W. D., 'Harold Arthur Prichard', *Dictionary of National Biography* (London: Oxford University Press, 1941–50), 697–8.

The Times, (London), 'Prichard, Harold Arthur, Death, December 31', 2 Jan. 1947, 6–7. [W. D. Ross and the author of *Who was Who?* obituary report the date of death as 29 Dec. 1947. Price writes in his memorial 'He died at the end of December, 1947'. Ed.]

Who was Who?, iv (London: Adam and Charles Black, 1941–50; repr. 1967), 938.

BIBLIOGRAPHY

SECONDARY LITERATURE

Allen, Paul, *Proof of Moral Obligation in 20th Century Philosophy* (New York: Lang, 1988).
Alston, W., 'What's Wrong with Immediate Knowledge?', *Synthese*, 55 (1983), 73–95.
Armstrong, A. M., 'Usage and Duty', *American Philosophical Quarterly*, 2 (1965), 74–80.
Atiyah, P. S., *Promises, Morals and Law* (Oxford: Oxford University Press, 1983).
Atkinson, R. F., *Conduct: An Introduction to Moral Philosophy* (Toronto: MacMillan, 1969).
Aune, Bruce, 'Prichard, Action, and Volition', *Philosophical Studies*, 25 (1974), 97–115.
—— *Reason and Action* (Dordrecht: Reidel, 1977).
Austin, J. L., 'Agathon and Eudaimonia in the *Ethics* of Aristotle', in J. M. E. Moravcsik (ed.), *Aristotle: A Collection of Critical Essays* (New York: Anchor Books, 1967).
—— *Sense and Sensibilia* (reconstructed from the manuscript notes by G. J. Warnock) (Oxford: Clarendon Press, 1962).
Baier, K., 'Doing My Duty' *Philosophy*, (1951), 253–60.
—— *The Moral Point of View* (Ithaca, NY: Cornell University Press, 1958).
Baldwin, T., *G. E. Moore* (London: Routledge, 1992).
Blanshard, B., 'The Impasse in Ethics, and a Way Out', Howison Lecture, 1954 (Berkeley and Los Angeles: University of California Press, 1955).
—— *Reason and Goodness*, ch. 6 (London: George Allen & Unwin, 1966).
Blumfield, Jean Beer, 'Is Acting Willing?', *Nous*, 17, (1983), 183–95.
Bradley, F. H., *Ethical Studies* (Oxford: Clarendon Press, 1876; repr. 1962).
Brandt, R., *A Theory of the Good and the Right*, (Oxford: Clarendon Press, 1979).
Brink, David O., 'Moral Realism and the Sceptical Arguments from Disagreement and Queerness', *Australian Journal of Philosophy*, 62 (1984), 111–125.
Broad, C. D., *Broad's Critical Essays in Moral Philosophy*, ed. D. Cheney (London: George Allen & Unwin, 1971).
Campbell, C. A., 'Moral Intuition and the Principle of Self-Realization', Henriette Hertz Lecture, *Proceedings of the British Academy* (1948), 1–34.
Cargile, J., 'In Reply to a defense of Skepticism', *Philosophical Review*, 81 (1972), 229–36.
Carritt, E. F., *Theory of Morals* (Oxford: Oxford University Press, 1928).
—— *Morals and Politics* (Oxford: Clarendon Press, 1935).
—— *Ethical and Political Thinking* (Oxford: Clarendon Press, 1947).
Collingwood, R. G., *An Autobiography*, ch. III, 'Minute Philosophers'; ch. VI, 'The Decay of Realism' (Oxford: Oxford University Press Paperback, 1970).
Cook Wilson, J., *Statement and Inference, with Other Philosophical Papers*, ed. A. S. L. Farquharson, 2 vols. (Oxford: Clarendon Press, 1926; repr. 1969).
Copelston, F., *History of Philosophy*, viii (London: Burns and Oates, 1966), 383–6.
Cua, A. S., 'The Concept of Moral Intuition', *Philosophical Quarterly*, (India), 35 (1962–3), 151–66.
—— *Reason and Virtue: A Study in the Ethics of Richard Price*, 'Appendix On Arguments Re. Moral Intuition' (Athens, Ohio: University Press, 1966).
Cunningham, Stanley, 'Does Moral Philosophy Rest upon a Mistake Make an Even Greater Mistake?', *Monist*, 54 1 (1970), 86–99.
Dahl, N. O., 'Obligation and Moral Worth: Reflections on Prichard and Kant', *Philosophical Studies*, 50, (1986), 369–99.
Daly, C. B., 'Inter-War British Ethics: The Oxford Intuitionists', *Philosophical Studies* (Ireland), 14 (1965), 55–87.

Dancy, Jonathan, 'Two Conceptions of Moral Realism', *Proceedings of the Aristotelian Society*, suppl. 60 (1986), 167–88.
—— *Moral Reasons* (Oxford: Blackwell, 1993).
—— *Practical Reality* (Oxford: Blackwell, 2000).
Dicker, Georges, 'Seeing Bodies Move', *Personalist*, 54 (1973), 111–22.
Edwards, P. (ed.), *Encyclopedia of Philosophy*, 8 vols. (New York and London: Macmillan and Free Press, 1967).
Ewing, A. C., 'Reason and Intuition', *Proceedings of the British Academy*, (1941).
—— *The Definition Of Good* (London: Routledge and Kegan Paul, 1948).
—— *Ethics* (London: English Universities Press, 1953).
—— *Second Thoughts in Moral Philosophy* (New York: Macmillan, 1959).
Falk, W. D., ' "Ought" and Motivation', *Proceedings of the Aristotelian Society*, 48 (1948), 111–38.
—— *Ought, Reasons and Morality: The Collected Papers*, foreword by Kurt Baier (Ithaca, NY: Cornell University Press, 1986).
Fox, R. M., and DeMarco, J. P., *The Immorality of Promising* (Amherst, NY: Humanity Books, 2000).
Frankena, W. K., *Ethics* (Engelwood Cliffs, NJ: Prentice-Hall, 1963).
—— 'Prichard and the Ethics of Virtue', *Monist*, 54 (1970), 1–17.
—— 'The Carus Lectures', *Monist*, 63 (1980), 3–68.
Fried, Charles, *Contract as Promise* (Boston: Harvard University Press, 1981).
Gass, W. H., 'The Case of the Obliging Stranger', *Philosophical Review*, 68 (1957), 193.
Gauthier, D., *Practical Reasoning* (Oxford: Clarendon Press, 1963).
—— *Morals by Agreement* (Oxford: Clarendon Press, 1986).
Green, T. H., *Prolegomena to Ethics*, ed. A. C. Bradley (Oxford: Clarendon Press, 1884).
—— *Lectures on the Principles of Political Obligation* (London: Longmans, 1941; repr. 1963).
Gustafson, Don, 'Prichard, Davidson and Action', *Philosophical Investigations* (1991) 205–30.
Hamlyn, D. W., 'The Obligation to Keep a Promise', *Proceedings of the Aristotelian Society*, 62 (1962), 179–94.
Hanfling, O., 'Promises, Games and Institutions', *Proceedings of the Aristotelian Society*, (1974–5), 13–31.
Hardie, Frank, 'The Final Good in Aristotle's *Ethics*', in J. M. E. Moravcsik (ed.), *Aristotle: A Collection of Critical Essays* (New York: Anchor Books, 1967).
—— 'Willing and Acting', *Philosophical Quarterly*, 21 (1971), 193–206.
Hare, R. M., *The Language of Morals* (Oxford: Clarendon Press, 1952).
—— *Moral Thinking* (Oxford: Clarendon Press, 1981).
Harman, G., *The Nature of Morality* (New York: Oxford University Press, 1977).
Heintz, L. L., 'Excuses and "Ought" Implies "Can" ', *Canadian Journal of Philosophy*, 5 (1975), 449–62.
Hirst, R., 'Realism', in Edwards (ed.), *Encyclopedia of Philosophy*, vii. 77–83.
Hornsby, Jennifer, *Actions* (London: Routledge and Kegan Paul, 1980).
—— 'The Agent's Independence of the World', pt. II, *Proceedings of the Aristotelian Society*, suppl. 56 (1982), 37–50.
Hudson, W. D., *Ethical Intuitionism* (New York: St Martin's Press, 1967).
—— *Reason and Right* (San Francisco: Freeman Cooper, 1970).

BIBLIOGRAPHY

Hudson, W. D., *A Century of Moral Philosophy* (London: Lutterworth, 1980).
—— *Modern Moral Philosophy* (London: Macmillan, 1983).
Hunt, Lester, 'Generosity', *American Philosophical Quarterly*, 12 (1975), 235–44.
Johnson, O. A., *Rightness and Goodness: A Study in Contemporary Ethical Theory* (The Hague: Nijhoff, 1969).
—— *The Problem of Knowledge* (The Hague: Nijhoff, 1974).
—— 'Is Knowledge Definable?', *Southern Journal of Philosophy*, 9 (1971), 277–86.
Joseph, H. W. B., *Some Problems in Ethics* (Oxford: Oxford University Press, 2nd imp., corrected, 1933).
Kant, I., *Critique of Pure Reason*, trans. J. M. D. Meiklejohn (New York: P. J. Collier & Son, 1902).
—— *Fundamental Principles of the Metaphysic of Morals*, trans. T. K. Abbott, (London: Longmans, Green & Co., 10th edn., 1946).
Kekes, J., *The Morality of Pluralism* (Princeton: Princeton University Press, 1993).
Krutzen, R. W., 'In Defense of Common Moral Sense', *Dialogue*, 38 (1999), 235–69.
Langford, G., *Human Action* (New York: Anchor, 1971).
Laird, John, *Enquiry into Moral Notions* (New York: AMS Press, 1936; repr. 1970).
Lemos, Ramon, 'Duty and Ignorance', *Southern Journal of Philosophy*, 18 (1980), 301–12.
Lewis, D., 'Some Problems of Perceptions', *Philosophy of Science*, 37 (1970), 100–13.
Lucas, J., 'The Philosophy of the Reasonable Man', *Philosophical Quarterly*, 13 (1963), 97–106.
—— 'Ethical Intuitionism', *Philosophy*, 46 (1971), 1–10.
Mabbott, J. D., *An Introduction to Ethics* (London: Hutchinson University Library, 1966).
MacAdam, J., 'H. A. Prichard', in L. and C. Becker (eds.), *Encyclopedia of Ethics*, ii, (New York: Garland, 1992); repr. (New York: Routledge, 2001).
—— 'Harold Arthur Prichard 1871–1947', in Edward Craig (ed.), *Routledge Encyclopedia of Philosophy*, vii (London: Routledge, 1998).
MacIntyre, A., *A Short History of Ethics* (New York: Macmillan, 1968).
—— *After Virtue* (Notre Dame, Ind.: University of Notre Dame Press, 1981).
McKellar, Stewart J., 'Duty and Interest', *Australian Journal of Philosophy*, 7 (1929), 220–5.
Mackie, J., *Ethics, Inventing Right and Wrong* (Harmondsworth: Penguin, 1983).
Mackinnon, D. M., *A Study in Ethical Theory* (London: Adam & Charles Black, 1957).
McNaughton, David, *Moral Vision: An Introduction to Ethics* (Oxford: Blackwell, 1996).
—— 'An Unconnected Heap of Duties?', *Philosophical Quarterly*, 46 (1996), 433–47.
Martineau, J., *Types of Ethical Theory* (Oxford: Clarendon Press, 1885).
Melden, A. I., 'Willing', *Philosophical Review*, 69 (1960), 475–84.
—— 'Willing and Acting', *Philosophical Quarterly*, 21 (1971), 193–206.
Monson, C. H., Jun., 'Prichard, Green and Moral Obligation', *Philosophical Review*, 63 (1954), 74–87.
Moore, G. E., *Principia Ethica* (Cambridge: Cambridge University Press, 1903; repr. 1980).
—— *Ethics* (London: Oxford University Press, 1912; repr. 1949).
Mothersill, M., 'Duty' in Edwards (ed.), *Encyclopedia of History*, iv. 442–4.
Muirhead, J. H., *Rule and End in Morals* (Oxford: Clarendon Press, 1932).
—— 'The New Deontology', *Ethics*, 50 (1940), 441–9.

Murdoch, Iris, 'Vision and Choice in Morality', pt, II, *Proceedings of the Aristotelian Society*, suppl. 30 (1956), 32–58.

Nagel, T., 'The Limits of Objectivity', in S. Murrin (ed.), *The Tanner Lectures on Human Values*, i (Salt Lake City: University of Utah Press, 1980).

—— The View from Nowhere (New York: Oxford University Press, 1986).

Narveson, Jan, 'The Agreement to Keep our Agreements: Hume, Prichard, and Searle', *Philosophical Papers*, 23/2 (1994), 75–87.

Nielsen, K., 'Deontological Non-Naturalists, Ethics, History of', in Edwards (ed.), *Encyclopedia of Philosophy*, iii. 102.

Nowell-Smith, P. A., *Ethics* (Harmondsmith: Penguin, 1961).

Passmore, J. A., 'Cook Wilson and Oxford Philosophy', in *A Hundred Years of Philosophy* (London: Gerald Duckworth, 1957), ch. 10.

Pearl, Leon, 'Objective and Subjective Duty', *Mind*, 80 (1971) 413–17.

Pickard-Cambridge, W. A., 'Two Problems about Duty', pts I–III, *Mind*, 41 (1932), 72, 145, 311.

Price, H. H., 'The Appeal to Common Sense', pts I–II, *Philosophy*, 5 (1930), 24–35, 191–202.

Prior, A. N., 'The Virtue of the Act and the Virtue of the Agent', *Philosophy*, 26 (1951), 121–30.

—— *Logic and the Basis of Ethics* (Oxford: Clarendon Press, 1961).

Quinton, A., 'Contemporary British Philosophy', in D. J. O'Connor (ed.), *A Critical History of Western Philosophy* (London: Collier Macmillan, 1964), 533.

—— 'Cook Wilson School, British Philosophy', in Edwards (ed.), *Encyclopedia of Philosophy*, i. 392.

—— 'Is Knowledge Definable? Knowledge and Belief', in Edwards (ed.), *Encyclopedia of Philosophy*, iv. 348.

Raphael, D. D., *Moral Judgement* (London: George Allen & Unwin, 1955).

—— *Moral Philosophy* (Oxford: Oxford University Press, 1981).

—— 'Les Intuitionnistes d'Oxford', *Archives de philosophie*, 57/2 (1994), 281–93.

Rashdall, H., *The Theory of Good and Evil*, 2 vols. (Oxford: Oxford University Press, 1924).

Rees, D. A., 'The Idea of Objective Duty', *Proceedings of the Aristotelian Society*, 52 (1952), 71–94.

Robinson, N. H. G., 'The Moral Situation', *Philosophy*, 24 (1949), 335–41.

Ross, W. D., *The Right and the Good* (Oxford: Clarendon Press, 1930).

—— *Foundations of Ethics* (Oxford: Clarendon Press, 1939).

Scanlon, T. M., 'Self-Anchored Morality', in J. B. Schneewind (ed.), *Reason, Ethics, and Society: Themes From Kurt Baier* (Chicago: Open Court, 1996).

Scheffler, S., *The Rejection of Consequentialism* (Oxford: Clarendon Press, 1982).

Schilpp, P. A. (ed.), *Philosophy of Brand Blanshard* (La Salle, Ju.: Open Court, 1980).

Schneewind, J. B., *The Invention of Autonomy: A History of Moral Philosophy* (Cambridge: Cambridge University Press, 1998).

—— 'First Principles and Common-Sense Morality in Sidgwick's Ethics', *Archiv für Geschichte de Philosophie*, 45 (1963), 137–156.

Schwarz, S. D., 'Does Prichard's Essay Rest on a Mistake?', *Ethics*, 81 (1970–1971), 169–80.

Selby-Bigge, L. A. (ed.) *British Moralists*, 2 vols. (Oxford: Clarendon Press, 1897).

Sidgwick, H., *The Methods of Ethics* (London: Macmillan, 1874; repr. 1962).

Sidgwick, H., *Outlines of the History of Ethics* (London: Macmillan, 1902: repr. Indianapolis: Hackett, 1988).
—— *Lectures on the Ethics of T. H. Green, Mr. Herbert Spencer and J. Martineau* (London: Macmillan, 1902; New York: Kraus Reprint, 1968).
Sievert, D., 'Does Prichard's Essay Rest upon a Confusion?' *Ratio*, 14 (1972), 172–85.
Smith, T. V., *Beyond Conscience* (New York: McGraw-Hill, 1934).
Sinnot-Armstrong, W. and Timmons, M. (eds.), *Moral Knowledge?* (Oxford: Oxford University Press, 1996).
Stout, A. K., 'Ross, William David', in Edwards (ed.), *Encyclopedia of Philosophy*, vii. 216–17.
Stout, G. F., 'Mr. Prichard's Criticism of Psychology', *Mind*, 16 (1907), 236–43.
Stoutland, F. M., 'The Logical Connection Argument', *American Philosophical Quarterly*, 4 (1970), 117–30.
Strawson, P., 'Ethical Intuitionism', *Philosophy*, 24 (1949), 23–33.
Taylor, P. (ed.), *The Moral Judgment* (Englewood Cliffs, NJ: Prentice-Hall, 1965).
Urmson, J. O., 'Saints and Heroes', in A. I. Melden (ed.), *Essays in Moral Philosophy* (Washington: University of Washington, 1958).
—— 'A Defence of Intuitionism', *Proceedings of the Aristotelian Society*, 75 (1974–5), 111–19.
—— 'Prichard and Knowledge' in J. Dancy, J. M. E. Moravcsik, and C. C. W. Taylor (eds.), *Human Agency* (Stanford: Stanford University Press, 1988), 11–24.
—— 'Hare on Intuitive Moral Thinking', in D. Seanor and N. Fotion (eds.), *Hare and Critics*, (Oxford: Clarendon Press, 1988).
—— and Ree, J. 'Prichard, Harold Arthur', (1871–1947) in J. O. Urmson and J. Ree (eds.), *The Concise Encyclopedia of Western Philosophy & Philosophers* (London: Routledge, 1993), 266.
Warnock, G., *Contemporary Moral Philosophy* (New York: St Martin's, 1967).
Warnock, M., *Ethics since 1900* (London: Oxford University Press, 1960, 1978).
Wedar, Sven, *Duty and Utility: A Study in English Moral Philosophy* (Lund: Gleerup, 1952).
Welbourne, Michael, 'Knowing and Believing', *Philosophy*, 55 (1980), 317–28.
Whitely, C. H., 'On Duties', *Proceedings of the Aristotelian Society*, 53 (1952–3), 95–104.
Whittemore, Robert C., 'Does the Neo-Intuitionist Theory of Obligation Rest on a Mistake?', *Tulane Studies in Philosophy*, 6 (1957), 101–27.
Williams, B., *Morality: An Introduction* (London: Harper, 1972).
—— *Ethics and the Limits of Philosophy* (London: Fontana Paperback, 1985).
—— 'What does Intuitionism Imply?', in J. Dancy, J. M. E. Moravcsik, and C. C. W. Taylor (eds.), *Human Agency* (Stanford: Stanford University Press, 1988).
Winch, Peter, 'Trying and Attempting', *Proceedings of Aristotelian Society*, suppl. 45 (1971), 209–27.
Wong, D., *Moral Relativity* (Berkeley and Los Angeles: University of California Press, 1984).
Wolgast, E., 'Perceiving and Impressions', *Philosophical Review*, 67 (1958), 226–36.

Index

action, consciously originate a new state of affairs 1, conscious origination of something 12, 28, 66, 84–5, 96, direct vs. indirect 85, setting myself to 97, choice 39, decision 39, attitude 55, distinct from motive 8, 12, 21, 202, effecting 218, 277, Green 39, Aristotle 103, two senses 155, Joseph 199, deliberate action 39, 239, desire 253, 278, promising 257, takes time 268, willing 270, what is acting? 272, causing 272, is willing 274, willing is sui generis 274, my moving my hand and my hand moving 275, not originating or causing 277, trying 279

acts, kind of 12–13, 23, a particular action of a certain kind 29, 48, 77, 84–5, 121–2, 140–1, 180, 226, purpose 184

Aristotle 14, 16, 17, 22, 36, 47, 59, 61, 102–13, 114, 185, 187, happiness 170, 180–1, 183, 187, 190, 277, 280–1

Bentham, J. 183, 187, 189–90, 208
Bosanquet, B. 187
Bradley, F. H. 163
Butler, J. 8, 22, 27, 30, 33, 39, 125, 163, 170, moral knowledge versus self-interest 34–6, 130, 134, 170–2, 204, law 52, 121–2, motive 129, good 154, 208, virtue 160, 216

Clarke, S. 245, 246
common-sense morality, real moral convictions 2, moral convictions of ordinary life 24, 30, ordinary moral convictions 27, 29–30, 46, 91, 121, ordinary moral rules 50, current moral rules 84, ordinary unreflective moral convictions 130, of different races 124, doubt 125, test of 125, & Sidgwick 133, ordinary moral ideas 227, our ordinary convictions 230

consequence(s) 1, 12, 81, and intuition 137
Collingwood, R. G. 93
Cook Wilson, J. 26, 115, 253, 255, 272–4, 276, 279, 284
Cudworth, R. 245

Descartes, R. 8, 18, 124
duty 22, conflict of duties 77, 92, 252, if only one 78, claim 79, 252, ignorance of facts 80–1, objective 81–7, 92, form of moral rule 86, facts 87, only if able to do it 86, subjective 87–90, without knowing 88, form of moral rule 88, not in the sense that no acts are really right or wrong 89, consider circumstances 91–2, ordinary thought 94, the main questions 114, Plato & Aristotle 114, moral convictions 119, unreflective 119, sense of 129, political 226, prima facie 286–7, as much good as possible 286–7

goodness, maximum effect of 1, 9, act itself 3, 8, 9, 10, immediate apprehension of virtues and good dispositions 20, intrinsically good 11, common good 42, 193–6, 239, moral and virtuous 61, 218, Aristotle 106, 109, rational benevolence 146–9, Universal Good 147–51, right and good 151, good will 153, 160, two meanings 160, 172–6, criterion of 185, three views 208, 215,

225, public good 237, as much good as possible 286–7

Green, T. H. 21, 22, 36, 39, agrees with Plato 42–3, 45, & Aristotle 109, 113, 144, 153, 183, 187, 190–3, common good 193–6, 239, no common good unless individuals are identical 241, 243–4, 248, 249, Principles 226, totally inconsistent with our ordinary moral ideas 227, 230, Social Contract Theory 228, personal good 239, 242, 247, deliberate action 239, 274, 278, society 244, will, not force 249

Grote, J. 142

happiness 8, 9, 23, 110, replies to Sidgwick's general happiness 136, psychological hedonism, Hedonist 239

Hegel, G. W. F. 21

Hobbes, T. 169, 183, 236, 245, 246, 247–8, 249

Hume, D., virtuous motive 161–2, 164–5, 167–9, 216, 220–1, 262, 266, 274

Hutcheson, F. 8, 22, 116, virtue 154, 160–1, 162, 169, 208, 215, 216

intuition 4, the sense of obligation to do, or of the rightness of, an action of a particular kind is absolutely underivative or immediate 4, 6, 12–13, 20, 75, 100, 122, self-evident 4, 13, 20, sense of obligation, involves no purpose or end 14, of virtues and good dispositions 20, a particular obligation 63, greater duty 79, and Plato 33, consequences 137, and Sidgwick 137, & universals 201

James, W. 274–6, 277, 279–80

Jeans, Sir James 94

Joseph, H. W. B. 169, unconnected heap 185, 199–203, 209–11, 213–14, 222–3, 225

justice 2, 10, 22, 24, 30–1, 176, fairness 248

Kant, I., mistake 1, 3, 9, and good will 11, 153, good based on right 14, self-interest 22, 28–9, 37–8, 48–9, involves an inversion 29, 158, two meanings of 'ought' 34, 126–7, 165–7, 237, categorical & hypothetical 53–5, 74, 126, 129–30, 133, 134, 165–7, 237, holy will, untenable 55, never merely as a means 57, freedom 64, freewill vs. free choice 70, law 52–3, 116, 127, 154, 169, two meanings of law 71, sense of obligation, rational emotion 73, 129, good 153–60, 175, 208, 215, 219, if capable of action then duty 159, 175, 187, 208, 215, 216, inversion 219–20,

knowledge, direct apprehension 2, ascertaining by instances 2, 5, 18, 20, inevitable immediacy of 19, no Theory of Knowledge 18–19, parallel 18–19, unquestioning frame of mind 23, knowing vs. thinking 24, Cook Wilson, theory of knowledge 284, representation 284, cannot construct knowing 284–5, theory of, a fallacy 284–5

Laird, J. 47, 210, 213, 224

Locke, J. 115, 230, 244, 274, 278

Macmurray, J. 273, 275

Martineau, J. 11, 154, 161, 215, 216, 221

Mill, J. S. 8, morality needs a sanction 36, end 103, 109, 113, 143–4, 183, 184, 187, 190–1

mistake, no general answer 1, parallel 7, 17, 19, no common reason 1, no Theory of Knowledge 7, 284, not by an argument 13, no common character of duties 84, but important for theory 84, self-interest, only motive 130

Mitchell, W. 253, 255

Moore, G. E. 47, 152–3, 176, 208, 210–13, 217, 224

moral thinking 12–13, 19, 20, 77

morality, and virtue are independent 15–16, forms of moral rule 86, 88 motive, moral 3, 35–6, 'good' refers to 11, desire that moves us to act 15, in the strict sense 16, virtuously and morally 11, 16, 218, Kant and sense of duty 37–8, duty and virtue 160, Green 191, 198, Joseph 199, versus action 218

Muirhead, J. H., teleological, 186–9

obligation(s), what is in our power 3, 4, freedom of choice 67, morally bound 36, 115, 164, conflicting 6, 14, 77, over-ridden 64, 252, always particular, imply a principle 4, 63, not unreal 64, admits of degrees 6, 14, 78, 92, different kinds 13–14, to oneself 13, an unrelated chaos 14, self-evident 14, 20, 115, only to act 16, 95, 198, unreflective consciousness 19, sense of 12, 73, plurality of 77, 83, what is? 114, unreal question 115–16, of men of different races 124, *sui generis* 115–16, 169, teleological 185, unconnected heap 185, quasi-teleological 197, three theories 208, Price 215–16, not a characteristic of ourselves 222, political 226, not one common ground, 250–2, legal and moral 169, 227–8, natural rights and obligations 229, 245–6, promising 257, giving 257, exchanging 266–7, time of 268

ought, only from another 'ought' 9, 47, if ought then can 67, 77, refers to actions alone 10, what we ought, not as we ought 12, Kant 34, ought-to-be-doneness 99, two senses 34, 43, 123, 126–7, 143–5, 188, poisoner's dose 126, obligation, Hume 164–5, 215–16, ought-to-existness 168, 221, 223, 225, Social Contract 228–9, oughting 268, ought and willing 282–3

Paley, W. 8, 169
Paulsen, F., teleological 186

Plato 7, 8, 17, 21, 22–7, 42–3, 48, 125, 163, 192, underlying identity with Sophists 25, 30–6, 38, 39, 45, 120, law 52, end 103–4, 114, 120, 187, 188, 189, self interest 123, 130, motive 129, obligation 172, 176, justice 117, 176–80, personal happiness 102, 172, 181–3, 184, 241, Crito 251, desire 278

Pickard-Cambridge, W. A. 286
Price, R. 208, 215–16, oughtness 216
promise, seems to create an obligation 257, not 'expectation' 258–9, not 'resolve' 258–9, nor true or false 258, doing something 258, general promise 260, binding myself 260, 264, presupposes obligation, 261, without language 262–4, exchanging 266

Rashdall, H. 9, 208, 210, 213, 223–4
rightness, independent of motive 3, 11, 35–6, 59, dilemma of benevolence 11, concerns narrower and commoner sense, merely the conscious origination of something 11–12, two necessary preliminaries 12, thinking vs. knowing right 24, advantageousness and nothing else 27, Kant's criteria 56–8, not deduced from a principle 63, *sui generis* 116, implies oughtness 216, meaning of moral right 228

Ross, W. D., Letter 286
Rousseau, J. J. 234

self-interest, inconclusive and irrelevant 1–2, 22, 123, 128, 130, 181, and preachers 26, Butler's 'cool hour' 27, 121, 170, disinterestedness 37, 241, Kant 62–3, Aristotle, pleasure 102, 109, as psychological hedonist 113, fatal dilemma 122–3, Sidgwick 145–51, Ethical Hedonists 208, 239, Green 42, 109, 113, 239, 242, 247, Mill 109, 113, 239, Shakespeare, W. 16

Sidgwick, H. 124, 130–43, Universal Good & Egoism 147–51, teleological 186, quasi-teleological 197, 199, 203–7
Sophists 23, 30–4, 120
Spencer, H. 116
Spinoza, B. 233
Stewart, J. A. 21
Stout, G. 275–6

test of morality, correspond with our real moral convictions 2, actual moral convictions 10, at variance with our moral consciousness 10, 29, not by an argument 13, 47

truth, in philosophy, only via ruins of the false 1, in morals, the test of instances 216

Utilitarianism, in the broad sense 2, false 2, 14, generic sense 9, 10, and Sidgwick 131, 136, 142, Utilitarians 236

virtue(s) 17, self-evidence 20, parallel immediacy 20

Wallace, W. 21

The Start-Up Formula™

6 easy steps to start your own business

Christine Michaelis

Copyright © August 2016 Christine Michaelis

All rights reserved. No part of this book may be reproduced, stored in a retrieval system, or transmitted, in any form or by any means, electronic, mechanical, photocopying, recording or otherwise, without the prior written permission of the copyright owner.

ISBN-13: 9781537695976
ISBN-10: 1537695975

ENDORSEMENTS

"When you start out in business, you'll often get conflicting advice or feel confused about how to prioritise your activities. Christine's book gives you simple tools to set up the foundations for your business, get clear on your customers, and get to grips with your marketing. By working through the book, you'll find it easy to follow established processes, answer powerful questions and work through useful checklists. A great starting point for new businesses."
Karen Williams, The Book Mentor, Librotas
www.librotas.com

"Drawing on her 4 years as an entrepreneur and extensive experience in coaching and mentoring start-ups, the Start-Up Formula provides bags of encouragement and advice along with plenty of practical tools to help anyone start to set up their own business."
Dave Stanbury, Head of Employability, University of Essex www.essex.ac.uk/careers

"This book contains lots of helpful advice and ideas to structure your progression into starting your own business. Christine guides you through the maze of information and thought processes involved, to give you, the reader, clarity, focus and purpose."
Brenda Coombes, Director, Andraste Accounting
www.andraste-accounting.com

"Christine managed to put through the six steps of her new book all the contagious energy that people find when they speak with her. This is a book I will recommend to my students of Entrepreneurship which will certainly inspire the creation of new start-ups."
Lara Ligeiro, Entrepreneurship Office of NOVA University of Lisbon
http://www.unl.pt/en/entrepreneurship

"With the clever use of the acronym "CHANGE" - representing the six easy steps to start your own business - Christine develops in her book the positive, informative and personal journey an entrepreneur will travel when beginning the journey of setting up a new business from scratch. Christine's easy and flowing style is a thoroughly enjoyable read. It has many helpful suggestions as to how the entrepreneur can develop personal skills. What particularly resonated with me were the sections on clarity, having the right mindset, staying motivated, and holding onto your own values thus discovering your business values and creating a vision board.
Notwithstanding many years of business experience I took away several "golden nuggets" from the book to add to my knowledge base. I particularly liked the approach Christine took in writing the book using elements of Emotional Intelligence when describing the Entrepreneur's personal development."
Barry van Eupen, Director Meritin Management Limited**,** Mentor to Start Up businesses

DEDICATION

I dedicate this book to everyone who is **brave enough to start his or her own business**. Don't give up! It's worth it.

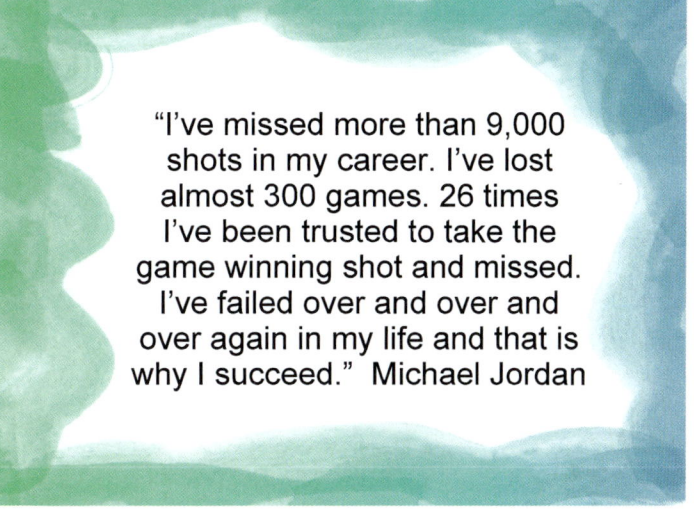

"I've missed more than 9,000 shots in my career. I've lost almost 300 games. 26 times I've been trusted to take the game winning shot and missed. I've failed over and over and over again in my life and that is why I succeed." Michael Jordan

CONTENT

Foreword	7
Acknowledgements	9
Introduction	10
Step 1 – Clarity	17
Step 2 – Hold on to your values	28
Step 3 – Analyse who you want to work with	38
Step 4 – Narrow down the steps involved	49
Step 5 – Grow your confidence	65
Step 6 – Engage your audience	79
About Christine	86
Further support	88

FOREWORD

Thank you for buying this book. I assume that you are about to start your own business or have already started, but are **overwhelmed** with it all? You don't know where to start? You have quit your current full-time job or are about to? You are looking for new challenges in your life and starting your own business seems like a good choice, but you are also **a bit scared** of it?

Believe me, I know how that feels. I was once at that point and I still am sometimes.

There is so much information out there and I want to **make it easy for you**. That's why I have developed **The Start-Up Formula™ 'CHANGE – 6 easy steps to start your own business.'**

Having your own business means a lot of work, but if you do something that you love and are passionate about, it is worth it.

By now, I have helped hundreds of individuals by validating their start-up idea and bringing it to life, as well as marketing it successfully.

The way to use this book is to read through it once to get a better understanding how it works and then start at the beginning again and work your way through it **step by step**, doing all the exercises. But it is totally up to you.

You might want to get stuck in right away and get started working your way through it step by step, rather than reading it first.

This book is designed to follow the steps in order. It is packed with lots of **practical tips and exercises.**

I hope this book will make it much **easier for you to start your own business** by breaking it down into manageable chunks.

Your marketing and creative start-up Coach – Christine

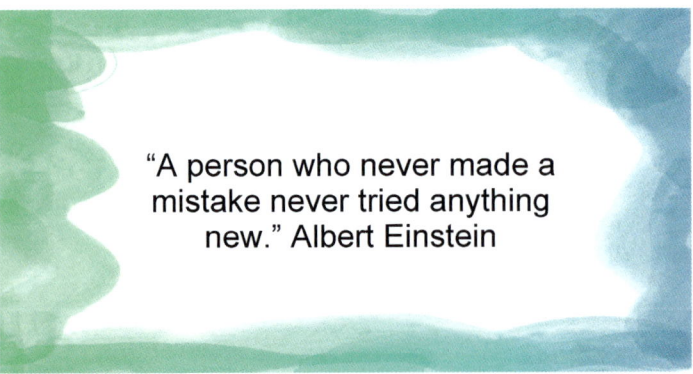

"A person who never made a mistake never tried anything new." Albert Einstein

ACKNOWLEDGEMENTS

First of all, I would like to thank my **mum, my dad and my sister** for their ongoing support. My family is amazing and is always there for me – no matter what life throws at me. They are all very strong and I am extremely proud of every single one of them. Especially my mum, who is basically superwoman.

A big thank you to **Brenda Coombes** who was kind enough to proof read the book.

Another acknowledgement goes to my friend **Magdalena Mahdy** whose opinion I highly value – for personal and professional matters. And a thank you to her for helping me with my book cover. She is a dear friend and colleague who helps wedding photographers in their start-up journey.
www.lovethatsmilephotography.com

Thank you, **Karen Williams** for the book 'Your book is the hook'. It was a massive help for me to get this book finished. And without your online course I would not have developed the six steps.

INTRODUCTION

1. WHY START YOUR OWN BUSINESS?

I would like to start this book with why it is great to start your own business, because once you think you want to do it, and evaluate if you really want to do it, you might get put off by everything that is involved. So, let me point out to you why it is great to start something by yourself.

BE YOUR OWN BOSS
This might be obvious but I would like to state it anyway. **You will be your own boss**; you won't work for someone else, as you will work for yourself. This keeps most people motivated when they hit the stage where it might not be going as planned.

SELF-EXPRESSION
It will give you the chance to **fully be yourself** and express yourself in ways you might not be able to when you are employed.

DO WHAT YOU LOVE
Most people that start their own business will do so out of a **passion**. They will do something that they love and they have found a way to make a living out of it. That is certainly what happened in my case.

INSPIRE
You have the chance to **impact** people directly through your work and **inspire** them. Being an inspiration to others is very rewarding.

throughout the book and links for **downloadable resources** for **further support**. This is a very **practical book** that will help you in the real world, rather than giving you the theory.

And here it is – **The Start-Up Formula™, 'CHANGE'** – an acronym standing for:

Clarity
Hold on to your values
Analyse who you want to work with
Narrow down the steps involved
Grow your confidence
Engage your audience

CLARITY
Find out what makes you **happy** and set yourself a **clear goal**, because having a clear goal helps you to achieve it and to identify when you have achieved it.

HOLD ON TO YOUR VALUES
Discover your **business values**. This will make your decision process much easier and is a good starting point for what you want to stand for.

ANALYSE WHO YOU WANT TO WORK WITH
Define your **ideal clients**, business partners and colleagues, define your tone of voice and know where to find them. It will be the basis for all your marketing activities.

NARROW DOWN THE STEPS INVOLVED
Starting your own business can be **overwhelming**. **Planning** and narrowing down the **steps involved** will help you get things done. It will give you a **good overview** of what is involved.

GROW YOUR CONFIDENCE
Everyone has a low point at some time with their business. You need to **stay motivated** and build up enough confidence to move forward.

ENGAGE YOUR AUDIENCE
Put a **1-year marketing plan** together and know what each marketing activity will cost – in time and money.

In this book, we will go through all the steps. **Enjoy!**

Your marketing and creative start-up Coach – Christine

STEP 1 – CLARITY

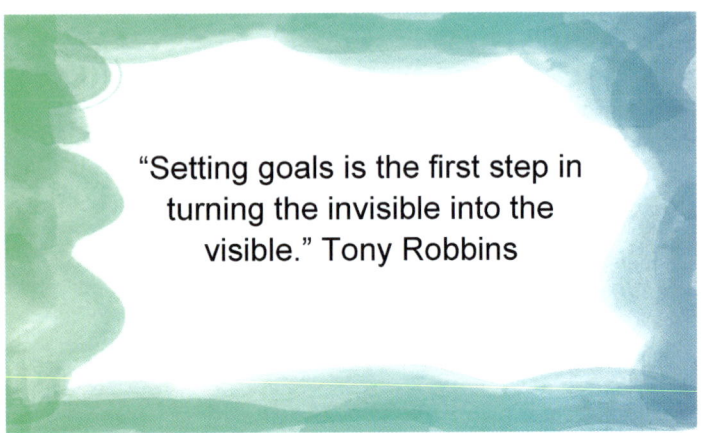

"Setting goals is the first step in turning the invisible into the visible." Tony Robbins

As mentioned in the foreword, the Start-Up Formula™ consists **of 6 easy steps to start your own business**, which are reflected in the acronym 'CHANGE'.

Step 1 of the Start-Up Formula™ is the 'C' in 'CHANGE', which stands for **'Clarity'**.

In this section you are **setting yourself a clear goal.**

1. WHAT DOES CLARITY MEAN?
Well, according to The Oxford English Dictionary:
- The quality of being **clear**
- The quality of being **coherent** and intelligible
- The quality of being **easy to see or hear**
- The quality of being **certain** or definite
- The quality of **transparency** or purity

2. WHY SET A GOAL?
There are different reasons why you should set yourself a goal.

CLARITY
Setting a goal in a 'proper' way will give you lots of **clarity**. You will know what you want, when you can achieve it and how you will achieve it.

PRODUCTIVITY
Having a clear goal helps you to put an **action plan** together and therefore, keeps you **focused** and makes you more productive.

REDUCING STRESS AND MOTIVATING YOU
Knowing what you want in life and what you don't want, will **reduce stress**. It will keep you **motivated** and give you a clear path to take.

WORK-LIFE-BALANCE
If you have set yourself a realistic goal, you will have put an achievable time frame on it, which will automatically lead to a **better Work-Life-Balance,** as

you don't feel the need to do everything at once in an unrealistic time frame.

ACCOUNTABILITY
Setting yourself a clear goal and communicating it, will hold you **accountable** and makes it more likely that you will actually achieve it.

CELEBRATION
When setting yourself a goal, you should also **set rewards for yourself** for achieving it. You should celebrate! Set rewards for milestones – both small and big. Whatever you feel is appropriate for you and what will keep you motivated.

3. WHAT HAPPENS IF YOU DON'T SET A GOAL?
Not having a goal means not knowing what exactly you want, not knowing when you want it and worst of all, not knowing when you have achieved it. You will feel **demotivated**, **lose focus** and work **less efficiently**.

4. HAVING THE RIGHT MINDSET
Setting yourself a goal is a good start. However, if you don't have the right mindset you might sabotage yourself from achieving it.

I have good news! You are in charge of your own mindset. Answer the following questions once you have set yourself a goal:
1. Do I deserve to achieve this goal?
2. Do I really want to achieve this goal?
3. Is this really my goal or someone else's?

If the answer is 'No' to any of these questions, ask yourself why you think this way. Go back to that moment that influenced you that way and change your thinking. Goals that you are setting should ALWAYS be **your own goals**, not somebody else's, because you would be less motivated to achieve them. Remember: You are in charge!

5. HOW TO SET A GOAL
There are different ways of setting a goal and different formulas you can use. You might have heard of the 'SMART' way to set a goal. I much prefer a different acronym as 'SMART', for me, is a bit too corporate.

The acronym I would like to introduce to you is **'ACHIEVE':**

As if now
Clear and specific
Hittable
In a positive direction
Exciting
Verifiable
Ecological

AS IF NOW
Write your goal **as if it has already happened.** Rather than saying 'I want a successful company' or 'I will have a successful company', say 'I have a successful company'. This will put your mind into the right mindset and supports you in subconsciously achieving it.

CLEAR AND SPECIFIC

There is no good setting a goal without including **specifics** because you will never know if you have achieved it. Be as clear and specific as you can.

Put in a **date** and **location**. Put in whom you want to achieve your goal with. Instead of saying you want a 'successful company' state **what kind** of 'successful company'. What **turnover** do you want? How many **staff** do you want? I think you get the gist of it, be **clear and specific**.

Looking at the goal that you have started phrasing 'I have a successful company' now becomes 'It is December 2020 and I have a profitable web design company in Auckland, New Zealand, with 5 staff members, a business partner (INSERT NAME) and a turnover of 500,000 NZD a year.'

You can see how much more specific and clear that is.

HITTABLE

Make sure your goal is **realistic**. Can you actually achieve it in the time frame? Do you have the skills and resources that you need to achieve it? If not, what do you need? Make sure you re-assess it and rethink the timeline. How much time can you invest achieving your goal? Are you still working full time or part-time elsewhere? Look at it from a realistic angle.

IN A POSITIVE DIRECTION
Always phrase your goal in a positive direction. This means, rather than stating what you don't want, you **state what you do want**. For example, don't say 'I don't want to be employed full time' but instead 'I have a profitable web design company...'

EXCITING
Your goal needs to excite you. I mentioned earlier that it always should be your own goal, not somebody else's. This has to do with **motivation**. You are much more motivated if it is your own goal. Have a look at the goal that you have written down and ask yourself: Is this exciting me? Will I be over the moon once I achieve it? If the answer is 'No', I suggest you rephrase it or find a new goal.

VERIFIABLE
Your goal needs to be verifiable. You need to be able to tell if you achieved it or not. This all comes down to how clear and specific you were. Again, once you have written down your goal, ask yourself 'Can I verify that goal? Will I be able to tell if I have achieved it or not?' If the answer is 'No', you need to be more specific.

ECOLOGICAL
Ecological means that you should have a **look at how your environment is affected** by you achieving your goal. Not just looking at material items such as money and your living situation, but also the people that are affected by it, your friends and family. If achieving your goal means, for example that you move to a different

country you have to think about the consequences for your family and friends. Are they ok with you moving to a different country? If not, is it ok for you that they are not ok with it?

6. WHAT TO DO WITH YOUR GOAL
First of all: **Write it down!** Write it down and have it printed off and hung up somewhere where you can see it regularly. Review your goal on a regular basis to see if it is still valid. Your goal is not written in stone. It is your goal and you can amend it or change it completely. It is totally up to you.

7. HOW TO STAY MOTIVATED
Once you have defined your goal, you want to ensure that you will actually achieve it. Here are a few tips to keep you motivated:

BREAK IT DOWN

Break your goal down into **smaller goals** and manageable tasks, whatever you want to call it. That way, your goal does not seem too big and you can start working towards it in smaller steps.

WHO CAN HELP YOU?

Have a think about **who** can help you achieve your goal? A friend, a mentor or an expert? Connect with those people and let them know what you would like them to help you with.

WHAT CAN HELP YOU?
What do you need to achieve your goal? Is there specific hardware or software that you need? Are there any skills you need to acquire and have some training for? Make a list and ensure you obtain them.

PLANNING
Plan things in advance. Once you have a plan in place you can **relax** a bit more and work towards your goal. Every time you think you are not moving forward fast enough, you can calm yourself down by saying 'That is ok, because I have a plan and this bit is planned for this month'.

WHAT IS YOUR BIG 'WHY'?
Why are you doing this? What made you set your goal? There will be a reason and reminding yourself of that reason from time to time will keep you motivated.

VISION BOARDING
Vision boarding is a great visual way to manifest your goal. A vision board is basically a paper flipchart full of things that represent you achieving your goal and showing off your big 'Why' (images, quotes etc.). **Create a vision board** for the goal that you have set yourself and hang it up for you to see.

CHECK YOUR GOAL REGULARLY
As mentioned before, your goal is not written in stone. Check it on a regular basis and make sure it is still **relevant and realistic.**

REPORT TO SOMEONE
Tell someone about your goal and check in with that person on a regular basis to advise them on what steps you have taken towards your goal. That person can be a friend, a family member or a professional, like a mentor or coach.

FEEDBACK SCRAPBOOK
Create a **feedback scrapbook**. This is a physical or digital scrapbook that you create, in which you collect **all positive feedback** that you receive. If you feel demotivated, have a look at it. It will pick you up straight away.

REVIEW YOUR SYSTEM
If you think you are not keeping on track towards your goal, make sure you review your system, the way you work. **You might want to tweak it to be more productive.**

As you can see, I had quite a lot to say about setting your goal, but you need to get this right to be able to move forward and start with Step 2.

Write down your goal here:

STEP 2 – HOLD ON TO YOUR VALUES

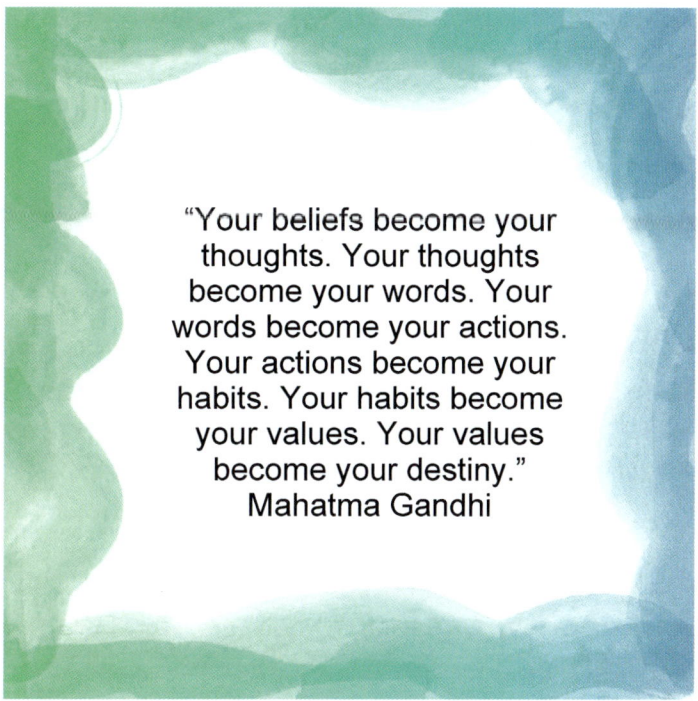

"Your beliefs become your thoughts. Your thoughts become your words. Your words become your actions. Your actions become your habits. Your habits become your values. Your values become your destiny."
Mahatma Gandhi

Step 2 of the Start-Up Formula™ is the 'H' in 'CHANGE', which stands for **'Hold on to your values'**.

In this section you are discovering your **business values.**

1. WHAT ARE VALUES?

According to The Oxford English Dictionary: Values are **principles** of standards of behaviours. They are one's **judgment** of what is important in life.

And another way to define values: They are the basis on which many of our decisions are made and **affect our thoughts and actions**. They define what you and your business stand for.

You can use the exercise that I explain here to discover your personal and your business values. But, as this book is about your start-up, I want you to **focus on your business values**. If the business consists of 'only' you, then your personal values might overlap with your business values. Make sure that you are focusing on your business values. One of my business values for example is 'Professionalism', which I would not have in my personal values.

2. WHY YOU SHOULD DEFINE YOUR VALUES

Knowing your business values will make the **decision processes much easier**. When you have to make a business decision, just ask yourself 'Will this align with my values?' If the answer is 'Yes' go ahead and give it a try. If the answer is 'No', don't do it. Simple.

Your values will also be **the basis for your branding**. It helps you to define what your business stands for.

3. DEFINING YOUR VALUES

I will now explain a way to define your values. This might take a moment to get your head around and I hope I have explained it well enough.

Take several **pieces of paper** or post it notes. **Brainstorm** your **values** and write each value on a different piece of paper/post it note. Ask yourself 'What do I value?' 'What is important to me?' and 'What do I want people to feel when they hear my business name?' Come up with **at least 15 values**.

1. Put the values in **order of importance** to you. Don't spend too much time on this, as it will most probably change.
2. Then take the values that are at position 1 (value 1) and position 2 (value 2). Look at them and ask yourself the question: 'I can have INSERT VALUE 1 but I can't have INSERT VALUE 2', then 'I can have INSERT VALUE 2 but I can't have INSERT VALUE 1'. You basically force yourself to **choose between the two values.** See which sounds right to you. If you can't be without value 2 and it sounds right, move it up a position. It is very important to ask yourself both ways and out loud to see which one sounds better as your brain will then make the decision easier for you.
3. You then take the value that is now at position 2 and the value that is at position 3 and ask yourself the same question again, in both ways. If value 3 moves up, you will then have to

compare it to value 1 to see if it moves up even further.
4. You always decide between the **two values that are next to each other**. And if a position changes, you compare the values that are then next to each other.
5. Once you have done that, you will have your **final order of values.**

4. EXAMPLES OF VALUES
It is important that you **brainstorm your own values first** before you 'get inspired' by other value lists. Otherwise you will limit your mind to the ones that are in front of you and you might forget a very important value.

My business values are:
- Happiness
- Authenticity
- Honesty
- Professionalism
- Passion
- Making a difference
- Integrity
- Fun
- Commitment
- Creativity

And here are a few more examples of values:

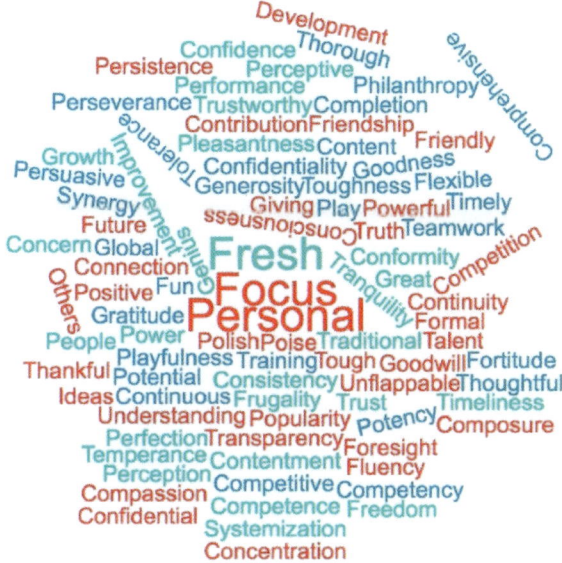

5. WHAT TO DO WITH YOUR VALUES

Once you have your values defined, focus on the **top 10 values** rather than all of them. You now have a good basis in place that will help you with your branding and define what your business stands for.

You can publicise your values in your marketing material so that it is easier for your target audience to understand what you value.

However, if you communicate your values, **make sure you always deliver** on them. There is nothing worse than creating expectations and then under-delivering. If one of your values is 'excellent customer service' and the customer service experience is really bad, it will damage your reputation from the beginning.

List your top 10 values here:

STEP 3 – ANALYSE WHO YOU WANT TO WORK WITH

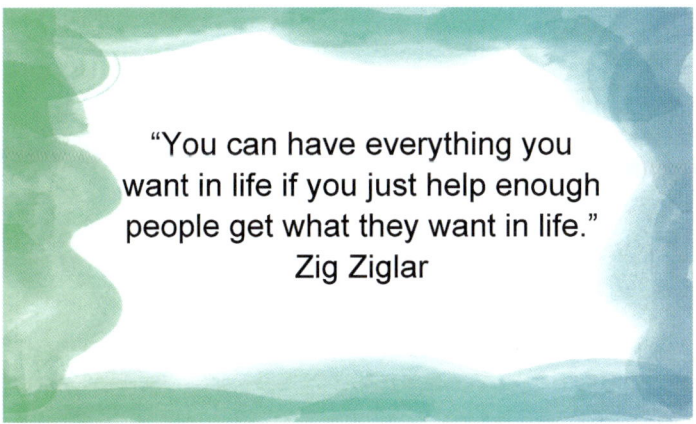

"You can have everything you want in life if you just help enough people get what they want in life."
Zig Ziglar

Step 3 of the Start-Up Formula™ is the 'A' in 'CHANGE', which stands for **'Analyse who you want to work with'**.

In this section you are defining your **ideal client**, business partner and employee.

1. WHY DEFINE YOUR IDEAL CLIENT?
When you know who your ideal client is, it will be **much easier to market** your products and services to your target audience. You will be able to define your **'tone of voice'** – how will you talk to them, what language will you use. It will be much easier to find your ideal client because you will know 'everything' about them. You will **stop wasting money and time** on marketing your products and services to people that will never buy your

products and services. Your ideal client will be the **basis for all your marketing activities.**

And don't worry about narrowing it down too much. Defining your ideal client doesn't mean that you won't work with anyone else; It just means you will attract more of the clients and customers that you ideally want to work with/want to sell your product to.

2. WHAT IF YOU HAVE MORE THAN ONE TARGET GROUP?

That is quite common. However, go through the exercise for all of the target groups separately, as you will reach one target group in a different way to the others. Let's say one of your target groups are CEO's of medium sized businesses and the other is Teenagers. You might reach the CEO's on LinkedIn, whilst you reach the Teenagers via Snapchat.

Just focus on **one target group at a time** in marketing your products and services. What target group to focus on first, you ask? Well, there are different ways to decide that. You might want to start with the most obvious one; maybe you can't target one group without having the other group on board? You might want to start with a particular group, or you have a group, which you already have connections with.

3. WHO IS YOUR IDEAL CLIENT?

Your ideal client is someone that is **in need of your product or service.** You have a **solution** to their problem. It is someone who **is ready** and can afford to

What do they do in their spare time?

What do they **want to do more** of in their spare time?

What do they value?

What is their biggest frustration?

What do they fear?

What do they want less of in their life?

What do they want in their life?

What do they want for their future?

What are their problems?

What are they thinking about themselves?

How can you make their lives better with what you offer?

What pain/problem will your product/service solve for them?

B2B (Business to Business) questions:

What type of organisation would you ideally work with and why?

What industry are they in?

What values do they have?

How many employees to do they have?

What is their turnover?

Where are they located?

What is the company's mission?

Anything else?

6. WRITE DOWN YOUR IDEAL CLIENT:

Write down your ideal client in a paragraph. Create an avatar, give your client a name, age etc. Everything that you have answered above…

STEP 4 – NARROW DOWN THE STEPS INVOLVED

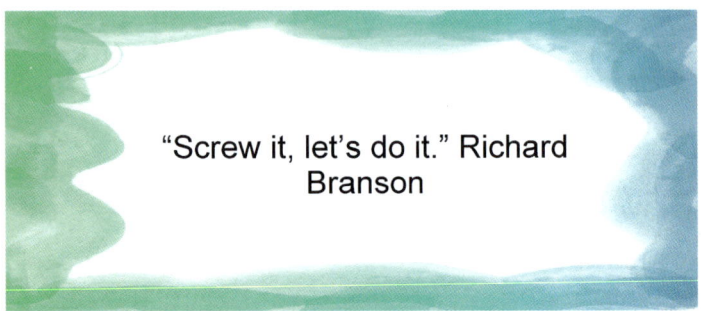

"Screw it, let's do it." Richard Branson

Step 4 of the Start-Up Formula™ is the 'N' in 'CHANGE', which stands for **'Narrow down the steps involved'**.

In this section we will look at the steps involved in starting up your own business.

1. WHAT DOES IT TAKE TO START YOUR OWN BUSINESS?

Starting up your own business is a great thing to do, as you have read in the introduction, but as we all know, it can be quite overwhelming. I will now mention a few points, which I think it takes to start your own business. Please note that this is by no means a complete list.

When starting your own business it helps to be multi-talented or at least be willing (or let me rephrase that) **eager to learn** new things. There is a lot of work involved and it can bring financial **insecurity** with it.

As things might not always go exactly as planned, you will need **passion** to keep **motivated** and high levels of **energy**. Self-determination and **problem solving** skills are essential in my view. You need to be willing to make personal sacrifice and have a **high-risk tolerance**. Self-motivation and **commitment** should go hand in hand with **curiosity** and **flexibility**.

Other useful skills include **networking** skills and **being organised**. A **supportive network** is a must-have. This should be a mixture of business associates, family and friends, as well as external contacts that you have made at networking events.

Don't worry if you don't have all those skills. You can either learn them or outsource things that you won't be able to or don't want to do. Although 'solopreneurs' tend to do everything themselves, it is worth looking into what you can **outsource**.

2. HOW TO NARROW DOWN THE STEPS INVOLVED

There are many methods that you can use. My preferred one is **mind-mapping**. It helps me to brainstorm and write down what pops into my head and then have it nicely structured. If you don't know how mind-mapping works, here is my attempt to describe it to you.

You start with your **central topic** in the middle of your piece of paper. Let's say 'Starting my own business'. From there you have **branches** going out with the different sections, i.e. 'Marketing', 'Finances', 'legal stuff' etc. From each of those branches you then write down what is related to the topic. For example for 'Marketing' you might want to add 'create Facebook account', 'email marketing' etc. and then you can go even further. Let's take 'email marketing'. From here you might want to add the steps involved in doing that, such as 'create newsletter sign up' etc.

This way you can easily write down what pops into your head and it will be organized into the right categories and will be **nicely structured**.

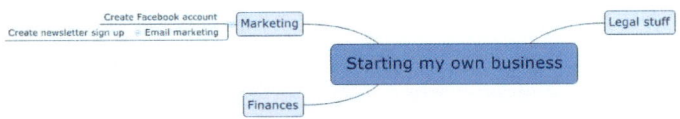

3. THE STEPS INVOLVED
Now, I would like to get into the **nitty gritty** and go through the steps involved. Please note that this is not a complete list but will give you a good start.

MARKET AND COMPETITORS
You need to look at your market and competitors to identify what the **market trends** are, discover **opportunities** and see if you are on the right track. Once you start with your research: **be flexible**. You might have an idea that you find won't work the way you thought it would. Be open to change your idea or

tweak it a bit. Looking at your **competitors** will show you how you can **stand out from the crowd**, finding your **USP (Unique Selling Point).** You can download more information about how to conduct a market and competitor analysis on my website: www.creativestartupacademy.com/freestuff

BUSINESS MODEL
After you have done some research about your competitors, market trends and your customers, you should have a better idea of what you are selling and what business model to use.
Look at your **business processes**, your purpose, what you are offering for what kind of price and what your organisational structure will be. What kind of policies will you have?

YOUR NAME
What will your **business name** be? Will it be something that helps everyone to understand at once what you are doing or does it need explanation? How can you stand out from your competitors with your name? What is appropriate for the industry you are in and your target audience?

VALUES
As you know from Step 2, you should define your **company's values.** It will be the basis for all your business decisions and your branding.

TARGET AUDIENCE

You need to know your target audience inside out. What do they **love**, what do they **hate**, **where** do they live and how much do they earn etc. The better you know them, the easier it will be for you to **target them**. You will have a **good understanding** by now as you went through Step 3.

BUSINESS PLAN

In my opinion, not everyone needs a comprehensive business plan, but everyone should go through certain sections of the business plan. The things I have outlined above are part of that. However, if you want to enter competitions or need investment, they will all ask for a **comprehensive business plan**. Everyone will have different parameters they want you to put in, so I suggest you create a comprehensive business plan that covers all aspects and then adjust it according to the guidelines of each one.

You can download a comprehensive business plan template on my website www.creativestartupacademy.com/freestuff

A good way to begin with your business plan is the **Business Model Canvas** – which is basically a one-page business plan. You can download your copy here: www.businessmodelgeneration.com/canvas

FUNDING
This is a massive topic on its own. You might need funding for your business. The main thing about it is that you **know exactly what you will need the funding for** and **how much** it will be. A **bulletproof** business plan is a must-have for getting funding. You need to know your numbers inside out, have done a good market and competitor analysis to prove that your idea will work and prove that you are the right person to invest in.

INSURANCE
Every business, no matter what legal entity, no matter what kind of products or services are offered, will need some kind of insurance. Make sure you are **covered for the worst-case scenario.**

Obvious ones would be contents insurance to insure all your equipment, possibly public liability and if you are offering advice indemnity insurance. Each industry will have its own insurance that you should have. Talk to more than one insurance broker and see what they think is the **minimum insurance** you should get and what would they **recommend**. What I have learned in the past is to ask a lot of questions to understand everything exactly. For example, I had public liability insurance that was covering me for £1 million. That might sound a lot, but it prevented me from running workshops in certain venues, as they wanted a cover of £2 million. What you don't always know is that if you would like £2 million cover rather than £1 million, it could be only a difference of £2 in the insurance premium (as in my case). **Ask questions** and get more than one quote with different levels of cover. I also recommend reading through all **Terms and Conditions** regardless of how large the document is. Go through them, understand them or ask questions if you don't. Here are a few insurances that might be applicable to you (there are lots more as mentioned above):

- Commercial liability
- Public liability
- Employer's liability
- Product liability
- Indemnity insurance
- Property insurance
- Fidelity guarantee
- Partnership protection
- Motor insurance
- Home insurance

BRANDING
To build **strong relationships** with your customers and to be recognisable, you need to build a strong brand. Branding is not just a logo, it is everything that you do, what you/your business represents, your colours, your way of speaking, your way of dealing with clients and your visual identity etc.

PRODUCTS AND SERVICES
You will need products and services developed that you can offer and charge for; otherwise it is not a business. Think of **different revenue streams and channels**. In my **online course 'Marketing made easy – 6 steps to**

become your own marketing expert', I am going deeper into that topic so that you can explore it a bit more: www.creativestartupacademy.com/courses

GETTING CLIENTS
There is no point of creating a business that is offering great products and services but has no clients. **Sales and marketing** are a massive factor in getting clients. How can you get people to know about you and how can you then **turn** their **interest into sales**?

DOCUMENTS
There are all kind of documents that you will need once you have clients. Things like code of conduct, agreements, contracts, invoice templates etc. Make a **list** of **everything** that you can think of that you might need.

LEGAL ENTITY
There are different legal entities that you can choose and they might be called differently in different countries. You need to **find out what will be best entity for you.** It all depends on how many people are involved in the business, what you are offering, where you are offering it and how much money is involved. Here are a few examples (based on UK legislation). Please have a look at your Government website to check for latest updates on rules and regulations regarding legal entities. Please note that this is not a complete list of legal entities and does not provide all rules and responsibilities.

SOLE TRADER
- You operate as a self-employed individual
- All profits go to you
- Personal liability for all debts
- Taxed as individual responsible for their own tax

LIMITED COMPANY
- At least one shareholder and one director
- Personal liability is limited to the shareholding in the company
- Company is liable for debts
- Pays corporation tax
- May be a more tax efficient entity

PARTNERSHIPS
- Run by more than one individual
- Unlimited liability for the partners
- Partners are taxed as individuals responsible for their own tax

LIMITED LIABILITY PARTNERSHIP
- Run by more than one individual
- Limited liability for the partners
- Partners are taxed as individuals responsible for their own tax

SOCIAL ENTERPRISE
- Operates for a social purpose
- Some of the profits are re-invested into the operation or the community

CHARITY
- Operates for a social purpose
- All the profits are re-invested into the operation or the community
- Mainly funded by grants

INTELLECTUAL PROPERTY
This is a topic that you should get **proper advice** on. Depending on what you are offering, you can protect your idea in different ways, and these can change from time to time. For UK businesses, you can go onto www.ipo.gov.uk to get some more information. Here are a few ways to protect your idea and the basics. Please note that this is not a complete list and is also not meant as legal advice. **Make sure you inform yourself** about what is the correct way for you to protect your idea and name.

COPYRIGHT
- For literary, artistic, dramatic and musical work
- Covers the way in which ideas are expressed
- Does not cover the idea as such
- The owner of the idea has the right to prevent others from using it by copyright

TRADEMARKS
- For brands, names, words, sounds and smells
- For symbols, words, shapes or anything capable of graphical representation
- Two types: registered or unregistered

PATENTS
- For technical solutions, new inventions and products
- Protects the rights of invention
- The idea must be novel, involve an inventive step and be capable of industrial application
- Patents are obtained for specific countries or groups of countries
- Cannot be obtained for an invention which has already been published or used in public previously

REGISTERED DESIGN RIGHTS
- Two types: registered and unregistered
- Protects shapes, textures, features, colours and contours of a product
- Must be new and have individual characteristics

ACCOUNTS/TAX RETURNS
Every business needs to prepare **accounts** and a **tax return** of some form or another. How and what you need to do depends on your legal entity. Make sure you **get your head around** what you have to do, when you have to do it and what records you have to keep. If you don't want to do it yourself, you can outsource it to an accountant.

PREMISES
You might want or need premises. There are different **options** available if you don't want to work from home. Have a look at **co-working** spaces, which are a great way to save costs and network with other businesses.

Make sure you have the insurance that you need if you do so.

MARKETING

If you don't tell anyone that you exist, no one will buy your products and services. Get a proper marketing strategy in place and have a marketing products created. My programme **'Marketing made easy – 6 easy steps to become your own marketing expert'** can help you with this. Have a look at the **online course**: www.creativestartupacademy.com/courses and get a **discount** by using the code **'CHANGEBOOK'**.

VAT REGISTRATION

Talk to an accountant to establish when you might want to **register for VAT** or when you are required by law to register for VAT. Every country has a different VAT threshold. And be aware of the **UK VAT MOSS** system that was introduced in 2015 for businesses that sell digital goods. It is important that you get this right so you don't get into trouble.

DATA PROTECTION ACT

As soon as you **handle client data** (names, addresses and contact details) you have to comply with the Data Protection Act. In the UK, you need to follow regulations and pay a fee to the Information Commissioner (www.ico.gov.uk). Make sure you check this for your particular country and comply.

PENSION PLAN
When you are self-employed/have your own business, you will have to think about your **pension provision**. You will have to sort this out yourself rather than relying on the company that you work for.

4. CHECKLIST

Here is a checklist to help you through this section. It is also downloadable on my website using this link bit.ly/checkliststeps. Again, please note that this is not a complete list but gives you a good overview of what you have to do.

- ☐ Have I validated my idea (market and competitor analysis)?

- ☐ Do I know my ideal client?

- ☐ Did I set myself a goal?

- ☐ Do I know what I want to stand for, what my values are?

- ☐ Are my prices and products defined?

- ☐ Have I decided on a business model?

- ☐ Do I have a company name?

- ☐ Do I know my finances?

- ☐ Do I have a business plan?

- ☐ Do I have branding in place?

- ☐ Are my insurances sorted?

- ☐ Am I aware of all the legal issues I need to comply with?

- ☐ Do I have a website?

- ☐ Do I have Terms and Conditions, Privacy and Cookie policies in place?

- ☐ Have I decided on a legal entity?

- ☐ Have I protected my idea?

- ☐ When do I need to register my business and with whom?

- ☐ Do I have a marketing strategy/plan in place?

- ☐ Do I have an accounting system in place?

- ☐ Have I signed up with the Information Commissioner (or similar)?

- ☐ Am I aware of the terminology that might have regulations attached to it? (For example you might not be allowed to call yourself a 'Coach' if you haven't done specific training for it)

- ☐ Do I have a pension plan in place?

STEP 5 – GROW YOUR CONFIDENCE

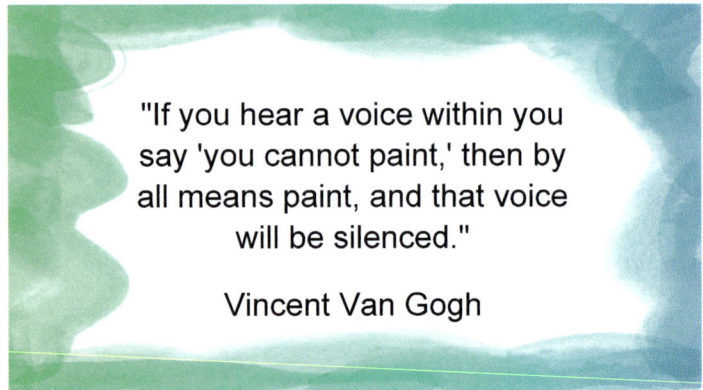

"If you hear a voice within you say 'you cannot paint,' then by all means paint, and that voice will be silenced."

Vincent Van Gogh

Step 5 of the Start-Up Formula™ is the 'G' in 'CHANGE', which stands for **'Grow your confidence'**.

In this section we will look at how you can grow your confidence.

1. WHY EVERYONE FEELS DOWN SOMETIMES
Every entrepreneur will feel a bit down sometimes, not confident enough. This might be due to some negative feedback that we received or self-doubt that is arising. Unfortunately not everything goes to plan all the time. Things might take longer than you thought or take a totally different route. Things change. **That is normal** and you are not alone!

2. WHAT IS CONFIDENCE?
Now, being confident **does not mean being arrogant**. At this point I would like to quote Colin Wright and his book 'Networking Fundamentals' which I recommend you read.

"Be confident but not arrogant.

This can be a thin line to walk, but the main difference between confidence and arrogance is that the first is about **answering to no one** because you feel justified in who and what you are, while the second is about **overcompensating** and tearing others down in order to make yourself feel big and important.

Even knowing this, it can be hard to distinguish the two sometimes, and some people stay away from being confident out of concern that they'll come across as arrogant.

The best way to distinguish yourself as confident rather than arrogant is to be **gracious, genuine and self-effacing**. Confidence means that you don't have to justify your presence or stride, so instead of telling people about how great you are, try putting the focus on someone else and building them up (in an honest way)"

I could not have said it better.

I would like to also quote another book called 'The Flinch' by Julian Smith. This book is about **overcoming fear** amongst other things.
"Look at the finish line now. It's far and it seems impossible. Maybe it's up in the clouds, and the journey is treacherous, or the mountain is too high. You imagine that you weren't meant for this. You think

you're not strong enough. In a sense, you're right. You're quitting before the pain even sets in. You're quitting out of fear of the flinch. What you are missing is that the path itself changes you. You're weak because you haven't stepped on the path. When you do, a process will begin. As you climb the mountain, you'll get stronger. Your plastic brain will be shaped by the path. You might think this path isn't for you, but it is – you'll just change along the way. The path itself will toughen you up for the end. Right now, you just need to start."

Being confident will help you **stay motivated** and also support you in your marketing activities, such as networking. People would rather talk to confident people who know what they are talking about than to people who seem to be unsure.

3. TECHNIQUES THAT CAN HELP

I would like to give you three techniques that you can use to build up your confidence. The three techniques are:
- Museum of old beliefs
- Timeline exercise
- Submodalities exercise

MUSEUM OF OLD BELIEFS

The 'museum of old beliefs' was developed by Robert Dilts and is used to change beliefs that are holding you back. For this exercise have several pieces of A4 paper ready with the following written on them:
- Meta
- Open to doubt
- Used to believe
- Museum of old beliefs
- Believe
- Trust

Put them all on the floor - in a circle around you, as you will start and finish in 'Meta'.

META
The Meta position is the neutral position and starting point. Step on the piece of paper saying 'Meta' and take a moment to **analyse how you feel right now.**

OPEN TO DOUBT
Now step onto the paper saying 'Open to doubt'. In this position, you need to go back to a time and **moment in your life in which you were open to doubt** and describe that feeling using all your senses. In which situation did someone tell you something that made you question your belief and you were open to it? What did you feel? What did you hear? What did you smell and what did you taste? Once you have established that feeling inside you again, you can step onto the next position.

USED TO BELIEVE
On this piece of paper, think about something that **you used to believe in but don't believe anymore**. Repeat the task above (feelings, sounds, tastes, smells). Once you have established that feeling, step onto the next position.

MUSEUM OF OLD BELIEFS
Think about a place that you would call **your personal 'Museum of old beliefs'.** It can be anything you like. It can be an actual building or it can be a different place. Describe it in detail. Again, everything you feel, hear, taste, smell. **Make it your own. Make it real.** Have it in front of your eyes. Now, take that belief you want to get rid of and put it into a little box or something. Then hide it in your museum of old beliefs. **Lock it away and throw away the key,** so you will never be able to get to it again.

Now rephrase the belief that you have just put away into a **positive belief** that will move you forward and step onto the next position.

TRUST
Go through everything that you feel, hear, taste and smell about what you now trust. Embrace this feeling fully and remain a while in that state. You have the **trust that it is possible.**

OPEN TO BELIEVE
Move onto the next position 'Open to believe'. Be open to **believe in yourself.** Find a situation in which you did

believe in yourself in the past and transfer this feeling into your new belief. Feel how you think it can be done, how it is possible.

BELIEVE
Once you have found the trust and opened yourself up to believing, step onto 'Believe'. Again, repeat the task above again and 'anchor' that feeling completely so that you are now in a **frame of mind that you actually believe in the newly phrased belief.**

META
Step back into the 'Meta' position and see **how you feel now.** You will feel full of energy and belief. You will be fully motivated again.

TIMELINE

In this exercise you will travel into the future. Put a **piece of paper on the floor saying 'Now'**, then put a piece of paper further down the room stating **your goal**, i.e. 'successful web design agency'. By now you know already what is involved in getting there. Have a couple of **milestones** written on different sheets of paper and put them in between your 'Now' and your achieved goal.

Step on the 'Now'. Close your eyes. Take in fully **how you feel right now**. How do you feel, what do you hear, taste and smell? Get fully engrossed by your present moment. You might feel excited but also a bit scared of what lies ahead. Just let the thoughts come into your mind and just be in the 'Now'. Open your eyes and **step on the next piece of paper** (first milestone). Do the same as before. You are now much closer to your end goal. **Repeat** with the next milestones.

Go to the **final piece of paper** (your **goal**) and do the same. The point of this exercise is to put you into the situation of achieving your goal. How will you feel when you have achieved it? What do you see? What do you hear, smell and taste? Go through all the senses.

SUBMODALITES

This works particularly well if it was a specific situation that made you feel doubt about yourself. Think about that moment and visualise it. Go through the **submodality checklist** (see below) and make notes. It works best if someone else will talk through the checklist whilst you close your eyes. The way it works is that you **imagine that situation** and the other person is asking you each point relating to the situation. Let me talk you through a few examples so you understand it better.

Associated or disassociated? Here you are asked to see if you are associated with the situation – you are yourself in the memory, or if you are disassociated – you observe yourself in the situation. The other person makes a note in the memory section.

Framed/panoramic – Do you see the situation in a limited frame or is it like a panorama view?

And so on. I explain the points a bit more in the checklist itself. Once you have been through the checklist, you then will **change your memory**. For example, if you have said you are associated with the situation, then the person will ask you to disassociate from it, meaning you will see yourself in the situation rather than being in it. Or the other way around, if your answer was that you are disassociated. You do this with every single point and the person guiding you through will make notes in the 'New' section. If you have seen the memory in black and white, you will now add colour to it. By doing this you are **reframing the memory** and make it more pleasurable. It will help you to see the situation in a different light and it will help you to be more **motivated** again and feel **more confident**.

SUBMODALITY CHECKLIST

Visual – everything that you can see	Memory	Now
Associated – are you yourself? Disassociated – do you see yourself in the situation?		
Framed/Panoramic view of the situation?		
3D/Flat – is the memory 3D or a Flat image?		
Colour or Black & White?		
Bright or Dim?		
Contrast – how much contrast is there?		
Intensity – low or high		
Focussed or unfocussed?		
Still/Motion – is the image still or moving?		

Auditory – everything that you can hear	Memory	Now
Volume – silence or do you hear things?		
Tempo – how fast is everything moving (if you had motion to it)		
Tonality – what is the tonality of the memory? Harsh or friendly?		
External/Internal – are the noises that you hear external or inside of you?		
Number of sources – how many sources make the noise?		

Kinaesthetic – everything that you can feel	**Memory**	**Now**
Temperature – hot, cold, warm...?		
Vibration – can you feel any vibration? How intense is it?		
Weight – do you feel heavy or light?		
Size – how tall or small do you feel?		
Movement – can you feel any movement?		

4. WHAT ELSE CAN BUILD YOU UP?
Some of these I have mentioned before but I would like to repeat them in this section, as they are great to build up your confidence.

Always remember **your big 'Why'**. Why are you doing this? Why did you want to start your business in the first place? If you feel less confident or motivated, remember that.

Keep the **feedback scrapbook** that I have mentioned on page 26.

Get a **Coach or mentor** that can help you build up the confidence that you need.

Make a list of all your **qualifications and any skills** that you have. There will be more than you think. List all the training that you have done, all the software that you are able to work with, all the other 'soft skills' that you have, such as being a good listener etc. You can also ask friends and family to see what they think you are good at.

STEP 6 – ENGAGE YOUR AUDIENCE

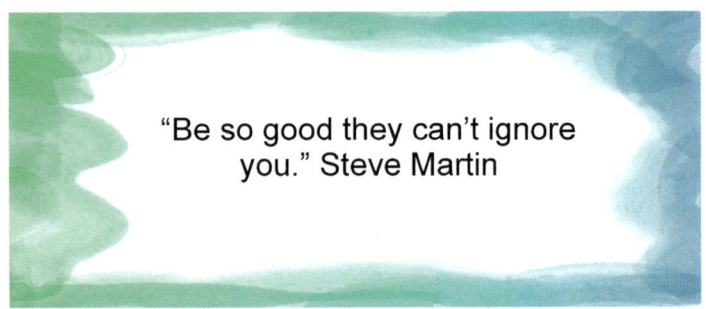

"Be so good they can't ignore you." Steve Martin

Step 6, the last one, of the Start-Up Formula™ is the 'E' in 'CHANGE', which stands for **'Engage your audience'**.

In this section you will put your **marketing plan** together.

By now you have done all the things that are involved starting your own business and you are now **ready to market** your business. Although you might still need to work through some of the steps involved as they come later in the process. You have set yourself a goal, you know your ideal client, you have an overview of the steps involved, have started working on them and you have tools that will help you grow your confidence when you need it.

1. RESULT – 6 STEPS TO BECOME YOUR OWN MARKETING EXPERT.

In addition to 'CHANGE – 6 steps to start your own business', I have developed **'RESULT – 6 steps to become your own marketing expert'**. 'RESULT' is also an acronym that helps you to remember the 6 steps easily:

- **R**ecognise yourself
- **E**valuate the market
- **S**how them what you've got
- **U**nite your knowledge
- **L**aunch your activities
- **T**alk about your business

You can learn more about the 6 steps above and put your 1-year marketing plan together in my **online course**: www.creativestartupacademy.com/courses. With the **code 'CHANGEBOOK'** you will get **discount** as a bonus for buying this book.

This course will make **marketing easy** for you.
You will:

- create a powerful marketing **mindset**
- review your business **values**
- review your ideal **client**
- look at your **market** and **competitors**
- create your **story**
- create your **products and prices** or review them
- get low and no cost **marketing ideas**
- create your **1-year marketing plan**
- get **time management** tips
- get **networking tips**

- create your perfect **elevator pitch**
- learn **how to build rapport** with body language and words

2. HOW TO CREATE A MARKETING PLAN

There is a **marketing plan template** that you can download on my website www.creativestartupacademy.com/freestuff

The first part of the marketing plan should be the summary of your **ideal client**.

The second page is your **mission statement**. What is your mission? Your mission statement should be concise and easy to understand. I will now give you two examples of mission statements:

AMAZON
We seek to be Earth's most customer-centric company for four primary customer sets: customers, sellers, enterprises, content creators.

AIR BNB
To help creating a world where you can belong anywhere and where people can live a place, instead of just travelling to it.

The next part is your marketing activities. Start with imagining that you have all the time and money in the world to spend on marketing. Brainstorm ideas and write them down. Look at them realistically. What can you really do with the resources you have? Write these down. Next, break every activity down into tasks. Next to every task write how much it will cost you in time and money.

I will give you an example (with example figures):
Having a website online:
- Decide on a URL name – 2 hours including research
- Buy URL and hosting – 0.5 hours, £25/year
- Design the website – 4 days, £35 for a nice design theme
- Write copy for the website – 5 days
- Find images for the website – 3 hours
- Buy images – 0.5 hours, £150
- Proof read website – £500 for a proof reader
- Test website – 1 day

Once you have **done this for every activity**, you can **evaluate** how much time you can spend per day/week/month. This obviously depends on whether you are also doing other things or have another job.

You can then put each activity **into time slots in your marketing plan**:

- 30 days
- 3 months
- 6 months
- 12 months

Having done this, you will now have a **realistic** marketing plan for an entire year!

This was the Start-Up Formula™ 'CHANGE – 6 easy steps start your own business'.

Congratulations! I hope you enjoyed working through each step and it made starting your own business easier for you.

3. WHAT'S NEXT?

Now you need to **get started with your marketing activities.**

I would like to support you with this, so don't forget to check out my **marketing online course:** www.creativestartupacademy.com/courses

In the next two sections, I will talk a bit more **about myself** and **further support** that you can get from me.

Your marketing and creative start-up Coach – Christine

ABOUT CHRISTINE

I was born and raised in Berlin, Germany and worked in marketing and design agencies for 7 years as a Strategic Consultant and Senior Account Manager. In 2009, I felt the need for a change. I quit my job, went travelling through New Zealand and Australia for 3 months before moving to London in 2010.

I started a new job as a Senior Account Manager in an agency. However, I knew I didn't want to do that for much longer. I was longing for something new, something that would be more rewarding. I have trained as a Coach and obtained a certificate in NLP (Neuro Linguistic Programming). Still not knowing exactly what I wanted to do, I called myself a 'Life Coach'. It soon turned out that I enjoy working with other **driven** individuals that are **starting up their own business** and following their **passion**. My purpose in life became clearer: **I want to help other people and I want to make them happy in what they do for a living.** I became the marketing and creative start-up Coach.

I now work with universities that pay me to help their students that want to start their own business. I work with individuals and small businesses that need help with starting their own business or marketing it successfully.

I run regular workshops, give talks about the '6 steps to start your own business' and the '6 steps to become your own marketing expert', run boot camps, competitions and work 1:1 with people – in person or via Skype. I started the **Creative Start-Up Academy** – an online course platform for start-ups: www.creativestartupacademy.com

My passions outside of work are cooking, travelling, Italy (everything about it – language, food, people, and the country itself), dancing salsa and doing exercise. I play the ukulele, which doesn't mean that I can sing, and enjoy spending time with friends, but also with myself.

If you would like to get in **contact** with me, send me an email: **hello@creativestartupacademy.com**

FURTHER SUPPORT

I hope this book gave you a good starting point and support for starting your own business. If you would like **further support** by me, there are many ways to get it.

Have a look at the **freebies** on my website:
www.creativestartupacademy.com/freestuff

Check out the **online courses** that I have:
www.creativestartupacademy.com/courses
You will receive a **discount** on every course. Just type in the **discount code 'CHANGEBOOK'** when you check out. Every online course comes with **personal support**, in the form of regular **live webinars**.

Have a look on www.christinethecoach.com for **personal support** and **workshops**.

I also run **free webinars** on a regular basis. Go to this website to see the latest dates and topics:
www.christinethecoach.com/webinar

Looking forward to talking to you. All the best!

Your marketing and creative start-up Coach – Christine

Printed in Germany
by Amazon Distribution
GmbH, Leipzig